READINGS IN
CANADIAN
HISTORY
POST~CONFEDERATION

R. DOUGLAS FRANCIS/DONALD B. SMITH

THIRD EDITION

Holt, Rinehart and Winston of Canada, Limited
Toronto

Canadian Cataloguing in Publication Data

Main entry under title:
Readings in Canadian history
3rd ed.
Includes bibliographical references.

Contents: [v. 1.] Pre-Confederation — [v. 2.] Post-Confederation.
ISBN 0-03-922691-3 (v. 1) ISBN 0-03-922692-1 (v. 2)

1. Canada — History.
I. Francis, R.D. (R. Douglas), 1944-   . II. Smith, Donald B., 1946-

FC164.R43 1990   971   C89-094789-9
F1026.R43 1990

Publisher: David Dimmell
Developmental Editor: Iris Coupe
Publishing Services Manager: Karen Eakin
Editorial Co-ordinator: Marcel Chiera
Copy Editor: Darlene Zeleney
Cover and Interior Design: John Zehethofer
Typesetting and Assembly: True to Type Inc.
Printing and Binding: Metrolitho Inc.

Cover: *Dayliner, Carleton Corner*, 1980, by Ken Tolmie. Private Collection, Halifax. Reproduced by permission.

Printed in Canada

1 2 3 4 5   94 93 92 91 90

Preface

In this third edition of our two-volume *Readings in Canadian History*, as in the previous two editions, our concern is to provide a collection of articles suitable for introductory Canadian history tutorials. This has meant selecting topics related to the major issues dealt with in such history courses, and providing useful readings of a general nature. We have once again included material that deals with the various regions of the country, and selected, whenever possible, readings that reflect new research interests among Canadian historians. Consequently, we have changed some of the topics, and many of the readings. Unfortunately, because of space limitations, these new additions have necessitated eliminating several worthwhile readings that appeared in the second edition. Still, we hope that this edition will continue to meet the needs of introductory students in Canadian history.

This volume includes two or three selections on each of fifteen topics, thus providing instructors flexibility in choosing readings. Short introductions to each topic set the readings in an historical context and offer suggestions for further readings. It is our hope that this reader will contribute to increased discussion in tutorials, as well as complement course lectures and, where applicable, textbooks.

In this edition we have included several popular historical articles from *Horizon Canada* and the National Museum of Civilization's Visual History Series. Although these essays appear in an undocumented form, we have chosen to include them because they provide good summaries of the respective topics and are written by experts in the field.

In preparing the reader, we and the publisher have both sought advice from a number of Canadian historians. Their comments have been generously given and have greatly improved the original outline. We would like in particular to thank Douglas Baldwin of Acadia University, Olive Dickason of the University of Alberta, Carol Wilton-Siegel of York University, John Eagle of the University of Alberta, and Hugh Johnston of Simon Fraser University for their detailed comments on our draft for the third edition. Many other individuals made valuable suggestions, and we are indebted to John Belshaw of Cariboo College, Margaret Conrad of Acadia University, Beatrice Craig of the University of Ottawa,

Chad Gaffield of the University of Ottawa, Marcel Martel of Glendon College, York University, Thomas Socknat of the University of Toronto, Robert Sweeny of Memorial University, Duncan McDowell of Carleton University, and Peter Ward of the University of British Columbia. Heartfelt thanks also go to Dave Dimmell, Steve Payne, Iris Coupe, John Caldarone, and Marcel Chiera of Holt, Rinehart and Winston for their help and constant encouragement towards the completion of this third edition and to Darlene Zeleney who edited the book. Finally, we wish to thank those Canadian historians who consented to let their writings be included in this reader. Their ideas and viewpoints will greatly enrich the study and appreciation of Canadian history among first- and second-year university students.

Douglas Francis
Donald Smith
Department of History
University of Calgary

Publisher's Note to Instructors and Students

This textbook is a key component of your course. If you are the instructor of this course, you undoubtedly considered a number of texts carefully before choosing this as the one that will work best for your students and you. The authors and publishers of this book spent considerable time and money to ensure its high quality, and we appreciate your recognition of this effort and accomplishment. Please note the copyright statement.

If you are a student, we are confident that this text will help you to meet the objectives of your course. You will also find it helpful after the course is finished, as a valuable addition to your personal library. So hold on to it.

And since we want to hear what you think about this book, please be sure to send us the stamped reply card at the end of the text. This will help us to continue publishing high-quality books for your courses.

Contents

List of Maps

Topic One

Consolidation of Confederation

Canada had just come into existence when it faced some critical challenges: the only British colony on the Pacific Coast debated whether it wanted to join Confederation; the tiniest British colony on the Atlantic made every effort to resist union with Canada; and one of the four original partners wanted to leave.

Nova Scotians had consistently opposed Confederation. They had been brought into the union largely through the efforts of the premier, Charles Tupper, who had refused to submit the question to a vote in the legislature. In the federal and provincial elections of September 1867, Nova Scotians recorded their disapproval — eighteen of the nineteen seats for the federal Parliament went to the separatists (with only Tupper retaining his seat for the pro-Confederationists) and provincially the electors almost eliminated Tupper's Conservative party, which retained only two of the thirty-eight seats. Part of this political protest consisted of an annexation movement ready to join the United States as an alternative to Confederation. Donald Warner, in "The Post-Confederation Annexation Movement in Nova Scotia," explains the reasons behind this dissatisfaction, and shows the continuity between the pre- and post-Confederation protest movements. He reveals the deep divisions within the annexation movement, both in personalities and principles, and analyzes the movement along geographical and class lines.

The fulfilment of the motto of the new nation, "from sea to sea," required the entry of British Columbia into Confederation. There was no assurance that British Columbia, a colony on the Pacific Ocean separated from Canada by the vast unsettled territory of the Northwest, would join. Yet despite considerable opposition, British Columbia did enter Confederation on July 20, 1871. Walter Sage explains the pro-Confederates' success in "British Columbia Becomes Canadian (1871–1901)."

In "How Much for the Island?" and "Confederation: The End of an Era," two selections from their book, *The Island and Confederation,* David Weale and Harry Baglole explain how Prince Edward Islanders held out against joining Confederation as long as possible, largely out of fear that union with Canada would end forever their traditional way of life as well as their independence.

The question of Nova Scotian protest at Confederation is examined in the context of later provincial protest movements in Colin D. Howell's "Nova Scotia's Protest Tradition and the Search for a Meaningful Federalism," in *Canada and the Burden of Unity*, ed. D. Bercuson (Toronto: Macmillan, 1977), 169–91. R.H. Campbell's "The Repeal Agitation in Nova Scotia, 1867–1869," Nova Scotia Historical Society, *Collections* 25 (1942), 95–130, is also of interest. George Rawlyk's *The Atlantic Provinces and the Problems of Confederation* (St. John's: Breakwater Press, 1979) provides a good overview of development in Atlantic Canada at the time of Confederation. K.G. Pryke discusses Nova Scotia's relations with the federal government in "The Making of a Province: Nova Scotia and Confederation," Canadian Historical Association, *Historical Papers* (1968), 35–48. The views of Joseph Howe, the leading opponent of Confederation in Nova Scotia, are presented in J. Murray Beck's *Joseph Howe*, vol. 2, *The Briton Becomes Canadian, 1848–1873* (Montreal: McGill-Queen's University Press, 1983), as well as in his *Joseph Howe: Anti-Confederate*, Canadian Historical Association, Historical Booklet no. 17 (Ottawa: CHA, 1965).

A useful contrast to Sage's interpretation of the British Columbia question is Margaret Ormsby's "Canada and the New British Columbia,"

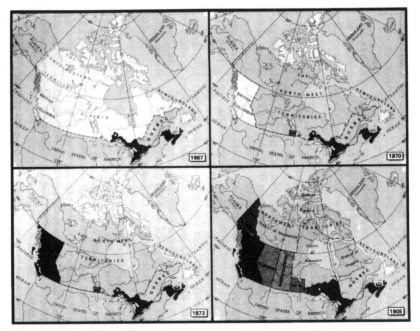

Energy, Mines and Resources Canada.

The territorial evolution of Canada from the original nation of four provinces in 1867 (Ontario, Quebec, Nova Scotia, and New Brunswick), to five in 1870 (Manitoba), seven by 1873 (British Columbia and Prince Edward Island), and nine by 1905 (Alberta and Saskatchewan).

Canadian Historical Association, *Report* (1948), 74–85. See also her book, *British Columbia: A History* (Toronto: Macmillan, 1958). The views of British officials in the colony of British Columbia are presented in M. Ormsby, "Frederick Seymour: The Forgotten Governor," and Robert Smith, "The Hankin Appointment"; both appear in *B.C. Studies* 22 (Summer 1974): 3–25 and 26–39, respectively. *British Columbia and Confederation*, ed. W. George Shelton (Victoria: University of Victoria Press, 1967), is a valuable collection of essays on this subject.

Francis Bolger presents a comprehensive treatment of Prince Edward Island's decision to join Canada in *Prince Edward Island and Confederation* (Charlottetown: St. Dunstan University Press, 1964) and in the chapters leading up to Confederation in *Canada's Smallest Province: A History of P.E.I.* (Charlottetown: P.E.I. Heritage Foundation, 1973). Ronald Tallman's "Annexation in the Maritimes? The Butler Mission to Charlottetown," *Dalhousie Review* 53 (Spring 1973): 97–112, describes the American influence which almost prevented Prince Edward Island from entering Confederation. John Reid examines Confederation's impact on the Maritime region as one of the topics in his *Six Crucial Decades: Times of Change in the History of the Maritimes* (Halifax: Nimbus Publishing, 1987).

James Hiller reviews Newfoundland's rejection of Confederation in "Confederation Defeated: The Newfoundland Election of 1869," in *Newfoundland in the Nineteenth and Twentieth Centuries: Essays in Interpretation* (Toronto: University of Toronto Press, 1980), 67–94, reprinted in *Readings in Canadian History: Pre-Confederation*, 3rd ed. (Toronto: Holt, Rinehart and Winston, 1990).

Suzanne Zeller looks at the role of science in the formation of a transcontinental nation in *Inventing Canada: Early Victorian Science and the Idea of a Transcontinental Nation* (Toronto: University of Toronto Press, 1987).

3

The Post-Confederation Annexation Movement in Nova Scotia*

DONALD F. WARNER

The story of the anti-Confederation movement in Nova Scotia and of Joseph Howe's part in it is an oft-told tale. Historians and biographers have related how this agitation was launched and how it rode out gales of denunciation only to founder on the rocks of adamant imperial opposition after the desertion of its captain, Howe. Thus the major outline of this story is well known. One aspect, however, has received too little

*From *Canadian Historical Review* 28 (1947): 156–65. Reprinted by permission of University of Toronto Press.

attention — the lively annexation movement which grew out of the agitation against Confederation. Some writers gingerly skirt this bog of treason barely acknowledging its existence. A few discuss it but seem, by brevity, to dismiss it as unimportant; they leave the impression that it was nothing more than an attempt on the part of a few desperate Nova Scotians to frighten the imperial government into permitting their province to secede from the Canadian Dominion as the price for keeping it in the British Empire. It is the purpose of this article to remedy the neglect by analysing this annexation movement, showing its causes and course, and demonstrating that, for a time, it did achieve some strength. To prove the sincerity of the annexationists is, of course, very difficult, involving as it does the nearly impossible problem of the exact analysis of human motives. It is probably true that most of the annexationists were "running a bluff." Yet contemporary evidence indicates that many of them, with their loyalty to the British Empire temporarily gone, viewed the question of joining the United States as a business proposition and were honestly convinced that they would gain materially from such a move. Certainly the alarm which this movement caused to the loyal elements in the province could not have been produced by an agitation which was entirely insincere.

Since the annexation movement had its origin in the agitation against Confederation, it is necessary, first, to glance at the latter. By 1864-65, the plan to unite British North America in a federation had aroused the opposition of the people of the Maritime colonies for several reasons. They realized that they would be a minority in the proposed union and that their interests might be subverted by the majority in Ontario and Quebec. Economically, the colonies by the sea also stood to lose by Confederation. They were, of necessity, wedded to free trade for they depended upon lumbering, mining, ship-building, and fishing for a livelihood, exporting their produce and importing much of what they consumed. Canada, on the other hand, was protectionist, and it seemed likely that its tariff wall would be stretched around the new Confederation.[1] Nova Scotia particularly disliked the financial terms of the union, fearing that its government would lose half of its income and would lack money to support such essential functions as education and public works.[2] For these and other reasons, most Nova Scotians preferred to remain as they were, a separate colony, rather than to join in the proposed union. A number of these "antis," as the opponents of federation were popularly called, formed the League of the Maritime Provinces to carry on the fight against Confederation. Joseph Howe, one of the greatest figures in the history of British North America, led this organization, partly, according to tradition, from personal motives. Nearly twenty years before, he had won the fight for responsible government in his province, and his victory had established him as the leader of Nova Scotia. Since then, however, he had accomplished little and his arch-enemy, Dr. Charles Tupper, had risen to dominate the province and to be the leader of its government. Howe, like most Nova Scotians, sincerely opposed Confederation; but he also astutely recognized in the "anti" movement an opportunity to regain his former prestige and to pay off old scores against Tupper, who favoured Confederation.

The first action of the "antis" was an attempt to prevent the passage of the British North America Act by the imperial Parliament, or at least to amend the Act so that it would not include Nova Scotia. For this purpose, the League sent Howe and other delegates to London. There the first mention of annexation occurred; for Howe was to hint to the Colonial Office that Confederation might cause "changes which none of us desire . . . and all of us deplore."[3] As instructed, Howe made the most of this weapon in his correspondence with Lord Carnarvon, the secretary of state for the colonies, by pointing out the "range of temptation" which political union with the United States offered to the Maritimes: they would have free trade with a market of 34 million people, access to American capital, and the benefit of American fishing bounties.[4] These broad hints did not impress the imperial government, which pushed the British North America Act through Parliament with little opposition. Thus Nova Scotia became part of the Dominion of Canada, for Tupper had pledged his province to enter Confederation without consulting the voters.

If Tupper expected the "antis" to accept this *fait accompli* without further ado, he was soon wiser. The "antis" turned from the attempt to prevent the formation of the Dominion to an attempt to withdraw Nova Scotia from it. The secession movement, already strong, was steadily gaining new adherents, largely because the formation of the Dominion coincided closely with the beginning of a severe depression. The termination, in 1866, of the Reciprocity Treaty of 1854 had had the immediate effect of halving the trade with the United States and bringing distress to the merchants, commercial cities, and producers of Canada. This depression was most severe in the Maritime Provinces whose staple exports of fish, coal, and lumber were subject to prohibitive duties after the end of the Treaty. To increase the discontent in these provinces, the fisheries of 1866 and 1867 proved to be complete failures, leaving thousands of families to struggle against hunger and privation.[5] At a time when income was declining, the federal government, as expected, extended the higher tariff of the old colony of Canada to the entire Dominion and considerably increased the price of necessities in the hardhit Maritime Provinces. This readjustment of the tariff was said to have cost the inhabitants of these provinces $356 000 a year;[6] even the lieutenant-governor and the confederationists in Nova Scotia felt compelled to condemn the tariff because of the hardship that it worked there.[7]

A final affliction to the depression-ridden Canadians was the spectacle of the United States which was, at this time, entering a frenzied post-war boom. The contrast was both vivid and suggestive.

It is not strange that the "antis" took advantage of these circumstances to argue that there was a direct connection between the formation of the Dominion and the coming of the depression. Nor is it strange that some Canadians envied the seeming prosperity of the United States and longed to share in it. The result of these factors was a double trend in the "anti" movement. As stated above, it grew steadily; and, secondly, some of its followers began to consider secession not as an end in itself but as a step toward annexation.

For a time, however, most of the "antis" regarded political union with the United States as a last resort and hoped to relieve their distress by other means. There was some foundation for this expectation. The first election in Nova Scotia under the new Dominion had resulted in an overwhelming victory for the opponents of Confederation. This made them confident that the British government would accede to their desire for secession from Canada and that a return to the status of a separate, self-governing colony would solve their economic and political problems. Nova Scotia could restore its revenue tariff, the income of its government would increase, and other provinces could not undermine its interests. More important, Nova Scotians were certain that the United States would be willing to negotiate a reciprocity treaty with their province if it were not part of the Dominion. This belief was based on the notion that the United States and Nova Scotia were complementary in production while the United States and Canada were competitive.

Thus secession was still the key to prosperity and the "antis" again set out to get it. The provincial assembly passed a series of resolutions urging the British government to release Nova Scotia from the Confederation. Howe embarked for London bearing this appeal, and the "antis" waited confidently for news that the British government had granted it. Talk of annexation almost disappeared.

Howe did not share the confidence of his followers that his mission would succeed. He knew from his previous experience in Great Britain that the home government was determined to have Confederation and would oppose the withdrawal of Nova Scotia, which might wreck the new union. This official British attitude was well expressed by Lord Monck, the governor-general of the Dominion, who pressed the colonial secretary to refuse Howe's request graciously but firmly. If the union broke up, wrote Monck, "I have no hesitation in expressing my opinion that . . . the maintenance of British power or the existence of British institutions in America will soon become impossible."[8] This advice from the man on the spot fortified the determination of the imperial government to deny the repeal of Confederation. Obviously, Howe had good reasons for admitting privately before he sailed that he expected his mission to fail,[9] and he was not mistaken. The colonial secretary, the Duke of Buckingham, proved to be courteous and willing to listen to the complaints of Nova Scotia but unmovable in his refusal to dissolve the Confederation or to permit the secession of any of the provinces. Early in June, he informed Monck that the imperial government "could not consider" this, or any other, request for repeal.[10]

The publication of this dispatch, bringing the frustration of their highest hopes, was a terrible blow to most of the "antis." A storm of protest arose in Nova Scotia, and bitter denunciations rained down upon the Canadian and British governments. One newspaper, typical of the organs that favoured repeal of Confederation, vented its wrath and sorrow in the following terms: "Nova Scotians have been proud of their connection with England. What have they to be proud of now? We feel assured that the people of Nova Scotia will never be loyal to the Dominion of Canada. They never have consented, never will consent to such an alliance. The Union, whilst it lasts, can only be one of force, so far as Nova Scotia is concerned."[11]

Many soon went beyond philippics and vowed that their loyalty to Great Britain was now gone. Prominent men and newspapers in the province came out openly for annexation.[12] These advocates of political union frankly stated that, with their hope of secession now blasted, their only remaining chance of rescue from the undesired federation was to join the United States.

This outburst of disloyalty frightened Howe, who realized how much he had helped to blow up this tempest. Even before leaving on his second mission to London, he had been uneasy over the extreme doctrines held by some of his followers; on his return to Halifax he became alarmed at the treasonable talk in the province. At once, he determined to check it. Calling a convention of the "anti" leaders, he lectured them sternly for their sedition. He pointed out that any attempt by Nova Scotia to secure annexation would be forcibly resisted with the whole power of the British Empire and would end in disaster.[13] This plain speaking seemed to have its effect; the convention resolved that the "antis" must continue to attempt to secure secession by "lawful and constitutional means."[14]

The conversion of some of the repealers to "lawful and constitutional means" proved to be very temporary. Soon they were again using violent language, advocating seditious action, casting strong hints that American aid would be forthcoming, and that annexation would result. Members of the provincial government and prominent newspapers led the way towards the edge of treason.[15] Howe soon realized that his efforts to secure secession and to quiet the extremists in his group had failed and that it would be a waste of time to repeat them. The repeal movement was in a *cul-de-sac*, and he faced the necessity of choosing between two lines of retreat: to abandon opposition to Confederation, or to attempt to bring Nova Scotia into the American union. To Howe, the former was distasteful and the latter abhorrent. Choosing the lesser of the two evils, he reluctantly decided to accept Confederation, the pain of transition being assuaged by the willingness of Macdonald to make concessions that would partially redress the grievances of Nova Scotia.[16] In November, 1868, Howe suddenly announced that he could no longer remain in the "anti" movement, which was becoming merely a cloak for annexationism.

Howe had apparently hoped and planned that his action would be imitated by many, if not most, of the advocates of the repeal of Confederation, and that the extremists would be driven to cover. His expectation was disappointed. The "antis" were stunned by this spectacular and unexpected about-face on the part of their leader. Some of the moderates followed him, but many others refused to do so, irked because he had not consulted or forewarned them. Even the confederationists in the province condemned Howe on the ground that his action would have been effective only if he had notified his moderate associates of his intentions, so that they might have been prepared to withdraw gradually from the secession movement and become confederationists with some show of consistency.[17] Contemporary observers, friendly to Howe, estimated that his action had important effects in only two counties — Queens and Lunenburg — where about half of the "antis" followed him out of the movement.[18] The rest, if anything, became more determined in opposition, and the tendency towards political union seemed to increase. Moreover, the tone of the annexationists was changing. In the beginning, they had been inspired by anger and had been hopeful of alarming the British government by the intemperance of their sentiments. But by this time, their wrath had cooled and so had their loyalty to the British Empire. With the hope of repeal gone and economic distress still prevalent, Nova Scotians began to view their future without sentiment and some of them concluded that annexation was the only cure for the depression from which they were suffering. It became the expression of cold self-interest, not of hot wrath.[19]

It is impossible to determine the extent of this movement with exactness. Contemporary evidence indicates, however, that it had considerable strength in some areas. Howe, who knew the political situation in Nova Scotia better than any other man, informed Macdonald that "a clear unfettered vote of the people might take it [Nova Scotia] into the American Union."[20] Three by-elections to the Dominion Parliament in 1869, in each of which annexation was a major issue, seemed to bear out this statement. Having accepted a post in the Dominion Cabinet, Howe was forced to stand for re-election, which he did in the constituency of Hants. Thereupon, both the annexationists and the confederationists determined to make this electoral contest a test of strength, and both strained every resource to win. The victory went to Howe because his personal prestige was highest in this, his home district, and because the Dominion government supported him with all of its resources in his "Holy War."[21] Even so, the margin of victory was not great.

The excitement in Hants partly obscured significant developments in the two other ridings where by-elections were being held. In Richmond a candidate, reputedly an annexationist, was returned after a canvass which seems to have excited almost no outside interest. The campaign in Yarmouth was more closely watched and contested. The confederationists were most anxious to carry this constituency which was known to contain many annexationists; and there, as in Hants, they raised a large campaign fund and secured aid from the Dominion government.[22] The annexationists nominated Frank Killam, a young merchant, and one of the wealthiest men in the province. Both the banks and every man of means in Yarmouth supported him.[23] The confederationists soon lost hope of defeating him at the polls and planned instead to "work on him" after his election.[24] The results of the polling proved the wisdom of this decision.[25]

9

Their success in two of the three by-elections greatly encouraged the advocates of political union. They were, by this time, numerous enough to control the League of the Maritime Provinces, which had been founded to fight Confederation, and in June, 1869, formally changed it to the Annexation League. This action was accompanied by the issuing of a manifesto which made the motivation of the annexationists clear: "Our only hope of commercial prosperity, material development, and permanent peace lies in closer relations with the United States. Therefore be it resolved that every legitimate means should be used by members of this convention to sever our connections with Canada and to bring about a union on fair and equitable terms with the American Republic."[26]

While these political unionists were fairly numerous, their strength, geographically and socially, was not uniformly distributed throughout the province. The movement apparently was strongest in the southern part of Nova Scotia, particularly about Yarmouth. This area was a centre for the fishing industry which wanted free access to American markets and hoped to attract capital from the United States.[27] The north-eastern portion of the province, including the adjacent counties of Cape Breton Island, also had numerous advocates of annexation. The coal industry of this area wanted duty-free entry into the United States; such a privilege, mine operators estimated, would increase their annual sales in that market from 200 000 to 11 million tons a year.[28] This industry had prospered during the years of the Reciprocity Treaty of 1854; now it was in the depths of depression, with thousands out of work.[29] Reopening of the American market, preferably on a permanent basis, seemed to be the only hope for restoring and maintaining prosperity. Finally, the commercial cities of the province, especially Halifax, contained many advocates of annexation. They were supplied mostly by the trading and shipping industries, which were then in a serious decline and were particularly anxious to qualify for participation in the lucrative American coasting trade, open only to citizens of the United States.[30]

It is also important to note that the movement in all centres was strongest among the more important economic classes in the province: merchants, ship captains, seamen, commission men, coal operators, and miners.[31] The moneyed interests of Nova Scotia, who had invested capital in the enterprises which would benefit from annexation, financed the movement.[32]

This agitation, however, began to decline as early as 1869 and was a thing of the past by 1872. The first defections took place in the coal region where the annexationist tide began to ebb in December, 1869, and soon disappeared.[33] The agitation was more persistent in southern Nova Scotia but there, also, its strength steadily waned. The *Yarmouth Herald*, most intransigent of the annexationist papers, sounded the death knell in December, 1870, when it declared that the time was not ripe for political union with the United States.[34]

10

The causes for this decline are not far to seek. As distress and depression had built up the annexation movement, so returning prosperity tore out its foundations. Exports from Canada to the United States, which had reached their nadir in 1867, were strongly reviving. The fisheries, after the complete failures of 1866 and 1867, yielded abnormal catches from 1869 to 1873, and the Treaty of Washington brought a new day of prosperity for the Maritime Provinces by admitting Canadian fish duty-free into the United States. At the same time, exports of coal from Nova Scotia increased greatly. The mine operators reaped heavy profits and were able to employ more men.[35] Finally, the annexationists of Nova Scotia realized that the British government would not stand idly by and see that province secede from the Dominion and join the United States. It seemed that an appeal to force would be necessary, and that it would be bound to fail unless the United States strongly assisted it. When it became apparent that there was no hope of such help, the political union agitation received its *coup de grâce*.[36]

Thus disappeared one of the strongest and most interesting of the Canadian annexation movements. Like most of them, it was born of discontent and it died when the conditions which produced that discontent had disappeared. Unlike most of the others, however, it had considerable and outspoken support and some financial backing. Indeed, for a time, it caused genuine alarm to the loyal majority in the province.

NOTES

[1] Public Archives of Canada (hereafter, P.A.C.), Howe Papers, vol. 26, pt. 1, Miscellaneous Papers on Confederation, 152–54.

[2] The normal annual income of the province, $1 500 000, would be reduced to $750 000 according to the *Yarmouth* (Nova Scotia) *Tribune*, June 27, 1866.

[3] Howe Papers, vol. 4, Letters to Howe, 1864–1873, Instructions to Howe from the League of the Maritime Provinces, July 5, 1866.

[4] British Parliament, *Accounts and Papers*, 1867, no. 48, 14–15, Howe to Lord Carnarvon, London, Jan. 19, 1867.

[5] *Yarmouth Tribune*, May 22 and Dec. 11, 1867 and Jan. 5, 1869.

[6] *Saint John* (New Brunswick) *Morning Freeman*, Sept. 7, 1868.

[7] P.A.C., Macdonald Papers, Nova Scotia Affairs, vol. 1, Lieutenant-Governor Hastings-Doyle to Sir John A. Macdonald, Halifax, Dec. 31, 1867, and P.S. Hamilton to Macdonald, Halifax, Feb. 24, 1868.

[8] P.A.C., Series G 573 A, Secret and Confidential Despatches, 1867–1869, Lord Monck to the Duke of Buckingham, Feb. 13, 1867.

[9] Howe Papers, vol. 37, Howe Letter Book, Howe to A. Musgrove, Halifax, Jan. 17, 1868.

[10] Macdonald Papers, Nova Scotia Affairs, vol. 111, Buckingham to Monck, London, June 4, 1868.

[11] *Yarmouth Herald*, June 18, 1868.

[12] Among the papers outspokenly advocating annexation, the most persistent were the *Yarmouth Herald* and the *New Glasgow Eastern Chronicle*. Others, including the *Halifax Morning Chronicle*, were more reserved but discussed annexation favourably. Among the annexationists of whom I have found mention were Marshall, the former chief justice of the province, and Underwood, a member of the Dominion Parliament. Most of the members of the provincial government frequently spoke favourably of annexation, especially Martin Wilkins, the attorney-general and real leader of the Cabinet. His sincerity, however, seems open to some question, for he likewise protested his loyalty to the Empire when questioned by Hastings-Doyle.

[13] Howe Papers, vol. 38, Howe Letter Book, Howe to Livingston, Halifax, Aug. 12, 1868.

[14] *Saint John Morning Freeman*, Aug. 11, 1868.

[15] Macdonald Papers, Nova Scotia Affairs, vol. 1, Hastings-Doyle to Macdonald, Halifax, Sept. 4 and 5, 1868.

[16] Macdonald addressed a repeal convention in Halifax in August, 1868, and promised that Nova Scotia would have better terms of union. Macdonald Papers, Nova Scotia Affairs, vol. 3, Macdonald to Lord Monck, Sept. 4, 1868.

[17] Macdonald Papers, Nova Scotia Affairs, vol. 3, Hastings-Doyle to Macdonald, Halifax, Feb. 25, 1869.

[18] Howe Papers, vol. 4, Letters to Howe, 1861–1873, R. Huntington to Howe, Yarmouth, Dec. 24, 1868.

[19] For typical expressions of this view, see M.N. Jackson to F. Seward, Halifax, Aug. 29, 1868. National Archives of the United States, Consular Despatches to the Department of State, Halifax, vol. 9. See also *Halifax Morning Chronicle*, Sept. 16, 1868, and *New Glasgow Eastern Chronicle*, Jan. 9, 1869.

[20] Macdonald Papers, Nova Scotia Affairs, vol. 2, Howe to Macdonald, Halifax, Oct. 29, 1868 and Nov. 16, 1868.

[21] The expression "Holy War" is Macdonald's. The federal government made 400 appointments to aid Howe in this campaign. See Howe Papers, vol. 4, Letters to Howe, 1864–1873, Macdonald to Howe, Ottawa, Jan. 12, Mar. 8, and Mar. 16, 1869. Also Macdonald Papers, Nova Scotia Affairs, vol. 1, Hastings-Doyle to Macdonald, Halifax, Mar. 5 and 30, 1869.

[22] Macdonald Papers, Nova Scotia Affairs, vol. 3, A.W. Savary to Macdonald, Halifax, Dec. 3, 1868. P.A.C., Macdonald Letter Books, vol. 12, Macdonald to Savary, Ottawa, December 14, 1868.

[23] Macdonald Papers, Nova Scotia Affairs, vol. 3, J.A. McClellan to Macdonald, Halifax, Feb. 23,1869.

[24] Howe Papers, vol. 38, Howe Letter Book, Howe to Macdonald, Halifax, Mar. 30, 1869. Series G 573 A, Secret and Confidential Despatches, 1867–1869, Young to Granville, Apr. 8, 1869.

[25] Killam had a majority in every district in the riding and, in Yarmouth County, polled 1220 votes to 598 for his opponent. *Saint John Morning Freeman*, Apr. 22, 1869.

[26] *Saint John Morning Freeman*, June 24, 1869.

[27] *Yarmouth Herald*, Apr. 15, 1869 and Apr. 14, 21, 26, and 30, 1870.

[28] *New Glasgow Eastern Chronicle*, Nov. 25, 1869.

[29] *Boston Daily Advertiser*, Oct. 17, 1868.

[30] Series G 573 A, Secret and Confidential Despatches 1867–1869, Young to Granville, Apr. 8, 1869.

[31] Secret and Confidential Despatches 1867–1869, Young to Granville, Apr. 8, 1869.

[32] Macdonald Papers, Nova Scotia Affairs, vol. 3, J. McClellan to Macdonald, Halifax, Feb. 23, 1869.

[33] The last annexation meeting in the region seems to have taken place in Feb., 1870. *Yarmouth Tribune*, Feb. 9, 1870.

[34] *Yarmouth Herald*, Dec. 5, 1870.

[35] *Saint John Morning Freeman*, Nov. 13, 1869.

[36] There were annexationists in the United States, but they were in the minority and very few of them were willing to fight Great Britain in order to obtain Canada or any part of it. See L.B. Shippee, *Canadian-American Relations, 1849–1874* (New Haven, Toronto, and London, 1939).

11

British Columbia Becomes Canadian (1871–1901)*

WALTER N. SAGE

In an impassioned speech against federation delivered in the Legislative Council of British Columbia in March, 1870, Dr. John Sebastian Helmcken uttered these prophetic words:

> No union between this Colony and Canada can permanently exist, unless it be to the mutual and pecuniary advantage of this Colony to remain in the union. The sum of the interests of the inhabitants is the interest of the Colony. The people of this Colony have, generally speaking, no love for Canada; they care, as a rule, little or nothing about the creation of another Empire, Kingdom, or Republic; they have but little sentimentality and care little about the distinctions between the forms of Government of Canada and the United States.
>
> Therefore no union on account of love need be looked for. The only bond of union outside of force — and force the Dominion has not — will be the material advantage of the country and the pecuniary benefit of the inhabitants. Love for Canada has to be acquired by the prosperity of the country, and from our children.[1]

12

The last four words are more than prophetic. They are a stroke of genius! Probably in his old age the good doctor was fated to hear the schoolchildren of British Columbia singing:

> Our fair Dominion now extends
> From Cape Race to Nootka Sound.

The children and children's children were in the process of becoming Canadians. It was not a speedy evolution. At Confederation British Columbians were *not* Canadians. By 1901 Canadianism had spread and penetrated the province. But there were still many in the older age groupings who remembered the colonial period and were still definitely British Columbians. The youngsters were Canadians, but Canadians with a difference. The barrier of the Rocky Mountains had conditioned them. Their outlook was towards the Pacific and not towards the Atlantic nor even towards Hudson Bay. They were not well acquainted with Ontario and knew little of the prairies or the Maritimes, and probably still less about Quebec. None the less they were becoming increasingly conscious that they were a part of Canada.

*From *Queen's Quarterly* 52 (1945): 168–83. Reprinted by permission of the editors.

Dr. Helmcken was right. Love for Canada was at first not a spontaneous or a natural growth in British Columbia. It did not spring from the native soil of the province as did love for British Columbia. In the colonial days and even for a time after Confederation "Canadians" were unpopular. They were known as "North American Chinamen" — a tribute to their thrift. They sent their money home and did not spend it so freely as did the open-handed Americans. But British Columbia could not thrive without the aid of the rest of Canada. She was cut off from American markets by the tariff laws of the United States. Until the completion of the Canadian Pacific Railway in 1885 there was no direct link through Canadian territory between the Coast and Eastern Canada. It is true that during the critical years from 1866 to 1871 British Columbia might have followed "Manifest Destiny" and as the Territory of Columbia have become a weaker edition of Washington Territory — weaker because, in spite of her huge expanse, she had a smaller and more widespread population. But British Columbia had made her decision. She would remain British even though it entailed paying the high price of becoming Canadian. The only other course open to her was to remain a bankrupt British colony on the edge of nowhere!

13

A glance at the early history of the British colonies on the Northwest Coast and especially at the so-called critical period between 1866 and 1871 will show that British Columbia was much more British and American in outlook than it was Canadian. In fur-trading days before 1849 there was relatively little Canadian influence. There had been some when the North West Company was operating west of the Rockies, but the union of 1821 left the Hudson's Bay Company in complete control. Very few of the company's officers were from Canada, although there were many French-Canadians among the *voyageurs*. The Colony of Vancouver Island was a British, not a Canadian, venture. The gold-seekers of 1858 were from California. A few of them were Canadians who had been attracted to the placer mines of the Golden State and were now following the paystreak north. The miners' meetings stemmed from California and even "Ned McGowan's War" had its roots in the troubles between the Vigilantes and the Law and Order Group, rival California organizations, members of which had come north to Fraser River.[2] The United States was omnipresent. The British Isles were half the world away, and Canada, although geographically nearer than Great Britain, was even farther away in spirit. There was a sentimental tie with the Mother Country but as yet practically none with Canada. Joseph Despard Pemberton, former Colonial Surveyor, in a letter to the Victoria *British Colonist* early in 1870, summed up the situation neatly in verse:

True Loyalty's to Motherland
And not to Canada,
The love we bear is second-hand
To any step-mama.

At first sight it would seem that American influences preponderated in British Columbia. The economic tie was with California, and this tie remained until the completion of the Canadian Pacific Railway. As the late Marcus Lee Hansen has penetratingly observed:

> The new province of British Columbia, although firmly attached to the empire by political, naval and military bonds, was in commerce and population a part of the Pacific region which had its center at San Francisco.[3]

Hansen also states that

> Fully three-fourths of the fifteen thousand miners who in 1864 made up the principal element in the population were Americans, and half of the business houses were branches of American establishments.[4]

14 The only regular steamship communication which British Columbia possessed with the outside world was by American vessels.[5] The express companies were of American origin, although local express was carried by British Columbian companies which maintained American connections. Postal service was through San Francisco. It was necessary for letters posted in British Columbia, destined for Great Britain, Canada, the United States, or elsewhere, to bear United States stamps in addition to their local postage. Governor Musgrave protested against this practice, but it was found impossible to change it.[6] Telegraph service with San Francisco, by way of Portland, Oregon, was established in 1865. The completion of the Union Pacific Railroad in 1869 provided British Columbia, through San Francisco, with railway connections with the Atlantic seaboard, and put an end to travel by the tedious, and often dangerous, Panama route.

From California the mining frontier spread eastward and northward to Nevada, Utah, Colorado, Wyoming, Montana, Idaho, and British Columbia. The gold rushes of 1858 to Fraser River and of 1862 to Cariboo stemmed from San Francisco. Later rushes to Omineca, the Stikine, Cassiar, and finally to Atlin and the Klondike were closely connected with California. Mining methods in British Columbia were similar to those in vogue in California, and the miners who came north were accustomed to "frontier justice." In British Columbia, however, they found Judge Begbie, but not "Judge Lynch."

American influences were economic, and, to a less degree, social and cultural. British influences were political and institutional and also social and religious. The political and legal structure of British Columbia was entirely British. The colonial governors were all of British origin. Most of the government officials had been born in the British Isles. In the Legislative Council of British Columbia, which in 1870 discussed terms of union with Canada, the majority had come from the Motherland.

The Royal Navy was another link with "Home." The part played by the Special Detachment of the Royal Engineers in the early development of the Crown Colony of British Columbia is too well known to demand more than a passing reference. The Church of England was also a link with the Mother Country. Bishop Hills, the first Bishop of Columbia, was consecrated in Westminster Abbey and set apart for his work in the far-off colony. In 1860 he arrived in Victoria, where he diligently upheld the traditions and dignity of his Church, but was unable to secure its establishment as the State Church of the colony. The first Presbyterian ministers came from Ireland, but the "Scottish Kirk" flourished under their ministrations, and for many years retained a close connection with the Established Church of Scotland. The Roman Catholics and the Methodists, on the other hand, had Canadian connections. The first Roman Catholic priests came from Canada to the Columbia in the 1830's, and later in the 1840's came north to Fort Victoria and the Fraser River. The Methodists were sent from Canada, in the late 1850's, to establish a mission in British Columbia.

15

Canadian influences were at first relatively weak, but they strengthened as the battle for Confederation was fought. The leading Confederationists were chiefly British North Americans: for example, Amor De Cosmos, John Robson, Dr. R.W.W. Carrall, Francis J. Barnard, and J. Spencer Thompson. Some Englishmen — for example, Robert Beaven and Alfred Waddington — also joined the cause of federation. George A. Walkem was Irish by birth but Canadian by adoption. Many of the Confederationist leaders had come to British Columbia by way of California. Their sojourn in the United States had, apparently, not dulled their affection for British institutions, but had strengthened rather than weakened their determination that British Columbia should join Canada.

A mining population is notoriously unstable. It is a case of "Here to-day and gone to-morrow." As a rule the American gold-seekers returned to the United States when they had "made their pile" or had become disgusted with the "Fraser River humbug." It was the British and the Canadians who remained and settled down in Cariboo, along the lower Fraser River, or on Vancouver Island. Unfortunately it is not possible to make an accurate check of the birthplace of British Columbians before 1871.[7] Some idea of the national origins of British Columbians at that date may, however, be obtained from a study of J.B. Kerr's *Biographical Dictionary of Well-Known British Columbians*, published in Vancouver in 1890. Of the 242 names listed in this publication, 178 were resident in British Columbia in 1871. An analysis of their birthplaces is rather enlightening: *British Isles*, 94, divided as follows: England, 57; Scotland, 21; Ireland, 16. *Dominion of Canada*: 45, — Nova Scotia, 7; New Brunswick, 3; Prince Edward Island, 1; Quebec, 5; Ontario, 29.[8] *British Columbia*, 7; *Other British possessions*, 5; United States, 12; Other Foreign Countries, 14; no birthplace, 1.

These figures clearly show that British Columbia was *British* in the broadest sense of the term. The Americans had come and gone. The British, including the Canadians, remained.

In the Canadianization of British Columbia from 1871 to 1901 three phenomena are clearly observable: political development, the building of the Canadian Pacific Railway, and the arrival as settlers of large numbers of Eastern Canadians. It must not be thought that British and American influences did not continue to be strong. What happened was that Canadian influence strengthened, especially after the completion of the Canadian Pacific Railway. The period divides naturally at 1886. The first regular transcontinental passenger train from Montreal arrived at Port Moody on July 4th of that year. Vancouver came into existence in April, and was burnt to ashes in June. But nothing could daunt the future Canadian metropolis of the West Coast. It arose triumphantly from its ashes and five years later had a population of 13 709 as compared with Victoria's 16 841. The census of 1901 showed that Vancouver had already surpassed Victoria in population — 29 432 as against 20 919.[9] Since Victoria was the centre of the British-born (natives of the British Isles), Vancouver's rapid advance was a sign of Canadianization. The roots of its people strike deep into Eastern Canada.

The political phase of Canadianization is concerned chiefly with the establishment of the provincial government and with the relations existing between the Lieutenant-Governor of British Columbia and the Government of Canada. Before federation British Columbia had possessed representative but not responsible government. Her political education was, therefore, not so far advanced as that of the eastern provinces. On the other hand, British Columbia had been the only Crown Colony west of the Great Lakes, and was rather more experienced than Manitoba in the art of self-government. Yet British Columbians in 1871 were still politically immature.

The Terms of Union with Canada provided for "the introduction of Responsible Government when desired by the Inhabitants of British Columbia."[10]

It was not, however, until after the first provincial elections had been held in October, 1871, that Lieutenant-Governor Joseph William Trutch could claim to have "established a Responsible Cabinet."[11] Actually, it may be doubted whether responsible government was fully established during the régime of John Foster McCreight, the first Premier of British Columbia. McCreight was a distinguished lawyer, Irish by birth, who had no previous political experience. Probably Trutch selected him because he was "a 'safe' man, one whom the Lieutenant-Governor could direct and guide."[12] Trutch virtually ruled British Columbia during the McCreight régime, 1871–1872. When Amor de Cosmos became premier in December, 1872, Trutch found his power challenged. De Cosmos, with his Nova Scotian tradition and his long political experience in British Columbia, was not prepared to yield the reins of power to any Lieutenant-

Governor, even though he had once held office in colonial days as Chief Commissioner of Lands and Works.

Trutch was in a unique position as regards Ottawa. He considered himself the accredited representative of the federal government in British Columbia. His letters to Sir John A. Macdonald and Macdonald's replies clearly indicate that he was definitely the *liaison* officer between Ottawa and Victoria during the period from July 20th to November 14th, 1871, that is, until the McCreight ministry was formally constituted. The real difficulty was that Trutch did not hand over full authority to McCreight. In his analysis of the situation, R.E. Gosnell saw very clearly:

> During the transition from Crown Colony government to Provincial autonomy there was a brief interregnum in which it was necessary for him [Trutch] to administer affairs on his own initiative, but he continued this rule much longer than was necessary, or than was constitutionally defensible.[13]

17

Part of Trutch's difficulties arose from his selection of McCreight as premier. Neither he nor McCreight had any real acquaintance with responsible government. The leading opponents of Trutch and McCreight — Amor De Cosmos and John Robson — possessed this experience. Either of them could, in all probability, have headed a real responsible ministry. In a rather pathetic passage in a letter to Sir John A. Macdonald, Trutch unburdened himself as follows:

> I am so inexperienced and indeed we all are in this Province in the practice of Responsible Govt. that we are initiating that I step as carefully and guardedly as I can — and whilst teaching others I feel constantly my own extreme need of instruction on this subject — which must account to you — if you please — for the trouble which I have put you to — and which I know I ought not to have imposed on you.[14]

De Cosmos, for his part, roundly denounced the Trutch-McCreight combination in an appeal addressed to "the Liberals of the Province":

> To rally round their old leaders — the men who have year after year fought their battles and have in no instance deserted the popular cause. To take any other course is to convict themselves of Treason to manhood, Treason to the Liberal party, that year by year for fourteen years have urged Responsible Government, Union of the Provinces, and Confederation with the Dominion. It is no Treason, no public wrong to ignore the nominees of Governor Trutch.[15]

The reference to the "Liberal party" is extremely interesting. Actually there were no political parties, in the federal sense of the term, in British Columbian provincial politics until 1903, when Richard McBride announced the formation of a Conservative ministry. De Cosmos, in his federal career, supported Macdonald and Mackenzie in turn. It is noteworthy, however, that as early as 1871 he could make his appeal to the "Liberals."

By the Terms of Union, British Columbia was entitled to three senators and six members of the House of Commons. The senators were Dr. R.W.W. Carrall, Clement F. Cornwall and W.J. Macdonald. Carrall was from Ontario, but the other two senators were born in the British Isles. The six Members of Parliament were J. Spencer Thompson, Hugh Nelson, Robert Wallace, Henry Nathan, Amor De Cosmos, and Charles F. Houghton. Two of them, Thompson and De Cosmos, both Canadians, had been prominent Confederationists. In Ottawa all six were classed as supporters of the Macdonald administration.

In the federal elections of 1872 Sir Francis Hincks was elected by acclamation for Vancouver Island. Six years later, in the well-known National Policy election, Sir John A. Macdonald, defeated in Kingston, Ontario, was elected for Victoria City. His colleague was Amor De Cosmos.

18

During the Macdonald régime from 1878 to 1891 the British Columbian Members of Parliament were Conservatives. They gave their political allegiance to the party which had promised to build the transcontinental railway. It must be confessed that, with the exception of Amor De Cosmos, the British Columbians do not seem to have played any large part at Ottawa. But their presence there showed that the Pacific province was part of the Canadian federation.

As has been noted, federal parties as such took no part in provincial politics until 1903. Political divisions in the provincial area were local rather than national. Until the population of the Mainland had surpassed that of Vancouver Island the division was Mainland vs. Island. But local issues in the 1870's and early 1880's were closely intertwined with the all-important railway question.

The greatest single Canadianizing force in British Columbia during the period 1871 to 1901 was the Canadian Pacific Railway. Its construction had been promised in the Terms of Union. Delay in carrying out those terms almost led to the secession of British Columbia from the Canadian federation in 1878. The change of government in 1873 and the attitude of the Mackenzie administration were largely responsible for this delay, but there is no denying that George A. Walkem in British Columbia made political capital out of the difficult situation. The return of Sir John A. Macdonald and the Conservatives to power in 1878 put an end to the secession movement and led to the chartering of the new company which built the railway. Over that railway from 1886 to 1901 came thousands of eastern Canadians who were to become the cement binding British Columbia more closely to the rest of the Dominion.

The well-known story of the building of the Canadian Pacific Railway need not here be retold. Its terminus was fixed at Port Moody, not Esquimalt. The so-called "Island section of the main line" became the Esquimalt and Nanaimo Railway, constructed not by the Canadian Pacific Railway Company, but by Robert Dunsmuir, the "coal king" of Vancouver Island, and the "Big Four" of the Southern Pacific Railway — Collis P. Huntingdon, Mark Hopkins, Leland Stanford, and Charles Crocker. The Yellowhead Pass route through the Rocky Mountains was abandoned in favour of the Kicking Horse. In 1887 the "branch" line from Port Moody to Vancouver was built.

From the vantage-point of nearly three-quarters of a century after the event the real wonder is that the railway was ever built at all. The total population of the Dominion, including Prince Edward Island, in 1871 was 3 689 257. Of this total 25 228 are listed for Manitoba, 36 247 for British Columbia, and 48 000 for the Northwest Territories.[16] The white population of Western Canada was probably short of 25 000. The four "original provinces" of Eastern Canada had a population of 3 225 761. It was a tremendous undertaking for Canada to build a transcontinental railway, and it is not surprising that others than Edward Blake had misgivings. But Sandford Fleming blazed the trails before the Canadian Pacific Railway Company was formed and that great group of railway builders who made up the new company built the road. James J. Hill withdrew from the directorate in 1883 when it became evident that the company was determined to build the Lake Superior section. Hill then began to plan the Great Northern Railway, which would invade the prairies and southern British Columbia.

The completion of the main line in 1886 did not, however, end the activities of the Canadian Pacific Railway in British Columbia. There was American competition to be faced, especially in the Kootenays and the Boundary country. In the 1880's and early 1890's the chief American competition was the Northern Pacific Railway, but in the late 1890's the Great Northern had seriously invaded the field. The Canadian Pacific Railway began to buy up, or lease, local lines in the Kootenays, especially the Columbia and Kootenay, the Columbia and Western, and the British Columbia Southern. Eventually the south line of the Canadian Pacific from Lethbridge, Alberta, through Crowsnest Pass and through the Kootenays and Boundary country was completed in 1916 by the construction of the Kettle Valley Railway. By that time the Great Northern had been worsted. The Trail smelter, which originally had been an American venture, was in the hands of the Consolidated Mining and Smelting Company of Canada, a subsidiary of the Canadian Pacific Railway. Thus did Canadian interests triumph over American in the Kootenays.

For many years there was a story current in British Columbia that an old-timer in Victoria addressed a newcomer from Eastern Canada as follows: "Before you Canadians came, you know, we never had to take the shutters down till ten o'clock." Whether apocryphal or not, the tale illustrates the clash between the early settlers, who usually had come from the British Isles, and the rather more hustling and energetic "Canadians." On the whole, this clash was more in evidence on Vancouver Island than on the Mainland. Cariboo had never been so "English" as Victoria, and the lower Fraser Valley after 1886 rapidly absorbed the newcomers from "the East." Vancouver was, *par excellence*, the Mecca of the men and women from Ontario and the Maritimes.

In a study of this sort there is no accurate yardstick by which the growth of Canadianism can be measured. Still, it is possible to detect certain tendencies. In 1871 Canadians in British Columbia had made their presence felt. Many of them had come from California during the early gold rushes. Others had come direct to British Columbia by way of Panama and San Francisco. One devoted band — "The Argonauts of 1862" — had come "the plains across" through British Territory from Fort Garry. But it was not until after the completion of the Canadian Pacific Railway that eastern Canadians came in large numbers to "the West beyond the West."

During the decade from 1871 to 1881 the population of British Columbia increased from 36 247 to 49 459. Manitoba's went up from 25 228 to 62 260. The next decade, 1881 to 1891, witnessed an increase in British Columbia from 49 459 to 98 173, but Manitoba shot up from 62 260 to 152 506. British Columbia from 1891 to 1901 increased from 98 173 to 178 657 and Manitoba from 152 506 to 255 211.[17] But even as late as 1901 British Columbia possessed only 3.33 per cent of Canada's total population. In 1901 only 12.02 per cent of Canadians lived west of the Ontario–Manitoba border. The proportion in 1941 was 28.30 per cent, roughly 3 250 000 out of 11 500 000.

The first Census of Canada contained figures dealing only with the four "original provinces." It was not until the 1880–1881 Census that information was published regarding Manitoba, British Columbia, and Prince Edward Island. The population of British Columbia is given as 49 459. According to birthplace this number was made up as follows:[18]

Born in British Columbia		32 175
Born in the British Isles		5 783
English	3 294	
Irish	1 285	
Scottish	1 204	
Born in other parts of Canada		2 768
Prince Edward Island	23	
Nova Scotia	379	
New Brunswick	374	
Quebec	396	
Ontario	1 572	
Manitoba	24	
Born in The Territories		14
Born in other British Possessions		211
Born in the United States		2 295
Born in other countries and at sea		5 462
Birthplace not given		751
Total		**49 459**

20

The Third Census of Canada, 1890–91, gave the population of British Columbia as 98 173, but apparently gave no statistics as regards the birthplaces of the people. It did, however, provide information regarding the numbers born in Canada and in foreign countries. In British Columbia 37 583 are classed as native, born of a native father; 19 268 as native, born of a foreign father; and 41 322 as foreign-born.[19] In this census, as in the previous one, the native Indians of British Columbia are included in the native-born totals. No attempt has been made to separate white men and Indians.

It is from the Fourth Census of Canada, 1900–1901, that most information is obtained regarding racial origins, nationalities, and the birthplaces of the people. The population of British Columbia was now 178 657. According to racial origins, 106 403 were of British birth (English, 52 863; Irish, 20 658; Scottish, 31 068), 25 488 were Indians, 532 Negroes, 19 482 Chinese and Japanese, and the remainder of continental European origins or "unspecified." On the basis of nationality, 144 989 are classed as Canadian, 10 088 as American, 14 201 as Chinese, 3516 as Japanese and the remainder from the continent of Europe. But it is Table 13 [of the Fourth Census] — "Birthplaces of the People" — which best tells the story. Of the 99 612 listed as born in Canada, 59 589 were born in British Columbia; 2203 in Manitoba; 2839 in New Brunswick; 4603 in Nova Scotia; 23 642 in Ontario; 1180 in Prince Edward Island; 4329 in Quebec; 991 in the North West Territories; and 236 in "Canada not given." The total of those born in the British Isles was 30 630 distributed as follows: English, 19 385; Irish, 3957; Scottish, 6457; Welsh, 710; Lesser Isles, 121. From the other British Possessions had come 1843. The foreign-born totalled 46 110, of whom 17 164 were from the United States.

From the statistics given above it is obvious that by 1901 the Canadianization of British Columbia was fairly well complete. A new generation had grown up west of the Rockies since 1871. No matter where their parents came from these young people were Canadians. To be sure, they were British Columbian Canadians, not quite the same as Canadians from the other provinces, nevertheless Canadians. Many of them were destined to prove their loyalty to Canada and to the British Empire in 1914. By 1901 east and west in Canada were really joined and "the West beyond the West" had become Canadian.

21

NOTES

[1] *Debate on the Subject of Confederation with Canada* (Victoria, 1878), 13.

[2] On this subject see F.W. Howay, *The Early History of the Fraser River Mines* (Victoria, 1926), viii–xvii.

[3] Marcus Lee Hansen and J. Bartlet Brebner, *The Mingling of the Canadian and American Peoples* (New Haven, 1940), 155.

[4] Hansen and Brebner, *The Mingling of the Canadian and American Peoples*, 155.

[5] For a discussion of this topic, see F.W. Howay, W.N. Sage, and H.F. Angus, *British Columbia and the United States* (Toronto: Ryerson, 1942), 184–86.

[6] Cf. A.S. Deaville, *The Colonial Postage Systems and Postage Stamps of Vancouver Island and British Columbia, 1849–1871*, Archives Memoir no. 8, (Victoria, B.C.: King's Printer, 1928), 137–43.

[7] *The Census of Canada, 1870–1871*, vol. 1, does not give figures for British Columbia. In *The Census of Canada, 1880–1881*, the total population of British Columbia, in 1871, whites, Indians, Chinese, and coloured is given, however, as 36 247. Of this number 25 661 were Indians. Cf. L.T. Marshall, *Vital Statistics of British Columbia* (Victoria, B.C.: Provincial Board of Health, [1932]), 192.

[8] Technically, of course, Prince Edward Island was not part of Canada till 1873, but this seems a hair-splitting distinction.

[9] *Canada Year Book, 1943–1944* (Ottawa: King's Printer, 1944), 125.

[10] *Journals of the Legislative Council of British Columbia, Session 1871* (Victoria, B.C., 1871), 6.

[11] J.W. Trutch to Sir John A. Macdonald, Nov. 21, 1871, P.A.C., Macdonald Papers, Trutch Correspondence, 1871–1873, p. 98.

[12] W.N. Sage, "John Foster McCreight, the first Premier of British Columbia," in the *Transactions of the Royal Society of Canada*, 3rd series, Sec. 2, vol. 34, (1940), 177.

[13] E.O.S. Scholefield and R.E. Gosnell, *British Columbia: Sixty Years of Progress* (Vancouver and Victoria, 1913), pt. 11, p. 15, n. 1.

[14] P.A.C., Macdonald Papers, Trutch Correspondence, 1871–73, pp. 101–102.

[15] Victoria *Daily Standard*, November 21, 1871.

[16] *Canada Year Book, 1943–44*, 79.

[17] *Canada Year Book, 1943–44*, 79, 80.

[18] *Census of Canada, 1880–1881*, (Ottawa: McLean, Roger & Co., 1882), 1: 396–9, Table 4.

[19] *Census of Canada, 1890–1891* (Ottawa: King's Printer, 1893), 2: 228.

22

The Island and Confederation: The End of an Era*

DAVID WEALE AND HARRY BAGLOLE

How Much for the Island?

... it would simply be selling ourselves for a larger sum, and I would not consent to sell ourselves at all.
James McLaren, Legislative Council, 1865, p. 63

The longer the Island stayed out of Confederation the more money it was offered to go in; and the terms which were finally received by the Island in 1873 were substantially better than those which had been offered in 1864. Consequently, it was possible for the Islanders to enter Confederation thinking of themselves as exceptionally adroit and successful bargainers. Even some of the previously rabid anti-Confederates assumed this attitude, and began to speak as though the events of 1873 had taken place in exact accordance with their long-range plans.

David Laird, for example, had been an opponent of Confederation for several years and had often blasted the scheme in his paper the *Protestant and Evangelical Witness*, and later in the *Patriot*. Nevertheless, when the day finally arrived for the Island to go into Confederation Laird managed to interpret his anti-Confederate role in such a way that he was able to take much of the credit for the generous terms. In the Assembly in 1873 he commented:

*From *The Island and Confederation: The End of an Era*, by David Weale and Harry Baglole. Copyright 1973 by David Weale. Reprinted by permission.

If it had not been for my opposition to Confederation in years gone by, we would to-day have the old spavined horse which the Hon. Colonial Secretary (T.H. Haviland) was willing to accept, and with that old horse we would now be limping and hobbling along. The eighty cents per head, and the debt equivalent, were all that were granted under the Quebec Scheme, and I am to-day proud that I opposed the scheme. The Better Terms of 1869, I also opposed, and I am glad I did so, as the terms secured by the former delegation were $14,000 better than they were.[1]

Taken at face value this type of statement would seem to indicate that the Islanders had never really been anti-Confederates in principle at all, but were merely shrewd political horse-traders who held out until they received the best possible deal. Donald Creighton, the outstanding Canadian historian, has adopted this interpretation in a recent book. The Island, he suggests, kept on postponing its entry into Confederation " . . . in the vague hope of getting a superlative bargain."[2]

23

Although the discussion of financial arrangements was an important part of the Confederation dispute, it is, nonetheless, a gross over-simplification of the matter to picture the Islanders as a canny and calculating lot whose only concern was to coax as much money as possible out of the Canadian treasury. There may have been a few Islanders who regarded the question in this way, but there were a great many more who made it quite clear that their resistance was not based exclusively — or even primarily — on financial considerations, and was not a tactic for inveigling better terms out of the Federal Government. In short, when the Islanders contemplated the generous terms of 1873 and began to congratulate themselves for being such patient and able negotiators, they were, to a great extent, being wise after the fact.

Throughout most of the period from 1864 to 1873 the majority of Islanders believed that the entry of their "country" into Confederation would necessitate drastic political sacrifices and precipitate many undesirable and far-reaching social changes. Confederation seemed like a "leap in the dark"[3] and many of the residents were uncomfortably aware that the Island just would not be the same afterwards. These fears and misgivings had little to do with the economic aspects of Union. In fact, on many occasions the Islanders emphasised clearly that money matters were of secondary importance.

In the House of Assembly in 1866 Emmanuel MacEachern observed that the terms devised at the Quebec Conference in 1864 were "unjust" to the Island, but added that " . . . the wrong done to us in that respect, would be light indeed when compared with the loss of our liberty — the loss of the power to regulate our own affairs."[4] And Cornelius Howatt, who represented 4th Prince for eighteen consecutive years, advised a public meeting in Summerside that Confederation was not an issue that should be evaluated in terms of pounds, shillings, and pence. He said that "figures could never tell" what scheme would be advantageous to the Island.[5]

Because of the belief that there were issues at stake which transcended economic considerations it was believed by some that the money being offered by Canada was little better than a bribe.[6] It was the "mess of pottage" which was being enticingly offered to separate Islanders from their birthright. Acceptance of terms or "better terms" was, it seemed, equivalent to selling out, and many Islanders were offended by the thought that the Island should have a price-tag on it or that they should be "bartered away to the Ottawa politicians."[7] In the Legislative Council in 1865 the Hon. James McLaren stated:

> . . . even supposing they could get more, or could get better terms — suppose they could get double as much for giving up our constitution and revenue to Canada — I would not consent to it, for it would simply be selling ourselves for a larger sum, and I would not consent to sell ourselves at all. We have a good constitution and let us keep it.[8]

George Beer, another member of the Legislative Council, also viewed the terms being offered by Canada as constituting, in effect, a purchase price. "Let the proposed Confederation be consummated," he warned, "and the now bountiful and flourishing Island of Prince Edward will be virtually sold to a large, extravagant absentee Proprietor named Canada."[9]

Beer knew what he was doing when he attempted to discredit Confederation by comparing it with the proprietary land system. For a period of one hundred years the Island community had chafed under the burden of absentee ownership and control. They had learned to despise the feelings of indignity and subservience which the system fostered, and were extremely reluctant to enter Confederation and find themselves in a comparable situation. They were afraid that if they accepted terms — which included funds to buy up the proprietor's lands — the Canadians might assume that they had "bought"[10] the Island, and there was little desire in the Colony to exchange one set of absentee landlords for another.

The belief that no set of terms, however handsome, could adequately compensate the Island for what it would lose by joining Confederation received formal expression in the Assembly in 1866 when Premier J.C. Pope introduced his famous "no terms" resolutions. The second of these resolutions stated adamantly that no terms of Union could possibly be devised " . . . that would prove advantageous to the interests and well-being of the people of the Island."[11]

Pope claimed that the extremity of these resolutions represented the true mood of the Island population, and the accuracy of his claim was confirmed during the spring and summer of that same year when public meetings right across the Island came out strongly and unequivocally against Confederation. Most Islanders at the time seemed to be in agreement with Assemblyman Francis Kelly who said regarding Pope's "no terms" resolutions that "if they could be made stronger, I would wish that they were."[12] Moreover, there was little in the sentiments expressed at the time which would suggest that the "no terms" position was in any way hypocritical. If it was a ploy, and if the Islanders were secretly looking forward to receiving a better deal later on, then they certainly disguised their true motives with consummate skill.

The "no terms" attitude was widespread on the Island until at least the early 1870's, and there were some who adhered unflinchingly to this position until the entry of the Island into Confederation in 1873. Moreover, neither the offer made to the Island in 1866, nor the terms proposed in 1869, did very much to change the Islanders' minds. And although the Colony experienced some hard times during this period — 1867 being a particularly bad year — there was little evidence of any kind of major swing towards Confederation.

During the election of 1867 the candidates on the hustings strained to outdo one another in their denunciation of Confederation. Liberal candidate S.F. Perry, in an address delivered in St. Eleanors, claimed that he "would die before surrendering to any foreign state our liberties and sacred privilege of self-government."[13] Later in the speech, apparently having forgotten that he had already said he would die in the defence of the Island's independence, Perry pledged that if Confederation came to the Island he "would sell out and emigrate to some other land."[14] In 1867 — despite the $800,000 offer of 1866 — these defiantly anti-Confederate pronouncements were still pleasing to the public ear.

The response of Islanders to the "better terms" of 1869 revealed that the "no terms" attitude, though perhaps less universal than it had been in 1866-67, was still extremely widespread. The anti-Confederates in the Assembly pointed out that although the latest terms were better monetarily, the scheme was just as threatening politically as it ever had been.[15] The members of the Legislative Council echoed these sentiments. Furthermore, amongst the population generally the "no terms" attitude was, if anything, even stronger than amongst the politicians. Several of the speeches made at a public meeting in Summerside in January, 1870, ended with the resolution that " . . . our representatives be requested to oppose Confederation on any terms,"[16] and during the debates of the Legislative Council in that same year, A.A. MacDonald reported that " . . . the verdict expressed at the public meetings in almost every settlement of the Island is that the people are opposed to the terms recently offered to us and, in fact, to the whole scheme of Confederation as far as it has reference to this Island."[17] Furthermore, as late as March, 1871, Lieutenant-Governor Robinson wrote in a memo that " . . . nine-tenths of the people are opposed to Confederation on almost any terms."[18]

Evidence of this type is difficult to reconcile with an interpretation which views the period from 1864 to 1873 as a time during which the Islanders haggled and dickered their way towards Confederation. The

25

evidence suggests, rather, that prior to 1873 a large portion of the Island population had little or no interest in discussing or negotiating terms. On those occasions when terms were offered, the Island people were, of course, obliged to consider them. However, during the intervals between these offers Islanders were for the most part preoccupied with more immediate local concerns. Apart from a small handful of pro-Confederates who were busily working behind the scenes to effect Confederation, Islanders had no desire to maintain a seat at the bargaining table or to keep the talks open. They were disposed, rather, to "hug"[19] their isolation in the hope that they could " . . . yet enjoy many a long year of isolated blessedness."[20] And when, in 1873, it finally became necessary for the Government of the Island to break this policy of isolationism and send a delegation to Ottawa to discuss terms, many Islanders were dismayed that such a course of action had finally become necessary.

It would be a mistake to suggest that the Islanders' response to the various offers and overtures was determined solely by "principle" and had nothing whatever to do with their pocketbooks. They were, of course, worried about terms, taxation, tariffs, and the prospect of having to help pay for the railways and canals of the "extravagant" Canadians. But that was by no means all that concerned them. They were also worried about their political institutions and traditions, and even about such sentimental and intangible matters as the identity and honour of the Island as an independent community, and the necessity of preserving the way of life which had evolved there.

These latter issues were mentioned at least as often as the economic aspects of Union — and generally with greater ardor. And while it is impossible to isolate the various ingredients of the Confederation debate so as to assess precisely their relative importance, it would appear that at its centre the anti-Confederation movement was not based on economic considerations, but rather on the Islanders' desire to maintain their established practice of looking after their own affairs in their own way.

If the Islanders had not been economically self-sufficient it would have been more difficult for them to behave as they did, and they undoubtedly would have expressed a much greater and earlier interest in procuring lucrative terms. The Colony was by no means wealthy, but because Islanders realized that they were capable of providing for themselves, and because they were generally contented with their way of life, they were for a time able to stand on their principles and declare that they would not barter away their independence for any amount of Canadian money.

Confederation: The End of an Era

We have sold our noble little ship and she now stands stripped of all the glory with which for one hundred years she was adorned.
A.E.C. Holland, Assembly Debates, *1873, p. 230.*

Confederation Terms!

THE subscriber has on hand a few barrels of

Prime Herring,

for family use, which he offers **CHEAP** for **CASH**,
previous to the Island entering the Dominion ! !
JAMES CALDWELL.
Summerside, Jan. 6, 1870.

During the late 1860's and early 1870's a kind of creeping fatalism was eating away at the Island's opposition to Confederation. The scheme was still tremendously unpopular, but there was a growing feeling that in its attempt to steer clear of Confederation the Island was working against insuperable odds and that, in the end, it would be unable to maintain its solitary course. In its editorial on December 6, 1869, the *Examiner* reported that even those who were most strenuously opposed to Confederation were beginning to say that the Island would "eventually be compelled to accept the Canadian overtures, and link its destiny to the new Dominion."[1] And there was a tone of plaintive resignation in the comments which appeared in the *Argus* on January 2, 1872: "We are sorry," lamented the writer, "that we cannot speak so hopefully of our 'own dear native land.' Our prospects are not so cheering as we could wish them to be."[2]

One of the principal causes of this feeling of futility and fatalism was the disapproving attitude of the British Government. The Mother Country made it quite clear to Islanders that in their attempts to retain an independent Colonial status they were becoming a nuisance and a burden. Various pressure tactics were used by the Home Government in its attempt to bring the headstrong little Colony into line, and soon Islanders became uncomfortably aware that behind the scenes the British Government was relentlessly "turning the screws" for Confederation.

Probably the best example of the manner in which the Home Government frustrated the Colony's efforts to go its own way was an episode which took place in late 1868 and early 1869. In the fall of 1868 the Islanders were tremendously pleased and flattered when the United States Congress sent a special delegation, headed by General Benjamin "The Beast" Butler, a colourful and controversial figure of Civil War fame, to the Island to discuss the possibility of working out some type of mutually beneficial trading agreement. The Reciprocity Treaty between the United States and the British North American Colonies, which had boosted the Island's economy in the late 1850's and early 1860's, had been abrogated in 1865 and Islanders now felt that it would be a tremendous coup if they alone in British North America were able to renegotiate the agreement.

27

The Congressional Delegation received an overwhelmingly enthusiastic welcome. Joseph Hensley, a member of the Assembly from 1st Kings, was pleased that Islanders were being treated "almost as if they were a strong nation,"[3] and Benjamin Davies, a member from 4th Queens, regarded the visit of the Congressional Committee as "one of the greatest honors ever bestowed upon the Colony."[4] The reaction of the editor of the *Examiner* was even more interesting and revealing. For him the visit of the Americans meant:

> . . . that Prince Edward Island is not such a very insignificant place after all. The Senate and House of Representatives of the Great Republic of the world have not considered reciprocity of trade with so small and so obscure a Colony unworthy of their attention. The name of Prince Edward Island has most likely for the first time in their lives been brought to the notice of many of the legislators of the United States. Charlottetown and Washington will be mentioned once more in the one sentence. . . . Well, it is pleasant to find that we are beginning to be of some consequence in the world.[5]

The visit of the Americans was extremely good for the Islanders' sagging morale, and was especially gratifying and reassuring in that it seemed to justify their rejection of Confederation. "We always contended," remarked the *Patriot* with obvious relish, "that so far as Reciprocity was concerned Canada was a drag upon Nova Scotia and Prince Edward Island, and now, we think, that point is settled beyond cavil."[6] And the editor of the *Progress* exultantly informed his readers that the Nova Scotians and New Brunswickers would enviously contemplate the Island's good fortune and say: "Look at Prince Edward Island, they had the good sense to keep aloof from Confederation. Its people now enjoy a free trade while we have it not."[7] For the moment, at least, Islanders were happily savouring their good fortune.

The Butler visit concluded with a "dejeuner" for approximately one hundred persons in the House of Assembly room of the Colonial Building. The banquet hall, it was reported, was "tastefully decorated" with "the folds of the Union Jack of Old England and the Star Spangled Banner of the United States being in a close fraternal embrace."[8] Accounts of the banquet indicated that the mood was extremely convivial, the cuisine sumptuous, the speeches numerous, and the liquor, like grace, sufficient for everyone's needs — one of the participants confessing later that he, "in company with many others, was a little too exhilarated with wine at the late banquet in Charlottetown."[9]

The next day the whirlwind tour ended and the American delegation departed. Islanders had been extremely impressed with their guests, and entertained high hopes that an agreement would soon be reached which would bolster their economy and, in so doing, put to silence those who were saying that they could not possibly survive on their own.

There was, however, one cloud which cast a dark shadow over these expectations. The Islanders realized that the British Government would probably take a dim view of the activities which had taken place and, consequently, a note of defiance began to creep into the tone of their comments. The *Herald*, for example, warned that "It would be very unwise on the part of the Dominion authorities or the Imperial Government to interfere in any way to thwart the movement which is now being made. . . . "[10] And a correspondent to the *Patriot* warned Lieutenant-Governor Dundas that he should not raise any "serious obstructions to a proposal so largely involving our prosperity."[11]

Unfortunately for the Islanders the Imperial authorities were little affected by the raised hackles of the intractable little Colony. On March 13, 1869, Lord Granville, the Colonial Secretary, sent an official despatch which expressed regret that the negotiations had ever taken place, and intimated strongly that the Island Government had impertinently overstepped its proper authority. The Islanders were furious! Reception of the despatch was like a bombshell, and a burst of protest, indignation, and resentment issued from every quarter.

29

It was a moment of supreme frustration for many Islanders, as, in the face of British opposition, they painfully recognized their helplessness. Alexander Laird, a member of the Assembly from 4th Prince, believed that "No Colony has ever been imposed upon as we have — no not even the thirteen colonies that raised the standard of resistance in what formed the nucleus of the great American Republic."[12] Many Islanders were, it seemed, almost angry enough to rebel — but they were not strong enough to give it a second thought. Henry Callbeck expressed the resulting mood of bitterness and pent-up frustration when he said: "We are only submitting to the demand of the British Government because we cannot help ourselves."[13]

The entire Butler affair illustrated clearly the determination of the Islanders to avoid Confederation, as well as the enormous and disheartening difficulties which they faced in attempting to follow that course. It is not surprising that after this setback an increasing number of them experienced the sinking feeling that ultimately they would be compelled to join the Union. The limits of their "independence" had been rudely impressed upon them; and the self-confidence of the community which had been so strong during the previous years had been badly shaken. In April, 1869, the *Examiner* described poignantly the mood which had been created: "The pulse of our Island home beats low," it commented. "From all appearances we will soon cease to exist as a separate Colony."[14]

Yet, in spite of this discouragement, there was still considerable life and spirit remaining in the anti-Confederation cause. It was after the Butler affair that the Island turned down the "better terms" of 1869, and by the beginning of the 1870's it appeared as though the Colony would be able to maintain for many years its position of splendid isolation.

However, in 1871 the Island Government made a decision which, in a very short time, effectively undermined and destroyed the anti-Confederate position.

One of the most ironic facts in all of Island history is that there were Islanders in the early 1870's who believed that the economic and psychological benefits which would result from the construction of a railway would help to keep the Colony out of Confederation. They did not believe that the Island should go on in the "old jig-joy way,"[15] but, rather, that it should "move with the times."[16] Otherwise, they reasoned, Islanders would become envious of the neighbouring provinces and their railroads and want to join Confederation.[17] During the evening of the day that the first Railroad Bill was passed in April, 1871, there was a great torchlight parade which featured, among other attractions, a large flaming "RR" which was held aloft for all to see. The *Examiner* concluded its description of this celebration with the following observation: "In a word it [the Railroad] means that Prince Edward Island feels that she has taken a foremost stand amongst the provinces of British North America, and that she can go on and prosper without any political connection with them further than she now enjoys."[18]

Not everyone held this view. In fact, there were others who were predicting that the construction of a railway would have exactly the opposite effect. They said it would sink the Island into such a deep financial rut that it would become necessary to reach out for the terms being offered by Canada as the only means of escape. Some even suggested that there was a definite "plot" or conspiracy involved, and that certain prominent Confederates were deliberately promoting the railway as a means of getting the Island into Confederation. In their eyes the railway was " . . . an amiable plan for plundering the country to such a point of beggary and misfortune, that even the misrule of Canada would prove a relief."[19]

In April, 1871, a letter to the editor of the *Examiner* captured something of this anti-railroad sentiment, which was extremely strong in certain sections of the Colony. It read:

> . . . I met an old gentleman in Belfast, it was storming dreadfully, he invited me in, and the first words he asked were "Well friend, are they goin' on with the Railroad?" Yes I believe they are. "Oh! They'll ruin the country; it's a scheme of the Popes to get us into Confederation." I said that I heard in town that they instructed their representatives to vote for it. This was too much for my host who used such strong language . . . that I thought he would do something desperate.[20]

Also, about this time the following brief but trenchant conversation was reported to have taken place in the Mink River area:

> "And did you hear are they going on with the Railroad?"
>
> "Yes sir, you will soon see the Iron Horse."
>
> "May they crack their necks."[21]

In spite of the fact that such feelings were expressed in anti-railroad meetings held in many sections of the Island, the Government of Premier J.C. Pope decided to go ahead with the project. In April, 1871, the first Railway Bill received assent; in May tenders were called for; in October the first sod was turned and the crews went to work; in the winter the work proceeded to the accompaniment of a swelling chorus of criticism regarding the shady dealings which appeared to be involved; in April, 1872, a new Government under R.P. Haythorne was formed; in June this new government introduced the Railway Extension Bill which provided for the construction of new branch lines; during the summer work continued; by the fall the Island found itself in severe economic difficulty; and in February, 1873, R.P. Haythorne and David Laird, with railway debts in pocket, embarked for Canada to negotiate regarding the entry of the Island into Confederation. The Island Government had built itself a railway, and the tracks led straight to Ottawa.

The entire incident was something of a fiasco. The planning, contracting, and construction phases were all hastily — and in some cases surreptiously — conducted, and bitter accusations of graft, bribery, and intrigue were flying in every direction throughout the period. This was partly attributable to the fact that by the early 1870's the Island political situation was in a shambles. The parties were not coherent entities, but unstable and heterogeneous coalitions comprised of factions which were divided over such explosive issues as religion, education, Confederation, and the railway. Politicians, and even the newspapers, were sliding around from one political position to another — continually aligning and realigning — in an attempt to discover some winning combination. In November, 1871, the editor of the *Argus* commented:

31

> It can hardly be said that we have pure party government to-day. . . . Now we find on one side an advanced school of Conservatives, anti-Conservatives, Grants and anti-Grant men. On the other side we find Conservatives of the old school, ultra-Liberals, Confederates and antis, Grant and anti-Grant men. The present government can scarcely be said to be a Railroad government. . . . The present opposition cannot claim to be an Anti-railroad party.[22]

Thus, while it has often been said that it was the railway that got the Island into Confederation, the political imbroglio which existed at the time — by muddying the issues, and precluding the possibility of a clear expression of public opinion — was also an important contributing factor.

Although the economic plight which resulted from the construction of the railway was very grim, not all Islanders were prepared to concede that Confederation was the only recourse. Indeed, it is possible that if a plebiscite had been conducted, the entry of the Island into Confederation might have been delayed even longer. There were still a great many unyielding anti-Confederates who were proclaiming that if Islanders put their "shoulders to the wheel"[23] they could surmount their financial difficulties and retain their independence.

However, a great many other Islanders, including the majority of the Island politicians, grudgingly concluded that Confederation had become unavoidable. They would have preferred "to manage their own affairs as in times past,"[24] but were convinced that this was no longer possible. Consequently, the Island's entry into the Union was a faltering and half-hearted step, accompanied by little enthusiasm or fanfare. The Islanders' determination to go their own way had gradually been worn down, and by the time of the railway crisis in 1873 there simply was not enough energy and will left to hold the door shut against Confederation any longer.

The British Government was pleased; the Canadians were pleased; and Lieutenant Governor Robinson, who had worked so hard — and in some instances so deviously — to bring about Confederation on the Island, was extremely pleased. Most of the Islanders themselves, however, simply attempted to put the best possible face on the situation and, in the words of the Halifax *Colonist*, were "determined to show no sulky humour."[25]

Nonetheless, in spite of the attempt to accept their fate graciously, it is clear that for many the entry of the Island into Confederation represented an unfortunate abortion of the Island's historical development. Cornelius Howatt viewed Confederation as an almost tragic end to "one hundred years" of autonomy,[26] and A.E.C. Holland, another stalwart anti-Confederate, commented glumly that Islanders had sold their "noble little ship" and that it was soon to be "stripped of all the glory with which for one hundred years she was adorned."[27] For both these men the coming of Confederation clearly represented not the beginning, but the end of an era.

In the eyes of men like John A. Macdonald and D'Arcy McGee the Confederation of the British North American Colonies into one nation represented a magnificent vision and destiny. However, in the 1860's Prince Edward Islanders had their own vision of what the future should hold, and it was a vision which was in many ways impossible to reconcile with the great Canadian dream. It went against their established habit of thinking to contemplate the absorption of the Island into a larger national unit. As inveterate isolationists, and as participants in a one hundred year old tradition of political independence, they were inclined to think in terms of a far different political destiny for the Island. Thus, although the eventual entry of the Island into Confederation was part of the unfolding of the great Canadian National Dream, it also in many ways represented the disintegration of the Island Dream.

For many years after the coming of Confederation, Islanders continued to look back on the pre-Confederation period — the days of Coles and Whelan[28] — as the golden age in Island history. In this regard it was perhaps symbolic that during the Assembly debates in 1873 a motion was put forward by Premier J.C. Pope for five hundred dollars to be given to George Coles "in recognition of his past services to his country," and also for a grant "to the widow of the late Hon. Edward Whelan, who is in rather poor circumstances."[29] Whelan had died suddenly in 1867, the same year in which Coles had begun to show signs of serious mental deterioration. These men had dominated Island political life throughout much of the 1850's and 1860's, and their names were intimately associated with the progress and growth of these years. The Hon. George Howlan suggested, therefore, that, in addition to the financial aid,

> . . . a monument . . . be erected to George Coles and Edward Whelan, both of whom deserved to be held by their countrymen in grateful remembrance. Such an act on the part of the people would be the means of raising the ambitions of our young men to perform similar deeds for their country.[30]

33

It was somehow fitting that in the year of their Confederation Islanders should have been contemplating the erection of a monument in memory of two Island heroes and a proudly remembered past.

NOTES

How Much for the Island?

[1] Cited in Bolger, *Prince Edward Island and Confederation* (Charlottetown: St. Dunstan University Press, 1964), 281.

[2] Donald Creighton, *Canada's First Century* (Toronto: Macmillan, 1970), 21.

[3] *Patriot*, August 31, 1867.

[4] *Assembly Debates* (1866), 113.

[5] Summerside *Journal*, January 27, 1870.

[6] It was felt that Union should depend on the "free and unbiassed consent and approval of the contracting parties" and that the Island should not enter as a "bribed constituency." *Minutes of the Executive Council*, February 4, 1870.

[7] *Argus*, December 31, 1872.

[8] *Debates of the Legislative Council* (1865), 63.

[9] *Debates of the Legislative Council* (1866), 46.

[10] *Assembly Debates* (1870), 127. (George Howlan).

[11] *Assembly Debates* (1866), 101.

[12] *Assembly Debates* (1866), 101.

[13] Summerside *Progress*, February 25, 1867.

[14] Summerside *Progress*, February 25, 1867.

[15] See Bolger, *Prince Edward Island and Confederation*, 210.

[16] Summerside *Journal*, January 27, 1870.

[17] *Debates of the Legislative Council* (1870), 92.

[18] Cited in Frank MacKinnon, *The Government of Prince Edward Island* (Toronto: University of Toronto Press, 1951), 131.

[19] *Patriot*, September 26, 1867.

[20] *Argus*, May 9, 1971.

Confederation: The End of an Era

[1] *Examiner*, December 6, 1869.

[2] *Argus*, January 2, 1872.

[3] Cited in D.C. Harvey, "Confederation in Prince Edward Island," *Canadian Historical Review* (1933), 158.

[4] *Assembly Debates* (1869), 59–60.
[5] *Examiner*, July 27, 1868.
[6] *Patriot*, July 30, 1868.
[7] Summerside *Progress*, September 7, 1868.
[8] *Patriot*, September 3, 1868.
[9] *Examiner*, September 21, 1868.
[10] *Herald*, July 29, 1868.
[11] "Nor-Wester" to the *Patriot*, August 13, 1868.
[12] *Assembly Debates* (1869), 150.
[13] *Assembly Debates* (1869), 156.
[14] *Examiner*, April 5, 1869.
[15] *Debates of the Legislative Council* (1871), 160. (Colonial Secretary).
[16] *Debates of the Legislative Council* (1871), 176. (W.G. Strong).
[17] *Debates of the Legislative Council* (1871), 176.
[18] *Examiner*, April 17, 1871.
[19] Cited in *Argus*, October 31, 1871.
[20] *Examiner*, April 24, 1871.
[21] *Examiner*, April 17, 1871.
[22] *Argus*, November 28, 1871.
[23] *Assembly Debates* (1873), 37. (Cornelius Howatt).
[24] *Assembly Debates*, (1873), 203. (James Rowe).
[25] Cited in *Argus*, July 15, 1873.
[26] *Assembly Debates* (1873), 38.
[27] *Assembly Debates* (1873), 232.
[28] *Patriot*, December 31, 1887. Also *Examiner*, January 28, 1887.
[29] *Assembly Debates* (1873), 283.
[30] *Assembly Debates* (1873), 284.

Topic Two

The National Policy

Considerable debate has centred on the National Policy since its inception. Why was it implemented? Was it designed to benefit certain classes or regions at the expense of others? To what extent was the policy truly national? Did Canada survive for over a century because or in spite of the National Policy?

John A. Macdonald's Conservative government implemented the National Policy, a policy of tariff protection, in 1879. It imposed a tariff of more than 17½ percent on many manufactured goods coming into the country from the United States. The policy, aimed at stimulating the growth of Canadian industries, appeared to Conservative politicians to be a logical solution to the problem of the depressed Canadian economy in the mid-1870s. Britain had abandoned the mercantile system of trade with her colonies in the late 1840s in favour of free trade, while the United States had adopted its own highly protectionist policy toward Canada after the abrogation of the Reciprocity Treaty in 1866. Certain Canadian leaders, forced to look within for a solution to their problems, believed that a policy of high protection would foster Canadian industrial growth.

The National Policy of tariff protection was part of a broader national policy, one that included the building of a transcontinental railway, and large-scale immigration to the West. The logic went as follows: the railway would promote east–west trade, while the growing population of the West would provide the necessary markets for Canadian manufactured goods and a ready source of raw materials for the growing industries of central Canada. The high tariff would force Canadians to buy Canadian products, thus encouraging industrial growth within the nation. From 1879 to the implementation of the new free-trade agreement with the United States in 1989, our economic policy was largely protectionist.

Craig Brown, in "The Nationalism of the National Policy," explains the policy's popularity in its time by showing it in a larger historical and international context. In "Canada's National Policies," John Dales questions the logic of the National Policy in terms of its long-range benefits for Canadians. T.W. Acheson examines the negative impact of the National Policy on the Maritime region in "The National Policy and the Industrialization of the Maritimes, 1880–1910."

Craig Brown presents his argument in greater detail in *Canada's National Policy, 1883-1900: A Study in Canadian-American Relations* (Princeton: Princeton University Press, 1964). John Dales elaborates on his position in *The Protective Tariff in Canada's Development* (Toronto: University of Toronto Press, 1966). Donald Creighton's works contain the traditional defence of the National Policy: see, for example, *Canada's First Century* (Toronto: Macmillan, 1970). Ben Forster analyses the events leading up to the adoption of the National Policy in *A Conjunction of Interests: Business, Politics, and Tariffs, 1825-1879* (Toronto: University of Toronto Press, 1986). The negative impact of the National Policy on developments in the hinterlands of the Maritimes and the West can be found in *Canada and the Burden of Unity*, ed. D. Bercuson (Toronto: Macmillan, 1977). Kenneth Norrie's "The National Policy and Prairie Economic Discrimination, 1870-1930," in *Canadian Papers in Rural History*, ed. Donald Akenson (Gananoque: Langdale Press, 1978), 13-33, questions whether western farmers had legitimate grievances against the National Policy. The Fall 1979 issue of the *Journal of Canadian Studies* (vol. 14) is devoted to "The National Policy, 1879-1979."

36

The Nationalism of the National Policy*

CRAIG BROWN

Debating nationalism is the great Canadian national pastime. Since Confederation it has been the pre-eminent preoccupation of politicians, journalists, scholars, and plain ordinary citizens. All have wrestled diligently with the problem that Canadian nationalism — if such there be — does not fit any of the classic definitions of nationalism. Common language, religion, and ethnic origin must obviously be rejected. Except for the disciples of Harold Adams Innis, geography provided few satisfactory clues to the Canadian identity. And a common historical tradition, in the words of Mill, "the possession of a national history and consequent community of recollections, collective pride and humiliation, pleasure and regret, connected with the same incidents in the past," raises more questions about a Canadian "nationality" than it answers. There is no great national hero who cut down a maple tree, threw a silver dollar across the St. Lawrence, and then proceeded to lead a revolution and govern the victorious nation wisely and judiciously. There are no great Canadian charters of freedom or independence expressing the collective will of the people. But the search goes on. Historians and retired Gov-

*From *Nationalism in Canada*, edited by Peter Russell for the University League for Social Reform. McGraw-Hill Ryerson, 1966. Reprinted by permission of the University League for Social Reform.

ernors General laboriously attempt to define "the Canadian identity" or "being Canadian." Many nations have manifested their nationalism through great public acts; Canada has asserted its nationalism by looking for it.

Yet there is abundant evidence that Canadians have both thought and acted like contemporary nationalists in other countries. Much, though by no means all, of the evidence is provided by the politicians.[1] The evidence is mundane, for seldom have Canadian politicians been political theorists or philosophers. Rather, their concerns have been with everyday problems of government. But within this framework their thoughts and acts have been decidedly nationalist in character. A brief look at the men who implemented and carried out the National Policy may serve to illustrate the point.

Writing to a Conservative editor in 1872, Sir John A. Macdonald noted in a postscript that "the paper must go in for a National policy in Tariff matters, and while avoiding the word 'protection' must advocate a read-justment of the tariff in such a manner as incidentally to aid our man-ufacturing and industrial interest."[2] In this obvious afterthought at the conclusion of a letter devoted to the necessity for finding an appropriate label for Macdonald's party, is the origin of the National Policy. The context is significant. Macdonald was looking for a policy that would attract, at one and the same time, voters and dollars to his party, and the National Policy would do both. The manufacturers would contribute to the party war-chest and the simplicity of the title and concept of the National Policy would appeal to an electorate looking to fulfill the promise of Confederation. Moreover, as a transcontinental railway, im-migration, and opening of the Northwest were added to the tariff as items in the National Policy, it took on a strikingly familiar complexion that added to its political attractiveness. It was in most respects a du-plication of a similar "national policy" designed for continental expansion in the United States. It was "a materialistic policy of Bigness"[3] in an age when expansionism appealed to nationalist sentiment. Canadians could take pride in their ability to compete with their neighbours in the conquest of the continent.

The National Policy was equally attractive because a policy of tariff protection meant another step in the long path from colony to nation within the Empire. As early as 1859, Galt argued for protection less on its economic merits than on the grounds that tariff autonomy was implicit in responsible government. Referring to Imperial objections to the Cayley-Galt tariff of that year, the crux of Galt's argument was that "self-government would be utterly annihilated if the views of the Imperial Government were to be preferred to those of the people of Canada."[4] With tariff autonomy not only achieved but emphasized by protection, in 1911 the ardent nationalist John S. Ewart proudly summed up the elements of "Canadian Independence" by pointing first to the fact that "we are fiscally independent." "By that I mean that we make our own tariffs; that we frame them as we wish; that we tax British and other goods as we please; and that neither the Colonial Office nor the British Parliament has any right whatever to interfere."[5]

That the National Policy was politically attractive, is, then, evident. By 1886 the Liberal party had been driven so far into a "me too" position that Blake in essence declared his party's policy to be, to borrow a phrase, the National Policy if necessary, but not necessarily the National Policy. It is true that in 1891, with a new leader and the new policy of Unrestricted Reciprocity with the United States, the Liberals came closer to victory than they had at any time since 1874. But within two years the Liberals had again revised their policy to "freer trade" and in 1897 the Liberal Government admitted the futility of attempting to destroy Macdonald's brainchild. "I not only would not retire from the Government because they refused to eliminate the principle of protection from the tariff, but I would not remain in the Government if they did eliminate the principle of protection entirely from the tariff," wrote Clifford Sifton. He added that "the introduction of a tariff from which the principle of protection would be entirely eliminated would be fraught with results that would be most disastrous to the whole Canadian people."[6] In 1911, Sifton and 17 other "revolting" Liberals issued their manifesto against reciprocity "believing as we do that Canadian nationality is now threatened with a more serious blow than any it has heretofore met with."[7] Robert Borden simply added that "we must decide whether the spirit of Canadianism or of Continentalism shall prevail on the northern half of this continent."[8]

In short, the idea of protection embodied in the tariff became equated with the Canadian nation itself. The National Policy, by stressing that Canadians should no longer be "hewers of wood and drawers of water" for the United States, as Tilley put it, recalled and reinforced that basic impulse of survival as a separate entity on this continent that had been born of the American Revolution, made explicit in Confederation, and remained the primary objective of Canadian nationalists. Protection and the National Policy, then, took on a much larger meaning than mere tinkering with customs schedules.

The same idea was evident in the building of the Canadian Pacific Railway and the opening of the Northwest. The Northwest was the key to the future of both the National Policy and the nation, and an expensive and partially unproductive railway through Canadian territory was the price Canada had to pay to "protect" it from American penetration and absorption. It was to be the great market for Canadian industry and the foundation of a "Canadian economy." Emphasizing that building the railway was "a great national question," Sir Charles Tupper remarked that "under the National Policy that Canada has adopted we must look forward not only to building up thriving centres of industry and en-

terprises all over this portion of the country, but to obtaining a market
for these industries after they have been established; and I say where
is there a greater market than that magnificent granary of the North-
west?"[9] He added that upon the success of the venture "the rapid progress
and prosperity of our common country depends."

The United States played an interesting role in the National Policy
that emphasized its nationalistic assumptions. Fundamental to the thinking of the framers of the policy was the idea that the United States
was much less a friendly neighbour than an aggressive competitor power
waiting for a suitable opportunity to fulfill its destiny of the complete
conquest of North America. The National Policy was intended to be
the first line of defence against American ambitions. And this, I think,
is the reason any Canadian alternative to it was unsuccessful. It was
the "national" implications of the National Policy that hindered the Liberals in their attempt to formulate an opposition policy before 1896. They
could not accept Commercial Union because it meant the total surrender
of tariff autonomy. Unrestricted Reciprocity was adopted as a compromise that retained autonomy. But its distinction from Commercial Union
was too subtle for much of the electorate to grasp and left the party
open to skillful exploitation by Macdonald's "loyalty" cry. More important, the very indefiniteness of what the Liberals meant by Unrestricted Reciprocity caused confusion and disruption in party ranks and
eventually led to the revelation that Unrestricted Reciprocity did not
mean the complete free interchange of all Canadian and American products after all. Rather, most Liberals simply wanted a more extensive
reciprocity agreement with the United States than the Conservatives.
Or, to put it another way, the Liberals were only interested in somewhat
less protection from American competition than their opponents. W.S.
Fielding's budget speech in 1897 had a very familiar ring to Canadian
ears: "If our American friends wish to make a treaty with us, we are
willing to meet them and treat on fair and equitable terms. If it shall
not please them to do that, we shall in one way regret the fact but shall
nevertheless go on our way rejoicing, and find other markets to build
up the prosperity of Canada independent of the American people."[10]

Other problems in Canadian–American relations in the latter part of
the nineteenth century were related to the nationalism of the National
Policy. With the abrogation of the fishery articles of the Treaty of Washington by the United States, Canada was forced to adopt what can properly be called a "protectionist" policy for her inshore fisheries. The fisheries and the commercial privileges extended to Americans by the treaty
were considered a national asset by Canadians. The object of their Government was to use that asset for the benefit of the whole of Canada,
not simply the Maritime Provinces. It was for this reason that from 1871
on the fishery question was always related to reciprocity. On each occasion
when Canada participated in negotiations the policy was always the same:

39

Canada's exclusive and undoubted rights in the inshore fisheries would be bargained for the free exchange of natural products.

A different and more complex problem was presented by the Behring Sea dispute arising out of the seizure of Canadian pelagic sealers by United States revenue cruisers. The central problem was one of international law involving the doctrines of freedom of the seas and *mare clausum*. And because the Canadian vessels were of British registry, the British Government assumed a much more active negotiating role than was the case in some other disputes. But Canadian participation was far from negligible, and Sir Charles Hibbert Tupper and Sir Louis Davies made a point of protecting Canadian interests. Significantly, they argued that despite the legal technicalities, it was a Canadian industry that was threatened with destruction by the illegal acts of the United States Government and that the Mother Country had a clear duty to protect that industry.

40 The Alaska Boundary question also illustrated the relationship between the National Policy and Canada's relations with the United States. All of the evidence available suggests that the Canadian case was hopelessly weak and members of the Canadian Government (Laurier and Sifton) as much as admitted it both privately and in public. Why, then, was the case pressed with such vigour? Part of the answer, it seems to me, is that when the Alaska Boundary question became important for Canadians after the Yukon gold rush began, those responsible for Canadian policy, led by Clifford Sifton, regarded the question less as one of boundary definition than of commercial competition with the United States. Definition of the boundary was important because it was related to control of the growing Yukon trade. The intricate legal details of the boundary dispute were generally ignored by the Canadian Government. Writing during the meetings of the joint High Commission in 1898, Lord Herschell complained to Lord Salisbury that "I found that the question had not been thoroughly studied or thought out by any Canadian official."[11] The urgent and ill-considered introduction of the Yukon Railway Bill of 1898 providing for a "Canadian" route to the Yukon — a route which was dependent upon trans-shipment privileges at the American customs port at Fort Wrangel and on navigation rights on the American portion of the Stikine River — illustrates the same point. The "imperative reason for immediate action" was that the Yukon trade was at stake, as the Minister of Railways and Canals explained to the House of Commons: "The importance of securing that trade and preserving it to Canada becomes a national question of the greatest interest. . . . It is ours, it is within our own borders and of right belongs to us, if, by any legitimate or proper means we can secure it for the people of our own country."[12]

Again, in the negotiations at the joint High Commission of 1898–99 the Canadians insisted that if the boundary question went to arbitration,

Pyramid Harbour should be reserved for Canada to match American insistence that Dyea and Skagway be reserved for the United States. While both sides thus rejected an unqualified and impartial arbitration, it must be admitted that Dyea and Skagway were established and settled communities under American control; Canada could make no such claim regarding Pyramid Harbour. Pyramid Harbour, as a Canadian outlet to the sea with a corresponding Canadian land corridor to the interior, had not arisen in negotiations until the meetings of the joint High Commission and, as before, the Canadian claim was based primarily on the desire to secure control of the Yukon trade.

Ultimately, of course, Canadian indignation knew no bounds when Lord Alverstone reportedly suddenly changed his mind and awarded Pearse and Wales Islands to the United States in 1903. The settlement of 1903 was unquestionably diplomatic rather than "judicial." Theodore Roosevelt's pressure tactics before and during the meeting of the so-called "judicial tribunal" were certainly deplorable and these factors, combined with the apparent sacrifice of Canadian interests by Great Britain, have supplied grist for the mills of Canadian nationalists ever since. But too often the emphasis in Canadian historiography on this point has been misplaced by concentrating solely on the alleged British sellout. The more interesting point in all the clamour surrounding the Alaska Boundary decision is that, once again, National Policy interests were considered to be threatened by the decision. Alverstone's agreement with Lodge and Root, that Pearse and Wales Islands belonged to the United States, threatened the Laurier Government's first venture in transcontinental railway building. The projected terminus of the Grand Trunk Pacific, chartered just a few short months before, was Port Simpson on Observatory Inlet; Pearse and Wales Islands, which the Canadians believed could be armed by the United States, commanded the shipping lanes into Port Simpson. Thus, though the Yukon trade had drastically declined in value by 1903, from first serious consideration of the problem to final settlement, the National Policy — an "all Canadian" trade route to the Yukon or a secure terminus for a new Pacific railway — dominated Canadian consideration of the Alaska Boundary dispute.

41

I have tried to suggest that the National Policy was a manifestation of Canadian national sentiment. Its basic assumptions, protection against the United States, the need for a "Canadian economy" with a strong industrial base and secure markets, and the implicit assumption of achieving greater autonomy within the Empire all crystallized that ill-defined, but deeply felt, sense of difference that set Canadians apart from both their neighbours to the south and the mother country. But why did this desire to proclaim a national identity take its form in economic terms?

Perhaps a part of the answer rests in the dilemma posed at the beginning of this paper. Appeals to a common language, a common cultural tradition, or a common religion were simply impossible for Canadians and when they were attempted they were rightly regarded by French Canadians as a violation of their understanding of Confederation. Most Canadians, especially those who built or paid for the building of the transcontinental railways, argued that the Canadian nation would have to be built in spite of its geography and regarded their efforts as "the price of being Canadian." Appeals to national history could also be a divisive rather than a unifying factor for, as often as not, the two ethnic groups disagreed as to what, in their historical tradition, was a matter of pride or of humiliation. What was necessary, then, as Cartier put it in the Confederation debates, was to "form a political nationality." And it is not at all surprising that the political nationalism of the early decades of Confederation was expressed in terms of railways and tariffs.

It is a commonplace to equate the politics of North America in the latter part of the nineteenth century with self-seeking capitalism. But we might remind ourselves that the age of Darwinism and of industrialism was also a great age of nationalism. The nationalism of the large assertive states of the age, the United States, Germany, and Great Britain, was assuredly economic in its emphasis. In the United States, in particular, nationalism was equated with the problems of industrialism and industrial expansion. In keeping with Darwinian assumptions, bigness was a virtue for a nation state, and industrialism was the key to bigness. At the very time their own nation was being born, Canadians reasoned that industrialism was the determining factor in the victory of the North in the Civil War and in the apparent reunification of the United States. Industrialism meant power; power to withstand the pressures from the south and power to expand and consolidate the Canadian nation. And a political programme that emphasized expansion and industrialism had the added advantage of ignoring the potentially divisive issues that would disrupt a "political nationality."

In sum, then, the National Policy, a policy for a "Canadian economy" and a "Big Canada," a materialistic policy for a materialistic age, was the obvious policy to give expression to Canadian national sentiment. That policy was adopted in 1878 and accepted by the Liberal party in 1896. Three years later J.I. Tarte urged Laurier to do more than simply accept the National Policy, to expand upon it with more railways, canals, and harbour improvements (and presumably with higher tariffs). "Voilà," he observed, "le programme le plus national et le plus populaire que nous puissons offrir au pays."[13]

NOTES

[1] Carl Berger, "The True North Strong and Free," in *Nationalism in Canada* (Toronto, 1966), 3ff.
[2] *Macdonald Papers*, (P.A.C.) Macdonald to T.C. Patteson, February 27, 1872.
[3] John Dales, "Protection, Immigration and Canadian Nationalism," in *Nationalism in Canada*, 167–70.
[4] A. B. Keith, *Selected Speeches and Documents on British Colonial Policy, 1763–1917* (London, 1953), 60.

[5] J.S. Ewart, *The Kingdom Papers*, vol. 1 (Ottawa, 1912), 3.
[6] Sifton Papers, (P.A.C.) Sifton to James Fleming, March 13, 1897.
[7] *Manifesto of Eighteen Toronto Liberals on Reciprocity*, February 20, 1911; cited, *Canadian Annual Review* (Toronto, 1911), 49.
[8] Henry Borden, ed., *Robert Laird Borden: His Memoirs*, vol. 1 (Toronto, 1938), 327.
[9] *House of Commons Debates*, April 15, 1880, pp. 1424–25.
[10] *House of Commons Debates*, April 22, 1897.
[11] Cited in R.C. Brown, *Canada's National Policy, 1883–1900* (Princeton, 1964), 379.
[12] *House of Commons Debates*, February 8, 1898, pp. 191–92.
[13] *Laurier Papers* (P.A.C.), Tarte to Laurier, April 3, 1899.

Canada's National Policies*

JOHN DALES

I

To the infant industry argument for protectionism Canadians have added an infant nation argument. Among Canadian academic historians, journalists, and citizens at large there seems to be a dangerous unanimity of opinion that Canada is a transparently artificial entity whose very existence has always depended on something called a national policy. Canada, in this view, is a denial of geography and a travesty of economics that stands as living proof of the primacy of politics in the affairs of men. Critical comment to the effect that most Canadian manufacturers still depend on protective tariffs is very apt to be greeted first by astonishment that anyone would think the comment worth making, and then by patient explanation that of course many parts of the Canadian economy — not only manufacturing — have always depended on government bounty in one form or another, and that Canada simply would not exist as a nation if public support were not continuously made available to key sectors of the economy. Such a policy is necessary, the explanation continues, both in order to overcome the outrageous geography of the country and in order to defend the nation's economy against the formidable efficiency, and thus the natural expansionism, of the American economy. In Canada infant industries are not *expected* to grow up.

I reject this view of Canada. It seems to me to be subversive not only of the nation's wealth but also of the nation's pride. National pride and economic performance I believe to be positively, not negatively, correlated; both efficiency and honour, as the parable of the talents teaches, come from making the most of what one has, not from having the most. And yet Canadian economic policy — and, what is more important, the economic policy of so many developing nations today — aims consistently at maximizing the purse, gross national product, rather than the performance, gross national product per citizen.

43

Sir John A. Macdonald gave us our first national policy, and our first lessons in the irrelevance of economics. Western lands, he argued, must be controlled by the Dominion because provincial land policies "might be obstructive to immigration," i.e., provinces might actually try to sell land rather than give it away. Canadian railways, in Macdonald's view, were not to be thought of primarily as business enterprises; they were instruments of national development and served this end by providing both attractive objects of government expenditure and reliable sources of party support. As for the tariff, Macdonald rang all the changes on the protectionist fallacies and promised that *his* tariff would benefit everyone, the teachings of the dismal science notwithstanding. Macdonald was the first great Canadian non-economist.

It is hard to believe, though, that Macdonald deserves the whole credit for the low esteem in which economics and economists are held in Canada today. Macdonald has in any event had powerful support from Canadian historians, of both the political and economic persuasions, who have rationalized his national policy and have encouraged Canadians to believe that by disregarding economics they could build a nation that would represent a victory over mere materialism. The national policy originally consisted of government support for three main ventures: railway building, Western settlement, and manufacturing development. (We adopt the original convention of using "national policy" for the famous trinity of Canadian nation-building policies, and of reserving "National Policy" for the protective tariff policy.) The mutual consistency of Western settlement and railway building was perhaps fairly obvious; land grants helped to finance railways, and railway companies encouraged settlement. From an economist's point of view, however, the rationalization has been carried a little far. The government has been praised for using valuable lands as a loss-leader, while the C.P.R. has been praised for selling land to immigrants at prices considerably below those charged by other land owners, and for showing great initiative in developing uneconomic irrigation projects.

What was at first difficult for historians to discover was the consistency between Macdonald's tariff policy and the other two prongs of his national policy. The late Professor H.A. Innis seems to have provided the connecting argument. The role of the tariff in the Canadian economy, he taught, was to inhibit Canadian–American trade, to promote east–west trade in Canada, and in this way to provide revenue for Canadian transcontinental railways. Though I cannot resist a long footnote on the subject, I do not want to make a full textual analysis of Innis' writings in order to try to find out whether he believed that his tariff–railway link was (a) the *ex post* result of the two policies — the way things worked out — or (b) the *ex-ante* design — the way things were intended to work out — or (c) either or both of these combined with the opinion that the link was felicitous.[1] I wish only to suggest that once the Innis

44

45

A circular prepared for the federal election of 1891. According to the National Policy's supporters, protectionism meant jobs and prosperity for the working man; free trade meant unemployment and poverty.

link was forged the way was wide open for a full-scale rationalization of the national policy. Thus D.G. Creighton:

> [The tariff] was intimately and vitally related to the other national policies. By means of the tariff, the settlement of the west would provide a national market; and this national market would supply east–west traffic for Canadian transcontinental railways and areas of exploitation for eastern Canadian industry.[2]

And J.B. Brebner:

> Looking backward from the present, it is easy to see that the very existence of both the Province and the later Dominion of Canada as entities separate from the United States has depended on such expensive transportation services that a large proportion of their cost has had to be met from the public purse. . . . it was [in the exuberant 1850s] that Canadians . . . began systematically to adopt the *only* procedure by which they could surmount this handicap, that is, the imposition of quite high tariffs on manufactured goods.[3]

W.T. Easterbrook and H.G. Aitken:

> [The detailed program of Canadian nation building] appeared slowly and in piecemeal fashion but by 1879 . . . the parts of the comprehensive and more or less complete pattern had fallen into place: a transcontinental railway, protective tariffs, land settlement policy, the promotion of immigration.[4]

And the present author, who providentially has written very little on the subject:

> The Dominion immediately proceeded to fulfil its purposes. A transcontinental railway system was constructed, an energetic settlement policy was adapted to the needs of the West, and the tariff was designed to develop Canadian industry and stimulate Canadian trade. These policies proved effective in the period of prosperity which began towards the end of the nineteenth century.[5]

Two features of the historians' stereotype of the national policy should be noted. First, much emphasis is placed on the consistency of the three pillars of the program, while inconsistencies are either ignored or glossed over. Among the authors I have consulted, several mention the regional inconsistency inherent in the policy. V.C. Fowke, in particular, interpreted the national policy as a program designed by and for central Canadians. The national policy is therefore seen not as national at all but rather as a policy of central Canadian imperialism. Fowke comes dangerously close to shattering the whole myth of the national policy, yet in the end he refuses to be an iconoclast. Thus his glosses that the national policy was "prerequisite to western development" and that "the groundwork [for western development] . . . was laid . . . by the institution of the 'National Policy' or tariff protection . . . "[6] seem wildly inconsistent with his main position, particularly in view of his insistence that Macdonald's railway policy was *not* prerequisite to western development: "As far as the western provinces are concerned . . . Canadian railways are expensive alternatives to American railways rather than to no railways at all."[7] Brebner and Careless both hint at the logical inconsistency inherent in protectionism, namely, the attempt to build a wealthy nation by lowering the standard of living of its population. Thus Careless notes that "A protective tariff plainly meant that goods would cost more to buy in Canada," yet after a token flirtation with this line of reasoning he surrenders to the stereotype on the following page and concludes that "as far as Canada is concerned the protective tariff system that was adopted under Macdonald . . . did much in the long run to develop the wealth and encourage the industry of the Dominion."[8] He then goes on to paint the usual picture of the wonderful consistency among Canada's railway, settlement, and tariff policies.

None of the authors I have examined has flatly challenged the national stereotype of the beneficence of the national policy. W.A. Mackintosh, however, writes very cautiously about this subject. He outlines the "Basic National Decisions" and their interrelations in chapter 2 of his *The Economic Background of Dominion–Provincial Relations*,[9] but adds at the end of the chapter (p. 21): "It is not suggested that these national decisions were taken by governments, or still less by electorates, in full consciousness of their implications, nor that the inter-relations among them were fully appreciated. They were in large measure the outcome of conflicts of interest and, to some extent, of political expediency." Later (p. 37) he notes the regional conflicts occasioned by the national policies, and the tendency of these policies to rigidify the economy by creating "vested interests, regional and sectional, which would resist readjustment." Also two other authors, both political historians, have distinguished themselves by refusing to have anything to do with the standard patter. Chester Martin disdains even to mention the tariff in his *Foundations of Canadian Nationhood*;[10] A.R.M. Lower bluntly refers to the National Policy as being a "frank creation of vested manufacturing interests living on the bounty of government," and in exasperation writes that "Macdonald's way of imposing the new tariff was simple: he just invited anyone who wanted a duty to come to Ottawa and ask for it."[11]

The stereotype of the national policy is powerful enough not only to bridge logical inconsistencies but also to abridge time. To its defenders the national policy was both a well-designed and a powerful engine of nation-building. Yet it refused to function for some twenty or thirty years. Many authors simply ignore this awkward gap in timing, as I did myself in the quotation above. Others mention it and then ignore it, as for example Easterbrookand Aitken: "The three decades following Confed-

47

eration . . . seemed to many a prolonged period of marking time. . . . Not until the turn of the century did the program of nation-building begin to pay off . . . " (p. 381). After a long account of the Time of Troubles in both its economic and political aspects, Careless finds himself concluding that "conservative nationalism was played out," and thus in imminent danger of rending the stereotype beyond repair. But he draws back at the very brink of the abyss, and proclaims in strident tones that "Macdonald nationalism had not failed. It was the age that had failed . . . " (p. 295).

Why can we not bring ourselves to say quite simply that the national policy was a dismal failure? Everyone admits, for example, that the land settlement policy was a failure before 1900. After 1900 the demand for western land was so brisk, and the C.P.R. and various land companies so zealous in attracting settlers to the region, that it is hard to believe that the homestead policy was in any sense necessary as a means of settling the West. It was, indeed, probably undesirable. After writing of the efficiency and enterprise of the private land companies, Martin notes that "The general opening of 'Dominion lands,' even- and odd-numbered sections alike, to homestead entry after 1908 brought a deluge of less selective migration to Western Canada. In vain the government had sought to reserve vast areas with marginal rainfall in 'Palliser's triangle' for grazing and other purposes. In the queues which formed up at the land offices prospective settlers, as one observer records, 'held their place in the line day and night for two or three weeks to enable them to file on certain lands,' and places in the queue were frequently bought and sold for 'substantial sums of money.'" Uneconomically low prices inevitably produce queues. No one, I suggest, really believes that without the homestead policy in particular, and the settlement policy in general, the West would not have been settled. These policies were powerless to promote settlement before 1900; after 1900 their chief effect was to promote not settlement but *rapid* settlement, and there is much evidence to suggest that the rapidity of settlement did much short-term and long-term harm in Western Canada. Martin's trenchant criticism of the homestead system certainly permits one to believe that Canada would have been better off without this member of the national policy trilogy.

As with land settlement policy so with tariff policy; the burden of the argument suggests that we would have been much better off still if we had never tangled with the National Policy. Historically, it need only be noted that manufacturing was developing in Canada well before the tariff of 1879; Mackintosh notes that the "Census of 1871 reveals that Canada had made some progress along the path of industrialization," and that "The new protectionist policy intensified, broadly speaking, industrial trends already visible."[12] Moreover, Canadian manufacturing grew less rapidly than American manufacturing both before and after the tariff and net emigration from Canada was a feature of the decades both before and after 1879. To the extent that the National Policy was intended to reverse, or even toreduce, the disparity in Canadian and American growth rates it was clearly a failure. After 1900 the Canadian economy, including Canadian manufacturing, grew more rapidly than the American economy for a dozen years, and Canadian historians have not hesitated to attribute this surge to the beneficial, if somewhat delayed, effects of the National Policy. As Careless wrote,[13] it was the "age that had failed" before 1900 and the rise of a prosperous age after 1900 that "spelt success at long last for the National Policy. . . . " In Canadian history it is heads the National Policy wins, and tails the age loses.

There remains the curious case of the C.P.R. While a Canadian trans-continental railway, as Fowke argues, was not prerequisite to western development, economists and political scientists can agree that as a matter of political economy such a railway was an essential adjunct of nationhood for the new Dominion. The railway had to be built for political reasons, whatever the subsidy involved; sensible economic policy required only that the subsidy be kept as low as possible. The C.P.R. was in fact heavily subsidized. Still, given the lack-lustre performance of Canadian settle-ment and tariff policies before the middle 1890s one might have expected, on the basis of the national policy stereotype in general and the Innis link in particular, that the C.P.R. would have been unable to survive its first bleak decade. Surely no one would wish to argue that the population of Western Canada in 1895 (perhaps a third of a million people, an in-crease of something over 100,000 since the completion of the C.P.R.) was able to supply either enough wheat or a large enough market for man-ufactured goods to make a paying proposition out of even so heavily subsidized a transcontinental railway as the C.P.R. Yet the C.P.R. was prof-itable from the minute it was completed and began to pay dividends on its common stock in 1889. The Wheat Boom that began in the closing years of the century was only the frosting on the cake that allowed the Company to raise dividends from 4% in 1897 to 10% in 1911, despite large decreases in railway rates around the turn of the century. The chronology of C.P.R. earnings thus raises a nagging doubt about whether the C.P.R. ever *needed* to be subsidized indirectly by the tariff as well as directly by grants of money and a kingdom in land. Professor Fogel's conclusion that the Union Pacific Railway would have been profitable *without* subsidies, despite unanimous opinion, before the fact, that it would not be,[14] suggests a need for testing the hypothesis that the C.P.R. would have been profitable with direct subsidies alone, or even, sub-versive thought, without *any* subsidy! Careful analysis of this matter seems to be an urgent necessity. The core of the national policy has always been the protective tariff, and although today the tariff is more and more often brazenly defended simply on the grounds that we must protect the vested interests we have built up, the argument of last resort

49

is still that the tariff is the defender of the railways, and thus of the east–west economy. The defence retains its appeal since the railways still carry a great deal of freight, if not many passengers, and the Innis link remains persuasive. If it were possible to deny the validity of the Innis argument that without the tariff there would be no C.P.R., it would be much more difficult for present-day nationalists to argue that if there were no tariff there would be no Canada.

There are, therefore, reasonable grounds for questioning the validity of the historians' stereotype of the national policy. To stress the consistency of the national policy as an interrelated whole is to ignore all too cavalierly its inconsistencies. And to write as if the wisdom and power of a nation-building program that is ineffective for two or three decades is somehow "proved" or "demonstrated" by a subsequent period of great prosperity is to mislead the public with a monstrous example of the *post hoc ergo propter hoc* fallacy. Moreover, the whole tortuous exercise is so unnecessary, for a much more reasonable, and very much simpler, explanation of the Great Canadian Boom is also standard fare in our textbooks. This explanation runs in terms of a number of world events and developments in the last decade of the nineteenth century, all of which reacted favourably on the Canadian economy — the "closing" of the American frontier, rising world prices, falling shipping rates, the development of the gradual reduction process for milling wheat, and the development of the technique of making paper from wood pulp are perhaps the principal items in the list. None of these factors owed anything to the national policy.

Why, then, do historians insist on overdetermining their explanation of the Great Boom by trying to fit a perfectly straightforward argument into the national policy stereotype, as Fowke, for example, does when he writes that "This conjuncture of world circumstances created the opportunity for Canadian expansion, but a half-century of foundation work along the lines of the national policy had prepared Canada for the opportunity."[15] Economic man does not need to be prepared by government policy before he reacts to opportunities for making profits. Is it crude hero worship, or an unconscious human predisposition to human explanations of history that leads Canadians to believe that what success they have enjoyed "must" reflect Macdonald's wise nation-building policies? Or are we all of us merely prisoners of our own history — as it has been written? It is very odd that, enjoying one of the highest standards of living in the world, Canadians in all walks of life should nevertheless believe that their economy is a frail, hothouse creation, whose very survival depends on the constant vigilance of a government gardener well provided with props and plant food. Who but historians could have created this chasm between reality and belief? It is high time that someone should write the history of Canada since Confederation as a triumph of the forces of economic and political development over the national policies of Macdonald and his successors.

50

II

Our national policies were laid down when Canada was young, both politically and economically. The country looked forward to a long period of what I shall call *extensive* economic growth — a combination of geographical expansion, immigration, the exploitation of new resources, railway building, and the extension of manufacturing and service industries to keep pace with the growth of the national economy. The national policies were adopted to facilitate this "natural" growth process; they were designed to increase natural resources through political expansion, human resources through immigration, social capital by railway building, and private capital by means of the tariff. This "vision" of growth was surely not unreasonable in 1870, even though, as things turned out, it failed to materialize during the next generation. In retrospect it is easy enough to see why the expectation was premature: world demand for wheat had not yet grown to the point where, even with rail transportation, *51* wheat could be profitably exported from the Canadian prairies; technology had not yet released the wealth of the Canadian Shield in terms of base metals, pulpwood, and waterpower; and the absence of cheap coal and iron ore hampered manufacturing development. It was only with the "conjuncture" around 1900 that natural economic expansion gave the national policies something to facilitate. For a generation thereafter, extensive growth was the stuff of Canadian economic development.

Extensive growth, which is essentially a process of increasing the quantity of resources, provides the sort of massive economic development that fascinates economic historians. Yet from an economic point of view it is such a simple type of growth that it holds almost no interest for economic theorists, who concern themselves primarily with the efficient use of *a given quantity* of resources, and who therefore tend to think of economic progress not in terms of amassing resources but in terms of making better use of existing resources. Fortunately, however, economic historians and economic theorists *do* have a common interest in an improvement of resource *quality* as a third path to the wealth of nations. Historians have long manifested an interest in technological change, which may be considered as a means of improving the quality of capital resources, and in such things as health, diet, training, and a wide range of institutional factors that affect the quality of human resources. Only recently have economic theorists invaded in force the fields of technology, health, education, recreation, and governmental activities, but already the power of economic analysis is beginning to make itself felt in public policies relating to these matters.

Both better resource allocation and resource improvement, but especially the latter, result in what I shall call *intensive* economic growth, a type of growth that has little to do with the mere multiplying of resources that is the basic characteristic of extensive economic growth. Intensive growth, as against extensive growth, involves better job opportunities rather than more job opportunities, more highly trained people rather than more people, better use of capital and land rather than more capital and land — in brief, a better performance rather than a larger one. Extensive growth implies primary concern with the GNP growth rate; intensive growth implies primary concern with the GNP per capita growth rate. What must now be asked is whether the roughhewn concepts of extensive and intensive growth have any operational significance, and if so whether national policies designed for extensive growth have any place in an age of intensive growth.

It is, of course, true that it would be hard to find historical examples of either pure intensive or pure extensive growth. The important question is whether it is legitimate to characterize certain periods as periods of *predominantly* intensive or extensive growth. Both traditional history and Professor Gallman's quantitative work suggest that for the United States it is meaningful to distinguish between the extensive growth of the last half of the nineteenth century and the intensive growth of the first half of the twentieth. Thus Gallman found that "the rate of increase of commodity output over the first fifty years of the twentieth century was very far below the rate for the last sixty years of the nineteenth," but "the average rate of change of commodity output per capita was about the same in the twentieth as in the nineteenth century."[16] That twentieth-century economic growth in the United States has been mainly of the *intensive* variety is made clear by Gallman's findings that "the twentieth century average decade rate of increase of gainful workers in commodity production was only . . . slightly more than one-fifth as large as that of the nineteenth. The twentieth-century increases in commodity output were largely productivity increases. . . . Productivity advance in commodity production was sufficiently high to maintain a high rate of growth of commodity output per member of the population, despite the fact that a sharply declining share of the population was engaged in commodity production."[17]

In Canada we have only the beginnings of a statistical history of our economic growth before 1926 and we cannot with confidence argue from the statistical record. Nevertheless the Canadian GNP data, based on Firestone's figures for the pre-1926 period, fail to show any evidence of retardation in the growth of GNP since 1900, or even since 1880, and clearly suggest some modest acceleration of GNP growth in the period since the Second World War. Taken at face value — and I find it hard to believe that the general trends of the data are misleading — the suggestion is that Canada has remained in a period of extensive economic growth for the past sixty or seventy years. Qualitative evidence, however, is clearly at odds with this hypothesis. Most economic historians would agree with Fowke's suggestion that 1930 marked "the end of the establishment phase of the wheat economy and the completion of the first national policy"[18] and would even go farther by using 1930 to mark the end of the period of extensive growth that started in Canada in the mid-1890s. By this time the West had been settled, the railways built, and the pulp and paper, hydroelectric, and mining industries established.[19] It is true that since the Second World War there have been some dramatic new mining developments in Canada — petroleum, iron ore, uranium, and potash — but the industries built on these new resources have been neither land-intensive nor labour-intensive and they have had a much smaller impact on the postwar economy than the earlier "staple industries" had on the pre-1930 economy. In retrospect, there seems as much reason to have expected some retardation in the growth of GNP in Canada after 1930 as there was to expect a slowing down of the GNP growth rate in the United States after 1900, that is to say, for a replacement of predominantly extensive growth by predominantly intensive growth.

Yet our growth statistics are still those of a period of extensive growth. In part, the statistics reflect the postwar resource discoveries mentioned above, and in part, I think, the likelihood that the expansion in manufacturing in Canada after 1940 was unusually large not only because of the war but also because normal growth had been suspended in the 1930s. In a sense, those technological trends that were differentially favourable to Canadian manufacturing had just begun to take hold in the 1920s, were submerged by the depression of the 1930s, and only became fully apparent in the 1940s and 1950s. But when this has been said, there still remains a strong suspicion that Canadian *policy* has had much to do with the perpetuation of very high GNP growth rates characteristic of a period of extensive growth long after our period of extensive growth apparently came to an end.

53

The change in "national policies" after 1930 was not, perhaps, as sharp as Fowke suggested.[20] Indeed two out of three of the main pillars of the old national policy — tariff protection and the promotion of immigration — are as much a feature of present-day Canadian policy as they were of Canadian policy sixty years ago. As has been argued throughout, the Canadian tariff and Canadian immigration policy operate jointly to "force the pace" of manufacturing growth and, more generally, of growth in population and GNP. The danger is that in a period of intensive growth, when the growth in natural resources is slower than the growth in population, part of the growth in GNP will be at the expense of growth in GNP per person. American adjustments to the "closing" of their "frontier" included, one might suggest, a rapid extension of birth control practices, severe limitations on immigration, land conservation policies, and, more recently, growing concern for the wise use of air and water. Some of these adjustments have also been in evidence in Canada. But our *national* economic policies today are substantially those of 1900 — more factories, more people, more cities, more GNP. Is it not time to consider whether these are appropriate policies for a country whose "frontier" was "closed" a generation ago?

NOTES

[1] The Innis link was derived from Galt's argument, made in reply to protests from British manufacturers against his raising of the Canadian tariff in the late 1850s, that increased tariff revenue was necessary to help pay for Canadian canals and railways that could not be profitably built by private concerns, and that British manufacturers ought to be pleased with the arrangement because the cheaper cost of transportation would lower the price of British manufactured goods in Canada and thus increase the market for them. (Innis accepted as profound this economic doubletalk of a suave politician, though with a certain amount of incredulity about its source: " . . . whether or not [Galt's] explanation was one of rationalization after the fact, or of original theoretical analysis, reliance on the customs was undoubtedly the only solution.") Surely it was not the only solution; if the canals had been paid for by domestic taxation, or by import duties that were no heavier than domestic excise duties, the British manufacturers would have been at least as well off, and Canadians would have been better off. A subsidy is always to be preferred to a tariff on both economic grounds and political grounds; on economic grounds because direct payments distort resource allocation less than indirect payments, and on political grounds because direct payments involve less deception than indirect payments.

Galt was talking *mainly* of revenue tariffs. Innis extended the Galt argument to tariffs that were mainly protective, and thereby compounded Galt's error. "The National Policy was designed not only to increase revenue from customs [as in Galt's argument] but also to increase revenue from traffic from the standpoint of the railways. The increasing importance of railways has tended to emphasize the position of protection rather than revenue." As economic theory this is absurd, not only because the railways, like the canals, could have been financed more efficiently by subsidy than by tariff, but also because a tariff cannot at the same time maximize both protection and revenue; the greater the protective effect of a tariff the less the revenue it will provide. The charitable interpretation of this passage is that Innis was indulging in "rationalization after the fact." In the article in which these passages occurred, Innis at any rate doubted the *future* application of his argument: "Dependence on the application of mature technique, especially in transport, to virgin natural resources must steadily recede in importance as a basis for the tariff. It will become increasingly difficult to wield the tariff as the crude but effective weapon by which we have been able to obtain a share of our natural resources."

All of the above quotations are taken from an article by Innis published in 1931, and reprinted in H.A. Innis, *Essays in Canadian Economic History* (Toronto, 1956), 76–77. Two years later Innis was in a deep quandary about the effect of the Canadian tariff. "Inflexibility of the tariff downward contributed to the difficulties during the period of prosperity which began . . . in 1896 . . . " (p. 91). On the following page he wrote that "During a period of prosperity the tariff should be raised to act as a brake. . . . If railroad rates are lowered at the beginning of a period of prosperity tariff rates should be raised accordingly. . . . Lowering the tariff during the period of a depression and raising the tariff during a period of prosperity might do much to alleviate the problem of a staple-producing area" (pp. 92–93). The only way I can see of resolving the contradiction between these two quotations is to suppose that in the first Innis was thinking of the combined effect on C.P.R. revenues of the wheat boom and the continued support of the tariff, and the consequent effect of swollen railway revenues in promoting a new, and uneconomically large, railway building program in Canada: had the tariff been lowered, and the C.P.R.'s profits thereby dampened, the incentive to build *two* new transcontinental railways in Canada would have been reduced; and that in the second he was thinking of the Western farmer: the wheat boom might have been dampened by raising farm costs by means of *increased* tariff rates in order to offset the advantages that farmers gained by lowered railway rates. Since the final part of the second quotation recommends a counter-cyclical tariff policy (Innis must have know how politically impracticable *this* was!), with no qualification about how railway rates should be changed, one can only make sense out of this passage by supposing that by 1933 Innis was willing to sacrifice the railways to the farmers during depression and the farmers to the railways during prosperity; his recommended policy would be counter-cyclical for farmers and pro-cyclical for railways! Perhaps the subtlety, or the confusion, was covering a retreat. Realizing that a high tariff may "become inadequate" during depressions (p. 91), and suggesting that the period of resource expansion in Canada had ended, Innis in fact repudiated his linking of the National Policy and railways by reverting to the lesser economic confusions of Galt's position: "Assuming relative stability in the production of raw materials as a result of exhaustion of natural resources the tariff must assume to an increasing extent the position of a toll, as Galt originally planned, and should approximate the deficit on transportation finance" (p. 93). Unfortunately the damage had been done, for textbook writers cannot spare the time to assess qualifications to, or second thoughts on, powerful generalizations.

[2] D.G. Creighton, *Dominion of the North* (Toronto, 1944), 346.

[3] J.B. Brebner, *North Atlantic Triangle* (New Haven and Toronto, 1945), 158. My italics.

[4] W.T. Easterbrook and H.G. Aitken, *Canadian Economic History* (Toronto, 1956), 383.

[5] J.H. Dales, *Engineering and Society*, pt. 2 (Toronto, 1946), 246.

[6] V.C. Fowke, *Canadian Agricultural Policy* (Toronto, 1946), 8. Fowke may mean that the national policy was a prerequisite from central Canadians' point of view, i.e., that central Canada would not have "invested" in the West without it. At the same time he would not argue that eastern investment was a *sine qua non* of western development; see note 7.
[7] V.C. Fowke, *The National Policy and the Wheat Economy* (Toronto, 1957), 69.
[8] J.M.S. Careless, *Canada* (Toronto, 1953), 277-78.
[9] W.A. Mackintosh, *The Economic Background of Dominion-Provincial Relations* (Ottawa, 1939).
[10] Chester Martin, *Foundations of Canadian Nationhood* (Toronto, 1956).
[11] A.R.M. Lower, *Colony to Nation* (Toronto, 1946), 373-74.
[12] Mackintosh, *Economic Background*, 17 and 20.
[13] Careless, *Canada*, 295 and 312.
[14] R.W. Fogel, *The Union Pacific Railroad* (Baltimore, 1960), *passim*.
[15] Fowke, *The National Policy and the Wheat Economy*, 70.
[16] R.E. Gallman "Commodity Output, 1839-1899," in *Trends in the American Economy in the Nineteenth Century* (Princeton, 1960), 18 and 20.
[17] Gallman, "Commodity Output," 20.
[18] V.C. Fowke, "The National Policy — Old and New," in *Canadian Journal of Economics and Political Science* (August 1952), 277-78.
[19] See J.H. Dales, *Hydroelectricity and Industrial Development* (Cambridge, Mass., 1957), ch. 8, esp. p. 166.
[20] Fowke, "The National Policy — Old and New."

The National Policy and the Industrialization of the Maritimes, 1880-1910*

T.W. ACHESON

The Maritime provinces of Canada in 1870 probably came the closest of any region to representing the classic ideal of the staple economy. Traditionally shaped by the Atlantic community, the region's industrial sector had been structured to the production and export of timber, lumber products, fish, and ships. The last was of crucial significance. In terms of the balance of trade, it accounted for more than one-third of New Brunswick's exports at Confederation. In human terms, the manufacture of ships provided a number of towns with large groups of highly skilled, highly paid craftsmen who were able to contribute significantly to the quality of community life. Against this background, the constricting British market for lumber and ships after 1873 created a serious economic crisis for the area. This was not in itself unusual. Throughout the nineteenth century the region's resource-based economy had suffered a series of periodic recessions as the result of changing imperial policies and world markets. Yet, in one respect, this crisis differed from all earlier; while the lumber markets gradually returned in the late 1870's, the ship market did not. Nova Scotians continued to build their small vessels for the coasting trade, but the large shipbuilding industry failed to revive.

*From *Acadiensis* 1, 2 (Spring 1972): 3-28.

In the face of this uncertain future the National Policy was embraced by much of the Maritime business community as a new mercantilism which would re-establish that stability which the region had enjoyed under the old British order. In the first years of its operation the Maritimes experienced a dramatic growth in manufacturing potential, a growth often obscured by the stagnation of both the staple industries and population growth. In fact, the decade following 1879 was characterized by a significant transfer of capital and human resources from the traditional staples into a new manufacturing base which was emerging in response to federal tariff policies. This development was so significant that between 1881 and 1891 the industrial growth rate of Nova Scotia outstripped all other provinces in eastern Canada.[1] The comparative growth of the period is perhaps best illustrated in St. John. The relative increase in industrial capital, average wages, and output in this community significantly surpassed that of Hamilton, the Canadian city whose growth was perhaps most directly attributable to the protective tariff.[2]

56

Within the Atlantic region the growth of the 1880's was most unequally distributed. It centred not so much on areas or sub-regions as upon widely scattered communities.[3] These included the tradional Atlantic ports of St. John, Halifax, and Yarmouth; lumbering and shipbuilding towns, notably St. Stephen and New Glasgow; and newer railroad centres, such as Moncton and Amherst. The factors which produced this curious distribution of growth centres were human and historical rather than geographic. The one characteristic shared by them all was the existence in each of a group of entrepreneurs possessing the enterprise and the capital resources necessary to initiate the new industries. Strongly community-oriented, these entrepreneurs attempted, during the course of the 1880's, to create viable manufacturing enterprises in their local areas under the aegis of the protective tariff. Lacking the resources to survive the prolonged economic recessions of the period, and without a strong regional metropolis, they acquiesced in the 1890's to the industrial leadership of the Montreal business community. Only at the century's end, with the expansion of the consolidation movement, did a group of Halifax financiers join their Montreal counterparts in asserting an industrial metropolitanism over the communities of the eastern Maritimes. This paper is a study in that transition.

I

The Maritime business community in the 1870's was dominated by three groups: wholesale shippers, lumber and ship manufacturers, and the small scale manufacturers of a variety of commodities for purely local consumption. As a group they were deeply divided on the question of whether the economic salvation of their various communities was to be found in the maintenance of an Atlantic mercantile system, or in a programme

TABLE 1   Industrial Development in Principal Maritime Centres, 1880–1890

	Population	Industrial Capital	Employees	Average Annual Wages	Output	Industry Output, 1891
Halifax (1880)	39,886	$2,975,000	3,551	$303	$6,128,000	Sugar**
Dartmouth (1890)	43,132	6,346,000	4,654	280	8,235,000	Rope*
						Cotton
						Confectionery
						Paint
						Lamps
St. John (1880)	41,353	2,143,000	2,690	278	4,123,000	Lumber**
(1890)	39,179	4,838,000	5,888	311	8,131,000	Machinery***
						Smelting
						Rope**
						Cottons
						Brass*
						Nails*
						Electric Light**
New Glasgow (1880)	2,595	160,000	360	255	313,000	Primary Steel*
(1890)	3,777	1,050,000	1,117	355	1,512,000	Rolling Mills**
						Glass
St. Stephen (1880)	4,002	136,000	447	314	573,000	Cottons
Milltown (1890)	4,826	1,702,000	1,197	320	1,494,000	Confectionery
						Fish Canning
						Soap
						Lumber
Moncton (1880)	5,032	530,000	603	418	1,719,000	Sugar
(1890)	8,765	1,134,000	948	333	1,973,000	Cottons
						Woolens
						Rolling Stock
Fredericton- (1880)	7,218[a]	1,090,000[a]	911[a]	221[a]	1,031,000[a]	Cottons
Marysville (1890)	8,394	2,133,000	1,526	300	1,578,000	Lumber
						Foundry Products
Yarmouth (1880)	3,485	290,000	211	328	284,000	Cotton Yarn*
(1890)	6,089	783,000	930	312	1,234,000	Fish Canning
						Woolens
Amherst (1880)	2,274	81,000	288	281	283,000	Foundry Products
(1890)	3,781	457,000	683	293	724,000	Shoes
						Doors

[a] Estimates. Marysville was not an incorporated town in 1880, and totals for that date must be estimated from York County figures.
* Leading Canadian Producer; ** second; *** third.

Source: Canada, *Census* (1891), vol. 3, Table 1; (1901), vol. 3, Tables 20, 21.

of continentalist-oriented industrial diversification. A wedding of the two alternatives appeared to be the ideal situation. While they had warily examined the proposed tariff of 1879, most leading businessmen accepted its philosophy and seriously attempted to adapt it to their community needs.[4]

For a variety of reasons the tariff held the promise of prosperity for the region's traditional commercial activities and, as well, offered the possibilities for the development of new manufacturing industry. For most Nova Scotian business leaders the West Indies market was vital to the successful functioning of the province's commercial economy. It was a major element in the region's carrying trade and also provided the principal market for the Nova Scotia fishing industry. These, in turn, were the foundations of the provincial shipbuilding industry. The successful prosecution of the West Indies trade, however, depended entirely upon the ability of the Nova Scotia merchants to dispose of the islands' sugar crop. The world depression in the 1870's had resulted in a dramatic decline in the price of refined sugar as French, German, British, and American refineries dumped their surplus production on a glutted world market. By 1877 more than nine-tenths of Canadian sugar was obtained from these sources,[5] a fact which threatened the Nova Scotia carrying trade with disaster. A significant tariff on foreign sugar, it was felt, would encourage the development of a Canadian refining industry which would acquire all of its raw sugar from the British West Indies. Through this means, most Nova Scotian wholesalers and shippers saw in the new policy an opportunity both to resuscitate the coastal shipping industry of the province and to restore their primacy in the West Indies.

Of the newer industries which the National Policy offered, the future for the Maritimes seemed to lie in textiles and iron and steel products. The optimism concerning the possibilities of the former appears to have emerged out of a hope of emulating the New England experience. This expectation was fostered by the willingness of British and American cotton mill machinery manufacturers to supply on easy terms the necessary duty-free equipment, and by the feeling of local businessmen that the market provided by the tariff and the low quality labour requirements of such an enterprise would guarantee that a profitable business could be erected and maintained by the efforts of a single community. Behind such reasoning lay the general assumption that, despite major transportation problems, the Maritimes, and notably Nova Scotia, would ultimately become the industrial centre of Canada. The assumption was not unfounded. The region contained the only commercially viable coal and iron deposits in the Dominion, and had the potential, under the tariff, of controlling most of the Montreal fuel sources. Under these circumstances the development of textiles and the expansion of most iron and steel industries in the Atlantic area was perhaps not a surprising project.

Despite a cautious enthusiasm for the possibilities offered by the new federal economic dispensation, there was considerable concern about the organizational and financial problems in creating a new industrial structure. The Maritimes was a region of small family firms with limited capital capabilities. Other than chartered banks, it lacked entirely the financial structure to support any large corporate industrial entity. Like the people of Massachusetts, Maritimers were traditionally given to placing their savings in government savings banks at a guaranteed 4 percent interest rather than in investments on the open market.[6] Regional insurance, mortgage and loan, and private savings corporations were virtually unknown. The result was to throw the whole financial responsibility for undertaking most manufactories upon the resources of individual entrepreneurs.

Since most enterprises were envisioned as being of general benefit to the community at large, and since few businessmen possessed the necessary capital resources to single-handedly finance such an undertaking, most early industrial development occurred as the result of co-operative efforts by groups of community entrepreneurs. These in turn were drawn from a traditional business elite of wholesalers and lumbermen. In Halifax as early as May, 1879, a committee was formed from among the leading West Indies shippers "to solicit capital, select a site and get a manufacturing expert" for the organization of a sugar refinery.[7] Under its leadership $500,000 was raised, in individual subscriptions of $10–20,000, from among members of the Halifax business community. This procedure was repeated during the formation of the Halifax Cotton Company in 1881; more than $300,000 was subscribed in less than two weeks, most of it by thirty-two individuals.[8]

The leadership in the development of these enterprises was taken by young members of traditional mercantile families. The moving spirit in both cases was Thomas Kenny. A graduate of the Jesuit Colleges at Stonyhurst (England) and St. Gervais (Belgium), Kenny had inherited from his father, the Hon. Sir Edward Kenny, M.L.C., one of the largest wholesale shipping firms in the region. In the early 1870's the younger Kenny had invested heavily in shipyards scattered throughout five counties of Nova Scotia, and had even expanded into England with the establishment of a London branch for his firm. Following the opening of the refinery in 1881, he devoted an increasingly large portion of his time to the management of that firm.[9] Kenny was supported in his efforts by a number of leading merchants including the Hon. Robert Boak, Scottish-born president of the Legislative Council, and John F. Stairs, Manager of the Dartmouth Rope Works. Stairs, who had attended Dalhousie University, was a member of the executive council of Nova Scotia, the son of a legislative councillor, and a grandson of the founder of the shipping firm of William Stairs, Son and Morrow Limited.[10]

In contrast to Halifax, St. John had always been much more a manufacturing community and rivalled Ottawa as the principal lumber manufacturing centre in the Dominion. Development in the New Brunswick city occurred as new growth on an existing industrial structure and centred on cotton cloth and iron and steel products. The New Brunswick

Cotton Mill had been erected in 1861 by an Ulster-born St. John shipper, William Parks, and his son, John H. Parks. The latter, who had been trained as a civil engineer under the tutelage of the chief engineer of the European and North American Railroad, assumed the sole proprietorship of the mill in 1870.[11] In 1881 he led the movement among the city's dry goods wholesalers to establish a second cotton mill which was incorporated as the St. John Cotton Company.

The principal St. John iron business was the firm of James Harris. Trained as a blacksmith, the Annapolis-born Harris had established a small machine shop in the city in 1828, and had expanded into the foundry business some twenty-three years later. In 1883, in consequence of the new tariff, he determined to develop a completely integrated secondary iron industry including a rolling mill and railway car plant. To provide the resources for the expansion, the firm was reorganized as a joint stock company with a $300,000 capital most of which was raised by St. John businessmen. The New Brunswick Foundry, Rolling Mills and Car Works, with a plant covering some five acres of land, emerged as the largest industrial employer in the Maritimes.[12] The success of the Harris firm induced a group of wholesale hardware manufacturers under the leadership of the Hon. Isaac Burpee, a former member of the Mackenzie Government, to re-establish the Coldbrook Rolling Mills near the city.

Yet, despite the development of sugar and cotton industries and the expansion of iron and rope manufactories, the participation of the St. John and Halifax business communities in the industrial impulse which characterized the early 1880's can only be described as marginal. Each group played the role of participant within its locality but neither provided any positive leadership to its hinterland area. Even in terms of industrial expansion, the performance of many small town manufacturers was more impressive than that of their city counterparts.

At the little railway centre of Moncton, nearly $1,000,000 was raised under the leadership of John and Christopher Harris, John Humphrey, and Josiah Woods, to permit the construction of a sugar refinery, a cotton mill, a gas light and power plant, and several smaller iron and textile enterprises. The Harris brothers, sons of an Annapolis shipbuilder of Loyalist extraction, had established a shipbuilding and shipping firm at Moncton in 1856.[13] Under the aegis of their firm they organized the new enterprises with the assistance of their brother-in-law John Humphrey, scion of Yorkshire Methodist settlers of the Tantramar, longtime M.L.A. for Westmorland, and proprietor of the Moncton flour and woolen mills. They were financially assisted in their efforts by Josiah Wood (later Senator) of nearby Sackville. The son of a loyalist wholesaler, Wood first completed his degrees B.A., M.A.) at Mount Allison, was later admitted to the New Brunswick bar, and finally entered his father's shipping and private banking business.[14] The leadership of the Moncton group was so effective that the owner of the *Monetary Times*, in a journey through the region in 1882, singled out the community for praise:

> Moncton has industrialized . . . business people only in moderate circumstances but have united their energies . . . persons who have always invested their surplus funds in mortgages are now cheerfully subscribing capital for the Moncton Cotton Co. Unfortunately for industrial progress, there are too many persons [in this region] who are quite content with receiving 5 or 6% for their money so long as they know it is safe, rather than risk it in manufactures, even supposing it yielded double the profit.[15]

At St. Stephen the septuagenarian lumber barons and bankers, James Murchie and Freeman Todd, joined the Annapolis-born shipbuilder, Zechariah Chipman, who was father-in-law to the Minister of Finance, Sir Leonard Tilley, in promoting an immense cotton concern, the St. Croix, second largest in the Dominion at the time. The son of a local farmer, Murchie, whose holdings included more than 200,000 acres of timber lands — half of it in Quebec — , also developed a number of smaller local manufactories.[16] At the same time two young brothers, Gilbert and James Ganong, grandsons of a Loyalist farmer from the St. John Valley, began the expansion of their small confectionery firm,[17] and shortly initiated construction of a soap enterprise in the town.

At Yarmouth a group of shipbuilders and West Indies merchants led by the Hon. Loran Baker, M.L.C., a shipper and private banker, and John Lovitt, a shipbuilder and member of the Howland Syndicate, succeeded in promoting the Yarmouth Woolen Mill, the Yarmouth Cotton Manufacturing, the Yarmouth Duck Yarn Company, two major foundries, and a furniture enterprise.[18] The development was entirely an internal community effort — virtually all the leading business figures were third generation Nova Scotians of pre-Loyalist American origins. A similar development was discernible in the founding of the Windsor Cotton Company.[19]

A somewhat different pattern emerged at New Glasgow, the centre of the Nova Scotia coal industry. Attempts at the manufacture of primary iron and steel had been made with indifferent results ever since Confederation.[20] In 1872, a New Glasgow blacksmith, Graham Fraser, founded the Hope Iron Works with an initial capital of $160,000.[21] As the tariff on iron and steel products increased in the 1880's so did the vertical expansion of the firm. In 1889, when it was amalgamated with Fraser's other enterprise, the Nova Scotia Forge Company, more than two-thirds of the $280,000 capital stock of the resulting Nova Scotia Steel and Coal Company was held by the citizens of New Glasgow.[22] Fraser remained as president and managing director of the corporation until 1904,[23] during which time it produced most of the primary steel in the

61

Dominion,[24] and remained one of the largest industrial corporations in the country.[25]

Fraser was seconded in his industrial efforts by James Carmichael of New Glasgow and John F. Stairs of Halifax. Carmichael, son of a prominent New Glasgow merchant and a descendant of the Scottish founders of Pictou, had established one of the largest shipbuilding and shipping firms in the province.[26] Stairs' investment in the New Glasgow iron and steel enterprise represented one of the few examples of inter-community industrial activity in this period.

The most unusual pattern of manufacturing development in the region was that initiated at Fredericton by Alexander Gibson. Gibson's distinctiveness lay in his ability to impose the tradition and structure of an earlier semi-industrial society onto a changing pattern of development. A St. Stephen native and the son of Ulster immigrants, he had begun his career as a sawyer, and later operated a small lumber firm at Lepreau. In 1865 he bought from the Anti-Confederationist government of A.J. Smith extensive timber reserves on the headwaters of the Nashwaak River,[27] and at the mouth of that river, near Fredericton, built his own mill town of Marysville. Freed from stumpage fees by his fortunate purchase, the "lumber king of New Brunswick" was producing as much as 100,000,000 feet of lumber annually by the 1880's — about one third of the provincial output. His lumber exports at times comprised half the export commerce of the port of St. John.[28]

One of the wealthiest industrial entrepreneurs in the Dominion, Gibson determined in 1883 to undertake the erection of a major cotton enterprise entirely under his own auspices.[29] He erected one of the largest brickyards in the Dominion and personally supervised the construction of the plant which was opened in 1885.[30] In that same year he employed nearly 2,000 people in his sundry enterprises.[31] By 1888 his sales of cotton cloth totalled nearly $500,000.[32] That same year the Gibson empire, comprising the cotton mill, timber lands, saw mills, lath mills, the town of Marysville, and the Northern and Western Railroad, was formed into a joint stock company, its $3,000,000 capital controlled by Gibson, his brother, sons, and son-in-law.

Several common characteristics distinguished the men who initiated the industrial expansion of the 1880's. They were, on the whole, men of substance gained in traditional trades and staples. They sought a substantial, more secure future for themselves within the framework of the traditional community through the instrumentality of the new industrial mercantilism. Averaging fifty-four years of age, they were old men to be embarking upon new careers.[33] Coupled with this factor of age was their ignorance of both the technical skills and the complexities of the financial and marketing structures involved in the new enterprises.

The problem of technical skill was overcome largely by the importation of management and skilled labour, mainly from England and Scotland.[34]

The problem of finance was more serious. The resources of the community entrepreneurs were limited; the costs of the proposed industry were almost always far greater than had been anticipated. Moreover, most businessmen had only the vaguest idea of the quantity of capital required to operate a large manufacturing corporation. Promoters generally followed the normal mercantile practice and raised only sufficient capital to construct and equip the physical plant, preferring to finance operating costs through bank loans — a costly and inefficient process. The Halifax Sugar Refinery perhaps best illustrated these problems. When first proposed in 1879 it was to have been capitalized at $300,000. Before its completion in 1881 it was re-capitalized twice to a value of $500,000.[35] Even this figure left no operating capital, and the refinery management was forced to secure these funds by loans from the Merchants Bank of Halifax. At the end of its first year of operation the bank debt of the corporation totalled $460,000,[36] which immediately became a fixed charge on the revenues of the infant industry. Fearing bankruptcy, the stockholders increased their subscriptions and kept the business functioning until 1885 when they attempted a solution to the problem by issuing debenture stock to a value of $350,000 of which the bank was to receive $200,000 in stock and $50,000 cash in settlement of debts still owed to it.[37]

While many industries received their initial financing entirely from local capitalists, some projects proved to be such ambitious undertakings that aid had to be sought from other sources. The St. Croix Cotton Company at St. Stephen, for example, was forced to borrow $300,000 from Rhode Island interests to complete their huge plant.[38] Some industries came to rely so heavily on small community banks for perpetual loans for operating expenses that any general economic crisis toppled both the industries and the banks simultaneously. The financing of James Domville's enterprises, including the Coldbrook Rolling Mills, was a contributing factor in the temporary suspension of the Maritime Bank of St. John in 1880,[39] while such industrial loans ultimately brought down the Bank of Yarmouth in 1905.[40]

II

The problem of industrial finance was intricately tied to a whole crisis of confidence in the new order which began to develop as the first enthusiastic flush of industrial expansion paled in the face of the general business downturn which wracked the Canadian economy in the mid-1880's. At the heart of this problem was a gradual deterioration of the British lumber market, and the continued shift from seaborne to railroad commerce. Under the influence of an increasingly prohibitive tariff and an extended railroad building programme a two cycle inter-regional trading pattern was gradually emerging. The westward cycle, by rail into the St. Lawrence basin, left the region with a heavy trade imbalance as the central Canadians rapidly replaced British and American produce in the Maritime market with their own flour and manufactured materials.[41] In return, the region shipped to Montreal quantities of primary and primary manufactured products of both local and imported origins. The secretaries of the Montreal and St. John boards of trade estimated the extent of this inter-regional commerce at about $15,711,000 in 1885, more than 70 percent of which represented central Canadian exports to the Maritimes.[42] By contrast the external trade cycle moved in traditional fashion by ship from the principal Maritime ports to Great Britain and the West Indies. Heavily balanced in favour of the Maritimes, it consumed most of the output of the region's resource industries. The two cycles were crucially interdependent; the Maritime business community used the credits earned in the external cycle to meet the gaping deficits incurred in the central Canadian trade. The system worked as long as the equilibrium between the two could be maintained. Unfortunately, as the decade progressed, this balance was seriously threatened by a declining English lumber market.[43]

In the face of this increasingly serious trade imbalance, the Maritime business community became more and more critical of what they regarded as the subversion of the National Policy by central Canadian interests. Their argument was based upon two propositions. If Canadian transportation policy was dedicated to creating an all-Canadian commercial system, then this system should extend not from the Pacific to Montreal, but from the Pacific to the Atlantic. How, in all justice, could the Montreal interests insist on the construction, at a staggering cost, of an all-Canadian route west of that city and then demand the right to export through Portland or Boston rather than using the Maritime route? This argument was implicit in almost every resolution of the Halifax and St. John boards of trade from 1880 onward.[44]

The second proposition maintained that, as vehicles of nationhood, the railways must be considered as a means of promoting national economic integration rather than as commercial institutions. The timing of this doctrine is significant. Before 1885 most Maritime manufacturers were competitive both with Canadian and foreign producers. Nails, confectionery, woolens, leather, glass, steel, and machinery manufactured in the Maritimes normally had large markets in both central Canada and the West.[45] The recession of 1885 reached a trough in 1886.[46] Diminishing demand coupled with over-production, particularly in the cotton cloth and sugar industries, resulted in falling prices, and made it increasingly difficult for many Maritime manufacturers to retain their central Canadian markets. The *bête noir* was seen as the relatively high freight rates charged by the Intercolonial Railway. The issue came to a head late in 1885 with the closing of the Moncton and the two Halifax sugar refineries. The response of the Halifax manufacturers was immediate and decisive.

Writing to the Minister of Railways, John F. Stairs enunciated the Maritime interpretation of the National Policy:

> Four refineries have been set in operation in the Lower Provinces by the policy of the Government. This was right; but trade having changed so that it is now impossible for them to work prosperously it is the duty of the Government to accommodate its policy to the change. The reduction in freight rates asked for is necessary to this. . . . If in answer to this you plead that you must manage so that no loss occur running the I.C.R., we will reply, we do not, and will not accept this as a valid plea from the Government . . . and to it we say that the people of Nova Scotia, nor should those of Ontario and Quebec, for they are as much interested, even admit it is essential to make both ends meet in the finance of the railroad, when it can only be done at the expense of inter-provincial trade, and the manufacturers of Nova Scotia. . . . How can the National Policy succeed in Canada where such great distances exist between the provinces unless the Government who control the National Railway meet the requirements of trade . . . [47]

At stake, as Stairs later pointed out in a confidential memorandum to Macdonald, was the whole West Indies trade of Nova Scotia.[48] Equally as important and also at stake was the entire industrial structure which had been created in the region under the aegis of the National Policy.

The Maritimes by 1885 provided a striking illustration of the success of that policy. With less than one-fifth of the population of the Dominion, the region contained eight of the twenty-three Canadian cotton mills — including seven of the nineteen erected after 1879[49] — , three of five sugar refineries, two of seven rope factories, one of three glass works, both of the Canadian steel mills, and six of the nation's twelve rolling mills.

Although Stairs succeeded in his efforts to have the I.C.R. sugar freight rates reduced,[50] the problem facing the Maritime entrepreneur was not one which could be solved simply by easier access to the larger central Canadian market; its cause was much more complex. In the cotton industry, for example, the Canadian business community had created industrial units with a production potential sufficient to supply the entire national market. In periods of recession many American cloth manufacturers were prepared to cut prices on exports to a level which vitiated the Canadian tariff; this enabled them to gain control of a considerable portion of the Canadian market. The problems of the cotton cloth manufacturers could have been solved by a further increase in the tariff — a politically undesirable answer — , by control of railway rates, or by a regulated industrial output.

From a Maritime regional viewpoint the second of these alternatives appeared to be the most advantageous; the limitations of the tariff could then be accepted and, having attained geographic equality with Montreal through a regulated freight rate, the more efficient Maritime mills would soon control the Montreal market. Such was the hope; there was little possibility of its realization. Such a general alteration in railway policy would have required subsidization of certain geographic areas — districts constituting political minorities — at the expense of the dominant political areas of the country, a prospect which the business community of Montreal and environs could hardly be expected to view with equanimity. Apart from the political difficulties of the situation, most Maritime manufactories suffered from two major organizational problems: the continued difficulty faced by community corporations in securing financing in the frequent periods of marginal business activity,[51] and the fact that most firms depended upon Montreal wholesale houses to dispose of their extraregional exports.[52] Short of a major shift in government railway or tariff policy, the only solution to the problem of markets which seemed to have any chance for success appeared to be the regulation of industrial production, a technique which was to bring into the Maritimes the Montreal interests which already controlled the major part of the distributive function in eastern Canada.

66

III

The entry of Montreal into the Maritime region was not a new phenomenon. With the completion of the Intercolonial Railway and the imposition of coal duties in 1879, Montreal railway entrepreneurs moved to control both the major rail systems of New Brunswick and the Nova Scotia coal fields. A syndicate headed by George Stephen and Donald Smith had purchased the New Brunswick Railroad from Alexander Gibson and the Hon. Isaac Burpee in 1880,[53] with the intention of extending it to Rivière du Loup. This system was expanded two years later by the purchase of the New Brunswick and Canada Railroad with the ultimate view of making St. John the winter port for Montreal.

In the same year, another Montreal group headed by John McDougall, David Morrice, and L.-A. Sénécal acquired from fifteen St. John bondholders, four-fifths of the bonds of the Springhill and Parrsboro Railroad and Mining Company,[54] and followed this up in 1883 with the purchase of the Springhill Mining Company, the largest coal producer in Canada.[55] The following year another syndicate acquired the International Mine at Sydney.[56] The coal mine takeovers were designed to control and expand the output of this fuel source, partially in an effort to free the Canadian Pacific Railways from dependence upon the strike-prone American coal industry. By contrast, the entry of Montreal interests into the manufacturing life of the Maritimes aimed to restrict output and limit expansion.

The first serious attempts to regulate production occurred in the cotton industry. Although informal meetings of manufacturers had been held throughout the mid-1880's, the business depression of 1886 and the threatened failure of several mills resulted in the organization of the first formal national trade association. Meeting in Montreal in the summer of 1886, representatives of sixteen mills, including four from the Maritimes, agreed to regulate production and to set standard minimum prices for commodities. The agreement was to be renegotiated yearly and each mill provided a bond as proof of good faith.[57] The arrangement at least stabilized the industry and the agreement was renewed in 1887.

The collapse of the association the following year was precipitated by a standing feud between the two largest Maritime mills, the St. Croix at St. Stephen and the Gibson at Marysville. Alexander Gibson had long been the maverick of the organization, having refused to subscribe to the agreement in 1886 and 1887. During this period he had severely injured his larger St. Stephen competitor in the Maritime market. By the time Gibson agreed to enter the association in 1888, the St. Croix mill, faced with bankruptcy, dropped out and reduced prices in an effort to dispose of its huge inventory. The Gibson mill followed suit. With two of the largest coloured cotton mills in the Dominion selling without regulation, the controlled market system dissolved into chaos, and the association, both coloured and grey sections, disintegrated.[58] The return to an unregulated market in the cotton industry continued for more than two years. A business upswing in 1889 mercifully saved the industry from what many manufacturers feared would be a general financial collapse. Even so, only the mills with the largest production potential, regardless of geographic location, escaped unscathed; most of the smaller plants were forced to close temporarily.

In the summer of 1890 a Montreal group headed by A.F. Gault and David Morrice prepared the second attempt to regulate the cotton market. The technique was to be the corporate monopoly. The Dominion Cotton Mills Company, with a $5,000,000 authorized capital, was to bring all of the grey cotton producers under the control of a single directorate. In January 1891, David Morrice set out on a tour of Maritime cotton centres. On his first stop, at Halifax, he accepted transfer of the Nova Scotia Cotton Mill to the syndicate, the shareholders receiving $101,000 cash and $101,000 in bonds in the new corporation, a return of 25 cents on the dollar of their initial investment.[59] The following day Morrice proceeded to Windsor, "to consummate the transfer of the factory there,"[60] and from there moved on to repeat the performance at Moncton. Fearful of total bankruptcy and hopeful that this stronger organization would provide the stability that earlier efforts had failed to achieve, stock-holders of the smaller community-oriented mills readily acquiesced to the new order. Although they lost heavily on their original investment, most owners accepted bonds in the new corporation in partial payment for their old stock.

The first determined opposition to the cotton consolidation movement appeared in St. John. Here, John H. Parks, founder and operator of the thirty-year-old New Brunswick Cotton Mill, had bought the bankrupt St. John Cotton firm in 1886 and had proceeded to operate both mills. Despite the perennial problem of financing, the Parks Mills represented one of the most efficient industrial operations in the Dominion, one which had won an international reputation for the quality of its product. The company's major markets were found in western Ontario, a fact which made the continued independence of the firm a particular menace to the combination. The firm's major weakness was its financial structure. Dependent upon the Bank of Montreal for his operating capital, Parks had found it necessary to borrow more heavily than usual during the winter of 1889–90. By mid-1890 his debts totalled $122,000.[61]

At this point two events occurred almost simultaneously: Parks refused to consider sale of the St. John Mills to the new corporation, and the Bank of Montreal, having ascertained that the Montreal syndicate would buy the mills from any seller, demanded immediate payment in full of the outstanding debts of the company[62] — a most unusual procedure. Claiming a Montreal conspiracy to seize the company, Parks replied with an open letter to the dry goods merchants of greater St. John.

> . . . I have made arrangements by which the mills of our company will be run to their fullest extent.
>
> These arrangements have been made in the face of the most de-termined efforts to have our business stopped, and our property sold out to the Montreal syndicate which is endeavouring to control the Cotton Trade of Canada. . . . I now propose to continue to keep our mills in operation as a St. John industry, free from all outside control. l would therefore ask you gentlemen, as far as your power, to support me in this undertaking —
>
> It remains with you to assist the Wholesale Houses in distributing the goods made in St. John in preference to those of outside man-ufacture so long as the quality and price of the home goods is satisfactory.
>
> The closing of our mills . . . would be a serious calamity to the community, and you, by your support can assist materially in pre-venting it. I believe you will.[63]

Parks' appeal to community loyalty saved his firm. When the bank foreclosed the mortgage which it held as security for its loans, Mr. Justice A.L. Palmer of the New Brunswick Supreme Court placed the firm in receivership under his control until the case was resolved. Over the strongest objections of the bank, and on one legal pretext after another, the judge kept the mill in receivership for nearly two years.[64] In the meantime he forced the bank to continue the provision of operating capital for the mill's operations, and in conjunction with the receiver, a young Fredericton lawyer, H.H. McLean, proceeded to run an efficient and highly profitable business. When the decision was finally rendered in December 1892, the firm was found to have cleared profits of $150,000 during the period of the receivership. Parks was able to use the funds to repay the bank debts and the mill continued under local control.[65]

The St. John experience was unique. Gault and Morrice organized the Canadian Coloured Cotton Company, sister consolidation to the Dominion Cotton Mills, in 1891. The St. Croix Mill entered the new organization without protest early in 1892,[66] and even the Gibson Mill, while retaining its separate corporate structure, agreed to market its entire output through the new consolidation. By 1893 only the St. John Mills and the small Yarmouth plant remained in the hands of regional entrepreneurs.

69

The fate of the Maritime cotton mills was parallelled in the sugar industry. In 1890 a syndicate of Scottish merchants, incorporated under English laws as the Halifax Sugar Refinery Ltd., bought up the English-owned Woodside Refinery of Halifax.[67] The ultimate aim of the Scottish group was to consolidate the sugar industry into a single corporate entity similar to Dominion Cotton. Failing in this effort because of the parliamentary outcry against combines, they turned their efforts to regional consolidation. With the assistance of John F. Stairs, M.P., they were able, in 1894, to secure an act of incorporation as the Acadia Sugar Refineries which was to amalgamate the three Maritime firms. Unlike the Cotton Union, the new consolidation worked in the interests of the regional entrepreneurs, the stockholders of all three refineries receiving full value for their holdings. Equally important, the management of the new concern remained in the hands of Thomas Kenny, M.P.

The consolidation movement of the early 1890's swept most of the other major Maritime manufactories. In some cases local entrepreneurs managed to retain a voice in the direction of the new mergers — John Stairs, for example, played a prominent role on the directorate of the Consumers Cordage Company which swept the Halifax and St. John rope concerns into a new seven-company amalgamation in 1890.[68] On the other hand, the Nova Scotia Glass Company of New Glasgow disappeared entirely in the Diamond Glass consolidation of that same year.[69] On the whole, saving only the iron and steel products, the confectionery, and the staple export industries, control of all mass consumption industries in the Maritimes had passed to outside interests by 1895. Thus, in large measure the community manufactory which had dominated the industrial growth of the 1880's ceased to exist in the 1890's. Given the nature of the market of the period, some degree of central control probably was inevitable. The only question at stake was whether it would be a control effected by political or financial means, and if the latter, from which centre it would emanate.

The failure of any Maritime metropolis to achieve this control was partly a result of geography and partly a failure of entrepreneurial leadership. The fear of being left on the fringes of a national marketing system had been amply illustrated by the frenetic efforts of the St. John and Halifax business communities to promote political policies which would link the Canadian marketing system to an Atlantic structure with the Maritime ports serving as the connecting points.[70]

The question of entrepreneurial failure is more difficult to document. In part the great burst of industrial activity which marked the early 1880's was the last flowering of an older generation of lumbermen and wholesale shippers. Having failed to achieve their position as the link between central Canada and Europe, and faced with the dominant marketing and financial apparatus of the Montreal community, they drew back and even participated in the transfer of control. This failure is understandable in the smaller communities; it is more difficult to explain in the larger. In the latter case it may well be attributable to the perennial failure of most Maritime communities to maintain a continuity of industrial elites. The manufacturing experience of most families was limited to a single generation: Thomas Kenny's father was a wholesale merchant, his son a stockbroker. John F. Stairs was the son of a merchant and the father of a lawyer. Even in such a distinguished industrial family as that of John Parks, a second generation manufacturer, the son attended the Royal Military College and then entered the Imperial service. Commerce and the professions provided a much more stable milieu, and while many participants in both of these activities were prepared to make the occasional excursion into manufacturing, usually as part of a dual role, few were willing to make a permanent and sole commitment to an industrial vocation.

IV

The lesson brought home to the Maritime entrepreneur by the industrial experience between 1879 and 1895 was that geography would defeat any attempt to compete at parity with a central Canadian enterprise. In response to this lesson, the truncated industrial community of the region turned increasingly to those resource industries in which geography gave them a natural advantage over their central Canadian counterparts. In the 1890's the thrust of Maritime industrial growth was directed toward the processing and manufacturing of primary steel and of iron and steel products. In part, since these enterprises constituted much of the industrial machinery remaining in the hands of regional entrepreneurs, there was little choice in this development. At the same time, Nova Scotia contained most of the active coal and iron deposits in the Dominion and had easy access to the rich iron ore deposits at Belle Isle. In any event, most competition in these industries came from western Ontario rather than Montreal, and the latter was thus a potential market.

Iron and steel development was not new to the region. Efforts at primary steel making had been undertaken successfully at New Glasgow since 1882. Yet production there was limited and would continue so until a more favourable tariff policy guaranteed a stable market for potential output. Such a policy was begun in 1887 with the passage of the "iron" tariff. Generally labelled as a Nova Scotia tariff designed to make that province "the Pennsylvania of Canada"[71] and New Glasgow "the Birmingham of the country,"[72] the act provided an effective protection of $3.50 a ton for Canadian-made iron, and imposed heavy duties on a variety of iron and steel products.[73] Protection for the industry was completed in 1894 when the duty on scrap iron, considered a raw material by secondary iron manufacturers, was raised from $2 to $4 a ton, and most rolling mills were forced to use Nova Scotia–made bar iron rather than imported scrap.[74]

The growth of the New Glasgow industries parallelled this tariff development. In 1889 the Nova Scotia Steel Company was united with the Nova Scotia Forge Company to form a corporation capable of manufacturing both primary steel and iron and steel products. In the same year, to provide the community with its own source of pig iron, a group of Nova Scotia Steel shareholders organized the New Glasgow Iron, Coal and Railroad Company with a capital of $1,000,000.[75] Five years later, following the enactment of the scrap iron duty, New Glasgow acquired the rich Wabana iron ore deposits at Belle Isle — some eighty-three acres covered with ore deposits so thick they could be cut from the surface. This was followed the next year by the union of the Nova Scotia Steel and Forge and the New Glasgow Iron companies into a $2,060,000 corporation, the Nova Scotia Steel Company. Containing its own blast and open hearth furnaces, rolling mills, forges, foundries, and machine shops, the firm represented the most fully integrated industrial complex in the country. The process was completed in 1900 when the company acquired the Sydney Coal Mines on Cape Breton Island, developed new steel mills in that area and reorganized as the Nova Scotia Steel and Coal Company with a $7,000,000 capital.[76]

The development of the Nova Scotia Steel and Coal corporation had begun under the direction of a cabal of Pictou County Scottish Nova Scotians, a group which was later enlarged to include a few prominent Halifax businessmen. Aside from Graham Fraser, its leading members included James D. McGregor, James C. MacGregor, Colonel Thomas Cantley, and John F. Stairs. All four were third generation Nova Scotians, the first three from New Glasgow. Saving only Cantley, all were members of old mercantile families. Senator McGregor, a merchant, was a grandson of the Rev. Dr. James McGregor, one of the founders of the Presbyterian Church in Nova Scotia; MacGregor was a partner in the large shipbuilding concern of Senator J.W. Carmichael, a prominent promoter of Nova Scotia Steel. Cantley was the only member of the group of proletarian origins. Like Graham Fraser, he spent a lifetime in the active service of the company, having entered the newly established Nova Scotia Forge Company in 1873 at the age of sixteen. Promoted to sales manager of the amalgamated Nova Scotia Steel Company in 1885, he had been responsible for the introduction of Wabana ore into England and Germany. In 1902 be succeeded Graham Fraser as general manager of the corporation.[77]

Aside from its value to the New Glasgow area, the Nova Scotia Steel Company was of even greater significance as a supplier of iron and steel to a variety of foundries, car works, and machine mills in the region. Because of its unique ability to provide primary, secondary, and tertiary steel and iron manufactures, it was supplying most of the Maritime iron and steel needs by 1892.[78] In this respect, the industrial experience of the 1890's differed considerably from that of the previous decade. It was not characterized by the development of new industrial structures, but rather by the expansion of older firms which had served purely local markets for some time and expanded in response to the demand created by the tariff changes of the period.[79]

The centres of the movement were at New Glasgow, Amherst, and St. John, all on the main lines of the Intercolonial or Canadian Pacific railroads. At New Glasgow, the forge and foundry facilities of the Nova Scotia Steel Company consumed half the company's iron and steel output. At Amherst, Nathaniel Curry (later Senator) and his brother-in-law, John Rhodes, continued the expansion of the small woodworking firm they had established in 1877, gradually adding a door factory, a rolling mill, a railroad car plant, and an axle factory, and in 1893 bought out the Harris Car Works and Foundry of St. John.[80] At the time of its incorporation in 1902, Rhodes, Curry & Company was one of the largest secondary iron manufacturing complexes in the Dominion.[81] Curry's industrial neighbour at Amherst was David Robb. Son of an Amherst foundry owner, Robb had been trained in engineering at the Stevens Institute of New Jersey and then had entered his father's foundry. Specializing in the development of precision machinery, he expanded his activities into Massachusetts in the 1890's and finally merged his firm into the International Engineering Works of South Framingham of which he remained managing director.[82]

If under the aegis of a protective government policy the iron and steel industry of the Maritimes was rapidly becoming a viable proposition for local entrepreneurs, it was also increasingly attracting the interest of both Boston and Montreal business interests. There was a growing feeling that,

72

once a reciprocal coal agreement was made between Canada and the United States, Nova Scotia coal would replace the more expensive Pennsylvania product in the New England market. Added to this inducement was the fact that Nova Scotia provided the major fuel source on the Montreal market — the city actually consumed most of the coal produced in the Cape Breton fields.[83] With its almost unlimited access routes and its strategic water position midway between Boston and Montreal, Nova Scotia seemed an excellent area for investment.

In 1893 a syndicate headed by H.M. Whitney of Boston and composed of Boston, New York, and Montreal businessmen, including Donald Smith, W.C. Van Horne, and Hugh McLennan, negotiated a 119-year lease with the Nova Scotia government for most of the existing coal fields on Cape Breton Island.[84] The new Dominion Coal Company came into formal being in March of that year, with David MacKeen (later Senator) as director and general manager, and John S. McLennan (later Senator) as director and treasurer. The son of a Scottish-born mine owner and member of the legislative council, MacKeen had been an official and principal stockholder in the Caledonia Coal Company which had been absorbed in the new consolidation.[85] McLennan was the second son of Hugh McLennan of Montreal, a graduate of Trinity College, Cambridge, and one of the very few entrepreneurs who made the inter-regional transfer in this period.[86] The success of the Dominion Coal syndicate and the growing feeling that the Canadian government was determined to create a major Canadian primary steel industry led Whitney in 1899 to organize the Dominion Iron & Steel Company. The date was significant. Less than two years earlier the government had announced its intention to extend bounty payments to steel made from imported ores.[87] The $15,000,000 capital of the new company was easily raised, largely on the Canadian stock market,[88] and by 1902 the company was employing 4,000 men in its four blast and ten steel furnace works.[89] Graham Fraser was induced to leave Nova Scotia Steel to become general manager of the new corporation,[90] and J.H. Plummer, assistant general manager of the Bank of Commerce, was brought from Toronto as president.

The primacy of American interests in both the Dominion Steel and Dominion Coal companies was rapidly replaced by those of Montreal and Toronto after 1900. The sale of stocks added a strong Toronto delegation to the directorate of the steel company in 1901.[91] In that same year James Ross, the Montreal street railway magnate, bought heavily into the coal corporation, reorganized its management, and retained control of the firm until 1910.[92]

V

The increasing reliance on the stock market as a technique for promoting and securing the necessary financial support to develop the massive Nova

Scotia steel corporations emphasized the growing shift from industrial to financial capitalism. Centred on the Montreal stock market, the new movement brought to the control of industrial corporations men who had neither a communal nor a vocational interest in the concern.

In emulation of, and possibly in reaction to the Montreal experience, a group within the Halifax business and professional communities scrambled to erect the financial structure necessary to this undertaking. The city already possessed some of the elements of this structure. The Halifax stock exchange had existed on an informal basis since before Confederation.[93] The city's four major banking institutions — the Nova Scotia, the Union, the Merchants (which subsequently became the Royal Bank of Canada), and the Peoples — were among the soundest in the Dominion. The development of Halifax as a major centre for industrial finance began in 1894, at the height of the first Montreal-based merger movement, when a syndicate headed by J.F. Stairs founded the Eastern Trust Company.[94] The membership of this group was indicative of the change that was occurring in the Halifax business elite. Although it contained representatives of the older mercantile group, such as Stairs, T.E. Kenny, and Adam Burns, it also included manufacturers and coal men, notably J.W. Allison and David McKeen, a stockbroker, J.C. MacKintosh, and lawyers such as Robert L. Borden and Robert E. Harris.

Until his death in 1904, the personification of the new Halifax finance capitalism was John Stairs. It was Stairs who arranged the organization of Acadia Sugar in 1894, who initiated the merger of the Union bank of Halifax with the Bank of Windsor in 1899, and who led the Halifax business community back into its traditional imperium in the Caribbean with the organization of the Trinidad Electric and Demerara Electric corporations.[95] After 1900, it was Stairs who demonstrated to this same group the possibilities for industrial finance existing within the Maritimes. With the assistance of his young secretary, Max Aitken, and through the medium of his own holding company, Royal Securities, he undertook the reorganization of a number of firms in the region, most notably the Alexander Gibson Railroad and Manufacturing Company which was recapitalized at $6,000,000.[96] The scope of his interests, and the changes which had been wrought in the Maritime business community in the previous twenty-five years, were perhaps best illustrated in the six corporation presidencies which Stairs held in his lifetime, five of them at his death in 1904: Consumers Cordage, Nova Scotia Steel, Eastern Trust, Trinidad Electric, Royal Securities, and Dalhousie University.

Yet, while promotion of firms such as Stanfield's Woollens of Truro constituted a fertile field of endeavour,[97] the major industrial interest of the Halifax finance capitalists was the Nova Scotia Steel Company. In its search for additional capital resources after 1900, the entrepreneurial strength of this firm was rapidly broadened from its New Glasgow base. The principal new promoters of the company were Halifax men, notably

James Allison, George Campbell, and Robert Harris. The New Brunswick–born nephew of the founder of Mount Allison University, Allison
had entered the chocolate and spice manufactory of John Mott & Company of Halifax in 1871, and had eventually been admitted to a partnership
in the firm. He had invested heavily in several Nova Scotia industries
and sat on the directorates of Stanfields Woollens, the Eastern Trust,
and the Bank of Nova Scotia in addition to Nova Scotia Steel.[98] George
Campbell, the son of a Scottish gentleman, had entered the service of
a Halifax steamship agency as a young man and ultimately became its
head. Like Allison he was deeply involved in a number of Nova Scotian
firms including Stanfields, the Silliker Car of Amherst, the Eastern Trust,
and the Bank of Nova Scotia.[99]

By far the most significant figure in the Nova Scotia Steel Corporation
after Stairs' death was Mr. Justice Robert Harris. The Annapolis-born
scion of a Loyalist family, Harris shared the same antecedents as the
Moncton and St. John entrepreneurs of the same name. After reading   75
law with Sir John Thompson, he was called to the Nova Scotia bar in
1882 and rapidly became one of the leading legal figures in the province.
In 1892 he moved his practice to Halifax and there became intimately
involved in the corporate promotions of the period, ultimately serving
on the directorates of thirteen major corporations including the Eastern
Trust, Eastern Car, Bank of Nova Scotia, Maritime Telegraph and Telephone, Acadia Sugar, Robb Engineering, Brandram-Henderson Paint,
and held the presidencies of Nova Scotia Steel, Eastern Trust, Demerara
Electric, and Trinidad Electric.[100]

Despite the continuing need for additional capital, the Nova Scotia
Steel Company found little difficulty obtaining most of this support from
the Halifax business community.[101] In turn, the corporation remained
one of the most efficiently organized industrial firms in the country. In
striking contrast to the larger Dominion Steel enterprise, Nova Scotia
Steel's financial position remained strong, its performance solid and its
earnings continuous. It was generally credited with being the only major
steel company which could have maintained its dividend payments without the aid of federal bounties.[102]

As the first decade of the twentieth century wore to a close, the Halifax
business elite appeared to have succeeded in establishing a financial hegemony in the industrial life of an area centred in eastern Nova Scotia
and extending outward into both southern New Brunswick and peninsular
Nova Scotia. Yet, increasingly, that hegemony was being challenged by
the burgeoning consolidation movement emanating from Montreal. The
most serious threat was posed in 1909 when Max Aitken, with Montreal
now as the centre for his Royal Securities Corporation, arranged the amalgamation of the Rhodes, Curry Company of Amherst with the Canada
Car and the Dominion Car and Foundry companies of Montreal to form
the Canadian Car and Foundry Company. The union marked a triumph

as much for Nathaniel Curry as for Aitken — he emerged with the presidency and with nearly $3,000,000 of the $8,500,000 capital stock of the new corporation.[103] The move was a blow to the Halifax capitalists, however, as it placed the largest car manufactory in the country, an Amherst plant employing 1,300 men and annually producing $5,000,000 in iron and steel products,[104] firmly in the Montreal orbit of the Drummonds and the Dominion Steel and Coal Corporation. Tension was heightened by the feeling that this manoeuvre was a prelude to the creation of a railroad car monopoly. The reaction was swift. To prevent the takeover of the other Amherst car works, the Silliker Company, a Halifax-based syndicate bought up most of the Silliker stock and organized a greatly expanded company, Nova Scotia Car Works, with a $2,625,000 capital.[105] The following year Nova Scotia Steel organized its own $2,000,000 car subsidiary, the Eastern Car Company.

The contest between Montreal and Halifax finance capitalism reached its climax at the annual meeting of the Nova Scotia Steel Company of New Glasgow in April, 1910. Fresh from the triumph of the Dominion Coal and Steel merger, Montreal stockbrokers Rudolphe Forget and Max Aitken determined to extend the union to include the smaller steel firm, a proposal which the Scotia Steel president, Robert Harris, flatly refused to consider. Arguing that the firm was stagnating and that a more dynamic leadership in a reorganized corporation would yield greater returns, Forget launched a major effort to acquire proxies with a view to taking control from the Nova Scotia directors. Using the facilities of the Montreal Stock Exchange, he bought large quantities of Scotia stock at increasingly higher prices, an example followed by Robert Harris and his associates at Halifax. At the April meeting, Harris offered Forget a minority of the seats on the directorate; Forget refused. In the voting which followed, the Montreal interests were narrowly beaten. The *Monetary Times*, in a masterpiece of distortion, described this victory as the triumph of "the law . . . over the market place,"[106] and proclaimed that "New Glasgow prefers coal dust to that of the stock exchange floor."[107] In fact, it marked a victory, albeit a temporary one, for New Glasgow industrial capitalism and Halifax financial capitalism. More important, it marked the high point of a late-developing effort on the part of the Halifax business community to create an industrial region structured on that Atlantic metropolis. It was a short-lived triumph. By 1920 the Halifax group made common cause with their Montreal and London counterparts in the organization of the British Empire Steel Corporation, a gigantic consolidation containing both the Dominion and the Nova Scotia Steel companies. This event marked both the final nationalization of the region's major industrial potential and the failure of its entrepreneurs to maintain control of any significant element in the industrial section of the regional economy.

VI

The Maritimes had entered Canada very much as a foreign colony. As the least integrated part of the Canadian economy, it was the region most dependent upon and most influenced by those policies designated to create an integrated national state. The entrepreneurs of the 1880's were capable men, vividly aware of the problems involved in the transition from an Atlantic to a continental economy. The tragedy of the industrial experiment in the Maritimes was that the transportation lines which linked the region to its new metropolis altered the communal arrangement of the entire area; they did not merely establish a new external frame of reference, they re-cast the entire internal structure. The Maritimes had never been a single integrated organic unit; it was, in fact, not a "region" at all, but a number of British communities clustered on the Atlantic fringe, each with its separate lines of communication and its several metropolises — lines that were water-borne, flexible, and changing. In this sense the railroad with its implications of organic unity, its inflexibility, and its assumption that there was a metropolitan point at which it could end, provided an experience entirely alien to the Maritime tradition. The magnitude of this problem was demonstrated in the initial attempts at industrialization; they all occurred in traditional communities ideally located for the Atlantic market, but in the most disadvantaged positions possible for a continental one.

Central to the experience was the failure of a viable regional metropolis to arise to provide the financial leadership and market alternative. With its powerful mercantile interests and its impressive banking institutions Halifax could most easily have adopted this role, but its merchants preferred, like their Boston counterparts, to invest their large fortunes in banks and American railroad stocks than to venture them on building a new order. Only later, with the advent of regional resource industries, did that city play the role of financial metropolis.

Lacking any strong regional economic centre, the Maritime entrepreneur inevitably sought political solutions to the structural problems created by the National Policy; he consistently looked to the federal government for aid against all external threats and to his local governments for aid against Canadians. Since the regional politician was more able to influence a hostile environment than was the regional businessman, the latter frequently became both. In many respects the National Policy simply represented to the entrepreneur a transfer from a British to a Canadian commercial empire. Inherent in most of his activities was the colonial assumption that he could not really control his own destiny, that, of necessity, he would be manipulated by forces beyond his control. Thus he produced cotton cloth for the central Canadian metropolis in precisely the same manner as he had produced timber and ships for the British.

In so doing he demonstrated considerable initiative and considerable courage, for the truly surprising aspect of the whole performance was that he was able, using his limited community resources, to produce such a complex and diversified industrial potential during the last two decades of the nineteenth century. The inability of the Canadian market to consume his output was as much a failure of the system as of the entrepreneur; the spectacle of a metropolis which devoured its own children had been alien to the Maritime colonial experience. Ultimately, perhaps inevitably, the regional entrepreneur lost control to external forces which he could rarely comprehend, much less master.

NOTES

[1] Nova Scotia's industrial output increased 66 percent between 1880 and 1890; that of Ontario and Quebec by 51 percent each. Canada, *Census* (1901), 3: 272, 283. Bertram estimates that the per capita value of Nova Scotia's industrial output rose from 57.8 percent to 68.9 percent of the national average during the period. Gordon Bertram, "Historical Statistics on Growth and Structure of Manufacturing in Canada, 1870–1957," Canadian Political Science Association Conference on Statistics, 1962 and 1963, *Report*, 122.

[2] Canada, *Census* (1901), 3: 326–29. The increase between 1880 and 1890 was as follows:

	St. John	Hamilton
Population	-3%	34%
Industrial Capital	125%	69%
Industrial Workers	118%	48%
Average Annual Wage	12%	2%
Value of Output	98%	71%

[3] See Table 1.

[4] For a sampling of business opinion on the National Policy see K.P. Burn's reply to Peter Mitchell in the tariff debate of 1883, Canada, House of Commons, *Debates* (1883), 551–52; the opinion of Josiah Wood, *Debates* (1883), 446–48; and the view of John F. Stairs, *Debates*, (1885), 641–49.

[5] Quoted by J.F. Stairs in the tariff debate of 1886, Canada, House of Commons, *Debates* (1886), 775.

[6] *Monetary Times*, 4 June, 6 September 1886. Forty-five of the fifty savings banks in the Dominion were located in the Maritimes.

[7] *Monetary Times*, 16 May 1879.

[8] *Monetary Times*, 20 May 1881.

[9] George M. Rose, ed., *Cyclopedia of Canadian Biography* (Toronto, 1886–88), 2: 729–31 (henceforth cited as *CCB*).

[10] *Encyclopedia of Canadian Biography* (Montreal, 1904–1907), 1: 86; *CCB* 2: 155; W.J. Stairs, *History of Stairs Morrow* (Halifax, 1906), 5–6.

[11] *Canadian Biographical Dictionary* (Montreal, 1880–81), 2: 684–85 (henceforth cited as *CBD*); Parks Family Papers, F, no. 1, New Brunswick Museum.

[12] *CBD* 2: 684–85; *Monetary Times*, 27 April 1883, 22 June 1888.

[13] *CCB* 2: 186–87, 86.

[14] *CBD* 2: 354–55; *CBD* 2: 693; Henry J. Morgan, ed., *Canadian Men and Women of the Time* (Toronto, 1898), 1000.

[15] *Monetary Times*, 16 December 1882.

[16] *CCB* 2: 221–22; *CBD* 2: 674–75; Harold Davis, *An International Community on the St. Croix (1604–1930)* (Orono, 1950), ch. 18; *Monetary Times*, 1 August 1890.

[17] Canada, *Sessional Papers*, 1885, no. 37, pp. 174–97.

[18] *Monetary Times*, 11 December 1885; *Canadian Journal of Commerce*, 3 June 1881; *CBD* 2: 409–10, 510; *Canadian Men and Women of the Time* (1898), 44.

[19] Canadian Journal of Commerce, 10 June 1881.

[20] W.J.A. Donald, *The Canadian Iron and Steel Industry* (Boston, 1915), ch. 3.

[21] *Monetary Times*, 28 April 1882.

[22] *The Canadian Manufacturer and Industrial World*, 3 May 1889 (henceforth cited as *Canadian Manufacturer*).

[23] Henry J. Morgan, ed., *Canadian Men and Women of the Time* (Toronto, 1912), 419; C.W. Parker, ed., *Who's Who and Why* (Vancouver, 1916), 6 & 7: 259 (hereafter cited as *WWW*).

[24] *Canadian Manufacturer*, 1 April 1892.

[25] *Canadian Manufacturer*, 7 March 1890.

[26] *CBD* 2: 534–35.

[27] A.G. Bailey. "The Basis and Persistence of Opposition to Confederation in New Brunswick," *Canadian Historical Review* 23 (1942): 394.

[28] *Monetary Times*, 9 January 1885.

[29] *Monetary Times*, 11 May 1883.

[30] *Our Dominion: Historical and Other Sketches of the Mercantile Interests of Fredericton, Marysville, Woodstock, Moncton, Yarmouth, etc.* (Toronto, 1889), 48–54.

[31] Canada, *Sessional Papers*, 1885, no. 37. pp. 174–97.

[32] Canada, Royal Commission on the Relations of Labour and Capital (1889), *Evidence* 2: 448.

[33] American industrial leaders of the same period averaged 45 years. See W.F. Gregory and I.D. New, "The American Industrial Elite in the 1870's: Their Social Origins," in William Miller, ed., *Men in Business* (Cambridge, 1952), 197.

[34] Canada, Royal Commission on the Relations of Labour and Capital, *Evidence* 2: 256, 458 and 3: 78, 238, 249; *Canadian Manufacturer*, 24 August 1883; *Monetary Times*, 17 June 1887.

[35] *Monetary Times*, 18 March 1881.

[36] *Monetary Times*, 17 February 1882.

[37] *Monetary Times*, 19 March 1886.

[38] *Canadian Journal of Commerce*, 26 October 1883.

[39] *Monetary Times*, 18 October 1880.

[40] *Monetary Times*, 10 May 1905.

[41] *Monetary Times*, 8 January 1886.

[42] *Monetary Times*, 30 January 1885. Principal Maritime imports from central Canada included flour, shoes, clothing, textiles, alcoholic beverages, and hardware; exports to Quebec and Ontario centred on sugar, coal, cotton cloth, iron, and fish.

[43] Exports of New Brunswick lumber declined from 404,000,000 board feet in 1883 to 250,000,000 feet in 1887. *Monetary Times*, 9 January 1885, 2 and 7 January 1887, 21 January 1898.

[44] See particularly, *Proceedings of the Ninth Annual Meeting of the Dominion Board of Trade* (1879), 65–73; *Monetary Times*, 27 January 1882; Minute Book of the St. John Board of Trade (1879–87), 14 October 1887, New Brunswick Museum.

[45] Canada, *Sessional Papers*, 1885, no. 34, 86–125.

[46] Bertram, *Historical Statistics on Growth*, 131.

[47] J.F. Stairs to J.M. Pope, 10 September 1885, Macdonald Papers, 50080-5, Public Archives of Canada.

[48] J.F. Stairs to Macdonald, 5 February 1886, Macdonald Papers, vol. 155.

[49] *Monetary Times*, 5 October 1888.

[50] *Monetary Times*, 12 February 1886.

[51] See the problems faced by John Parks and the N.B. Cotton Mills. Parks Family Papers, F, New Brunswick Museum.

[52] Montreal *Herald*, 15 October 1883.

[53] *Monetary Times*, 8 October 1880.

[54] *Monetary Times*, 15 December 1882.

[55] *Monetary Times*, 8 June 1883.

[56] *Monetary Times*, 16 November 1884.

[57] *Monetary Times*, 13 August 1886; *Canadian Manufacturer*, 20 August 1887.

[58] *Canadian Journal of Commerce*, 7 September 1888.

[59] Thomas Kenny in Canada, House of Commons, *Debates*, (1893), 2522.

[60] *Monetary Times*, 16 January 1891.

[61] St. John *Globe*, 1 May 1891.

[62] E.S. Clouston to Jones, 25 April 1891, Bank of Montreal, General Managers Letterbooks, vol. 8, Public Archives of Canada.

[63] 15 December 1890, Parks Papers, Scrapbook 2, New Brunswick Museum.

[64] Clouston to Jones, 13, 22 April, 23 May 1891, Bank of Montreal, General Managers Letterbooks, vol. 8, Public Archives of Canada.

[65] St. John *Sun*, 28 December 1892.

[66] *Monetary Times*, 18 March 1892.

[67] *Monetary Times*, 24 October 1890.

[68] *Canadian Journal of Commerce*, 22 March 1895.

[69] *Monetary Times*, 24 October 1890.

[70] *Monetary Times*, 12 June 1885, 22 April 1887, 22 August 1902; Minutes of the St. John Board of Trade, 1 December 1979, 8 November 1886, New Brunswick Museum.

[71] *Monetary Times*, 20 May 1887.

[72] *The Canadian Journal of Commerce*, 29 April 1887.

[73] Canada, Statutes, 50-1 Victoria C.39.

[74] Simon J. MacLean, *The Tariff History of Canada* (Toronto, 1895), 37.

[75] *Nova Scotia's Industrial Centre: New Glasgow, Stellarton, Westville, Trenton. The Birthplace of Steel in Canada* (n.p., 1916), 45–46.

[76] *Monetary Times*, 9 March 1900; *Industrial Canada*, 20 July 1901.

[77] *www* 6 & 7: 927, 1075–76.

[78] R.M. Guy, "Industrial Development and Urbanization of Pictou Co., N.S. to 1900" (unpublished M.A. thesis, Acadia University, 1962), 120–123.

[79] *Canadian Manufacturer*, 20 April 1894.

[80] *Monetary Times*, 30 June 1893.

[81] *Industrial Canada*, March, 1910; *Canadian Men and Women of the Time* (1912), 290.

[82] *CCB* 2: 183; *CBD* 2: 506–507; *www* 6 & 7: 997; *Canadian Men and Women of the Time* (1912), 947.

[83] *Monetary Times*, 26 November 1896. The St. Lawrence ports imported 88,000 tons of British and American coal in 1896, and 706,000 tons of Nova Scotia coal. The transport of this commodity provided the basis for the Nova Scotia merchant marine of the period.

[84] *Monetary Times*, 3 February 1893.

[85] *Canadian Men and Women of the Time* (1912), 698–99; *www* 6 & 7: 1118.

[86] *www* 6 & 7: 1322.

[87] Donald, however, argues that Whitney had been determined to go into steel production even if no bounty had been granted. See Donald, *The Canadian Iron and Steel Industry*, 203.

[88] Partly, the *Canadian Journal of Commerce* (15 March 1901) suggested, on the promise of the promoters that the Company would receive bonuses of $8,000,000 in its first six years of operation.

[89] *Industrial Canada*, May 1902.

[90] J.H. Plummer to B.E. Walker, 3 December 1903. Walker Papers, University of Toronto Archives.

[91] *Annual Financial Review* 1 (1901): 92; 3 (1903): 158–60.

[92] *Monetary Times*, 3 August 1907.

[93] *Monetary Times*, 17 April 1903.

[94] *Monetary Times*, 23 February 1894.

[95] *Annual Financial Review*, 23 (1923): 682, 736.

[96] *Monetary Times*, 5 December 1902.

[97] *Monetary Times*, 22 April 1911.

[98] *Canadian Men and Women of the Time* (1912), 19; *www* 6 & 7: 762; *Annual Financial Review* 3 (1903): 174–76.

[99] *Canadian Men and Women of the Time* (1912), 192; *www* 6 & 7: 803.

[100] *Canadian Men and Women of the Time* (1912), 505; *www* 6 & 7: 1107; *Annual Financial Review* 3 (1903): 174–76.

[101] Most of the stock in this concern was held by Nova Scotians who also bought up two-thirds of the $1,500,000 bond which the company put out in 1904. L.M. Jones to B.E. Walker, 5 August 1904, Walker Papers; *Monetary Times*, 15 August 1902.

[102] *Monetary Times*, 9 March 1907.

[103] *Monetary Times*, 8 January 1910.

[104] *Industrial Canada*, August 1913.

[105] *Monetary Times*, 29 October 1910.

[106] *Monetary Times*, 2 April 1910.

[107] *Monetary Times*, 9 April 1910.

Topic Three

The Rise of Western Alienation

Roughly 25 000 Indians and 10 000 mixed-bloods, or Métis, lived in the Prairie West in 1867. The Métis had developed their own sense of nationality and had established their own way of life based on agriculture and the buffalo hunt. The majority of the Métis lived in the Red River colony at the junction of the Red and Assiniboine rivers (present-day Winnipeg), the only major permanent settlement in the entire region.

The newly formed Canadian government purchased Rupert's Land (which incorporated all of the present-day prairies) from the Hudson's Bay Company in 1869, for a cash payment of £300 000 plus one-twentieth of the fertile area of the prairies. This new colony would be administered by a federally appointed lieutenant governor and council, until the granting of provincial status. Without consulting the local western population, the Canadian government arranged for the new lieutenant governor and a group of surveyors to go west to prepare the way for settlement and the building of a transcontinental railway. Donald Swainson, in "Canada Annexes the West: Colonial Status Confirmed," provides an overview of the history of the Canadian West in the nineteenth century from the perspective of western alienation.

The Métis resisted the Canadian takeover under the leadership of Louis Riel, a Red River Métis who had been educated in Quebec. They formed their own provisional government to defend their interests and to present their views. Armed conflict arose between the settlers who had recently arrived in the Red River colony from Ontario (and whose interests initially paralleled those of the federal government) and the Métis. Out of the Riel uprising of 1869 emerged the terms for the incorporation of Manitoba as a province the following year. In his historiographical article "The Myth of Louis Riel," Douglas Owram outlines and explains the different perceptions of this important figure in the writing of Canadian history from the 1880s to the 1960s and 1970s.

The Canadians' takeover of the Métis's homeland adversely affected other groups as well. The Indians, the original inhabitants, also had to adjust to the new conditions. Traditionally, historians have favourably regarded the Canadian government's policy of negotiating treaties with the Indians and settling them on reserves, but historian John Tobias offers an alternative viewpoint in "Canada's Subjugation of the Plains Cree, 1879–1885." Looking at this critical period in western Canadian

Indian history from the Indians' vantage point, he argues that their sub-jugation came only after much resistance, and as a result of policies both unjust and dishonourable.

For a short overview of the Métis see D.B. Sealey and A.S. Lussier's *The Métis: Canada's Forgotten People* (Winnipeg: Métis Federation Press, 1975). A growing literature exists on Louis Riel and the Métis in 1869–70 and 1885. The five-volume *Collected Writings of Louis Riel/Les Écrits complets de Louis Riel* (Edmonton: University of Alberta Press, 1985), under the general editorship of George F.G. Stanley, is currently available. Secondary studies include G.F.G. Stanley's *The Birth of Western Canada: A History of the Riel Rebellion* (Toronto: University of Toronto Press, 1961; first published in 1936); Thomas Flanagan's *Louis 'David' Riel: 'Prophet of the New World'* (Toronto: University of Toronto Press, 1979); H. Bowsfield's *Louis Riel: The Rebel and the Hero* (Toronto: Oxford University Press, 1971) and his recent edited collection, *Louis Riel: Selected Readings* (Toronto: Copp Clark, 1987); Joseph Kinsey Howard's *Strange Empire* (New York: William Morrow, 1952); and, for the uprising of 1885, B. Beal and R. Macleod's *Prairie Fire: A History of the 1885 Rebellion* (Edmonton: Hurtig, 1984). Hugh Dempsey presents one Indian leader's response in his *Big Bear* (Vancouver: Douglas and McIntyre, 1984). For a critical view of the Métis position see T. Flanagan, *Riel and the Rebellion: 1885 Reconsidered* (Saskatoon: Western Producer Books, 1983). The opposite viewpoint is presented in D.N. Sprague, *Canada and the Métis, 1869–1885* (Waterloo: Wilfrid Laurier University Press, 1988). Douglas Owram presents the central-Canadian view of the West in *The Promise of Eden: The Canadian Expansionist Movement and the Idea of the West, 1856–1900* (Toronto: University of Toronto Press, 1980).

George F.G. Stanley reviews the various interpretations of Riel in "The Last Word on Louis Riel — The Man of Several Faces," in *1885 and After*, ed. F. Laurie Barron and James B. Waldram (Regina: Canadian Plains Research Centre, 1986), 3–22. George Melnyk's *Radical Regionalism* (Edmonton: NeWest Press, 1981) examines the roots of western protest, and its relationship to regional identity.

82

Canada Annexes the West: Colonial Status Confirmed*

DONALD SWAINSON

The early history of the Canadian West[1] is characterized by dependence and exploitation. The area and its resources were controlled from outside,

*From *Federalism in Canada and Australia: The Early Years*, ed. Bruce W. Hodgins et al. Copyright 1978 by Wilfrid Laurier University Press, Waterloo, Ontario. Reprinted by permission.

for the benefit of several distant centres, whose relative importance changed from time to time. London, Montreal, and Toronto, the major and competing metropolises, were flanked by such lesser competitors as Minneapolis–St. Paul, Benton, and Vancouver. A prime result of this pattern of development has been a continuing resistance to outside controls. At the same time, the character of western people and institutions has been heavily influenced by forces outside western control. Even indigenous peoples were largely defined by the forces that controlled the region. The interplay of these factors has played a large part in moulding the character of the West and in determining fundamentally its role in Canadian federalism.

I

The pattern of dependence preceded federal union and for the West is the context within which federalism must be viewed. It began in the seventeenth century when English traders established themselves in posts around Hudson Bay. Chartered in 1670 as the Hudson's Bay Company, this "Company of Adventurers of England tradeing [sic] into Hudson Bay"[2] tapped an enormously profitable trade in furs. To this prestigious and powerful firm the Crown delegated vast responsibilities and valuable privileges:

83

> [T]he Company was granted the "sole Trade and Commerce of all those Seas Streightes Bayes Rivers Lakes Creekes and Soundes in whatsoever Latitude they shall bee that lye within the entrance of the Streightes commonly called Hudsons Streightes together with all the Landes and Territoryes upon the Countryes Coastes and confynes of the Seas Bayes Lakes Rivers Creekes and Soundes aforesaid that are not actually possessed by or granted to any of our Subjects or possessed by the Subjects of any other Christian Prince or State". They were to be the "true and absolute Lordes and Proprietors" of this vast territory, and they were to hold it, as had been envisaged in the grant of October 1669, in free and common socage. . . . These lands were to be reckoned as a plantation or colony, and were to be known as Rupert's Land; and the Company was to own the mineral and fishing rights there as well as the exclusive trade and the land itself.[3]

For two hundred years, the Hudson's Bay Company was the (more or less) effective government of Rupert's Land, an enormous territory stretching from Labrador through the shield and the prairies and into the Arctic tundra in the West. It included most of what are now the provinces of Manitoba, Saskatchewan, and Alberta. Control over the West was thus vested in a firm centred in London and exercised in the interests of commerce.

Montreal businessmen (whether French before the Conquest, or British after) refused to recognize the HBC's trade monopoly, and wanted to share in the profits. In spite of enormous overhead costs French traders penetrated the West in the middle of the eighteenth century, and entered into competition for the favour of the Indian fur gatherers. After the Conquest Montreal's challenge to the Hudson's Bay Company's monopoly was even more serious. Numerous Montreal-based traders entered the field, but the most famous and effective were organized late in the eighteenth century as the North-West Company. This marvel of capitalist organization exploited the wealth of the shield and the prairies. It opened the rich Athabasca country and its agents penetrated north to the Arctic and west to the Pacific. The Nor'Westers introduced the influence of Montreal into the mainstream of western life. The vicious competition between Montreal and London for the control of the western trade, however, proved too costly; in 1821 the Hudson's Bay Company and the North-West Company amalgamated. But both Montreal and London continued to exercise great influence in the West. And, of course, the officers and men of the reorganized Hudson's Bay Company remained a powerful force in the West until Canada annexed the area in 1870.

84

Children of mixed white and Indian blood were an inevitable result of the presence of fur traders in the West. By the late eighteenth century these people were a numerous group on the prairies. They can be very roughly divided into two sub-groups: English-speaking half-breeds and French-speaking Métis. The former tended to be relatively settled and to have close ties with the white communities in the Red River Valley. The Métis were more autonomous and distinctive. During this period, they developed into a powerful force.

As a people, the Métis were very much a product of the fur trade. Like many other unsophisticated and indigenous peoples, they were manipulated by the great business firms that exploited the natural resources of their area. The North-West Company employed them first as labourers and hunters. The trade war between the fur trading giants increased their utility, especially after Lord Selkirk established his famous settlement in the Red River Valley in 1811–12. Selkirk's colony and the HBC functioned as interdependent units, and challenged the viability of the NWC operations west of the Red River. The NWC could not declare war on one without fighting the other. Consequently it declared war on both, and the Métis became its prime weapon. The leaders of the NWC encouraged the growth of a primitive nationalism; the Métis were encouraged to believe that the Red River settlers threatened their claim to western lands, a claim inherited from their Cree and Saulteaux mothers. Cuthbert Grant, a Scottish-educated half-breed, was appointed Captain of the Métis by the North-West Company, and his followers became a small private army. They harassed the Selkirk settlers, a process that culminated in 1816 in the battle of Seven Oaks where Grant's men massacred Governor Robert Semple and twenty of his settlers. But in spite of its superior military strength, the NWC, primarily for geographical reasons, could not sustain a protracted campaign against the Red River colonists and the HBC. Consequently, the firms united in 1821; the West was pacified.

The four-year struggle (1812–1816) against the Selkirk settlers was a decisive event in western history. It marked the beginning of the Métis as an organized and self-conscious group. After 1821, they continued to accept Grant's leadership. They founded Grantown on the Assiniboine River west of the restored Selkirk settlement and made that village their capital; for the next seventy years they were at the centre of prairie history.

After the union of the firms, Cuthbert Grant and his people were coopted by the controlling interests. The Métis defended the growing and prosperous community of Selkirk settlers, their former enemies, from the Sioux. In 1828, Grant was made Warden of the Plains of Red River, with responsibility for enforcing the Hudson's Bay Company trade monopoly. During these quiet years of the 1820s and 1830s the Métis of Grantown organized and refined their most important institution, the famous buffalo hunt, which provided important food reserves for settlers and traders alike, and an economic base for the Métis.[4] The implications of the hunt were endless. It was organized along military lines and was easily adaptable to military and political purposes. The Métis, self-confident about their identity and proud of their place in western society, referred to themselves as the "New Nation" but nonetheless they remained dependent on buffalo and fur traders.

The Métis were created as a people only after the arrival of white traders in the West; the Indians had peopled the prairies for several millennia. It might be argued, however, that European influences recreated Indian society; these forces certainly revolutionized Indian history. When white men first came to North America the Indians who inhabited the western plains lacked horses and guns. The acquisition of these items, combined with trade, radically altered Indian society. In some instances, and for a brief period, the result was startling. A recent historian of Alberta illustrates:

> For a few vivid decades Blackfoot culture, based upon horses, guns and unlimited buffalo, rose rapidly into the zenith of the rich, colourful and glamorous life which many regard as the apogee of plains culture. Prior to 1730, during the long era which the Blackfoot called the dog-days, they travelled on foot and used dogs for transport. About that year, the acquisition of horses and guns swept them rapidly onward and upward until slightly over a century later they were at the peak of their spectacular horse-based culture. . . . Though horses and guns had made the Blackfoot aggressive, they also provided the leisure which led to the flowering of their social life.[5]

Revolutionized Indian societies were highly vulnerable to external forces. They could not manufacture either guns or ammunition; traders could (and did) cause social calamities through the introduction of liquor and

85

a variety of diseases; trading patterns could not be controlled by Indians. More important, the buffalo could be liquidated and settlement could destroy the basis of Indian independence. In the mid-nineteenth century these successful western Indian societies were in a delicately balanced position. European contacts had changed the very character of their society; at the same time they were dependent upon and vulnerable to white society. Further white encroachment in the West could destroy them. That encroachment of course quickly occurred, and in the 1870s the western Indians were swamped. A recent student of Canadian Indians comments: "For the sake of convenience, and recognizing the arbitrariness of the choice, we may use the date 1876, that of the first Indian Act, as the beginning of what we call the "colonial" period. From the point of view of the European, the Indian had become irrelevant."[6]

The full complexity of mid-nineteenth-century prairie society cannot be revealed in a few paragraphs. The main characteristics, however, can

be delineated. The West was inhabited by French-speaking Métis, English-speaking half-breeds, officers and men of the Hudson's Bay Company, Selkirk settlers and a handful of missionaries, retired soldiers and free-traders. Except for the Indians, these groups were all centred around the forks of the Red and Assiniboine Rivers, where a pluralistic society emerged. Reasonable amity usually prevailed, although the Métis could not be controlled against their will by the aging and increasingly ineffective HBC regime. This was a civilized society, with its own churches, schools, and law courts. Its various components produced their own indigenous middle-classes, leaders, institutions, and traditions. Several religions were sustained within the settlement and promoted amongst the Indians.

At the same time these diverse western societies were fragile and derivative. W.L. Morton describes the Selkirk settlers as "Scottish crofters on the banks of the Red."[7] Indian society had been recreated through European contact and persons of mixed blood were a product of liaisons between fur traders and Saulteaux and Cree women. Employees of the HBC were often of British birth. None of these groups had sufficient cultural integrity or autonomy to retain their distinctiveness and independence without a considerable degree of isolation from the larger North American society. As Bishop Taché observed about immigration into the West: "[T]he movement [of immigration] is an actual fact, and we must cease to be what we have hitherto been, an exceptional people."[8]

They were dependent on more than isolation. Economically they needed the fur trade and the buffalo hunt. Buffalo products were sold to traders, settlers, and Americans at Minneapolis–St. Paul. The fur trade supplied cash, employment, and markets. Agriculture, "subsistent, riparian, and restricted,"[9] was nonetheless an important enterprise. Markets were obviously extremely limited. The large-scale export of commodities was hardly reasonable and, even within the West, Red River

Valley farmers had no monopoly on food production as long as the buffalo survived. The agricultural sector of the western economy thus remained modest.[10]

Within the West some of these groups, particularly HBC officials, Indians, and Métis, could exert tremendous authority; their futures, however, were in the hands of forces that could not be contained. They had sufficient group-consciousness to defend collective interests, and to varying degrees they were all willing to resist encroachments from the outside. The Métis revolted against the locally enforced trade monopoly; HBC officials became dissatisfied with the treatment meted out to them by their London superiors. The Scots settlers resented the suggestion that the area could be disposed of without prior consultation. A willingness to resist in spite of dependence and relative weakness was a striking western characteristic long before the West was annexed by Canada. It is an important component of the western context of federalism.[11]

87

II

The Central Canadian context is equally important. French-Canadian explorers penetrated the West in the eighteenth century, and thereafter the West was always a concern of at least some Central Canadians. The connection became somewhat tenuous after the union of the fur companies in 1821, but it was never lost; there was always full cognizance of the fact that Rupert's Land was British territory.

A more pointed interest became evident in the late 1840s, and the nature of that interest illuminates Central Canadian attitudes about what the West was, what it should become and how it should relate to what was then the Province of Canada. This interest, while by no means partisan in nature, centred in the Upper Canadian Reformers. It can be illustrated by an examination of two of its representative manifestations: the campaign of the Toronto *Globe* to annex the West and the organization of the North-West Transportation Company.[12]

The *Globe* was the organ of George Brown, who emerged in the 1850s as the Upper Canadian Reform leader. It was a Toronto newspaper that spoke to the farmers of what became western Ontario, but at the same time represented many of the metropolitan interests of Toronto's business elite. Its interest in the North-West tended to be economic and exploitative. Underlying this early tentative interest in the West was the assumption that the West would become an economic and social adjunct of Upper Canada. On 24 March 1847, for example, Brown reprinted Robert Baldwin Sullivan's lecture, "Emigration and Colonization." While primarily concerned with Upper Canada, Sullivan also discussed settlement possibilities in the North-West. He viewed the West as a potential settlement area for Upper Canadians. In 1848 the *Globe* claimed the West for Canada, and dismissed the rights of the Hudson's Bay Company. The West, it argued, was "capable of supporting a numerous population. This wide region nominally belongs to the Hudson's Bay Company, but in point of fact it does not seem to be theirs."[13] The *Globe*'s interest petered out in 1850, but revived after a few years. In 1856 it published a series of revealing articles by an anonymous correspondent, "Huron": "I desire to see Canada for the Canadians and not exclusively for a selfish community of traders, utter strangers to our country; whose only anxiety is to draw all the wealth they can from it, without contributing to its advantages even one farthing."[14] He pronounced the charter of the Hudson's Bay Company "null and void" and declared that "[t]he interest of Canada require that this giant monopoly be swept out of existence. . . . " "Huron" was emphatic on this point:

> The formation of a Company in opposition to the Hudson's Bay Company would advance the interests of Canada; it would consolidate and strengthen the British power on the continent. . . . In the organization of [opposition to the HBC], every patriot, every true Canadian, beholds results the most important to his country.

According to the *Globe*, westward expansion was an urgent need because of a shortage of settlement land "south of Lake Huron." "[Canada] is fully entitled to possess whatever parts of the Great British American territory she can safely occupy. . . . "[15]

Interest in westward expansion was by no means confined to the *Globe*. In 1856 the Toronto Board of Trade indicated interest in western trade.[16] Various politicians took up the cause and the matter was aired in both houses of parliament.[17]

In 1858 a Toronto-based group made a "quixotic" and "abortive"[18] attempt to penetrate the West through the incorporation of the North-West Transportation, Navigation and Railway Company (known as the North-West Transit Co.).[19] The project, designed to link Central Canada and the Red River Valley by a combination of rail and water transport, was premature and unsuccessful, but its promoters' attitudes towards the West were both representative and persistent.[20] The objects were the exploitation of such likely and unlikely western possibilities as buffalo hides, furs, tallow, fish, salt, sarsaparilla, and cranberries, "the opening [of] a direct communication between Lake Superior and the Pacific . . . ," and the opening of trade with the Orient. "[W]e place before us a mart of 600 000 000 of people [in China] and [our project will] enable us geographically to command them; opening the route, and leaving it to the guidance of commercial interests, Canada will, sooner or later, become the great tollgate for the commerce of the world." By "Canada," of course, was meant Toronto, and these promoters dreamed of controlling a great empire: "Like the Genii in the fable [the East Indian trade] still offers the sceptre to those who, unintimidated by the terms that surround it, are bold enough to adventure to its embrace. In turn

88

Phoenicia, Carthage, Greece, Rome, Venice, Pisa, Genoa, Portugal, Holland and lastly England, has won and worn this ocean diadem; Destiny now offers [the East Indian trade] to us."

During the 1850s a dynamic and expansive Upper Canada saw the North-West as its proper hinterland. It was regarded as a huge extractive resource, designed to provide profit for the businessman, land for the farmer, and power for Toronto.

While cultural attitudes are sometimes difficult to identify, it was probably assumed that the North-West would be culturally as well as economically dependent on the St. Lawrence Valley. J.M.S. Careless, for example, suggests that "Brown used the North-West agitation to complete the reunification of Upper Canada's liberal party, merging Toronto urban and business leadership with Clear Grit agrarian strength in a dynamic party front."[21] Brown's "party front," which wanted "French Canadianism entirely extinguished,"[22] was dedicated to majoritarianism and the sectional interests of Upper Canada. While the nature of Reform attitudes towards French Canada is debatable, it is hardly likely that the same men who strove to terminate duality in Central Canada sought to extend it to the North-West. Some Lower Canadian leaders (both French- and English-speaking), especially those identified with Montreal business, were interested in westward expansion for economic reasons. There was, however, little French-Canadian enthusiasm for expansion westward.[23] French-Canadian attitudes emanated from the nature of Lower Canadian society, which was profoundly conservative and lacked the buoyant and dynamic qualities of Upper Canada: "Not movement but stasis, enforced by the very nature of the task of 'survival', was the keynote of French-Canadian society."[24] French Canadians lacked confidence in the economic viability of the North-West, in major part because of pre-Confederation missionary propaganda that emphasized difficulties related to the West. It was generally assumed that "western settlement was the sole concern of Ontario"[25] and that large-scale French-Canadian emigration would threaten French Canada's ability to survive. Thus there existed no Lower Canadian force to counterbalance Upper Canada's drive westward or Upper Canadian assumptions about how the West should be used. The only additional British North American region that could have possessed western ambitions consisted of the Atlantic colonies: New Brunswick, Nova Scotia, Prince Edward Island, and Newfoundland. Their traditional orientation was towards the Atlantic, not the interior. The Atlantic colonies were not about to launch an imperialistic venture in the 1860s.

Apart from Montreal business ambitions, the field was clear for Upper Canada, but little could be done until a new political order was established in Central Canada. The constitutional settlement embodied in the Act of Union of 1840 broke down during the 1850s. The complexities of Central Canadian politics during the 1850s are not germane to this

89

discussion, although it should be noted that a prime reason for the break-down of Canadian government was the incompatibility between the un-controllable dynamism and expansionism of Upper Canadian society on the one hand, and the conservative and inward-looking society of Lower Canada on the other.

The new order was worked out by the Great Coalition of 1864 that was committed to the introduction of "the federal principle into Canada, coupled with such provision as will permit the Maritime Provinces and the North-West Territory to be incorporated into the same system of government."[26] The solution was Confederation, which was established by the British North America Act of 1867. It created a highly centralized federation that included the Province of Canada (divided into Ontario and Quebec), Nova Scotia, and New Brunswick, and that made explicit provision for the inclusion of the remaining British North American territories:

90

> It should be lawful for the Queen, by and with the Advice of Her Majesty's Most Honourable Privy Council, on Addresses from the Houses of the Parliament of Canada, and from the Houses of the respective Legislatures of the Colonies or Provinces of Newfound-land, Prince Edward Island, and British Columbia, to admit those Colonies or Provinces, or any of them, into the Union, and on Ad-dress from the Houses of the Parliament of Canada to admit Rupert's Land and the North-western Territory, or either of them, into the Union. . . . [27]

Confederation was thus the constitutional framework within which the West was destined to relate to Central Canada.

The nature of the new Confederation had profound implications for the West. The system was highly centralized, so much so that in con-ception it hardly qualified as a federation in the classic sense. The Fathers of Confederation wanted a strong state that could withstand American pressure. Heavily influenced by trade considerations, they saw federation in mercantilistic terms. As children of the empire as it existed prior to the repeal of the corn laws, it is not surprising that their federal model was the old colonial system, modified to involve "the citizens of the prov-inces . . . in the government of the whole entity":[28]

> The purpose of the Fathers of Confederation — to found a united and integrated transcontinental Dominion — was comparable with that of the mercantilists: and in both designs there was the same need that the interests of the parts should be made subordinate to the interest of the whole. The Dominion was the heir in direct succession of the old colonial system. It was put in possession of both the economics and political controls of the old regime. On the one hand, it was given the power to regulate trade and commerce,

which had been the chief economic prerogative of Great Britain; on the other hand, it was granted the right to nominate provincial governors, to review provincial legislation and to disallow provincial acts, the three powers which had been the chief attributes of Great Britain's political supremacy.[29]

In his more optimistic moments, John A. Macdonald went so far as to predict the demise of the provinces: "If the Confederation goes on, you, if spared the ordinary age of man, will see both local parliaments and governments absorbed in the general power. This is as plain to me as if I saw it accomplished."[30]

It is true that Lower Canada and the Atlantic colonies were part of the new dominion, but the effective pressure for the new settlement came from Upper Canada. French Canada realized the inevitability of change, but generated little enthusiasm for Confederation. She could offer no better alternative and hence acquiesced (not without considerable protest) in the new arrangement.[31] The creative role was played by Upper Canada, *91* and for that section Confederation was a great triumph. The new system was posited on the abandonment of dualism and, through representation by population in the House of Commons, the acceptance of majoritarianism, albeit with limited guarantees for French-Canadian culture within the Province of Quebec. Majoritarianism was very much to the advantage of Ontario, which, according to the 1871 census, had 1 600 000 persons — or 46 per cent of Canada's 3 500 000 people. This translated into 82 of 181 seats in the House of Commons. The first prime minister was an Ontarian, as were the leading lights of the opposition — George Brown, Edward Blake, and Alexander Mackenzie. In the first cabinet Ontario, the wealthiest province, had 5 of 13 places. Even the capital was an Ontario city.

The Ontario Liberals became the leaders of the nineteenth-century provincial rights agitation and Ontario emerged as the bastion of provincial rights sentiment, but while the federal scheme was being defined most of Ontario's leaders, regardless of party, concurred on the utility of this "quasi federal" scheme.[32] This is hardly surprising. The Reformers or Liberals were the larger of the two Ontario parties, and doubtless looked forward to a great future as the rulers of *both* Ontario and the Dominion. Although they realized this aim by 1873 and ruled simultaneously in Toronto and Ottawa for five years, they suffered humiliating defeats in 1867 at both levels. The deep autonomist drives within Ontario society quickly reasserted themselves and Ontario's Liberals began their protracted assault on Macdonald's constitutional edifice. This should not obscure the fact that quasi-federalism met with little Ontario opposition during the mid-1860s.

The acquisition of the North-West would take place within the context of Canadian federalism. The Fathers of Confederation tended to assume that the "'colonial' relationship with the provinces was a natural one. . . . It therefore seems more appropriate to think of the dominion–provincial relationship at that time as similar to the relationship of the imperial government with a colony enjoying limited self-government."[33] Ontario Liberals quickly adopted a different approach to federalism; federal Conservatives did not. The West was to be "annexed as a subordinated territory."[34] Ontario's leaders were anxious that expansion take place quickly, and assumed that Ontarians would benefit through the creation of a miniature Ontario in the West. At the same time the settled portion of the West, shaken by the breakdown of its isolation and possessing a tradition of resistance to outside control, was accustomed to colonial status, exploitation and dependency.

III

92

Canada's first Confederation government was anxious to honour its commitment to annex the West. William McDougall and George Cartier went to London in 1868 to negotiate the transfer to Canada of Rupert's Land and the North-West Territory. Their mission was successful. The Hudson's Bay Company agreed to transfer its territory to Canada; the dominion agreed to compensate the company with one-twentieth of the fertile area in the West, land surrounding HBC posts, and a cash payment of £300 000. The initial transfer was to be to the Crown, which would immediately retransfer the area to Canada.

In preparation for the reception of this great domain, Canada passed "An Act for the temporary Government of Rupert's Land and the North-Western Territory when united with Canada."[35] This short act provided that the West, styled "The North-West Territories," would be governed by federal appointees — a lieutenant governor assisted by a council. It also continued existing laws in force and public servants in office until changes were made by either the federal government or the lieutenant governor. The act was to "continue in force until the end of the next Session of Parliament."

It has been suggested that this statute does not reveal much about the intent of the federal authorities because it was preceded by such phrases as: "to make some temporary provision" and "until more permanent arrangements can be made."[36] At the same time P.B. Waite notes that it was not a temporary provision at all. After the creation of Manitoba, "the rest of the vast Northwest Territories remained under the Act of 1869, that 'temporary' arrangement. It was re-enacted in 1871 as permanent without any alteration whatever."[37] There is no reason to assume that in 1869 Macdonald and his colleagues intended any very radical future alteration in the statute, which, with the appointments made thereunder, revealed much about Ottawa's attitude toward the West. The area, not a crown colony in 1869, was to join Confederation as a federally controlled territory — not as a province. It was not assumed that the West was joining a federation; rather, Canada was acquiring a subservient territory. Local leaders were neither consulted nor considered. These assumptions emerge even more clearly when the initial appointments under the act are studied. Ontario's ambitions to control the West were symbolized by the appointment of William McDougall as Lieutenant Governor. He was a former Clear Grit who represented Ontario Reformers in the first Confederation government. An imperious and sanctimonious expansionist, he had neither the ability nor the desire to take local leaders, especially those who were not white, into his confidence. Certainly the federal government's request that he search out westerners for his council[38] would hardly inspire local confidence. McDougall was regarded as anything but impartial.[39] Initial executive appointments were not likely, with the possible exception of J.A.N. Provencher,[40] to inspire local confidence in a regime that was organized in Central Canada. Two appointments were flagrantly political. A.N. Richards was the brother of a minister in Sandfield Macdonald's Ontario government and Captain D.R. Cameron was Charles Tupper's son-in-law. Even if one accepts the argument that the "temporary" act was indeed temporary, it is difficult to argue that Lieutenant Governor McDougall, Attorney General Richards, or Chief of Police Cameron were temporary.

93

These various decisions made in distant capitals caused an upheaval in the Red River settlement, the only really settled part of Rupert's Land. Red River was, in fact, on the verge of explosion — a point forcibly made to federal and imperial authorities by Anglican Bishop Machray, HBC Governor of Assiniboia Mactavish, and Roman Catholic Bishop Taché.[41] The unsettled state of Red River was a product of many factors. By the end of the 1840s the commercial authority of the HBC had been irretrievably eroded. During the 1850s the isolation of the area was just as irretrievably lost. American traders pushed up from St. Paul and by the late 1850s a Canadian party, allied with the anti-HBC agitation in Canada, had emerged in the settlement. These Canadians, whose attitudes had been previewed in the 1840s by Recorder Adam Thom and were later to merge with those of Canada First, were arrogant, threatening, and racist. They led a concerted assault on the authority of the company, and were instrumental in producing political chaos at Red River during the 1850s. To the Métis especially they represented a threat to their rights and way of life. These justified fears[42] were confirmed by Canadian government officials who entered the area prior to the transfer and offended local sensibilities. Instability was abetted by a "breakdown of the traditional economy of the Settlement" during the late 1860s. In 1868 Red River "was threatened by famine."[43]

The people of Red River could assess Canadian intentions only on the basis of Canadian activities, appointments, and laws. The response was resistance, spearheaded by the Métis but reluctantly supported to varying degrees (or at least tolerated) by most people at Red River, except the members of the Canadian party: "Riel's authority, although it originated in armed force, came within a few months to be based on the majority will of the community."[44]

The details of the resistance of 1869–1870 are well known and are not germane to this paper. What is important is that Louis Riel's provisional government was in such a strong strategic position that it was able to force the federal authorities to negotiate on terms of entry. The results were embodied in the Manitoba Act that created the Province of Manitoba.

Provincehood was a victory (more, it might be noted, for the Métis than for the other sections of the Red River community), but Manitoba nonetheless entered Confederation as a dependency, not as a full partner with a federal system. Two broad circumstances explain the continuation of "subordinate"[45] status. First, Manitoba was not constitutionally equal to the other provinces. The Métis leaders and their clerical advisors placed great emphasis on cultural problems. Anticipating an influx of Ontarians, they demanded and obtained educational and linguistic guarantees. The federal authorities were concerned primarily with such larger issues as the settlement of the West and the construction of a transcontinental railroad. To facilitate these policies, in the formulation of which Manitoba had no say, Ottawa retained control of Manitoba's public lands and natural resources "for the purposes of the Dominion."[46] Professor Eric Kierans comments:

> The ownership of the land and the resources belong [sic] to the people collectively as the sign of their independence and the guarantee of their responsibility. By British law and tradition, the ownership and control of the public domain was always handed over to the political authority designated by a community when the citizens assumed responsibility for the government of their own affairs. . . . During the . . . hearings [related to the *Report of the Royal Commission on the Transfer of the Natural Resources of Manitoba* (Ottawa, 1929)] Professor Chester Martin . . . testified: "The truth is that for 35 years, (i.e., until the creation of the Provinces of Saskatchewan and Alberta), I believe that it will be correct to say, Manitoba was the solitary exception within the British Empire to accepted British practice with regard to control of the crown lands and it still remains in respect of public lands, literally not a province but a colony of the Dominion." . . . In substance, any attempt to grant responsible government to a province or state, while retaining for the Imperial or Federal authority the control of crown lands and revenues, was held to be a "contradiction in terms and impossible."[47]

Just as serious as Manitoba's inferior constitutional position was her effective status. She was in no way equipped to function as a province with the full paraphernalia of responsible government. She was ridiculously small, limited in 1870 to some 12 000 persons and 13 500 square miles. The province had an extremely limited tradition of representative government and, to complicate matters further, several of her key leaders were fugitives from justice because of their roles in the resistance. As Lieutenant Governor A.G. Archibald explained in 1872: "You can hardly hope to carry on responsible Government by inflicting death penalties on the leaders of a majority of the electors."[48] Perhaps even more important, provincial finances were hopelessly inadequate; the federal government granted "provincial status to an area which was essentially primitive; and it gave financial terms modelled improperly upon those given to the older provinces."[49] Under the Manitoba Act the province received $67 104 per annum in grants. Her own revenue came to only about $10 000. Even by 1875, 88 per cent of provincial revenues were federal subsidies. "During the whole period from 1870 to 1885 Manitoba was little more than a financial ward of the federal government. . . . "[50] The province could not even afford public buildings to house the lieutenant governor and assembly until Ottawa advanced the necessary funds. In 1871 about one-third of provincial expenditures were used to cover legislative expenses.

95

Thus provincehood was granted prematurely to a jurisdiction that could sustain neither its responsibilities nor the kind of status it ought to have occupied with a federal state. The primary fault lay with the federal leaders: "[T]he Manitoba Act bears on its face evidence both of the inexperience of the delegates from the Red River settlement and of the lack of mature consideration given to the measure by the federal government. The former circumstance was unavoidable; the latter can hardly be condoned."[51] During the early years of Manitoba's history even the outward trappings of real provincehood were absent. For several years the province's immaturity prevented the development of responsible government and the first two lieutenant governors, A.G. Archibald and Alexander Morris, functioned as effective governors rather than as constitutional monarchs. Until 1876 the lieutenant governors even attended cabinet meetings.

Early Manitoba was a colony of Central Canada because of constitutional discrimination and because she had neither the maturity nor resources to support provincehood. But that was not all. With the advent of formal provincial status came an influx of settlers from Ontario, a process that started with the arrival of the Anglo-Saxon Ontarian hordes that dominated Colonel Garnett Wolseley's expeditionary force of 1870. That small army had no real military function. It was sent west in 1870 to appease Ontario — to serve as symbolic compensation for the inclusion in the Manitoba Act of cultural guarantees for the Métis. In extreme form, the expeditionary force was a model of what the later Central Canadian influx was to mean. Local traditions were shunted aside as agriculture was commercialized and society revolutionized. The Indians were unable to assimilate themselves; many Métis sold the land they had been granted to unscrupulous speculators and moved into the North-West Territories. In a symbolic action a group of Ontarians who arrived in 1871 seized some Métis land on the Rivière aux Ilets de Bois. In spite of Métis protests they kept the land and sharpened the insult by renaming the river "the Boyne"! Some Scots settlers sympathized with the Canadians, but like the HBC traders they had to watch the old society die. Within a few years Manitoba was a colony of Ontario demographically as well as constitutionally, politically, and economically.

The Province of Manitoba was only a miniscule portion of the territory annexed by Canada. The remaining enormous area was organized as the North-West Territories. With virtually no permanent white settlement, it received even shorter shrift than Manitoba. Its initial government was provided under the "temporary Government" act. That statute was "reenacted, extended and continued in force until . . . 1871" by the Manitoba Act.[52] Prior to its second automatic expiry in 1871 it was again reenacted without major change, this time with no expiry date. Until 1875, therefore, government for the North-West Territories was provided under the initial legislation of 1869. During these six years the administration of the territories was somewhat casual. There was no resident governor — that responsibility was simply added to the duties of the Lieutenant Governor of Manitoba. Most of the members of the council were Manitobans who did not live in the territories. The Indians, the largest group of inhabitants, were managed not consulted.

The Mackenzie government overhauled the administration of the North-West in 1875 by securing the passage of "The North-West Territories Act." Although not "fully thought out"[53] it did provide a fairly simple system of government consisting of a separate governor and a council that was initially appointed but that would become elective as a non-Indian population grew. The capital was established at Battleford until 1882 when it was moved to Regina. Mackenzie appointed David Laird, a federal cabinet minister from Prince Edward Island, as the first full-time Lieutenant Governor of the North-West Territories. His first council included neither an Indian nor a Métis who resided in the NWT. There was no elected councillor until 1881.

Prior to 1869 the West was a dependent area, ruled (if at all) in a casual, chaotic, but paternalistic manner for the benefit of a huge commercial firm centred in London. Westerners feared that the transfer involved simply a change of masters, not a change of status. The Métis feared that in the process they would lose their life style and culture through an inundation of Ontario settlers. The result was a movement of resistance led by the Métis, but with broad support within the Red River settlement. For the bulk of the West the resistance resulted in no change whatsoever. For a small district on the Red River the result was a tiny, anemic province incapable of functioning as a viable partner within a federal system.

IV

After 1867 Macdonald and his colleagues were not able to maintain "quasi-federalism" over the original components of Confederation, but for the West annexation to Canada involved the confirmation of colonial status. The fifteen years after the transfer was the launching period for the West in Confederation. During those years federal sway on the prairies was virtually unchallengeable.

Ottawa's most powerful instrument was federal possession of the West's public lands "for the purposes of the Dominion." This enabled Ottawa to implement two policies that were crucial to the Canadianization of the West: rapid settlement and the construction of a transcontinental railroad. Extreme difficulties did not prevent the execution of these policies. Public lands were made available to settlers in a variety of ways. Although settlement did not proceed as quickly as the federal authorities desired, Manitoba experienced rapid growth during the 1870s and 1880s. Within a generation of the transfer the territories west of Manitoba had been populated by Ontarians, Americans, and Europeans. Consequently the provinces of Saskatchewan and Alberta were established in 1905. The federal authorities had recognized from the outset that a transcontinental railroad was required if the West was to be properly Canadianized. After several false starts, the Canadian Pacific Railway was chartered in 1880. The CPR was heavily subsidized, receiving from the federal government some $38 000 000 worth of track constructed at public expense, $25 000 000 in cash, a railroad monopoly in western Canada for twenty years, and 25 000 000 acres of prairie land. The land grant was considered indispensable to the line's success and the success of the railroad was one of the fundamental "purposes of the Dominion." The federal government designed its transportation policies to suit the needs of Central Canadian business, and was not particularly tender towards western interests. As Charles Tupper, Minister of Railroads, put it in 1883: "The interests of this country demand that the Canadian Pacific Railway should be made a success. . . . Are the interests of Manitoba and the North-West to be sacrificed to the interests of Canada? I say, if it is necessary, yes."[54]

Federal Conservative strategists, who were in power during 1867–73 and 1878–96, tied tariff policy to settlement and transportation. They saw the West as Central Canada's economic hinterland. The area was to be settled quickly and become an exporter of agricultural products and an importer of manufactured goods. Central Canada was to be the manufacturing centre. The CPR was to haul eastern manufactured goods

97

into the West and western agricultural produce to market. High tariffs were designed to protect the manufacturing industries from foreign competition and at the same time guarantee freight traffic to the CPR by forcing trade patterns to flow along east–west, not north–south, lines. These basic decisions determined the nature of post-1870 western development. They were made by federal leaders to serve Central Canadian interests and they perpetuated the status of the West as a colonial region.

Federal management of the West during these years should be looked at in micro as well as macro terms, although it is clear that federal authorities had little interest in day-to-day western conditions. If settlement was to proceed in orderly and rapid fashion the Indian "problem" had to be solved. That task involved extinguishing Indian rights to the land and rendering the tribes harmless by herding them onto reserves. The instrument used for these purposes was the Indian "treaty." During the 1870s a series of agreements was negotiated between the crown and the prairie tribes. Through these treaties the Indians gave up their rights to their traditional lands in return for reserves and nominal concessions, payments, and guarantees. However, they tended to resist being forced onto reserves as long as the buffalo, their traditional source of food, remained plentiful. By 1885 the buffalo were on the verge of extermination and most Indians had been coerced to settle on reservations.

In 1873 Canada founded the North-West Mounted Police, another instrument of federal control.[55] The mounties constituted an effective federal presence on the prairies, chased American traders out of southern Alberta, policed the Indians and Métis, and symbolized the stability and order desired by white settlers. In bringing effective federal rule to southern Alberta they abetted the termination of the international aspect of Blackfoot life. This breakdown of regional international societies was part of the process of Canadianization.

The federal political structure also functioned as a control instrument. Until 1887 Manitoba's handful of MPs constituted the West's entire representation in the House of Commons. These members tended to support the government of the day because of its immense patronage and fiscal authority.

> Dependent upon federal largesse yet suspicious of eastern dictation, the western attitude towards national politics was often a curious mixture of ministerialism and defiance. Some papers seemed to believe that the electorate should always give a general support to the government, for such support would ensure a continuous supply of federal monies for western projects. At the same time these papers admitted the need to champion regional interests.[56]

During the 1870s and 1880s the West was Canadianized. By the end of the century massive immigration (which incidentally produced a distinctive population mix that helped differentiate the region from Central

Canada) combined with basic federal policies had produced a new West, but its status had changed little. The process generated resistance. The government of Manitoba challenged the CPR's monopoly and sought to obtain better financial terms. Farmers in Manitoba and along the Saskatchewan River organized unions and began their long struggle for a host of reforms including lower tariffs and a transportation system sensitive to their needs. Under Louis Riel's leadership a minority of Indians and Métis rose in 1885 in a pathetic and ill-led rebellion. Territorial politicians crusaded for representation in parliament and responsible government for the North-West Territories.

By the end of the century western resistance to federal control and leadership was a well-established tradition. The West, however, was not strong enough to challenge Canada's great national policies successfully. Consequently the West has remained a subordinate region; the Canadian federation retains its imperialistic characteristics. As W.L. Morton suggested: "For Confederation was brought about to increase the wealth of Central Canada, and until that original purpose is altered, and the concentration of wealth and population by national policy in Central Canada ceases, Confederation must remain an instrument of injustice."[57]

99

NOTES

[1] In this essay the "West" refers to the territories that became the provinces of Manitoba, Saskatchewan, and Alberta. Rupert's Land consisted of the Hudson's Bay Company territories. The North-West Territory included the other British lands in the northwest. British Columbia was separate and is not considered in this essay.

[2] E.E. Rich, *Hudson's Bay Company, 1670-1870*, 3 vols. (Toronto, 1960): 1:53.

[3] Cited in Rich, *Hudson's Bay Company* 1: 53-54.

[4] For a superb account of the buffalo hunt, see Alexander Ross, *The Red River Settlement* (London, 1856), ch. 18.

[5] James G. MacGregor, *A History of Alberta* (Edmonton, 1972), 17, 24. For further illustrations see Stanley Norman Murray, *The Valley Comes of Age: A History of Agriculture in the Valley of the Red River of the North, 1812-1920* (Fargo, 1967), 13: "By 1800 the Sioux and Chippewa tribes also had acquired horses. Because these animals made it possible for the Indians to hunt the buffalo over great distances, these people soon spent most of the summer and fall roaming the vast prairie west of the Red River. As they became more nomadic, the Indians placed less emphasis upon agriculture, pottery making, weaving, and the idea of a fixed dwelling place. In years when the buffalo were numerous, they could live from the hunt alone. Such was the case between 1800 and 1840 when the Sioux and Chippewa experienced degrees of luxury and leisure they had never known."

[6] E. Palmer Patterson, *The Canadian Indian: A History since 1500* (Don Mills, 1972), 39-40. Different dates apply in different areas: "Thus, by 1865 the plight of the Indians in the Red River Valley was a pathetic one, and for the most part their culture no longer had any effect upon this area" (Murray, *Valley Comes of Age*, 15).

[7] W. L. Morton, "Introduction to the New Edition" of Alexander Ross, *The Red River Settlement* (Edmonton, 1972), xx.

[8] Cited in A.I. Silver, "French Canada and the Prairie Frontier, 1870-1890," *CHR* 50 (March 1969): 13.

[9] W.L. Morton, "Agriculture in the Red River Colony," *CHR* 30 (December 1949): 321.

[10] Murray, *Valley Comes of Age*, 44 and 48: "[T]here can be little question that the economy of the Selkirk colonies stagnated soon after they were able to produce a surplus. The major reason for stagnation in Red River agriculture was the limited market for farm produce, and this situation developed primarily out of the economic prerogatives of the Hudson's Bay Company. . . . [I]t continued to rely upon supplies brought from England and pemmican furnished by the métis hunters." In short, "agriculture did not become really commercial under the fur company regime. . . . " Morton points out that Red River agriculture lacked both "an export staple and transportation" ("Agriculture in the Red River Colony," 316).

11 There has recently been considerable discussion of western "identity." Debate on this question will doubtless continue. It can be argued that this persistent willingness to resist is one of the most distinctive western characteristics and is certainly a part of any western "identity," and that it long antedates Confederation. P.F.W. Rutherford, however, dismisses Métis influence: "Unlike other regions in the dominion, the western community was essentially a product of events set in motion by Confederation" ("The Western Press and Regionalism, 1870-96," *CHR* 52 [September 1971]: 287). Morton, however, comments: "Louis Riel was a more conventional politician than William Aberhart . . . " and "[t]his was the beginning of the bias of prairie politics. The fears of the Métis had led them to demand equality for the people of the Northwest in Confederation" ("The Bias of Prairie Politics," in *Historical Essays on the Prairie Provinces*, ed., Donald Swainson [Toronto, 1970], 289 and 293). What is more "western" than this recurring "demand" for "equality"?

12 For a more detailed discussion by the present author see *Ontario and Confederation*, Centennial Historical Booklet no. 5 (Ottawa, 1967) and "The North-West Transportation Company: Personnel and Attitudes," Historical and Scientific Society of Manitoba, *Transactions*, Series 111, no. 26. 1969-70.

13 *Globe* (Toronto), 14 June 1848.

14 Quotations from articles by "Huron" are from *Globe*, 18 and 31 October 1856.

15 *Globe*, 10 December 1856.

16 *Globe*, 4 December 1856.

17 Province of Canada, *Journals of the Legislative Council of the Province of Canada*, Being the 3rd Session of the 5th Provincial Parliament, 1857, vol. 15, pp. 60, 80, 184, 195; Province of Canada, *Appendix to the Fifteenth Volume of the Journals of the Legislative Assembly of the Province of Canada*, Being the 3rd Session of the 5th Provincial Parliament, 1857, vol. 15, Appendix 17.

18 Joseph James Hargrave, *Red River* (Montreal, 1871), 143.

19 Province of Canada, *Statutes*, 1858, pp. 635ff.

20 Material that follows is from *Memoranda and Prospectus of the North-West Transportation and Land Company* (Toronto, 1858): Allan Macdonnell, *The North-West Transportation, Navigation and Railway Company: Its Objectives* (Toronto, 1858) and *Prospectus of the North-West Transportation, Navigation and Railway Company* (Toronto, 1858).

21 J.M.S. Careless, *The Union of the Canadas: The Growth of Canadian Institutions, 1841-57* (Toronto, 1967), 206.

22 *PAC*, George Brown Papers, George Brown to Anne Brown, 27 October 1864, cited in Donald Creighton, *The Road to Confederation* (Toronto, 1964), 182.

23 For an analysis of French-Canadian attitudes see Silver, "French Canada and the Prairie Frontier."

24 Silver, *French Canada*, 29.

25 Silver, *French Canada*, 15.

26 Cited in Chester Martin, *Foundations of Canadian Nationhood* (Toronto, 1955), 314.

27 British North America Act, Section 146.

28 Bruce W. Hodgins, "Disagreement at the Commencement: Divergent Ontarian Views of Federalism, 1867-1871," in *Oliver Mowat's Ontario*, ed. Donald Swainson (Toronto, 1972), 55.

29 Donald Creighton, *British North America at Confederation* (Ottawa, 1939), Appendix 2, *The Royal Commission on Dominion-Provincial Relations* (Ottawa, 1940), 83.

30 *PAC*, John A. Macdonald Papers, 510. Macdonald to M.C. Cameron, 19 December 1864, cited in Creighton, *The Road to Confederation*, 165.

31 See Jean Charles Bonenfant, *The French Canadians and the Birth of Confederation*, Canadian Historical Association, Historical Booklet no. 10 (Ottawa, 1967).

32 See Hodgins, "Disagreement at the Commencement."

33 J.R. Mallory, "The Five Faces of Federalism," in *The Future of Canadian Federalism*, ed. P.-A. Crepeau and C.B. Macpherson (Toronto, 1965), 4.

34 W.L. Morton, "Clio in Canada: The Interpretation of Canadian History," in *Approaches to Canadian History*, ed. Carl Berger, Canadian Historical Readings 1 (Toronto, 1967), 44.

35 This act is reprinted in W.L. Morton, ed., *Manitoba: The Birth of a Province* (Altona, 1965), 1-3.

36 See Ralph Heintzman, "The Spirit of Confederation: Professor Creighton, Biculturalism, and the Use of History," *CHR* 52 (September 1971): 256-58. Heintzman comments: "Now even a cursory examination of the text of this Act of 1869 would cast serious doubt upon the worth of this argument" (p. 256) — i.e., that the act revealed the "real intentions of the federal government" (p. 247). "The purely temporary character of the Act is made clear in the preamble. . . . But all of this informed speculation is quite unnecessary. We have an explicit statement of the intentions of the government from the mouth of John A. Macdonald himself. Macdonald told the House of Commons flatly that the 1869 Act was 'provisional' and 'intended to last only a few months' . . . " (p. 257). Heintzman's chief concerns are educational and linguistic rights.

37 P.B. Waite, *Canada 1874-1896: Arduous Destiny* (Toronto, 1971), 65. See also Lewis Herbert Thomas, *The Struggle for Responsible Government in the North-West Territories, 1870-97* (Toronto, 1956), 48. It is clearly possible to debate the implications of the act, but a document that Macdonald's government made the permanent constitution for the North-West Territories cannot simply be dismissed as meaningless. It is interesting to note that when the statute was made permanent in 1871, with only insignificant modifications, and, of course, the exclusion from its provisions of the new Province of Manitoba, it was justified in its preamble as follows: "whereas, it is expedient to make provision

for the government, after the expiration of the Act first above mentioned [i.e., An Act for the temporary government of Rupert's Land], of the North-West Territories, that being the name given . . . to such portion of Rupert's Land the North Western Territory as is not included in . . . Manitoba . . . " (An Act to make further provision for the government of the North-West Territories, 34 Vict. Cap. 16).

38 "Instructions issued to Hon. Wm. McDougall as Lieutenant Governor of the North West Territories, Sept. 28, 1869," in The Canadian North-West: Its Early Development and Legislative Records, ed. E.H. Oliver (Ottawa, 1914-15), 2: 878-79.

39 For his earlier hopeless insensitivity concerning Red River see W.L. Morton, "Introduction" to Alexander Begg's Red River Journal (Toronto, 1956), 23.

40 Provencher, a nephew of Bishop J.N. Provencher of St. Boniface (1847-53), was a Central Canadian newspaperman. He had only a minimal contact with the West and was described by Alexander Begg, an intelligent and representative citizen of Red River, as "a pleasant sort of a man who had come up altogether wrongly informed regarding this country. . . . " (Alexander Begg's Red River Journal, 176). Provencher's relationship with the Bishop was his only tie with the West, unless it is assumed that the Métis were French Canadians and therefore identified closely with other French Canadians. The Métis, of course, assumed no such thing, regarding themselves as a New Nation. To assume that the Métis were French Canadian is to commit a sort of historiographical genocide. Heintzman, "Spirit of Confederation," 253, for example, comments: "This awareness of the 'canadien' community at Red River was one reason to rejoice in the annexation of the North-West: it meant that the French of the west would be welcomed back into the fold and raised the possibility that colonists from Lower Canada would find themselves 'at home' on the prairies." Presumably, for Heintzman, these "canadiens" included the Métis. Alexander Begg held the members of McDougall's party in very low esteem. McDougall was characterized as "overbearing," "distant," "unpleasant," and "vindictive." Richards "does not appear to be extraordinarily [sic] clever on Law Subjects although appointed Attorney General." Cameron was "a natural ass" and Dr. Jacques "an unmannerly young fellow" (W.L. Morton, "Introduction," Alexander Begg's Red River Journal, 176). Is it any wonder that Canada's initial attitude toward the North-West was looked at through a jaundiced eye?

41 George F.G. Stanley, The Birth of Western Canada: A History of the Riel Rebellions (Toronto, 1936), 63-64.

42 Morton, "Introduction," Alexander Begg's Red River Journal, 29, 40-42, 45.

43 Morton, "Introduction," Alexander Begg's Red River Journal, 17.

44 M.S. Donnelly, The Government of Manitoba (Toronto, 1963), 10.

45 Morton, "Clio in Canada," 44.

46 Manitoba Act, Section 30.

47 Eric Kierans, Report on Natural Resources Policy in Manitoba (Winnipeg, 1973), 1. The severity of this kind of analysis has been questioned. See, for example, J.A. Maxwell, Federal Subsidies to the Provincial Governments in Canada (Cambridge, Mass.: 1937).

48 Cited in Donnelly, Government of Manitoba, 16.

49 Maxwell, Federal Subsidies to the Provincial Governments, 37.

50 Donnelly, Government of Manitoba, 161.

51 Maxwell, Federal Subsidies to the Provincial Governments, 37-38.

52 Section 36.

53 R.G. Robertson, "The Evolution of Territorial Government in Canada," in The Political Process in Canada (Toronto, 1963), 139 note.

54 Cited in Chester Martin, "Dominion Lands" Policy (Toronto, 1938), 470.

55 See S.W. Horrall, "Sir John A. Macdonald and the Mounted Police Force for the Northwest Territories," CHR 53 (June 1972). Horrall notes, pp. 182-83: "To Macdonald the problem of policing the Northwest resembled that faced by the British in India."

56 Rutherford, "Western Press and Regionalism," 301.

57 Morton, "Clio in Canada," 47.

101

The Myth of Louis Riel*

DOUGLAS OWRAM

In recent years Louis Riel has become somewhat of a Canadian folk hero. At the official, scholarly, and popular levels the rebel hanged in

*From Canadian Historical Review 63, 3 (1982): 315-36. Reprinted by permission of University of Toronto Press.

1885 has become the subject of much attention. Manitoba and Saskatchewan, the site of his two uprisings, have commemorated him in statue while the federal government which allowed his execution to take place in the 1880s has, in the 1980s, designated Batoche a national historic site. Canadian government money has also provided a half million dollar grant designed to allow the compilation and publication of all of Riel's writings. Such scholarly and official interest is complemented by popular interest. Plays, poems, television dramas, and even an opera have been written about him. Riel has assumed mythical stature.

Such attention is a relatively recent phenomenon. In fact, the evolving historiography of Louis Riel might well serve as yet another illustration of Voltaire's dictum that history is a pack of tricks played upon the dead. For the mood in most of Canada in 1885 was to treat Riel as anything but a hero. Much of the nation then demanded and eventually secured the execution of this notorious rebel in spite of vociferous objections from many French Canadians. If the generation of 1885 had been able to nominate heroes for perpetuity it would not have been the rebel who went to the scaffold but the young "citizen soldiers" who marched out to subdue rebellion on the frontier. Yet a century later the militia have been reduced to a supporting role and the rebel of 1885 has become the mythical figure.

Such changes in historical mythology do not occur by accident. They develop because they fulfil a perceived need in the minds of the community or because they are thought useful to those creating the myth.[1] As one writer has put it, "the identification of an historical event (or historical individual) and, conversely, the transmutation of an historical event into an historical ideal" rests at the basis of myth-making.[2] The identification of Jackson with the American frontier, of Wellington with the glories of the British empire, of Napoleon with the destiny and power of France all serve as examples of this sort of identification of the individual with the ideal or the larger community.[3] If Riel is a hero, then the question might legitimately be asked: What community values does he represent for Canadians and what historical ideals are his actions thought to represent? Why has this individual, hanged for his activities against the nation, become such a national figure in recent years?

Given the controversy surrounding Riel, such a question is not easy to answer. In general, however, Louis Riel has been interpreted within two broad frameworks. One framework has stressed the idea of cultural conflict, whether as a part of the French–English duality of Canada or as part of the frontier experience. The alternative has emphasized not the clash of cultures but the clash of regions. This interpretation has seen the real significance of Riel in his position as a westerner defending his region and its people from the arrogance and indifference of the East. Writers have drawn on these themes to varying degrees and combinations to explain the significance of Riel's life until he has come

102

103

Glenbow Archives, Calgary.

One of the most dramatic moments in a Canadian courtroom — a photograph of Louis Riel taken during his trial in Regina. He spoke in his own defence in leading the resistance of 1885 against the Canadian government.

to be looked at "in a seemingly infinite number of ways."[4] The result has been a very complex myth or series of myths. In order to sort these out it is necessary to trace their evolution, for, as will be argued, the myth has developed layer by layer. Only by looking at the historiography and folklore surrounding Riel through the years will the Riel myth become understandable.

Given the important role which Riel has assumed in recent years, the most striking aspect of late nineteenth- and early twentieth-century writing on the rebellions is the lack of interest in Riel himself. There were, of course, a flurry of accounts, government reports, and other material flowing from the events of 1869–1870 and 1885. Once the investigations had been made, however, and the controversy allowed to die down somewhat, Riel faded very much into the background of Canadian history. While, for example, there were some seventy-five different items published on him between 1885 and 1887, practically nothing appeared on the rebellions or their leader by the early 1890s.[5] This tendency was to continue, especially in English Canada, and when, for example, the *Chronicles of Canada* series was published during World War I, no volume was thought necessary on Riel or his rebellions.[6]

This is not to say that Riel disappeared completely. The events in which he was involved were important parts of Canadian history and he was discussed in works dealing with the Red River insurrection and the Northwest rebellion. He was, however, not considered a dominant or even major figure in Canadian history. Even in the context of the Canadian West he would seem to have ranked as only one thread in a varied tapestry of history. He was neither hero nor anti-hero so much as non-hero.

Even had he been more important, Riel would not have developed into a myth in these years. Among English Canadians Riel was simply not thought to symbolize anything positive for Canada. Neither the man nor the activities in which he was involved were considered deserving of commendation from those who wrote on the subject in later years. In fact, in English Canada there would seem to have been a remarkable degree of unanimity, if one can judge from the writings, concerning the nature of Riel and the events of his life. From the late 1880s through to the later 1930s this unanimity remained generally unbroken.

First, with regard to the Red River resistance, or rebellion as it was then commonly called, a fairly clear chain of argument was developed. This argument, interestingly, did not rest on the assumption that Canadian involvement in Red River had been totally beneficent. It was generally admitted, as one historian put it, that there were "blunders" on the part of Canada.[7] Writers agreed that the Canadian government should have been aware of the concerns that existed in Red River and have worked to calm them before the event. Equally, the Canada party is often seen as a turbulent group, and it is generally accepted that the people in Red River had reason for complaint as the transfer approached. It is, however, one thing to be upset and quite another to use armed force. Only the Métis, these writers point out, of all the groups in Red River, thought it necessary to threaten force and violence to resolve their concerns. Whether this was attributed, as in a 1905 work, to their "fiery disposition"[8] or blamed on the presence of various individuals with influence, such as the Catholic priest, Father Richot, the important fact remained that the Métis were seen as acting alone.[9]

Moreover, these English-language writers argued, the Métis remained alone, for they were never able to broaden their base of support in any significant way among the settlers of Red River. There may have been times when they came close to an agreement, as in November 1869 and February 1870, but, for various reasons, such agreement failed to materialize or lasted for only the briefest periods of time. Events through the winter of 1869–70 led writers to the unvaried conclusion that Riel's provisional government was never the legitimate authority in Red River. The references talked of the "so-called Provisional Government" or "Provisional Government" in quotation marks. Some writers argued that whatever the possibilities of a provisional government in constitutional terms, it failed to eventuate when Riel lost the support of the English-speaking settlers. From that point on Riel was thought to head not a government, even a temporary one, but "a dictatorship of the Métis."[10]

105

The refusal to see the provisional government as legitimate or as supported by a wide segment of the population is important to the overall assessment of the rebellion and its leader. For without the legitimacy of government, even provisional government, Riel's capture of Fort Garry, seizure of Hudson's Bay Company funds, and imprisonment of individuals all become illegal acts. The most severe criticism, however, came for a deed "for which nothing can be said in condonation, extenuation, excuse or apology for its enormity."[11] This was, of course, the execution or, as these writers unanimously concluded, the "wanton murder" of Thomas Scott.[12] Tried by a mock court martial in a language he did not understand, "the brutal murder of Scott aroused as much horror and indignation among the majority of the French and Métis settlers as it did among those of English blood."[13] Quite aside from the questions of procedure or the reaction among the population, the condemnation of Scott's execution flowed naturally from the denial of the legitimacy of the provisional government. For if the government was illegal, then so too was its use of sovereign power. Riel had committed murder and as a criminal he thus fled the country when Wolseley's troops approached. Those troops marked not the anger of Ontario Orangeism but "peace and order" being brought to "the little prairie province."[14]

The interpretation of the events of 1885 by these writers was even more critical. Riel was seen as the cause of the rebellion at least in the sense that without him there would not have been violence. "Riel himself could doubtless have prevented the outbreak," H.A. Kennedy concluded in 1928, but he did not.[15] In the minds of English-Canadian historical writers, Riel's motives also distinguished the 1885 rebellion from that of 1869–70. Looking at the events of 1869, they had been forced to concede that Riel's motives may have been sincere, at least in part. In 1885, however, he was seen to be a "wretched malefactor" actuated by personal ambition and by a delusory mission leading a people into a rebellion against their, by now, undoubted constitutional government.[16]

In addition, no doubt was expressed in any of the writings surveyed that Riel was insane by 1885. The insanity simply confirmed the accusations of those who felt that Riel was not only to blame for the rebellion but that the very reasoning that lay behind the rebellion was irrational or distorted. There may have been grievances, but to turn to violence only made matters worse for the Métis. As R.G. MacBeth said, "rebellion was rampant with a madman at its head."[17] Madmen, or for that matter cold blooded murderers, do not make for mythic history.

In the late nineteenth and first third of the twentieth century, English-Canadian historians and chroniclers thus rejected Louis Riel as a possible hero for Canadians or symbol to them. Both in the lack of attention given him and the way in which his actions were described they saw him as their predecessors had seen him at the time of the rebellions.

English Canadians did have heroes in the West, and in work after work names do appear which were obviously thought more appropriate than Riel to portray the significance of the West in Canadian history. This pantheon of heroes ranges from early explorers like La Vérendrye to Sir Alexander Mackenzie and Sir George Simpson. The traders and explorers of the North-West and Hudson's Bay companies seemed to represent the spirit of early Canada in their efforts to open the continent. The most dominant of Canadian mythic figures, however, was an organization rather than an individual. In works like E.J. Chambers, *The Royal Northwest Mounted Police* (1906), A.L. Haydon, *Riders of the Plains* (1910), R.G. MacBeth, *Policing the Plains* (1921), and in numerous memoirs and works of fiction the Northwest Mounted Police, the men who fought Riel at Duck Lake, were glorified as the truest examples of the Canadian historical epic.[18]

A collection of myths which ranges from early French explorers through fur traders and the Northwest Mounted Police may seem rather discursive. There was, however, a certain continuity in the Canadian choice of heroes in these years. The men and the organizations treated with such sympathy by these historians were all, in some fashion, involved in opening the West to civilization. Explorers, fur traders, leaders of settlement, and the men who brought British law to the West exemplified a myth of development and expansion. Civilization's spread under the trusteeship of Canada was, in an age of imperial expansion and glorification, the real focus of Canadian writers in these years. A man who stood in the way of that expansion, even if with some reason, was not the sort of figure to become a Canadian folk hero.

Behind this glorification of the spread of civilization was another very deeply held assumption. English Canadians, even as late as the interwar period, generally looked to the British empire as a positive force in history. Mistakes had been made but, this Whig view of history argued, generally the expansion of British systems or British institutions was also the expansion of an enlightened form of government and social conduct. As has been reasoned with regard to the Northwest Mounted Police, they were maintaining not just the law but the "right."[19] Equally, as a part of this process, Canadian expansion into the West was thought fundamentally correct. The truly important story was the orderly expansion of just and civilized institutions. Such errors as existed were unintentional and the controversy surrounding them was only a secondary aspect of the more important process of expansion. Louis Riel was ultimately on the wrong side of history not because he lost but because he had misunderstood the forces around him. The forces represented by the citizen soldiers of 1885 remained important in an age which still gloried in the conquest of the frontier by British civilization and justice.

107

While the English-Canadian view of Riel remained consistent, so too did the minority dissent from that view. By 1885 French Canadians had already to a great degree adopted the Métis Louis Riel as one of their own.[20] The half century that followed saw that tradition cemented by an era of French–English confrontation over such issues as imperial relations, education, and conscription. In particular three men, all of whom had lived in Manitoba, worked hard to preserve the memory of an heroic Louis Riel. The assessments of his life by Auguste-Henri Trémaudan (1874–1929), Georges Dugas (1833–1928), and A.G. Morice (1859–1938) reflected the belief that Riel was a martyr to their race and religion and, thus, deserved not only to be remembered but to be celebrated. And where the Métis were interpreted by English Canadians in the context of imperial expansion, French-Canadian writers dealt with events in Red River and after in the context of the long-standing controversy between Protestant English and French Catholic in North America.

From this perspective there was no reason to doubt the necessity for Métis resistance at Red River. After all, did not more recent experience confirm the intolerance of the English Protestant community? "In view of what we know of the illegal abolition of the separate schools of Manitoba," wrote Morice in 1935, "and especially when we remember the brazen lies and broken promises which made abolition possible," there was no reason to doubt the necessity of Riel's stand.[21] It was not the turbulence of the Métis but the fanaticism of the English that created the troubles at Red River.

Further, that English fanaticism was thought to have emanated from a small group of troublemaking Canadians for, it was argued, Riel quickly gained the support of most long-time English-speaking residents of Red

River.[22] Even the Hudson's Bay Company which "connaissant la bonne foi et l'honnêteté des Métis et redoutant au contraire la sournoiserie et l'ambition du Dr. Schultz et de ses partisans" was thought secretively supportive of the Métis movement.[23] Given the turbulence in the settlement and the need to establish order, this interpretation would have it that Riel had no real choice but to impose a provisional government. The settlers were supportive of the action because some step was necessary to prevent anarchy. Governor McTavish recognized as much as Riel that the rule of the Hudson's Bay Company was finished. "La colonie ne pouvait rester sans gouvernement dans une situation confinant à l'anarchie; elle se donna donc une administration complète, régulière, bien que provisoire, tout en maintenant son allégeance à la Couronne Britannique."[24] This claim of legitimacy for the provisional government was as central to the French-Canadian interpretation of Riel as was its denial to English-Canadian writers. As Morice concluded, "the legality of Scott's execution depends on the legitimacy of the Provisional Government." Both English and French Canadians would have agreed with this statement, but only the French tradition accepted Morice's next statement that "this legitimacy has been abundantly proven."[25] The death of Thomas Scott was, whether politically wise or not, an execution at the hands of a government after a fair trial. Wolseley's expedition was unnecessary and Riel should never have had to flee into exile as a result of events at Red River.

The histories of the 1885 rebellion were more ambiguous in their interpretations though they remained more charitable than their English counterparts. The ambiguity resulted from the role of religion in the interpretation of Riel among French-Catholic writers. Riel was considered a martyr not only to his French language and culture but as well to the Catholic religion. He was, in other words, fighting not only against English vindictiveness but also against Protestant bigotry. The heresies of Riel in 1885 thus created very real difficulties for those who would picture him as the hero of Catholicism.

Trémaudan showed one approach to the problem by simply ignoring the heresies and controversies with the priests.[26] Most writers, however, felt it necessary to deal with the subject of Riel's religious delusions. The favourite means of reconciling Riel's actions with his myth was to depict him as the victim of temporary insanity in the hectic months of the 1885 rebellion. This insanity is further seen as having been brought on specifically by the pressures of his attempts to help his people. With the end of the rebellion the pressure eased, the insanity disappeared, and Louis Riel, faithful Catholic, returned to the bosom of mother church.[27] Nevertheless, one is left with the impression that the religious activities of Riel in 1885 distinctly tarnished his otherwise strong reputation in the minds of French-Catholic writers, and it is instructive that at least one writer practically ignored the activities of Riel during these months while concentrating instead on the missionaries of the region.[28]

In sum, then, those writing on Riel tended to refight the battles and controversies of the 1880s. English-Protestant writers largely ignored him, as befitted a criminal, or when they did discuss him portrayed him as "a little Napoleon."[29] French-Catholic writers, in contrast, adopted him as a faithful, if slightly unstable, son of the church and protector of the culture. As a result Louis Riel the Métis became Louis Riel the French-Catholic and his cause a defence of the true faith and of the minority language rather than a defence of a way of life or a frontier people. In fact, the religious implications of the Red River resistance and of Riel's life may have been one of the most important factors dividing writers in these years. Many of those writing in both the English and French traditions were ordained members of a church[30] and they tended to expand the issues beyond the immediate and obvious to a more fundamental attempt to condemn the ethics, goals, and procedures of the opposing denomination.

109

The nature of Canadian historiography on Riel underwent important changes in the later 1930s, especially in English Canada. These changes were largely the results of the work of a new generation of professional and more secularly oriented historians seeking to introduce English-Canadian readers to a balanced and more thoroughly researched discussion of Riel. The most important work in this new tradition was G.F.G. Stanley's *Birth of Western Canada*, published in 1936 and still perhaps the best general work on the era. Also worth noting as reflective of this new tradition were A.S. Morton's massive *A History of the Canadian West to 1870–71*, a doctoral thesis done at Stanford University by Jonas Jonasson, "The Riel Rebellions" (1933), and, in French, Marcel Giraud's *Le Métis canadien* (1945).

These works constitute an important contribution to Canadian historical writing and mark a distinct phase in the interpretation of Riel. It would be a mistake, however, to see them as beginning the mythification of Riel in English Canada or as marking the reconciliation of the two views of Riel. Riel was far from a hero in any of the English-language works while Giraud continued the French-language tradition of high praise for the Métis leader.[31] Even more importantly, these were the works of a scholarly élite and there is no indication that the reinterpretations reflected a parallel shift in popular English-Canadian perceptions of Riel. None of the writings had a major impact on the public or, for that matter, on the average college student. Jonasson's thesis, except for a brief article,[32] did not reach publication, while Morton's massive tome of more than 900 pages was obviously designed for the specialist audience and his careful narrative was hardly designed to create myths. Stanley's experiences with the *Birth of Western Canada* are even more revealing. Published in the United Kingdom in the middle of the Depression the book, in Stanley's words, "was virtually ignored" in Canada in the first years after publication — the lack of interest itself indicative of the indifference to Riel. Then, with large numbers of copies unsold, the warehouse in which the stock was stored was destroyed in the London blitz.[33] Not until 1960 was it thought worthwhile to reissue the work. For the twenty intervening years there were no more than three to four hundred copies of the book in existence. The later 1930s are thus important in that they saw a new viewpoint toward Riel develop among English-Canadian scholars. There was, however, no parallel shift in general public opinion. Louis Riel still remained far from a mythical figure.

Yet even if the 1930s are looked at purely in the context of the eventual evolution of the myth of Riel, the scholarly re-evaluations of the decade are of tremendous significance. Until that time Louis Riel had been interpreted solely within the context of the debate over French–English relations. His rejection by English Canadians and acceptance by French Canadians had left no room for a generalized Canadian myth. In the 1930s, however, a variation on the cultural conflict thesis was developed by Stanley, and later pursued by Giraud.[34] This variation saw at least part of the reason for the troubles of the Riel period as stemming not from language or religion but from his leadership of a semi-nomadic "nation" caught between two ancestries and faced with an uncertain future. It was, as Stanley said, the story of a clash between "primitive and civilized peoples."[35] Giraud argued in a similar vein that "sans principe cultural solide" the Métis faced disintegration in the wake of rapid change.[36] This new emphasis did not replace, or even contradict, earlier views of the Red River and Northwest rebellions as examples of conflict between the French and English Canadians. It did, however, open the way for reinterpretations of Riel, especially on the part of English Canadians. Once removed, at least in part, from Ontario-Quebec controversies, Louis Riel began to be viewed by writers who saw his importance as deriving from other factors in his leadership of the Métis. In their scholarly manner, the works of Stanley, A.S. Morton, and Giraud had prepared the way for Riel's mythification.

It was not until after World War II that popular opinion appears to have been receptive to major changes in the interpretation of Riel. The war itself had created a new awareness of the dangers of racial injustice and had made the former casual assumptions about race less acceptable. Equally, the previous orientation toward the expansion of the might of the British empire as a perspective for the writing of Canadian history began to seem less relevant as the Commonwealth faded in importance relative to Canada's bilateral relations with the United States. Finally, Canadians were absorbing more and more of their cultural standards and images from south of the border. Radio, newspapers, magazines, and even comic books brought home to Canadians the relative abundance of American heroes like Davey Crockett, Stonewall Jackson, and, of course, the ubiquitous American cowboy.

In such an atmosphere it is not surprising that the image of Louis Riel should have been reconsidered not by a Canadian but by an American. For the publication in 1952 of *Strange Empire: The Story of Louis Riel* by Joseph Kinsey Howard marks the real beginning of the mythification of Riel for English Canadians. Howard wrote of Riel in terms of his frontier, cultural milieu and Indian ancestry, and did so in a way designed to have an appeal far beyond the community of professional historians. "Here," said Bernard de Voto in an Introduction, "are primitive emotion and primitive dream. Here is the American primitive, his participation as a person and a society in the events of history, and his world reaching its final collapse. In the whole expanse of American historiography there is very little writing about the Indians of quality comparable with this."[37] Louis Riel had, in a quite literal sense, been Americanized. He had been transformed from a Catholic French Canadian into a representative of the North American Indian's struggle against European domination. Howard had turned the theme of primitive versus civilized societies into an epic struggle of innocence versus corruption, good versus evil. Stanley had also viewed the Métis with sympathy and regretted the passing of their civilization, but at the same time he retained elements of the older Canadian tradition and sensed the importance of the expansionary process to Canada as a whole. For him it was thus a matter of trying to reconcile two conflicting goals. Howard felt no need for such reconciliation. Canadian expansion and the treatment of minorities in the West were, to him, negative aspects of history and, in fact, recalled more contemporary horrors. "There were no gas chambers then," he writes in his Introduction, "but there was malevolent intention."[38]

Howard's story is thus a very black-and-white treatment. To him the Métis are the perfect examples of romantic primitivism, "a new people, wild and free and in love with their land."[39] As for Louis Riel, he was the symbol of that spirit: " . . . he was their voice: the only man they had ever produced who could fashion a philosophy from the crude materials of their semi-primitive way of life, the only one whose eloquence would become a sort of alchemy, transmuting frontier expedients into eternal human values, shaping standards out of habits. . . . Out of the struggle the Métis hero emerged: Louis Riel, symbol and spokesman of the oppressed but gallant minority; revolutionist, leader and lord."[40] Patrick Henry had come to Red River.

In fashioning the story of the rebellions, Howard makes Riel's mission a democratic one, portraying Red River as containing a "new ideal of social equality." Riel's actions in stopping McDougall, in capturing Fort Garry, and in establishing a provisional government are all seen as the

111

efforts of the people to protect their rights in the face of totalitarian imperialism. Their aim, he argues, was merely to obtain better terms from Canada and guarantees of their own rights in the future. Howard also portrays a grander, if unrealized, dream. Riel is at one point depicted as looking "out over the shivering thousand, over the snow and the great buffalo plain. . . . He glanced at the fort and the flag he had designed: the golden symbol of medieval France on the pure white banner which had been borne westward by Champlain. He thought of the new nation whose flag it might have been: haven for the wanderers of the wilderness, red or brown or white — the Cree who watch the ghost dancers in the winter night, a dainty and dauntless grandmother, Marie Lagimodiere, the hunters and voyageurs, and dusty wagon men."[41] This was the material of mythology indeed.

Howard's portrayal of Métis actions as part of the larger panorama of the fight of the native people for freedom means that it is consistent for him to continue the heroic tradition through the 1885 rebellion. It does not really matter that the Canadian government is now the clearly constitutional government of the region for that status was obtained in Howard's eyes through theft and was thus owed no respect by the native population. "The War for the West, begun fifteen years ago on Red River, had entered its final desperate phase."[42]

Nevertheless, the question of Riel's sanity still had to be confronted, and it is his handling of that subject that most clearly reveals the mythmaker at work. Howard was quite willing to portray the eccentricities of Riel's character in such a way as to make the man appear unbalanced, especially in religious matters. However, unlike French-Catholic writers, Howard is under no compulsion to portray these religious delusions as central to the man's purpose or role in 1885. He may have had religious delusions but this, in Howard's eyes, did not affect the nature of the cause or his heroism in defending his people. Louis Riel became the "John Brown of the Half-Breeds," and like Brown the justness of the cause was more important than the mental problems that plagued him.[43]

What Howard did, in essence, was adapt the thesis first presented by Stanley and popularize it, removing the shades of grey in favour of a black-and-white treatment. It is a theme which has since become a constant in the writings on Riel. Most obviously, the Métis themselves began in the 1960s to write their own interpretation of Riel's life and career. Not surprisingly, Louis Riel is to them a symbol of both the wrongs of the Canadian government and a means of defending their claim to recognition as a distinct group in Canadian society. Riel was an unqualified hero.[44] Riel's close association with native concerns has seen a reinterpretation of his religious heresies and his actions during the rebellion in terms of native customs and traditions. Most recently, a scholarly work by Thomas Flanagan has developed this theme by emphasizing the ties of Riel's messianic thoughts to native religion.[45] If

112

this argument is accepted, then Riel may have been thought insane largely because he was not as completely Europeanized as many had assumed.

A variant of this theme of Riel as a defender of his primitive people was developed in the politically conscious 1960s. In essence the symbol of Riel was generalized until skin colour and the non-industrial state of his followers became more important than the specific historical setting. As one playwright put it, "I see the leader and the rebellions which he led as precursors of later and present uprisings all over the world, particularly the so-called Third World."[46] Riel became important to some because he was an anti-imperialist. His activities could even be seen as a resistance to American capitalism and continentalism: "The aspirations of the people of the new land for self-government, for an identity distinct from that of 'the States,' for material advance and a partnership of the national communities founded on equality: these came into collision with the entrenched interests of great property in power."[47] Riel had become a sort of northern Che Guevera searching for the people's socialist utopia on the northern plains.[48]

The development of the concept of a clash between frontier and civilization by writers in the 1930s and its subsequent extension and popularization by Howard illustrates one branch of the evolving Riel myth. Another branch may be shown by looking at an important work published in 1956. W.L. Morton's excellent study of the Red River resistance is especially interesting in that it remains within the mainstream of English-Canadian writing on Riel while simultaneously avoiding the obvious bias and anger which marked so many earlier writings. Morton's overall tone is one of scholarly detachment but he is able to give the reader a sense of sympathy for the nervous Métis and for their young leader. Nevertheless, he continually stresses two points which bring into question the rationale for the resistance. First, he points out that there were no evil designs emanating from Ottawa and that the Métis were mistaken in many of their fears.[49] Secondly, while he admits that the government of the Northwest was in a state of near collapse, he nevertheless feels the actions of the Métis to have been illegal and rebellious.[50] Moreover, he further divorces himself from the French-Catholic tradition by remaining conspicuously aloof from the basic aim of the Métis which he sees as obtaining a position in the West "similar to that which the French of Quebec had won for themselves in Canada."[51] Louis Riel emerges neither as hero nor villain but as a capable, if erratic and naive, individual caught up in events which he understood only a little better than his followers and which controlled him as much as he controlled them: "It would seem then that the pattern of Resistance was a common one, the leader an enthusiastic, partially educated, unemployed young patriot, the following a mass movement of simple and easily persuaded men, accustomed to tough ways in dispute and to bearing arms. And there are indications that the rougher element of the Métis formed the backbone of Riel's forces, men who might be persuaded but could not be disciplined except by superior force."[52] Patrick Henry may indeed have come to Red River, as Howard imagined, but the conservative from Gladstone, Manitoba, had a different view of such an event.

While Morton does reassert some of the traditional English-Canadian views challenged by Howard, there are also points of sympathy with Riel, especially in his anger with arrogant Upper Canadian attitudes. In one instance, for example, Morton expresses sympathy with the priests in their concern with Upper Canadian attitudes.[53] The implicit argument contained in these passages, however, was only made explicit in a separate article published the year before. In his "Bias of Prairie Politics," Morton identified Riel with a western political tradition of grievance against the east. Louis Riel, the argument went, was the first in a long line of western leaders of protest movements. "In his aims," he concluded, "Louis Riel was a more conventional politician than William Aberhart, but both were prairie politicians."[54]

114

The link Morton made was an important one for there was a strong potential for myth in his association of Riel with western grievance. There are also indications that Morton was elevating a popular viewpoint to scholarly respectability rather than initiating a new interpretation. Riel seems to have been a part of western folklore before he was either a western hero or a national figure. G.F.G. Stanley has indicated that his interest in the rebel grew in part from stories heard at his grandmother's knee.[55] The memory of the Northwest field force remained strong and local historical associations kept alive the story of 1885, even if from the expeditionary force's point of view.[56] In other words, Riel had long been seen as a part of the western story.

Riel was not yet a part of the western mythology, however. Two preconditions were necessary, it would seem, before Louis Riel could emerge as a symbol to westerners. First, the West itself had to develop a sense of regional identity which would make it view the expansionist process in a regional manner. Although that process was begun in the later nineteenth century and by the 1920s was forcefully expressed in a series of political protest movements, Riel was far from a hero in the West. This may have been because the second condition was absent. While the West had a regional perspective on Canadian history, it was also a region in which the society considered itself predominantly English and Protestant. So long as Louis Riel was thought of in terms of a defence of French Catholicism, western writers would not adopt him as one of their own. Only as professional and secular scholars such as Stanley began to reassess Riel as a symbol of native rather than of French-Catholic resistance was Riel likely to be acceptable to western Canadians. The decline of religious controversy in the years after World War II further relegated traditional concerns to a less important position. The denominational issues which had seemed so important to earlier generations became less relevant in an increasingly secular nation. Riel as a westerner was thus able to supplant Riel as Catholic.

Certainly the 1950s marked the beginning of a series of publications, statues, speeches, and political rhetoric which continues unabated to the present day. The same year that saw the appearance of "Bias of Prairie Politics" brought the publication of work actually written during the protest-filled years of the 1920s but unpublished until 1955. William Davidson's portrayal of Riel heartily scorns the "Upper Canadians" who "aspired to own a Crown Colony of their own."[57] In 1961 E.B. Osler combined the view that Riel was defending the native population with the western regional view in a romanticization of the old order of the West and its defence against intruders.[58] More recently a work concerned with western grievances described the 1885 uprising as "the most violent expression of western alienation."[59] Riel has gone from being a piece of western folklore to a symbol of western grievance.[60]

Emphases on western regionalism and native rights thus became important parts of the writings on Riel by the 1960s. Louis Riel had become, to varying degrees, a symbol of Canada's unjust treatment of its native peoples, man's injustice to his fellow man, and the mistreatment of the West at the hands of the East. Yet the most important addition to the symbolism behind Riel came not because a new meaning was assigned to him but because there was a reassessment of an older interpretation. It was the adoption and adaptation by many English Canadians of the long-standing French-Canadian belief that Riel had been defending his culture and language. As has been noted, this sort of argument had been viewed with little sympathy in English Canada through much of the century. In the 1960s, however, new currents of thought caused many in English Canada to reassess their attitudes. The election of Jean Lesage's Liberals in Quebec in 1960, the beginning of the Quiet Revolution, and the rise of terrorist groups led to commissions on bilingualism and biculturalism and a new sensitivity on the part of many English Canadians to the fact that either Quebec and French Canada generally would have to be treated differently or Canada might not survive. At the same time, however, there was resistance to this idea from other English Canadians who saw familiar societies being swept away by the vast changes taking place or expected to take place. In this atmosphere Louis Riel became a weapon. His story could be used as a message by those who urged reform to remind others of the previous injustices against French Canada. Acceptance of Riel was, in a way, a deliberate rejection of the "imperialist" and "jingoist" aspects of Canada's past which seemed, to the degree they survived, to threaten the necessary reforms. As such his symbolism became national in scope: while easterners may not have had much interest in Louis Riel's meaning as a westerner, they were very much concerned with the implications of his lesson to French–English relations in Canada as a whole. The new concern with

115

Riel as a French Canadian is clearly illustrated in a 1965 edition of Howard's work. In an introduction by Hartwell Bowsfield, de Voto's concern is replaced with a more Canadian preoccupation: " . . . the effect of his career was of significance, for the resistance of the métis people at Red River proved a stimulus to French Canadian nationalism which to this day still gives the Canadian political experience its unique and challenging aspect. Riel would have understood and thrived in the current debate as to the meaning of Canadian federalism."[61]

This reattachment of Riel to the concerns of French–English relations in Canada has continued. It has also proved extremely adaptable. In 1979, for instance, the Canadian Broadcasting Corporation portrayed Riel's fight for justice as an alternative to an Ontario fanaticism that would breed separatism. Bilingualism, it was urged by one actor, was the ultimate solution.[62] Louis Riel, one is tempted to comment, had ceased to be Patrick Henry and had become instead an official languages commissioner.

116

This interpretation of Riel meant that for the first time since 1869 French and English Canadians held essentially similar views. For in French Canada Riel had remained a standard and sympathetically treated figure in school texts, historical works, and novels.[63] Generally, however, there has been very little original scholarship on Riel in French since 1950. French-Canadian historians, it would appear, have become increasingly preoccupied with the history of Quebec. Louis Riel remains a symbol of injustice, it is true, but the geographic location of that injustice makes him somewhat irrelevant to an intellectual community beginning to discuss the idea of a separate Quebec nation. Thus, ironically, English Canada's concern with cultural duality has tended to make Riel more an English-Canadian hero than a French one.[64]

Through the later 1950s and into the 1960s two things became apparent. First, there was a growing interest in Riel. In 1957 R.E. Lamb's *Thunder in the North* and G.H. Needler's *Louis Riel* furthered interest in the subject, while in 1960 the University of Toronto Press gave recognition to the new importance of Riel by reissuing Stanley's *Birth of Western Canada*, this time in paperback. It has remained in print ever since. In 1963 Stanley published his full biography, *Louis Riel*. A.I. Silver and Marie-France Valleur's *North-West Rebellion* followed in 1967 and two years later Hartwell Bowsfield's *Louis Riel: Rebel of the Western Frontier or Victim of Politics?* appeared.[65] While Riel gained in importance those earlier heroes, La Vérendrye, Selkirk, and Simpson faded into the background. Even the Northwest Mounted Police were not the dominant figures they had once been. In fact, 1950 saw the last publication of a full-length history of the police for twenty years.[66] The story of the opening of the Canadian West had been replaced with that of the defence of the older order. English Canadians had identified with Riel's cause and he was thus, whatever his flaws, on the right side of history. Like Mackenzie and Papineau before him, and the Loyalists before them, he had become one of Canada's special losers.

Secondly, by the 1960s there was a similar outlook in both the scholarly and popular writings on Riel. The former, it was true, tended to be more qualified in their praise for Riel and more cautious in their judgments generally. For the most part, however, scholars readily accepted the elevation of Riel to historical status, perhaps thankful to have at least one portion of Canadian history viewed with interest by the general public and students. Many works, in fact, sought to bridge the traditional gap between academic and public. Hartwell Bowsfield's brief and readable biography of Riel provides one such example and even G.F.G. Stanley's full-length biography of Riel was popular enough to go through six printings in six years.[67] More recently Thomas Flanagan's study of Riel has received widespread publicity and has been put on the lists of a major book club.[68] Riel, it would seem, has become not only a symbol to Canadians but a subject of fascination for them.

With his reputation secure in the annals of scholarly writings, Louis Riel became a subject for repeated popular historical and fictional treatment in the years after 1960. The works published in response to this public interest, whether fictional or historical, varied greatly in quality and style. There were, nevertheless, certain recurrent themes which revealed the existence of a Riel myth as well as any of the specific historiographic interpretations which have been discussed. For in these writings Louis Riel's character, career, and motives have been interpreted with an eye to his legend. He has become an almost classic hero, possessed of great nobility and, as in the Greek tragedy, belaboured by tragic flaws. In their judgments on him, recent writings reveal much of the nature of the Riel myth.[69]

The first judgment made of Riel in much of the literature is that of motive. Earlier works have debated what mixture of egoism, insanity, and altruism shaped Riel's activities. More recent popular works have continued the debate but have shifted the emphasis. Riel's motives in leading his people are seen as essentially sincere. The myth seems to have demanded that Riel be freed of any taint of personal ambition in his decision to lead the Métis. His leadership tends to be portrayed as a reluctant one in which he is imposed upon, in both 1869 and 1885, to take up the burden of his people. Given such reluctance, Riel's reputed offer to leave the country in 1885 if paid enough by the Canadian government is either dismissed or viewed in a light favourable to Riel.[70] Finally, the "right" of Riel to lead his people is emphasized and his leadership seen as springing from the people themselves. Louis Riel,

117

the reader is continually reminded, was one of those he led and his selection was a popularly demanded one as befitted a hero in a democratic age.

With Riel's motives established, the next step for most writers is to vindicate his cause. This is relatively easy as historians have always accepted the fact that the Canadian government had made errors and that the Canada party in Red River had created tensions within the settlement. Scholarly works, such as those by Stanley and Morton, had carefully documented these difficulties and the popularizers really had to do little new to explain the reason for the Métis resistance. Nevertheless, there is a tendency among some popularizers to simplify issues and to make the Canadians more villainous than was actually the case. All the Canadians involved in the Red River and Northwest rebellions have had their reputations suffer with the exception of the seemingly invulnerable Macdonald. The Canadian party has been portrayed as "bully boys,"[71] "bigoted intellectuals,"[72] and "rowdies,"[73] while Thomas Scott, William McDougall, and John Christian Schultz have tended to become cardboard caricatures of everything that was wrong with English Canada.[74] It is not enough, it would appear, to have Riel in opposition to indifference and ignorance. The hero must fight positively evil forces for only then can his struggle take on the symbolism demanded.

A third essential attribute for mythical status is usefulness. This does not mean that Riel had to be seen as succeeding for, after all, many heroic figures failed. Rather, it meant that Riel must have contributed to the cause which he led and, at the very least, not have made things worse. Interestingly, this seems to be the most vulnerable spot in the Riel legend. Most writers assert that Riel made positive gains for the Métis in obtaining the provincial status for Manitoba in 1869–70 and at least made the government aware of the problems that existed along the North Saskatchewan in 1885. There remains, however, a nagging doubt about Riel's decision to begin a rebellion initially and then, having done so, failing to utilize the Métis forces to best advantage. Louis Riel's military tactics can be seen as the positive act of a peace-loving man[75] but they also tend to be seen as either "naïveté"[76] or, worse yet, a sign that his mind was losing its grip on reality. The result is that in recent years an alternate hero has shown signs of emerging to complement Riel. Gabriel Dumont, plains fighter and military strategist, has been the subject of a full-length and admiring work recently, while various works have taken liberties with fact by making Dumont a major figure at Red River as well as in the 1885 rebellion.[77]

Finally, in the classic tradition of heroes, Louis Riel died for his cause. This is important, for unlike two other rebels in Canadian history, William Lyon Mackenzie and Louis-Joseph Papineau, Riel's reputation was not to suffer because later years were to make him an irrelevant figure. He died at the height of his power and with controversy swirling around him. The debate over the trial has simply added to the imagery and accentuated the sense of martyrdom which pervades his execution. The decision of Macdonald to allow the law to take its course at Regina inadvertently contributed to the myth of the man who caused him so much difficulty in life.

Collectively, the writings of the last two decades, while assigning certain heroic attitudes to Riel, do not yield a straightforward answer to the question posed at the beginning of the paper: What national ideal is Riel thought to represent? Indeed, the evolution of the myth and the nature of its appeal would indicate that Riel's legendary status rests on the different meanings which he has assumed in the eyes of various communities within Canada. As a defender of French-Catholic rights, Métis culture, or western identity Riel would appeal to only a small portion of Canada. By being portrayed as a defender of all these things, however, he appeals to a great number of Canadians. In fact, given the complex nature of the Riel myth, with various groups adopting him for different reasons, it is tempting to argue that Riel gives us one more piece of evidence that Canada is a land of "limited identities."[78] Riel, in other words, has become a national myth only because he has evolved as a pluralistic symbol.

119

The particular significance attached to Riel by various communities would seem to reinforce this argument. Riel is as close as Canada comes to a national myth yet the symbolism that has evolved is extremely divisive. The lessons emphasized are those of historical injustice; French against English, East against West, Anglo-Saxon civilization against a nomadic people. Louis Riel may not be a symbol of Canadian values so much as a form of national penitence for our shortcomings. Perhaps Louis "David" Riel, the unstable prophet of the new world, has been vindicated in his myth — martyred for the sins of society. As one writer said, "Louis Riel is Canada's Joan of Arc."[79]

Yet the myth of Riel as it has evolved is not merely a complex religious allegory of sin and martyrdom. The martyr is too flawed and his religious delusions remain, in most works, the tragic flaw in the hero's character. Rather, the story of Riel is also a civics lesson of a peculiarly Canadian nature. The writings on him are both a reminder of the continuous frictions within Canadian life and of the delicate nature of the Canadian nation. Those who would forget the necessity for compromise within Canada, as the Canadian government did in 1869 or as Riel did in 1885, invite disaster. Riel's "insane" pretensions of founding a new nation along the North Saskatchewan and Macdonald's failure to show mercy after Riel was defeated led to disaster for both of them. "Where, in Riel's actions at this time, was the harmony or the proportion he had shown on occasion before, the harmony and proportion that distinguish reasonable ambition from the blind compulsion of a madman?"[80] The celebration of rebellion is not a part of the myth of the peaceable kingdom.

NOTES

My thanks to the Universiy of Calgary for the opportunity to present an earlier version of this paper.

[1] See Joseph Campbell, *The Hero with a Thousand Faces* (New York, 1949); Dixon Wecter, *The Hero in America Society* (New York, 1941).

[2] J.T. Marcus, "The World Impact of the West: The Mystique and the Sense of Participation in History," in Henry Murray, ed., *Myth and Mythmaking* (New York, 1960), 222.

[3] See "The Myth of Napoleon," *Yale French Studies* 26; Pieter Geyl, *Napoleon: For and Against* (New Haven, 1949), ch. 3. William Ward, *Andrew Jackson: Symbol for an Age* (New York, 1953).

[4] Donald Swainson, "Rieliana and the Structure of Canadian History," *Journal of Popular Culture* 14, 2 (Fall 1980): 20.

[5] The main source for bibliographic references on Riel has been Bruce Peel, *A Bibliography of the Prairie Provinces*, 2nd ed. (Toronto, 1973).

[6] The *Chronicles of Canada* series was edited by G.M. Wrong and H.H. Langton and appeared between 1914 and 1916. See Carl Berger, *The Writing of Canadian History* (Toronto, 1976), 14.

[7] F.H. Schofield, *The Story of Manitoba*, vol. 1 (Winnipeg, 1913), 227.

[8] R.G. MacBeth, *The Making of the Canadian West* (Toronto, 1905), 30-31.

[9] Chester Martin, "The Red River Settlement," in *Canada and Its Provinces*, vol. 19, *The Prairie Provinces*, 1 (Toronto, 1914), 69-70, 72-73.

[10] E.E. Kreutzweiser, *The Red River Insurrection: Its Causes and Events* (Garden Vale, Que., 1936), 100.

[11] Kreutzweiser, *Red River Insurrection*, 132.

[12] MacBeth, *The Making of the Canadian West*, 81.

[13] Schofield, *Story of Manitoba*, 274.

[14] Schofield, *Story of Manitoba*, 274. See also G.M. Wrong, *Canada: A Short History* (Toronto, 1921), 311.

[15] Howard Angus Kennedy, "Louis Riel and the North-West Rebellion," in F.W. Howay, *Builders of the West* (Toronto, 1929), 47.

[16] Sir Joseph Pope, *The Day of Sir John Macdonald* (Toronto, 1915), 128.

[17] MacBeth, *Making of the Canadian West*, 144.

[18] See, on the Mounties, two articles in Hugh Dempsey, ed., *Men in Scarlet* (Calgary, 1973): Dick Harrison, "The Mounted Police in Fiction," 163-74, and Henry Klassen, "The Mounties and the Historians," 175-86.

[19] Harrison, "The Mounted Police in Fiction," 165.

[20] See Arthur Silver, "French Quebec and the Métis Question," in R. Cook and C. Berger, eds., *The West and the Nation* (Toronto, 1976).

[21] A.G. Morice, *A Critical History of the Red River Insurrection* (Winnipeg, 1935), 63-64.

[22] Morice, *Critical History*, 243-44; see also A.H. Trémaudan. *Histoire de la nation métisse dans l'ouest canadien* (n.p., 1935), 213-14.

[23] Trémaudan, *Histoire de la nation métisse*, 181.

[24] Soeur St Léandre, *L'oeuvre véridique de Louis Riel* (Montreal, 1934), 49. S. Puchniak, "Riel's Red River Government: A Legislative Government" (MA thesis, University of Ottawa, 1933), 38.

[25] Morice, *Critical History*, 298.

[26] Trémaudan, *Histoire de la nation métisse*, 181.

[27] St Léandre, *L'oeuvre véridique*, 129-34, 169.

[28] St Léandre, *L'oeuvre véridique*, 132-35.

[29] A.C. Garrioch, *First Furrows: A History of the Early Settlement of the Red River Country* (Winnipeg, 1932), 205.

[30] The Reverend Morice, Trémaudan, MacBeth, and George Bryce serve as examples, as does Soeur St Léandre.

[31] G.F.G. Stanley, *The Birth of Western Canada* (London, 1936), 68. Marcel Giraud, *Le Métis canadien* (Paris, 1945), 1100, 1103.

[32] Jonas Jonasson, "The Background of the Riel Rebellions," *Pacific Historical Review*, 3, 3 (1934): 270-79.

[33] Riel Project Bulletin no. 5, April 1981. The loss of stock is mentioned in the foreword to the University of Toronto Press edition (1960).

[34] This emphasis is probably connected to the then prevalent interest in social and economic forces in history. See Berger, *The Writing of Canadian History*, 137.

[35] Stanley, *Birth of Western Canada*, vii.

[36] Giraud, *Le Métis canadien*, 1100.

[37] Joseph Kinsey Howard, *Strange Empire* (New York, 1952), Introduction by Bernard de Voto, 9-10.

[38] Howard, *Strange Empire*, 23.

[39] Howard, *Strange Empire*, 85.

[40] Howard, *Strange Empire*, 133.

[41] Howard, *Strange Empire*, 151–52.

[42] Howard, *Strange Empire*, 329–30.

[43] Howard, *Strange Empire*. This is the title of Chapter 17.

[44] See Terry Lusty, *Louis Riel: Humanitarian* (Edmonton, 1975); Association of Métis and Non-Status Indians of Saskatchewan, *Justice Must Be Done* (Winnipeg, 1979); Duke Redbird, *We Are Métis: A Métis View of the Development of the Canadian People* (Toronto, 1980).

[45] Thomas Flanagan, *Louis "David" Riel: "Prophet" of the New World* (Toronto, 1979).

[46] John Coulter, *The Crime of Louis Riel* (Toronto, 1976), Foreword.

[47] Stanley Ryerson, "Riel vs. Anglo-Canadian Imperialism," *Canadian Dimension* 7, 1 (July 1970), and his *Unequal Union* (Toronto, 1973).

[48] See also Léandre Bergeron, *Petit manuel d'histoire du Québec* (Editions Québécoises), who combines the radical view with a focus on cultural dualism.

[49] W.L. Morton, ed., *Alexander Begg's Red River Journal* (Toronto, 1956), Introduction, 3, 44.

[50] Morton, ed., *Alexander Begg's Red River Journal*, 48, 68, 77.

[51] Morton, ed., *Alexander Begg's Red River Journal*, 31.

[52] Morton, ed., *Alexander Begg's Red River Journal*, 53.

[53] Morton, ed., *Alexander Begg's Red River Journal*, 143–44, 43.

[54] W.L. Morton, "The Bias of Prairie Politics," *Transactions of the Royal Society of Canada* 49 (June 1955), 57.

[55] *Riel Project Bulletin* no. 5 (April 1981), 4.

[56] Aside from the recounting of 1885 in the various police histories, there were a number of memoirs and stories of the militia units and specific histories of the rebellion from the military perspective. See, as examples, George Dunlop, *Tales of the North-West Rebellion* (Edmonton, 1934); Neil Brodie, *Twelve Days with the Indians* (Battleford, 1932); and Prince Albert Old Timers, *Reminiscences of the Riel Rebellion of 1885* (Prince Albert, 1935).

[57] W.M. Davidson, *Louis Riel, 1844–1883* (Calgary, 1955), 26.

[58] E.B. Osler, *The Man Who Had to Hang* (Toronto, 1961).

[59] Owen Anderson, "The Unfinished Revolt," in Anderson, ed., *The Unfinished Revolt* (Toronto, 1971), 36.

[60] This writer's favourite use of the Riel myth came during the Ottawa–Alberta energy wars when a politician, one who will remain unnamed, argued that Riel's fight had been one for the provincial ownership of natural resources.

[61] Howard, *Strange Empire*.

[62] "Riel," George Bloomfield director, screenplay by Ray Moore.

[63] Jean-Jules Richard, *Louis Riel, Exovide* (Montreal, 1972), serves as an example of a recent novel. Recent texts include J. Lacoursière, J. Provencher, and D. Vaugeois, *Canada/Québec synthèse historique* (Montreal, 1978), 409–410, 437–39, and P.A. Linteau, René Durocher, and J.C. Robert, *Histoire du Québec* (Quebec, 1979). The latter, interestingly, adopts a frontierist approach.

[64] Both Osler (1964) and Bowsfield's (1973) biographies have been translated into French.

[65] Hartwell Bowsfield, *Louis Riel* (Toronto, 1969); G.F.G. Stanley, *Louis Riel* (Toronto, 1963).

[66] J. Turner, *The North-West Mounted Police, 1873–1893* (Ottawa, 1950).

[67] Hartwell Bowsfield, *Louis Riel: The Rebel and the Hero* (Toronto, 1971); Stanley, *Louis Riel*.

[68] Flanagan, *Louis "David" Riel*.

[69] The following paragraphs are drawn from a series of post-1960 works: Pierre Berton, *The National Dream* (Toronto, 1970); Canadian Broadcasting Corporation, "Riel"; Peter Charlebois, *The Life of Louis Riel* (NC Press, 1975); Association of Métis and Non-Status Indians of Saskatchewan, *Justice Must Be Done;* Harry Somers, *Louis Riel: Music Done in Three Acts;* Lusty, *Louis Riel: Humanitarian;* George Woodcock, *Gabriel Dumont* (Edmonton, 1975); Osler, *The Man Who Had to Hang;* R.W. Robertson, *The Execution of Thomas Scott* (Toronto, 1968); Frank Rasky, *The Taming of the Canadian West* (Toronto, 1967).

[70] For such a favourable interpretation see Charlebois, *Life of Louis Riel*.

[71] Osler, *The Man Who Had to Hang*, 9.

[72] Charlebois, *Life of Louis Riel*, 32.

[73] Rasky, *Taming of the Canadian West* (Toronto, 1967), 202.

[74] Good examples of this include Harry Somers, *Riel* 1: 50; Osler, *The Man Who Had to Hang;* and Rudy Wiebe, *The Scorched-Wood People* (Toronto, 1977). One exception is the short study by R. Robertson, *The Execution of Thomas Scott* (Toronto, 1968), which portrays Scott in a rather kindly light.

[75] Association of Métis and Non-Status Indians, *Justice Must Be Done*, 48.

[76] Rasky, *The Taming of the Canadian West*, 231.

[77] Woodcock, *Gabriel Dumont*. See also the revealing comments of Margaret Laurence in her review of Woodcock's *Dumont*, in *Canadian Forum* (Dec. 1975), 28–29.

[78] J.M.S. Careless, "'Limited Identities' in Canada," *Canadian Historical Review* 50, 1 (1969): 1–10.

[79] Hector Coutu, *Lagimodière and their Descendants* (Edmonton, 1980), 63.

[80] Osler, *The Man Who Had to Hang*, 241.

Canada's Subjugation of the Plains Cree, 1879–1885*

JOHN L. TOBIAS

One of the most persistent myths that Canadian historians perpetuate is that of the honourable and just policy Canada followed in dealing with the Plains Indians. First enunciated in the Canadian expansionist literature of the 1870s as a means to emphasize the distinctive Canadian approach to and the unique character of the Canadian west,[1] it has been given credence by G.F.G. Stanley in his classic *The Birth of Western Canada*,[2] and by all those who use Stanley's work as the standard interpretation of Canada's relationship with the Plains Indians in the period 1870–85. Thus students are taught that the Canadian government was paternalistic and far-sighted in offering the Indians a means to become civilized and assimilated into white society by the reserve system, and honest and fair-minded in honouring legal commitments made in the treaties.[3] The Plains Indians, and particularly the Plains Cree, are said to be a primitive people adhering to an inflexible system of tradition and custom, seeking to protect themselves against the advance of civilization, and taking up arms in rejection of the reserve system and an agricultural way of life.[4] This traditional interpretation distorts the roles of both the Cree and the Canadian government, for the Cree were both flexible and active in promoting their own interests, and willing to accommodate themselves to a new way of life, while the Canadian government was neither as far-sighted nor as just as tradition maintains. Canada's principal concern in its relationship with the Plains Cree was to establish control over them, and Canadian authorities were willing to and did wage war upon the Cree in order to achieve this control.

Those who propagate the myth would have us believe that Canada began to negotiate treaties with the Indians of the West in 1871 as part of an overall plan to develop the agricultural potential of the West, open the land for railway construction, and bind the prairies to Canada in a network of commercial and economic ties. Although there is an element of truth to these statements, the fact remains that in 1871 Canada had no plan on how to deal with the Indians and the negotiation of treaties was not at the initiative of the Canadian government, but at the insistence of the Ojibwa Indians of the North-West Angle and the Saulteaux of the tiny province of Manitoba. What is ignored by the traditional interpretation is that the treaty process only started after Yellow Quill's band of Saulteaux turned back settlers who tried to go west of Portage

*From *Canadian Historical Review* 64 (December 1983): 519–48. Reprinted by permission of the author and the University of Toronto Press.

la Prairie, and after other Saulteaux leaders insisted upon enforcement of the Selkirk Treaty or, more often, insisted upon making a new treaty. Also ignored is the fact that the Ojibwa of the North-West Angle demanded rents, and created the fear of violence against prospective settlers who crossed their land or made use of their territory, if Ojibwa rights to their lands were not recognized. This pressure and fear of resulting violence is what motivated the government to begin the treaty-making process.[5]

Canada's initial offer to the Saulteaux and Ojibwa Indians consisted only of reserves and a small cash annuity. This proposal was rejected by the Ojibwa in 1871 and again in 1872, while the Saulteaux demanded, much to Treaty Commissioner Wemyss Simpson's chagrin, farm animals, horses, wagons, and farm tools and equipment. Simpson did not include these demands in the written treaty, for he had no authority to do so, but he wrote them down in the form of a memorandum that he entitled "outside promises" and which he failed to send to Ottawa. Thus, the original Treaties 1 and 2 did not include those items the Saulteaux said had to be part of a treaty before they would agree to surrender their lands. Only in 1874, after the Indian leaders of Manitoba became irate over non-receipt of the goods that Simpson had promised them, was an inquiry launched, and Simpson's list of "outside promises" discovered and incorporated in renegotiated treaties in 1875.[6] It was only in 1873, after the Ojibwa of the North-West Angle had twice refused treaties that only included reserves and annuities, that the government agreed to include the domestic animals, farm tools, and equipment that the Ojibwa demanded. After this experience Canada made such goods a standard part of later treaties.[7]

Just as it was pressure from the Indians of Manitoba that forced the government of Canada to initiate the treaty process, it was pressure from the Plains Cree in the period 1872–75 that compelled the government of Canada to continue the process with the Indians of the Qu'Appelle and Saskatchewan districts. The Plains Cree had interfered with the geological survey and prevented the construction of telegraph lines through their territory to emphasize that Canada had to deal with the Cree for Cree lands.[8] The Cree had learned in 1870 about Canada's claim to their lands, and not wanting to experience what had happened to the Indians in the United States when those people were faced with an expansionist government, the Cree made clear that they would not allow settlement or use of their lands until Cree rights had been clearly recognized. They also made clear that part of any arrangement for Cree lands had to involve assistance to the Cree in developing a new agricultural way of life.[9]

In adopting this position, the Cree were simply demonstrating a skill that they had shown since their initial contact with Europeans in 1670. On numerous occasions during the fur trade era, they had adapted to

123

changed environmental and economic circumstances, beginning first as hunters, then as provisioners and middlemen in the Hudson's Bay Company trading system, and finally adapting from a woodland to parkland-prairie buffalo hunting culture to retain their independence and their desired ties with the fur trade.[10] Having accommodated themselves to the Plains Indian culture after 1800, they expanded into territory formerly controlled by the Atsina, and as the buffalo herds began to decline after 1850, the Cree expanded into Blackfoot territory.[11] Expansion was one response to the threat posed by declining buffalo herds; another was that some Plains Cree bands began to turn to agriculture.[12] Thus, when the Cree learned that Canada claimed their lands, part of the arrangement they were determined to make and succeeded in making was to receive assistance in adapting to an agricultural way of life. So successful were they in negotiating such assistance that when the Mackenzie government received a copy of Treaty 6 in 1876 it accepted the treaty only after expressing a protest concerning the too-generous terms granted to the Cree.[13]

124

While willing to explore the alternative of agriculture, three Cree leaders in the 1870s sought means to guarantee preservation of the buffalo-hunting culture as long as possible. Piapot (leader of the Cree-Assiniboine of the region south of Qu'Appelle River), and Big Bear and Little Pine (leaders of two of the largest Cree bands from the Saskatchewan River district) led what has been called an armed migration of the Cree into the Cypress Hills in the latter 1860s. All three men were noted warriors, and Big Bear and Piapot were noted religious leaders, but their prowess was not enough to prevent a Cree defeat at the Battle of the Belly River in 1870,[14] and as a result they explored the alternative of dealing with the government of Canada, but in a manner to extract guarantees for the preservation of Cree autonomy. They were determined to get the government to promise to limit the buffalo hunt to the Indians — a goal that Cree leaders had been advocating since the 1850s.[15] When Big Bear met with Treaty Commissioner Alexander Morris at Fort Pitt in September 1876, he extracted a promise from Morris that non-Indian hunting of the buffalo would be regulated.[16]

Big Bear refused to take treaty in 1876, despite receiving Morris's assurances about the regulation of the hunt. Little Pine and Piapot also did not take treaty when the treaty commissions first came to deal with the Cree. Oral tradition among the Cree maintains that all three leaders wished to see how faithful the government would be in honouring treaties,[17] but equally important for all three leaders was their belief that the treaties were inadequate and that revisions were necessary. Piapot thought Treaty 4 (the Qu'Appelle Treaty) needed to be expanded to include increased farm equipment and tools, and to stipulate that the government had to provide mills, blacksmith and carpentry shops and tools, and instructors in farming and the trades. Only after receiving assurances that Ottawa would consider these requests did Piapot take treaty in 1875.[18] Big Bear and Little Pine objected to Treaty 6 (Fort Pitt and Carlton) because Commissioner Morris had made clear that in taking treaty the Cree would be bound to Canadian law. To accept the treaties would mean being subject to an external authority of which the Crees had little knowledge and upon which they had little influence. Neither Big Bear nor Little Pine would countenance such a loss of autonomy.

Big Bear had raised the matter of Cree autonomy at Fort Pitt in 1876 when he met Commissioner Morris. At that time Big Bear said: "I will make a request that he [Morris] save me from what I most dread, that is the rope about my neck. . . . It was not given to us to have the rope about our neck."[19] Morris and most subsequent historians have interpreted Big Bear's statements to be a specific reference to hanging, but such an interpretation ignores the fact that Big Bear, like most Indian leaders, often used a metaphor to emphasize a point. In 1875, he had made the same point by using a different metaphor when he spoke to messengers informing him that a treaty commission was to meet with the Cree in 1876. At that time Big Bear said: "We want none of the Queen's presents: when we set a foxtrap we scatter pieces of meat all around, but when the fox gets into the trap we knock him on the head; we want no bait. . . . "[20] A more accurate interpretation of Big Bear's words to Morris in 1876 is that he feared being controlled or "enslaved," just as an animal is controlled when it has a rope around its neck.[21] In 1877, when meeting with Lieutenant-Governor David Laird, Little Pine also stated that he would not take treaty because he saw the treaties as a means by which the government could "enslave" his people.[22]

The importance of these three leaders cannot be underestimated, for they had with them in the Cypress Hills more than fifty per cent of the total Indian population of the Treaty 4 and 6 areas. By concentrating in such numbers in the last buffalo ranges in Canadian territory, the Cree were free from all external interference, whether by other Indian nations or by the agents of the Canadian government — the North-West Mounted Police.[23] Recognizing that these men were bargaining from a position of strength, Laird recommended in 1878 that the government act quickly to establish reserves and honour the treaties. He was aware that the Cypress Hills leaders had the support of many of the Cree in treaty, and that many of the Cree leaders were complaining that the government was not providing the farming assistance promised. As the number of these complaints increased, so did Cree support for Big Bear and Little Pine.[24]

The Cree were concerned not only about the lack of assistance to farm, but when Canadian officials were slow to take action to regulate the buffalo hunt, Big Bear, Piapot, and Little Pine met with Blackfoot leaders and with Sitting Bull of the Teton Sioux in an attempt to reach agreement among the Indian nations on the need to regulate buffalo hunting.[25] These councils were also the forum where Indian leaders discussed the need to revise the treaties. On learning about the Indian council, the non-Indian populace of the West grew anxious, fearing establishment of an Indian confederacy which would wage war if Indian demands were rejected.[26] However, an Indian confederacy did not result from these meetings, nor was agreement reached on how the buffalo were to be preserved, because the Cree, Sioux, and Blackfoot could not overcome their old animosities towards one another.[27]

When in 1879 the buffalo disappeared from the Canadian prairies and Big Bear and Little Pine took their bands south to the buffalo ranges on the Milk and Missouri rivers, most of the other Cree and Assiniboine bands also went with them. The Cree who remained in Canada faced starvation while awaiting the survey of their reserves and the farming equipment that had been promised. Realizing that many of the Cree were dying, the government decided that those who had taken treaty should be given rations. As well, the government appointed Edgar Dewdney to the newly created position of Commissioner of Indian Affairs for the North-West Territory; a farming policy for the western reserves was introduced; a survey of Cree reserves was begun; and twelve farming instructors were appointed to teach the Indians of the North-West.[28]

The new Indian Commissioner quickly sought to use rations as a means of getting control over the Cree. In the fall of 1879 he announced that rations were to be provided only to Indians who had taken treaty. To get the Cree into treaty more easily and to reduce the influence of recalcitrant leaders, Dewdney announced that he would adopt an old Hudson's Bay Company practice of recognizing any adult male Cree as chief of a new band if he could induce 100 or more persons to recognize him as leader. He expected that the starving Cypress Hills Cree would desert their old leaders to get rations. As a means of demonstrating Canada's control over the Cree, Dewdney ordered that only the sick, aged, and orphans should receive rations without providing some service to one of the government agencies in the West.[29]

Dewdney's policies seemed to work, for when the Cree and Assiniboine who had gone to hunt in Montana returned starving, their resolve weakened. Little Pine's people convinced their chief to take treaty in 1879, but when Big Bear refused to do the same, almost half of his following joined Lucky Man or Thunderchild to form new bands in order to receive rations.[30]

Taking treaty to avoid starvation did not mean that the Cree had come to accept the treaties as written; rather they altered their tactics in seeking revisions. Believing that small reserves were more susceptible to the control of the Canadian government and its officials, Big Bear, Piapot, and Little Pine sought to effect a concentration of the Cree people in an Indian territory similar to the reservation system in the United States. In such a territory the Cree would be able to preserve their autonomy, or at least limit the ability of others to control them; they would be better able to take concerted action on matters of importance to them.[31]

Soon after taking treaty Little Pine applied for a reserve in the Cypress Hills, twenty-seven miles north-east of the North-West Mounted Police post of Fort Walsh. Piapot requested a reserve next to Little Pine's, while ten other bands, including most of the Assiniboine nation, selected reserve sites contiguous to either Little Pine's or Piapot's and to one another.[32] If all these reserve sites were granted, and if Big Bear were to take treaty and settle in the Cypress Hills, the result would be concentration of much of the Cree nation and the creation of an Indian territory that would comprise most of what is now south-western Saskatchewan.

Unaware of the intention of the Cree and Assiniboine leaders, Canadian officials in the spring of 1880 agreed to the establishment of a reserve for all the Canadian Assiniboine and reserves in the Cypress Hills for each of the Cree bands that wished them. In 1880, the Assiniboine reserve was surveyed, but the other Indian leaders were told that their reserves would not be surveyed until the following year.[33] In the interim, most of the Cree went to the buffalo ranges in Montana.

The Cree effort to exploit the remaining American buffaloranges caused them much trouble. The Crow, the Peigan, and other Indian nations with reservations in Montana were upset by competition for the scarce food resource, and these people threatened to wage war on the Cree if the American authorities did not protect the Indian hunting ranges. These threats were renewed when the Cree began to steal horses from the Crow and Peigan. To add to their difficulties, American ranchers accused the Cree of killing range cattle. American officials, not wishing trouble with their Indians and wishing to placate the ranchers, informed the Cree that they would have to return to Canada. Most Cree bands, aware that if they did not leave voluntarily the American government would use troops to force them to move north, returned to the Cypress Hills.[34]

They returned to find that Canadian officials were now aware of the dangers to their authority posed by a concentration of the Cree. A riot at Fort Walsh in 1880, which the police were powerless to prevent or control, assaults on farming instructors who refused to provide rations to starving Indians, and rumours that the Cree were planning a grand Indian council to discuss treaty revisions in 1881 all caused the Indian Commissioner much concern.[35] To avoid further difficulties over rations, in late 1880 Dewdney ordered that all Indians requesting rations be given them, regardless of whether the supplicant was in treaty.[36] There was little that the government could do at this time about the proposed Indian council or the concentration of Cree in the Cypress Hills.

In the spring of 1881, Cree bands from all regions of the Canadian prairies left their reserves to go south to meet with Little Pine and Big Bear. Even the new bands Dewdney had created were going to the council in American territory. What was also disconcerting to Canadian officials were the reports that Big Bear and Little Pine, who had gone to Montana to prepare for the council, had reached an accommodation with the Blackfoot and had participated in a joint raid on the Crow. To all appearances the Blackfoot, the Indian confederacy the Canadian government most feared, would be part of the Indian council.[37]

The Indian council was not held because the raid on the Crow led American officials to intervene militarily to force the Cree to return to Canada. With Montana stockmen acting as militia units, the American army prevented most Cree and Assiniboine bands from entering the United States. As well, the American forces seized horses, guns, and carts, and escorted the Cree to Canada.[38] The Cree–Blackfoot alliance did not materialize, for soon after the raid on the Crow, young Cree warriors stole horses from the Blackfoot and thereby destroyed the accord that Little Pine and Big Bear were attempting to create.[39]

128

The actions of the American military in 1881 were extremely beneficial to Canada. Not only did the Americans prevent the holding of the Indian council, but by confiscating the guns and horses of the Cree, the Americans had dispossessed the Cree of the ability to resist whatever measures the Canadian authorities wished to take against them. The Canadian authorities also benefited from Governor-General Lorne's tour of the West in 1881, for many of the Cree bands that had gone to the Cypress Hills in the spring went north in late summer to meet Lorne to impress upon him the inadequacy of the treaties and the need to revise them.[40] Thus, Lorne's tour prevented the concentration of most of the Cree nation in the Cypress Hills.

The threat posed to Canadian authority in the North-West by concentration of the Cree was clearly recognized by Dewdney and other Canadian officials in late 1881. They saw how the Cree had forced officials to placate them and to ignore their orders in 1880 and 1881. This convinced both Dewdney and Ottawa that the Cree request for contiguous reserves in the Cypress Hills could not be granted. Dewdney recognized that to grant the Cree requests would be to create an Indian territory, for most of the Cree who had reserves further north would come to the Cypress Hills and request reserves contiguous to those of the Cypress Hills Cree. This would result in so large a concentration of Cree that the only way Canada could enforce its laws on them would be via a military campaign. To prevent this, Dewdney recommended a sizeable expansion of the Mounted Police force and the closure of Fort Walsh and all government facilities in the Cypress Hills. This action would remove all sources of sustenance from the Cree in the Cypress Hills. Dewdney hoped that starvation would drive them from the Fort Walsh area and thus end the concentration of their force.[41]

Dewdney decided to take these steps fully aware that what he was doing was a violation not only of the promises made to the Cypress

Hills Indians in 1880 and 1881, but also that by refusing to grant reserves on the sites the Indians had selected, he was violating the promises made to the Cree by the Treaty Commissions in 1874 and 1876, and in the written treaties. Nevertheless, Dewdney believed that to accede to the Cree requests would be to grant the Cree de facto autonomy from Canadian control, which would result in the perpetuation and heightening of the 1880–81 crisis. Rather than see that situation continue, Dewdney wanted to exploit the opportunity presented to him by the hunger crisis and disarmament of the Cree to bring them under the government's control, even if it meant violating the treaties.[42]

In the spring of 1882 the Cree and Assiniboine were told that no further rations would be issued to them while they remained in the Cypress Hills. Only if the Indians moved north to Qu'Appelle, Battleford, and Fort Pitt were they to be given assistance, and at those locations only treaty Indians were to be aided. The Mounted Police were ordered to stop issuing rations at Fort Walsh and the Indian Department farm that had been located near Fort Walsh was closed. Faced with the prospect of starvation, without weapons or transport to get to the Montana buffalo ranges, and knowing that if they were to try to go south the Mounted Police would inform the American military authorities, many Cree and all the Assiniboine decided to go north.[43] Even Big Bear discovered that his people wanted him to take treaty and move north. In 1882, after taking treaty, he, along with Piapot and Little Pine, promised to leave the Cypress Hills.[44]

129

Only Piapot kept his promise and even he did not remain long at Fort Qu'Appelle. By late summer of 1882, Piapot was back in the Cypress Hills complaining about how he had been mistreated at Qu'Appelle, and making the Cree aware of how they could lose their autonomy if the government could deal with them as individual bands.[45] On hearing this report, the other Cree leaders refused to leave the Fort Walsh region and insisted upon receiving the reserves promised them in 1880 and 1881. North-West Mounted Police Commissioner Irvine feared a repetition of the incidents of 1880 if he refused to feed the Cree and believed that the hungry Cree would harass the construction crews of the Canadian Pacific Railway for food, which would lead to a confrontation between whites and Indians which the police would be unable to handle and which in turn might lead to an Indian war. Therefore Irvine decided to feed the Cree.[46]

Dewdney and Ottawa were upset by Irvine's actions. Ottawa gave specific instructions to close Fort Walsh in the spring of 1883. When Irvine closed the fort, the Cree faced starvation. As it was quite evident that they could not go to the United States, and as they would not receive reserves in the Cypress Hills, the Cree moved north. Piapot moved to Indian Head and selected a reserve site next to the huge reserve set aside for the Assiniboine. Little Pine and Lucky Man moved to Battleford and selected reserve sites next to Poundmaker's reserve. Big Bear went to Fort Pitt.

The move to the north was not a sign of the Cree acceptance of the treaties as written, nor of their acceptance of the authority of the Canadian government. Big Bear, Little Pine, and Piapot were aware that the other Cree chiefs were dissatisfied with the treaties, and were also aware that if they could effect concentration of the Cree in the north they would be able to preserve their autonomy, just as they had done in the Cypress Hills in the 1879–81 period. Therefore, the move to the north was simply a tactical move, for no sooner were these chiefs in the north than they once again sought to effect a concentration of their people.

By moving to Indian Head, Piapot had effected a concentration of more than 2,000 Indians. This number threatened to grow larger if the council he planned to hold with all the Treaty 4 bands to discuss treaty revisions were successful. Commissioner Dewdney, fearing the results of such a meeting in 1883, was able to thwart Piapot by threatening to cut off rations to any Indians attending Piapot's council and by threatening to arrest Piapot and depose any chiefs who did meet with him. Although Dewdney, in 1883, prevented Piapot holding a large council by such actions, Piapot was able to get the Treaty 4 chiefs to agree to meet in the late spring of 1884 for a thirst dance and council on Pasquah's Reserve, near Fort Qu'Appelle.[47]

While Piapot was organizing an Indian council in the Treaty 4 area, Big Bear and Little Pine were doing the same for the Treaty 6 region. Little Pine and Lucky Man attempted to effect a concentration of more than 2,000 Cree on contiguous reserves in the Battleford district, by requesting reserves next to Poundmaker, whose reserve was next to three other Cree reserves, which in turn were only a short distance from three Assiniboine reserves. Another 500 Cree would have been located in the Battleford area if Big Bear's request for a reserve next to Little Pine's site had been granted. Only with difficulty was Dewdney able to get Big Bear to move to Fort Pitt.[48] However, he was unable to prevent Big Bear and Little Pine from sending messengers to the Cree leaders of the Edmonton, Carlton, and Duck Lake districts to enlist their support for the movement to concentrate the Cree.[49]

Dewdney was convinced that the activities of Big Bear, Piapot, and Little Pine were a prelude to a major project the Cree planned for the following year, 1884. He was also aware that his ability to deal with the impending problem was severely limited by decisions taken in Ottawa. The Deputy Superintendent-General of Indian Affairs, Lawrence Vankoughnet, was concerned about the cost of administering Dewdney's policies, and he ordered reductions in the level of assistance provided to the Cree and in the number of employees working with the Cree.[50] In making these decisions, Ottawa effectively deprived Dewdney of his major sources of intelligence about the Cree and their plans. It also deprived Dewdney of a major instrument in placating the Cree — the distribution of rations to those bands which co-operated.

Vankoughnet's economy measures led to further alienation of the Cree. In some areas, notably in the Fort Pitt, Edmonton, and Crooked Lakes regions, farming instructors were assaulted and government storehouses broken into when Indians were denied rations. The incident on the Sakemay Reserve in the Crooked Lakes area was quite serious, for when the police were called upon to arrest those guilty of the assault, they were surrounded and threatened with death if they carried out their orders. Only after Assistant Indian Commissioner Hayter Reed had agreed to restore assistance to the Sakemay band to the 1883 level and had promised not to imprison the accused were the police allowed to leave with their prisoners.[51]

The violence that followed the reductions in rations convinced Dewdney that starving the Cree into submission was not the means to control them. He wanted to use coercion, but this required an expansion of the number of police in the West. Therefore, he recommended that more men be recruited for the Mounted Police. In addition, Dewdney wanted to ensure that jail sentences were given to arrested Indians so that they would cause no further problems. Having seen the effects of incarceration on Indians, Dewdney was convinced that this was the means to bring the Cree leaders under control. However, what was needed in his opinion were trial judges who "understood" Indian nature at first hand and who would take effective action to keep the Indians under control. Therefore, Dewdney wanted all Indian Department officials in the West to be appointed stipendiary magistrates in order that all Indian troublemakers could be brought to "justice" quickly. As Dewdney stated in his letter to Prime Minister John A. Macdonald: "The only effective course with the great proportion [of Indian bands] to adopt is one of sheer compulsion. . . ."[52]

131

Dewdney used the policy of "sheer compulsion" for only a few months in 1884. He found that his efforts to use the Mounted Police to break up the Indian councils and to arrest Indian leaders only led to confrontations between the Cree and the police. In these confrontations the police were shown to be ineffectual because they were placed in situations in which, if the Cree had been desirous of initiating hostilities, large numbers of Mounted Police would have been massacred.

The first incident which called the policy of compulsion into question was the attempt to prevent Piapot from holding his thirst dance and council in May 1884. Assistant Commissioner Hayter Reed, fearing that the council would result in a concentration of all the Treaty 4 bands, ordered Police Commissioner Irvine to prevent Piapot from attending the council. Irvine was to arrest the chief at the first sign of any violation of even the most minor law. To be certain that Piapot broke a law, Reed promised to have an individual from Pasquah's reserve object to the council being held on that reserve in order that the accusation of trespass could be used to break up the meeting, which all the bands from Treaty 4 were attending.[53]

With a force of fifty-six men and a seven-pounder gun, Irvine caught up with Piapot shortly before the chief reached Pasquah's reserve. Irvine and the police entered the Indian camp at 2 A.M., hoping to arrest Piapot and remove him from the camp before his band was aware of what happened. However, when they entered the camp, the police found themselves surrounded by armed warriors. Realizing that any attempt to arrest the chief would result in a battle, Irvine decided to hold his own council with Piapot and Reed. This impromptu council agreed that Piapot should receive a new reserve next to Pasquah, in return for which Piapot would return to Indian Head temporarily.[54]

The agreement reached between Piapot and Irvine and Reed was a victory for Piapot. By getting a reserve at Qu'Appelle again, Piapot had approximately 2,000 Cree concentrated on the Qu'Appelle River, and he was able to hold his council and thirst dance, for after going to Indian Head, he immediately turned around and went to Pasquah's. Reed and Irvine were aware of Piapot's ruse, but did nothing to prevent his holding the council, for they were aware that the Cree at Qu'Appelle were prepared to protect Piapot from what the Indians regarded as an attack on their leader. Realizing the effect that an Indian war would have on possible settlement, and that the police were inadequate for such a clash, the Canadian officials wished to avoid giving cause for violent reaction by the Cree.[55] Piapot acted as he did because he realized that if any blood were shed the Cree would experience a fate similar to that of the Nez Percés, Blackfoot, and Dakota Sioux in those peoples' conflicts with the United States.

Dewdney and the police were to have a similar experience when they attempted to prevent Big Bear from holding a thirst dance and council at Poundmaker's reserve in June 1884. Dewdney feared that Big Bear's council, to which the old chief had invited the Blackfoot and all the Indians from Treaty 6, would result in a larger concentration of Cree than Little Pine had already effected at Battleford. Dewdney also believed that he had to undo what Little Pine had accomplished, and refused to grant Little Pine and Lucky Man the reserve sites they had requested next to Poundmaker. Big Bear was again told that he would not be granted a reserve in the Battleford district. Dewdney believed that the Cree chiefs would ignore his order to select reserve sites at some distance from Battleford, and that this could be used as a reason for arresting them. To legitimize such actions on his part, Dewdney asked the government to pass an order-in-council to make it a criminal offence for a band to refuse to move to a reserve site the Commissioner suggested.[56] In order to avoid violence when he attempted to prevent Big

132

Bear's council and ordered the arrests of Lucky Man and Little Pine, Dewdney instructed the Indian agents at Battleford and Fort Pitt to purchase all the horses, guns, and cartridges the Cree possessed. He increased the size of the police garrison at Battleford and ordered the police to prevent Big Bear from reaching Battleford.[57]

All Dewdney's efforts had little effect, for Big Bear and his band eluded the police, reached Battleford, and held their thirst dance. The Cree refused to sell their arms, and even the effort to break up the gathering by refusing to provide rations had no result other than to provoke another assault on a farm instructor on 17 June 1884. When the police sought to arrest the farm instructor's assailant, they were intimidated into leaving without a prisoner. When a larger police detachment went to the reserve on 18 June, the police were still unable to make an arrest for fear of provoking armed hostilities. Only on 20 June, when the thirst dance had concluded, were the police able to arrest the accused and only then by forcibly removing him from the Cree camp. This was done with the greatest difficulty for the police were jostled and provoked in an effort to get them to fire on the Cree. That no violence occurred, Superintendent Crozier, in charge of the police detachment, attributed to the discipline of his men and to the actions of Little Pine and Big Bear, who did all that was humanly possible to discourage any attack on the police.[58]

The events at Battleford frightened all parties involved in the confrontation. Big Bear was very much disturbed by them, for he did not want war, as he had made abundantly clear to Dewdney in March 1884, and again to the Indian agent at Battleford, J.A. Rae, in June. However, he did want the treaties revised and establishment of an Indian territory.[59] Agent Rae was thoroughly frightened and wanted Dewdney and Ottawa to adopt a more coercive policy designed to subjugate the Cree. Superintendent Crozier argued for a less coercive policy, for unless some accommodation were reached with the Cree, Crozier believed that out of desperation they would resort to violence.[60]

On hearing of the events of May and June 1884, Ottawa decided that Dewdney, who was now Lieutenant-Governor in addition to being Indian Commissioner, was to have complete control over Indian affairs in the North-West Territories. As well, the Prime Minister informed Dewdney that more police were being recruited for duty in the West and that the Indian Act was being amended to permit Dewdney to arrest any Indian who was on another band's reserve without the permission of the local Indian Department official.[61] Dewdney was thus being given the instruments to make his policy of compulsion effective.

Dewdney did not, however, immediately make use of his new powers. He still intended to prevent concentration of the Cree, and rejected the requests Big Bear, Poundmaker, Lucky Man, and others made for a reserve at Buffalo Lake, and later rejected Big Bear's, Little Pine's, and

133

Lucky Man's renewed requests for reserves next to Poundmaker's.[62] However, rather than following a purely coercive policy, Dewdney adopted a policy of rewards and punishments. He provided more rations, farming equipment, oxen, ammunition, and twine, and arranged for selected Cree chiefs to visit Winnipeg and other large centres of Canadian settlement. If the Cree were not satisfied with his new approach, he would use force against them. To implement this new policy, Dewdney increased the number of Indian Department employees working on the Cree reserves, for he wanted to monitor closely the behaviour of the Indians, and, if necessary, to arrest troublesome leaders.[63]

While Dewdney was implementing his new policy, the Cree leaders continued their efforts to concentrate the Cree in an exclusively Indian territory. Little Pine went south to seek Blackfoot support for the movement.[64] Big Bear, Lucky Man, and Poundmaker went to Duck Lake for a council with the Cree leaders of the Lower Saskatchewan district. The Duck Lake council, attended by twelve bands, was initiated by Beardy and the chiefs of the Carlton District. Beardy, who acted as spokesman for the Carlton chiefs, had been relatively inactive in the Cree movements in the 1881–83 period. He, however, had been the most vehement critic of the government's failure to deliver the farm materials promised by the treaty commissioners. In the 1877–81 period, Beardy was a man of little influence in the Carlton area, but when Mistawasis and Ahtahkakoop, the principal Cree chiefs of the Carlton District, came to share his views, Beardy's standing among the Carlton Cree rose dramatically.[65]

The Duck Lake Council, called by Cree leaders who Dewdney thought were loyal and docile, and of which the Commissioner had no foreknowledge, was a cause of much concern. Especially vexing was the detailed list of violations of the treaty for which the Cree demanded redress from the government. The Cree charged that the treaty commissioners lied to them when they said that the Cree would be able to make a living from agriculture with the equipment provided for in the treaties. However, rather than provide all the farming goods, what the government did, according to the Cree, was to withhold many of the cattle and oxen; send inferior quality wagons, farm tools, and equipment; and provide insufficient rations and clothes, and no medicine chest. The petition closed with the statement expressing the Cree sentiment that they had been deceived by "sweet promises" designed to cheat them of their heritage, and that unless their grievances were remedied by the summer of 1885, they would take whatever measures necessary, short of war, to get redress.[66]

Dewdney originally assumed, as did some newspapers across the West, that the Duck Lake Council was part of a plot by Louis Riel to foment an Indian and Metis rebellion. Dewdney's assumption was based on the fact that the Duck Lake Council was held a short time after Riel had returned to Canada. It was also known that Riel had attended it, and that he had advocated such an alliance and a resort to violence when he had met the Cree in Montana in 1880.[67] Further investigation, however, made quite clear that Riel had little influence on the Cree. To allay the growing concern about the possibility of an Indian war, Dewdney had Hayter Reed issue a statement that nothing untoward was happening and that there was less danger of an Indian war in 1884 than there had been in 1881. Privately Dewdney admitted to Ottawa and his subordinates in the West that the situation was very serious.[68] After both he and Dewdney had met with Cree leaders throughout the West and after carefully assessing the situation, Hayter Reed stated that the government had nothing to fear from the Cree until the summer of 1885. What Reed and Dewdney expected at that time was a united Cree demand to renegotiate treaties.[69]

What Reed and Dewdney had learned on their tours of the Battleford, Edmonton, Carlton, and Qu'Appelle districts in the fall of 1884 was that Big Bear, Piapot, and Little Pine were on the verge of uniting the Cree to call for new treaties in which an Indian territory and greater autonomy for the Cree would be major provisions. In fact, throughout the summer and fall of 1884 Little Pine attempted, with limited success, to interest the leaders of the Blackfoot in joining the Cree movement for treaty revision. Little Pine had invited the Blackfoot to a joint council with the Cree leaders on Little Pine's reserve scheduled for the spring of 1885.[70] If the Blackfoot joined the Cree, Ottawa's ability to govern the Indians and control the West would be seriously jeopardized.

135

At the moment that the Cree movement seemed on the verge of success, Big Bear was losing control of his band. As he told the assembled chiefs at Duck Lake in the summer of 1884, his young men were listening to the warrior chief, Little Poplar, who was advocating killing government officials and Indian agents as a means of restoring Cree independence. Big Bear feared that if Little Poplar's course of action were adopted the Cree would fight an Indian war that they were certain to lose.[71]

Dewdney was aware of Little Poplar's growing influence on the young men of Big Bear's and the Battleford Assiniboine bands; however, he wished to wait until after January 1885 before taking any action, because after that date the new amendments to the Indian Act would be in effect. These amendments could be used to arrest and imprison Little Pine, Little Poplar, Big Bear, and Piapot, and thereby, Dewdney hoped, destroy the movements these chiefs led.[72] In anticipation of confrontations in 1885, Dewdney ordered that the guns and ammunition normally allotted to the Cree so they could hunt for food be withheld. In addition, Indian councils were prohibited, including the one scheduled for Duck Lake in the summer of 1885, to which all the Cree in Treaty 6 had been invited. Arrangements were made to place the Mounted Police at Battleford under Dewdney's command, and serious consideration was given to placing an artillery unit there also.[73]

To get improved intelligence, Dewdney hired more men to work as Indian agents with the Cree. These men were given broad discretionary powers and were to keep the Commissioner informed on Cree activities. As well, English-speaking mixed-bloods, many of whom had worked for the Hudson's Bay Company and had the confidence of the Cree, were hired as farm instructors. There would now be a farm instructor on each Cree reserve, with explicit instructions to keep the Indian Agent informed of what was happening on his reserve. Staff who had personality conflicts with any of the Cree leaders were either transferred or fired. Only Thomas Quinn, Indian Agent at Fort Pitt and his farming instructor, John Delaney, were not removed before March 1885, although both were slated for transfer.[74]

136 Dewdney found that his most important staffing move was the employment of Peter Ballendine, a former Hudson's Bay Company trader much trusted by the principal Cree leaders. Ballendine's job was to ingratiate himself with Big Bear and report on that chief's comings and goings. Ballendine won the confidence of Big Bear and reported upon how wrong Dewdney's earlier efforts to break up Big Bear's band had been. Because so many of Big Bear's original followers either joined Lucky Man, Thunderchild, or Little Pine's bands, Big Bear by 1884 was left with only the most recalcitrant opponents of the treaty. These individuals were only lukewarm in support of their chief's non-violent efforts to get the treaty revised. They favoured instead the course of action advocated by Little Poplar. Ballendine believed that the government could expect trouble from the Big Bear and Little Poplar bands. However, Ballendine emphasized that there was little danger of a Cree–Metis alliance, for the Cree were refusing to meet with the Metis, and were rejecting all entreaties from the Metis suggesting the two should make common cause. Instead the Cree, under the leadership of Big Bear, Beardy, and Little Pine, were planning their own council for the summer of 1885.[75]

Ballendine also developed a new source of information in Poundmaker, who was also acting as a police informer. It was from Poundmaker that Dewdney and the police learned that Little Pine was attempting to involve the Blackfoot in the summer of 1884, and wanted to do so in January 1885, but was prevented from doing so because of temporary blindness — a possible sign of malnutrition from the hunger that most Cree experienced in the extremely harsh winter of 1884–85. Little Pine had sought to get Poundmaker to encourage Crowfoot to join the Cree movement but Poundmaker refused to aid Little Pine, and when Little Pine recovered from his blindness, he went south to meet with Crowfoot.[76]

While Little Pine met with Crowfoot, Big Bear was being challenged for the leadership of his band by his son Imases, also called Curly, and by one of his headsmen, Wandering Spirit. These two men were spokesmen for the younger men of Big Bear's Band, and wanted to work with

Little Poplar. In the winter of 1885, Little Poplar was journeying constantly between Pitt and Battleford enlisting support for his plan of action. Although Ballendine could not get precise information on Little Poplar's plans, he did report that by March 1885 Big Bear had asserted himself and that the influence of Imases and Wandering Spirit had seemed to wane.[77]

On the basis of these and similar reports, Dewdney and the police were convinced that, although a number of councils were expected in 1885, no violence was to be anticipated from the Cree. Nevertheless, Dewdney wished to prevent the Cree from holding their councils. His strategy was to make the Cree satisfied with the treaties. He therefore admitted in February 1885 that the government had violated the treaties and ordered delivery to the Cree of all goods the treaties had stipulated. In addition, he ordered a dramatic increase in their rations. If this failed to placate them he planned to arrest their leaders, use the police to keep the Cree on their reserves, and to depose any chief who attempted to attend an Indian council.[78]

137

Dewdney had the full support of Ottawa for his policy of arresting Cree leaders. The only reservations the Prime Minister expressed were that Dewdney have sufficient forces to make the arrests and that he provide enough evidence to justify the charges of incitement to an insurrection. Macdonald also volunteered to communicate with the stipendiary magistrates to assure their co-operation in imposing long prison terms for any Cree leader convicted of incitement.[79] Macdonald was willing to provide his assistance because Dewdney had earlier complained that he could not use preventive detention of Indian leaders because the magistrates "only look at the evidence and the crime committed when giving out sentences," rather than taking into consideration the nature of the man and the harm that he might do if he were released at an inopportune time.[80] All these preparations were complete when word reached Dewdney of the Metis clash with the Mounted Police at Duck Lake in March 1885.

The Riel Rebellion of 1885 provided Dewdney with a new instrument to make his coercive policy effective. The troops sent into the North-West to suppress the Rebellion could be used to destroy the Cree movement for an Indian territory. The Cree themselves would provide the excuse Dewdney needed virtually to declare war on the bands and leaders who had led the Cree movement for treaty revision. During March 1885, the Cree did engage in some acts of violence that Dewdney chose to label acts of rebellion.

These acts were unrelated to the Cree movement for treaty revision. In fact, the acts that led to the subjugation of the Cree were committed by persons not involved with the Cree movement for autonomy. It is one of the ironic quirks of history that the leaders of the Cree movement had little or nothing to do with the events which would destroy that movement to which they had devoted ten years of their lives. Nevertheless, they would be held responsible for the actions of their desperate and hungry people. To heighten the irony, it was the Metis movement, from which the Cree had held aloof, which would give Dewdney the excuse to use military force to subjugate the Cree.

The Duck Lake clash coincided with a Cree Council on Sweetgrass Reserve. The council of the Battleford area Cree had been called to consider how they could press for increased rations. When word reached the Cree at Sweetgrass of the clash at Duck Lake, they felt that circumstances would make Indian Agent Rae willing to grant them more rations. Thus the Cree, taking their women and children with them to demonstrate their peaceful intent, set out for Battleford. Fear and panic prevailed at Battleford, for on learning of the Crees' approach, the town's citizens assumed that the Cree had thrown in their lot with the Metis. The town was evacuated; most townspeople took refuge in the Mounted Police post.[81]

138

When the Cree arrived at Battleford they found the town abandoned. They sent word to the police that they wished to speak to the Indian Agent, who refused to leave the safety of the post. The Cree women, seeing the abandoned stores and houses filled with food, began to help themselves. Then, fearing arrest by the police, the Cree left town. On the way back to their reserves, as well as on their way to town, the Cree assisted a number of Indian Department employees and settlers to cross the Battle River to get to the police post, thus demonstrating the pacific nature of their intentions.[82]

Rather than returning to their individual reserves, the Cree went to Poundmaker's, for as the leader in the Battleford district to whom the government had shown much favour in the past, Poundmaker was seen as the man best able to explain to the government what had happened at Battleford. A second significant reason was the deaths of two prominent Cree leaders: Red Pheasant, the night before the Cree left for Battleford, and Little Pine, the night they returned. As it was the practice for the Cree to leave the place where their leaders had expired, both bands left their reserves and went to Poundmaker's, who, given the fears the whites had concerning a Cree and Metis alliance, might possibly defuse any crisis. Thus, in March 1885, Poundmaker became the spokesman of the Battleford Cree.[83]

No sooner were the Cree at Poundmaker's than they were joined by the local Assiniboine, who insisted that a soldier's (war) tent be erected, for events at the Assiniboine reserves convinced them that an attack on the Indian camp was imminent. The Assiniboine explained that when word had reached them of the Duck Lake fight, a few of their young men sought revenge on farming instructor James Payne, who was blamed for the death of a girl. The girl's male relatives killed Payne and murdered farmer Barney Tremont. The Assiniboine now assumed that the Canadian authorities would behave in a similar manner to the Americans and blame all Indians for the actions of a few individuals.[84]

Erection of the soldier's tent meant that the warriors were in control of the camp and that Poundmaker and the civil authorities had to defer to them. It was at this time that the Metis appeal for aid was received. The Cree refused to assist the Metis, although they expected an attack on their camp. Watches were set on the roads, and protection was offered to the Metis at Bresaylor for the settlers there had earned the enmity of the Batoche Metis. As long as no military or police forces came towards the Cree camp, the Cree remained on their reserves and did not interfere with anyone going to or leaving Battleford. The Mounted Police detachment from Fort Pitt and Colonel Otter's military unit arrived in Battleford without encountering any Indians. Nevertheless, reports from the police and local officials maintained that the town was under siege.[85]

While the Battleford Cree were preparing their defences, Big Bear's band was making trouble for itself. Big Bear was absent from his camp when the members of his band heard about the fight at Duck Lake. Wandering Spirit and Imases sought to use the opportunity presented by the Metis uprising to seek revenge for the insults and abuses perpetrated against the Cree by Indian Agent Thomas Quinn and Farming Instructor Delaney. Quinn had physically abused some of the Indian men, while Delaney had cuckolded others before he brought a white bride to Frog Lake in late 1884. Big Bear's headmen demanded that the two officials open the storehouse to the Cree, and when they refused to do so, they were murdered. This set off further acts of violence that resulted in the murder of all the white men in the camp save one.[86]

On his return to camp Big Bear ended further acts of violence. Although unable to prevent a minor skirmish between his young men and a small police patrol, he convinced his warriors to allow the police detachment at Fort Pitt to withdraw from the post without being attacked and to guarantee safety to the civilian residents of the Frog Lake and Fort Pitt regions. Big Bear then led his people north, where he hoped they would be out of harm's way and not engage in further acts of violence.[87]

Beardy also lost control of his band. He and the neighbouring One Arrow band had reserves next to Batoche. Before the clash with the police, the Metis had come to the One Arrow Reserve, captured Farming Instructor Peter Tompkins, and threatened the Cree band with destruction unless the Cree aided the Metis. Some of the younger men of One Arrow's band agreed to do so.[88] The Metis made the same threat against Beardy and his band, and although a few of his young men joined the Metis, Beardy and most of his people remained neutral.[89] It is doubtful that the Cree would have aided the Metis without the threat of violence. Earlier, the Cree of the Duck Lake region had threatened hostilities against the Metis, for the Metis had settled on One Arrow's Reserve

139

and demanded that the government turn over to them some of One Arrow's Reserve. Ottawa, fearing the Metis more than the Cree in 1880, acquiesced. Over the next four years, one task of the local Indian Agent and the police was to reconcile the Cree with the Metis of the Batoche region.[90]

The Cree acts of violence in March 1885 were the excuse Dewdney needed to justify the use of troops against them. He maintained that the Battleford, Fort Pitt, and Duck Lake Cree were part of the Riel Rebellion. Privately, Dewdney reported to Ottawa that he saw the events at Battleford and Frog Lake as the acts of a desperate, starving people and unrelated to what the Metis were doing.[91] In fact, Dewdney had sought in late March to open negotiations with the Battleford Cree, but Rae refused to meet the Cree leaders. Subsequent efforts to open negotiations ended in failure because there was no way to get a message to Poundmaker, and after Colonel Otter's attack on the Cree camp any thought of negotiations was dropped.[92]

Publicly Dewdney proclaimed that the Cree were part of the Metis uprising. He issued a proclamation that any Indian who left his reserve was to be regarded as a rebel.[93] As well, to intimidate Piapot and the Treaty 4 Cree, Dewdney stationed troops on their reserves. To prevent an alliance of Blackfoot and Cree, Dewdney announced that he was stationing troops at Swift Current and Medicine Hat. Dewdney took these steps, as he confided to Macdonald, because he feared that the Cree might still attempt to take action on their own cause, and he was concerned because in the previous year the Cree had attempted to enlist the Blackfoot in the movement to revise the treaties.[94]

The military commander in the North-West, General F.D. Middleton, was not as concerned about the problems with the Cree. He wanted to concentrate his attention on the Metis. Although he did send troops under Colonel William Otter to Swift Current, he refused to order them to Battleford to lift the alleged siege until he received word of the Frog Lake massacre. Otter was then ordered to lift the "siege" and protect Battleford from Indian attack, but he was not to take the offensive. At the same time General Thomas Strange was ordered to bring Big Bear under control.

Otter reached Battleford without seeing an Indian. He was upset that he and his troops would not see action. He therefore proposed that he attack the Indian camp at Poundmaker's Reserve. Middleton vetoed the plan, but Dewdney welcomed it as a means to bring the Cree under government control. Taking the Lieutenant-Governor's approval to be paramount to Middleton's veto, Otter launched his attack. The engagement, known as the Battle of Cut Knife Hill, almost ended in total disaster for Otter's force. Only the Cree fear that they would suffer the same fate as Sitting Bull after the Battle of the Little Big Horn saved Otter's troops from total annihilation.[95]

The tale of the subsequent military campaigns against the Cree by Strange and Middleton and the voluntary surrenders of Poundmaker and Big Bear is found in detail in Stanley's *Birth of Western Canada* and Desmond Morton's *The Last War Drum*. With Big Bear and Poundmaker in custody, Dewdney prepared to use the courts in the manner he had planned before the Riel Rebellion. Both Cree leaders were charged with treason-felony, despite Dewdney's knowledge that neither man had engaged in an act of rebellion. Eyewitnesses to the events at Fort Pitt, Frog Lake, and Battleford all made clear that neither chief was involved in the murders and looting that had occurred. In fact, many of these people served as defence witnesses.[96] As Dewdney informed the Prime Minister, the diaries and letters of the murdered officials at Frog Lake showed that until the day of the "massacre" there was "no reason to believe that our Indians were even dissatisfied much less contemplated violence."[97] Ballendine's reports indicated that there were no plans for violence, that the Cree were not involved with the Metis, and that they planned no rebellion. Dewdney believed that the Cree had not "even thought, intended or wished that the uprising would reach the proportion it has. . . . Things just got out of control."[98] As Dewdney related to the Prime Minister, had the people living in the region not been new settlers from the East, and had they not fled in panic, much of the "raiding" and looting would not have occurred. In regions where people had not abandoned their homes no raiding occurred.[99] Therefore, the charges against Big Bear and Poundmaker were designed to remove the leadership of the Cree movement for revision of the treaties. They were charged to elicit prison sentences that would have the effect of coercing the Cree to accept government control. The trials were conducted to have the desired result, and both Big Bear and Poundmaker were convicted and sentenced to three years in Stoney Mountain Penitentiary.[100] Neither man served his full term, and both died a short time after their release from prison.

By the end of 1885, Dewdney had succeeded in subjugating the Cree. Big Bear was in prison, Little Pine was dead, and Piapot was intimidated by having troops stationed on his reserve. Dewdney had deprived the Cree of their principal leaders and of their autonomy. He used the military to disarm and impoverish the Cree by confiscating their horses and carts; he increased the size of the Mounted Police force, and used the police to arrest the Cree leaders who protested against his policies; he broke up Cree bands, deposed Cree leaders, and forbade any Indian to be off his reserve without permission from the Indian Agent.[101] By 1890, through vigorous implementation of the Indian Act, Dewdney and his successor, Hayter Reed, had begun the process of making the Cree an administered people.

The record of the Canadian government in dealing with the Cree is thus not one of honourable fair-mindedness and justice as the traditional interpretation portrays. As Dewdney admitted in 1885, the treaties' promises and provisions were not being fulfilled, and Dewdney himself had taken steps to assure Canadian control over the Cree, which were themselves violations of the treaties. Thus, he had refused to grant the Cree the reserve sites they selected; he had refused to distribute the ammunition and twine the treaties required. His plans for dealing with the Cree leaders were based on a political use of the legal and judicial system, and ultimately he made use of the military, the police, and the courts in a political manner to achieve his goals of subjugating the Cree. Only by ignoring these facts can one continue to perpetuate the myth of Canada's just and honourable Indian policy from 1870 to 1885.

NOTES

[1] Doug Owram, *Promise of Eden: The Canadian Expansionist Movement and the Idea of the West, 1856-1900* (Toronto, 1980), 131-34.

[2] G.F.G. Stanley, *The Birth of Western Canada: A History of the Riel Rebellions* (Toronto, 1960).

[3] Stanley, *The Birth of Western Canada*, 206-215.

[4] Stanley, *The Birth of Western Canada*, vii-viii, 196, 216-36. It should be noted that the traditional interpretation of a Cree rebellion in association with the Metis has been challenged by R. Allen, "Big Bear," *Saskatchewan History* 25 (1972); W.B. Fraser, "Big Bear, Indian Patriot," *Alberta Historical Review* 14 (1966): 1-13; Rudy Wiebe, in his fictional biography *The Temptations of Big Bear* (Toronto, 1973) and in his biography of Big Bear in the *Dictionary of Canadian Biography* [DCB] vol. 11, 1881-90 (Toronto, 1982), 597-601; and Norma Sluman, *Poundmaker* (Toronto, 1967). However, none of these authors deals with Canada's Indian policy, and none examines what the Cree were doing in the period 1876-85.

[5] Alexander Morris, *The Treaties of Canada with the Indians of Manitoba and the North-West Territories* (Toronto, 1880), 37; Public Archives of Manitoba, Adams G. Archibald Papers (hereafter cited as PAM Archibald Papers, letters).

[6] Public Archives of Canada, Record Group 10, Indian Affairs Files, vol. 3571, file 124-2, also vol. 3603, file 2036 (hereafter cited as PAC, RG 10, vol. file). See also Morris, *Treaties of Canada*, 25-43 and 126-27, for a printed account of the negotiations and the texts of the original and renegotiated treaties, pp. 313-20, 338-42. Two articles by John Taylor, "Canada's Northwest Indian Policy in the 1870's: Traditional Premises and Necessary Innovations" and "Two Views on the Meaning of Treaties Six and Seven," in *The Spirit of Alberta Indian Treaties* (Montreal, 1980), 3-7 and 9-45 respectively, provide a good account of the Indian contribution and attitude towards the treaties.

[7] Morris, *Treaties of Canada*, 44-76; on pp. 120-23 Morris demonstrates how he had to make Treaty 3 the model for the Qu'Appelle Treaty to get the Saulteaux and Cree of the Qu'Appelle River region to accept what he originally offered them. Compare Treaties 1-6 to see what the government was forced to concede. Also see Taylor's "Traditional Premises" for Indian contributions to the negotiation process.

[8] PAC, RG 10, vol. 3586, file 1137, Lieutenant-Governor Morris to Secretary of State for the Provinces, 13 Sept. 1872; PAC, RG 10, vol. 3576, file 378 entire file; vol. 3609, file 3229; vol. 3604, file 2543; vol. 3636, 6694-1.

[9] PAC, RG 10, vol. 3612, file 4012, entire file; PAM Archibald Papers, W.J. Christie to George W. Hill, 26 Apr. 1871; Archibald to Secretary of State for the Provinces, 5 Jan. 1872; also letters in note 15; William Francis Butler, *The Great Lone Land* (Rutland, Vermont, 1970), 360-62, 368; PAC, Manuscript Group 26A, John A. Macdonald Papers, vol. 104, entire volume (hereafter cited as PAC, MG 26A, letters), PAM, Archibald Papers, Joseph Howe to Archibald, 30 June 1872; PAM, Alexander Morris Papers, Lt Governor's Collection, Morris to Minister of the Interior 7 July 1873 (hereafter cited as PAM, Morris Papers, letter); PAC, RG 10, vol. 3625, file 5366, Morris to Minister of the Interior, David Laird, 22 July and 4 August 1875; RG 10 vol. 3624, file 5152, Colonel French, Commissioner of the NWMP to the Minister of Justice, 6 and 19 August 1875; Morris, 170-1, RG 10 vol. 3612, file 4012, entire file; Adams G. Archibald Papers, Petition of James Seenum to Archibald, 9 Jan. 1871, and attached letters of Kehewin, Little Hunter, and Kiskion; Archibald to Secretary of State for the Provinces, 5 Jan. 1872.

[10] Two excellent studies of the Cree in the pre-1870 era are those by Arthur J. Ray, *Indians in the Fur Trade: Their Role as Hunters, Trappers, and Middlemen in the Lands Southwest of Hudson Bay, 1660-1870* (Toronto, 1974), and David G. Mandelbaum, *The Plains Cree*, Anthropological Papers of the American Museum of Natural History, no. 37, pt. 2 (New York, 1940).

[11] See note 10 above. An excellent study of the Cree expansion is the unpublished MA thesis by John S. Milloy, "The Plains Cree: A Preliminary Trade and Military Chronology, 1670-1870" (Carlton University, 1972); also Henry John Moberly and William B. Cameron, *When Fur Was King* (Toronto, 1929), 208-212, describes part of the last phase of this movement. The shrinking range of buffalo and how the Cree reacted are also discussed in Frank Gilbert Roe, *The North American Buffalo: A Critical Study of the Species in Its Wild State* (Toronto, 1951), 282-333.

[12] Henry Youle Hind, *Narrative of the Canadian Red River Exploring Expedition of 1857 and of the Assiniboine and Saskatchewan Exploring Expedition of 1858* (Edmonton, 1971), 1: 334; Irene Spry, *The Palliser Expedition: An Account of John Palliser's British North American Expedition, 1857-1860* (London, 1964), 59-60; Viscount Milton and W.B. Cheadle, *The Northwest Passage by Land, Being the Narrative of an Expedition from the Atlantic to the Pacific* (Toronto, 1970), 66-67; Edwin Thompson Perry, *Five Indian Tribes of the Upper Missouri: Sioux, Arickaras, Assiniboine, Crees, Crow* (Norman, Oklahoma, 1969), 99-137; J. Hines, *The Red Indians of the Plains: Thirty Years' Missionary Experience in Saskatchewan* (Toronto, 1916), 78-80, 88-91.

[13] Morris, *Treaties of Canada*, 77-123 and 168-239, discusses the negotiations of Treaties 4 and 6 with the Cree and how he was forced to modify his offer. Also described is the Cree concern about their land. The reaction of the Mackenzie government is detailed in PAC, RG 10 vol. 3636, file 6694-2 and in particular, Minister of the Interior Report to Privy Council, 31 Jan. 1877 and order-in-council, 10 Feb. 1877.

[14] Milloy, "The Plains Cree," 250-62; Alexander Johnson, *The Battle at Belly River: Stories of the Last Great Indian Battle* (Lethbridge, 1966).

[15] Henry Youle Hind, *Narrative* 1: 334, 360-61, carries reports of Mistickoos or Short Stick's comments on a council of Cree leaders that resolved to limit white and Metis hunting privileges. Viscount Milton and W.B. Cheadle, *The Northwest Passage by Land, Being the Narrative of an Expedition from the Atlantic to the Pacific*, 66, 67, contains comments on the Cree determination to limit non-Indian involvement in the hunt. PAM, E. Adams Archibald papers, letter #200, Macdonald to Archibald, 14 Feb. 1871; letter #170, English halfbreeds to Archibald, 10 Jan. 1871, all stress that Cree were taking action to limit non-Indian involvement in the buffalo hunt.

[16] Morris, *Treaties of Canada*, 241.

[17] Interview with Walter Gordon, Director of the Indian Rights and Treaties Program, Federation of Saskatchewan Indians, Mar. 1974. Poundmaker made a similar statement in an interview quoted in "Indian Affairs," *Saskatchewan Herald*, 2 Aug. 1880. The importance of Big Bear, Piapot, and Little Pine cannot be underestimated, for of those Cree chiefs who took treaty only Sweetgrass had the standing of these men, and Sweetgrass died within a few months of taking treaty.

[18] Morris, *Treaties of Canada*, 85-87. More detailed information on the adhesions of Piapot and Cheekuk is to be found in PAC, RG 10, vol. 3625, file 5489; W.J. Christie to Laird, 7 Oct. 1875.

[19] Morris, *Treaties of Canada*, 240, for the quotation. See p. 355 for the clauses in Treaty 6 respecting acceptance of Canadian laws.

[20] Morris, *Treaties of Canada*, 174.

[21] Fraser, "Big Bear, Indian Patriot," 76-77, agrees that Big Bear was not referring specifically to hanging but to the effect the treaty would have on the Cree.

[22] PAC, RG 10, vol. 3656, file 9093, Agent Dickieson to Lt-Gov. Laird, 14 Sept. 1877.

[23] PAC, RG 10, vol. 3648, file 8380; vol. 3655, file 9000, Laird to Minister of the Interior, 9 May 1878.

[24] PAC, RG 10, vol. 3655, file 9000, Laird to Minister of the Interior, 9 May 1878; vol. 3636, file 9092, Laird to Superintendent-General, 19 Nov. 1877; PAC, RG 10, vol. 3670, file 10,771 Laird to Minister of the Interior, 12 Nov. 1878. PAC, RG 10, vol. 3672, file 10,853, Dickieson to Meredith, 2 Apr. 1878; vol. 3656, file 9092, Inspector James Walker to Laird, 5 Sept. 1877. Department of Indian Affairs and Northern Development, Ottawa, file 1/1-11-3, Laird to Minister of the Interior, 30 Dec. 1878; Dickieson to Laird, 9 Oct. 1878; Walker to Laird, 4 and 26 Feb. 1979 (hereafter cited as DIAND, file, letter).

[25] PAC, RG 10, vol. 3655, file 1002, Laird to Minister of the Interior, 9 May 1878; vol. 3672, file 19,853, Dickieson to Vankoughnet, 26 July 1878; PAC, MG 26A, E.D. Clark to Fred White, 16 July 1879.

[26] "News from the Plains," *Saskatchewan Herald*, 18 Nov. 1878; "From the Plains," *Saskatchewan Herald*, 5 May 1879; "Contradictory News from the West," *Fort Benton Record*, 31 Jan. 1879.

[27] PAC, RG 10, vol. 3672, file 10,853, M.G. Dickieson to Vankoughnet, 26 July 1878; *Opening Up the West: Being the Official Reports to Parliament of the North-West Mounted Police from 1874-1881* (Toronto, 1973), Report for 1878, p. 21.

[28] PAC, RG 10, vol. 3704, file 17,858, entire file; vol. 3648, file 162-2, entire file; vol. 3699, file 16,580, order-in-council, 9 Oct. 1879; vol. 3766, file 22,541; E.T. Galt to Superintendent-General of Indian Affairs, 27 July 1880; vol. 3730, file 26,279, entire file; vol. 3757, file 21,397, entire file.

[29] House of Commons, Ottawa, *Sessional Papers* 17 (1885), Report No. 3, 157 (hereafter cited as CSP, vol., year, report); Edward Ahenakew, *Voices of the Plains Cree*, ed. Ruth Buck (Toronto, 1973), 26. Dewdney in adopting this tactic simply copied what the fur-trading companies had done in the past. The Cree tolerated such practices because they improved the opportunities to have better access to European goods. See Arthur J. Ray and Donald Freeman, *"Give Us Good Measure": An Economic Analysis of Relations between the Indians and the Hudson's Bay Company before 1763* (Toronto,

143

1978), *passim*. Ray, *Indians in the Fur Trade, passim*, deals with the same practice in the post-1763 period. Mandelbaum, *The Plains Cree*, 105–110, discusses the nature of Cree political organization and leadership that explains their acceptance of such practices.

[30] Morris, *Treaties of Canada*, 366–67. DIAND, Treaty Annuity Pay Sheets for 1879. More than 1,000 Plains Cree took treaty for the first time in 1879 under Little Pine, Thunderchild, and Lucky Man. Others from Little Pine's and Big Bear's bands had already taken treaty a year earlier as part of Thunder Companion's band, while others joined Poundmaker, and the three Cree bands settled in the Peace Hills. A portion of the Assiniboine also took treaty under Mosquito in 1878, while many of the northern Saulteaux who had followed Yellow Sky took treaty in 1878 under the leadership of Moosomin.

[31] PAC, RG 10, vol. 3745, file 29506-4, vol. 2. Ray to Reed, 23 Apr. 1883; vol. 3668, file 9644, Reed to Commissioner, 23 Dec. 1883. Although these materials refer to events in the Battleford district, as will be demonstrated, the tactics in 1883–84 were similar, if not exactly the same as those used in the Cypress Hills between 1879 and 1882. That they were not better recorded for the earlier period is due to the fact that the government had fewer men working with the Indians, and did not have as effective supervision in the 1879–82 period as it did at Battleford. Also much of the police and Indian Affairs material relating to this region in the 1879–82 period has been lost or destroyed.

[32] PAC, RG 10, vol. 3730, file 36,279, entire file; vol. 3668, file 10,440, Agent Allen to L. Vankoughnet, 11 Nov. 1878, CSP, vol. 16 (1883), Paper no. 5, p. 197. *Settlers and Rebels: Being the Reports to Parliament of the Activities of the Royal North-West Mounted Police Force from 1882–1885* (Toronto, 1973), Report for 1882, pp. 4–6 (hereafter cited as *Settlers and Rebels*).

144

[33] PAC, RG 10, vol. 3730, file 26,219, Report of surveyor Patrick to Superintendent-General, 16 Dec. 1880; vol. 3716, file 22,546, Assistant Commissioner E.T. Galt to Superintendent-General, 27 July 1880; vol. 3757, files 31,393 and 31,333; vol. 3757, file 20,034. PAC, MG 26A, vol. 210, Dewdney to Macdonald, 3 Oct. 1880.

[34] RG 10, vol. 3652, file 8589, parts 1 and 2, entire file; vol. 3691, file 13,893, entire file. The *Benton Weekly Record* throughout the spring and summer of 1880 carried reports of Cree and Assiniboine horse-stealing raids, and reports of what the Cree were doing in Montana. On 7 May 1880, the paper carried an article entitled "Starving Indians," which was a strong denunciation of Canada's Indian policy and the effect it had on the Cree.

[35] PAC, MG 26A, vol. 210, Dewdney to Macdonald, 29 Oct. 1880; *Saskatchewan Herald*, 14 Feb. 1881.

[36] PAC, MG 26A, vol. 210, Dewdney to Macdonald, 26 Oct. 1880 and 23 Apr. 1880; *Saskatchewan Herald*, 14, 28 Feb. 1881.

[37] PAC, MG 26A, vol. 210, Dewdney to MacPherson, 4 July 1881; vol. 247, Galt to MacPherson, 14 July 1881; "Edmonton," *Saskatchewan Herald*, 12 Nov. 1881.

[38] See note 37 above; also PAC, MG 26A, vol. 210, Dewdney to Macdonald, 19 June 1881; vol. 247, Galt to Vankoughnet, 16 July 1881. PAC, RG 10, vol. 3739, file 28, 748-1, Dewdney to Macdonald, 3 Apr. 1882; Fred White to Minister of the Interior, 9 June 1882; Freylinghausen to Sackville-West, 9 June 1882. *Saskatchewan Herald*, 1 Aug. 1881; "Starving Indians," *Benton Weekly Record*, 14 July 1881; 25 Aug., 1 Sept., and 13 Oct. 1881.

[39] PAC, RG 10. vol. 3739, file 28,478-1, C.G. Denny to Commissioner, 24 Oct. 1881; vol. 3768, file 33,642; vol. 3603, file 20,141, McIlree to Dewdney, 21 June 1882. Glenbow Institute, Calgary, Edgar Dewdney Papers, vol. 5, file 57, Irvine to Dewdney, 24 June 1882 (hereafter cited as Dewdney Papers, vol., file, letter). *Saskatchewan Herald*, 24 June 1882; *Edmonton Bulletin*, 17 June 1882.

[40] PAC, RG 10, vol. 3768, file 33,642, entire file.

[41] PAC, MG 26A, vol. 210, Dewdney to Macdonald, 19 June 1881; vol. 247, Galt to Vankoughnet, 16 July 1881. *Saskatchewan Herald*, 1 Aug. 1881. "Starving Indians," *Benton Weekly Record*, 14 July 1881. See also *Benton Weekly Record*, 25 Aug., 1 Sept., and 13 Oct. 1881.

[42] Morris, *Treaties of Canada*, 205, 218, 352–53.

[43] PAC, RG 10, vol. 3604, file 2589, entire file. See also *Settlers and Rebels*, 1882 Report. See also Dewdney Papers, vol. 5, file 57, White to Irvine, 29 Aug. 1882, RG 10, vol. 3604, file 2589. "The Repatriated Indians," *Saskatchewan Herald*, 5 Aug. 1882. "From the South," *Saskatchewan Herald*, 21 May 1882; "Back on the Grub Pile," *Saskatchewan Herald*, 24 June 1882.

[44] Dewdney Papers, vol. 5, file 57, Irvine to Dewdney, 24 June 1882 and 25 Sept. 1882. *Settlers and Rebels*, 1882 Report, pp. 4, 5. CSP, 16 (1883), Paper no. 5, p. 197, RG 10, vol. 3604, file 2589. "Repatriated Indians," *Saskatchewan Herald*, 5 Aug. 1882.

[45] See note 44 above; Dewdney Papers, vol. 4, file 45, White to Dewdney, 12 Oct. 1882, *Saskatchewan Herald*, 14 Oct. 1882. "Big Bear and Others," and the "I.D.," *Edmonton Bulletin*, 21 Oct. 1882.

[46] Dewdney Papers, vol. 4, file 45, White to Dewdney, 17 Oct. 1882, PAC, MG 26A, vol. 289, Vankoughnet to Macdonald, 2 Nov. 1882.

[47] PAC, MG 26A, vol. 11, Dewdney to J.A. Macdonald, 2 Sept. 1883. PAC, RG 10, vol. 3682, file 12,667, Dewdney to Superintendent-General, 28 Apr. 1884.

[48] PAC, RG 10, vol. 3668, file 10,644, Reed to Commissioner, 23 Dec. 1883. Robert Jefferson, *Fifty Years on the Saskatchewan* (Battleford, 1929), 103.

[49] PAC, RG 10, vol. 3668, file 10,644, Reed to Commissioner, 23 Dec. 1883. *Edmonton Bulletin*, 9 Feb. 1884; *Saskatchewan Herald*, 24 Nov. 1883.

[50] PAC, MG 26A, vol. 289 Vankoughnet to Macdonald, 4, 10 Dec. 1883; vol. 104, Deputy Superintendent-General to T. Quinn, 21 Sept. 1883; Dewdney to Superintendent-General, 27 Sept. 1883; Deputy Superintendent-General to Reed, 10 Apr. 1884; vol. 212, Dewdney to Macdonald, 2 Jan. 1883 [sic! Given the contents of the letter, it is obvious Dewdney forgot that a new year had begun the previous day], vol. 91, Dewdney to Macdonald, 24 July 1884, another letter but without a date, which was probably written in the first week of Aug. 1884; vol. 107, entire file. PAC, RG 10, vol. 3664, file 9843, entire file.

[51] PAC, RG 10, vol. 3616, file 10, 131. Burton Deane, *Mounted Police Life in Canada: A Record of Thirty-One Years in Service, 1883-1914* (Toronto, 1973), 140-53. Isabell Andrews, "Indian Protest against Starvation: The Yellow Calf Incident of 1884," *Saskatchewan History* 28 (1975): 4-52. *Edmonton Bulletin*, 7 Jan., 3 Feb., 7, 28 July, and 4 Aug. 1883.

[52] Dewdney Papers, vol. 5, file 58, Dewdney to Superintendent-General, 29 Feb. 1884; PAC, MG 26A, vol. 211, Dewdney to Macdonald, 6 Oct. 1883; vol. 212, Reed to Dewdney, 15 Feb. 1884; Dewdney to Macdonald, 16 Feb. and 9 Apr. 1884.

[53] PAC, RG 10, vol. 3682, file 12,667, Dewdney to Superintendent-General, 28 Apr. 1884; vol. 3686, file 13,168, entire file; vol. 3745, file 29,506-4(2), Reed to Colonel Irvine, 18 May 1884.

[54] PAC, RG 10, vol. 3745, file 29,506-4(2), Reed to Irvine, 18 May 1884; Irvine to Comptroller Fred White, 27 May 1884; White to Vankoughnet, 19 May 1884.

[55] PAC, RG 10, vol. 3745, file 29,506-4(2), Agent Macdonald to Commissioner, 29 May 1884; vol. 3655, file 026, Dewdney to Superintendent-General, 13 June 1884.

[56] PAC, RG 10, vol. 3745, file 29,506-4(2), Reed to Superintendent-General, 19 Apr. 1884. Similar report in vol. 3576, file 309B, PAC, MG 26A, file 37, Dewdney to Macdonald, 3 May 1884. Dewdney's request and actions were contrary to what the Cree had been told about how reserve sites could be chosen, as were the government's actions in denying the Cree reserves in the Cypress Hills and forcing them to move north. See Morris, *Treaties of Canada, passim.* PAC, RG 10, vol. 3576, file 309B, Vankoughnet to Dewdney, 10 May 1884; MG 26A, vol. 104, Dewdney to Superintendent-General, 14 June 1884. Campbell Innes, *The Cree Rebellion of 1884: Sidelights of Indian Conditions Subsequent to 1876* (Battleford, 1926), "Fine Day Interview," 13-15. *Saskatchewan Herald*, 19 Apr. and 17 May 1884.

[57] PAC, RG 10, vol. 3576, file 309B, Reed to Superintendent-General, 19 Apr. 1884. Reed to Vankoughnet, 19 Apr. 1884; Ray to Commissioner, 23 Apr. 1884; Reed to Superintendent-General, 20 May 1884. Dewdney Papers, vol. 3, file 36, Dewdney to Macdonald, 12 June 1884.

[58] PAC, RG 10, vol. 3576, file 309B, Ray to Commissioner, 19, 21 June 1884; Crozier to Dewdney, 22 June 1884. Jefferson, 108-109, Innes, *The Cree Rebellion of 1884*, 13-17, 29.

[59] PAC, RG 10, vol. 3576, file 309B, Ray to Commissioner, 28 June 1884; see also Ray to Dewdney, 9 June 1884, Innes "McKay Interview," 44. PAC, RG 10, vol. 3576, file 309B, Dewdney to Ray, 5 July 1884.

[60] PAC, RG 10, vol. 3576, file 309B, Ray to Dewdney, 23 June 1884; Crozier to Dewdney, 23 June 1884.

[61] Dewdney Papers, vol. 3, file 37, Macdonald to Dewdney, 18 July 1884, 11 Aug. 1884, and 2 Sept. 1884; vol. 4, file 45, Macdonald to White, 15 Sept. 1884. PAC, RG 10, vol. 3576, file 309A, Vankoughnet to Dewdney, 27 July 1884.

[62] PAC, RG 10, vol. 3576, file 309B, Ray to Commissioner, 30 June 1884; file 309A, Ray to Commissioner, 24, 29 July 1884. PAC, MG 26A, vol. 212, Dewdney to Macdonald, 14 July 1884; J.A. MacRae to Commissioner, 7 Aug. 1884; vol. 107, Ray to Commissioner, 29 July 1884.

[63] PAC, RG 10, vol. 3745, file 29,506-4(2), Dewdney to Superintendent-General, 7 Aug. 1884; vol. 3576, file 309A, Ray to Dewdney, 19 July 1884. PAC, MG 26A, vol. 104, Dewdney to Department, 19 July 1884.

[64] PAC, RG 10, vol. 3576, file 309B, Ray to Commissioner, 30 June 1884; file 309A, Ray to Commissioner, 24, 29 July 1884. PAC, MG 26A, vol. 212, Dewdney to Macdonald, 14 July 1884; J.A. MacRae to Commissioner, 7 Aug. 1884; vol. 107, Ray to Commissioner, 29 July 1884.

[65] PAC, MG 26A, vol. 107, Ray to Commissioner, 29 July and 2 Aug. 1884; J.A. MacRae to Commissioner, 29 July 1884.

[66] PAC, RG 10, vol. 3697, file 15,423, J.A. MacRae to Dewdney, 25 Aug. 1884.

[67] Ibid., Reed to Superintendent-General, 23 Jan. 1885; Reed to Dewdney, 22, 25 Aug. 1884. PAC, MG 26A, vol. 107, J.A. MacRae to Commissioner, 29 July 1884; J.M. Ray to Commissioner, 2 Aug. 1884; MacRae to Commissioner, 5 Aug. 1884; vol. 212, MacRae to Commissioner, 7 Aug. 1884. PAC, RG 10, vol. 1756, file 309A, J.M. Ray to Commissioner, 24, 25 July 1884. "Big Bear Rises to Speak," *Saskatchewan Herald*, 5 Aug. 1882. *Saskatchewan Herald*, 25 July and 9 Aug. 1884.

[68] See note 67 above; PAC, RG 10, vol. 3576, file 309A, Commissioner to Ray, 7 Aug. 1884. Ray to Commissioner, 29 July 1884; see also in PAC, MG 26A, vol. 107. Dewdney Papers, vol. 6, file 69, Crozier to Comptroller, NWMP, 27 July 1884. PAC, MG 26A, vol. 212, Dewdney to Macdonald, 8 Aug. 1884.

[69] PAC, MG 26A, vol. 107, Reed to Dewdney, 23, 24, 25 Aug., 4 Sept. 1884; Dewdney to Macdonald, 5 Sept. 1884.

[70] PAC, RG 10, vol. 3576, file 309A, Begg to Commissioner, 20 Feb. 1885; "Indian Affairs," *Saskatchewan Herald*, 31 Oct. 1884.

145

[71] Dewdney Papers, vol. 6, file 66, Reed to Dewdney, 4 Sept. 1884.

[72] Statutes of Canada, 43 Vict. i, cap. 27, "An Act to Amend the Indian Act, 1880," 12 Apr. 1884. PAC, MG 26A, vol. 107, Dewdney to Macdonald, 24 Aug. 1884.

[73] PAC, MG 26A, vol. 212, Reed to Dewdney, 7 Sept. 1884; vol. 107, Dewdney to Macdonald, 24 Aug. 1884.

[74] PAC, RG 10, vol. 3576, file 309A, Reed to Dewdney, 12 Sept. 1884; vol. 3745, file 29,506-4(2), Reed to Dewdney, 14 Sept. 1884; vol. 3704, file 17,799, entire file; vol. 3664, file 9834 and 9843; vol. 3761, file 30,836, entire file; Dewdney Papers, vol. 4, file 45, Reed to Dewdney, 12 Sept. 1884; vol. 4, file 47, Crozier to Comptroller NWMP, 4 Nov. 1884; vol. 5, file 57, Crozier to Dewdney, 30 Jan. 1885.

[75] PAC, RG 10, vol. 3582, file 749, Ballendine to Reed, 8 Nov. and 26 Dec. 1884.

[76] PAC, RG 10, vol. 3582, file 949, P. Ballendine to Reed, 20 Nov., 26 Dec., 2 Jan., 1885: J.M. Ray to Commissioner, 27 Dec. 1884; Crozier to Commissioner, NWMP, 14 Jan. 1885; vol. 3576, file 309A, Magnus Begg to Dewdney, 20 Feb. 1885. PAC, MG 26A, extract of Ray to Dewdney, 24 Jan. 1885, Ray, Ballendine, and Crozier when they reported on Little Pine mentioned that their principal source of information was Poundmaker, although Ballendine did get some of his information directly from Little Pine himself.

[77] PAC, RG 10, vol. 3582, file 949, Ballendine to Reed, 10 Oct. and 26 Dec. 1884, and 2 Jan. and 16 Mar. 1885: Ballendine to Dewdney, 19 Mar. 1885. PAC, MG 26A, vol. 107, extract of Ray to Dewdney, 24 Jan. 1885. PAC, Manuscript Group 27I C4, Edgar Dewdney Papers, vol. 2, Francis Dickens to Officer Commanding, Battleford, 27 Oct. 1884 (hereafter cited as PAC, MG 27I C4, vol., letter).

[78] PAC, MG 26A, vol. 177, Dewdney to Macdonald, 9 Feb. 1885. PAC, RG 10, vol. 3676, file 309A, Dewdney to Vankoughnet, 12 Feb. 1885.

[79] PAC, RG 10, vol. 3705, file 17,193, Vankoughnet to Dewdney, 5 Feb. 1885; Vankoughnet to Macdonald, 31 Jan. 1885; vol. 3582, file 949, Vankoughnet to Reed, 28 Jan. 1885. Dewdney Papers, vol. 3, file 38, Macdonald to Dewdney, 23 Feb. 1885.

[80] PAC, RG 10, vol. 3576, file 309A, Dewdney to Vankoughnet, 12 Feb. 1885.

[81] Jefferson, Fifty Years on the Saskatchewan, 125.

[82] Jefferson, Fifty Years on the Saskatchewan, 126–28. PAC, MG 26A, deposition, William Lightfoot to J.A. MacKay, 31 May 1885.

[83] Jefferson, Fifty Years on the Saskatchewan, 127, 130, 138.

[84] Innes, "Fine Day Interview," 185. Sluman, Poundmaker, 199–200, 184–85. Jefferson, Fifty Years on the Saskatchewan, 130–38.

[85] Desmond Morton, The Last War Drum (Toronto, 1972), 98–102. Jefferson, Fifty Years on the Saskatchewan, 125–40.

[86] PAC, RG 10, vol. 3755, file 30,973, Reed to Commissioner, 18 June 1881; see also material cited in note 72 above. William B. Cameron, Blood Red the Sun (Edmonton, 1977), 33–61, vividly describes the slaughter at Frog Lake.

[87] Cameron, passim.

[88] Charles Mulvaney, The History of the North-West Rebellion of 1885 (Toronto, 1885), 212–16. Settlers and Rebels, 1882 Report, pp. 22, 26–7. PAC, RG 10, vol. 3584, file 1130, p. 1, Superintendent Herchmer to Dewdney, 5 Apr. 1885.

[89] See note 88 above.

[90] PAC, RG 10, vol. 3697, file 15, 446, entire file; vol. 598, file 1411, entire file; vol. 7768, file 2109-2; vol. 3794, file 46 584.

[91] PAC, MG 27I C4, vol. 7, letters, Dewdney to White, Mar.–Apr. 1885. This correspondence reveals that in early Apr. Dewdney believed that he had to deal with an Indian uprising. However, he did not admit that this impression was based on scanty and often faulty or false information. By mid-Apr., Dewdney makes clear to White, the NWMP Comptroller, that he did not believe that he was dealing with either an Indian uprising or a rebellion.

[92] PAC, MG 27I C4, vol. 1, Dewdney to Begg, 3 May 1885; vol. 4, Dewdney to Middleton, 30 Mar. 1885. RG 10, vol. 3584, file 1130, Dewdney to Ray, 7 May 1885 Jefferson, Fifty Years on the Saskatchewan, 128–33.

[93] PAC, RG 10, vol. 3584, file 1120. Proclamation of 6 May 1885.

[94] MG 26A, vol. 107, Dewdney to Macdonald, 6 Apr. 1885.

[95] Morton, The Last War Drum, 96–110.

[96] Cameron, Blood Red the Sun, 195–204. Sandra Estlin Bingman, "The Trials of Poundmaker and Big Bear," Saskatchewan History 28 (1975): 81–95, gives an account of the conduct of the trials and raises questions about their conduct, particularly the trial of Big Bear. However, Bingman apparently was unaware of Dewdney and Macdonald's efforts to use the courts and whatever other means possible to remove Cree leaders.

[97] PAC, MG 26A, vol. 107, Dewdney to Macdonald, 3 June 1885.

[98] See note 97 above.

[99] See note 97 above.

[100] Bingman, "The Trials of Poundmaker and Big Bear," 81-95.

[101] A very good account of Dewdney's actions to bring the Cree under government control after 1885 is to be found in Jean Lamour, "Edgar Dewdney and the Aftermath of the Rebellion," *Saskatchewan History* 23 (1970): 105-116. For a discussion of the use of the Indian Act as a means of destroying Indian cultural autonomy see John L. Tobias, "Protection, Civilization, Assimilation: An Outline History of Canada's Indian Policy," *The Western Canadian Journal of Anthropology* 6 (1976). For a discussion of specific use of this policy against the Cree, and how the Cree reacted see John L. Tobias, "Indian Reserves in Western Canada: Indian Homelands or Devices for Assimilation," in *Approaches to Native History in Canada: Papers of a Conference held at the National Museum of Man, October, 1975*, ed. D.A. Muise (Ottawa, 1977), 89-103.

147

Topic Four

Political and Cultural Conflict in Late Nineteenth-Century Canada

In late nineteenth-century Canada, numerous political and cultural disputes arose, particularly in the area of dominion–provincial relations. Prime Minister John A. Macdonald had worked to create a highly centralized nation with major powers in the hands of the central government. In his view provincial governments should rank as little more than glorified municipalities under the supervision of the federal government in Ottawa.

Ontario opposed Macdonald's conception. George Brown and his Clear Grits (later known as the Liberals) had favoured Confederation, but only for the possible benefits it could bring to the province. Oliver Mowat, one of Brown's followers and premier of Ontario for twenty-four years (from 1872 to 1896), became the "champion of provincial rights" and the chief opponent of Macdonald's centralized view of the nation. He challenged Macdonald on two fronts: the nature of Canadian federalism and the extent of Ontario's lands and resource rights. In "Ontario on the Rise," Donald Swainson highlights Mowat's achievements in the area of dominion–provincial relations and reviews the province's expansion in agriculture, education, and social programs under Mowat's regime. By his retirement in 1896, Mowat had developed Ontario "into the overwhelmingly dominant economic unit within the Canadian federation."

Tension also surfaced between English- and French-speaking Canadians in the late nineteenth century. The question of French Canadian educational and linguistic rights outside Quebec became contentious. Initially, Macdonald's scheme of achieving "political unity" through a centralized economic program of territorial expansion, a National Policy, and regional integration had worked, and unity prevailed. By the 1880s, however, that unity began to be undermined by three forces: political opportunism, economic stagnation, and theories of national unity based on language and culture rather than on economic co-operation. In "Unity/Diversity: The Canadian Experience; From Confederation to the First World War," J.R. Miller explains the shift from the concept of "unity in diversity" to "diversity into unity," and the resulting political alienation of French-speaking Quebec from English-speaking Canada.

On the provincial-rights movement in Ontario see J.C. Morrison, "Oliver Mowat and the Development of Provincial Rights in Ontario: A Study in Dominion–Provincial Relations, 1867–1896," in *Three History Theses* (Toronto: Ontario Department of Public Records and Archives, 1961), and Christopher Armstrong, *The Politics of Federalism: Ontario's Relations with Federal Government, 1867–1942* (Toronto: University of Toronto Press, 1981).

The literature on the question of Canadian duality is extensive. Perhaps the most complete overview of relations between French and English Canadians in the late nineteenth century is to be found in Volume 1 of Mason Wade's *The French Canadians*, 2 vols. (Toronto: Macmillan, 1977). A short, lively summary of the issue is presented in Susan Mann Trofimenkoff's *The Dream of Nation: A Social and Intellectual History of Quebec* (Toronto: Gage, 1982), and a more detailed account can be found in P.B. Waite's *Canada 1874–1896: Arduous Destiny* (Toronto: McClelland and Stewart, 1971). The rise of a militant Anglo-Canadian Protestant movement agitating to make Canada into a unilingual country, and the French Canadian response to it, are described in J.R. Miller, *Equal Rights: The Jesuits' Estate Act Controversy* (Montreal: McGill-Queen's University Press, 1979). Miller reviews the ideas and the activities of D'Alton McCarthy, regarded as the leading advocate for the assimilation of the French Canadians, in "D'Alton McCarthy, Equal Rights, and the Origins of the Manitoba School Question," *Canadian Historical Review* 54 (December 1973): 369–92, and "'As a Politician He Is a Great Enigma': The Social and Political Ideas of D'Alton McCarthy," *Canadian Historical Review* 58 (December 1977): 399–422. The French Canadians' changing attitude toward Confederation is explored by A.I. Silver in *The French-Canadian Idea of Confederation, 1864–1900* (Toronto: University of Toronto Press, 1982). Ramsay Cook reviews the idea of Confederation as a compact of provinces or cultures in *Provincial Autonomy: Minority Rights and the Compact Theory, 1867–1921* (Ottawa: Queen's Printer, 1969).

Considerable attention has been given by historians to the issue of French-language rights in western Canada. Donald Creighton has argued that John A. Macdonald did not wish to protect French in Manitoba and the Northwest: see his article "John A. Macdonald, Confederation and the Canadian West," *Historical and Scientific Society of Manitoba*, series 3, no. 23 (1966–67), reprinted in D. Creighton, *Towards the Discovery of Canada: Selected Essays* (Toronto: Macmillan, 1972), 229–37. Ralph Heintzman takes the opposite view in "The Spirit of Confederation: Professor Creighton, Biculturalism, and the Use of History," *Canadian Historical Review* 52 (September 1971): 245–75. D.J. Hall enters the debate, essentially on Professor Creighton's side, in " 'The Spirit of Confederation': Ralph Heintzman, Professor Creighton and the Bicultural Theory," *Journal of Canadian Studies* 9 (November 1974): 24–43. For specific information on the major issue of the Manitoba Schools

149

Question in the 1890s, consult Lovell Clark, *The Manitoba School Question: Majority Rule or Minority Rights?* (Toronto: Copp Clark, 1968), and Paul Crunican, *Priests and Politicians: Manitoba Schools and the Election of 1896* (Toronto: University of Toronto Press, 1974). Cornelius Jaenen has completed a review of the language question in "The History of French in Manitoba: Local Initiative or External Imposition?" *Language and Society* 13 (Spring 1984): 3–16. Donald B. Smith reviews the Alberta situation in "A History of the French-speaking Albertans" in *Peoples of Alberta*, ed. Howard and Tamara Palmer (Saskatoon: Western Producer Prairie Books, 1985), 84–108.

Ronald Rudin, *The Forgotten Quebecers* (Québec: Institut québécois de recherche sur la culture, 1985) provides a history of the English-speaking population of Quebec from 1759 to 1980.

---

150 Ontario on the Rise*

DONALD SWAINSON

Oliver Mowat may have learned his law from John A. Macdonald, but he looked elsewhere for his political inspiration. Repelled by the Tory leader's blatant use of political patronage and corruption, Mowat set up as a Liberal to practise the politics of "virtue." And as premier of Ontario for 24 years, he fought John A.'s centralizing view of federalism and championed provincial rights, establishing a solid claim to be considered Canada's most famous and most important provincial premier of the 19th century.

Like Macdonald, Mowat grew up in the Scots Presbyterian community in Kingston, Upper Canada, where he was born in 1820 — the year Macdonald arrived in the area as a five-year-old immigrant from Glasgow. Young Oliver was educated at Rev. John Cruickshank's private school, graduating to Macdonald's office to study law. On being called to the bar in 1841, he moved to Toronto where he quickly established a large and lucrative practice.

Oliver's Twist

The product of a Conservative town, a Conservative family, and Conservative legal training, Mowat showed little interest in politics as a young man. In the early 1850s, he regarded himself as an Independent, but he maintained his ties with Macdonald, then the rising Tory star. The connection proved useful — John A. made him a Queen's Counsel in 1855 and a government commissioner in 1856.

*From *Horizon Canada* 66 (1986): 1561–67. Reprinted by permission.

On Oct. 21, 1872, Vice Chancellor Mowat received Premier Blake, Treasurer Mackenzie, and his former leader, George Brown, at his home on Simcoe Street in Toronto. They offered him the leadership of the Ontario Liberal party and the post of premier. He considered the offer with care, accepted, and was sworn in as Ontario's third premier. A riding was opened for him and by the end of the year, he was premier, attorney general, and member for North Oxford in the Ontario legislature.

Starting Something

Mowat — Sir Oliver after 1892 — never again left public life. He remained premier of Ontario from 1872 to 1896, easily winning six successive general elections. Sir Wilfrid Laurier made him a Senator and federal Minister of Justice in 1896, but the following year, he returned to Toronto as lieutenant governor of Ontario, a post he retained until his death in 1903.

152

Mowat's long tenure as premier of Canada's largest province is enough to make him an important Ontarian and a major Canadian public figure. But his importance goes beyond that normally associated with a powerful premier. Mowat played a key role in structuring the country as a whole.

John A. Macdonald conceived of Canada as a highly centralized state. Financially and politically, he saw Ottawa's role as dominant. The provincial governments were to be minor affairs, with little money and little authority. He explained his position to a friend in 1864: "If the Confederation goes on, you, if spared the ordinary age of man, will see both local parliaments and governments absorbed in the general power. This is as plain to me as if I saw it accomplished." That was not Oliver Mowat's view of Canada, or of Ontario's place in Confederation.

Mowat wanted Ontario to develop into a modern society with a sophisticated economy, and as premier he set out to bring that about. Agriculture, for example, was modernized. Mowat's government was very imaginative in educational and scientific areas related to agriculture, and he himself took this sector of the economy so seriously that he did not hesitate to pursue improvements substantially in advance of public opinion.

Hence he proceeded to permit the provincial agricultural college to award degrees, even as *The Globe*, powerful supporter of Mowat and the Liberal party, scoffed: "It would strike a farmer as a ludicrous thing to have his son come home as a full blown 'Doctor of Agriculture,' or 'Master of Artificial Manures,' or 'Bachelor or Livestock' . . . "

While farmers were becoming substantially more competitive and productive, Ontario underwent tremendous urbanization, industrialization, and population growth. Major adjustments were required to meet these

Mowat now made a decisive career decision. He concluded that acting as a lone gun was no way to win the political influence he desired. He also decided that he preferred not to be a Tory, because he was appalled by Macdonald's brand of politics. So he joined George Brown's Reform party.

Elected to the Parliament of the United Canadas, his obvious abilities and his capacity for hard work immediately made him a Reform leader. He served in George Brown's pathetic two-day "Short Administration" in August 1858, and in the government of John Sandfield Macdonald and Antoine-Aimé Dorion in 1863–64.

He followed Brown into the great Confederation Coalition of Reformers and Tories in 1864, serving as postmaster general. He attended the Quebec Conference in October 1864, thus becoming one of the Fathers of Confederation, but in November, he retired from politics to become a judge as vice-chancellor of Upper Canada.

Needless to say, John A. Macdonald was less than amused by the emergence of his former pupil and protégé as one of George Brown's most influential and effective lieutenants. John A.'s resentment boiled over in April 1861 when Mowat had criticized him in Parliament. "You damned pup," he roared, "I'll slap your chops for you!" John Sandfield Macdonald had to step in bodily to prevent a fistfight on the House floor.

151

In the Wings

But now Mowat had withdrawn from all that. He remained away from politics for several years. Confederation came, Sir John A. Macdonald became Canada's first prime minister, while John Sandfield Macdonald took over as the first premier of Ontario. And after being routed in 1867, the Liberal party, as the Reform movement was known after Confederation, was rejuvenated by Edward Blake and Alexander Mackenzie.

The first major Liberal success came in 1871 with the toppling of the Ontario government of J.S. Macdonald. Blake became premier, with Mackenzie as his provincial treasurer. But these two had bigger fish to fry. Their major objective was the overthrow of Sir John A. Macdonald's national Conservative government. Establishing a Liberal power base in Toronto was but a step in the strategy; that task completed, they wanted to leave the provincial scene and focus all their energies on national politics.

Of course, they wanted to leave a trusty Liberal in charge in Toronto, so they sought a first-rate public figure who could step into Blake's shoes as premier and govern Ontario with ability and success. Mowat was their choice.

fundamental shifts. Big-city problems had to be faced, and trade unions had to be accepted as a fact of life.

Advances by Consensus

Mowat's government moved further and further into the field of government regulation. Significant legislation was passed to protect industrial workers. By the end of the Mowat period, an embryonic welfare state existed, placing Ontario at least a generation ahead of the other provinces. Increasingly sophisticated forms of education were required, and in this area the Mowat record was brilliant. The judicial system was reorganized and the law of the province codified, reforms reflecting the growth of statute law and the need for a more efficient administration of justice. Statistics began to be collected in a systematic way, providing the kind of material that was of enormous use to a government that was becoming increasingly rationalized and bureaucratic.

153

The Mowat regime did much to encourage economic growth. It was responsible for the completion of numerous railways in both northern and southern Ontario. These lines were extremely important: They stimulated development within the older part of the province and opened up large sections of northern Ontario; and they helped mold the province's diverse regions into a whole.

By the end of the century, the Ontario economy and social structure, as we know it, was emerging. At the same time, the provincial administration was becoming ever more modern, better able than any other regime in Canada, federal or provincial, to accommodate the tremendous and dynamic developments of 20th-century Canadian society.

Mowat's liberalism, broad and pragmatic, performed an indispensable function in late 19th-century Ontario history, and materially assisted the province in its rise to dominance. It permitted the maintenance of a provincial consensus during a crucial period of economic and social growth. It set the tone for a party that could accommodate a variety of elements which in other provinces, other governments, provoked discord and instability.

For example, after campaigning on the divisive slogan of "Mowat and the Queen," or "Morrison and the Pope," in his first election in 1857, Mowat, as premier, was able to incorporate into the Liberal party most types of Protestants and large numbers of Roman Catholics. During his premiership, he was also able to retain prohibitionists and representatives of the liquor interests within his party. Businessmen and trade unionists, farmers and urbanites, eastern Ontarians and peninsular Grits, promoters and unemployed, old-fashioned partisans and third-party advocates, liberals and conservatives — his party encompassed them all.

The Good Fight

Mowat's stubborn refusal to allow his Liberals to become at any time a single-issue party muted dissension within the province. While the province of Quebec, to cite a dramatic example, was being torn apart by infighting within the Conservative party and vicious assaults on liberalism, Mowat was able to focus the energies of Ontarians on the basic

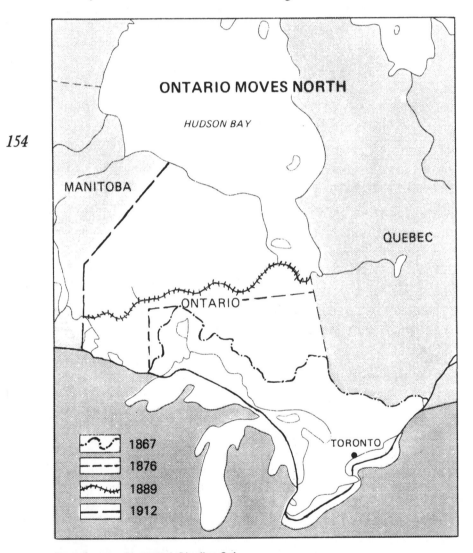

154

Dept. of cartography, CEGEP de Limoilou, Qué.

Northern empire. Ontario has profited enormously from the valuable natural resources of its northern territory, much of which was secured in court cases during Mowat's period.

work of adjusting to industry and urbanization, modernizing agriculture, opening the North, absorbing the political and social energies of trade unionism, and developing Ontario into the overwhelmingly dominant economic unit within the Canadian federation.

It is doubtful that Ontario society would have matured so quickly, or the economy grown so dramatically, without Mowat's consensus-style liberalism. At the same time, the most famous examples of strife in Mowat's day aided rather than harmed Ontario's development. Mowat is best known in Canadian history for his bitter feuds with Sir John A. Macdonald. The warfare between the two was particularly nasty in the years after Macdonald's return to power in 1878.

The feud revolved around two broad problems — the nature of Canadian federalism, and lands and resources.

Mowat refused to accept Macdonald's notion of quasi- federalism in which the provinces were to be subordinate to the federal authority. He held to the view that each level of government was sovereign within its sphere of jurisdiction as defined by Canada's Constitution. Mowat dealt with this problem through the courts, fighting all the way to the Judicial Committee of the Privy Council, which was then the highest court for all British colonies. He won a sweeping victory; his view, not Macdonald's, prevailed and became the basis for Canada's constitutional evolution.

155

The second major point in dispute between Toronto and Ottawa concerned the physical dimensions of Ontario. Macdonald wanted Ontario kept as small as possible in order to retain federal control over the lands and resources of as much territory as he could manage. Mowat wanted an enlarged Ontario, in order to obtain ownership of the wealth of the North.

The province, as it existed in 1867, was much smaller than it is today. It consisted essentially of what is now southern and eastern Ontario, plus an extension northward in the timber lands of the upper Ottawa River watershed, and a strip north of Georgian Bay and lakes Huron and Superior. The western frontier was in the Thunder Bay area, and the province did not possess the vast northern regions that are part of the watershed of Hudson Bay and James Bay.

Holding His Ground

Ottawa and Toronto both recognized that serious legal questions existed concerning Ontario's borders, so negotiations began. They were protracted and difficult, and ultimately failed. The matter was finally decided by the Judicial Committee of the Privy Council in important cases in 1884 and 1888. Mowat personally represented Ontario and won another sweeping victory.

In the west, Ontario's boundary was extended some 440 km; in the northeast, the province's frontier was pushed all the way to James Bay. Mowat had secured for Ontario 285,000 sq. km more, a resource-rich territory more than five times the size of Nova Scotia.

Mowat's victory over Macdonald was complete. Is it any wonder that the prime minister hated the premier of his home province and could say: "Mr. Mowat, with his little soul rattling like a dried pea in a too large pod — what does he care if he wrecks Confederation and interferes with the development of Canada so long as he can enjoy his little salary as Attorney-General?"

Mowat's legacy is modern Ontario and to a substantial extent, modern Canada. His policies led to the development of a provincial society that was productive, advanced, well-educated, stable, and wealthy. Those attributes, plus the extension of the province's borders, made Ontario a resource giant and the dominant social, economic, and political unit within Canada. And he imposed on Canada his view of federalism as a system in which powerful and wealthy provinces could easily act as counterweights to federal authority. He was, without a doubt, a key architect of the Canadian nation.

Unity/Diversity: The Canadian Experience; From Confederation to the First World War*

J.R. MILLER

I

While everyone conceded in the 1860's that the object of the Fathers of Confederation was to produce the bases of one political entity, no one anticipated that this task would be performed by imposing uniformity on the diverse peoples and regions of British North America. Indeed, had such a goal been sought, it would have proved impossible of attainment. The various colonies, with their unique historical development, their different religious denominations, and their distinct nationalities, could not have been homogenized culturally as they were joined politically. The peculiarities of language, creed, and regional identity had to be maintained, for several good and compelling reasons.

Diversity was both desirable and unavoidable, first, because the existing differences were simply too strong to be dismissed. This was true

*Originally published in the *Dalhousie Review* 55, 1 (Spring 1975): 63–81.

not just in the case of the French Canadians, but even with the local autonomists of Ontario, the Grits, and, most especially, in the Maritimes. The *Acadian Recorder* lamented: "We don't know each other. We have no trade with each other. We have no facilities or resources or incentives to mingle with each other. We are shut off from each other by a wilderness, geographically, commercially, politically and socially. We always cross the United States to shake hands." Joseph Howe, as usual, put it more pungently: "Take a Nova Scotian to Ottawa, away above tidewater, freeze him up for five months, where he cannot view the Atlantic, smell salt water, or see the sail of a ship, and the man will pine and die."[1] Diversity was a force too powerful to be exorcised.

Even were it possible to assimilate all British North Americans, to what would you assimilate them? Unlike the United States, a community created by revolution and compact, the proposed Canada was to be produced as the result of an evolutionary process by an act of an external authority, the United Kingdom. Rather than a society of revolution and consensus, Canada was to be a community of evolution and allegiance. The society of allegiance did not require conformity to any one model; the Canadians had no object of assimilation.[2] If they copied anything at all, it was the British pattern, which, since the days of imperial expansion and Catholic Emancipation, meant not something monolithic, Protestant, and Anglo-Saxon, but a number of things more diversified. Canadians could not, at Quebec and Charlottetown, have sought unity at the expense of diversity because there was nothing to which they could conform, and no imperative of revolution to force them to make such a compact.

Finally, Canadian unity was not purchased at the price of homogenization because the colonial politicians who produced it had no intention of creating problems for themselves by debating something as abstract and theoretical as the cultural basis of the new state. These were practical politicians with painfully real problems. Their attention was devoted to solving the difficulties created by deadlock, acquisition of the Northwest, inadequate defences, and promotion of intercolonial commerce, not to searching for new ones. They were, as Donald Creighton has observed, "as far away from the dogmas of the eighteenth-century Enlightenment as they were from twentieth-century obsession with race, and with racial and cultural separatism." These men "saw no merit in setting out on a highly unreal voyage of discovery for first principles."[3] In short, the delegates at Quebec were not about to open a new can of worms by debating the place of various cultural and religious groups in Canada. Such a discussion was as undesirable as it was unnecessary.

These were the reasons why the British North American colonies, as Arthur Lower pointed out, "were carpentered together, not smelted."[4] Or, as G.F.G. Stanley observed: "The Canadian Confederation came into being not to crush but to reconcile regional diversities. . . . Union,

157

not unity, was the result."[5] As one might expect, it was the French-Canadian leader, George Etienne Cartier who expressed the idea of unity in diversity most clearly:

> In our own Federation we should have Catholic and Protestant, English, French, Irish and Scotch, and each by his efforts and his success would increase the prosperity and glory of the new Confederacy. . . . They were placed like great families beside each other, and their contact produced a healthy spirit of emulation. It was a benefit rather than otherwise that we had a diversity of races. . . .
>
> Now, when we were united together, . . . we would form a political nationality with which neither the national origin, nor the religion of any individual, would interfere. It was lamented by some that we had this diversity of races, and hopes were expressed that this distinctive feature would cease. The idea of unity of races was utopian — it was impossible. Distinctions of this kind would always exist. Dissimilarity, in fact, appeared to be the order of the physical world and of the moral world, as well as of the political world.[6]

158

The key words were "a political nationality": the unity that Confederation was to produce was union at the political level, not cultural. While "carpentering" political unity, British North Americans would retain regional, religious, and cultural diversity; Canada was founded on unity in diversity. And, in passing, one might note the type of diversity intended — "Catholic and Protestant, English, French, Irish and Scotch." This was a very Britannic mosaic.

II

Of course, the formula "Unity in diversity" raised as many questions as it answered. What did the concept mean? How did you hold a diverse country together? Specifically, what were the rights and privileges of the most distinctive minority, the French Canadians? More specifically still, what was to become of the principle of cultural and political *duality* that had evolved in the Province of Canada (the future Ontario and Quebec) between 1841 and 1867? It would take a decade and more to work out the first set of answers to these riddles; and, then, the first essay at a resolution of them would come under attack and be modified substantially.

The first question dealt with was the fate of the duality of the Canadian union. Here the answer was starkly simple: duality would be eliminated. This did not mean any tampering with the official status of the French language that was protected by Section 133 of the British North America Act in the courts and Parliament of Canada, as well as in the courts and Legislature of Quebec. However, in succeeding years it was evident that Canadians were not prepared to foster the expansion of this limited, pragmatic recognition of French into a great principle of *duality* throughout the land. Although French was officially countenanced in Manitoba and the Northwest Territories, under special and pressing circumstances, it was not enshrined in the other new provinces of British Columbia and Prince Edward Island. Indeed, in New Brunswick, the Acadian minority suffered the loss of an important cultural bulwark in the 1870's, when their Legislature deprived them of public support for their denominational schools. In short, the first generation of Canadian politicians was prepared to grant French culture official status where temporary exigencies and local pressures made it politically expedient to do so, and nowhere else. They certainly were not about to erect linguistic duality into a great principle of the federation.

Moreover, other aspects of dualism, the double political and administrative institutions that had developed in the United Province, were deliberately removed. Governor General Monck's invitation to John A. Macdonald to form the first Dominion Cabinet explicitly forbade the continuation of the dual premiership. Sectional equality in the Cabinet was replaced by a careful balancing of regional, economic, religious, and cultural interests in Macdonald's first ministry, and in almost all that have succeeded. Duality of administrative posts was also abolished, essentially because the unsatisfactory quasi-federalism of the Union was replaced by a real federation and division of powers between levels of government. There were for example no longer two Superintendents of Education because the schools were now the responsibility of the provinces. Similarly, two Attorneys-General were not needed because French Canada's peculiar civil law was to be controlled by Quebec. And so it went. Institutional duality, whether at the political or civil service level, was eradicated because it was unnecessary and unwanted.

159

Whatever else the first decade demonstrated, it proved that unity in diversity did not mean the retention of any more duality than was essential. There still remained the more difficult question: if unity in diversity did not mean duality, what did it mean? How was it to be formalized, embodied, made concrete? How did you tack together "a political nationality" out of diverse elements?

The first indication of the means that would be used to hold the country together came in 1868, in Minister of Justice Macdonald's memorandum on the federal power of disallowance. Macdonald laid down guidelines for the federal veto of provincial legislation that were sweeping. They were so general as almost to be unqualified, as was suggested by the provision that provincial statutes "as affecting the interests of the Dominion generally" could be struck down if Ottawa wished.[7] This was Macdonald's instinctive reversion to the eighteenth-century Tory tradition of centralized governmental power. Under his leadership, the first government after Confederation followed a highly centralist policy, one suspects because he regarded such centralization as being as essential to the well-being of the fragile union as it was congenial to his Conservative temperament.

Gradually during the 1870's the rest of the apparatus for ensuring the unity of the state was put into place. The policy of pushing the Indians out of the arable lands of the prairie West and replacing them with white, agricultural settlers was one such project. The gargantuan task of binding the newly acquired and sparsely populated West to the rest of the country with a transcontinental railroad was another. And the policy of forcing economic diversification and regional specialisation of economic function through the imposition of the protective tariff was the final means chosen to produce enduring unity out of diversity and distance. The objective of these national policies of expansion and development was to provide an economic *raison d'être* for the political state; or, if you prefer, it was the means of putting the flesh of economic self-interest on the bare bones of the constitutional skeleton. The West, once filled, would produce agricultural products for export and would serve as a captive market for Canadian manufacturers. Central Canada would manufacture goods, protected and encouraged by the tariff; would fuel her industries with Nova Scotian coal; and would sell her products to Maritimers and Westerners alike. The whole scheme would be facilitated by the network of railways that was so essential to the Canadian federation: the Grand Trunk, Intercolonial, and Canadian Pacific. And, finally, the scheme of economic nationalism — the encouragement of a transcontinental economy of diverse, but integrated economic regions — would be supervised and protected by a powerful central government.

Now, the formulation of these policies was undoubtedly much more accidental than the foregoing sketch suggests. The steps toward adoption of the various pieces were often hesitant, taken out of a sense of constitutional obligation (the promise of a railway to B.C.), and motivated more by partisan political calculations than nation-building ambitions. And, yet, what seems striking is the fact that the pieces fit, that they made up a coherent, compelling, and politically appealing programme of national self-defence through economic expansion and integration. Furthermore, when the pieces are put together, they provide an answer to the question of how unity could be maintained amidst diversity. The answer was that diverse regions, religious groups, and nationalities could stay united politically while remaining different culturally because they had a programme of economic development from which they could all benefit. And, moreover, these policies meant that the focus of political life at the federal level would not be on sensitive issues of religion and nationality, but on economic issues that cut across regional, religious, and cultural lines. Macdonald's nationalism would make unity in diversity possible by concentrating on those things that united Canadians, or, at least, did not divide them according to religion and language. The

160

recipe was: diversity locally, but political unity in pursuit of common economic objectives.

Not the least significant feature of this concoction is the fact that, to a large extent, it succeeded. The French Canadians participated in the scheme as enthusiastically as anyone else. There were no more fervent Protectionists than Quebec's leaders, who saw the industrialization of the Townships as the alternative to the continuing hemorrhage of French-Canadian youth to the detested United States. Ontario was satisfied, for the key to Macdonald's scheme was the realisation of Ontario's traditional dream of opening and developing the West in Ontario's image and for Toronto's pecuniary benefit. The national policies embodied Ontario imperialism. And the Maritimes benefited too, although the advantages were offset by the general deterioration of the Atlantic economy in the waning years of wind and wood transportation. There was substantial growth in the Nova Scotian coal industry, as the industrialization encouraged by the tariff created markets for the fuel in urban Quebec.[8] *161* The only region that did not benefit very much from the scheme was the West. There the response to centralization and the national policies was protest: formation of the Manitoba and Northwest Farmers' Union, Riel's second Rebellion, the provincial autonomy campaign in Manitoba, and the steady intonation on the litany of grievances (freight rates, elevators, and tariffs) that was to become so familiar. But, frankly, no one worried much about western complaints, for colonies were only supposed to produce wealth, not be happy. Western grievances aside, however, the Tory scheme of unity through economic expansion was quite successful.

III

This unity based on pursuit of common economic goals under the direction of a strong central government began to erode in the 1880's as the result of three corrosive influences. Political opportunism inspired an attack on centralization by the Liberal parties at the federal and provincial levels. The economic stagnation that returned after 1883 destroyed the rosy dreams of prosperity and unity. As is normally the case in difficult times, economic discontent led to internal bickering: the provinces *versus* Ottawa; and Ontario against the rest, especially Quebec, when the provinces succeeded in extorting "better terms" from the Conservative federal government. Finally, the desired unity within the country was eroded by the influence in Canada of radically new theories of national unity that focused upon language and culture, rather than economic cooperation, as essential criteria for unification.

The new theories which sought unity at the expense of cultural diversity were represented in the 1880's and 1890's by such men as D'Alton

McCarthy and Goldwin Smith. McCarthy, an Anglo-Saxon supremacist, imperialist, and tariff reformer, was worried about the lack of cohesion in Canada and anxious about the declining power of the central government. To him the villain of the piece seemed to be the French Canadian who insisted on having his own way, thereby preventing fusion:

> My own conviction is that it is not religion which is at the bottom of the matter but that it is a race feeling. There is no feeling so strong — no feeling which all history proves so strong — as the feeling of race. Don't we find the French today in the province of Quebec more French than when they were conquered by Wolfe upon the plains of Abraham? Do they mix with us, assimilate with us, intermarry with us? Do they read our literature or learn our laws? No, everything with them is conducted on a French model; and while we may admire members of that race as individuals, yet as members of the body politic I say that they are the great danger to the Confederacy.[9]

In McCarthy's view, "It was the language of a people that moulded its nationality."[10] The "science of language" demonstrated "that there is no factor equal to language to band people together, and . . . as is demonstrated in our own case, that nothing is more calculated to keep people asunder."[11] If McCarthy's analysis was correct, then it followed that Canadian unity could be achieved only through the imposition on Canada of one language: unity was to be achieved, not through diversity, but through cultural uniformity brought about by assimilation. His programme for national unity was summarized in his resolution calling for the abolition of the official use of French in the Northwest Territories: that it was "expedient in the interest of national unity that there should be community of language among the people of Canada."[12]

Goldwin Smith, free trader, continentalist, and Anglo-Saxon racist, advocated a slightly different programme to achieve the same end. He believed that French Canada was an obstacle to unity not just because of its language, but also because of its obscurantism and economic backwardness, both of which were the results of clerical domination:

> Quebec is a theocracy. While Rome has been losing her hold on Old France and on all the European nations, she has retained, nay tightened, it here. The people are the sheep of the priest. He is their political as well as their spiritual chief and nominates the politician, who serves the interest of the Church at Quebec or at Ottawa. . . . Not only have the clergy been the spiritual guides and masters of the French Canadians, they have been the preservers and champions of his nationality, and they have thus combined the influence of the tribune with that of the priest.[13]

> The French province, the people of which live on the produce of their own farms and clothe themselves with the produce of their spinning, is uncommercial, and lies a non-conductor between the more commercial members of the Confederation.[14]

Unlike McCarthy, Smith did not seek a solution to this problem in Canada, because he believed the political parties were totally and irrevocably the tools of the Quebec clergy. To Smith it was "perfectly clear that the forces of Canada alone are not sufficient to assimilate the French element or even to prevent the indefinite consolidation and growth of a French nation."[15] The answer, then, was obvious: "French Canada may be ultimately absorbed in the English-speaking population of a vast Continent; amalgamate with British Canada so as to form a united nation it apparently never can."[16] Canada should join the Americans to form an Anglo-Saxon republic of North America in which the French Canadians would drown.

There is a two-fold significance in the emergence of such advocates *163* of Anglo-Saxon cultural uniformity as McCarthy and Smith. The first is that they are evidence that in English Canada, for a variety of reasons, many people had by the 1890's rejected the pursuit of unity in diversity. The second is that the country as a whole rejected the extreme prescriptions put forward by continentalists and cultural assimilationists alike for coercive uniformity. Parliament's response to McCarthy's call for linguistic uniformity was a compromise resolution that said that nothing had happened since Confederation to justify taking from the French Canadians the guarantees they received at the time of union, while allowing the populace of the Northwest Territories itself to decide the fate of the official use of French on the prairies.[17] And in the 1890's such annexationist schemes as Smith's Continental Union Association were rejected by the electorate.

Though McCarthy and Smith failed, they were not without lingering influence. French Canadians, seeing assimilationist movements such as the Equal Rights Association, Equal Rights League, Protestant Protective Association, and Continental Union Association, found renewed cause for anxiety about their future as a distinct cultural entity within the Canadian "political nationality." This disquiet was aggravated by a new phenomenon of the late 1890's and early 1900's, massive European immigration to the Canadian West. As French-Canadian leaders quickly perceived, this demographic change made Cartier's doctrine of diversity a source of danger.

IV

The problem arose because of English-Canadian reaction to the immigration of the Laurier period. As thousands of Poles, Russians, Germans,

Italians, Scandinavians, and Ukrainians flooded the West, middle-class, Anglo-Saxon Canadians began to join working-class critics of extensive immigration. Whereas the old trade union criticism of immigration was essentially economic in character,[18] the new critique was fundamentally concerned with the cultural effects of immigration. Stephen Leacock observed disapprovingly that the new immigration was "from the Slavonic and Mediterranean peoples of a lower industrial and moral status," and consisted of "herds of the proletariat of Europe, the lowest class of industrial society."[19] Principal Sparling of Wesley College, Winnipeg, warned that Canadians "must see to it that the civilization and ideals of Southeastern Europe are not transplanted to and perpetuated on our virgin soil."[20] While Ralph Connor fictionalized Sparling's injunction in *The Foreigner*,[21] a poet, of sorts, expressed similar ideas in verse:

They are haggard, huddled, homeless, frightened at — they know
not what:
With a few unique exceptions they're a disappointing lot;
But I take 'em as I get 'em, soldier, sailor, saint and clown
And I turn 'em out Canadians — all but the yellow and brown.[22]

In the era of the Laurier Boom many Canadians recoiled from the tidal wave of immigration, sorrowfully concluding that they could "not make a nation by holding a basket at the hopper of an immigration chute."[23]

The English-Canadian answer to these cultural dangers was a drive to assimilate the "foreigner" by inculcating in him the values of British-Canadian civilization. What precisely that meant, and the danger it portended, manifested itself in the prescriptions critics of immigration put forward for the solution of the problem. "One of the best ways of Canadianizing, nationalizing, and turning all into intelligent citizens," said one Protestant clergyman in 1913, "is by means of a good English education. . . . "[24] When J.S. Woodsworth asked himself how "are we to break down the walls which separate these foreigners from us?" his conclusion was that first and foremost was "the Public School. Too great emphasis cannot be placed upon the work that has been accomplished and may — yes, must — be accomplished by our National Schools."[25] Linguistic uniformity imposed by the schools was the answer:

If Canada is to become in any real sense a nation, if our people are to become one, we must have one language. . . . Hence the necessity of national schools where the teaching of English — our national language — is compulsory.

The public school system was "the most important factor in transforming the foreigners into Canadians."[26]

French Canada, not unnaturally, took alarm at such programmes, which drew no distinction between the worthy French Canadian and the despised "Galician." The emerging champion of French-Canadian nationalism, Henri Bourassa, protested that the Fathers of Confederation had never intended "to change a providential condition of our partly French and partly English country to make it a land of refuge for the scum of all nations."[27] Bourassa's complaint was that diversity, by which Canadians had meant a mixture of English, French, and Scot, now seemed to mean Ukrainian, German, and Italian; and that English Canadians, in reacting to this new form of diversity, attacked French-Canadian rights as well as the pretensions of the European "scum." Bourassa knew whereof he spoke, for, in the early years of the twentieth century, Woodsworth's prescription (and Bourassa's nightmare) was realized. In 1901 and 1905 on the prairies, and in 1912 in Ontario, unilingual education was imposed in an effort to assimilate all minorities, including the French Canadians. In the era of massive European immigration Cartier's "multicultural argument could only accelerate, not retard the unilingual process."[28]

Bourassa's, and French Canada's, response to this danger was to work out a new theory of Canadian unity that protected rather than jeopardized French-Canadian cultural rights. The new spokesman of French Canada found his justification of his culture in Providence and History. God, he argued, had placed the Latin culture of French Canada in North America as a spiritual beacon in the materialistic, Anglo-Saxon darkness. And what God planted, not even the Canadian Parliament ought to root out. Furthermore, he insisted, Canadian history was the record of the preservation of cultural duality. The Royal Proclamation of 1763 and Quebec Act of 1774 had ensured the survival of the primary agency of French Canada, the Roman Catholic Church. A political process stretching from the Constitutional Act of 1791 to the struggle over responsible government of the 1840's had expanded the limited eighteenth-century guarantees into semi-official recognition of duality. Confederation, in Bourassa's historical recitation, became the adoption by the new Dominion of Canada of biculturalism and bilingualism. Hence, French Canada should be respected because it was a co-ordinate partner with a special providential mission to perform. Not even the infringements of the Confederation compact in the West and Ontario between 1890 and 1912 could alter that fact. "The Canadian nation," Bourassa argued, "will attain its ultimate destiny, indeed it will exist, only on the condition of being biethnic and bilingual, and by remaining faithful to the concept of the Fathers of Confederation: the free and voluntary association of two peoples, enjoying equal rights in all matters."[29] In other words, in flight from the vulnerability of diversity, Bourassa had erected duality as a new line of defence. Bourassa and biculturalism had replaced Cartier and diversity as the theoretical justification of French Canada's right to exist.

In the first half-century of Confederation, then, Canadians' concept of their political community as a unity in diversity had come under attack

165

on two fronts. English assimilationists had argued for cultural homogenization as an answer to disunity, and French-Canadian nationalists had responded with a messianic and historical defence of cultural duality. The two conflicting viewpoints were the subject of much public discussion in the early years of the twentieth century, as each struggled for mastery. As it turned out, with the coming of the Great War the English-Canadian assimilationist model triumphed. Several provinces terminated the official use of French; Ontario refused to soften the assimilationist thrust of its 1912 policy; and Quebec, as a result of the language issue and the conscription crisis, was politically isolated and alienated.

NOTES

1. *Acadian Recorder*, quoted in Ricker, Saywell, and Cook, *Canada: A Modern Study* (Toronto, 1963), 101; J. Howe, quoted in J.M. Beck, *Joseph Howe: Anti-Confederate* (Ottawa, 1956), 15.
2. W.L. Morton, *The Canadian Identity* (Madison and Toronto, 1961), 100-107, 110-12.
3. D.G. Creighton, *The Road to Confederation* (Toronto, 1964), 141-42.
4. A.R.M. Lower, *Canadians in the Making* (Don Mills, 1958), 289.
5. G.F.G. Stanley, "Regionalism in Canadian History," *Ontario History* 51 (1959): 167.
6. P.B. Waite, ed., *Confederation Debates in the Province of Canada/1865* (Carleton Library edition, Toronto, 1963), 51 and 50.
7. Quoted in J.M. Beck, ed., *The Shaping of Canadian Federalism* (Toronto, 1971), 159.
8. P.B. Waite, *Canada, 1874-1896: Arduous Destiny* (Toronto, 1971), 184.
9. Quoted in F. Landon, "D'Alton McCarthy and the Politics of the Later Eighties," Canadian Historical Association, *Report of the Annual Meeting, 1932*, 46.
10. Stayner Speech, 12 July 1889, *Toronto Daily Mail*, 13 July 1889.
11. *Speech of Mr. D'Alton McCarthy delivered on Thursday, 12 December 1889 at Ottawa* (n.p., n.d.),
12. *Debates of the House of Commons*, Fourth Session, Sixth Parliament, vol. 29 (1890), columns 674-75.
13. G. Smith, *Canada and the Canadian Question* (Toronto, 1891), 5-6.
14. Smith, *Canada and the Canadian Question*, 206-207.
15. Smith, *Canada and the Canadian Question*, 275.
16. Smith, *Canada and the Canadian Question*, 215.
17. *Debates of the House of Commons* (1890), columns 881-82 and 1017-18.
18. With the exception, of course, of British Columbia, where the objections had been based on both economic and racial arguments. See J.A. Munro, "British Columbia and the 'Chinese Evil': Canada's First Anti-Asiatic Immigration Law," *Journal of Canadian Studies* 6 (1971): 42-49.
19. S. Leacock, "Canada and the Immigration Problem," *The National Review* 52 (1911): 317 and 323.
20. Principal Sparling, "Introduction" to J.S. Woodsworth, *Strangers Within our Gates, or Coming Canadians* (Toronto, 1909).
21. R. Connor [C.W. Gordon], *The Foreigner: A Tale of Saskatchewan* (Toronto, 1909), especially 23-25 and 37-41. This theme in Connor's work has been analysed carefully in J.L. Thompson and J.H. Thompson, "Ralph Connor and the Canadian Identity," *Queen's Quarterly* 79 (1972): 166-69.
22. R.J.C. Stead, "The Mixer" (1905), quoted in R.C. Brown and R. Cook, *Canada, 1896-1921: A Nation Transformed* (Toronto, 1974), 73.
23. Leacock, "Canada and the Immigration Problem," 318.
24. Rev. W.D. Reid, in R.C. Brown and M.E. Prang, eds., *Confederation to 1949* (Scarborough, 1966), 84.
25. J.S. Woodsworth, *Strangers Within Our Gates*, 281.
26. J.S. Woodsworth (1905), quoted in Brown and Cook, *Canada, 1896-1921*, 73.
27. H. Bourassa (1904), quoted in Brown and Cook, *Canada, 1896-1921*, 74.
28. A. Smith, "Metaphor and Nationality in North America," *Canadian Historical Review* 51 (1970): 268. This paper owes far more than this isolated quotation to Professor Smith's stimulating analysis, as students of the topic will realize.
29. H. Bourassa (1917), quoted in R. Cook, *Canada and the French-Canadian Question* (Toronto, 1966), 51.

Topic Five

Imperialism, Continentalism, and Nationalism

A growing number of Canadians in the late nineteenth and early twentieth centuries debated their country's future position in the world: Should they seek greater unity with Britain through an imperial federation? Closer union with the United States in a form of continental union? Or independence for Canada itself? All three possibilities were, in their own ways, forms of Canadian nationalism, debated in light of the advancement of Canadian interests.

The idea of an imperial federation or closer union of Britain and Canada was born in the depressed and ethnically divided atmosphere of the late nineteenth century. Some twenty years after Confederation, Canada appeared to some Canadians to be a dismal failure. The National Policy had not stimulated economic growth; the expected population explosion had not occurred; and the nation was racked with political, cultural, social, and regional dissent. At the same time the rival German nation and empire, and an expanding American nation, challenged Britain's world supremacy. A group of imperial enthusiasts in both Canada and Britain dreamt of a consolidated British Empire which would bring glory to Britain and a "sense of power" to Canada. Carl Berger outlines the ideas of Canadian imperialists in his introduction to *Imperialism and Nationalism, 1884–1914: A Conflict in Canadian Thought*.

While the majority of English-speaking Canadians favoured some form of imperial federation or continental union, a significant group of French-speaking Canadians looked towards the possibility of Canadian independence. Henri Bourassa, the grandson of Louis-Joseph Papineau (the fiery leader of the *Parti Patriote* before the Lower Canadian Rebellions of 1837/38), spoke for those French Canadians who felt Canada should weaken its ties to Britain. Between the beginning of the Boer War in 1899 and the ending of the First World War in 1918, Bourassa fought tirelessly for Canadian independence and a bilingual Canada. Joseph Levitt summarizes the ideas of this important and influential French Canadian thinker in his introduction to *Henri Bourassa on Imperialism and Bi-culturalism, 1900–1918*.

Carl Berger analyses English-Canadian imperial thought in greater detail in *The Sense of Power: Studies in the Idea of Canadian Imperialism, 1867-1914* (Toronto: University of Toronto Press, 1970). For a different perspective on Canadian imperial thought see Robert Page, "Canada and the Imperial Idea in the Boer War," *Journal of Canadian Studies* 5 (February 1970): 33-49. Also useful is a collection of essays entitled *Imperial Relations in the Age of Laurier*, ed. Carl Berger (Toronto: University of Toronto Press, 1969).

Students are also encouraged to read Goldwin Smith's book, *Canada and the Canadian Question*, first published in 1891 but still relevant today. Elisabeth Wallace's *Goldwin Smith: Victorian Liberal* (Toronto: University of Toronto Press, 1957) is a full-scale study of his life and ideas.

Henri Bourassa's ideas on national questions are analyzed in M.P. O'Connell's "The Ideas of Henri Bourassa," *Canadian Journal of Economics and Political Science* 19 (1953): 361-76; S.M. Trofimenkoff's *The Dream of Nation: A Social and Intellectual History of Quebec* (Toronto: Gage Publishing, 1983), 167-83; and Mason Wade's *The French Canadians, 1760-1945* (Toronto: Macmillan, 1955), 447-539. See as well Joseph Levitt's pamphlet, *Catholic Critic*, Canadian Historical Association, Historical Booklet no. 20 (Ottawa: CHA, 1976).

Imperialism and Nationalism, 1884-1914: A Conflict in Canadian Thought*

CARL BERGER

Introduction

Imperialism in Canada presented many faces and its story has been told from various perspectives. Its aim was to consolidate the British Empire through military, economic, and constitutional devices. Those Canadians who supported imperial unity, or imperial federation, believed that Canada could attain national status only by maintaining the connection with the Empire and by acquiring an influence within its councils. Their opponents were convinced that imperialism was incompatible with Canada's national interests, internal unity, and self-government. The conflict between these two forces was a major theme in Canadian life in the thirty years before the First World War, and the struggle was bitter and divisive. It was fought out in many arenas, in Parliament, at Colonial and Imperial

*Introduction to *Imperialism and Nationalism, 1884-1914: A Conflict in Canadian Thought*, ed. Carl Berger (Toronto: Copp Clark, 1969), 1-5. Reprinted with permission.

Conferences, and in polemical literature, and it centred upon several issues — commercial policy, participation in the Boer War, and military and naval preparedness. But it was above all fought out in the minds of Canadians, and it is from this point of view, as a problem in Canadian intellectual history, that it is presented in this book. The questions raised here do not concern, at least not primarily, elections, the formulation of tariff policy, or the problems of military co-operation. These readings are intended rather to bring into sharper focus the guiding ideas and divergent conceptions of the Canadian future that underlay the clash between imperialism and nationalism.

Imperialism and nationalism are vague words which must be defined in terms of their historical context. The organized movement for imperial unity originated in the later 1880's. The cumulative impact of the long depression, the failure of Macdonald's National Policy to generate prosperity and economic integration, and the cultural crisis that followed the execution of Louis Riel, produced a widespread feeling of pessimism about Canada's future. The commitment of the Liberal party to unrestricted reciprocity, or free trade with the United States, climaxed the fears of those who, rightly or wrongly, identified such a policy with continentalism. It was at this point — in 1887 and 1888 — that branches of the Imperial Federation League, an organization founded in England in 1884, were set up in Canada, and they quickly became the centres of a perfervid British Canadian patriotism. As a countermeasure to reciprocity, the supporters of imperial unity advocated the idea of an economic union of the Empire to be secured through preferential tariffs. Imperial preference remained the central plank in the agenda of Canadian imperialism long after unrestricted reciprocity was defeated in the election of 1891, and long after the Liberal party rejected it in 1893. Canadian imperialists were far more emphatic on the commercial aspects of imperial unity than were their counterparts in England. In fact the difference of opinion between those who stressed imperial preference and those who placed their faith in military and naval co-operation was one of the chief reasons why the Imperial Federation League disintegrated in 1893. Its branches in Canada, however, were simply reconstituted as organs of the British Empire League. When in 1897 the new Liberal government of Wilfrid Laurier extended a preference on British manufactured commodities entering Canada, the action was widely hailed as a practical implementation of the imperial ideal.

Imperial unity was as much a state of mind as a political platform, and the appeals of those who underlined the necessity for Canada to maintain and strengthen the British connection customarily transcended commercial and economic arguments. The leading spokesmen of imperial unity — Colonel George T. Denison of Toronto, a police magistrate and military thinker, George R. Parkin, a New Brunswick born teacher and writer, and Rev. George M. Grant, Principal of Queen's University

169

170

THE OLD FLAG.
THE OLD POLICY,
THE OLD LEADER.

McCord Museum of Canadian History, Montreal.

During the election of 1891, the Conservatives championed continued association with Britain under "the old flag," the "old policy" of national protection, and the "old leader." By implication the Liberals offered close association with the United States, and free trade, under an unknown and untried leader (Wilfrid Laurier).

— all believed that Canada could only grow and survive if it held fast to the imperial connection. They were convinced, or they convinced themselves, partly through their reading of Goldwin Smith's plea for continental union, *Canada and the Canadian Question* (1891), that though unrestricted reciprocity might bring prosperity it would also ultimately end in political extinction. As a consequence, their arguments against a particular trade policy moved away from a discussion of the comparative prices of eggs in Toronto and Pittsburg to an attempt to awaken an appreciation for, and an attachment to, those traditions and institutions which in their minds made the Canadian nationality worthy of preservation. In this sense imperial unity began as a defence of Canada.

In the later eighties and early nineties imperial unity found its main support in the older section of English Canada and particularly among the descendants of the United Empire Loyalists. Both Denison and Parkin traced their roots back to the Loyalists who were described, in the mythology of the day, as "Canada's Pilgrim Fathers." Though the Imperial Federation League in 1889 counted one quarter of the members of the Dominion Parliament in its ranks, its most vocal and devoted supporters were drawn from a narrow group of politicians, lawyers, teachers, and Protestant ministers. It received no support from labour or the farming population, and in French Canada its progress was viewed firstly with indifference, then alarm, and finally with massive hostility. This is hardly surprising. Members of the Orange Order, who interpreted imperial federation to mean Protestant supremacy, were often members of the League, and D'Alton McCarthy, the leader of the Equal Rights Movement which endeavoured to limit French language rights and separate schools to Quebec alone, was prominent among the adherents of imperialism. Not all imperialists, of course, were supporters of Orangeism and Equal Rights. One of the most sympathetic defences of the state-supported separate schools of Manitoba was penned by G.M. Grant, who had been instrumental in deposing McCarthy from his position in the League because he had jeopardized the cause of imperial unity. Yet in general, the obvious racial overtones of the imperial sentiment, and the strange allies with whom the imperialist consorted, were enough to alienate French Canada.

Born in a period of doubt and despair, imperialism by the late 1890's had become more impatient, assertive and bellicose. The appointment of Joseph Chamberlain to the Colonial Office in 1895 signalized the increasing seriousness of purpose of British imperialism. In 1899, in spite of his own personal predisposition to remain uninvolved, Laurier was forced by public pressure in English Canada to dispatch Canadian soldiers to fight in the Boer War. This action was in itself a testimony to the growing strength of the imperial cause. Fourteen years before, Macdonald had shrugged off similar suggestions that Canada aid Britain in the Soudan and his reaction was endorsed by Denison, one of the

171

most militant of Canadian imperialists who was never one to miss a war if he could help it. The Boer War was the decisive event in the history of Canadian imperialism. To many English Canadians it was not a matter of aiding England. For them that experience was invested with all the enthusiasm of nationalism. Canada's participation, niggardly though some thought it was, marked the entry of the Dominion into world politics. She had become a force within the Empire and her path forward was straight and clear. Now that Canadians had demonstrated their willingness to support the Empire with more than emotional speeches, was it not only fair that they be accorded some influence over the direction of imperial foreign policy? French Canadians saw the matter very differently. The spectacle of Canadians fighting in so remote a war, one waged against a non-British minority with which they so easily identified themselves, generated an imperialist reaction which grew and gained momentum. Some time before, the nationalist Premier of Quebec, Honoré Mercier, had warned that the imperial federationists wanted "us to assume, in spite of ourselves, the responsibilities and dangers of a sovereign state which will not be ours. They seek to expose us to vicissitudes of peace and war . . . ; to wrest from our arms our sons, . . . and send them off to bloody and distant wars, which we shall not be able to stop or prevent."[1] And the prophecy had come true. In 1899 Henri Bourassa left the Liberal Party charging that Laurier had capitulated to pressure from the Colonial Office and had thereby established a precedent, fatal to Canadian self-government, that Canada must fight in all imperial wars. In 1903, in conjunction with a group of young French Canadian nationalists, Bourassa founded the *Ligue Nationaliste* to combat the imperial menace. The zest with which imperialists had supported the South African war was proof to them of the essentially colonial-minded character of English Canada.

These two extremes, the one demanding that Canada take up imperial obligations and be accorded a voice in Empire affairs, the other insisting on Canadian neutrality and freedom from such burdens, were not easily reconciled, and for some time Laurier did not try to reconcile them. He turned aside Chamberlain's suggestions at the Colonial Conference of 1902 that co-operation be institutionalized. Though he declared in the same year that Canada must take some steps to ensure her security, and though in 1903, after the unpopular Alaska Boundary decision, he also urged that the Dominion make her own foreign policy, Laurier made no fundamental decisions in either direction, except for taking over the management of the naval bases at Halifax and Esquimalt. The imperial question lay quiescent until the "naval scare" of 1909 made postponement impossible. The threat that the German ship-building programme would undermine the supremacy of British seapower set off a wide-ranging and acrimonious debate over what stand Canada should take. The imperialists contended that Canada, now strong and prosperous, should help sustain the force upon which her own security depended; to the anti-imperialists this appeared as the payment of tribute to the motherland whose interests were very different from Canada's. In reality the debate was more complex than this, for even imperialists were in disagreement about the exact extent and nature of Canada's contribution to imperial defence. But Laurier's proposal for the creation of a Canadian navy which in times of crisis would become part of the British fleet angered both extremes and in part accounted for his defeat in 1911. Long before this time Bourassa had come to think of Laurier as the main instrument of the imperialist conspiracy. On July 13, 1911, he wrote in *Le Devoir*: "English and African soldiers fell on the veldt for the glory of Chamberlain; women and children died of shame and misery for the grandeur of Laurier; children's entrails were cut out in the Concentration camps for the honour of the Empire." From the imperialist Stephen Leacock, on the other hand, came this greeting at the news of Laurier's defeat:

173

> Sir Wilfrid, it may be said, with all the gentleness of speech which is becoming in speaking of such a man on such an occasion, touched in this election upon the one point on which he never fully enjoyed the confidence of the Canadian people — our relations to the British Empire. It has been his fortunate lot to represent us on great occasions. He has ridden for us in coaches of State, to the plaudits of a London multitude. He has coined phrases for us, of summoning us to Imperial councils and the like, grandiloquent in the utterance, but meaning less and less as they recede into retrospect. That he never really understood the feelings of his English-speaking fellow citizens of Canada towards their Mother Country, that he never really designed to advance the cause of permanent Imperial unity — these things may well be doubted. . . . We are . . . groping for something which we desire but still seek in vain. The great problem of our common future is to find an organic basis of lasting union.[2]

Such was the burden of the two extremes which tore apart the man who searched for the fragile consensus.

In the thirty years before 1914, the difference between nationalism and imperialism was much more complicated than the desire for Canadian autonomy on the one hand and a willingness to live under Downing Street rule on the other. Not even the anti-imperialists thought it was that simple. John Ewart, for example, who defined nationalism as the end of subordination of one state to another, remarked that those Canadian imperialists with whom he was acquainted were really Canadian nationalists. And within the terms of his own definition he was right. What divided those who called themselves nationalists from those who preferred to be known as imperialists was not the question of whether Canada should manage her own affairs and have the power to formulate

a foreign policy expressive of her interests; what divided them was disagreement over how these powers were to be acquired and for what purposes they were to be employed. The imperialists saw the British Empire
as the vehicle in which Canada would attain national status; the anti-
imperialists were so convinced of the incompatibility of imperial and
Canadian interests that they saw all schemes for co-operation as reactionary and anti-national. In a fundamental sense, therefore, the differences between, say, Stephen Leacock and Henri Bourassa stemmed
from their very different ideas about Canada, her history, and place in
the world. The only way to understand the conflict between the positions
these two men embodied is to understand the divergent conceptions
which underlay them.

There are some limitations to the purpose of this volume as well as
some particular problems that are raised by such an approach. It is not
intended as a self-contained presentation of every facet and ramification
of the nationalist–imperialist conflict. Such a project would require several more volumes. Nor does the approach suggest that intellectual history offers some magical key that will unlock all the puzzles and problems
raised by the theme. And certainly it is not intended to supersede all
other approaches. Someone has said that the practice of intellectual history is like trying to nail jelly to the wall, and indeed the entities that
are subject to examination are nebulous and intangible. Any exact and
scientific way of measuring the force and impact of ideas, furthermore,
has yet to be devised, and the question must always arise as to the connection between ideas and the motives of those active men of power
who made the crucial decisions. Yet when all this is said our understanding of Canadian history would be narrow indeed if we left out of
account the climate of opinion in which the battle between imperialism
and anti-imperialism took place. In the accounts of the Boer War crisis
or the naval debate, for example, one invariably encounters allusions to
the "imperialist pressure from English Canada" for this or that policy;
yet one often comes away with the impression that we are told a good
deal more about how extreme positions were accommodated or com-
promised at the centre than we learn about the extremes themselves.
If we want to understand what imperialism and nationalism meant we
must look to those who were the exponents and interpreters of these
beliefs and try to grasp what these convictions meant to them. Only
by doing so can we appreciate why their opposition was so fundamental
and why Canadian historians are still divided as to the meaning of imperialism as a factor in Canadian history.

The selections from the historians in Part Three [of *Imperialism and
Nationalism, 1884–1914*] have been chosen with certain criteria in mind.
The secondary literature on imperialism and imperial relations in Canada
is vast in bulk and for the most part is devoted to investigations of tariff
policy, specific crises like the Boer War, or, more generally, the impact

of imperial problems in politics. Since the focus of this volume is on the ideas of nationalism and imperialism, few of these works, some of them very excellent studies, were directly and immediately appropriate. Because of this fact, and also because of the lack of scholarly studies in intellectual history, the selections presented here are therefore intended to illustrate the different ways in which historians have looked at the imperial-nationalist theme in a general and reflective way. They are also meant to suggest what happened to these ideas in the long run and how historians, looking back over a couple of generations, have weighed their significance.

NOTES

¹ Quoted in George R. Parkin, *Imperial Federation: The Problem of National Unity* (London, 1892), 85-86.
² Stephen Leacock, *The Great Victory in Canada* (reprint from *The National Review*, London, 1911), 12.

Henri Bourassa on Imperialism and Bi-culturalism, 1900-1918*

J. LEVITT

Henri Bourassa: Canadian Intellectual

Henri Bourassa had a clear vision of how to bring about Canadian nationhood, and with unbelievable stubbornness he struggled to persuade both French and English Canadians to accept his ideas. Although not an original thinker, he was well read, highly intelligent, and had absorbed the principles of three of the most important ideologies of late nineteenth century Western Europe: Catholicism, nationalism, and liberalism. These he integrated into the coherent world outlook which underlay his conception of a Canadian nation.

Bourassa's ideas penetrated the consciousness of his contemporaries because they dealt with the fundamental difficulties that confronted the builders of a Canadian nation: the relations between Canada and Great Britain, the relations between French and English Canadians, and the economic and social relations between rich and poor in an industrial and capitalist society. This book will present Bourassa's ideas on the first two problems.

*Introduction to *Henri Bourassa on Imperialism and Bi-culturalism, 1900-1918*, by J. Levitt. Copyright 1970 by Copp Clark Limited. Reprinted by permission.

The reception that Bourassa's contemporaries gave his ideas was enhanced by Bourassa's formidable forensic talent and massive personality. The article by John Boyd, included in this book, describes Bourassa as a great orator who skillfully articulated the aspirations of his French Canadian audiences. Bourassa's power as a writer is striking even today. On the one hand, with very few exceptions, he used meticulously documented facts to appeal to reason (see his pamphlets *Great Britain and Canada* and *Que Devons-Nous à l'Angleterre*); on the other, by always giving his ideas an ethical basis, he aroused moral passion. To Bourassa a policy was always either morally *right* or morally *wrong*.

Bourassa had unusual political gifts: forceful personality; keen intellect; eloquence. When he first entered Parliament, some believed that he would succeed Laurier as the most prominent French Canadian in the Liberal party. But Bourassa possessed characteristics fatal to any politician. In him were combined a dread of forcing a decision on his reluctant supporters and a positive distaste for exercising power. "I am of such a temperament that I never feel like being a whip," he commented. "I have enough trouble in keeping myself in line: I have no desire to keep others in line."[1] He had little or no tolerance for other people's opinions. He was totally unable to compromise. This made him hopeless as a politician but superb as a critic. Because he had no need to cope with political realities, his proposals were straightforward, clear, consistent with one another and suffused with moral rectitude.

Although Bourassa accepted the parliamentary system, he believed that party leaders, corrupted by their love of power, too often sacrificed principle to keep themselves in office; party policy was dictated by political advantage rather than concern for the good of the country. The only way to offset this weakness in parties was to arouse public opinion to the point where it would compel politicians anxious to win elections to take up patriotic policies. It was as such an educator of public opinion that Bourassa saw himself and indeed acted. Working outside Parliament and through his newspaper, *Le Devoir*, he won the following of enough French Canadians to make the policies he advocated of pivotal importance in the elections of 1911 and 1917. As the feat of an individual, this accomplishment is unmatched in twentieth century Canadian politics.

BOURASSA AND CANADIAN NATIONHOOD

Nationalist, Catholic, and liberal values all went into Bourassa's conception of Canadian nationhood. Accepting the nationalist nineteenth century idea that each nation had been given a specific task by God, he believed that French Canada's mission was to build the ideal society on Catholic principles and by its example win back to the Church millions of Protestants and free-thinkers in North America. The situation of

French Canadians was complicated: not only were they under British rule, but they also lived with Anglo-Canadians, more numerous than they, in the same confederation. But Bourassa was able to reconcile his patriotism to French Canada with a genuine loyalty to Canada, a British Dominion, because he was a cultural nationalist. He wished French Canada to have a culture separate from that of English Canada, but not to be a sovereign state of its own. Thus he was both a French Canadian nationalist and a Canadian nationalist at the same time.

Bourassa desired amity between English and French Canadians. He wished to see an Anglo-French Canadian nation, one in which each group would keep its own culture but would be united with the other "in a sentiment of brotherhood in a common attachment to a common country."[2] The necessary legal framework for such a bi-cultural country was possible only on the basis of liberal principles: Canada must be free to choose her foreign policies on the sole basis of her own interests, not those of the British Empire, and French Canada must be free to develop her culture everywhere in the Dominion. But Bourassa's aspirations were frustrated by the majority of Canadians who believed that Canada ought to co-operate with Great Britain in imperial defence and by an English Canada that refused to accept cultural duality.

177

IMPERIAL DEFENCE

The turn of the century saw the heyday of the imperialist movement in England. Of the many causes of this complex phenomenon, we are concerned with only one: the growing vulnerability of the Empire to powerful rivals. Faced with potential threats, Imperial defence planners turned to the Dominions for help. They wished the Dominions to contribute to a system of Imperial defence controlled centrally in London. But colonial politicians saw things differently. Previously, a colony had been responsible only for its own defence while Great Britain protected the rest of the Empire. Now a centralized defence would mean that the colonies were contributing large amounts of money to further policies over which they had no control.

Canadian politicians stood firm in defence of their military autonomy. At the Imperial conference of 1902 Laurier rejected any proposals for defense centralization, "not so much from the expense involved," but because it represented "an important departure from the principles of colonial self-government."[3] In 1904 his government placed all Canadian military affairs under the command of a Militia Council which itself was under the direct control of the Canadian Minister of Militia. Then in 1907, Canada helped to persuade the British General Staff to agree that dominion officers whom it trained would be responsible to their own cabinet ministers and not to British officials; this implied that the principle in defence relations was to be co-operation and not automatic commitment. Two years later the Laurier government was an important influence in the admiralty's decision to concede the principle of naval decentralization for the Empire. Yet while insisting on defence co-operation, Laurier did not neglect military reform. New training schemes for officers were begun and military institutions in the country were made more efficient. Such was the progress that the government accepted a plan for the dispatch of a Canadian contingent overseas if necessary.

The government's defence policy, however, aroused passionate controversy on two occasions: once in 1899 over the sending of troops to South Africa, and then again in 1910 over its decision to found a Canadian navy. At first Laurier did not believe that Canada should participate in the Boer War. He stated publicly that soldiers could not be legally sent to South Africa because the Boers did not present a threat to Canadian security. Many Anglo-Canadians, including members of his own cabinet, would not accept his decision and compelled him to change his mind; the Cabinet authorized the dispatch of troops to South Africa but emphasized that this action was not to be taken as a precedent. Bourassa, however, because he believed that the government's action was a serious step towards Canada's being automatically committed to take part in every British war, resigned from his seat in the Commons. Laurier, on the other hand, was criticized for not fully supporting the Imperial cause since Canadian troops once in South Africa were to be paid by Great Britain.

As a response to the "dreadnought" crisis which had blown up in 1909 over the possibility of the German fleet catching up to the British, Laurier proposed forming a small navy which the Cabinet could turn over to the Admiralty if it thought necessary. Bourassa and his supporters opposed the Naval Bill, arguing that it would commit Canada to every British war. Many Anglo-Canadians, however, objected to Laurier's proposal for exactly the opposite reasons; it gave the Cabinet the alternative of not sending the navy and thus undermined the principle of "One King, One Fleet, One Flag." But in Quebec Bourassa's attack on Laurier's federal naval policy was so popular that candidates whom he supported in the 1911 Federal election won sixteen seats from the Liberals. This loss of Quebec support contributed to the defeat of the Laurier government and the election of a Conservative administration headed by Robert Borden.

Although Canada was automatically committed to war in 1914, there was almost unanimous sentiment for participation. This did not, however, end the speculation over imperial relations. It was clear that as a consequence of their taking part in the War, the Dominions would demand a voice in Imperial foreign policy; and denial of this claim would result in the shattering of the Empire. This was the thesis of a book by Lionel Curtis, the leader of a group of thoughtful imperialist-minded people devoted to building imperial unity through the exchange of information and propaganda. But it was not only these intellectuals of the Round Table (the name of a quarterly founded by Curtis in which he expounded his ideas) who were concerned with the fate of the Empire. Even while leading the Canadian war effort, Prime Minister Borden found the question important enough to help set up in London an Imperial War Conference, composed of overseas prime ministers and British cabinet ministers, to chart the future of the Empire.

BOURASSA AND THE BRITISH CONNECTION

The roots of Bourassa's disagreement with Laurier over Imperial defence lay in their differing concepts of the British Empire. To Laurier, the British Empire represented liberty and justice;[4] to Bourassa, all empires, including the British, were "hateful," and stood in the way of "liberty and intellectual and moral progress." Bourassa believed that the Empire imposed serious constraints on the life of nationalities, preventing them from achieving the destiny that God had planned for them; thus it was necessary to choose between "British ideals and British domination."[5]

179

Bourassa was convinced that the aim of British Imperialists was to assure the military, commercial, and intellectual supremacy of the Anglo-Saxon race. Since this could be achieved only by force, the British were led to demand military aid from the Dominions. To ensure that this help was forthcoming, Imperialists like Joseph Chamberlain, the British Colonial Secretary, and Lord Grey, the Governor General of Canada, were plotting to revolutionize imperial defence relations so that Great Britain would continue to control foreign policy but would be able to commit the colonies, including Canada, to her wars — hence the danger of Laurier accepting the premise that when Great Britain was at war Canada was at war.[6] Canada, Bourassa insisted, could go to war only by its own consent and not by some Imperial act. This reaction was anti-imperialist, not pacifist. He was ready to agree to Canada's going to war, but only if she were directly attacked or if her vital interests were in jeopardy.

Laurier's decision to send troops to South Africa had raised in Bourassa's mind the question of Canadian responsibilities in British wars. What made Laurier's action even more reprehensible to Bourassa was that Laurier had knowingly violated the existing law. Under pressure from London Laurier had set a precedent which, if followed, would mean that Canadian forces would be automatically put at the disposal of the British in all their future wars. The consequences would be very grave for Canada: "If we send 2000 and spend $2,000,000 to fight two nations, aggregating a population of 250,000 souls, how many men shall we send and how many millions shall we expend to fight a first class power, a coalition of powers?"[7]

Bourassa was going too far to claim that a precedent had been set, even though he offered as proof the fact that Chamberlain regarded the Canadian action as such. Influential Anglo-Canadians believed that although Canada had sent troops to fight the Boers, she had not given up the right to choose whether she would engage in British wars or not. They supported Laurier when he rejected Chamberlain's plea to Canada to accept the principle of centralized defence at the Imperial Conference of 1902.

Laurier's intention to develop a Canadian navy posed the same issue. He believed that British naval supremacy was necessary to protect the Empire and all the values it stood for; if it were threatened, Canada must aid Great Britain with all her force. But he wished the Canadian cabinet to decide whether or not the navy should be turned over to the Admiralty. Bourassa, though, viewed the question from an entirely different perspective. The fact that the proposed fleet was to include cruisers and destroyers suggested to him that its purpose was not to defend Canadian coastal waters but to form part of the British fleet in time of war. Laurier claimed he would put the Canadian fleet under British control only if he believed the danger to Britain great enough, but Bourassa maintained that he would in fact do this for all wars in which Great Britain became involved. Bourassa did not trust Laurier: the Prime Minister was bound to cave in under Imperial pressure in an emergency, even as he had done in 1899 over the Boer War. To emphasize his point Bourassa implied that at the Imperial Conference of 1909 Laurier had agreed that in time of war the fleet would automatically come under British control and that this commitment had been given the force of law by the Naval Bill of 1910. This was an unfair presentation of Laurier's position.

It was natural that Bourassa would be interested in the discussion on post-war Imperial relations. He believed that by their contribution to the Imperial war effort the Dominions had left behind their colonial status. They should not put up with less say on British foreign policy than a "single cab driver in London";[8] if the Canadian people insisted on taking part in British wars they ought to have some control over the way in which their men and money were used.

Still, for Bourassa such Imperial partnership was even at best a poor alternative to complete Canadian independence. Independence would mean that Anglo-Canadians would acknowledge for once and for all that Canada and not Great Britain was their homeland. This would eliminate the major reason for quarrels between the two Canadian peoples. In foreign affairs Canada's position would be safer, for she would not be exposed to attacks from British enemies. She would have a national personality of her own and would make her decisions about war and peace for her own interests.

Such practical advantage reinforced Bourassa's ideological conviction that it was right for Canada to become independent. He believed that the natural evolution of human societies was towards nationhood. A centralized Empire was ultimately impossible because each part separated from the other by the ocean would develop in its own way according to its geographical situation, its economic needs, and its temperament. Canada, like the other communities in the Empire, was progressing towards nationhood, the achievement of which would be marked by independence — the only status that could satisfy the aspirations of a free people.

In becoming independent, Canada would be also fulfilling God's design. Bourassa believed that God had wished Canada to separate herself from the old world by breaking the imperial tie to fulfill her destiny chosen by Him in North America. That Canada, by taking part in European wars because of Imperial membership, was not carrying out this mission was no small reason for Bourassa's ardent desire for her independence.

181

Bourassa's desire to see Canada a nation was similar to that of English-speaking Liberals like John Dafoe, the editor of the *Winnipeg Free Press*, or of French-speaking ones like Wilfrid Laurier. But Dafoe believed that it was possible for the Empire to be based on the principle of autonomy and that Canada could be a greater nation for being part of it; Bourassa considered Canadian autonomy or freedom and her membership in the Empire to be mutually exclusive. Laurier, too, differed from Bourassa in his conviction that autonomy was not necessarily incompatible with retaining the British connection. To Laurier Imperial sentiment in Canada, whether reasonable or not, was a force which responsible leaders must accommodate. To Bourassa it was precisely this loyalty to the Motherland that was the main barrier to Anglo-Canadians and French Canadians co-operating to build a nation and therefore this loyalty must be opposed.

FRENCH CULTURAL RIGHTS

In the decade before the war, French cultural rights outside of Quebec become a burning issue: non-French-speaking immigration to the West and French Canadian immigration to Ontario provoked a great public debate on whether one of the functions of the schools in these areas was to further French Canadian culture.

Responding to the demands of settlers, the Laurier government decided to form two new Western provinces. Written into the Autonomy Bill of 1905 was the legal framework for a school system that many people, including Clifford Sifton, the Minister of the Interior, believed substituted denominational for what should have been public schools. A public uproar arose; some regarded it as an attack on the autonomy of the new provinces; militant Protestants objected to turning over the direction of any schools to the Church; many Westerners favoured the idea of the melting pot and opposed a school system which would further divide a population already fragmented by ethnic origin. To satisfy these critics, Laurier rewrote the offending clause: the schools would be run by the provincial government, not by religious institutions. Catholics were free to set up a separate school in districts where they were a *minority*; however, since they clustered together, they were usually the majority in their district and thus were compelled to attend public schools. In 1905 there were only nine Catholic "separate" schools in the Northwest. French Canadians were granted two other concessions in the new provinces. They were allowed religious instruction for a half-hour after half-past-three, and could have a primary course in the French language if they desired it.

182
In 1912 the separate school question was briefly revived in the West when the territory of Keewatin was joined to Manitoba. A demand arose that one of the conditions of annexation would be the guarantee of the territory's right to separate schools. But Robert Borden, then Prime Minister, made no provision for such rights in his annexation bill and public interest soon petered out.

French cultural rights became a burning issue when the movement of French Canadians into Eastern Ontario changed the relative positions of French and English in the schools. Although still the legal language of instruction, English became just another subject on the curriculum; French became the real means of communication. Towards the end of 1910 opposition to this arrangement arose in Ontario: Canadian nationalists were convinced that a common Canadian consciousness could not be created unless English were the common language.[9] Orangemen feared that the spread of French would undermine the Anglo-Saxon character of the province and so injure the Empire; Irish Catholics believed that the identification of separate schools with French would prejudice their schools receiving public grants. What these three groups had in common was a conviction that everybody must learn English and a determination to reject any legal status for French. This point of view was accepted by the two major provincial parties, the Conservatives and the Liberals.

In September 1910 at the Eucharistic Congress in Montreal, Archbishop Bourne of Westminister sparked public debate by declaring that if the Catholic Church wished to make progress in Canada, it ought to be English-speaking. Bourassa's rebuttal came in his most celebrated speech, *Religion, Langue, Nationalité*. The excitement aroused by this clash led the French Canadian press to reveal the details of a well-kept secret: that Bishop Michael Francis Fallon, the Bishop of London, had undertaken to eliminate French in the Catholic schools of his diocese on the grounds that students were learning neither English nor French.

The subsequent public furor caused the government to assign Dr. F.W. Merchant, an official of the Ontario Department of Education, to investigate the schools where French was the language of instruction. After the Merchant report found that much was lacking in the teaching of English in these schools, the Conservative provincial government issued Regulation 17 late in 1912. Regulation 17 was to apply only to certain schools, designated each year as English–French schools. In these schools French was permitted as a language of instruction only for the first two years of school. Where French had "hitherto" been a subject of study, instruction in the French language for no more than one hour each day might be provided. (Many French Canadians, including Laurier, took this to mean that French would be prohibited in all future schools.) Any school which did not comply with Regulation 17 would no longer be entitled to public funds.

Although the government claimed to be interested only in improving the quality of the English spoken by Franco-Ontarians, the majority of French Canadians saw Regulation 17 as a prelude to the complete removal of French from Ontario schools. Franco-Ontarian teachers in the Ottawa Valley refused to comply with the Regulation and their students walked out of schools. In 1915 some hundred and fifty schools outside of Ottawa refused to accept the Regulation and gave up the provincial grant. In Ottawa itself the majority of the Separate School Board defied the Department of Education. The government responded by appointing a commission to take over its duties. Meanwhile important Quebec personalities, including Church dignitaries, led a campaign to raise funds for "les blessés d'Ontario." The Quebec legislature, asserting that the Ontario government did not understand British principles, authorized local Catholic commissions to contribute officially to the fund.

Outside intervention helped to ease the crisis. In October 1916 Pope Benedict XV issued an encyclical which most Catholics interpreted as supporting the position of Bishop Fallon: the study of French was not to be pushed to the point where it endangered Catholic schools in Ontario. Significantly, Bourassa was silent on the encyclical. A month later, the Privy Council in London established the basis for a compromise by ruling that Regulation 17 was legal, but the commission which had taken over the duties of the Separate School Board was not.

For four years the controversy had raged, becoming especially violent after the Great War began. Many French Canadians believed the majority of Ontarians hypocritical in supporting a war for freedom while repressing French at home. Armand Lavergne, a colleague of Bourassa's, spoke for many of his compatriots when he cried out in the Quebec legislature, "I ask myself if the German regime might not be favourably compared with the Boches of Ontario."[10] On their side, Anglo-Ontarians continued to support Regulation 17 because they wished Ontario to be exclusively English. Many of them believed that the French Canadians

183

were using the question of French in Ontario schools as an excuse for not giving full support to the war and they resented what they regarded as an attempt of French Canada to compel them to change the Regulation by threatening to slow down the war effort. Either Regulation 17 or the war would have strained relations between the English and French; the conjunction of the two exacerbated hostility to a level of bitterness hitherto unknown between the two peoples.

BOURASSA AND BI-CULTURALISM

Bourassa became the most prominent spokesman of French Canadian resentment. Deeply convinced that Catholics should control the schools their children attended to ensure the teaching of religious values, he also believed God had bestowed on French Canadians a particular genius, character, and temperament which could be fully expressed only through the French language. They were something more than British subjects who happened to speak French. Bourassa exhorted his compatriots to fight for French Canadian culture. If they meekly accepted that it had no legal rights in English Canada, on what basis would they oppose the application of this false principle to Quebec itself?

For Bourassa, faith and language were inextricably united. He vehemently rejected the contention of English-speaking Catholics that it would be better for the Church to present an English image: it was the natural right of everyone to speak his maternal tongue; to use the Church as an instrument of assimilation would be "odious." There were other practical reasons for the Church to reject the argument: English-speaking Catholics themselves were open to the social influences of Protestant and free-thinking North Americans, while apostasy was rare among French Canadians, whose language served as a barrier to heretical influences.

But such Catholic and racial values, although acceptable to significant segments of French Canadian opinion, made little impression in English Canada where the majority was Protestant. Yet French Canadian culture could only survive outside Quebec if Anglo-Canadians accepted cultural duality. To persuade them, Bourassa advanced two main propositions: the constitution was based on the principle of cultural duality and the Canadian confederation could not survive unless such bi-culturalism was accepted by English Canada. These arguments were not mere debating tricks with Bourassa; he believed them with total sincerity.

Bourassa viewed Confederation as the result of an agreement between English and French to accept the equal rights of each culture throughout the Dominion. The Fathers of Confederation had envisaged Canada as a bi-cultural country. If their behests had been followed, then the West, acquired "in the name of and with the money of the whole Canadian people,"[11] would have been French as well as English, Catholic as well

184

as Protestant. It would have been made clear to all immigrants that the West was Anglo-French.

In the first years after Confederation, maintained Bourassa, the federal government affirmed the bi-cultural nature of the country by the Manitoba Act of 1870 and the North West Territories Bill of 1875, each of which accepted French as one of the official languages and established a denominational school system. But in 1890, Ottawa had permitted the territorial government of the North West to extinguish the legal status of French. Two years later, the school system began to be modified until in 1901 it was, in fact, a state school system.[12] Because the ordinances of the Territorial Government which had changed the school system violated the spirit and text of the 1875 law passed by the federal government, a government superior in authority to that of the North West Territories, Bourassa considered them illegal. By accepting the Sifton amendment in 1905, the government legitimized these illegal school ordinances and ratified the limitations of the rights of Western French Canadians to schools of their own.

185

The bi-cultural compact implied the right not only to separate schools but also to instruction in French. By giving both French and English official status in Parliament, the Fathers had made it clear that they wished both languages to co-exist everywhere in public life: in church, in court, and in government. These rights would be meaningless if the English provinces prevented French Canadian children from acquiring a perfect knowledge of their own language.

Bourassa also insisted that cultural duality was necessary if Confederation were to last. The materialist ethos of the United States was penetrating Canada; the unchecked consequence of the invasion of such values would lead to the slow absorption of Canada into the United States. The greatest barrier to "l'américanisme"[13] was French Canada, because being Catholic, it rejected materialism and the American way of life. But if French Canadians continued to be humiliated, they would no longer resist Americanization, for they could see no advantage to remaining British.

Refusal to accept cultural duality threatened Confederation in yet another way. French Canadians would never feel that Canada was their homeland unless their culture was free to develop. Thus national unity was conditioned on cultural duality. The alternative was constant instability and crisis. Confederation, Bourassa maintained, would not survive without the reciprocal respect of the rights of the two races.

Such was Bourassa's general attitude towards cultural duality. He also had a number of specific points to make about each issue. The Autonomy Bill specifically forbade Catholics from organizing separate schools where they were a majority in the district. Yet they would reconcile themselves more easily to sending their children to a government school if it were called "separate" and not "public"; Catholic school boards would hire

Catholic teachers and thus all lessons would be infused with a Church spirit. The new bill compelled most Catholic children to attend public schools where they could not be protected should the Minister of Education decide to suppress religious or French teaching. The advantages to Catholics of attending schools that could be called separate even though they were essentially controlled by the government were so important to Bourassa that he declared that if the Catholics were allowed to set up such "separate" schools he would withdraw his opposition to the new bill.

Bourassa denied that instruction in French in Ontario schools would harm national unity. Even if proficient in French, French Canadians had no more intention of becoming attached to France than Americans had of becoming British colonists again. Nor did it mean, if French were granted official status in English Canada that the languages of the immigrants ought to receive similar recognition: the French claim, after all, was based on the bi-cultural compact. Bourassa also denied that a bilingual people could not form a homogeneous nation, arguing that discord would stem only from the attempts of the majority to force their language on the minority.

Then too there were some practical advantages to French.

Outside the English-speaking world French was useful in commerce and diplomacy. More important it was the language of cultivated minds. When Canada had developed sufficiently to appreciate art and literature, claimed Bourassa, it would turn to French as an instrument of communication with the best of European civilization.

Bourassa's claim that Confederation was based on a bi-cultural pact is debatable. True, the Fathers had recognized the separateness of the French Canadians of Lower Canada: the predominately French Canadian province would still control its French Catholic schools, and French would be an official language in the federal parliament and courts. Such measures would enable French Canadians in Quebec both to develop their own culture and take part in the public life of the new Dominion. But on the other hand, the Fathers made no provision for the legal status of French in provinces other than Quebec; the constitution furnished no protection for the Acadians. Professor Donald Creighton has shown that the Manitoba Act of 1870 and the Territorial Act of 1875 were not conscious steps in a plan to extend bi-culturalism to the West; instead, they were passed because of fortuitous circumstances and indeed were then quickly reversed.[14] Thus the Fathers did not object to cultural duality but neither did they determine to make Canada a bi-cultural country.

However, Bourassa's proposition that Confederation would not survive without cultural duality has been accepted by a large number of English-speaking Canadians. Many feel guilty about the shabby treatment given to French outside of Quebec. More important, many believe such cultural equality necessary if Quebec is to remain in Confederation.

CONSCRIPTION

As the war went on, it became clear that there was a great difference of opinion between French and English over Canada's responsibility to the Allied side. Great numbers of Anglo-Canadians believed that Canada should be ready to fight to the end of her resources in both men and money. French Canadians, however, indicated by their markedly low rate of enlistment that they thought Canada should play a relatively minor role. This issue came to the fore over the proposal of the Borden government in the spring of 1917, to conscript men for overseas service. Voluntary enlistments, which were falling due to war-weariness, could not fill the gaps left by the high casualty rate suffered by Canadian troops on the Western front since the first of the year.

Borden asked Laurier to join him in a coalition government on a program of introducing conscription. The latter refused for a number of reasons: conscription was repugnant to him personally; if he took part in a coalition he would become responsible for a policy that he had no share in making; he suspected that it was a trick to split the Liberal party. But equally important, as he emphasized to friends, if he accepted conscription, he would be breaking his promise to Quebec and thus would virtually be handing over the province to Bourassa and his friends. Borden, however, succeeded in inducing a number of Liberals to join him in a "union" government which defeated Laurier in the federal election of December 1917. In contrast to the election of 1911, Bourassa now threw his support behind Laurier.

187

Bourassa had no objection to conscription as such. His attitude to it was conditioned by what he thought about the war. Although in 1914 he had supported Canadian participation, by 1916 he had come to modify his opinion: the war was supposedly being fought for the right of small nations to live, but in fact the great powers were smashing up the small nationalities. He followed the lead of Pope Benedict XV in calling for an end to the war, for a negotiated peace in which neither side would emerge solely victorious. Since he believed that there was no real Canadian interest involved in the war, he was logically consistent to claim that those who opposed conscription were the most patriotic Canadians; and that if French Canadians adopted this stand, it was because they were very clear in their minds that they owed their patriotism to Canada and Canada alone, unlike Anglo-Canadians whose focus of loyalty shifted between Canada and Great Britain.

BOURASSA'S ACHIEVEMENTS

Many Canadian historians have been critical of Bourassa, presenting him as the spokesman for narrow French Canadian clerical and racial elements that had refused to do their part in building Canadian unity (see

Clash of Opinion). Yet it would be difficult to find any statement of his in support of Canadian autonomy within the Empire or of French Canadian rights outside of Quebec that was not logically consistent with his program of achieving Canadian nationhood.

What his critics object to, however, is not Bourassa's program but the consequence of his determination to promote it. In 1911, by attacking Laurier, he helped bring the "more Imperialist of the two national parties"[15] to power. And since many of the Quebec members who had been elected because they had been endorsed by Bourassa gave their support to the Conservative naval program, French Canadians in Borden's Cabinet soon lost popularity in French Canada. Without influence in Quebec, their voices in Ottawa became feeble. Thus the manpower crisis was met by a government that was to all intents and purposes Anglo-Canadian.

Again Bourassa used rhetoric that was so strong about the French language issue during the war that he substantially embittered French–English relations and thereby contributed to the emotional climate out of which came the storm around conscription. In sum, the charge against Bourassa is that he went too far, that he was an extremist.

Yet from his own point of view, Bourassa's tactics made good sense. What he was trying to do in 1911, he said, was to send to Ottawa a block of members (whom he called Nationalists) who would hold the balance of power between the two parties and thus force the new government to revise the Naval Bill. What is more, he would have achieved his purpose if Borden had won a few seats less in Ontario and the Nationalists a few more in Quebec.[16] Even with the number of seats the Nationalists did win, they would have formed an important force within the Conservative government had Bourassa accepted a Cabinet position. But he was not prepared to undertake the tough responsibility of political leadership.

It was only natural for Bourassa to take advantage of the Anglo-Canadians' claim that they were fighting for freedom abroad to demand that they show good faith by granting equal rights to Franco-Ontarians at home. If as a consequence Canada's war effort were to slacken, it would not be too serious since Canada's role was a minor one and the Allies ought to be aiming at negotiating a just peace and not at winning the war.

Bourassa then had some grounds for believing that his tactics would be successful. But even without such hopes he would have acted the same way. He was not pragmatic: that he might not succeed in persuading Anglo-Canadians to do the right thing was no reason for not trying. It was on this point that Laurier differed profoundly from him. Although Laurier agreed with a great deal of Bourassa's program of Canadian nationalism, he did not defy Anglo-Canadian opinion because he wished the Liberal party to be the instrument of building unity between French and English. As an independent critic, Bourassa proclaimed what Anglo-Canadians ought to do; as a politician with responsibilities, Laurier proposed only what they would agree to do.

Many who are sympathetic with Laurier fail to see that even if he was right to contend that satisfactory relations between English and French must be founded on the possible rather than the ideal, it does not mean that left to himself he would have found the right point of compromise. Laurier's most significant action for Canadian unity was to reject conscription and refuse to join the Union coalition. This left the way open for the preservation of the Liberal party as an effective forum for the reconciliation of English and French in the post-war decade in Canada. But, as Professor Ramsay Cook has argued, Laurier's primary motive for these actions was his fear of handing Quebec over to Bourassa.[17] Because Bourassa would not compromise, Laurier was unable to compromise; it was the tension between the critic and the politician that determined the fate of the Liberal party.

189

Bourassa did a great deal to turn Canadian public opinion against any form of centralization of Imperial foreign policy and defence. His greatest accomplishment, however, was to convince succeeding generations of French Canadians that their language ought to have the same rights as the English language. Thus he, more than any other individual, was responsible for making his dictum that Canada could only survive as a bi-cultural country much truer now than when he first enunciated it at the turn of the century.

NOTES

[1] H. Bourassa, *Canada: House of Commons Debates*, Feb. 19, 1900, p. 500.

[2] H. Bourassa, "Réponse amicale à la vérité," *La Nationaliste*, April 3, 1904.

[3] Quoted in R. Preston, *Canada and Imperial Defense* (Toronto, 1976), 305.

[4] H.B. Neatby, "Laurier and Imperialism," Canadian Historical Association, *Report* (1955), 25.

[5] H. Bourassa, *Canadian Nationalism and the War* (Montreal, 1916), 14.

[6] Bourassa usually ignored Laurier's qualifications. What Laurier said was this: "If England is at war, we are at war and liable to attack. I do not say that we shall always be attacked, neither do I say that we would take part in all the wars of England. That is a matter that we must be guided by the circumstance upon which the Canadian Parliament will have to pronounce, and will have to decide in its own best judgement." O.D. Skelton, *Life and Letters of Sir Wilfrid Laurier* (Toronto, 1965), 11: 125.

[7] Henri Bourassa, *Canada House of Commons Debates*, March 13, 1900, p. 1802.

[8] H. Bourassa, *Independence or Imperial Partnership*, (Montreal, 1916), 47.

[9] C.B. Sissons quotes a small English boy to a French teacher: "This country does not belong to France and you must all learn English; my grandpa says so." C. B. Sissons, *Bilingual Schools in Canada* (London, 1917), 66.

[10] *Canadian Annual Review, 1916* (Toronto, 1917), 34.

[11] H. Bourassa, *Canada, House of Commons*, July 5, 1905, p. 8848.

[12] In the same speech Bourassa did not refer to the abolition of the rights of French culture in Manitoba, probably because he had supported Laurier's position on the Manitoba School question in 1896.

[13] H. Bourassa, *La langue française et l'avenir de notre race* (Quebec, 1913), 17.

[14] D.G. Creighton, "John A. Macdonald, Confederation, and the Canadian West," in C. Brown, *Minorities, Schools and Politics* (Toronto, 1969), 8.

[15] H.B. Neatby, *Laurier and a Liberal Quebec: A Study in Political Management* (unpublished Ph.D. thesis, University of Toronto, 1956), 350.

[16] J.M. Beck, *Pendulum of Power* (Scarborough, 1968), 133.

[17] Ramsay Cook, "Dafoe, Laurier, and the Formation of Union Government," *Canadian Historical Review* 42, 3 (September 1961): 197.

Topic Six

Immigration and Western Settlement

Between 1896 and 1914 over two million immigrants arrived in Canada, the majority of them settling in the West.

Changed world conditions partially explain the expansion of immigration to Canada. With the best homestead land in the American West settled by the 1890s, immigrants began considering the Canadian prairies — "the last best West" — as a viable alternative. The worldwide prosperity of the turn of the century enabled more immigrants to come to Canada. The efforts of the Liberal government of Wilfrid Laurier, elected in 1896, also helped to settle the West. Under the leadership of Clifford Sifton, the minister of the interior, the Liberals vigorously recruited immigrants. Sifton doubled, then redoubled, the expenditures of the Immigration Branch. He sent government agents to Britain, the United States, and various European countries armed with propagandist literature on western Canada. In Europe the Canadian government offered special bonuses to steamship agents booking immigrants to Canada. Immigration officials assured various ethnic and sectarian groups that they could establish bloc settlements and retain their customs in the New World.

A large proportion of the new immigrants came from Britain and the United States and thus assimilated easily into Canadian society. A significant number, however, arrived from continental Europe and found it difficult to adjust because of cultural and linguistic differences. Howard Palmer examines the negative response of the dominant Anglo-Canadian community to these "foreign" newcomers in "Reluctant Hosts: Anglo-Canadian Views of Multiculturalism in the Twentieth Century." In his novel *Under the Ribs of Death* (from which an excerpt is included here), John Marlyn imaginatively re-creates the immigrant's difficulties and frustrations in trying to fit into, and be accepted in, the dominant Anglo-Canadian community.

For an overview of immigration to western Canada, see the chapter "Opening Up the Land of Opportunity," in R.C. Brown and R. Cook's

Canada, 1896-1921: A Nation Transformed (Toronto: McClelland and Stewart, 1974), 49-82. Pierre Berton's *The Promised Land: Settling the West, 1896-1914* (Toronto: McClelland and Stewart, 1984) is a popular treatment.

Elizabeth B. Mitchell's *In Western Canada before the War* (Saskatoon: Western Producer Prairie Books, 1981; first published in 1915) is a contemporary look at western settlement. David Jones recounts the settlers' experience in the dry-belt area of southern Alberta and southern Saskatchewan in the 1920s in *Empire of Dust: Settling and Abandoning the Prairie Dry Belt* (Edmonton: University of Alberta Press, 1987). Gerald Friesen provides an overview of the subject of western immigration and settlement in "Immigrant Communities, 1870-1940: The Struggle for Cultural Survival" in his *The Canadian Prairies: A History* (Toronto: University of Toronto Press, 1984), 242-73. *Immigration and the Rise of Multiculturalism*, ed. H. Palmer (Toronto: Copp Clark, 1975), contains a good selection of primary readings on the subject of immigration. An *191* important study is Donald Avery's *Dangerous Foreigners: European Immigrant Workers and Labour Radicalism in Canada, 1896-1932* (Toronto: McClelland and Stewart, 1979). Howard Palmer reviews the Anglo-Albertans' reaction to "foreign" immigrants in *Patterns of Prejudices: A History of Nativism in Alberta* (Toronto: McClelland and Stewart, 1982). The immigrant's viewpoint is portrayed in John Marlyn's novel *Under the Ribs of Death* (Toronto: McClelland and Stewart, 1971) and in R.F. Harney and H. Troper's *Immigrants: A Portrait of the Urban Experience, 1890-1930* (Toronto: Van Nostrand Reinhold, 1975). The Department of the Secretary of State has published individual histories of several ethnic groups in Canada. In the series' introductory volume, *Coming Canadians: An Introduction to a History of Canadian Peoples* (Toronto: McClelland and Stewart, 1988), Jean Burnet and Howard Palmer survey ethnic relations in Canada. On Clifford Sifton's role in promoting immigration to the West see D.J. Hall's two-volume biography, *Clifford Sifton*, vol. 1, *The Young Napoleon, 1861-1900* (Vancouver: University of British Columbia Press, 1981), vol. 2, *A Lonely Eminence, 1901-1929* (Vancouver: University of British Columbia Press, 1985), and his "Clifford Sifton: Immigration and Settlement Policy, 1896-1905," in *The Settlement of the West*, ed. H. Palmer (Calgary: University of Calgary Comprint Publishing Co., 1977), 60-85. Two articles provide an overview of work in Canadian immigration and ethnic history: H. Palmer, "Canadian Immigration and Ethnic History in the 1970's and 1980's," *Journal of Canadian Studies* 17 (Spring 1982): 35-50; and Roberto Perin, "Clio as Ethnic: The Third Force in Canadian Historiography," *Canadian Historical Review* 64 (December 1983): 441-67.

Reluctant Hosts: Anglo-Canadian Views of Multiculturalism in the Twentieth Century*

HOWARD PALMER

Introduction

The way in which Anglo-Canadians have reacted to immigration during the twentieth century has not simply been a function of the numbers of immigrants or the state of the nation's economy. The immigration of significant numbers of non-British and non-French people raised fundamental questions about the type of society which would emerge in English-speaking Canada; hence, considerable public debate has always surrounded the issue of immigration in Canada. The questions which have repeatedly been raised include the following: Were the values and institutions of Anglo-Canadian society modelled exclusively on a British mold and should immigrants be compelled to conform to that mold? Or, would a distinctive identity emerge from the biological and cultural mingling of Anglo-Canadians with new immigrant groups? Would cultural pluralism itself give English-speaking Canada a distinctive identity? These three questions reflect the three theories of assimilation which have dominated the twentieth century debate over immigrant adjustment.

The assimilation theory which achieved early public acceptance was Anglo-conformity. This view demanded that immigrants renounce their ancestral culture and traditions in favour of the behaviour and values of Anglo-Canadians. Although predominant prior to World War II, Anglo-conformity fell into disrepute and was replaced in the popular mind by the "melting pot" theory of assimilation. This view envisaged a biological merging of settled communities with new immigrant groups and a blending of their cultures into a new Canadian type. Currently, a third theory of assimilation — "cultural pluralism" or "multiculturalism" — is vying for public acceptance. This view postulates the preservation of some aspects of immigrant culture and communal life within the context of Canadian citizenship and political and economic integration into Canadian society.[1]

There has been a recent burgeoning of historical and sociological research on Anglo-Canadian attitudes toward ethnic minorities. Much of

192

*Adapted from *Multiculturalism as State Policy*, 1976 Canadian Consultative Council of Multiculturalism, Department of Secretary of State for Canada. Reprinted with permission of the Minister of Supply and Services Canada, 1989.

this research contradicts the view which has been advanced by some Anglo-Canadian historians[2] and politicians that Anglo-Canadians have always adopted the "mosaic" as opposed to the American "melting pot" approach. Much of this rhetoric has simply been wishful thinking. Perhaps immigrant groups did not "melt" as much in Canada as in the United States, but this is not because Anglo-Canadians were more anxious to encourage the cultural survival of ethnic minorities. There has been a long history of racism and discrimination against ethnic minorities in English-speaking Canada, along with strong pressures for conformity to Anglo-Canadian ways.

The "Settlement" Period and the Predominance of Anglo-conformity: 1867–1920

Among the several objectives of the architects of the Canadian confederation in 1867, none was more important than the effort to accommodate the needs of the two main cultural communities. There was virtually no recognition of ethnic diversity aside from the British–French duality. This is, of course, somewhat understandable since at the time of confederation, only eight percent of the population of three and one half million were of non-British[3] or Non-French ethnic origin. There were, however, significant numbers of people of German and Dutch origin, well-established black and Jewish communities, as well as a few adventurers and entrepreneurs from most European ethnic groups now in Canada.

193

The proportion of people of other than British, French, or native origin in Canada remained small until nearly the turn of the century; the United States proved more attractive for most European emigrants. In fact it was attractive for many Canadians as well, and the Dominion barely maintained its population. But with the closing of the American frontier which coincided with improving economic conditions in Canada and an active immigration promotion campaign by Wilfrid Laurier's Liberal government, many immigrants began to come to the newly opened land of western Canada in the late 1890s.[4] Immigration policy gave preference to farmers, and most non-British immigrants came to farm in western Canada. However, some immigrants ended up working in mines, laying railway track, or drifting into the urban working class.[5] During this first main wave of immigration between 1896 and 1914, three million immigrants, including large numbers of British laborers, American farmers, and eastern European peasants, came to Canada. Within the period of 1901 to 1911, Canada's population rocketed by 43 percent and the percentage of immigrants in the country as a whole topped 22 percent. In 1911, people of non-British and non-French origin formed 34 percent of the population of Manitoba, 40 percent of the population of Saskatchewan, and 33 percent of the population of Alberta.

Throughout the period of this first large influx of non-British, non-French immigrants (indeed up until World War II), anglo-conformity was the predominant ideology of assimilation in English-speaking Canada.[6] For better or for worse, there were few proponents of either the melting pot or cultural pluralism. Proponents of anglo-conformity argued that it was the obligation of new arrivals to conform to the values and institutions of Canadian society — which were already fixed. During this period when scarcely anyone questioned the verities of God, King, and country, there was virtually no thought given to the possibility that "WASP" values might not be the apex of civilization which all men should strive for.

Since at this time the British Empire was at its height, and the belief in "progress" and Anglo-Saxon and white superiority was taken for granted throughout the English-speaking world, a group's desirability as potential immigrants varied almost directly with its members' physical and cultural distance from London (England), and the degree to which their skin pigmentation conformed to Anglo-Saxon white. Anglo-Canadians regarded British and American immigrants as the most desirable.[7] Next came northern and western Europeans who were regarded as culturally similar and hence assimilable. They were followed by central and eastern Europeans, who in the eyes of Clifford Sifton and immigration agents, had a slight edge on Jews and southern Europeans, because they were more inclined to go to and remain on the land. These groups were followed in the ethnic pecking order by the "strange" religious sects, the Hutterites, Mennonites, and Doukhobors, who were invariably lumped together by public officials and the general public despite significant religious and cultural differences between them. Last, but not least (certainly not least in the eyes of those British Columbians and their sympathizers elsewhere in the country who worried about the "Asiatic" hordes), were the Asian immigrants — the Chinese, Japanese, and East Indians (the latter of whom were dubbed "Hindoos," despite the fact that most were Sikhs). Running somewhere close to last were black immigrants, who did not really arise as an issue because of the lack of aspiring candidates, except in 1911, when American blacks were turned back at the border by immigration officials because they allegedly could not adapt to the cold winters in Canada — a curious about-face for a department which was reassuring other American immigrants that Canadian winters were relatively mild.[8]

As might be expected, prevailing assumptions about the relative assimilability of these different groups were quickly transformed into public debate over whether immigrants whose assimilability was problematic should be allowed into the country. During this first wave of immigration, considerable opposition developed to the entry of central, southern, and eastern European immigrants, Orientals, and to the three pacifist sects. Opposition to these groups came from a variety of sources, for a variety of reasons. But one of the most pervasive fears of opinion leaders was that central, southern, and eastern Europeans, and Orientals would wash away Anglo-Saxon traditions of self-government in a sea of illiteracy and inexperience with "free institutions."[9] Many English-Canadian intellectuals, like many American writers at the time, thought that North Amer-

195

Vancouver Public Library (7641).

These Sikh lumber workers were a few of the South Asians allowed into Canada in the pre-World War I era. Many were turned back, like the shipload of Indians on the *Komagata Maru* who were prevented from docking at Vancouver harbour. Once here South Asians met racial discrimination by the dominant Anglo-Canadian population.

ica's greatness was ensured so long as its Anglo-Saxon character was preserved. Writers emphasized an Anglo-Saxon tradition of political freedom and self-government and the "white man's" mission to spread Anglo-Saxon blessings.[10] Many intellectuals and some politicians viewed Orientals and central, southern, and eastern European immigrants as a threat to this tradition and concluded that since they could not be assimilated they would have to be excluded. The introduction in Canada of a head tax on Chinese immigrants, a "gentlemen's agreement" with Japan which restricted the number of Japanese immigrants, the passing of orders-in-council which restricted immigration from India, the gradual introduction of restrictive immigration laws in 1906, 1910, and 1919 relative to European immigration, and the tightening of naturalization laws were based in considerable part on the assumptions of anglo-conformity — immigrants who were culturally or racially inferior and incapable of being assimilated either culturally or biologically would have to be excluded.[11] Those who rose to the immigrants' defence argued almost entirely from economic grounds: immigration from non-British sources was needed to aid in economic development, not because it might add anything to Canada's social or cultural life.

196

Although the trend toward restrictionism during the early 1900s seemed to indicate a government trend toward anglo-conformity in response to public pressure, for the most part between 1867 and 1945, there was no explicit federal government policy with regard to the role of non-British and non-French ethnic groups in Canadian society. It was generally assumed, however, that immigrants would eventually be assimilated into either English-Canadian or French-Canadian society. A recent careful study of Clifford Sifton's attitudes toward immigrant groups in Canadian society concludes Sifton assumed that central and eastern Europeans " . . . would be 'nationalized' in the long run through their experience on the land. . . . "[12] The federal government's concern was tied to the economic consequences of immigration, while schools, the primary agents of assimilation, were under provincial jurisdiction. The federal government had encouraged Mennonites and Icelanders to settle in blocks in Manitoba during the 1870's and had given them special concessions (including local autonomy for both and military exemptions for the Mennonites) to entice them to stay in Canada rather than move to the United States.[13] But this was not because of any conscious desire to make Canada a cultural mosaic, nor was it out of any belief in the value of cultural diversity. Block settlements, by providing social and economic stability, were simply a way of getting immigrants to settle in the west and remain there.[14] The government policy was pragmatic and concerned primarily with economic growth and "nation building"; there was little rhetoric in immigration propaganda picturing Canada as a home for oppressed minorities who would be able to pursue their identities in Canada.

Provincial governments were faced with the problems of assimilation more directly than the federal government since the provinces maintained jurisdiction over the educational systems. The whole question of the varying attitudes of provincial authorities toward assimilation is much too complex to outline in this article; suffice it to say that with some notable exceptions (like the bilingual school system in Manitoba between 1896 and 1916, and the school system which was established for Hutterites in Alberta), anglo-conformity was the predominant aim of the public school system and was an underlying theme in the textbooks.

Anglo-conformity was most pronounced during World War I as nationalism precipitated insistent hostility to "hyphenated Canadianism" and demanded an unswerving loyalty. For many Anglo-Canadians during the war, loyalty and cultural and linguistic uniformity were synonymous. During the war, western provincial governments acted to abolish the bilingual schools which had previously been allowed.[15] The formation of the Union government of Conservatives and Liberals during the First World War was an attempt to create an Anglo-Saxon party, dedicated to "unhyphenated Canadianism" and the winning of the war; even if this meant trampling on the rights of immigrants through press censorship and the imposition of the War Time Elections Act which disfranchised "enemy aliens" who had become Canadian citizens after March 21, 1902.[16] Various voluntary associations like the YMCA, IODE, National Council of Women, Canadian Girls in Training, Girl Guides, Big Brothers and Big Sisters Organizations, and Frontier College, as well as the major Protestant denominations, also intensified their efforts to "Canadianize" the immigrants, particularly at the close of the war when immigrant support for radical organizations brought on anti-radical nativist fears of the "menace of the alien."[17] The pressures for conformity were certainly real, even if English-Canadians could not always agree completely on the exact nature of the norm to which immigrants were to be assimilated.

All the major books on immigration prior to 1920, including J.S. Woodsworth's *Strangers Within Our Gates*, J.T.M. Anderson's *The Education of the New Canadian*, Ralph Connor's *The Foreigner*, Alfred Fitzpatrick's *Handbook for New Canadians*, C.A. Magrath's *Canada's Growth and Some Problems Affecting It*, C.B. Sissons, *Bilingual Schools in Canada*, and W.G. Smith, *A Study in Canadian Immigration*, were based on the assumptions of anglo-conformity. To lump all these books together is of course to oversimplify since they approached the question of immigration with varying degrees of nativism (or anti-foreign sentiment), and humanitarianism. Nor were all of the voluntary organizations' attempted "Canadianization" work among immigrants motivated solely by the fear that immigrants would undermine the cultural homogeneity of English-speaking Canada. Many of these writers and organizations saw their work with the immigrants as a means of fighting social problems and helping immigrants achieve a basic level of political, social, and economic integration into Canadian society. But it cannot be denied that their basic assumption was that of anglo-conformity. Cultural diversity was either positively dangerous, or was something that would and should disappear with time, and with the help of Anglo-Canadians.

Perhaps it should be emphasized that the individuals advocating anglo-conformity were not just the reactionaries of their day. Protestant Social Gospellers (including J.S. Woodsworth, later one of the founders of the CCF) who played such a prominent role in virtually all the reform movements of the pre-World War I period (including women's rights, temperance, and labor, farm, and penal reform) believed that immigrants needed to be assimilated to Anglo-Canadian Protestant values as part of the effort to establish a truly Christian society in English-speaking Canada.[18] Women's groups pushing for the franchise argued that certainly they deserved the vote if "ignorant foreigners" had it, and joined in the campaign to Canadianize the immigrants who "must be educated to high standards or our whole national life will be lowered by their presence among us."[19]

198

But there was a central contradiction in Anglo-Canadian attitudes toward ethnic minorities. Non–Anglo-Saxon immigrants were needed to open the west and to do the heavy jobs of industry. This meant not only the introduction of culturally distinctive groups, but groups which would occupy the lower rungs of the socioeconomic system. The pre-1920 period was the period of the formation of, and the most acute expression of, what was later called the "vertical mosaic." Anglo-Canadians were not used to the idea of cultural diversity, nor the degree of class stratification which developed during this period of rapid settlement and industrialization. The answer to all the problems of social diversity which the immigrants posed was assimilation. The difficulty however with achieving this goal of assimilation was not only the large numbers of immigrants, or the fact that not all (or even a majority) of them wanted to be assimilated. One of the major factors preventing assimilation was discrimination by the Anglo-Canadian majority.

The basic contradiction, then, of Anglo-Canadian attitudes as expressed through the "Canadianization" drives was the tension between the twin motives of humanitarianism and nativism — between the desire to include non-British immigrants within a community and eliminate cultural differences and the desire to stay as far away from them as possible because of their presumed "undesirability." This contradiction was graphically revealed at the national conference of the IODE in 1919. The women passed one resolution advocating a "Canadianization campaign" to "propagate British ideals and institutions," to "banish old world points of view, old world prejudices, old world rivalries and suspicion" and to make new Canadians "100 percent British in language, thought, feeling, and impulse." Yet they also passed another resolution protesting "foreigners" taking British names.[20]

It does not appear that this was simply a case of the Anglo-Canadian majority being divided between those who wanted to pursue a strategy of assimilation and those who wanted to pursue a strategy of subordination and segregation. Certainly there was some division along these lines, but as suggested by the IODE resolutions, discrimination and anglo-conformity were often simply two different sides of the same coin — the coin being the assumption of the inferiority of non–Anglo-Saxons.

What developed throughout English-speaking Canada during this period was a vicious circle of discrimination. Non–Anglo-Saxons were discriminated against because they were not assimilated, either culturally or socially, but one of the reasons they were not assimilated was because of discrimination against them. As one researcher noted in a 1917 report on "Social Conditions in Rural Communities in the Prairie Provinces," the group "clannishness" of immigrants which was so widely deplored by the public was caused as much by the prejudice of the "English" as it was by the groups' desire to remain different.[21]

199

There is no need to catalogue here the extensive patterns of social, economic, and political discrimination which developed against non–Anglo-Saxons.[22] Patterns of discrimination parallelled preferences of immigrant sources, with northern and western Europeans encountering relatively little discrimination, central and southern Europeans and Jews encountering more discrimination, and non-whites encountering an all-pervasive pattern of discrimination which extended to almost all aspects of their lives. Discrimination was one of the main factors which led to the transference (with only a few exceptions) of the same ethnic "pecking order" which existed in immigration policy to the place each group occupied in the "vertical mosaic," with the British (especially the Scots) on top, and so on down to the Chinese and blacks who occupied the most menial jobs.[23] Non-British and non-French groups not only had very little economic power; they also would not even significantly occupy the middle echelons of politics, education, or the civil service until after World War II.

The ethnic stereotypes which developed for eastern European and Oriental groups emphasized their peasant origins. These stereotypes played a role in determining the job opportunities for new immigrants and functioned to disparage those who would climb out of their place. Opprobrious names such as "Wops," "Bohunks," and especially "foreigner" indicated class as well as ethnic origin and these terms were used as weapons in the struggle for status. The very word "ethnic" carried, for many people, such an aura of opprobrium that even recently there have been attempts to expurgate the use of the word. Ethnic food and folklore were regarded by most Anglo-Canadians as not only "foreign," but "backward" and lower class. Folklorist Carole Henderson has aptly described the views of Anglo-Canadians toward folklore (views which continue to the present day): "Except for members of some delimited regional, and usually ethnic, subcultures such as Newfoundlanders or Nova Scotian Scots, most Anglo-Canadians simply fail to identify folklore with themselves, and tend to consider such materials to be the . . . unimportant possessions of the strange, foreign, or 'backward people in their midst.'"[24]

The 1920s and the Emergence of "Melting Pot" Ideas

The 1920s brought the second main wave of non-British and non-French immigrants to Canada and saw the emergence of the second ideology of assimilation, the "melting pot." During the early 1920s both Canada and the United States had acted to further restrict immigration from southern, central, and eastern Europe and from the Orient. Chinese were virtually excluded from Canada, and central, southern, and eastern Europeans were classified among the "non-preferred" and restricted category of immigrants. But by the mid-1920s several powerful sectors of Canadian society, including transportation companies, boards of trade, newspapers, and politicians of various political persuasions, as well as ethnic groups, applied pressure on the King government to open the immigration doors.[25] These groups believed that only a limited immigration could be expected from the "preferred" countries and that probably only central and eastern Europeans would do the rugged work of clearing marginal land. The railways continued to seek immigrants to guarantee revenue for their steamship lines, traffic for their railways and settlers for their land. With improving economic conditions in the mid-twenties, the Federal government responded to this pressure and changed its policy with respect to immigrants from central and eastern Europe.

While continuing to emphasize its efforts to secure British immigrants, in September 1925 the Liberal government of Mackenzie King entered into the "Railways Agreement" with the CPR and CNR, which brought an increased number of central and eastern Europeans. The Government authorized the railways to encourage potential immigrants of the "non-preferred" countries to emigrate to Canada and to settle as "agriculturalists, agricultural workers, and domestic servants."[26]

Through this agreement, the railways brought to Canada 165 000 central and eastern Europeans and 20 000 Mennonites. They represented a variety of ethnic groups and a diversity of reasons for emigrating. Most of the Ukrainian immigrants were political refugees. Poles, Slovaks, and Hungarians were escaping poor economic conditions. German-Russians and Mennonites were fleeing civil war, economic disaster, and the spectre of cultural annihilation in Russia.[27] Often they chose Canada since they could no longer get into the United States because of its quota system and the Canadian route was the only way they could get to North America. With this new wave of immigration, the proportion of the Canadian population that was not of British, French, or native origin rose to more than 18 percent by 1931.

In responding to this new wave of immigration, many opinion leaders held to an earlier belief that Canada should be patterned exclusively on the British model, and continued to advocate anglo-conformity. In national periodicals and newspapers during the 1920s, the emphasis which was placed on the need to attract British immigrants was related to this assumption that anglo-conformity was essential to the successful development of Canadian society. "Foreign" immigrants had to be assimilated and there needed to be enough Britishers to maintain "Anglo-Saxon" traditions.[28] R.B. Bennett, later to become the Conservative prime minister during the early 1930s, attacked melting pot ideas in the House of Commons and argued "These people [continental Europeans] have made excellent settlers: . . . but it cannot be that we must draw upon them to shape our civilization. We must still maintain that measure of British civilization which will enable us to assimilate these people to British institutions, rather than assimilate our civilization to theirs. . . . "[29]

201

The influx of new immigrants from central and eastern Europe during the mid and late twenties also aroused protests from a number of nativist organizations, such as the Ku Klux Klan, The Native Sons of Canada, and The Orange Order, who were convinced that Canada should "remain Anglo-Saxon."[30] Nativist sentiment in western Canada was most pronounced in Saskatchewan where one of its leading spokesmen was George Exton Lloyd, an Anglican bishop and one of the founders of the Barr colony at Lloydminster.

In a torrent of newspaper articles and speeches, Lloyd repeated the warning that Canada was in danger of becoming a "mongrel" nation: "The essential question before Canadians today is this: Shall Canada develop as a British nation within the empire, or will she drift apart by the introduction of so much alien blood that her British instincts will be paralyzed?"[31] According to Lloyd, Canada had but two alternatives: it could either be a homogeneous nation or a heterogeneous one. The heterogeneous or "melting pot" idea had not worked in the United States (as evidenced by large numbers of unassimilated immigrants at the outbreak of World War I), and could not, he argued, work in Canada. With Lloyd, as with other individuals and organizations promoting anglo-conformity at this time, one gets the distinctive feeling that they were on the defensive. Like other English-speaking Canadians who had a strong attachment to Britain and the Empire, Lloyd saw a threat to Canada's "British" identity, not only in the increasing numbers of "continental" immigrants, but also in the declining status of things British as Canadians moved towards a North American based nationalism which did not include loyalty to the British Empire as its primary article of faith.[32]

During the late 1920s, a new view of assimilation, the melting pot, developed greater prominence. This view of assimilation, which arose partly as a means of defending immigrants against nativist attacks from people like Lloyd, envisioned a biological merging of Anglo-Canadians with immigrants and a blending of their cultures into a new Canadian type. Whereas Lloyd and other nativists argued that since immigrants could not conform to Anglo-Canadian ideals they should be excluded, a new generation of writers argued that assimilation was indeed occurring, but to a new Canadian type.[33] Since assimilation was occurring, nativist fears were unwarranted. Indeed, immigrants would make some valuable cultural contributions to Canada during the process of assimilation. Although these writers did not all use the "melting pot" symbol when discussing their view of assimilation, one can lump their ideas together under the rubric of the "melting pot" because they did envisage the emergence of a new society which would contain "contributions" from the various immigrant groups.

Most of these writers who defended "continental" European immigration did not seriously question the desirability of assimilation. Robert England, a writer and educator who worked for the CNR, had read widely enough in anthropological sources to be influenced by the cultural relativism of Franz Boas and other anthropologists and did in his writing question the desirability of assimilation.[34] But most of these writers were concerned primarily with attempting to promote tolerance toward ethnic minorities by encouraging their assimilation, and many became involved in programs to facilitate this assimilation.

Advocates of anglo-conformity and the melting pot both believed that uniformity was ultimately necessary for unity, but they differed on what should provide the basis of that uniformity. Advocates of the melting pot, unlike the promoters of anglo-conformity, saw assimilation as a relatively slow process, and saw some cultural advantages in the mixing that would occur.

There was not, however, always a clear distinction between anglo-conformity and the melting pot. Rhetoric indicating that immigrants might have something more to offer Canada than their physical labor was sometimes only a thinly veiled version of anglo-conformity; the melting pot often turned out to be an Anglo-Saxon melting pot. For example, John Blue, a prominent Edmonton promoter and historian, wrote in his history of Alberta in 1924 that the fears about foreign immigration destroying Canadian laws and institutions had proved groundless. "There is enough Anglo-Saxon blood in Alberta to dilute the foreign blood and complete the process of assimilation to the mutual advantage of both elements."[35]

There were a variety of reasons for the development of melting pot ideas during the 1920s.[36] The growth during the 1920s of an autonomous Canadian nationalism helped the spread of melting pot ideas. Some English-Canadian opinion leaders began to discuss the need for conformity to an exclusively Canadian norm rather than a "British" norm.

202

One of the arguments that John W. Dafoe, the influential editor of the *Winnipeg Free Press*, and J.S. Ewart, a constitutional lawyer, used in support of their view of Canadian nationalism was that non-British immigrants could not be expected to feel loyalty to the British Empire.[37]

Melting pot advocates tended to be people who had some personal experience with immigrants, and recognized both the intense pride that immigrants had in their cultural backgrounds as well as the rich cultural sources of those traditions. But they also lived in a time when recognition of ethnicity meant mostly Anglo-Canadian use of ethnicity as a basis of discrimination or exploitation. It was also a time when some ethnic groups were still close enough to their rural peasant roots that ethnic solidarity was often not conducive to upward mobility. The view of most melting pot advocates that the disappearance of ethnicity as a basis of social organization would increase the mobility opportunities of the second generation was based on a sound grasp of the realities of the day. The life-long campaign of John Diefenbaker for "unhyphenated Canadianism" and "one Canada" grew out of this experience with ethnicity as something that could be used to hinder opportunities, and was consistent with his emphasis on human rights, rather than group rights.[38]

203

The 1930s

Although immigration was severely cut back during the depression of the 1930s, the role of ethnic minorities in English-speaking Canada continued to be a major public concern. Paradoxically, although the depression witnessed the high point of discrimination against non–Anglo-Saxons, it was also during the 1930s that the first major advocates of cultural pluralism in English-speaking Canada began to be heard.

The depression affected non–Anglo-Saxon immigrants more than most other groups in the society. These immigrants, because of their language problems and lack of specialized skills, were concentrated in the most insecure and therefore most vulnerable segments of the economy. Since immigrants were the last hired and the first fired, a large proportion were forced onto relief. Government officials were gravely concerned about the way immigrants seemed to complicate the relief problem. Calls by some officials for deportation as the solution to the relief problem were heeded by the federal government; sections 40 and 41 of the Immigration Act (still essentially the same act as the one which existed in 1919) provided for deportation of non-Canadian citizens on relief and government officials took advantage of the law to reduce their relief rolls.

While there was some continuing concern over the assimilation of non-British and non-French immigrants during the 1930s, most Anglo-Canadians were more concerned about protecting their jobs.[39]

Prior to the depression, most Anglo-Saxons were content to have the "foreigners" do all the heavy work of construction, and the dirty work of the janitors and street sweepers. But as the economy slowed down, these jobs became attractive. Whereas the pre-depression attitude was "let the foreigners do the dirty work," the depression attitude became "how come these foreigners have all of our jobs?" The 1930s also saw the high point of anti-semitism in English-speaking Canada as the patterns of discrimination which had hindered the desires of second generation Jews for entry into the professions were extended into a vicious and virulent anti-semitism by fascist groups.[40]

Barry Broadfoot's book *Ten Lost Years* also makes it very clear that discrimination and prejudice flourished during the depression. In the transcripts of his interviews with the "survivors" of the depression, one is struck by the all-pervasiveness of derogatory ethnic epithets in interviewees' recollections of their contact with immigrants. One does not read of Italians, Chinese, or Poles. One reads of "Dagos," "Wops," "Chinks," "Polacks," "Hunyaks."[41] One "survivor" of the depression, waxing philosophical, gives explicit expression to the prevailing attitudes of the time. He compares how the depression affected people from R.B. Bennett down to "the lowest of the low," "some bohunk smelling of garlic and not knowing a word of English. . . . "[42] Another "survivor" recalls that her boy had great difficulty finding work during the depression, and went berserk because of the blow to his self-esteem when the only job he could find was "working with a bunch of Chinks. . . . "[43]

The vicious circle of discrimination became perhaps even more vicious during the 1930s as non–Anglo-Saxons' political response to the depression further poisoned attitudes toward them. The discrimination and unemployment which non–Anglo-Saxons faced was an important factor in promoting the support of many for radical political solutions to the depression, in either communist or fascist movements. Indeed the vast majority of the support for the communists throughout Canada, and for the fascists in western Canada, came from non–Anglo-Saxons.[44] Ethnic support for these two movements, and the conflict between left and right within most central and eastern European groups and the Finns was seen as further evidence of the undesirability of non–Anglo-Saxons. The existence of fascist and communist movements in Canada was not of course due simply to the presence of immigrants bringing "old world" ideas. The leaders in both movements were predominantly of British origin,[45] and their "ethnic" support came more from immigrants reacting to depression conditions than from immigrants bringing to Canada "old world" ideas. But the depression gave further support to the notion of non–Anglo-Saxons being unstable politically; one more proof along with immigrant drinking, garlic eating, and the legendary violence at Slavic weddings, that non–Anglo-Saxons were in dire need of baptism by assimilation. Deporting immigrant radicals was seen as one alternative to assimilation and the federal government did not hesitate to use this weapon.[46]

The relationship in the public mind between ethnicity, lower social class origins, and political "unsoundness" explains why during the late 1920s so many second generation non–Anglo-Saxons who were anxious to improve their lot economically made deliberate attempts to hide their ethnic background, such as changing their names. Ethnic ties were clearly disadvantageous for those non–Anglo-Saxons seeking economic security or social acceptance. The experience of the second generation in English-speaking Canada was similar to the second generation experience as described by a historian writing about ethnic groups in the United States. "Culturally estranged from their parents by their American education, and wanting nothing so much as to become and to be accepted as Americans, many second generation immigrants made deliberate efforts to rid themselves of their heritage. The adoption of American clothes, speech, and interests, often accompanied by the shedding of an exotic surname, were all part of a process whereby antecedents were repudiated as a means of improving status."[47]

205

Despite the continuing dominance of the old stereotypes concerning non–Anglo-Saxons and the continuing dominance of assimilationist assumptions, the 1930s also saw the emergence of the first full blown pluralist ideas in somewhat ambiguous form in John Murray Gibbon's book, *The Canadian Mosaic*, and in the writings of Watson Kirkconnell, then an English professor at the University of Manitoba. These writers were much more familiar than earlier writers with the historical backgrounds of the ethnic groups coming to Canada, and they were influenced by a liberalism which rejected the assumptions of Anglo-Saxon superiority. Gibbon, a publicity agent for the Canadian Pacific Railway, wrote his book as an expansion of a series of CBC radio talks on the different ethnic groups of Canada. He traced the history of each group and related their "contributions" to Canadian society. Although he was concerned with the preservation of folk arts and music, he also went out of his way to alleviate fears of unassimilability by discussing individuals' assimilation as well as the "cement" of common institutions which bound the Canadian mosaic together. Although Gibbon was not the first writer to use the mosaic symbol, he was the first to attempt to explore its meaning in any significant way.

Kirkconnell was an essayist, poet, and prolific translator of European verse from a number of European languages. His writing on ethnic groups was based on a different approach than Gibbon's. He tried to promote tolerance toward "European Canadians" by sympathetically portraying the cultural background of the countries where the immigrants originated and by demonstrating the cultural creativity of European immigrants in Canada through translating and publishing their creative writing.[48]

In his writing he attacked the assumptions of anglo-conformity, and advocated a multicultural society which would allow immigrants to maintain pride in their past:

> . . . it would be tragic if there should be a clumsy stripping-away of all those spiritual associations with the past that help to give depth and beauty to life. . . . If . . . we accept with Wilhelm von Humboldt "the absolute and essential importance of human development in its richest diversity," then we shall welcome every opportunity to save for our country every previous element of individuality that is available.[49]

Kirkconnell was not advocating complete separation of ethnic groups so that they might be preserved. He believed that assimilation needed to occur in the realm of political and economic values and institutions but he hoped that some of the conservative values and folk-culture of immigrants could be preserved.

Kirkconnell did not ignore the political differences within ethnic groups. Indeed, with the outbreak of World War II he wrote a book in which he attempted to expose and combat both fascist and communist elements in different ethnic groups.[50] But he was also active in attempts to bring various other factions of eastern European groups together in order to alleviate public criticism of divisions within ethnic groups.[51]

These advocates of pluralism believed that ethnic diversity was not incompatible with national unity. Unity need not mean uniformity. They believed that recognition of the cultural contributions of non–Anglo-Saxon groups would heighten the groups' feeling that they belonged to Canada and thus strengthen Canadian unity. But Gibbon and Kirkconnell were voices crying in the wilderness — a wilderness of discrimination and racism.

After World War II: The Emergence of Multiculturalism

The war period and early post-war period was a transitional time with respect to attitudes toward immigration and ethnicity. Although the war brought renewed hostility toward enemy aliens, a number of developments during the war eventually worked to undermine ethnic prejudice. During the arrival of the third wave of immigration in the late 1940s and 1950s, many pre-war prejudices lingered, and ethnic minorities encountered considerable pressures for conformity. But for a variety of intellectual, social, and demographic reasons, the ideology of cultural pluralism has been increasingly accepted in the post–World War II period. The post-war decline of racism and the growing influence of theories about cultural relativism opened the way for the emergence of pluralist ideas. The arrival of many intellectuals among the post-war political refugees from eastern Europe and the growth in the number of upwardly mobile second- and third-generation non–Anglo-Canadians, some of whom felt that they were not being fully accepted into Canadian society, increased the political pressures at both federal and provincial levels for greater recognition of Canada's ethnic diversity. Some suggested that this could be achieved through the appointment of senators of a particular ethnic origin, or through the introduction into the school curriculum of ethnic content and of ethnic languages as courses (and sometimes as languages of instruction).[52]

These demands for greater government recognition of "other ethnic groups" increased during the 1960s in response to the French-Canadian assertion of equal rights and the Pearson government's measures to assess and ensure the status of the French language and culture. In 1963 the Royal Commission on Bilingualism and Biculturalism was appointed to "inquire into and report upon the existing state of bilingualism and biculturalism in Canada and to recommend what steps should be taken to develop the Canadian Confederation on the basis of an equal partnership between the two founding races, taking into account the contribution made by the other ethnic groups to the cultural enrichment of Canada." Many non-British, non-French groups, but particularly Ukrainians, opposed the view that Canada was bicultural. By 1961, 26 percent of the Canadian population was of other than British or French ethnic origin; over two hundred newspapers were being published in languages other than French and English; there were fairly well-defined Italian, Jewish, Slavic, and Chinese neighbourhoods in large Canadian cities, and there were visible rural concentrations of Ukrainians, Doukhobors, Hutterites, and Mennonites scattered across the western provinces: thus, how was it possible for a royal commission to speak of Canada as a *bi*cultural country?

This feeling that biculturalism relegated all ethnic groups who were other than British or French to the status of second-class citizens helps explain the resistance some of these groups expressed to the policies and programs that were introduced to secure the status of the French language in Canada. The place of the so-called "other" ethnic groups in a bicultural society became a vexing question for federal politicians, who had originally hoped that steps to ensure French-Canadian rights would go a long way towards improving inter-ethnic relations in Canada. The partial resolution of this dilemma was the assertion in October 1971 by Prime Minister Trudeau that, in fact, Canada is a *multi*cultural country and that steps would be taken by the federal government to give public recognition to ethnic diversity through the introduction of a policy of multiculturalism. Several provinces with large numbers of non-Anglo Canadians have also initiated their own policies of multiculturalism.

Although most political leaders in English-speaking Canada have accepted and proclaimed the desirability of Canada's ethnic diversity, the

207

Canadian public has not given unanimous support to pluralism. The debate over the place of ethnic groups in Canadian life continues, focusing on such questions as: Does the encouragement of pluralism only serve to perpetuate the vertical mosaic, in which class lines coincide with ethnic lines, or does it help break down class barriers by promoting acceptance of the legitimacy of cultural differences? Are the goals of current government policy — cultural pluralism and equality of opportunity — mutually compatible? Does the encouragement of ethnic group solidarity threaten the freedom of individuals in these groups, or can ethnic groups provide a liberating, rather than a restricting, context for identity? Does the encouragement of cultural diversity serve to perpetuate old-world rivalries, or will the recognition of the contributions of Canada's ethnic groups heighten their feeling that they belong in Canada and thus strengthen Canadian unity? Is government talk of multiculturalism just a way to attract the "ethnic vote," or is positive action necessary to preserve cultural pluralism when cultural diversity throughout the world is being eroded by the impact of industrial technology, mass communication, and urbanization? Does the encouragement of multiculturalism simply heighten the visibility of the growing numbers of non-whites in the country and hinder their chances of full acceptance as individuals into Canadian life, or is a public policy of multiculturalism essential to an effective campaign against racism? The nature of these arguments suggests that the prevailing assumptions about immigration and ethnicity have changed over time in English-speaking Canada. They also suggest that the discussion about the role of immigration and ethnic groups in Canadian life is still an important, and unfinished, debate.

NOTES

[1] For a discussion of these three ideologies of assimilation in the United States, see Milton Gordon, *Assimilation in American Life* (New York, 1964).

[2] L.G. Thomas, "The Umbrella and the Mosaic: The French–English Presence and the Settlement of the Canadian Prairie West," in J.A. Carroll, ed., *Reflections of Western Historians* (Tucson, Arizona, 1969), 135–52; Allan Smith, "Metaphor and Nationality in North America," *Canadian Historical Review* 51, 3 (September 1970).

[3] The Canadian census has consistently classed the Irish as part of the "British" group.

[4] Howard Palmer, *Land of the Second Chance: A History of Ethnic Groups in Southern Alberta* (Lethbridge, 1972); Norman Macdonald, *Canada Immigration and Colonization, 1841–1903* (Toronto, 1967); Harold Troper, *Only Farmers Need Apply* (Toronto, 1972).

[5] Donald Avery, "Canadian Immigration Policy and the Foreign Navy," Canadian Historical Association, *Report* (1972); Edmund Bradwin, *Bunkhouse Man* (New York, 1928); H. Troper and R. Harney, *Immigrants* (Toronto, 1975).

[6] Donald Avery, "Canadian Immigration Policy, 1896–1919: The Anglo-Canadian Perspective" (unpublished Ph.D. thesis, University of Western Ontario, 1973); Cornelius Jaenan, "Federal Policy Vis-à-Vis Ethnic Groups" (unpublished paper, Ottawa, 1971); Howard Palmer, "Nativism and Ethnic Tolerance in Alberta, 1880–1920" (unpublished M.A. thesis, University of Alberta, 1971); Palmer, "Nativism and Ethnic Tolerance in Alberta, 1920–1972" (unpublished Ph.D. thesis, York University, 1973).

[7] H. Palmer, "Nativism and Ethnic Tolerance in Alberta, 1880–1920" (unpublished M.A. thesis, University of Alberta, 1971), ch. 1 and 2; H. Troper, *Only Farmers Need Apply* (Toronto, 1972); D.J. Hall, "Clifford Sifton: Immigration and Settlement Policy, 1896–1905," in H. Palmer, ed., *The Settlement of the West* (Calgary, 1977), 60–85.

[8] H. Troper, "The Creek Negroes of Oklahoma and Canadian Immigration, 1909–11," *Canadian Historical Review* (September 1972), 272–88.

[9] Rev. George Bruce, "Past and Future of Our Race," *Proceedings*, Canadian Club of Toronto, 1911, pp. 6-7; C.A. Magrath, *Canada's Growth and Problems Affecting It* (Ottawa, 1910); Goldwin Smith in *Weekly Sun*, Feb. 1, 1899, Sept. 17, 1902, Sept. 23, 1903, May 18, 1904, Aug. 16, 1905; W.A. Griesbach, *I Remember* (Toronto, 1946), 214-17, 220-21.

[10] Carl Berger, *Sense of Power* (Toronto, 1970), 117-88.

[11] Morton, *In a Sea of Sterile Mountains* (Vancouver, 1974); W.P. Ward, "The Oriental Immigrant and Canada's Protestant Clergy, 1858-1925," *B.C. Studies* (Summer 1974), 40-55; Ted Ferguson, *A White Man's Country* (Toronto, 1975).

[12] D.J. Hall, "Clifford Sifton: Immigration and Settlement Policy: 1896-1905," in H. Palmer, ed., *The Settlement of the West* (Calgary, 1977), 79-80.

[13] W.L. Morton, *Manitoba: A History* (Toronto, 1957), 161, 162.

[14] J.B. Hedges, *Building the Canadian West* (New York, 1939); Frank Epp, *Mennonites in Canada, 1786-1920* (Toronto, 1974).

[15] Cornelius J. Jaenen, "Ruthenian Schools in Western Canada, 1897-1919," *Paedagogica Historica: International Journal of the History of Education* 10, 3 (1970): 517-41. Donald Avery, Canadian Immigration Policy," 374-420.

[16] Avery, "Canadian Immigration Policy," 408.

[17] Kate Foster, *Our Canadian Mosaic* (Toronto, 1926); J.T.M. Anderson, *The Education of the New Canadian* (Toronto, 1918); C.B. Sissons, *Bi-Lingual Schools in Canada* (Toronto, 1917); W.G. Smith, *Building the Nation* (Toronto, 1922). For a discussion of some of the concrete activities involved in these "Canadianization" programs, see R. Harney and H. Troper, *Immigrants*, ch. 4.

[18] J.S. Woodsworth, *Strangers Within our Gates* (Winnipeg, 1909); Marilyn Barber, "Nationalism, Nativism and the Social Gospel: The Protestant Church Response to Foreign Immigrants in Western Canada, 1897-1914," in Richard Allen, ed., *The Social Gospel in Canada* (Ottawa, 1975), 186-226.

[19] Quoted in Barbara Nicholson, "Feminism in the Prairie Provinces to 1916," (unpublished M.A. thesis, University of Calgary, 1974), 71. For the views of womens' groups on immigration and the role of immigrants in Canadian society, see pp. 83-85, 86, 114, 121, 133, 165-69, 186-87.

[20] Reported in *Lethbridge Herald*, May 29, 1919.

[21] J.S. Woodsworth, "Social Conditions in Rural Communities in the Prairie Provinces," Winnipeg, 1917, p. 38.

[22] For a fairly extensive chronicling of patterns of discrimination against a number of minority groups see Morris Davis and J.F. Krauter, *The Other Canadians* (Toronto, 1971).

[23] For an analysis of the various causes of ethnic stratification (settlement patterns, time of arrival, immigrant and ethnic occupations, ethnic values, language barriers, and discrimination and exploitation) see Book 4, *Report of the Royal Commission on Bilingualism and Biculturalism*, Ottawa, 1969, ch. 2.

[24] Carole Henderson, "The Ethnicity Factor in Anglo-Canadian Folkloristics," *Canadian Ethnic Studies* 7, 2 (forthcoming).

[25] *Canadian Annual Review* (1923), 264-65; (1924-25), 190-92.

[26] *Canada Year Book* (1941), 733.

[27] Olha Woycenko, *The Ukrainians in Canada* (Winnipeg, 1967); Victor Turek, *Poles in Manitoba* (Toronto, 1967), 43; J.M. Kirschbaum, *Slovaks in Canada* (Toronto, 1967), 101; Edmund Heier, "A Study of German Lutheran and Catholic Immigrants in Canada formerly residing in Czarist and Soviet Russia" (unpublished M.A. thesis, University of British Columbia, 1955), ch. 3.

[28] R.B. Bennett, House of Commons *Debates*, June 7, 1929, p. 3925-27.

[29] Bennett, House of Commons *Debates*, 3925-27.

[30] H. Palmer, "Nativism in Alberta, 1925-1930," Canadian Historical Association, *Report* (1974), 191-99.

[31] G.E. Lloyd, "National Building," *Banff Crag and Canyon*, Aug. 17, 1928.

[32] A.R.M. Lower, *Canadians in the Making* (Don Mills, Ontario, 1958), ch. 22, 27.

[33] J.S. Woodsworth, "Nation Building," *University Magazine*, 1917, pp. 85-99. F.W. Baumgartner, "Central European Immigration," *Queen's Quarterly* (Winter 1930), 183-92; Walter Murray, "Continental Europeans in Western Canada," *Queen's Quarterly* (1931); P.M. Bryce, *The Value of the Continental Immigrant to Canada* (Ottawa, 1928); E.L. Chicanot, "Homesteading the Citizen: Canadian Festivals Promote Cultural Exchange," *Commonwealth* (May 1929), 94-95; E.K. Chicanot, "Moulding a Nation," *Dalhousie Review* (July 1929), 232-37. J.H. Haslam, "Canadianization of the Immigrant Settler," *Annals* (May 1923), 45-49; E.H. Oliver, "The Settlement of Saskatchewan to 1914," *Transactions of the Royal Society* (1926), 63-87; Agnes Laut, "Comparing the Canadian and American Melting Pots," *Current Opinion* 70 (April 1921), 458-62; Kate Foster, *Our Canadian Mosaic* (Toronto, 1926). Robert England, "Continental Europeans in Western Canada," *Queen's Quarterly* (1931).

[34] Robert England, *The Central European Immigrant in Canada* (Toronto, 1929).

[35] John Blue, *Alberta Past and Present* (Chicago, 1924), 210.

[36] There were some advocates of the melting pot prior to 1920, but it did not gain widespread acceptance until the 1920s. See H. Palmer, "Nativism in Alberta, 1880-1920," ch. 1. Marilyn Barber, "Nationalism, Nativism, and the Social Gospel."

[37] Douglas Cole, "John S. Ewart and Canadian Nationalism," Canadian Historical Association, *Report* (1969), 66.

[38] John Diefenbaker, *One Canada* (Toronto, 1975), 140, 141, 218-19, 274.

[39] H. Palmer, "Nativism in Alberta, 1920-1972," ch. 3.

[40] James Gray, *The Roar of the Twenties* (Toronto, 1975), ch. 11; Lita-Rose Betcherman, *The Swastika and the Maple Leaf* (Don Mills, Ontario, 1975).

[41] Barry Broadfoot, *Ten Lost Years*, 25, 70, 76, 132, 156-64, 186, 279.

[42] Broadfoot, *Ten Lost Years*, 132.

[43] Broadfoot, *Ten Lost Years*, 186.

[44] Ivan Avakumovic, *The Communist Party in Canada: A History* (Toronto, 1975), 66-67; Lita-Rose Betcherman, *The Swastika and the Maple Leaf*, ch. 5.

[45] See note 44 above.

[46] H. Palmer, "Nativism in Alberta, 1920-1972," ch. 3.

[47] M.A. Jones, *American Immigration* (Chicago, 1960), 298. For fictional treatments of the second generation's repudiation of the ethnic past in an attempt to become accepted see John Marlyn, *Under the Ribs of Death* (Toronto, 1951) and Magdalena Eggleston, *Mountain Shadows* (New York, 1955), 122. See also *Change of Name* (Toronto: Canadian Institute of Cultural Research, 1965).

[48] Watson Kirkconnell, *The European Heritage: A Synopsis of European Cultural Achievement* (London, 1930) and *Canadian Overtones* (Winnipeg, 1935). For a complete listing of Kirkconnell's work, see the list in his memoirs, *A Slice of Canada* (Toronto, 1967), 374-75. For an assessment of his work see J.R.C. Perkin, ed., *The Undoing of Babel* (Toronto, 1975).

[49] W. Kirkconnell, trans., *Canadian Overtones*, preface.

[50] Watson Kirkconnell, *Canada, Europe, and Hitler* (Toronto, 1939).

[51] W. Kirkconnell, *A Slice of Canada*.

[52] For documentary evidence of changing ethnic attitudes in the post-war era and the emergence of multiculturalism as an idea and as a governmental policy, see H. Palmer, *Immigration and the Rise of Multiculturalism* (Toronto, 1975), ch. 3.

Under the Ribs of Death*

JOHN MARLYN

For hours on end he sat on the roof of the woodshed silently contained within himself, re-living Saturdays that had come and gone, lost in unfolding fantasies that formed themselves sometimes about Eric, sometimes about his mother. He moved from the far circumference of her life to its centre. He related himself to her, subjected her to a thousand perils and saved her from them all — and sighed at their unlikelihood. Her presence hovered about him. Enough that she liked cleanliness; he washed himself half a dozen times a day: that she had once frowned at his manner of speech, and she accomplished by the mere lowering of a brow what school teachers and his father and Mr Crawford had tried in vain to do.

The outer aspects of his life receded. He held himself proudly aloof from the affairs of his family. He moved through his neighbourhood with unseeing eyes.

The summer holidays arrived. He remained alone, snug and secure in the cocoon he had woven about himself.

One night, sitting in his accustomed place, he overheard his parents talking in the yard below. With an air of supreme condescension he raised his head and listened. It appeared that his father had made the last payment on Onkel Janos' ticket. Sandor curbed his excitement. It was undignified and out of keeping with his highborn rôle.

*Chapter 6 of *Under the Ribs of Death*, by John Marlyn. Used by permission of the Canadian Publishers, McClelland and Stewart, Toronto.

But a week or so later he became aware that his mother was planning a party, and from the evidence that had begun to accumulate, a party such as Henry Avenue had never known.

The attitude he had imposed upon himself began to show signs of strain. A telegram from his uncle shattered it.

Early that Sunday morning on which his uncle was to arrive, the kitchen began to fill with women — friends and acquaintances who had been invited to the party and had come to help. It was sweltering outside; in the kitchen the heat was almost unbearable. The women moved around in their petticoats, long shapeless affairs with flounces and lace, black and purple and yellow — an amusing sight to Sandor who stood in a corner laughing until his mother sent him upstairs to make sure that his uncle's room was in order. Mr Schwalbe had consented to sleep in the outer attic so that Frau Hunyadi's brother would have a room to himself, for the first few days at least.

In the doorway of the attic, Sandor paused. All the beds had been covered with thick flannel sheets and on them, sucking their thumbs in sleep, squalling, pink and gurgling or blue with moist anger, lay the babies. Watching over them were the grown-up daughters of the women downstairs.

Once he might have stopped to listen to them. Now he simply looked into Mr Schwalbe's cubicle and passed them by. They reminded him too much of the maids he had seen in Eric's neighbourhood. They laughed too loud and too long. Their clothes were too bright and too fancy.

He went into the toilet, took a small fragment of mirror out of his hiding-place under the floorboards and, holding it at arm's length, examined his new blue serge sailor-suit which his mother had bought — by instalments — with the money he had earned. He straightened the collar and continued to look at himself until he heard his mother calling to him from the foot of the stairs. It was time to go. He was to meet his father at the station.

A few minutes later he was on his way. He came to the hotel and reverting to his former rôle, passed proudly and sedately below the windows of the lobby.

Then he saw the crowd moving toward the station and became Sandor Hunyadi again, pressing excitedly and eagerly to the great doors. He saw his father standing there in his best black suit which he wore at Christmas and New Year. It was like new. Whenever he removed it from the closet, he smiled and stroked it and clicked his tongue at Old-Country craftsmanship.

Sandor waved to him. His father waved back. They had been on good terms ever since the summer holidays had started. His father took him by the hand.

They followed the crowd into the vast echoing cavern to a rope barrier. Sandor had been here before and it had always been crowded, but now for the first time he sensed the expectancy of the people around him. Now and then the station reverberated to the jargon of the train-caller. On the platform above, he heard the familiar, ponderous clatter of the engines. The suppressed excitement of the crowds began to affect him. He heard his father call out a greeting to a friend and realized that his father was as excited as he was. His father did not quite approve of Onkel Janos. Was it only because he was an adventurer, or were there other hidden reasons?

From the upper level came the interminable slow creak and groan of a train coming to a stop. Behind him the crowd strained forward, pressing him against the rope barrier. All was still. There reached them the shrill cry of a child; a voice in English giving directions. Then the long-awaited tramp of feet, growing louder and louder, reaching the head of the stairs, and finally the first of the new arrivals emerged from the gates and looked about them timidly and fearfully, bent under the weight of their belongings. Reluctantly they moved forward, pushed ahead by those who came behind.

Sandor turned pale at the sight of them. They stood there, awkward and begrimed, the men in tight-fitting wrinkled clothes, with their wrists and ankles sticking out, unshaven and foreign-looking, the women in kerchiefs and voluminous skirts and men's shoes . . . exactly the way his grandmother looked in that picture in the front room. And it was this that was frightening. They were so close to him. Only a few months or years — a few words and recently acquired habits — separated his parents from them. The kinship was odious. He knew how hard it was for his parents to change their ways. But they were changing. They used tinned goods sometimes at home now, and store-bought bread when they had enough money. English food was appearing on their table, the English language in their home. Slowly, very slowly, they were changing. They were becoming Canadians. And now here it stood. Here was the nightmare survival of themselves, mocking and dragging them back to their shameful past.

Sandor looked up at his father. His lips trembled at the expression on his father's face. It was as though the embers of something long forgotten had been stirred into flame by the sight of these people and now cast an ardent glow upon his features. His eyes half-closed, he murmured something to himself in his native tongue. Sandor tugged at his arm. His father never noticed. Sandor turned back and glanced at the newcomers. The foremost among them had faltered and finally come to a stop at the sight of the crowd in front of them.

The two groups stared at one another. Then a man's voice cried "Ilonka!" The new arrivals wavered. A woman shifted the child in her arms and waved. The man called to her again, and before they were in each other's arms the barrier was down and the two groups were

212

one. The station echoed their gladness in many tongues. They touched one another and cried. They embraced and smiled and stood apart and stared into eyes familiar and yet grown strange.

Sandor scowled. There were probably dozens of people here who could call his father "landsmann." As he followed his father with reluctant steps to the foot of the stairs, he wondered with a sudden shudder of disgust whether his uncle was as foreign-looking and as dirty as these others. Off to one side of him, he heard someone calling his father by his first name. He caught sight of a tall, dark man moving towards them, with an enormous wickerwork trunk on his shoulders and a miscellaneous array of packages and boxes in his hand. His teeth against dark lips and a swarthy complexion flashed in a dazzling smile. Onkel Janos, Sandor thought with a sinking heart. He was unshaven; he wore a collarless shirt, and a faded green jacket that looked as though it had once been part of a uniform. Ten feet away he shouted a greeting at them, dropped his belongings, and sprang forward to meet them with outstretched hands.

213

"By gollies, hullo," he shouted, and laughed uproariously.

The two men began shaking hands and talking excitedly in Hungarian. Sandor caught the sound of his mother's name, and once, while his uncle's glance swept appraisingly over him, his own. He stood still while his uncle patted him on the head and shouted "Kolossal." For his uncle everything was evidently "kolossal." Sandor crept around behind his father and waited. The only thing to look forward to now was the food and possibly, though not very probably, his uncle's present.

The two men began collecting the parcels and boxes. On the street, Sandor dropped a few paces behind them. Gollies hullo, he moaned. So this was the Pirate Uncle. This was how an adventurer looked and smelled. This was the man who had fought the Turks — who had been captured by the Arabs and who had been a millionaire several times over.

He had arrived just in time. With his ticket paid for they were just beginning to lay aside a little money every week. Now they would probably have to buy him clothes and feed him until he found a job.

Half a dozen steps or so behind them, Sandor stood still while his uncle looked about him. He drew a little nearer when he discovered that they were speaking German. His uncle wanted to know if there was a place where he could wash and shave before going on. Joseph Hunyadi explained that he had already thought of that. He hoped Janos wouldn't mind; he had taken the liberty of buying him a few things: underwear, a shirt, a pair of socks.

Yeah. That's how it was with his father, Sandor thought. He could make a gesture worthy of a millionaire and borrow the money to do it.

There was a place only a few blocks away, his father continued, where Janos could have a bath and a shave.

Sandor walked on behind until they reached the barber shop.

His father and his uncle went downstairs. He sat down despondently in the empty pool room until a barber who had once lived with them as a non-paying boarder called to him and asked him if he wanted a haircut. The boss was out, he explained. Sandor nodded, and thanked him as he walked back into the barber shop. He sat down and closed his eyes. It was warm and quiet here, the air filled with the odours of the lotions and the soap. A fly droned on the ceiling. From the basement came the faint hiss of escaping steam; above him, the rhythmic snick of the scissors.

He had been up since early morning. He nodded and fell into a light slumber, from which he was awakened by the sound of laughter. He opened his eyes to discover his father, two barbers, and a stranger, all smiling at him. Sandor blinked, smiled back weakly, and felt his hair. It was cool and moist. He blinked again, and then turned back to the stranger, who was still laughing. He was tall and elegantly dressed. There was an air of distinction about him.

Sandor rubbed his eyes. The stranger laughed uproariously and cried, "Kolossal!" It was a complete transformation. His uncle was a foreigner no longer. He reminded Sandor strongly of the men in the hotel lobby.

He jumped to his feet. "Onkel Janos!" he cried.

His uncle bent down and with a swoop raised him aloft.

"Hullo," he roared.

"Hullo," Sandor cried joyfully.

"By gollies, hullo hullo, hullo," his uncle echoed. "I spik English? You will learn me, ya?"

Sandor nodded, too happy to speak.

He felt as though he were walking on air as they left the barber shop. The wickerwork trunk had been left behind to be picked up later. But the shoe-box, Onkel Janos said as he thrust it into Sandor's hands with a promising wink, this box was to be handled carefully. Sandor winked back and tucked it under his arm; it felt reassuringly heavy and solidly packed. He took his uncle's hand as they turned down Logan Avenue.

He snorted impatiently as his father and uncle began talking Hungarian again. Finally, he caught his uncle's eye. "Onkel Janos," he said, "please talk German. I can't understand."

"You don't speak Hungarian?"

Sandor shook his head. "I've forgotten."

"I've tried to teach him Hungarian," Joseph Hunyadi said.

"Maybe when he's a little older . . . "

"But you speak English?" Onkel Janos asked, turning to Sandor.

"I talk English very well," Sandor said, and repeated it in German.

"Of course, you speak English. And why not? This is an English-speaking country isn't it? You want to get on. I can see just by looking at you that you're the kind of boy who's going to get ahead."

He turned away from Sandor and looked across at Joseph Hunyadi. "What does the boy want with Hungarian?" he asked. "Take my advice, Joseph, don't addle his brains."

Sandor tightened his grip on his uncle's hand. They turned down Henry Avenue, and walked on. A few hundred feet from the house, Onkel Janos suddenly raised his head. "I smell goulash," he roared, and lengthened his stride.

"The back way," Sandor cried, tugging at his hand. "Ma said to use the back door."

The back yard was full of children. On the roof of the woodshed sat the sons of the invited guests, taunting those who now gathered below, having nosed their way to the origin of the odours that had been drifting through the neighbourhood all morning. In their midst stood Frau Hunyadi handing out cookies. The invited urchins screamed. They were not being given any on the fantastic ground that it would spoil their appetites. From their perch on the roof they yelled down their defiance and threats.

As Frau Hunyadi turned back to the screen door, she caught sight of her brother. In an instant she was in his arms. "Ach, Janos, Janos." She held him close to her. They embraced and beheld each other at arm's length as well as their tears would allow. The children grew silent. Sandor shifted uncomfortably. His mother and Onkel Janos began to talk to one another in Hungarian.

Now a woman's face appeared at the window, and then another. Frau Hunyadi, catching sight of them, whispered something to her brother. To Sandor's relief they spoke German. It was very hot in the kitchen, his mother explained. And the front room was filled with tables and chairs. They had arranged a little party. Would Janos mind . . .

Onkel Janos kissed her. The women streamed into the back yard from the kitchen, red and smiling. And behind them came their husbands, their hands and faces burned dark with the sun, painters and carpenters and sewer-diggers; and a pale shoe-maker, a Hegelian philosopher and close friend of Joseph Hunyadi.

The women began gathering around Onkel Janos, to be introduced. Sandor grinned from ear to ear at his uncle's performance. He had drawn himself erect. Now he twirled the ends of his moustache, and with a faint click of his heels and a slight bow, bent over and kissed Frau Szabo's hand. Frau Szabo flushed and giggled. Then Frau Gombos.

Their husbands smiled indulgently. The kids on the roof looked on in silent delight. Sandor laughed to himself. He felt he was beginning to understand. His uncle had a way with him that made people smile.

When the introductions were over, the women returned to the house; there were still a few things to be done in the kitchen. The men had been told to stay where they were. They pulled some logs off the woodpile and settled down to a comfortable smoke.

Sandor followed his mother and uncle upstairs into Mr Schwalbe's cubicle. He remained in the doorway while they seated themselves on the cot. To his annoyance they began to talk in Hungarian again, and they talked for a long time. He caught the names of other uncles and distant relations. His mother began to cry. Sandor shifted impatiently. Finally his uncle noticed him, reached out, and took the shoe-box from him.

"Guess what?" he asked as he broke the string.

Sandor smiled and shook his head. This was going to be something, a real present. He knew it. Everything his uncle did exceeded one's expectations.

Onkel Janos opened the box and handed him a long shining cardboard tube, gaily decorated with laughing fishes and mermaids, with sailing ships and benign, droll monsters cavorting in a sky-blue sea.

Sandor eyed it with dismay. It looked like a kid's toy. From the expression on his uncle's face, he suspected that a joke was being played on him. "What is it?" he asked.

"Kolossal!" his uncle shouted, and burst into laughter.

"It's a joke," Sandor cried. "It's not my present at all."

Onkel Janos slapped his knees and roared with laughter. "Here, I'll show you," he said at last. "It's called a kaleidoscope. Look." He took the tube, held it up to the light, and peered through it. "So," he said, and handed it back.

Sandor placed his eye to the peep-hole and gasped.

"Turn it," his uncle said.

He turned it. There was a click, and behold, a new world. Another turn and another in a riot of colour, like a splintered rainbow; cool, deep-green gems, and frivolous pink ones, water-blue and orange jewels in triangles and squares and crescents glittering and flashing before his eye, ever changing, ever new.

He set it aside, finally, and gazed across at his uncle with a look of deep affection.

"Thank your uncle, Sandor," his mother said.

"Ho, something for you too," Onkel Janos cried, handing her a small leather case.

She opened it. A slow flush came over her cheeks. Sandor craned his neck and saw a pair of gold ear-rings with small red stones, and a brooch. She kissed her brother tenderly. "You shouldn't have done this, Janos," she said. "You know you shouldn't. But they are beautiful."

Onkel Janos was already engrossed in pulling out more shredded paper from his shoe-box. "For Joseph," he said, extracting an amber-stemmed pipe. "I'll give it to him later."

"You really shouldn't have done this, Janos. You've spent all your money, haven't you? . . . And a new suit," she exclaimed. "I never even noticed. It's very becoming."

216

Onkel Janos grasped her hand. "Here. Feel," he said. "English tweed."

"It reminds me of so many things to see you sitting here like this," she said quietly. "You haven't changed a bit."

"And neither have you. You're as beautiful as ever, Helena."

Sandor's eyebrows rose. He watched the colour ebb and flow on his mother's cheeks.

She laughed softly and shook her head. Her laughter had a girlish trill. Sandor's incredulity grew. He had never heard his mother laugh like this.

"The whole village went into mourning the day Joseph took you away," Onkel Janos continued. "At least, the young men did . . . The girls? Hmm!" He rolled his eyes, raised his right hand, and gave his moustache a twirl.

Frau Hunyadi laughed.

Sandor looked on in astonishment. His mother's lips, always so tightly pressed together, were now parted softly in a smile. He scarcely knew her. She looked strange and beautiful. He shifted uneasily.

217

As she raised her arm to fit her ear-rings in place, he bent over impulsively, threw his arms about her, and kissed her.

"Why, Sandor!" she said in surprise. He drew away, embarrassed, and looked at his uncle, who merely laughed and caught him between his knees and rumpled his hair some more.

His mother rose to her feet. "There's so much to talk about, I don't know where to start," she said. "But I'll have to go downstairs now . . . Come, Sandor. Onkel Janos is going to have a little nap."

Sandor wandered about the kitchen until his mother asked him to leave. The men in the yard were talking about the Old Country. With the exception of Willi Schumacher, the kids on the roof were all too young to play with. He went into the lane and looked into his kaleidoscope until his arm grew numb holding it to his eye. He smiled to himself as he lowered it. Next Saturday he would take it along and show it to Eric, and maybe even lend it to him for a week.

As he walked back into the yard, Willi Schumacher called down to him, asking him what he was carrying. Sandor paused. The thought that flashed across his mind was fully developed by the time he was up on the roof.

Five minutes later he was doing a roaring business. None of his customers had any ready money, but their fathers were down there in the yard below and feeling in an expansive mood. A few of the boys came back with nickels. These were permitted to hold the tube in their own hands. Some, who had been able to raise only a few coppers, found their exclamations dying in their throats, the tube was snatched away so fast.

When it was over, Sandor thrust his hand into his pocket and let the coins trickle through his fingers. In fifteen minutes, he had made forty-three cents — almost as much as he earned for a morning's work. As he climbed down, he caught sight of his father and Onkel Janos looking down at him from the attic window. Onkel Janos was smiling. But in that brief glance at his father, he knew that there was going to be trouble. His father motioned to him to come upstairs.

Sandor walked slowly through the yard, wondering what was wrong. He shrugged his shoulders and went upstairs. They were waiting for him behind Mr Schwalbe's cubicle. If he was going to be shamed, he thought, at least it was not going to be in the presence of all those girls. . . .

His father turned on him the moment he appeared. His face was livid. He raised his hand, dropped it — and Sandor, looking straight ahead, saw the clenched fingers in a convulsive fist, darkly veined, opening and closing and opening again.

"You demand money of your friends before you would let them see your gift?" his father asked in German.

Sandor looked up at him in astonishment.

"Sure," he said. "Why not?"

"You're not ashamed," his father asked, "to make your friends pay?"

"They're not my friends," Sandor replied. "And anyway, what did I do that's wrong? They'da done the same to me if they were in my place . . . "

"They are our guests," his father shouted. "You sent them down to their parents for money to pay you. Have you no shame at all? Your gift has not been an hour in your possession and already you have turned it into something dirty by contaminating it with money."

Sandor lowered his head. To be humiliated like this in front of his uncle, on the day or his arrival, and for no reason that he could understand!

"I didn't do anything wrong," he cried tearfully. "Anybody woulda done the same as I did." He saw his uncle shaking his head at him, but with a faint sympathetic smile on his lips. "It's my present, isn't it?" he shouted. "I can do what I like with it."

He fled into Mr Schwalbe's cubicle. At the door, he saw Onkel Janos remonstrating with his father, and as he closed it, caught a glimpse of his brother on one of the beds outside, lying peacefully there on his back, playing with his toes.

Poor little punk, he thought. He doesn't know yet what kind of a family he's in . . .

He lay down on the cot, his eyes tight against the threatening tears, his mind filled with the familiar pain and pleasure of crushing his father and humiliating him as he himself had been humiliated. Then he thought of how things might have been if he had been older. And he remembered that Eric too had trouble with his father. It was something you had to bear until you were grown up. He thought of how his uncle had taken his part. He wiped his eyes.

The door opened suddenly and his uncle entered the room. He sat down, sighed, and removed his shoes. Then he yawned, flinging out his arms as far as they would go, which was not very far, for the cubicle was only five feet wide and as a result the knuckles of his left hand struck the beaverboard partition a blow that seemed to Sandor to rock the entire attic. The plaster between the sheets of beaverboard shot out against the far wall. Sandor began to smile. His uncle merely raised his eyebrows and asked Sandor to move over. The springs groaned under his weight.

"Your father has great plans for you," he began. "A fine life is in store for you. A good education, an established position. Some day people will call you Herr Doktor. You will be a wealthy man. Does this please you?"

Sandor shook his head. "Pa doesn't want me to be rich," he cried. "He wants me to be like him, instead of like other people. He thinks everything that's got anything to do with money is wrong. Honest-to-God, Onkel Janos," he continued passionately, "Pa won't ever make enough money for me to go to University. He just talks like that. . . . And even if I could go, I wouldn't. You don't have to go to University to get rich."

His uncle stared up at the ceiling for a long time. "But your father works very hard," he said at last.

Sandor raised himself on one elbow. "Pa works hard," he admitted. His voice broke. "But he doesn't make enough," he continued. "And what makes Ma so mad is that he takes in boarders even when they don't pay."

His uncle turned and looked at him in silence. "I see," he said.

"Some day, I'm going to make a lot of money," Sandor said.

"And Ma won't have to worry any more. I won't let her take in any boarders, and Pa won't have to work. I'll look after the whole family."

His uncle smiled and nodded. "So? That's fine," he said. "It's good to hear such things. But how will you earn this money?"

Sandor flushed. "I'm going to quit school as soon as I can, and get a job. In an office. That's how people get rich in this country. Working in offices. And I'm already earning money," he added. "A dollar every week, cutting grass for rich people. Next week maybe I'll be making a dollar and a half when I get another customer."

"But that's a great deal of money," his uncle said.

"That's how things are in this country," Sandor explained.

Onkel Janos sighed and pulled a package of cigarettes and a box of matches from his pocket. He flicked the package open and popped a cigarette into his mouth, then lit it and letting the cigarette dangle from his lower lip, he gave a snort and blew at the flame of the match in a great sweeping gust that quite extinguished it and sent a shower of sparks and ashes into the air intermingled with the smoke from the bright-glowing end of the cigarette.

219

Sandor looked at him, hungrily intent upon the mighty inhalation which caused the cigarette so visibly to shorten, almost tasting the long-drawn, thin blue smoke streaming slowly and deliciously out of his uncle's hairy nostrils. His uncle had a way about him, a special way. Everything he did was just right. You felt that the way he did a thing was the only way it could ever be done.

He lay on his back watching the smoke trickle out of his uncle's nostrils. He watched until he could stand it no longer. "Onkel Janos," he pleaded, "give me a puff, will you?"

His uncle raised his eyebrows. "You smoke already?"

"I've been smoking for years."

His uncle looked at him thoughtfully as he handed him a cigarette. "And girls, too," he said. "I suppose you know all about girls."

"What is there to know?" Sandor asked. "They're all the same, aren't they?"

"You think so?" his uncle inquired, and nodded. "Maybe you're right," he said.

Sandor felt himself flushing. Out of the corner of his eyes he glanced at his uncle to see if he was laughing at him. But Onkel Janos was very soberly crushing the remains of his cigarette in the lid of a jam tin.

"So you're already earning a dollar and a half a week," he said. "You've been smoking for years and you know all about girls. It is as I said to your father. He doesn't have to worry about you. You're the kind of boy who's going to get along in this country."

"And so will you," Sandor cried. "You look like an English millionaire in your new suit. Nobody could tell you just came to Canada a few hours ago."

Onkel Janos laughed. Grabbing him by the middle he lifted him in the air for a moment, then dropped him on the cot and pretended to wrestle with him. Sandor screamed with pleasure.

He was weak with laughter when his uncle finally let him go.

He was about to retrieve his cigarette which had fallen to the floor when he heard the sound of footsteps on the lower front stairs. He listened intently and crushed his cigarette in the jam-tin lid. "It's Ma," he said.

His uncle grinned. "Go and tell her you'll wake me," he whispered, and winked. Sandor winked back. He opened the door and ran down the steps to the first landing. His mother stopped and looked up at him.

"You want me to call Onkel Janos, Ma?"

"Yes, call him Sandor. Everything's ready now."

Sandor ran back upstairs. Onkel Janos was lying on his side, breathing heavily. Sandor smiled softly.

"Onkel Janos. It's all right now," he said.

His uncle rose, combed his hair, and put on his shoes. They went downstairs.

Sandor's mouth fell open as he entered the living-room. All the tables they had borrowed from their neighbours that morning had been placed end to end. With wedges under their legs they were now all the same height, and since they were covered with several white tablecloths whose edges overlapped, the whole thing looked like one table, long and immense in the little room. The linen gleamed, the dishes sparkled. But Sandor's attention was fastened upon the head of the table where, in all its splendour, stood the Hunyadi geranium. For the occasion, the jam tin in which it stood was covered with a piece of green crepe.

Sandor looked at it in astonishment. Against the cool crisp background, where everything glistened so invitingly, it seemed to have taken on fresh colour and life. Its blood-red blossoms gave an air of festivity to the room. How it had ever managed to survive at all was a mystery. Year in and year out, it stood on the front-room window-ledge. In winter, the panes froze over; in summer they were black with rain-smeared grime. The Hunyadis had not only to water the plant, but also, since the window faced the freight-yards, to dust its thick limp leaves and blow away the specks of soot that lay like so many black sins upon its petals. Sometimes, they forgot to water it; sometimes in the winter when they were short of coal for the frontroom stove it was kept above the kitchen range. His mother had tried to grow other things, delicate fragile things with subtle odours and gracious forms, but one season on Henry Avenue and they were dead. Only the geraniums survived. And in window after window on Henry Avenue they stood, earthy and sturdy, throwing up leaves so that they might blossom and give their colour in lonely splendour to a neighbourhood whose only workaday tone was an abiding grey.

Now it stood at the head of the table to welcome Onkel Janos who, as he passed by, plucked a blossom and stuck it in his lapel.

Sander followed suit and trotted after his uncle into the kitchen.

A moment later he heard the strains of an accordion in the back yard. The screen door banged as Long Thomas, a neighbour, entered with his accordion, flanked on either side by one of the Nemeth twins. Long Thomas was well over six feet tall, sad and gaunt. The great bald nodding heads of the twins came scarcely to his elbows. With their fiddles under their arms, they walked sedately beside him, their dark eyes infinitely guileless. Upon a few rare occasions Sandor had visited them in their shack by the river. In the winter they made raffia baskets; in the summer, willow flower-stands. But no matter what the season, there was always time for music. No party was complete without them. By long-established custom their fee had come to consist of all the beer they could drink and as much food as they could eat.

Behind them swarmed the children, screaming with laughter. Long Thomas stopped, flung an incredibly long leg into the air, did a short little jig, and walked into the front room.

As though guided by some infallible sense, the twins made straight for the corner where the beer barrel stood. They drank in a way that made Sandor's mouth water even though he hated the smell of beer.

When they had finished, they sat down with their mugs of beer beside them, adjusted their instruments, and began to play. They played with verve, gusto, sweat, and love. Their eyes closed, their bodies swayed, their pink domes nodded, their fingers flew. Long Thomas finished his beer and joined them.

But now without warning the song changed to a Hungarian dance. Played by the Nemeth twins to a houseful of Hungarians, it was irresistible. From the kitchen came the sound of shouting and laughing and the impatient clacking of heels. Then to the loud delight of Sandor and the children, who had gathered around the musicians, Onkel Janos came waltzing into the front room with Frau Szabo in his arms. Sandor could not make up his mind whether to look at his uncle or receive the admiring glances of those around him for possessing such a relative. For Onkel Janos did not merely dance. There were times when Sandor could have sworn that neither Onkel Janos nor his partner had their feet on the ground. He spun her around, did a series of weird little sidesteps and then, while she whirled alone, leaped up, snapped his fingers, clicked his heels in mid-air, and shouted incomprehensible rhymes in Hungarian. Frau Szabo's face grew flushed. She smiled happily. Her bosom strained alarmingly against the fabric of her bodice.

The twins, watching them, nodded and grinned. Then their eyes and their mouths closed simultaneously and sublime smiles settled on their faces. The tempo of their playing became frenzied. More and more of the guests came from the kitchen and back-yard; a man would laugh, look shyly at his wife, and step out. The room grew so crowded one could scarcely move. The narrow aisle between the wall of children and the row of tables was filled with people dancing.

But no one danced as his uncle did, Sandor thought. Everything he did became appropriate, but only because he himself had done it.

When the music stopped, Sandor followed him to the corner where the twins were. With a few words, he had them laughing uproariously. They looked droll with their pink tongues flickering in the dark caverns of their mouths.

But now the guests were beginning to respond to Frau Hunyadi's pleas. They were gradually seating themselves at the table. Frau Hunyadi's friends helped her to serve.

Sandor pushed his way forward to the table set up for the older children. He sat down where he could watch his uncle.

The food arrived, the hot steaming fragrance of it filling the room, savoury and varied and as spicy as an adventure, rich with the treasured cooking-lore of the whole of Europe. Crumb by crumb the women had garnered the skills and details, the piquant flavours and the subtle aromas from a thousand sources — small ingenuities that came from poverty,

222

recipes taken from the vanquished and imposed by conquerors, graciously given by neighbours or stolen from friends, handed down from mother to daughter so that at last in Frau Hunyadi's kitchen there came to fruition an age-long process, proudly, lovingly, and painstakingly fulfilled.

Soup came first. But this was merely to prepare the guests for the more serious business of eating. Immediately after, there appeared an enormous bowl of chicken goulash, steaming hot in its red sauce of paprika, with great fat globules floating on the surface. As a side dish for soaking up the gravy there was a mound of home-made noodles, accompanied by small green gherkins with flesh clear as glass from their long immersion in brine, with the pungent aroma of dill and garlic and the young tender leaves of horse-radish. And there were pickled red peppers — for the adults who knew how to get them into their mouths without touching their lips — and horse-radish grated into crushed beetroot that went with the sausages, which were made by a landsmann who had been a butcher in the Old Country and who could be depended upon to season them liberally with paprika and garlic among other things.

223

Sandor rose after every course, with twitching nostrils breathing in the food that was carried past him, following it with his eyes to the adults' table, listening to his uncle's exclamations and the remarks of guests with a deep feeling of pride. This was a party. Not one — not one guest — had been asked to bring anything. The pickles and preserves and things were offered out of friendship. Their equivalent would some day be returned. A fleeting image of the Kostanuiks, Mary and her mother and father, came to him. He saw them, their long-drawn hungry faces pressed to the front room window, their eyes imploring him for food. "Yeah," he muttered, "that would be good for them."

He sat down, satisfied, only to spring up again as the aroma of another dish came to him. Sarma, it was called, made of ground meat and rice flavoured with paprika and chopped onions, wrapped in sauerkraut leaves. The thought of the paprika seeping through the finely shredded kraut almost made him swoon. He sat down. When he had finished the last course, he closed his eyes.

The clatter around him slowly diminished. Above the murmuring voices he heard his uncle's laughter. The twins began once more to play. He smelled coffee — real coffee with no chicory in it. His eyes opened.

The dishes had been cleared away; the cakes and pastry were brought in, heaping platters of kupfel, the bright outer pastry caressingly flaked around apricot, cherry, or plum centres. Mohn strudel — ground poppy seeds with sugar and raisins, enfolded in a pastry like a jelly-roll. Then apfel strudel and other tidbits, crisp bubbles of fruit-sugar and egg-white beaten to a froth and browned, with a walnut or an almond in the centre.

And last of all, the crowning achievement, the Torte, made of ground hazelnuts and a few spoonfuls of flour with five whipped-cream layers and a glazed dark chocolate covering. Sandor bit into it ecstatically. He felt as though he were eating his way into heaven. A few gulps later it was gone. He sipped his coffee and discovered that there was real cream in it.

At the adults' table, the men were getting up and beginning to smoke. Sandor got to his feet, just as the change of shift occurred at his table. The children were told to go outside and play. The girls who had been watching the babies upstairs, and the women who had helped to serve, seated themselves while the neighbours waited on them. Sandor sauntered slowly to the corner where the men were talking.

He sat down on the floor beside his uncle and listened, and watched the coming and going of people, and leaned back against his uncle's chair, contented.

Unfortunately, his uncle was speaking Hungarian. He got up after a time, passed a woman, a neighbour from across the way, who alone among the guests did not appear to be enjoying herself, and glared at her ferociously as he passed by.

The kitchen was full of women washing dishes and cleaning up. He helped himself to a handful of assorted pastries. Beside the dish stood a decanter and a brandy bottle with a few thimblefuls left at the bottom. He uncorked it and a sweet pungent odour reached his nostrils. He had never tasted brandy. His mouth began to water. He unbuttoned his blouse, thrust the bottle into it, and ran happily upstairs into his uncle's cubicle. He sat down, smoked the remainder of his cigarette, and then, raising the bottle to his lips, swallowed its contents in a gulp that suddenly sent him leaping to his feet to go reeling and gasping around the cubicle, clutching his throat. In trying to get cold air into his lungs, he tore open the door and staggered across the attic and down the stairs.

At the bottom, just as suddenly, he stopped. From the pit of his stomach there began to spread the most agreeable feeling he had ever known, a warm, satisfying glow that rose languidly to his head and darted like little tongues of flame in his veins, slowly to his loins. He sat down and grinned vacantly. A great peace came over him. Above he heard the sound of footsteps. He turned and saw two girls come mincing down the stairs, one of them Emma Schumacher. Emma's name had been a byword in the gang. Fragments of sex lore flashed through his mind, but most of them had become established as neighbourhood fact only so that they might fit into the sorry scheme of some dirty joke or other, and they only made things more confusing. He looked up. He caught a glimpse of the margin of Emma's black cotton stockings and above them the pink flesh of her thighs. Emma was small and slender, but the size of her thighs was appalling. He grew frightened lest in some future time he should prove unequal to what would be demanded of him. But then he remembered. The last time he had gone swimming with the gang, it had not escaped his notice that he was almost as big as Hank and certainly as big as Louis.

Emma's skirt swished past his ears and for the first time in his life he felt an unmistakable tremor in his loins, as though of a power long dormant now stirring at last to brief wakefulness, to fill him with a delight that was indescribable, that seemed to transport him to a region deep within him, where his passionate affection for himself, far from laughter and derision, could unfold and flower.

As though entranced he returned to the front room to his place beside his uncle's chair. Distantly he heard the party coming to life. He felt his uncle's hand on his head and fell asleep.

When he awoke, it was to the sound of his uncle's voice singing a Hungarian song. Onkel Janos stood in the centre of the room, keeping time with a glass of beer to the music. The refrain consisted of a few bars of laughter. His uncle's voice, Sandor thought, no less than his laughter, was deep and rich and splendid. It was fine to see him standing there.

The assembled guests clapped loudly when he had finished. He lowered his glass and in bowing caught sight of Sandor who had risen to his feet to applaud. With a shout Onkel Janos swooped down on him, caught him under the armpits, and raised him to his shoulders.

225

"A toast," he cried; the rest was a Hungarian rhyme.

And Sandor looked down at the smiling, friendly faces upturned to him, all happy, all willing to raise their glasses to him, and thought that it was only fitting that they should do so, that they should look up at him. Somehow he felt he had deserved it. He saw his parents smiling up at him and in that moment he forgave them everything.

Topic Seven

The Impact of Industrialization and Urbanization

Canada's prolonged depression, which began in the early 1870s, finally ended in the late 1890s. The economy expanded because of increased worldwide demand for Canadian agricultural and mineral resources and increased private and public investment. The structures set in place by the National Policy could finally be put into effect. Western settlement became a reality, as did large-scale industrialization, notably in southern Ontario and Quebec. In a chapter from their *Quebec: A History, 1867–1929* entitled "Urbanization," P.-A. Linteau, R. Durocher, and J.-C. Robert show industrialization's impact on the urban centres — particularly on Quebec's two dominant cities, Montreal and Quebec City.

Industrialization and urbanization increased the wealth and the power held by a small group of successful entrepreneurs. It also lead to a significant growth of the working class, and labourers in construction, railway building, and factory production came to represent the majority of the "urban poor." What kind of life did they experience in the core of the new industrial city? How did they develop their own consciousness as working-class people? In "Joe Beef of Montreal: Working-Class Culture and the Tavern, 1869–1889," Peter DeLottinville reconstructs life in Montreal's Joe Beef's tavern, the centre of an evolving working-class consciousness and culture.

On urbanization see J.M.S. Careless' pamphlet *The Rise of Cities in Canada before 1914*, Canadian Historical Association, Historical Booklet no. 32 (Ottawa: CHA, 1978) and his collection of essays, *Frontier and Metropolis in Canada: Regions, Cities, and Identities in Canada before 1914* (Toronto: University of Toronto Press, 1989). *The Canadian City: Essays in Urban History*, ed. G.A. Stelter and A.F.J. Artibise (Toronto: McClelland and Stewart, 1977; 2nd ed., Carleton Library, 1984) provides a very good anthology of articles in Canadian urban history and contains a good bibliography organized by regions. The National Museum of Civilization (formerly the National Museum of Man) is publishing a series of illustrated histories of Canadian cities. To date the following have appeared: J.M.S. Careless, *Toronto to 1918* (1984); James Lemon, *Toronto since 1918* (1985); Patricia Roy, *Vancouver* (1980); Max Foran, *Calgary* (1978); Alan Artibise, *Winnipeg* (1977); and John Weaver, *Hamilton* (1982). A major reference work is A.F.J. Artibise and G. Stelter, *Canada's Urban Past: A Bibliography to 1980 and Guides to Canadian Urban Studies* (Vancouver: University of British Columbia Press, 1981). Also consult the journal *Urban History Review/Revue d'histoire urbaine* (*UHR/RHU*), for recent articles in urban history.

Michael Bliss' *Northern Enterprise: Five Centuries of Canadian Business* (Toronto: McClelland and Stewart, 1987) provides a comprehensive history of Canadian business. Bliss has examined the attitudes of Canadian businessmen in *A Living Profit: Studies in the Social History of Canadian Business, 1883-1911* (Toronto: McClelland and Stewart, 1974). For a fine study of one notable Canadian businessman — Joseph Flavelle — see Bliss, *A Canadian Millionaire* (Toronto: Macmillan, 1978). For a good overview of the rise of business at the turn of the century in English- and French-speaking Canada respectively see "The Triumph of Enterprise" and "French Canada and the New Industrial Order," in R.C. Brown and R. Cook, *Canada, 1896-1921: A Nation Transformed* (Toronto: McClelland and Stewart, 1974). On the rise of public utilities as big business see Christopher Armstrong and H.V. Nelles, *Monopoly's Moment: The Organization and Regulation of Canadian Utilities, 1830-1930* (Toronto: University of Toronto Press, 1988).

Three excellent primary sources exist for a study of the impact of industrial growth in Canada at the turn of the century. The first is *The Royal Commission on the Relations of Labour and Capital, 1889*. An abridged version has been published under the title *Canada Investigates Industrialism*, edited and with an introduction by Greg Kealey (Toronto: University of Toronto Press, 1973). The other two sources are collections of documents: *The Workingman in the Nineteenth Century*, ed. M.S. Cross (Toronto: Oxford University Press, 1974), and *The Canadian Worker in the Twentieth Century*, ed. I. Abella and D. Millar (Toronto: Oxford University Press, 1978). Two worthwhile collections are *Essays on Canadian Working Class History*, ed. G. Kealey and P. Warrian (Toronto: McClelland and Stewart, 1976), and *Canadian Labour: Selected Readings*, ed. D.J. Bercuson (Toronto: Copp Clark, 1987). Terry Copp provides an in-depth study of working-class life in Montreal in his *The Anatomy of Poverty: The Conditions of the Working Class in Montreal, 1897-1929* (Toronto: McClelland and Stewart, 1974). A counterpart to Copp's work is Greg Kealey's *Toronto Workers Respond to Industrial Capitalism, 1867-1892* (Toronto: University of Toronto Press, 1980). A second valuable study on Toronto is Michael Piva, *The Conditions of the Working Class in Toronto, 1900-1921* (Ottawa: University of Ottawa Press, 1979). For a discussion of working-class culture see Bryan Palmer's *A Culture in Conflict: Skilled Workers and Industrial Capitalism in Hamilton, Ontario,*

1860-1914 (Montreal: McGill-Queen's University Press, 1979), and his *Working-Class Experience: The Rise and Reconstitution of Canadian Labour, 1800-1980* (Toronto: Butterworth and Co., 1983).

On working women see selected essays in the following anthologies: Janice Acton et al., ed., *Women at Work: Ontario, 1850-1930* (Toronto: Women's Educational Press, 1974); L. Kealey, ed., *A Not Unreasonable Claim: Women and Reform in Canada, 1880s-1920s* (Toronto: Women's Educational Press, Martin, 1976); and S.M. Trofimenkoff and A. Prentice, eds., *The Neglected Majority* (Toronto: McClelland and Stewart, 1977).

Urbanization*

P.-A. LINTEAU, R. DUROCHER, J.-C. ROBERT

228

Because industrialization brings workers together in factories, the growth of cities and changes in the living conditions of urban populations are among its effects. In examining these effects, however, urbanization and industrialization should not be confused. Urbanization refers to a social process in which people are grouped together in cities; in that sense it is a very old phenomenon, but one whose characteristics change over time and vary from one economic system to another. Industrialization does not create urbanization, but rather speeds up its pace and changes some of its characteristics.

General Characteristics

To describe and explain the growth of cities, geographers have developed the concept of urban function. An urban function is an economic activity that distinguishes a city, employs a significant portion of its population, and has a product that is intended for use outside the city. Until the middle of the nineteenth century, the function of Quebec's cities was essentially commercial. They were trading posts with a double role, covering both international trade, as the major staples — furs, lumber, and wheat — were brought there to be shipped out, and internal distribution, as they provided goods and services to a growing rural hinterland.

Quebec's dominant urban centres, Montreal and Quebec City, are also among its oldest. The importance of these two cities, their control of economic activity and political power, and their attraction for a significant part of the population have been evident from the seventeenth century to the present day. As the area of Quebec under cultivation expanded

*From *Quebec: A History, 1867-1929*, by P.-A. Linteau, R. Durocher, and J.-C. Robert. Copyright 1983 by James Lorimer & Co. Reprinted by permission.

in the late eighteenth and early nineteenth centuries, a network of villages — points of communication between city and country — appeared, forming the skeleton of Quebec's future urban network. The dominant position of Montreal and Quebec City was not the only characteristic of the urban network that was already apparent in the commercial era; the geographer Louis Trotier has pointed out others as well. Urban centres grew up primarily along the banks of the St. Lawrence and its tributaries, and were most densely concentrated and most clearly organized into a hierarchy in the Montreal plain (Map 1).

The 1850s and 1860s were a transition period in several respects. In those decades, the first effects of industrialization began to be felt, especially in Montreal. Montreal's growth took off, and it definitively replaced Quebec City as the nerve centre of Quebec's economic life. The population gap between the two cities widened steadily from then on. In Quebec as a whole, the organization of the urban network was changed radically by the coming of the railway. The Grand Trunk main line became a second spinal column (after the St. Lawrence) through which part of Quebec's urban system was linked together. Thanks to the railway, some villages — Saint-Hyacinthe, Sherbrooke, Lévis, Rivière-du-Loup — became intermediate centres of regional significance and experienced a period of rapid growth. As urban areas grew, it became necessary to establish political structures on the local level. Between 1840 and 1870, a series of acts set up the municipal government system as it exists today.

After 1870, the industrial function clearly became the driving force behind urban growth in Quebec. Factories began to dot Quebec's ter-

229

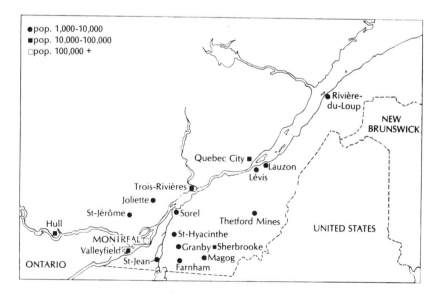

MAP 1: Quebec's Urban Network, 1901.

ritory, draining a portion of the surplus rural population towards the cities. The commercial function did not disappear, but rather remained a significant economic base for most of Quebec's urban centres. Its effects, however, were overshadowed by those of the new industrial establishments, which were generally built in already existing towns and villages, giving them a new impetus. Very few new towns were established in this period as a direct result of industry, and there was no radical change in the existing urban network. Rather, industrial centres were superimposed on commercial ones, and urban development became even more concentrated in the Montreal plain and its neighbouring region, the Eastern Townships.

The Urban Population

230   As a result of industrialization, the concentration of Quebec's population in cities increased, as can be seen by looking at the percentage of the population living in urban areas in a succession of census years (Table 1). The census definition of an urban area is an incorporated municipality with a population of 1,000 or more; in 1851, a little under fifteen per cent of Quebecers lived in urban areas, while fifty years later the figure was more than a third. The growth of the urban population began to accelerate in the decade 1871–81.

The degree of urbanization in Quebec followed a similar pattern to that of Canada as a whole. Table 1 shows no evidence of a lag in the urbanization of Quebec in relation to that of Canada, and the percentage of Quebec's population living in urban areas was higher than the Canadian percentage for every census year except 1891. There is a clearer gap between Quebec and its neighbouring province, Ontario. In the middle of the nineteenth century the two provinces showed a similar level of urbanization, but after 1871 Ontario clearly outpaced Quebec as a result of its more favourable economic circumstances.

Table 1 shows that Quebec underwent a significant change in the second half of the nineteenth century. But in giving us snapshots at a succession of fixed points in time, these figures can be misleading and do not always do justice to the complexity of the real world. It could be argued, for instance, that Quebec's population also underwent another process of urbanization. Throughout this period, the surplus population of the countryside flowed to the cities. Some of those who left rural Quebec remained in agriculture, in the American mid-west or western Canada, but cities were the destination for the largest part of Quebec's rural exodus. The weakness of Quebec's industrial structure relative to that of the United States made it impossible for Quebec cities to absorb all the surplus population. Those who were not absorbed within Quebec experienced urbanization outside Quebec, in the industrial towns of New England.

TABLE 1 Percentage of the Population Living in Urban Areas, Quebec, Ontario, and Canada, 1851–1901

Year	Quebec	Ontario	Canada
1851	14.9	14.0	13.1
1861	16.6	18.5	15.8
1871	19.9	20.6	18.3
1881	23.8	27.1	23.3
1891	28.6	35.0	29.8
1901	36.1	40.3	34.9

Source: L.O. Stone, *Urban Development in Canada*, 29.

As was pointed out in chapter 2, migration was characteristic of North America as a whole in the second half of the nineteenth century, and it led to another phenomenon of continental significance. Much of the urban population of the time consisted of transients, either from overseas or from the rural hinterland, for whom the city was only a temporary place of residence. In a context of great geographical mobility, as people left, new arrivals came to take their place, so that the total number of people who lived in a city in a ten-year period was much larger than the population figure that showed up in a census. As major relay points in the continental communications network, Quebec City and Montreal saw part of their population periodically replaced in this way. The scope of the phenomenon has not been measured, but the geographer Raoul Blanchard examined the case of the Irish of Quebec City. For a few decades in the middle of the nineteenth century, they represented a significant proportion of the population of the city. Around 1871, with Quebec City in a period of economic stagnation, they left en masse, some for Montreal, some for other parts of North America.

231

Urbanization was brought about by these population movements as well as by industrialization. In the last few decades of the nineteenth century, the process was clearly under way in Quebec and could not be reversed. All regions of the province were affected by it, but its pace and scope differed from one region to another.

The Major Cities

MONTREAL

At the time of Confederation, Montreal was unquestionably the metropolis not only of Quebec but of Canada as a whole, and it maintained its dominant position throughout succeeding decades. During the period, it registered a consistently high rate of population increase, with the most rapid growth occurring between 1881 and 1891 (Table 2). In 1861, Montreal was a city of 90,000 people; adding the population of its still semi-rural suburbs gives a figure of almost exactly 100,000. At the end of the century Montreal proper, which now covered an expanded area, had a population of more than a quarter of a million, and adding the suburban municipalities brought the total to about 325,000, or half the urban population of Quebec.

As Raoul Blanchard pointed out, Montreal's rise was due to industry. A first period of industrial growth had occurred in the 1850s and 1860s, and was concentrated in the southwestern part of the city, especially along the Lachine Canal. Around 1867, Montreal's industrial structure was characterized by the presence of five major industries: sugar refining, flour milling, ironmaking, wood processing, and shoemaking. In the 1880s, a second wave of manufacturing investment rounded out this early structure. Additional enterprises were founded in the existing sectors, while new ones such as meat curing, textiles, clothing, railway rolling stock, and tobacco emerged. By the end of the nineteenth century Montreal had become an important industrial centre and accounted for half the value of Quebec's manufacturing production. Illustrations from the era show a landscape dominated by factory smoke in the southwestern and eastern parts of the city.

232

TABLE 2 Population of Major Urban Centres in Quebec, 1861–1901

Municipality	1861	1871	1881	1891	1901
Montreal Region					
City of Montreal	90,323	107,225	140,247	216,650	267,730
Montreal and suburbs[1]	100,723	126,314	170,745	250,165	324,880
Saint-Jérôme	—	1,159	2,032	2,868	3,619
Joliette	—	3,047	3,268	3,347	4,220
Sorel	4,778	5,636	5,791	6,669	7,057
Saint-Hyacinthe	3,695	3,746	5,321	7,016	9,210
Saint-Jean	3,317	3,022	4,314	4,722	4,030
Valleyfield	—	1,800	3,906	5,551	11,055
Quebec City Region					
City of Quebec	42,052	59,699	62,446	63,090	68,840
Lévis	—	6,691	5,597	7,301	7,783
Lauzon	—	—	3,556	3,551	3,416
Eastern Townships					
Sherbrooke	5,899	4,432	7,227	10,110	11,765
Magog	—	—	—	2,100	3,516
Granby	—	876	1,040	1,710	3,773
Thetford Mines	—	—	—	—	3,256
Coaticook	—	1,160	2,682	3,086	2,880
Farnham	—	1,317	1,880	2,822	3,114
Others					
Hull	—	3,800	6,890	11,264	13,993
Trois-Rivières	6,058	7,570	8,670	8,334	9,981
Chicoutimi	—	1,393	1,935	2,277	3,826
Rivière-du-Loup	—	1,541	2,291	4,175	4,569

[1]A suburb is defined here as a town or village on Montreal Island bordering Montreal.
Source: Censuses of Canada.

The advantages accruing to Montreal from its position at the centre of the transportation system were another factor in its growth. It benefited from the substantial investments in infrastructure made in the nineteenth century. The St. Lawrence River canals, the ship channel, and the city's new harbour facilities made Montreal the focal point of water transportation. It was also the base of operations for the two major railway systems, the Grand Trunk and the Canadian Pacific, which established their administrative offices and maintenance shops there, and the centre of a web of railway lines extending in many directions. Transportation was an essential factor in the marketing and distribution of the goods that were manufactured in the city. Because Montreal was so well endowed with means of transportation, the concentration of industry in the city increased and its status as a metropolis for all of Canada was enhanced.

Towards the end of the nineteenth century, Montreal's capitalist class clearly dominated the economic activity of Canada as a whole. The most visible symbol of this domination was the ascendant Bank of Montreal–Canadian Pacific tandem. These two companies seemed to be almost ubiquitous in Canada. They were controlled by a close-knit group consisting of Donald Smith, George Stephen, R.B. Angus, William C. Van Horne, and others, whose interests extended to a large number of companies in the financial, commercial, industrial, and transportation sectors. *233*

Spatial extension was another aspect of Montreal's growth, as the area within the city limits was systematically occupied and the city began to overflow into the suburbs. Montreal's city limits had been officially designated in the late eighteenth century; within them were large areas that were not yet urbanized. These areas gradually became inhabited as the nineteenth century progressed; at the time of Confederation this progress was not yet completed. Three wards near the city limits grew substantially in the decades after Confederation — Saint-Antoine in the west end and Saint-Jacques and Sainte-Marie in the east (Map 2). By the late nineteenth century, occupation of the city's original territory was almost complete, and the overflow of population into the new suburban municipalities that had been established from the late 1860s on had begun. The most important of these new suburbs were the industrial towns of Saint-Gabriel, Sainte-Cunégonde, and Saint-Henri on the banks of the Lachine Canal to the west; Saint-Jean-Baptiste and Saint-Louis to the north; and Hochelaga and Maisonneuve to the east. Between 1871 and 1901, the population of these newly urbanized areas on Montreal Island grew from 11,000 to 130,000, or from four per cent to twenty per cent of the urban population of Quebec. At the end of the century, the largest part of the population increase in the metropolitan region was occurring in these new areas.

Montreal's municipal authorities wanted to adjust the region's political structures to these new demographic and economic realities, and tried to extend the city's territory by annexing suburban towns. The process

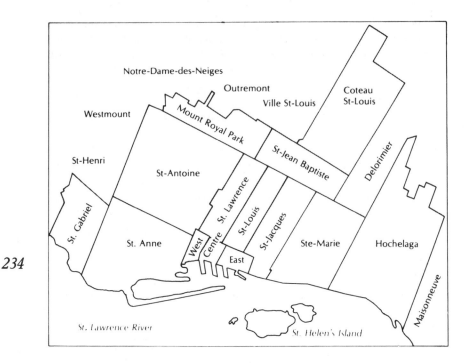

MAP 2: Montreal Wards in the Late Nineteenth Century.

began in 1883 with the annexation of Hochelaga; in the subsequent years, three more municipalities met the same fate. The phenomenon took on new dimensions in the early twentieth century, when the annexation of nineteen suburban municipalities in twelve years brought about a spectacular increase in Montreal's territorial size.

These small municipalities were typically the creation of a handful of real estate promoters who wanted to develop land that they owned. Towards this end, they would incorporate a small town, in which they would then control the town council. Through tax exemptions or cash subsidies, they attracted companies whose employees became residents of the new town. The promoters themselves also used tax exemptions to start development projects, which the municipality financed through borrowing, the burden of which was ultimately borne by small property owners and tenants. A few years or decades later, the municipality was heavily in debt, and annexation to Montreal seemed appealing as a solution to its financial problems.

The period was thus one of rapid growth and change for Montreal. One of the most significant changes was in the city's ethnic composition. Mid-nineteenth-century Montreal was culturally and politically a British city, with an English-speaking majority between 1831 and 1865; the English-speaking proportion of the population reached a peak of fifty-seven per cent in 1844. This British preponderance was reflected in the city council, where decisions were made in the interests of the English-speaking majority. The appearance of the city also changed, and in the 1840s British-style architecture started to replace the old French architecture that had characterized the city until then, although French architecture was never completely eliminated. The situation began to be reversed around 1865, when a French-speaking majority was re-established in the city as rural French Canadians came to work in the factories and immigration from the United Kingdom slowed down. Annexation of suburban municipalities with large French-speaking majorities intensified the process. However, it was almost twenty years before the change in ethnic composition was felt on city council, and much longer before it was reflected in the city's appearance and major cultural institutions.

By 1896, Montreal had become not only a financial and commercial metropolis but also a great industrial city. However, as a result of its rapid growth, a number of problems of adjustment affected living conditions in the city: crowding, deficient sanitary conditions, a high death rate.

235

QUEBEC CITY

The evolution of Quebec City during this period was very different from that of Montreal. Founded in 1608, Quebec City was the oldest city in the province, and had been the principal centre of New France and later of British North America. However, it had gradually lost its political pre-eminence to Ottawa, and at the time of Confederation it was entering a period of relative stagnation that lasted until the end of the century.

Quebec City's population grew by forty-two per cent between 1861 and 1871 (Table 2), but its growth in the three succeeding decades was very slow. A comparison between Quebec City and Montreal brings this slowdown into sharp focus. Throughout the first half of the nineteenth century, the population of the two cities was roughly the same. A clear gap began to appear in 1851, and by 1901, the Montreal urban area had a population five times as large as the Quebec City urban area. While twenty-two percent of Quebec's urban population lived in the Quebec City area in 1871, that figure had fallen to 10.5 per cent in 1901.

The transition from the commercial era to the industrial era was difficult for Quebec City. The difficulties the city experienced in the late 1860s were identified by Raoul Blanchard. Most significant was the decline of the timber trade. From the early nineteenth century, Quebec City was the port from which the largest part of Canadian lumber exports to England were shipped. But the replacement of squared timber by sawn lumber and the redirection of trade from Britain to the United States changed the lines of communication, so that Quebec City was no longer the pivot of wood exports. Ships built in Quebec City had carried Canadian timber to England, where the ships were resold; the slowdown in timber shipments thus adversely affected the city's shipbuilding industry. This industry was also hurt by changes in maritime technology, as the wooden vessel was replaced by the iron- or steel-hulled ship. From the 1870s on, Quebec City's shipyards declined rapidly. The port of Quebec City also experienced difficulties as a result of competition from Montreal. The dredging of the ship channel made it possible for ocean-going vessels to sail upriver as far as Montreal, and Quebec City gradually lost its importance as a terminus for transatlantic lines. Thus, as Blanchard pointed out, all of Quebec City's maritime activity was in decline, with thousands of workers losing their jobs and having to seek employment elsewhere.

Quebec City was also not well integrated into the railway system. With the Grand Trunk running along the south shore, it was the Lévis area rather than Quebec City that developed; it was not until the early twentieth century that the two banks of the river were linked by a bridge. It was only in 1879 that the North Shore Railway, connecting Quebec City with Montreal, was opened to traffic, and this long wait for railway service did not help the city get out of its slump. When the capital of Canada was established at Ottawa in 1867 there was an exodus of civil servants, which was followed by the departure of the British garrison in 1871.

While there were many unfavourable elements in Quebec City's situation, they were partly counterbalanced by the development of some compensating factors. Having lost its pre-eminence on a Canada-wide scale, Quebec City increasingly became a regional metropolis for eastern and central Quebec. Quebec City's immediate hinterland is fairly limited, so that new regions had to be brought under its influence and dominated, a task which occupied the Quebec City bourgeoisie during the last three decades of the century. Its main instrument was the railway. Thus, the Quebec and Lake St. John Railway allowed it to dominate the Saguenay region, the Lévis and Kennebec brought the Beauce within its orbit, and the North Shore Railway strengthened its links with the region to the west of the city. Also during this period, Quebec City attracted some industrial establishments, especially shoe factories. Some of the jobs lost through the decline of maritime activities were made up for by this industrial growth, but not enough to retain all the city's surplus population. An attempt was also made to breathe new life into the maritime sector by significantly enlarging the city's harbour facilities; this project was completed in 1890.

Thus, Quebec City's stagnation in the late nineteenth century was due to the decline of its traditional economic activities; their replacement by new activities did not occur quickly enough to stabilize its population.

This situation also had significant effects on the city's ethnic composition. In 1861, about forty per cent of its population was of British origin: by 1901 this figure had declined to fifteen per cent. The decline was just as dramatic in absolute numbers — from 23,000 to 10,000 in the same period. This population was mostly Irish and consisted primarily of labourers in the harbour or the shipyards; they were the first to feel the effects of the slowdown in economic activity and had no choice but to leave the city. Thus, Quebec City became increasingly French in the late nineteenth century. As Blanchard noted, this change affected the bourgeoisie as well, and there were a growing number of French Canadians among the owners of the major enterprises.

The growth of the population, limited as it was, nevertheless brought about an expansion of the city's inhabited area. This occurred in the eastern part of the city, the population of which doubled between 1861 and 1901, especially in the neighbourhoods of Saint-Roch, Saint-Sauveur, and Saint-Vallier, where new industries were established.

237

OTHER CITIES AND TOWNS

At the time of Confederation, Trois-Rivières was still the third largest city in Quebec, far behind Montreal and Quebec City; in the next three decades it was passed by Hull, Sherbrooke, and Valleyfield in succession. Like Quebec City, Trois-Rivières was in a period of stagnation, and its population grew only from 6,098 to 9,981 in forty years; between 1881 and 1891, it even declined slightly. The reason for this situation was the decline of the timber trade in the last quarter of the century. The economy of Trois-Rivières' hinterland was essentially agricultural or agroforest. It was not until the early twentieth century that hydroelectricity and the pulp and paper industry gave new impetus to the region's economy and brought about the development of an urban network (Cap-de-la-Madeleine, Shawinigan, Grand-Mère, La Tuque) for which Trois-Rivières was the bridgehead.

The situation was different in the Eastern Townships, where a relatively prosperous agricultural economy led to the growth of a network of villages. In the last quarter of the nineteenth century, factories were established in a number of these centres to make use of rural manpower, turning them into small towns, each with a population of barely 3,000 in 1901 — Magog, Granby, Coaticook, Farnham, Richmond, Windsor. Thetford Mines, whose growth was based on the asbestos-mining industry, was a special case. This little urban network was capped by a regional metropolis, Sherbrooke, which played a dominant role in the Eastern Townships during the period. Sherbrooke's location on the St. Francis River at its confluence with the Magog was advantageous, and it benefited further from being on the Grand Trunk Railway. It was both an industrial town and a service centre for the Eastern Townships as a whole.

There was also another regional network in Quebec, consisting of six satellite towns forming a ring around Montreal at a radius of about sixty kilometres — Saint-Jérôme, Joliette, Sorel, Saint-Hyacinthe, Saint-Jean, and Valleyfield. Their combined population was more than 18,000 by 1871, and it was 40,000 in 1901. Industrial and commercial functions and a role as service centres all contributed to their growth. The town of Joliette is a representative case. Founded in 1824, it developed slowly until the middle of the century. It was the site of a large sawmill, and the forest industry was its main economic base. When neighbouring townships were opened to settlement, it quickly became a regional service centre, a development which brought new kinds of establishments to the town and introduced a form of economic activity that was both commercial and industrial. Typical of this process was the gradual evolution of a small ironworks into a plant where farm machinery was manufactured; another ironworks offered its customers a wide variety of iron goods, from machine parts to saucepans by way of *ferrures de moulin à laver* (iron parts for wood-frame washing machines). The population of Joliette at the turn of the century was 6,000; creation of a diocese of Joliette in 1904 was testimony to its importance.

238

At the end of the period, the process of urbanization in Quebec was well under way. Montreal's ascendancy had grown, while a network of small towns had developed primarily in the Montreal plain and the Eastern Townships.

Joe Beef of Montreal: Working-Class Culture and the Tavern, 1869–1889*

PETER DeLOTTINVILLE

Montreal was a city of contrast. The casual tourist, following the advice of his *Strangers' Guide to Montreal*,[1] would spend days viewing florid Gothic and ornate Italian church architecture, the engineering marvel of Robert Stevenson's Victoria Bridge, and the various monuments to commercial power. This faithful *cicerone*, however, would not give the tourist the total picture of a nineteenth-century urban landscape. The official face of Canada's first city consisted of monuments to individual industry, public morality, and social harmony. Absent from the official guide were the inhabitants of the narrower streets — the factory workers, the frequenters of taverns, the waterfront street gangs, or the crowds of longshoremen outside the Allen Line office waiting for work. What the tourist needed to see was a monument to Montreal's working class. Had he accidentally wandered into Joe Beef's Canteen, the tourist might

*From *Labour/Le Travailleur* 8/9 (1981/1982): 9–40, with permission of the editor. Copyright Committee on Canadian Labour History.

have found it, where the rules and procedures of official Montreal had little value.

During the late nineteenth century, Joe Beef's Canteen was a notorious part of that underworld which existed in the Victorian city.[2] Located in the centre of the waterfront district, the Canteen was the haunt of sailors and longshoremen, unemployed men and petty thieves. Middle-class Montreal saw this tavern as a moral hazard to all who entered and a threat to social peace. Yet if critics called the Canteen's owner, Charles McKiernan, the "wickedest man" of the city, working-class residents along the waterfront claimed McKiernan as their champion. His tavern was a popular drinking spot, but also a source of aid in times of un-employment, sickness, and hunger. For its patrons, Joe Beef's Canteen was a stronghold for working-class values and a culture which protected them from harsh economic times.

Primarily, this essay describes the working-class culture which grew around Joe Beef's Canteen and analyzes that culture in terms of the community which supported it. The efforts of middle-class organizations to improve the conditions of the waterfront labourers are examined in the light of this culture. Finally, by placing this culture within the major developments influencing Montreal during the 1880s, the decline of Joe Beef's Canteen can be understood. Through this process a clearer understanding of the relationship between cultural change and historic development can be reached.

As the recent lively debate bears witness,[3] the concept of working-class culture in historical analysis is both fruitful and problematic, and before entering into a detailed discussion of the working-class tavern, it is necessary to define this concept and establish the limitations of its application. Working-class culture covers a wide range of recreational, social, and job-related activities from labour day parades and trade union picnics to charivaris and the secret ceremonies of the Knights of Labor. While each form of culture can only be understood within its specific time and place, there was a common thread which made particular cultures working-class cultures. As Raymond Williams has stated, working-class culture embodies "a basic collective idea and the institutions, manners, habits of thought and intentions which proceed from this."[4] By assuming an "active mutual responsibility"[5] between workingmen, working-class culture offered an alternative to the individualist, competitive philosophy of the nineteenth-century middle class. Nothing was as common as a tavern in nineteenth-century Montreal, and because of this, working-class taverns probably represented one of the most basic forums of public discussion. Drawing their customers from the neighbouring streets, such meeting places were the first to a sense change in mood, or experience the return of economic prosperity. Joe Beef's Canteen, while attracting a wider clientele than most taverns, was essentially the same

239

type of focal point for the dockyard workers. The uncommon aspect of the Canteen was the remarkable ability of Charles McKiernan, the tavern's owner, to transform this rather commonplace forum into a dynamic force for the working class of Montreal.

The depression which accompanied the 1870s had a great impact on those who, like the patrons of Joe Beef's Canteen, were at the bottom end of the economic scale. Gareth Stedman Jones, in his study of casual labour and unemployment, *Outcast London*, demonstrated that middle-class London saw the casual labourers of East London as unregenerated workers who had yet to accept the industrious habits of their fellow workingmen of the factories.[6] These "dangerous classes," much like the patrons of the Canteen, were perceived as a threat to social order. While Montreal's waterfront could not compare to the horrors of East London, Montreal's middle classes were concerned about a "dangerous class" united by a forceful, if eccentric, spokesman who articulated labourers' frustrations and demands. Joe Beef would have been taken much less seriously had his success not coincided with the increasing number of factory workers, both skilled and unskilled, who appeared on the streets of Montreal. Municipal authorities, encouraged by middle class reformers, paid more attention to questions of public order and morality in the face of such a mass of new residents. Drunkenness, blood sports, and street brawls associated with the waterfront taverns could not be permitted to flourish if all workers were to adopt the disciplined virtues of the new industrial society.

Charles McKiernan was born on 4 December 1835, into a Catholic family in Cavan County, Ireland. At a young age, he entered the British Army and, after training at the Woolwich gunnery school, was assigned to the 10th Brigade of the Royal Artillery. In the Crimean War, McKiernan's talent for providing food and shelter earned him the nickname of "Joe Beef," which would stay with him for the rest of his life. In 1864, McKiernan's Brigade was sent to Canada to reinforce the British forces at Quebec. By then a sergeant, McKiernan was put in charge of the military canteens at the Quebec barracks and later on St. Helen's Island. If army life had seemed an alternative to his Irish future, then McKiernan saw better opportunities in North America. In 1868, McKiernan bought his discharge from the Army and with his wife and children settled in Montreal, opening the Crown and Sceptre Tavern on St. Claude Street.[7]

By settling in Montreal, McKiernan joined an established Irish community which accounted for 20 per cent of the total population. Centred in Griffintown, the largely working-class Irish had their own churches, national and charitable societies, political leaders, and businessmen.[8] And as a tavern owner, McKiernan entered a popular profession in a city with a liquor licence for every 150 inhabitants.[9] The increasing number of taverns caused one temperance advocate to lament that if trends continued Montreal was destined to become "the most drunken city on the continent."[10] The Crown and Sceptre, commonly known as "Joe Beef's Canteen," had a central location, with Griffintown and the Lachine Canal to the east and the extensive dockyards stretching out on either side. Business was good for Charles McKiernan.

In spite of the large numbers of taverns, Joe Beef's Canteen had an atmosphere, and a reputation, which was unique. Located in the waterfront warehouse district and at night identified only by a dim light outside the door, the Canteen housed a fantastic assortment of the exotic and the commonplace. One visitor described it as "a museum, a saw mill and a gin mill jumbled together by an earthquake; all was in confusion."[11] The barroom was crudely furnished with wooden tables and chairs, sawdust covering the floor to make cleaning easier. At one end of the bar, great piles of bread, cheese, and beef supplied the customers with a simple meal. Behind the bar a large mirror reflected a general assortment of bottles, cigar boxes, and curios. One bottle preserved for public display a bit of beef which lodged — fatally — in the windpipe of an unfortunate diner. The quick-witted McKiernan served his patrons with an easy manner. An imposing figure with a military bearing and fierce temper, the owner had few problems with rowdyism.[12]

241

Joe Beef's Canteen had a special type of patron, and McKiernan aptly referred to his establishment as the "Great House of Vulgar People." His clientele was mostly working class. Canal labourers, longshoremen, sailors, and ex-army men like McKiernan himself were the mainstays of the business. Along with these waterfront workers, Joe Beef's Canteen attracted the floating population along the Atlantic coast. W.H. Davies, in his *Autobiography of a Super-Tramp*, remarked that, "not a tramp throughout the length and breadth of the North American continent . . . had not heard of [Joe Beef's Canteen] and a goodly number had at one time or another patronized his establishment."[13] McKiernan's tavern was also a well-known *rendezvous* for the "sun-fish" or "wharf-rats" of the harbour who lived a life of casual employment and poverty. Newspaper reporters often dropped into the tavern to check on petty criminals who mingled with the crowd. Unemployed labourers visited the Canteen in the early morning to look for a day's labour and often remained there throughout the day in the hope of something turning up. In all it was not a respectable crowd[14] and, no doubt, was shunned by the more self-respecting artisans of the neighbourhood.

For working-class Montreal, the tavern held attractions beyond the simple comforts of food and drink. With no public parks in the immediate area, and only occasional celebrations by national societies and church groups, their daily recreational activities were centred around places like Joe Beef's Canteen. McKiernan's tavern was exceptionally rich in popular recreations. A menagerie of monkeys, parrots, and wild cats of various kinds were from time to time exhibited in the Canteen, but it was McKiernan's bears which brought in the crowds. Joe Beef's first bear, named

Jenny and billed as the "sole captive" of the "courageous" 1869 expedition to the North West, never retired sober during the last three years of her life. One of her cubs inherited the family weakness. Tom, who had a daily consumption of twenty pints of beer, was often as "drunk as a coal heaver" by closing. Indeed, Tom was one of the regulars, usually sitting on his hind quarters and taking his pint between his paws, downing it without spilling a drop. Local temperance men had always pointed out that drink turned men into animals, but in observing Tom's habits Joe Beef could point out this curious reversal of behaviour which the Canteen produced.[15] Other bears were kept in the tavern's cellar and viewed by customers through a trap door in the barroom floor. Occasionally, McKiernan brought up the bears to fight with some of his dogs or play a game of billiards with the proprietor.

The tavern was not an ideal place for animals and one observer remarked on the mangy, dirty, and listless character of the bears.[16] Beatings

were often used to rouse the animals into their "naturally" ferocious state. Sometimes McKiernan was mauled during these demonstrations and once a buffalo on exhibit sent him to hospital for a number of days.[17] A Deputy Clerk of the Peace, inspecting the tavern to renew its licence, was bitten by one of Joe Beef's dogs.[18] There was little public outcry over these conditions. Montreal's Royal Society for the Prevention of Cruelty to Animals was still a fledgling organization in the 1870s which spent its time regulating butchers' practices and prosecuting carters for mistreatment of their horses. As long as they presented no public danger, McKiernan's menagerie was left undisturbed.

Although lacking formal education, Charles McKiernan considered himself a man of learning and regularly read the *New York Journal*, the *Irish American*, the *Irish World*, and local newspapers. He employed a musician (which was illegal under the terms of his licence) to entertain his customers. Regular patrons played the piano in the tavern. McKiernan, however, led much of the entertainment. Drawing on personal experience and varied readings, McKiernan eagerly debated topics of the day, or amused patrons with humorous poems of his own composition. He had a remarkable ability to ramble on for hours in rhyming couplets. Sometimes to achieve this end, he distorted the accepted English pronunciation beyond recognition. This disgusted some middle-class visitors to the Canteen, but regular customers clearly enjoyed these feats of rhetoric.[19] Behind the bar, two skeletons were hung from the wall and served as props for McKiernan's tales. From time to time, the skeletons represented the mortal remains of McKiernan's first wife, his relatives in Ireland, or the last of an unfortunate temperance lecturer who mistakenly strayed into Joe Beef's Canteen one night.

From the occasional poetry which McKiernan printed in the newspapers, the style and subjects of these evenings can be seen. Concentrating on the figures of authority in the workingman's life, the employer, the

Recorder, the landlord, or the local minister, McKiernan's humour allowed his patrons a temporary mastery over the forces which dominated their lives outside the Canteen doors. Inside the Canteen, the rights of the common man always triumphed. On local issues, McKiernan complained about the lack of municipal services for the waterfront community. He demanded,

Fair play for Sammy, Johnny and Pat as
well as the Beaver Hall Bogus Aristocrat![20]

Legal authority, most familiar to his patrons through the Recorder's Court, was also denounced, but feared. An engraving of the Recorder looked down on the patrons from above the bar, and wedged into the frame were a number of dollar bills and notes which served as a reserve fund. McKiernan used this fund to pay fines imposed upon his regular customers.[21] Since most depended upon day labour, even a short jail term could spell disaster for the labourers' families. Imprisonment in lieu of fines was a very contentious issue, as the vehemence of the following poem illustrates.

They have taken me from my father,
They have taken me from my mother,
They have taken me from my sister,
They have taken me from my brothers,
In this wintry season of woe
And for the sake of *one* paltry, lousy *Dollar*,
Down to jail, for to die, like a Dog, amongst *Bugs* and *Vermin*,
   I had to go.
I died amongst howling and laughter,
I died howling for a drink of water
But you living *Tyrants*, and *Two Legged Monsters* take warning and
   remember that cold, cold Saturday Morning!!!
For man's vengeance is swift, though God's vengeance is with
   some, rather slow.[22]

McKiernan himself was no stranger to the Recorder's Court. In July 1867, the tavern keeper faced charges from a disgruntled patron who had been roughly thrown into the street for rowdyism. On different occasions, McKiernan's musician and a former servant complained of beatings they had received for drunkenness on the job.[23] Along with the violations of his liquor licence, such incidents illustrated that Joe Beef's legal opinions were grounded in experience.

Another prominent subject in Joe Beef's Canteen was the economic depression which hovered over Montreal for much of the 1870s. As casual labourers, the Canteen's patrons were severely affected by commercial slumps. In "Joe Beef's Advice to Biddy, the Washerwoman," McKiernan wrote,

I must tell you that Kingston is dead, Quebec is
Dying and out of Montreal, Ottawa and Toronto hundreds are flying
In the country parts unless you can
Parlez-vous, There is nothing for you to do
And in John's office it is all the cry
No Union printers for work need apply
And if the landlord his rent you cannot
Pay your sewing machine he will take
Away. So in the fall God help the
Poor of Montreal.[24]

The unwillingness of the private and public authorities to provide adequate relief systems also attracted Joe Beef's notice. In a parody of the
economic theories of industrialists, McKiernan professed,

Joe Beef of Montreal, the Son of the People,
He cares not for the Pope, Priest, Parson or King
William of the Boyne; all Joe wants is the Coin.
He trusts in God in the summer time to keep him
from all harm; when he sees the first frost and
snow poor old Joe trusts to the Almighty Dollar
and good maple wood to keep his belly warm. . . . [25]

These were problems which his patrons had little difficulty in
understanding.

Central to all of McKiernan's pronouncements was the belief that the
common problems of casual labourers and the poor of Montreal should
overcome the religious and national differences which separated them.
Joe Beef did "not give a damn Whether he is an Indian a Nigger a
Cripple a Billy or a Mich"[26] when attempting to help the unemployed.
What the unemployed and casual labourer lacked, in McKiernan's opinion, was a common voice. Since no one else was likely to assume that
role, Joe Beef became the self-appointed champion of the waterfront
workers. His success was remarkable as he gained the confidence of his
neighbours and attracted the attention of many residents who were unaware of the poor conditions on their doorstep. Making friends with both
English and French journalists, Joe Beef's Canteen and the waterfront
community appeared regularly in the press. While such publicity was
good for the Canteen, few accused McKiernan of self interest. "Joe Beef"
became so well known that few knew precisely who Charles McKiernan
was. And despite his Irish background, Joe Beef had considerable appeal
to French Canadian workers as well, if one can judge popularity from
the coverage Joe Beef received in the French language press.

The recreational aspects of Joe Beef's Canteen covered only a narrow
spectrum of the interaction between the tavern owner and his patrons.
As the focal point of social activities, Joe Beef's Canteen also provided

the initiative for a number of social services which were a logical out-growth of the close relationship between McKiernan and his neighbour-hood. His role in alleviating problems of housing, job hunting, health care, and labour unrest indicated the possibility of a collective response to the common problems among casual labourers of Montreal's waterfront.

The most visible service which Joe Beef's Canteen offered was a cheap place to stay for transient and single workers. In the Crown and Sceptre, the barroom was situated next to a dining room and sleeping quarters. The sleeping area contained about 40 wooden sofas which served as beds. At eleven o'clock, boarders deposited ten cents at the bar and were handed a blanket. The men then spread a mattress over the wooden sofa, stripped off all their clothes, and went to sleep. McKiernan insisted that all his boarders sleep naked as a matter of cleanliness. Those found dirty were ordered upstairs to use one of the wash tubs. Each boarder also had to have his hair cut short, and those failing to meet the standards were sent to Joe Beef's "inspector of health," or barber, to comply. No con-versation was permitted after eleven o'clock and everyone was roused out of bed at seven sharp. These rules were enforced personally by McKiernan in his best British Army sergeant's manner. Three-quarters of the tavern's boarders were boys between the ages of 12 and 14 who earned their living selling newspapers. For 20 cents a day, they received their food and lodging and, although the conditions set down by Joe Beef might be draconian, they were clearly preferred to similar facilities offered by church organizations. Indeed, the Crown and Sceptre proved such a popular place that one of the prime reasons for moving to Common Street in 1876 was the lack of space. His waterfront location had room for 200 men.[27]

245

Fees for room and board were often waived for those without the means to pay such modest sums. McKiernan's tavern was also close to the sour-ces of casual employment which was an important consideration when a day's work might depend on arriving early on the job site. McKiernan often loaned shovels to men engaged in snow shovelling and other jobs. And as the natural resting place for all types of labourers on the docks, Joe Beef's Canteen was an ideal location to learn who might be hiring in the future. In this way, the tavern allowed transient workers to fa-miliarize themselves with the local labour market and to make a decision whether to stay in Montreal or move on.[28]

Other social services grew informally as local residents turned to McKiernan for assistance in times of trouble. When a Lachine canal la-bourer was injured during a blasting operation, fellow workers brought him to Joe Beef's to recuperate. After two men got into a drunken brawl and the loser stripped naked in the street, the crowd brought the man to Joe Beef's for care. A young immigrant who collapsed on the docks also ended up in the tavern for convalescence. While Joe Beef's served as a neighbourhood clinic, McKiernan's folk cures left much to be desired. The young immigrant was treated with a vinegar-soaked towel bound tightly around his head. McKiernan also professed faith in cayenne pepper and whiskey to cure cramps and Canadian cholera. All this in 20 minutes.[29] Still, many people in the nineteenth century attributed medicinal powers to alcohol, and McKiernan did state an intention to take courses at the Montreal General Hospital to improve his knowledge of basic medicine.

These experiences led the tavern owner to lobby established medical institutions to improve health care services for waterfront residents. In December 1879, he set up a collection box in his tavern for the Montreal General Hospital and invited his customers to contribute. Donating one-tenth of his receipts from all his dinners and a similar share of his boarding house income, McKiernan hoped to raise $500 a year. In the following years, McKiernan offered $100 to the Montreal General if they would provide a doctor to attend the poor in their homes. The hospital declined the offer. Unsuccessful in a more formal improvement of health care services, McKiernan continued to provide emergency relief. When the body of a suicide was buried in August 1883, the tavern keeper provided a tombstone.[30]

The question of class allegiance was most clearly defined by the incidents of labour unrest which periodically disrupted the city. In December 1877, over 1,000 labourers working on the enlargement of the Lachine Canal abandoned their picks and shovels after a reduction in wages. The Irish and French workers paraded behind a tricolour flag along the canal banks and drove off those who refused to participate in the strike. Following a riot at the offices of canal contractor William Davis, during which the strike leader was shot, the Prince of Wales Rifles were called out to protect the canal and those workers who continued to work at reduced wages.[31] The strikers demanded a wage increase to a dollar a day, a nine hour day, regular fortnightly payments, and an end to the "truck system" of payment.[32] Among the Montreal citizens, there appeared to be some sympathy with the poor working conditions of the labourers, notably from the *Montreal Witness* and local MP Bernard Devlin,[33] but the militant behaviour of the strikers was generally condemned.

Strongest support for the strikers came from the waterfront community. Practical in all things, McKiernan realized that strikers, like the army, travel on their stomachs. On the morning of 20 December, he sent 300 loaves of bread, 36 gallons of tea, and a similar quantity of soup. These supplies required two wagons to be delivered. In addition to feeding the strikers, McKiernan took in as many as the Canteen could hold. One night 300 people found shelter under his roof. Throughout the strike McKiernan was observed "carting loaves and making good, rich soup in mammoth boilers, as if he were a commissary-general with the resources of an army at his back."[34] No doubt his military training was put to the test in maintaining order in his kitchen. That background also made the tavern keeper aware of the awkward position of the Prince of Wales Rifles who had been hastily summoned to guard the canal. To ensure that the soldier ate as well as a striker, McKiernan despatched a wagon of bread to the men on duty. The soldiers saw the humour in Joe Beef's assistance and gave most of the bread away to the crowd.[35] Some of the tension between striker and soldier was successfully released.

McKiernan, of course, was not popular with the canal contractors for his whole-hearted support of the labourers. William Davis, pointing suspiciously to the 14 taverns in the immediate area, wrote that the strike was caused by outside trouble makers. Another contractor was more direct in his accusations. "All of the trouble which we have had on the canal this winter has been caused mostly by men that never worked a day on the canal and have been started in a low Brothel kept by one *Joe Beef* who seems to be at the head of it all."[36] Despite this claim, McKiernan had only a supporting role in the labourers' actions, but such comments indicated the success of McKiernan's efforts to aid the strike.

Besides using his Canteen to take care of the strikers' physical needs, McKiernan also used his skills as an orator to attract public attention to the strikers' demands. By 1877, Joe Beef was a figure of some notoriety in Montreal and the local press found that his exploits made good copy. His support of the strike was reported extensively in Montreal and even in one Ottawa newspaper. The strikers' first meeting took place outside Joe Beef's Canteen and the tavern owner was asked to say a few words. Those nightly discussions in the tavern had given McKiernan a remarkable ease with language, and his talent for speaking in rhyming couplets was not wasted. Most of his speech to the crowd was in rhyming form, which so impressed the *Montreal Witness* reporter that he apologized for only reporting the substance of the speech and not its form as well. McKiernan explained his actions in the following terms.

I have been brought up among you as one of yourselves since I was a boy running about bare-footed. When I heard of the strike on the Lachine Canal, I thought I would try to help you, for I knew that men employed there had much to put up with. So I sent you bread to help you hold out. I could not send you whiskey, because you might get drunk, and commit yourselves. In this way you might have injured your cause, and perhaps made the volunteers fire on you. (Laughter) . . . The greatest philanthropists in the world are in Montreal, and the public here will sympathize with you. They will not see you tyrannized over. But if you are riotous, depend upon it, as sure as you are men before me, the law will take it in hand and crush you. I have nothing against the contractors and you will succeed by speaking rightly to them. You will get your $1 a day for nine hours, or perhaps for eight hours (cheers) or perhaps more (loud cheers). But keep orderly; mind your committee.[37]

The speech was received with "deafening" cheers.

These mass meetings organized by the strike committee were an important part of their efforts to secure better working conditions. Since the canal enlargement was a federal project, Alexander Mackenzie's government was anxious to have it completed before the next election. Failure to live up to this previous election promise would cost the Liberals votes in Montreal.[38] By rallying public support for their cause, the strikers hoped that Ottawa would intervene on their behalf and compel the contractors to make concessions. As the strike continued, the size of the mass meetings grew. In Chaboillez Square 2,000 people assembled to hear McKiernan and other speakers. Joe Beef lectured on the theme of the "Almighty Dollar."

248

My friends, I have come here tonight to address you on "the Almighty Dollar." The very door bells of Montreal ring with the "Almighty Dollar." The wooden-headed bobbies nail you, and you have to sleep on the hard floor provided by the City Fathers, and the next morning the fat Recorder tells you: "Give me the 'Almighty Dollar,' or down you go for eight days." The big-bugs all have their eyes on the "Almighty Dollar," from the Bishop down, and if you die in the hospital, they want the almighty dollar to shave you and keep you from the students. No one can blame you for demanding the "Almighty Dollar" a day. The man who promises 90¢ a day and pays only 80¢ is no man at all. The labourer has his rights.[39]

Public support for the strikers did not alter the fact that the labourers were without income, and after eight days on strike, they returned to the canal at the old wages.[40]

The canal labourers, however, refused to admit defeat. In mid-January, a strike committee went to Ottawa with funds raised by McKiernan and others in order to plead their cause before Alexander Mackenzie. They reduced their demands to the single request that the contractors pay them every fortnight in cash.[41] Mackenzie was sympathetic but non-committal. When the committee returned to Montreal, the mass meetings became overtly political and the problems of the canal labourers were attributed to the inaction of the Liberal government.[42] Meanwhile, Mackenzie had ordered an investigation into the Lachine situation which revealed the widespread use of store payment which considerably reduced the real wages of the labourers. Sensing a political disaster in the making, the government ordered the contractors to end store payments.[43] All contractors complied immediately and the labourers won a modest victory. McKiernan's efforts, while not the only factor in this outcome, did help the strikers publicize their demands and eased their physical hardships. In doing so, he demonstrated the potential strength of a waterfront community united in a common cause.

The canal labourers' strike was McKiernan's most extensive effort in aiding strikers, but not his only involvement. During a strike against the Allen line, ship labourers used the Canteen as a rallying point and the flag they used in their parades came from the tavern. In April 1880, when the Hochelaga cotton mill workers struck, Joe Beef again assumed his role as people's commissary-general by supplying the strikers with bread.[44] Such incidents illustrated how the working-class culture which centred around the tavern could be mobilized to produce benefits for the Canteen's patrons. But in doing so, McKiernan also attracted the criticism of middle-class reformers who felt that such a culture encouraged workers in a dangerous behaviour which threatened the social stability of Montreal.

During the 1870s, middle-class reformers began to enter into the waterfront community to assist the workingman in overcoming his social and economic poverty. The YMCA, the Salvation Army, as well as local employers and clergy, all found themselves confronted by an existing culture and community services centred around Joe Beef's Canteen. Their response to McKiernan's activities illustrated the immense social differences between the middle and working class of Montreal. One visitor to the city described Joe Beef's Canteen as a "den of robbers and wild beasts" over which McKiernan presided, "serving his infernal majesty in loyal style." The patrons were "unkempt, unshaven, fierce-looking specimens of humanity," and "roughs of various appearances, ready apparently, either to fight, drink, or steal, if the opportunity offered." In conclusion, this visitor wrote, "As we came away from his canteen where we felt that dirt, bestiality, and devilment held high carnival, my friend said, 'I believe Joe is worse than his bears and lower down in the scale of being than his monkeys. No monkey could ever be Joe's ancestor, though he is the father of wild beasts that prey on society.' "[45] While Montreal's middle class did not engage in the "slumming parties" which were popular in London, portrait painter Robert Harris and his companion William Brymmer visited the Canteen to satisfy their curiosity.[46] The actions of middle-class men on the waterfront revealed a fundamental misunderstanding of the nature of the working-class behaviour which they observed.

The common middle-class picture of the waterfront community was one of drunkenness, immorality, and lawlessness. Waterfront taverns like the Canteen, or French Marie's, were described by the Montreal Police Chief as "hot beds of all that is vicious" whose patrons were "always on the look out for mischief, and whose chief and most relished pastime seems to consist in attacking the police, rescuing prisoners, and spreading terror."[47] Sub-Chief Lancy reported that the only reason why police did

249

not close down Joe Beef's Canteen was that "it is better to have all these characters kept in one place so that they might be dropped upon by the detectives."[48] Indeed, there was much truth to police complaints about public order on the waterfront, but they were less than candid in public statements about the role which men like Charles McKiernan played in the maintenance of order. The Black Horse Gang, composed of working-class youths, roamed the waterfront for years, extorting drinking money from lone pedestrians and robbing drunken sailors. Implicated in at least one death, the Black Horse Gang rarely faced prosecution because their violent reputation intimidated many witnesses from pressing charges. And the Black Horse Gang did frequent Joe Beef's Canteen, or at least until October 1876, when McKiernan threw four of its members out into the street for rowdiness. Ironically, one of the gang members attempted to lay charges against the tavern owner for injuries resulting from the incident.[49] The waterfront also harboured "Joe Beef's Gang" which in November 1878 was involved in a market square battle with local butchers.[50]

Violations of public order, however, must be distinguished from acts of criminality. Indeed, McKiernan was known to assist the police in their efforts to capture criminals. Police arrested ten men on charges of highway robbery in September 1880 following a tip from McKiernan. In minor cases, the tavern owner was called upon to give character references for waterfront residents. McKiernan's censure was enough to send a local street gang leader to two months' hard labour. When the prisoner tried to retaliate by charging Joe Beef's Canteen with violations of its liquor licence, the judge, grateful for the favour to the court, refused to admit the evidence.[51] McKiernan, like many working-class people, did not consider occasional drunkenness or acts of rowdyism sufficient cause to send men to jail, especially if imprisonment meant certain ruin for a labourer's family. The informal, if sometimes rough, justice which McKiernan enforced upon his patrons was obviously preferable to the legal penalties of the court. While not publicly admitting such an accommodation, the Montreal police found that such informal co-operation worked in their favour.

The difference between the middle-class attitude towards the police and that of the waterfront residents was illustrated by the experience of the YMCA's first venture into the area. As an alternative to the saloon, the YMCA established a reading room on Craig Street. In January 1877, eight men were arrested there for creating a disturbance, and the *Montreal Witness* accused McKiernan of offering a reward to the men who closed down the operation. The tavern owner refuted these charges by pointing out that the incident had occurred only because of the YMCA's mishandling of the situation. As McKiernan explained, "Joe Beef never called on one policeman to arrest any of those men who frequent *his* place. If those eight had only been sent to him he would have given them work and food and sent them back better behaved."[52] By using the police to settle their problems, the YMCA violated one of the unwritten rules of behaviour on the waterfront.

The influence of waterfront taverns upon sailors visiting Montreal was a constant concern amongst ship owners. Searches for deserting sailors often started with a visit to Joe Beef's Canteen and a quick check of its customers. As an alterative to the tavern, the Montreal Sailors Institute was established in 1869 "a stone's throw" from nine taverns. Open from May to November, the Institute had a reading room, writing desks, stationery, and sabbath services. Food, for a price, could be bought but not alcohol. In 1879, the Institute sold 4,885 cups of coffee and confidently concluded that "Every cup lessening much the demand for whiskey." Encouraging sailors to sign abstinence pledges, the Institute recognized that sober sailors were dependable sailors.[53] But like the YMCA, the Institute had little understanding or sympathy for the working-class culture of the neighbourhood. The Institute manager, Robert R. Bell, described tavern patrons as "the lowest and most depraved human beings."[54] Dock workers, in particular, he found "a class much given to alcoholic liquors."[55] Bell lamented the inability to enforce the Sunday liquor laws and suggested the local policemen were in league with the tavern keepers. In his attempts to save the waterfront workers from their own culture as well as from economic hardship, Bell was typical of the middle-class professionals who came into the area. With 60 per cent of the Institute's budget earmarked for the salary of Bell and his two assistants, and liberal contributions from local ship owners,[56] the motives behind such projects were viewed suspiciously by the waterfront workers.

251

The most ardent attempts to reform the moral and social habits of the waterfront workers came from Montreal's clergy. The importance of the church in nineteenth-century social welfare services need not be recounted here,[57] but the resources of Montreal's various churches dwarfed anything which the waterfront community could organize on its own. McKiernan's public attitude towards all denominations of clergy was openly hostile. He wrote that "Churches, Chapels, Ranters, Preachers, Beechers and such stuff Montreal has already got enough."[58] The cartoon from *Le Canard* illustrated quite clearly that Joe Beef would look almost anywhere for salvation before turning to the church. Respectable Montreal was shocked in 1871 when McKiernan buried his first wife. On leaving the cemetery, he ordered the band to play the military tune, "The Girl I Left Behind Me." This so outraged the *Montreal Witness* that its editor only described the funeral as a "ludicrous circumstance" without going into details.[59] And, probably to his great delight, McKiernan actually convinced the census taker in 1881 that he was a practising *Baptist!*[60]

Clergy who ventured onto the waterfront, however, were sometimes pleasantly surprised at McKiernan's behaviour. John Currie, a Presbyterian minister, ventured into Joe Beef's Canteen to preach to its patrons as an "act of Faith." After some initial heckling from the tavern owner, Currie was allowed to finish his sermon. On its conclusion, McKiernan offered any man who went to Currie's services a dinner and night's lodging for free.[61] The YMCA and a "Hot Gospeller" at different times held religious services in the dining room attached to Joe Beef's Canteen. The apparent contradiction in McKiernan's public and private behaviour originated with his general distrust of a clergy which was essentially middle class. Once he viewed individual ministers at close range and found them willing to treat his patrons as their equals — at least before the eyes of God — then the tavern keeper had no objection to their work. As Joe Beef reported to the press,

> A Preacher may make as many proselytes as he chooses in my canteen, at the rate of ten cents a head. That's my price . . . for if I choose to give myself the trouble I could make them embrace any faith or none at all or become free thinkers.[62]

252

Not all preachers received a welcome into Joe Beef's Canteen. Mr. Hammond, a travelling revivalist whose views on tobacco and drink were at odds with McKiernan's, was invited to the Canteen for a debate. Before the evening was out, Mr. Hammond had been chased around the Canteen by a pack of Joe Beef's bears and dogs to the general amusement of the taverns' patrons.[63] When the Salvation Army first appeared in Montreal, McKiernan supported them. With their military bearing and brass-band approach to salvation, they were a natural to play outside the Canteen, and McKiernan paid them to do so. This harmonious relationship abruptly ended when an Army officer called the Canteen "a notorious *rendez-vous* of the vicious and depraved."[64] Shortly afterwards the band was arrested for disturbing the peace and McKiernan was suspected of being behind the complaint.

These clashes between the local clergy, reform groups, the police, and Joe Beef were carefully chronicled by the editor of the *Montreal Witness*, John Dougall. Dougall founded the *Witness* to instruct the general public in the Christian way of life and frequently drew upon Joe Beef for examples of modern depravity. Dougall was not unsympathetic to the economic hardships of Montreal's working class. He gave extensive coverage to the 1877 canal labourers' strike and attacked industrialists for their lack of concern over the moral implications of modern industry upon employees. But Dougall was convinced that the working-class culture which centred around taverns was a dangerous influence for all workingmen. As one contemporary described Dougall, he was "a fighter in the cause of temperance, of political purity, of public morals, of municipal righteousness, of Free Trade and of aggressive Christianity."[65] The unyielding earnestness of Dougall's public statements made him a frequent target for Joe Beef's satires. A typical verse stated,

Bitter beer I will always drink,
and Bitter Beer I will always draw
and for John and his song singing
Ranters never care a straw.[66]

When the *Witness* dismissed six of its printers for belonging to the International Typographers Union, McKiernan naturally sided with the union's efforts to have the men reinstated.[67]

Dougall characterized Joe Beef as the "hunter for the souls of men"[68] and, instead of seeing the social services which surrounded the Canteen as a positive contribution to the community, believed that these were merely clever ways of entrapping unsuspecting workers into a world of drink and sin. The death of John Kerr in April 1879 confirmed Dougall's conviction. Kerr was a regular at the Canteen who made his living doing odd jobs around the docks. One day in April, Kerr did not go out to work and by nightfall had drank himself to death. During the Coroner's inquest, McKiernan explained his policy of never calling in the police. When men got rowdy, he simply put them in a room under the bar to sleep it off. Customers, McKiernan went on, were never treated roughly and they were "all in good health. We never club them; you know you can squeeze a man to make him do what you want, without beating him."[69] Kerr, a well-behaved man and often sick, was never treated in this manner. Yet the existence of the "Black Hole" (as the jury foreman described it) caught Dougall's attention. In a scathing editorial, the *Witness* charged that McKiernan preyed on the unemployed in a merciless way.

253

> What an empire within an empire is this, where law is administered and Her Majesty's peace kept without expense to Her Majesty. How joyfully should Government renew the licence of this carer of the poor, who can squeeze a man even to the last cent he wants, even to go uncomplainingly to prison, or to working for him all day with the snow shovel he provides, and bringing home his earning daily and nightly to hand over the counter for the poison which is his real pay.[70]

Dougall demanded the Canteen's licence be revoked. The coroner's jury, however, did not see anything illegal in the unconventional practices of Joe Beef.

"Into Africa" was the phrase that one visitor to the waterfront used to describe his experience, and the social isolation of the middle and working classes of Montreal in the 1870s was quite remarkable. Yet these initial failures for the reformers did not stop their efforts, and throughout the coming decades they continued to establish links between the waterfront and the rest of the city. McKiernan, though suspicious, was not entirely hostile to these men addressing themselves to the obvious problems of the casual labourers. Their working-class culture was still strong enough to ensure that social assistance did not mean social control. Forces beyond the control of the waterfront community, however, were already weakening that culture.

The world of Joe Beef, which developed during the 1870s, continued to function throughout the 1880s, but its dynamic qualities appeared to be on the wane. Joe Beef's public profile certainly declined in the 1880s. The eventual disintegration of this culture cannot be attributed to any single factor either within the working-class community or from some of the larger developments of the decade. A combination of factors, including a decasualization of dockwork, the rise of the Knights of Labor, plus new attitudes towards leisure and urban conditions, made the survival of Joe Beef's Canteen beyond the death of its owner unlikely.

As a waterfront tavern, Joe Beef's Canteen depended upon the patronage of the longshoremen who unloaded and loaded the ships in the Montreal harbour. Longshoremen worked irregular hours, sometimes as long as 36 hours at a stretch. Crews were hired by stevedores who contracted with a ship's captain to unload the vessel for a fixed price and provided the necessary equipment. Longshoremen, therefore, spent long periods of time on the docks either working, or contacting stevedores about the prospects for employment. With between 1,700 and 2,500 men competing for work, individuals had to spend much of their time ensuring that they earned the average wage of $200 per season.[71] Given these job conditions, the attraction of a waterfront tavern where one could eat, sleep, drink, and scout around for employment can not be underestimated.

The nature of employment on the docks began to change in the mid-1880s. H. & A. Allen Company, one of the larger shipping firms in the port, introduced a system of contract labour. Over 100 longshoremen signed contracts directly with the shipping company which guaranteed steady employment for the season. The contract specified that each contract employee would have to pay 1 per cent of his wages towards an accident insurance plan, as well as agree to have 10 per cent of his total wages held back until the end of the season. Any man who left before the term of his contract forfeited claim to these wages. With a rate of 25 cents per hour, the pay of the Allen contract employees was slightly better than that of regular longshoremen, but these relinquished their traditional rights to refuse work which did not suit them.[72] Longshoremen testifying before the 1889 Royal Commission on the Relations of Capital and Labour were certainly critical of the contract system, which most felt gave the company a guaranteed labour supply without contributing greatly to the welfare of the longshoremen.[73] While the contract system accounted for only a fraction of the total labour force on the docks, the Allen Company's desire to "decasualize" their labour force was an indication of the future. Such a system made a convenient tavern unnecessary.

It was no coincidence that the Allen Company attempted to introduce the contract system among longshoremen at the same time that labour organizations appeared on the waterfront. Edmund Tart told the Royal Commission that he belonged to a "secret trades organization" which existed on the docks.[74] Possibly a local of the Knights of Labor, the union had its own benefit plan to offset the Allen Company insurance scheme. Patrick Dalton, a longshoreman for the Allen Company, testified against the contract system. Pointing to the organization of the Quebec City longshoremen, Dalton stressed that only the organization of all longshoremen could guarantee higher wages. Dalton concluded by saying that labour unions were not fundamentally concerned with wages, but with bettering "the condition of the men, socially and morally."[75]

The rise of the Knights of Labor in the mid-1880s produced profound changes in the dynamics of working-class development, and the culture surrounding Joe Beef's Canteen was shaken up by their emergence. Along with lawyers, bankers, and capitalists, the Knights of Labor banned tavern owners from their ranks. Testifying before the Royal Commission on the Liquor Traffic, Louis Z. Boudreau, president of the Montreal Trades and Labour Council, reflected this attitude towards drink when he stated that "people we meet in the Trades and Labor Council are not drinking men as a whole. They are a good class of men."[76] As skilled workers accepted the need for temperance, the unskilled waterfront labourers might also re-examine the benefits of tavern life. This did not signal an alliance between organized labour and the temperance advocates who attacked Joe Beef in the 1870s. Spokesmen for organized labour criticized most of these temperance workers for failing to realize that much of the drunkenness among workingmen resulted from economic hardship. Clearly, William Darlington, a prominent Montreal Knight of Labor, shared McKiernan's distrust of the clergy's attempt to reform the workingman. Darlington told the Liquor Commission that "the workingmen feel that the church is a religious institution without Christianity, and that the clergy is simply a profession, got up for the purpose of making money in some instances, and in other, for preaching in the interest of capital against labour. . . . They find out in reality that the Knights of Labor preach more Christianity than the churches."[77] Despite such similarities, there was no room for Joe Beef in the Knights of Labor.

Outside of the working-class neighbourhoods, other forces were emerging which shaped public attitudes towards Joe Beef's Canteen. Throughout the 1880s, Montreal's middle-class residents grew more critical of the police force's inability to enforce the liquor laws. This new mood was captured by the Law and Order League (also known as the Citizens League of Montreal) which was formed in 1886. The League's purpose was to pressure police to enforce the liquor and public morality laws by publicizing open violations. Operating in co-operation with the Royal

Society for the Prevention of Cruelty to Animals, the League was able to effect a dramatic increase in the number of prosecutions against tavern owners.[78] Under such pressure, the police were less likely to work informally with Joe Beef on matters of public order.

New attitudes towards leisure activities were also coming to the fore during the 1880s. With the growth of the YMCA and the Amateur Athletic Associations, urban youths were encouraged to spend their time in organized sport and develop the socially useful traits of "teamwork, perseverance, honesty and discipline — true muscular Christianity."[79] As one YMCA lecturer told his audience, recreation had to "invigorate the mind and body, and have nothing to do with questionable company, being regulated by Christian standards."[80] While such campaigns were not designed to recruit former members of street gangs, but rather the middle-class youth and clerks from the new industrial factories, these new approaches to recreation did have an impact on general tolerance of the waterfront culture. Prize fighting, probably a favoured sport of Joe Beef's patrons, was publicly denounced as a barbaric and dangerous sport.[81] With the growing alliance between the RSPCA and the Law and Order League, the Canteen's menagerie could not have survived a public outcry. New recreational opportunities for working-class Montreal, such as the opening of Sohmer Park in the early 1890s,[82] indicated that the necessity to centre all recreational life around the tavern was diminishing.

There was also a perceptible shift in public attitudes towards poverty and the city slums. With the reformers' concentration on the physical aspects of their city — clean water, paved streets, public parks, and adequate fire protection — urban slums were no longer seen only as places for poor people to live, but as potential threats to public health. Herbert Ames, a pioneer in efforts to clean up Montreal, stated that in matters of public health a simple rule existed — "the nearer people live to each other, the shorter they live."[83] Such programmes as the Fresh Air Fund, which sent mothers and children of the slums to a country retreat for temporary escape from the noise and smoke of the city, testified to the concern among middle-class reformers about the dangerous effects of an industrial city.[84] The *Montreal Star* carried a series of reports on the terrible living conditions in Montreal's slums.[85] In 1885 during a smallpox epidemic, riots broke out when health authorities tried to vaccinate working-class people against the disease.[86] The great physical dangers which the slums created for the city, let alone the social danger, forced local authorities to take a closer look at the waterfront neighbourhoods.

Many of these fears and developments seem to have been familiar to the reporter who visited the Canteen in 1887. While the bears received the familiar treatment, the reporter was quite disturbed at the new attitude among the patrons. He wrote, "Nothing is more striking than the demeanor of the poor folk who fill the room. No oaths are uttered, no coarse jests, no loud talking, and never a laugh is heard. A very quiet,

256

not to say sombre, lot of men. One would like to see a little more animation and liveliness, to hear now and then a good hearty laugh."[87] Nor was this brooding silence unique to Joe Beef's Canteen, as the reporter found several other taverns similarly devoid of their regular good cheer. These dull vacant looks, the reporter went on, "are the kind of faces one meets in the east end of London and other similar districts; but we should hardly expect to find them here. They are here, though, you see."[88] The reporter's reference to East London was repeated a few years later by the author of *Montreal by Gaslight*, a muckraking study of the city's "underworld." For the local observer, the most frightening prospect for his city was to duplicate the urban miseries of the East End of London. In *Montreal by Gaslight*, the author warned against the social consequences of drink and crushing poverty. "Last and greatest of all, think you that the modern plague of London is not known to us? Are we not infected?"[89] Along the waterfront, the silence of the labourers was feared to be the incubation period of this great urban disease. Of its eventual outbreak, one author wrote, "It may be that some day labor will raise and demand that for which it now pleads. That demand will mean riot, strike, and even civil war."[90] *Montreal by Gaslight* was written as a warning that a solution must be found before it was too late. The general outcome of such fears was that middle-class Montreal began to pay more attention to its waterfront area just as the social and economic circumstances which gave rise to Joe Beef's Canteen were changing.

257

The rough life along the waterfront had its own hazards and on 15 January 1889 Charles McKiernan died of heart failure in his Canteen while only 54 years of age. His death was received with great sadness in many quarters of the city and the funeral attracted large crowds. As the *Gazette* reporter commented, "Every grade in the social scale was represented in those assembled in front of the 'Canteen.' There were well known merchants, wide awake brokers, hard working mechanics and a big contingent of the genus bum, all jostling one another for a glimpse of the coffin containing what remained of one, whatever may have been his faults, who was always the poor man's friend."[91] After a short Anglican service, McKiernan's body was carried out of the tavern and the procession started for Mount Royal Cemetery. Among those in the procession were representatives from 50 labour societies who acknowledged for the last time Joe Beef's support of the trade union movement. The exception to this general sympathy was the Montreal *Witness* which published its own death notice.

> Joe Beef is dead. For twenty five years he has enjoyed in his own way the reputation of being for Montreal what was in former days known under the pet sobriquet of the wickedest man. His saloon, where men consorted with unclean beasts was probably the most disgustingly dirty in the country. It has been the bottom of the sink

of which the Windsor bar and others like it are the receivers. The only step further was to be found murdered on the wharf or dragged out of the gutter or the river, as might happen. It was the resort of the most degraded of men. It was the bottom of the pit, a sort of *cul de sac*, in which thieves could be coralled. The police declared it valuable to them as a place where these latter could be run down. It has been actively at work over all that time for the brutalizing of youth — a work which was carried on with the utmost diligence by its, in that sense, talented proprietor.[92]

Perhaps more than any of Joe Beef's lampoons, this editorial showed the limits of the *Witness*'s Christian charity.

With McKiernan's death, Joe Beef's Canteen declined. The transient customers were the first to suffer. Thomas Irwin, a "protege" of the Canteen, was arrested a few days after McKiernan's death for stealing a piece of flannel. In explaining his crime, Irwin stated "There is no use for me trying to make my living now that poor old Joe is dead and gone. I must get a home somewhere in winter; won't you admit that? Well, I stole to get a lodging."[93] For the wharf-rats and sun-fish, Joe Beef's was closed. His bears met an ignoble end as well. In April police officers shot Joe Beef's bears on the request of McKiernan's widow. She planned to have them stuffed.[94] By 1893 the Canteen was gone. The Salvation Army bought the tavern and under the banner of "Joe Beef's Converted" continued many of the services to transient workers which McKiernan had pioneered. Masters at adapting popular culture to their religious beliefs, the Salvation Army transformed one of their most troublesome enemies into a prophet for bread and salvation.[95]

In assessing the significance of Charles McKiernan to the Montreal working class in the 1870s and 1880s, one must remember that when McKiernan arrived in 1868 he did not create the working-class culture associated with Joe Beef's Canteen. That culture, which had grown out of the daily routines of the casual labourers on the docks, already existed. What Joe Beef accomplished was to give that culture a public face and voice, a figure upon which the local press and reformers could focus. In doing so, Joe Beef saved that culture from the obscurity which generally surrounds work cultures. The material necessary for that culture was amply demonstrated by the numerous community services which grew up around the tavern. This waterfront culture possessed its own values of mutual assistance, hard work, good cheer, and a sense of manly dignity. The necessity to "act like men," which McKiernan urged upon striking canal labourers, was an important code of ethics which the tavern owner used as a measure of all things. Clergy who treated his patrons "as men" were allowed into the Canteen, but organizations which resorted to the police to settle problems deserved condemnation for such unmanly behaviour. Even McKiernan's denunciations of Montreal industrialists,

258

the "Big Bugs," or John Dougall were denunciations of individuals and not social classes. Indeed, the tendency to personalize every problem facing the waterfront community pointed out the necessity for longshoremen to find some larger institutional framework through which they could preserve the values that their work culture generated. The Knights of Labor provided this opportunity, but the Knights built upon the traditional values preserved and strengthened by Joe Beef.

While Joe Beef's controversies with the middle-class reformers who entered into his neighbourhood were genuine, the lasting influence of such incidents appeared small. For all his bluster, Joe Beef was a limited threat to the social order of Montreal. As a spokesman for rough culture, Joe Beef satirized only the pretensions and hypocrisy which he saw in the smooth behaviour of middle-class men. He did not advocate class antagonism, but a fair deal. For a short time, Joe Beef's influence was able to reach a fair deal with municipal authorities. What frightened some observers was the possibility that the growing numbers of unskilled factory workers, that unknown quantity of industrial transformation, would adopt the working-class culture of Joe Beef, with its violence and disregard for legal and moral authority. No doubt these observers were pleased that the new factory hands followed the lead of respectable skilled workers within the Knights of Labor.

259

The culture represented by Joe Beef was certainly different than that of the skilled tradesmen of Montreal. Only with difficulty can one imagine an experienced typographer making regular trips to the Canteen to see the bears. Though rough and respectable cultures interacted, they were clearly separate.[96] The culture surrounding the casual labourers grew out of a physically demanding life of marginal economic benefit, obtained through the common exertion of labour. In these respects, Joe Beef's world was closer to the world of Peter Aylen and the Shiners of the Ottawa Valley than to the typographers in the offices of the *Montreal Witness*, or the cotton mill workers of Hochelaga.[97] The waterfront world had its own internal hierarchy as Joe Beef vigorously defended his patrons against middle-class charges of drunken violence, but then threw them into the street when they got rowdy. While McKiernan's background, as his Irish verses confirm,[98] was rural, he lived in an industrial city and had to contend with the economic and social restrictions which this implied. Realizing the growing power of the police and social reformers to define the limits of acceptable behaviour, Joe Beef attempted to convince these men of the validity of working-class culture. He was not very successful. To the very end, McKiernan was rooted in the culture of his tavern and neighbourhood. For him, the liquor business was not a means of upward mobility and the tavern owner's sons remained working class.

Joe Beef's Canteen illustrated the complex nature of working-class culture. In the narrow, traditional sense of culture as artistic creation, the satiric verses, engravings or cartoons by McKiernan and others about Joe Beef contributed in a minor way to the nineteenth-century radical literature in Canada. Local historians of Montreal were well aware of this tradition left behind by Joe Beef.[99] In the broader sense of culture as popular culture, the tavern life of bears, debates, and songs acknowledged a recreational culture created by the working class and not for them. The coming of rational recreation would weaken this tradition, but McKiernan's death had little long term effect on this level. Finally, Joe Beef's Canteen represented a material culture of community services relating to the employment, housing, and health of the working-class neighbourhood. This culture was the most important manifestation of the Canteen in terms of class conflict.[100] All aspects of culture surrounding Joe Beef's Canteen demonstrated the integral nature of the life of the labouring men along the waterfront who would probably not have recognized distinctions between recreation and work, between a popular and material culture.

260

To label Joe Beef's Canteen a "pre-industrial" fragment in an industrial world obscures the fact that working-class culture was a fluid culture borrowing from its own past and from contemporary middle-class culture. Middle-class disgust at Joe Beef's antics largely grew out of his ability to parody their most pious thoughts. While Joe Beef rejected these new industrial virtues, this hardly distinguished him from thousands of other Montreal labourers and skilled workers. In many ways, the culture of Joe Beef had reached its own limits. Successful in bargaining social questions of public conduct and order, McKiernan played only a supporting role in the economic struggles in the factories and on the docks. The attempt to form new alliances between skilled and unskilled, men and women, tradesman with tradesman, would be made not by the Joe Beefs of the nineteenth century but by the Knights of Labor.

NOTES

I would like to acknowledge the advice and assistance of Peter Bailey, Doug Cruikshank, Greg Kealey, Danny Moore, and Bryan Palmer in writing this article.

[1] *Montreal Illustrated; or The Strangers' Guide to Montreal* (Montreal, 1875). For a more thematic guide to the city in the 1880s, see S.E. Dawson, *Hand-Book for the City of Montreal and its Environs* (Montreal, 1883). *Lovell's Historic Report of the Census of Montreal* (Montreal, 1891) is a good example of how the material progress of Montreal was equated with social and moral improvements. As Lovell stated, "Peace, happiness and prosperity abound, and brotherly love forms a link that might be prized in any city. The policeman is seldom needed. Intemperance is becoming a thing of the past." (45) Lovell's private census should not be confused with the Dominion census conducted that same year. *The Montreal Star*, in its 16 September 1886 issue, carried special stories on the city's capitalists and their contribution to social development.

[2] This underground Montreal is given a muckraker's treatment in *Montreal by Gaslight* (Montreal, 1889), which contains a chapter on Joe Beef's Canteen. Charles McKiernan's landlord, F.X. Beaudry, was closely connected with the local prostitution trade, as his obituary (*Montreal Witness*, 25 March 1885) details. On gambling dens, see *Montreal Witness*, 14 September 1876, and *Montreal Star*, 30 October 1889. The *Star*, 23 January 1872, carries an article on a local cockfight.

[3] The most recent contributions to this debate are Kenneth McNaught, "E.P. Thompson vs. Harold Logan," *Canadian Historical Review* 62 (1981): 141-68; Gregory S. Kealey's "Labour and Working-Class History in Canada: Prospects in the 1980s," and David J. Bercuson's "Through the Looking Glass of Culture," both from *Labour/Le Travailleur* 7 (1981): 67-94, 95-112. The history of Joe Beef hopefully shows some of the merits of a cultural approach to working-class history.

[4] Raymond Williams, *Culture and Society* (London, 1960), 327.

[5] Williams, *Culture and Society*, 330.

[6] Gareth Stedman Jones, *Outcast London* (Oxford, 1971). Comparisons between Montreal and London, at least on general terms, are not as tenuous as might first appear. Contemporary observers of the waterfront often compared these slums to those of East London. Herbert Ames' attempt to introduce model housing for the workingman was modelled on the efforts of Octavia Hill's plan to help the London poor (*The City Below the Hill* [Toronto, 1972], 114). McKiernan received his training at Woolwich, which William Booth studied before founding his Salvation Army. The Salvation Army was one of the more successful groups in the waterfront neighbourhood.

[7] *Montreal Star*, 16 January 1889. See also Edgar A. Collard's *Montreal Yesterdays* (Toronto, 1962) for a good general assessment of Charles McKiernan, and the Montreal City Archives clipping file-R. 3654.2 "*Rues*, Commune, Rue de la," for general press coverage of McKiernan by Collard and other Montreal historians.

[8] Dorothy Suzanne Cross, "The Irish in Montreal, 1867-1896," (M.A. thesis, McGill University, 1969) gives a general account of the Montreal Irish community. For contemporary descriptions, see John Francis Maguire's *The Irish in America* (Montreal, 1868), and Nicholas Flood Davin, *The Irishman in Canada* (Toronto, 1877).

[9] *Montreal by Gaslight*, 10. Other well known taverns were Tommy Boyle's The Horseshoe, which catered to those who followed prize fighting, and the Suburban which had a reputation for giving the poor man a helping hand (94-105).

[10] *Montreal Star*, 14 February 1888. Liquor licences, which included hotels, restaurants, saloons and groceries, increased from 723 in 1879 to 1,273 in 1887. Joe Beef's Canteen had a hotel licence.

[11] *Montreal Witness*, 4 April 1881.

[12] *Toronto Globe*, 14 April 1876; *Halifax Herald*, 28 June 1880; *Montreal Star*, 3 October 1887.

[13] W.H. Davies, *The Autobiography of a Super-Tramp* (London, 1964), 131, cited in Clayton Gray, *Le Vieux Montreal* (Montreal, 1964), 16.

[14] *Montreal Witness*, 4 April 1881. In an account of Joe Beef's encounter with the census taker, the problems of tracing the transient population were made clear. Of all the one-night guests which the Canteen provided for, only ten men were found by the census taker. Two of these, an Irish musician and a Spanish cook, were probably employees of the tavern. Also listed were an English coachmaker, an Irish blacksmith, an American barber, a Scottish commercial agent, an English (Quaker) leather merchant, an Irish accountant, an English labourer, and an Irish tanner. McKiernan's fifteen-year-old son was listed as a rivet maker and was likely serving an apprenticeship. See Public Archives of Canada, (hereafter PAC), RG 31, Census of Canada, 1881, Manuscript, Montreal, West Ward, Division 3, p. 1.

[15] *Toronto Globe*, 14 April 1876.

[16] *Montreal by Gaslight*, 115.

[17] *Montreal Star*, 10 September 1883; 11 September 1883; 3 October 1883.

[18] *Montreal Witness*, 17 March 1881; 22 March 1881.

[19] *Montreal Herald*, 21 April 1880; *Montreal Witness*, 6 August 1875. Jon M. Kingsdale, "The Poor Man's Club: Social Functions of the Urban Working Class Saloon," *American Quarterly* 25 (1973): 472-89, provides an excellent background to the discussion which follows and demonstrates that many of the Canteen's services were common to nineteenth-century taverns.

[20] *La Minerve*, 2 August 1873.

[21] *Toronto Globe*, 14 April 1876; *Halifax Herald*, 28 June 1880; *Montreal Star*, 3 October 1887.

[22] *La Minerve*, 20 January 1874.

[23] *Montreal Star*, 14 July 1876; *Montreal Witness*, 22 October 1873; 12 November 1877.

[24] *La Minerve*, 7 November 1873. John was John Dougall of the *Montreal Witness* who had recently dismissed some union employees. Although the Canteen was a male bastion, McKiernan was not unaware of the growing number of women workers in the Montreal labour force. For the employment of women, see Dorothy Suzanne Cross' "The Neglected Majority: The Changing Role of Women in Nineteenth Century Montreal," *Social History* 12 (1973): 202-203.

[25] *Montreal Yesterdays*, 273-74.

[26] *La Minerve*, 28 December 1878.

[27] *Toronto Globe*, 14 April 1876.

[28] The integration of transient labour into urban centres was very important and a failure to do so is described in Sydney L. Harring's "Class Conflict and the Suppression of Tramps in Buffalo, 1892-1894," *Law and Society Review* 11 (1977): 873-911. See also James M. Pitsula's "The Treatment of Tramps in Late Nineteenth-Century Toronto," *Historical Papers* (1980), 116-32.

[29] *Montreal Star*, 5 February 1877; *Witness*, 2 August 1876: *Star*, 3 October 1879.

[30] *Star*, 15 January 1878; 29 December 1879; 27 February 1880; 25 March 1880, 1 April 1880. H.E. MacDermot in his *History of the Montreal General Hospital* (Montreal, 1950) wrote that Joe Beef's

Canteen was "a particularly staunch supporter, and entries of donations from 'Proceeds of iron box, barroom, of Joe Beef' are frequent, or from 'his own skating Rink,' as well as contributions for the care of special patients." (55) MacDermot's work was cited in Edgar Collard's "All Our Yesterdays," *Montreal Gazette*, 9 January 1960. William Fox Beakbane, who drowned at Allan's wharf on 29 July 1883, was buried in the McKiernan family plot in Mount Royal Cemetery (*Star*, 10 August 1883).

31 *Witness*, 17 December 1877; 19 December 1877. Strike leader Lucien Pacquette spent several days in hospital recovering from his wound. For contractor William Davis, this was not the first time his workers reacted violently to his labour practices. A year earlier someone tried to blow up the contractor's house and severely damaged the building (*Witness*, 20 December 1877).

32 *Witness*, 17 December 1877.

33 *Witness*, 19 December 1877, 20 December 1877. Bernard Devlin (1824–80) came to Quebec in 1844 and published the *Freeman's Journal and Commercial Advertiser*. He ran unsuccessfully for the 1867 Parliament against Thomas D'Arcy McGee who accused Devlin of being secretly in support of the Fenians. Devlin served as a Liberal MP for Montreal West from 1875 to 1878. (*DCB* 10: 250).

34 *Star*, 20 December 1877; *Witness*, 24 December 1877.

35 *Star*, 19 December 1877.

36 PAC, Dept. of Public Works, RG11, B1(a), vol. 474, p. 2534, Whitney & Daly to F. Braun, 22 January 1878.

37 *Witness*, 21 December 1877.

38 *Witness*, 22 December 1877.

39 *Witness*, 21 December 1877.

40 *Witness*, 26 December 1877.

41 *Ottawa Citizen*, 18 January 1878. The *Citizen* carried a copy of a strikers' petition to Mackenzie which was signed by 122 people including McKiernan. Most of the signers were untraceable in local business directories, but some local grocers and dry goods merchants did support the strikers' demands and this suggests some degree of neighbourhood support. Original petition in PAC, RG11, B1(a), vol. 473, pp. 2514–20.

42 *Ottawa Citizen*, 24 January 1878. An admitted weakness of this study is the failure to document the political connections which McKiernan had with municipal politicians. Federally, McKiernan was a Conservative and this no doubt played some part in his attack on Mackenzie. During the 1872 election, McKiernan led a group of sailors into a Liberal polling station and began serenading them with a concertina. When surrounded by an angry crowd, McKiernan pulled out a pistol and fired into the air. In the tumult which followed McKiernan and his companions were beaten and had to be rescued by the police. *Montreal Witness*, 28 August 1872.

43 PAC, RG11, B1(a), vol. 473, pp. 2514–69. Not all contractors paid their workers in truck, and those who did argued that the workers benefited from the arrangement. Davis argued that monthly pay periods increased productivity. "On Public Works as a Rule, a large number of men lose time after pay day, and, thereby disarrange and retard the progress of the Works." (Davis to Braun, 21 January 1878, p. 2532). John Dougall of the *Montreal Witness*, however, published an account of the supplies given to a labourer instead of cash. For $1.75 owing in wages, the worker received whiskey, sugar, tobacco, cheese and bread valued at $1.05. The goods were on display throughout the strike at Joe Beef's Canteen (*Witness*, 22 January 1878).

44 *Star*, 17 April 1880; *Witness*, 21 April 1880.

45 *Halifax Herald*, 28 June 1880.

46 PAC, MG28, I 126, vol. 15, Royal Canadian Academy of Art scrapbook, *Montreal Gazette*, 7 February 1916, cited in *Montreal Yesterdays*, 271.

47 "Third Report of the Select Committee of the House of Commons respecting a Prohibitory Liquor Law," *House of Commons Journals*, 1874, Testimony of F.W. Penton, 9.

48 *Montreal Gazette*, 22 April 1880. The importance of battles between the police and working-class people is illustrated by Robert D. Storch in "The Policeman as Domestic Missionary: Urban Discipline and Popular Culture in Northern England," *Journal of Social History* 9 (1976): 481–509.

49 *Star*, 30 October 1876. The Black Horse Gang's activities are reported in the *Witness*, 26 May 1875; 27 May 1875; *Star*, 1 February 1876; *Witness*, 24 July 1880; 10 May 1882. Street gangs in general are discussed in the *Witness*, 31 May 1875.

50 *Witness*, 19 November 1878; 18 November 1878. The *Witness* story on the incident was protested by "Joe Beef's Gang" who turned up in the editor's office and claimed that they were "respectable mechanics and that the butchers are on the contrary not noted for their respectable behaviour."

51 *Witness*, 28 September 1880; 24 July 1879.

52 *Witness*, 8 February 1877.

53 *Annual Report of the Montreal Sailors Institute for the Year Ending January, 1870* (Montreal, 1870), 5; *Annual Report of the Montreal Sailors Institute of 1870* (Montreal, 1871), 8.

54 Royal Commission on the Liquor Traffic, *House of Commons Sessional Paper*, no. 21, 1894, 584.

55 *House of Commons Sessional Paper*, no. 21, 1894, 589.

56 *House of Commons Sessional Paper*, no. 21, 1894, 586.

57 The difference of religious sentiment was reflected in the organization of benevolent associations. Roman Catholic Montreal had its own hospitals and dispensaries, 13 benevolent institutions caring

for the aged, orphaned, and widowed. Nine Catholic charitable societies also contributed to the welfare of the impoverished citizens. Protestant Montreal, besides having its hospitals, had 16 benevolent institutions for the same clientele as the Catholic institutions as well as homes for female immigrants and sick servant girls. Religious differences were further complicated by the national origins of Montreal residents. To aid fellow countrymen there were several national societies including the St. George, St. Andrew, St. Patrick, St. Jean Baptiste, Irish Protestant, Italian, Welsh, Scandinavian, and Swiss benevolent organizations. See *Lovell's Historic Report of the Census of Montreal* (Montreal, 1891), 62–63, 72–73. See also Janice A. Harvey's "Upper Class Reaction to Poverty in Mid-Nineteenth Century Montreal: A Protestant Example," (M.A. thesis, McGill University, 1978) for descriptions of Protestant charities.

[58] *Montreal Yesterdays*, 273–74.
[59] *Montreal Star*, 29 September 1871; *Montreal Yesterdays*, 272–73. McKiernan's 25 year old wife Mary McRae and her baby died on 26 September 1871, and it is uncertain whether the contemporary accounts correctly interpreted McKiernan's actions. Interestingly enough, McKiernan's republican sentiments exhibited themselves on his wife's gravestone. Her inscription read in part,

> I leave a husband and four orphan babes
> To mouth their mother's loss
> Who will never return.
> But let that tree, which you see
> Be the tree of Liberty
> And in its stead never let the tree of [Bigotry]
> Be planted between them and me.

[60] *Montreal Witness*, 4 April 1881; PAC, RG31, Census of Canada, 1881 Manuscript, Montreal, West Ward, Division no. 3, p. 1.
[61] *Montreal Yesterdays*, 279–80.
[62] *Toronto Globe*, 14 April 1876; *Montreal Star*, 31 July 1876.
[63] *Halifax Herald*, 28 June 1880. For Mr. Hammond's preaching style see *Montreal Star*, 18 March 1880.
[64] Edgar Collard, "Of Many Things," *Montreal Gazette*, 28 February 1976. For the legal problems of the Salvation Army, see the *Montreal Star*, 19 August 1886; 3 September 1886; 14 September 1886.
[65] *Montreal Star*, 9 January 1911. See J.I. Cooper's "The Early Editorial Policy of the Montreal Witness," Canadian Historical Association, *Report* (1947), 53–62, and Dougall's obituary in the *Montreal Star*, 19 August 1886.
[66] *La Minerve*, 13 March 1873.
[67] *Montreal Star*, 26 November 1872; 27 November 1872; 28 November 1872.
[68] *Montreal Witness*, 8 February 1877.
[69] *Montreal Witness*, 4 April 1878.
[70] *Montreal Witness*, 5 April 1879.
[71] Royal Commission on the Relations of Capital and Labour, 1889, Quebec Evidence, vol. 1, pp. 150–86.
[72] Royal Commission on the Relations of Capital and Labour, Testimony of R.A. Smith, 156–60; James Urquhart, 173–75.
[73] Royal Commission on the Relations of Capital and Labour, Testimony of Patrick Dalton, 183–85.
[74] Royal Commission on the Relations of Capital and Labour, Testimony of Edmund Tart, 175–81.
[75] Royal Commission on the Relations of Capital and Labour, Testimony of Patrick Dalton, 186.
[76] Royal Commission on the Liquor Traffic, 512.
[77] Royal Commission on the Liquor Traffic, 583.
[78] *Montreal Star*, 28 January 1886. On the Law and Order League, see *Star*, 16 August 1887; 24 January 1889; 16 February 1889, 10 March 1887.
[79] Alan Metcalfe, "The Evolution of Organized Physical Recreation in Montreal, 1840–1895," *Social History* 21 (1978): 153. For the role of the YMCA in the new attitude towards leisure activities, see David Macleod, "A Live Vaccine: The YMCA and Male Adolescence in the United States and Canada, 1870–1920," *Social History* 21 (1978): 5–25. An excellent study of recreation in England is Peter Bailey, *Leisure and Class in Victorian England* (Toronto, 1978).
[80] *Montreal Star*, 15 November 1873.
[81] For denunciations of prize fighting see *Star*, 4 January 1887; 9 May 1887; 20 May 1887; 23 May 1887; 15 September 1887.
[82] *Montreal Star*, 6 June 1893; 13 July 1893. Richard Bell of the Montreal Sailors Institute preferred that sailors drink at Sohmer Park rather than in the waterfront taverns. Royal Commission on the Liquor Traffic, 584–89.
[83] Herbert B. Ames, "Why We Should Study the Municipal System of Our City," *Abstract of a Course of Ten Lectures on Municipal Administration* (Montreal, 1896), 7.
[84] *Montreal Star* contains several articles promoting the Fresh Air Fund, see 11 June 1887; 18 June 1887; 25 June 1887; 6 July 1887; On the Fresh Air Home, see *Star*, 23 June 1888.
[85] *Star*, 24 December 1883; 29 December 1883.
[86] *Star*, 29 September 1885.

263

[87] *Star*, 3 October 1887.

[88] *Star*, 3 October 1887.

[89] *Montreal by Gaslight*, 10.

[90] *Montreal by Gaslight*, 35.

[91] *Montreal Gazette*, 19 January 1889.

[92] *Montreal by Gaslight*, 119.

[93] *Star*, 24 January 1889.

[94] *Star*, 29 April 1889.

[95] *Star*, 26 May 1893; 27 May 1893. R.G. Moyles, in *The Blood and Fire in Canada* (Toronto, 1977), remarked that this was a new venture for the Salvation Army. "Whereas other men's hostels had been designed as rescue centres for ex-prisoners and for total derelicts, Joe Beef's was a hostel for transients, providing a cheap bed for the unemployed man with little money and a cheap meal for the poor city labourer." (69)

[96] Peter Bailey's "Will the Real Bill Banks Please Stand Up? Towards a Role Analysis of Mid-Victorian Working-Class Respectability," *Journal of Social History* 12 (1979) offers some interesting insights into the differences between rough and respectable workingmen.

[97] Michael S. Cross, "The Shiners' War: Social Violence in the Ottawa Valley in the 1830's," *Canadian Historical Review* 54 (1973): 1–26. For a description of an early Ottawa tavern see W.P. Lett, "Corkstown," *Recollections of Old Bytown* (Ottawa, 1979), 81–86.

[98] See the attitudes reflected in "Spurn Not the Poor Man," *La Minerve*, 7 January 1874; "I am Long Past Wailing and Whining," *La Minerve*, 27 January 1874; and "The Big Beggarman," *La Minerve*, 13 January 1874. Poetic style makes it unlikely that these verses are from McKiernan's pen, but by printing them with his advertisements he demonstrated a sympathy with their author.

[99] Frank W. Watt, "Radicalism in English Canadian Literature since Confederation," (Ph.D. thesis, University of Toronto, 1957). Watt does not mention McKiernan but Watt's description of a literature disillusioned with nation building and inclined to associate patriotic feelings with the motives and methods of capitalist exploitation could accommodate much of McKiernan's verse.

[100] Bryan D. Palmer's *A Culture in Conflict* (Montreal, 1979), contains the fullest discussion of the importance of culture in Canadian class conflict. See also, Gareth Stedman Jones, "Working-Class Culture and Working-Class Politics in London, 1870-1900," *Journal of Social History* 7 (1974): 460-508.

Topic Eight

Women's History

Women had to fight to gain rights enjoyed by men — including admission into professions such as medicine and law and into the universities themselves. The attempt to gain the provincial and federal franchises also involved women in a long campaign against the widely accepted notion that their "proper sphere" was in the home.

By the late nineteenth century, a growing number of middle-class women were demanding the right to vote. Some argued that they deserved the same political privileges as men; others argued in terms of women's special abilities. A philosophy of "maternal feminism" prevailed, which maintained that women had certain innate maternal instincts that could be applied effectively within society. Their obligation was to protect the home and the family, which required the reform of society to ensure the security and survival of these treasured institutions. In "'Singing up the Hill,'" Deborah Gorham reviews both arguments.

The desire for emancipation arose in part from women's demands (especially in English-speaking Canada) to control their own fertility, and thus to restrict the size of their families. Yet at the turn of the century only limited information on contraception was available to women. Self-help and medical literature discussed only "natural" means of birth control, not the use of "mechanical" contraceptives. Angus McLaren discusses the prevailing attitudes in "A Motherhood Issue."

The interwar years proved to be a turning point in women's progress towards emancipation. In the prosperity and optimism of the 1920s, women enjoyed greater freedom from social and cultural restraints. Yet even during this so-called decade of liberation, opportunities for women to break away from traditional stereotypes in a male-dominated society were limited. By the 1930s, the situation deteriorated again. Veronica Strong-Boag discusses these transitions in societal perceptions of women and girls during the interwar years in "Growing Up Female," a chapter from her award-winning book *The New Day Recalled: Lives of Girls and Women in English Canada, 1919–1939*.

Alison Prentice et al., *Canadian Women: A History* (Toronto: Harcourt Brace Jovanovich, 1988) provides a comprehensive overview of the role of women in Canadian society. For developments in Quebec see Micheline Dumont et al., *Quebec Women: A History* (Toronto: Women's Press, 1987), and Marta Danylewycz, *Taking the Veil: An Alternative to Marriage, Motherhood, and Spinsterhood in Quebec, 1840–1920* (Toronto: McClelland and Stewart, 1987). Two anthologies of women's history are *Rethinking Canada: The Promises of Women's History*, ed. V. Strong-Boag and Anita Clair Fellman (Toronto: Copp Clark, 1986); and *Canadian Women on the Move, 1867–1920*, ed. B. Light and J. Parr (Toronto: New Hogtown Press, 1983).

Wayne Roberts' " 'Rocking the Cradle for the World': The New Woman and Maternal Feminism, Toronto, 1877–1914," in *A Not Unreasonable Claim: Women and Reform in Canada, 1880s–1920s*, ed. Linda Kealey (Toronto: Women's Press, 1979), 15–45, explains the origins, nature, and ultimate decline of the "new woman" who provided the impetus behind the social-reform movements at the turn of the century. Carol Bacchi examines the ideas and activities of the English-Canadian suffragettes in *Liberation Deferred? The Ideas of the English-Canadian Suffragists, 1877–1918* (Toronto: University of Toronto Press, 1983). Wendy Mitchinson analyses the ideas of the members of the Women's Christian Temperance Union in "The W.C.T.U.: 'For God, Home and Native Land': A Study in Nineteenth-Century Feminism," in Kealey, ed., *A Not Unreasonable Claim: Women and Reform in Canada, 1880s–1920s*.

The period 1880 to 1902 witnessed the rise of a number of national women's organizations, which became forums for the women's social-reform zeal. Wendy Michinson's study of the Women's Christian Temperance Union can be supplemented by her article "The YWCA and Reform in the Nineteenth Century," *Histoire Sociale/Social History* 12 (1979): 368–84 and by Veronica Stong-Boag's "The Roots of Modern Canadian Feminism: The National Council of Women, 1893–1929," *Canada: An Historical Magazine* (December 1975): 22–33, and her " 'Setting the Stage': National Organization and the Women's Movement in the Late 19th Century," in *The Neglected Majority: Essays in Canadian Women's History*, ed. S.M. Trofimenkoff and A. Prentice (Toronto: McClelland and Stewart, 1977), 87–103. A useful bibliography on women's history is B. Light and V. Strong-Boag, *True Daughters of the North: Canadian Women's History: An Annotated Bibliography* (Toronto: Ontario Institute for Studies in Education, 1980).

On women and medicine see Angus McLaren and Arlene Tigar McLaren, *The Bedroom and the State: The Changing Practices and Politics of Contraception and Abortion in Canada, 1890–1980* (Toronto: McClelland and Stewart, 1986) and selected articles in *Essays in the History of Canadian Medicine*, ed. Wendy Mitchinson and Janice Dickin McGinnis (Toronto: McClelland and Stewart, 1988).

"Singing up the Hill"*

DEBORAH GORHAM

Outside the senate chamber in Ottawa can be found a bronze plaque commemorating the historic decision of the Judicial Committee of the Privy Council of Great Britain by which Canadian women were declared to be legally "persons" under the terms of the British North America Act. The date of that decision was October 18, 1929. In it, the British Empire's highest court of appeal overturned a decision handed down by the Supreme Court of Canada in 1928. The immediate practical effect of the Privy Council decision was to make women eligible to be appointed to the Senate, but its symbolic significance was equally important. Although the framers of the BNA Act had not in truth considered that women should be part of Canada's political community the Privy Council decision made them full participants in the constitution of the Dominion. And although in 1929 the Canadian woman's struggle for legal and institutional equality was not yet over (the major piece of unfinished business being the granting of the provincial suffrage to the women of Quebec) the successful conclusion of the Persons Case is a landmark in the history of Canadian feminism. When the law was made to acknowledge that women were "persons," a major undertaking begun by Canadian feminists in the nineteenth century, the task of achieving full citizenship for women, was symbolically completed.

267

In the late nineteenth and early twentieth centuries, Canada was experiencing a period of social and economic change, characterized by rapid urbanization, the pressures of immigration from non–Anglo-Saxon countries, increased industrialization and labour unrest, and changes in the pace of agricultural development. Major changes in women's social, political, and economic role were an important factor during this period, a factor which has been given too little consideration in the accounts of historians. This omission not only leaves the woman reader with the all-too-familiar feeling that her history has been left out of "Respectable" (male) History, it also distorts male history itself. The women's emancipation movement in Canada came about partly as a result of these social and economic developments but it was also a factor which served to shape them.

The women's suffrage movement, symbol of nineteenth and early twentieth-century feminism then and now, is the most visible manifes-

*From *Canadian Dimension*, a socialist news magazine, 801-44 Princess Street, Winnipeg, MB R3B 1K2. Volume 10, 8 (June 1975): 26-38. Reprinted by permission.

tation of women's emancipation, but it is merely the tip of the iceberg. Those who attacked women's suffrage were attacking much more than the idea that women as well as men should enter the polling booth. Unlike the opposition to a wider male suffrage, women's suffrage was opposed, not so much because people feared the effects women might have as voters, but because the idea of the woman voter challenged the ideal of womanhood which formed an essential part of a social order that many saw slipping away from them. As the *Toronto Mail & Empire* put it in 1909 in an editorial commenting on the arrival of Mrs. Pankhurst in North America,

> Nature has assigned to us all our duties in life. To the man has been given the task of supporting the woman, of sustaining the home, of fighting the battles and of governing the family, the clan or the nation. To woman has been committed the charge of the home and the duty of exercising a moderating influence over all its occupants. The Suffragettes . . . are at war with nature. They want the women to be too much like men.

268

More often than not, Canadian feminists gave wholehearted support to the belief that women had special duties. However they insisted that these very duties made it essential that they participate fully in public life: only then could they carry out their special mission, the protection of the home, the family of women and children. Thus they used in their own defense the view of womanhood expressed in the above extract quoted from a *Toronto Mail & Empire* editorial. Feminists in the U.S. and Britain used the same tactics. But this approach may have been a tactic of argument as much as it was a deeply felt belief. A. Kraditor, one of the most thoughtful commentators on the American movement, suggested in *Ideas of the Woman Suffrage Movement* that the U.S. suffragists' arguments were shaped not at their own initiative, but more often in response to the arguments of anti-suffragists. Tactically, it was wise, at least in the short run, to emphasize the woman's maternal role because this technique turned the arguments of the opposition against itself. But tactics are one thing, inner beliefs are another, and many American and British feminists were ambivalent about both their literal and their figurative maternal roles. If this was true in the U.S. (and in Britain) perhaps it was also true in Canada. Only as we come to know more about a larger number of Canadian feminists will we truly be able to judge. One of the best recent analyses of Canadian feminism is V. Strong-Boag's introduction to the new edition of Nellie McClung's *In Times Like These*. In it Strong-Boag argues that maternal feminism was dominant: I am suggesting here (and elsewhere in this paper) that she may have over-emphasized it.

In any case there were Canadian women who took the equal rights issue seriously, for its own sake. They firmly insisted that as human beings they had a *right* to full citizenship, and they fought for their rights as individuals and not merely for their duty to expand their maternal role into the public sphere. Equal rights feminism as well as maternal feminism was a reality in Canada.

If the Persons Case marks the symbolic end of the nineteenth century women's struggle for equal rights in Canada, where did that struggle begin? It had its origins in the European society out of which the new Canadian society developed. The most important institutions which formed the attitude of Canadian society toward women were those which were common to all of North America and were a direct result of the influence of the parent cultures on their Colonial offspring. European society was patriarchal, and the patriarchal nature of that society was upheld by those twin institutional pillars, the church and the law.

Of the two, religion was probably the more important because it shaped attitudes — attitudes of women as well as men. From its beginnings, Christianity has offered women both a negative and a positive message. *269* This double message is nowhere more openly expressed than in the Pauline Epistles. From Paul we learn that slave and free, male and female are equal in God's sight; but we are also told that wives are to obey their husbands and to remain silent in church. Institutionalized Christianity has tended to reinforce the negative message. It has been patriarchal, its central figures have been male, and its ritual has been almost exclusively in the hands of males. Throughout the history of Christianity, only the more radical heresies and sects have offered scope for the democratic Christian message.

Although the conflict between religious belief and feminism is less important today when few feminists are religious (in the church-going sense) and when religious institutions themselves are more open to change, the sexism of religion posed a problem for many religious feminists of an earlier era. Devout feminists attempted to resolve it by stressing the democracy of Christ's message, as Nellie McClung did when she insisted in *In Times Like These* that "Christ was a true democrat" but "the Christian Church has departed in some places from Christ's teachings — notably in its treatment of women." Unfortunately this sort of statement did nothing to alter the fact that religious belief was used to justify sexist legal, social, and political structures and was in fact one of the most powerful agencies of a patriarchal society.

The legal structure of European society certainly reinforced the inferior position granted to women by religious ideology. This legal structure was transported to the New World when the new colonies were established. The legal position of women in Canada as settlement began reflected the legal position of women in France and England and it is important to remember just how onerous the law was. The legal structure grew out of the patriarchal nature of society, and there is no question that the subservient status of women in the eyes of the law appeared to its supporters to be sanctioned by the patriarchal Christian tradition. The genuinely oppressive provisions of the law in both French and English Canada applied only to married women, but, since most women married, the freedoms allowed to unmarried adult women under the law were of minor importance.

What was the position of women under English common law at the beginning of the nineteenth century?

> The theoretical basis for the married woman's loss of legal rights was the feudal doctrine of coverture. Based in part upon biblical notions of the unity of flesh of husband and wife, the doctrine was described by Blackstone as follows: "By marriage, the husband and wife are one person in law; that is, the very being or legal existence of the woman is suspended during the marriage, or at least is incorporated and consolidated." In modern times, the doctrine has been described with greater candor as resting "on the old common-law fiction that the husband and wife are one . . . [which] has worked out in reality to mean . . . the one is the husband."
>
> — L. Kanowitz, *Women and the Law*

270

In concrete terms, what this meant was that a married woman had only a limited control over her own actions, and could not own property. Any property she brought to the marriage belonged to her husband, any wealth she acquired or produced was also his. Moreover, a mother also had no rights whatever concerning her children: " . . . a mother had no more legal relationship to her children than a stranger . . . the father was the sole guardian of his children until they reached the age of 21. He could educate them how and when he pleased, give them in adoption or bind them out as apprentices, and he was entitled to all their earnings," as Margaret MacLellan put it in one of the studies for the 1971 report of the Royal Commission on the Status of Women. No woman could vote in nineteenth century English Canada and the married woman enjoyed no right to a voice in the law courts. (It should be remembered that the issue of the suffrage was less important as it applied to women before the late eighteenth century, since the suffrage was confined to a small class of men, and was associated with property rather than with individual rights. Indeed, in some cases women, by virtue of being property owners, could exercise the suffrage. This was true in Quebec, for instance, in the late eighteenth and early nineteenth centuries.) In summary, then, in Canada, at the time of settlement, a married woman's "only basic legal right was the right to support by her husband with the necessities of life, according to his means," as MacLellan wrote in that same study.

Given these institutional constraints on their activities it is not difficult to understand that nineteenth-century Canadian women, like their American and British counterparts, had to begin by attacking the legal structures which hampered them. They could not begin by attacking the social and psychological barriers to women's freedom that the women's movement sees as central today, even though many nineteenth-century women were also concerned with these more subtle constraints.

When and where did the Canadian fight for equal rights for women begin? In Canada, the feminist movement was shaped by regional factors, although there are certain shared characteristics which manifested themselves in all areas of the country. The movement began in Ontario, but achieved the symbolic success of equal suffrage first in the prairie provinces. An active movement developed in British Columbia, but at a relatively late date. In the Maritimes it appears that only small numbers of women were involved in public activities and few indeed were concerned with the equal rights issue. In Quebec, French Canadian women were slow to involve themselves in any activities outside the home, and it appears that in the period before the achievement of the Dominion Suffrage, the equal rights movement in that province was in the hands of a small number of English-speaking women in Montreal.

271

There was considerable women's activity in Ontario in the last decades of the nineteenth century and at the beginning of this century, but most of it was not focussed directly on equal rights. By the 1870's the province was rich enough to support a significant number of middle-class women with sufficient leisure to devote themselves to concerns other than the immediate ones of raising a family and of managing a home. With this new-found time many women devoted themselves merely to a more elaborate social life. Those women who did seek other channels for their energies usually applied them to social welfare causes, thus fitting the model of "maternal feminism." This activity extended from Women's Institutes to temperance organizations, and found a central focus in the 1890's with the founding of the National Council of Women. But as early as the 1870's there was a small band of dedicated women who saw that the equal rights issue was one of central concern. The equal rights women were also concerned about temperance or slum clearance, or the evils of prostitution, but they were distinguished from others by the fact that they saw equal civil, economic, and educational rights. Because of their efforts, other socially concerned women, notably those for whom temperance was the major social issue, would gradually see that they too had to make a positive commitment to their own rights as citizens.

The equal rights advocates launched a Toronto suffrage society at a public meeting held in the city council chambers in 1883, but the origins of this suffrage society go back to a private club, the "Toronto Women's Literary Club" founded in 1876 by Dr. Emily Howard Stowe, Canada's first woman physician. Catherine Cleverdon in *The Woman Suffrage Movement in Canada* dates the beginnings of organized Canadian feminism from the founding of this club, and it is becoming commonplace to use this date as a signpost. Like the Seneca Falls Convention of 1848, which is usually taken to mark the beginning of an organized movement in the United States, the date of the founding of the literary club should be seen as a convenient landmark but should in no way be taken as a rigid or definitive starting point for the whole feminist movement. However, it is likely that it does mark the first attempt to publicize the equal rights issue.

Its founder, Dr. Emily Howard Stowe is a genuinely interesting and important figure. She was one of those nineteenth-century professional women who made her way to a career (in her case in medicine) in the face of severe practical and psychological opposition. Faced with a career versus motherhood dilemma, she proved herself committed enough to a career to leave her children in the care of a sister while undertaking her training. (See the account by Joanne Thompson in *Ontario History*, December, 1962.) Forced to receive her training outside the country (no medical school in Canada would admit her) she was exposed to feminist ideas during her stay in the United States. On her return to Toronto she felt the need to advocate the advancement of women in Canadian society. The Literary Club's innocuous name was apparently chosen intentionally, the founders believing that any overt mention of that chief of feminist causes, the suffrage, would arouse too much hostility.

The Literary Club in its early stages hardly represents a movement: only a few women were involved and it was primarily an individual educational experience for those who did attend its meetings. However, as we have seen, the Toronto Women's Literary Club did provide the nucleus for the first Canadian suffrage society, the Toronto Women's Suffrage Society which was launched at a public meeting in March of 1883, and this society also provided the base for the development of an attempt at a national organization, the Dominion Women's Enfranchisement Association (later the Canadian Suffrage Association). But the national society appears to have been national in name only, and remained largely a Toronto organization.

The equal rights movement in Ontario in the 1880's and 1890's seems to have been directed to two main areas, the suffrage and increased educational opportunities for women. It scored some notable successes, including the admission of women to the University of Toronto in 1886 and the establishment of the Ontario Medical College for Women in 1883. The Ontario legislature's response to the demand for political rights met with qualified success. The right to vote for school trustees had been granted to women with the necessary property qualifications in 1850. In 1884, the legislature granted the municipal franchise to unmarried women with the necessary property qualifications. In 1872, Ontario passed the first Married Women's Property Act in Canada. The pattern of granting local franchises, or of franchises specifically concerned with education, had parallels elsewhere. In England for instance the fran-

272

chise for the school boards set up by the Education Act of 1870 was granted to women. In the 1870's women were permitted to be poor law guardians and under the County Councils Act of 1888 they were admitted to participation in local government. Why were male legislatures so willing to grant these concessions? Because these tasks and responsibilities were housekeeping tasks and thus it was considered that women could participate in them without violating the accepted Victorian image of women.

When it came to granting the suffrage in jurisdictions which involved less restricted areas of activity, the Ontario legislature was to prove less open to woman suffrage. In spite of the fact that there was an active petition campaign in the 1880's (largely dominated by the temperance interests) and in spite of the fact that the women had gained a supporter in the legislature, the Liberal John Waters, who sponsored several suffrage bills in the 1880's and 1890's, these bills met with no success and little debate. There was not enough of a movement in the province to bring pressure on a legislative body most of whose members found the idea outlandish and ridiculous and were to do so for some time to come. The provincial suffrage was in fact not achieved in Ontario until 1917 and is said to have been a direct result of women's participation in the war effort.

273

Why did the struggle take so long in Ontario? Although Ontario was the first place in Canada in which sentiment for women's rights emerged, there is little doubt that those interested in women's rights were not able to secure mass public opinion in their favour, nor were they able to arouse sufficient numbers of women for sufficient lengths of time. Although they were earnest and dedicated, women like Emily Howard Stowe and the second-generation women like her daughter Augusta Stowe-Gullen and Flora MacDonald Denison appear to have been if not content, at least resigned to wait for public opinion to swing their way. In the first years of this century, they watched the progress of the English militants with benevolent interest, but with a sense of detachment, and they seemed to accept the views of their male supporters that although women's suffrage was "inevitable," in Canada it might be a long time in coming.

It was a characteristic of male supporters in Canada to qualify their support for the suffrage with comments about women's "apathy," and to insist that the suffragists garner an unrealistic amount of visible support: The *Toronto World*, for instance, which was a friend of the cause (Flora MacDonald Denison wrote a column for the Sunday edition) in 1909 urged the "apostles and evangelists of the movement [to] get the women of Ontario together and confront the provincial premier [Sir James Whitney] with a requisition signed by a majority of their number calling on him to fulfil his pledge." Whitney had agreed to support the suffrage if he saw "sufficient" public demand. When Augusta Stowe-

Gullen, as president of the Canadian Suffrage Association, wrote to the paper praising the editorial, she did not point out that this demand on the part of *The World* was both unnecessary and impossible to fulfil.

In Ontario, although the equal rights women played an essential role in providing a forum and a focus for the issue, the long time span of the movement in the province appears to have served to institutionalize non-success. By the early 1900's, support by enlightened voices in the province had become a substitute for full citizenship and only the success of the movement elsewhere brought the issue to a final conclusion in Ontario. And perhaps it was social and economic change which finally made success inevitable. Especially important was the rapid development of women's occupational roles which took place in Ontario in the last decades of the nineteenth century, and the first years of the twentieth century. Women established themselves in teaching; they began to enter office work and factory work, and the percentage of women gaining more education and entering professional fields increased considerably. Although they were still second class citizens in the labour market, their increased participation did make them more visible and gave them more power. This was the case even before the experience of World War I, during which women were employed in occupations and used in the military in greatly expanded areas.

From what we know of it at present, the Ontario women's rights movement would appear to have been largely middle-class in origin, allied to the temperance movement and centred in Toronto. When we turn to the prairie provinces, we find a picture which is notably different in several ways. At the beginning of this paper, it was suggested that the Persons Case marks a symbolic end to the equal rights struggle in English Canada. In the context of a discussion of feminism in the Prairies, it is significant that all five of the women whose names appeared as appellants of the Persons Case suit were residents of Alberta. Although one of the five was Nellie McClung, she was not in fact the leader of this particular struggle. The prime mover behind the Persons Case was another Alberta woman, Emily Murphy, who like Nellie McClung had been born in Ontario but had found full scope for her energies in the West. Emily Murphy, who moved to Alberta in 1907, distinguished herself as a journalist and in social service work and in 1916 she was appointed police magistrate for Edmonton. This was the first such appointment to be made not only in Canada, but in the British Empire.

Canada's first woman judge was appointed by an Alberta government; the first province to grant the suffrage to women was Manitoba, followed quickly by the other two prairie provinces. Feminism in the prairies won the wholehearted support of important interest groups including the farmers' organizations. Women were active in the political and social life of the prairies, in the radical movements, in the temperance movement. The use women made of their position in a new society is perhaps

274

the most outstanding difference between North American feminism and the European context to which it owes its origins. In Canada, historians have tended to see a regional division which relates to this factor: the suffrage came first in the prairies because the prairies were still a new society in which women and men worked together.

The equal rights movement in the Canadian prairie provinces did not follow a completely uniform pattern. The movement had an early phase in Manitoba, almost as early as the first stage of the movement in Ontario. In Saskatchewan and Alberta (which achieved provincial status only after the turn of the century) the movement really begin after 1910. Christine Macdonald writing in *Saskatchewan History* (October, 1948) points out that in Saskatchewan it was rural and small-town, whereas in Manitoba, Winnipeg was clearly the centre of the movement. It has also been pointed out by June Menzies in *Politics in Saskatchewan* (Toronto, 1968) that whereas in Manitoba, in the second phase of the struggle, the women had real opposition in the form of provincial premier Roblin, who was a personal opponent of women's suffrage, in Saskatchewan the women were faced with "support" from Premier Scott, but in the same form that we have seen it manifested in Ontario. Scott agreed that women should have the suffrage, but only if they could mobilize a widespread campaign to overcome "apathy." This sort of technique was actually much more difficult to deal with than outright opposition. The Manitoba women could answer Roblin's anti-suffrage arguments, but how were women to answer the demand that they overcome "apathy?" Why should it have been necessary in any case? If *some* women wanted the suffrage clearly any "supporter" of the suffrage ought to have been committed to giving it to them, even if they were in a minority.

275

Since Nellie McClung, to whom this book is dedicated, was a leading figure in the feminist movement in Manitoba, it seems fitting for us to examine the progress of the suffrage movement in that prairie province in some detail. The suffrage movement in Manitoba began in the 1890's. The first organized attempt to work for the suffrage in the prairies was launched by a group of Icelandic Manitoban women some time in the early 1890's. From these beginnings the Icelandic community in Manitoba apparently continued to work for the franchise from the 1890's until success was achieved in 1916. Although they communicated with English-speaking advocates, they maintained a separate campaign. English-speaking Manitoban women became involved in suffrage organizations through the Women's Christian Temperance Union which began actively advocating the suffrage in the 1890's. It was the WCTU which staged the first mock parliament in the history of the Canadian suffrage movement in Winnipeg in February 1893. A year later the Manitoban Equal Franchise Club was founded. However, in spite of these beginnings the suffrage movement in Manitoba made little headway in the nineties or in the first decade of this century. It was really only after 1910 that the movement began to gain momentum once again and it was only with the founding of the Winnipeg Political Equality league in 1912, with Lilian Beynon Thomas as its first leader, that real progress began to be achieved. But from then on, until January 1916 when Manitoba became the first Canadian province to enfranchise women, the movement progressed steadily towards success.

There are several factors of interest about this period of feminist history in Manitoba, and several explanations as to why the movement was such a success there after 1912. The chief explanation is to be found in the fact that the women who were involved in the suffrage cause and in allied movements in Manitoba were also very much involved in other movements which had a broad and firm base in the affairs and concerns of the province. This was true from the beginning of the movement in Manitoba: E. Cora Hind, for instance, a journalist and agricultural expert whose determination earned her a post on the *Winnipeg Free Press* after twenty years of persistence, was active in the WCTU from the 1890's and out of her temperance interests she became committed to women's suffrage. Suffrage was never her main concern, but the support of such a widely respected figure did much for the cause. The later group of feminists, including Nellie McClung herself, was similarly involved in a wide range of problems. This was also true in Ontario, but it appears that in the prairies, in contrast to Ontario, a commitment to equal rights was more widely disseminated among socially active women and, of equal importance, the women involved in social concerns had close connections with powerful forces in the region. It was vital to the feminist campaign in all three prairie provinces that the women had the support of the most influential of the farmers' groups, the Grain Growers Associations of Manitoba and Saskatchewan and the United Farmers of Alberta. The *Grain Growers' Guide*, the organ of all three of these farmers' organizations, was a strong and influential supporter of women's rights from its beginnings in 1908. However, the support of the farmers' organizations did have qualifications, and the qualifications indicate the limits the progress of women's rights had made in the Canada of the early twentieth century. The farmers' organizations were men's organizations, but both men and women were, after all, farmers in the prairie society, the women being vital to the farm economy. Yet although the farmers were willing to give support to "their women" in their cause, it was only in 1915 that the Manitoba association offered women entry into full membership in the association. As a concession, the women were to be admitted at half the dues paid by men. The women, realizing more than the men the limitations imposed by such a concession, accepted membership, but insisted on paying full dues, as Cleverdon documents.

A major base of support for the women's movement throughout Canada was the temperance movement, and specifically the WCTU. As a social cause, temperance seems rather unappealing in the mid-twentieth century and it is easy today to forget how deeply imbedded the temperance cause was in nineteenth- and early twentieth-century reform movements, not only in Canada but also in Britain and the United States. Temperance was a central issue for reformers whose other views covered a very wide spectrum, from Lord's Day Alliance people to Socialists like J.S. Woodsworth. There was good reason for this interest in temperance: the abuse of alcohol was a severe social problem in the nineteenth and early twentieth centuries. Although in England drunkenness usually appears as a problem connected with urbanization and industrialization, in Canada it was also perceived as a rural problem. And, as many temperance reformers pointed out, it was a problem which bore with particular severity on women. As Nellie McClung put it in *The Stream Runs Fast,* "no one could deny that women and children were the sufferers from the liquor traffic; any fun that came from drinking belonged to men exclusively, and the men themselves would be the first to admit that."

Given the circumstances of life in rural Canada, it is easily understandable that a specifically female temperance movement should have emerged. As with its counterparts in the United States and Britain, the temperance movement in Canada had strong links with evangelical religion and especially with the Methodist movement. It has also been pointed out by M.G. Decarie in *Ontario History* (March, 1974) that the movement had strong "nativist" elements — elements hostile to or at least suspicious of immigrant groups that were not Anglo-Saxon — and that the nativism of the prohibition movement in general and of the WCTU in particular may have limited the suffrage movement as well. The movement began in Canada in the 1870's and by the 1880's the WCTU had become a national organization. For many individual WCTU members and for the organization as a whole, the interest in temperance led them, sometimes unexpectedly, to the support of other reform causes — most notably, the cause of woman's suffrage, which many temperance advocates, male as well as female, began to see as a necessary step towards the achievement of prohibition.

During the last years of the suffrage campaign in Manitoba, Nellie McClung took as active a role as anyone in the movement. McClung was interested in the suffrage not as an empty symbol, but because she saw it as a means of achieving the kinds of social changes to which she was committed: the temperance measures, the protection of women workers, an end to corruption in government, a more sane, non-violent foreign policy.

The tone of the suffrage campaign in Manitoba, during these last years leading to final success, reflects the tolerance and the aversion to conflict that were such a strong part of Nellie McClung's character. Both the character of the suffragists and the character of their opposition determined that in Manitoba hostile confrontation simply was not necessary. Typical of the sort of technique that was used was the staging of a "mock parliament" in 1914. This piece of gentle theatrical satire can be said to represent both the height of McClung's career as a suffragist as well as the high point of this last phase of the Manitoba suffrage campaign.

This attitude of determined reconciliation worked through to the end of the struggle in Manitoba. During the 1914 election campaign in the province the opposition Liberals strongly endorsed the principle of woman suffrage and Nellie McClung and Lilian Thomas as representatives of the suffrage cause spoke to their convention and were a resounding success. The Conservatives on the other hand made their opposition to the suffrage a major part of their campaign. "Wifehood, motherhood and politics cannot be associated together with satisfactory results," said their campaign literature. The Conservatives won by a small margin in 1914; however, their government was short-lived. They were forced to resign because of a construction industry scandal in May, 1915, and the Liberals came to power in Manitoba. After a resounding Liberal victory in August, 1915, the success of woman suffrage in the province

278

British Columbia Archives & Records Service   (HP 39854).

Suffragists (L–R) Nellie McClung, Alice Jamieson, and Emily Murphy. McClung (writer, reformer, and women's advocate) and Murphy (the first woman magistrate in the British Empire) were two of the five women involved in the 1929 "Persons Case": a successful legal challenge to the 1928 Supreme Court of Canada decision that women were not legally "persons" and consequently were not eligible to be appointed to the Senate.

was assured. The measure was introduced in January of 1916, and received Royal Assent on January 28.

This success in Manitoba was parallelled by similar successful campaigns in the other two prairie provinces, both of which granted the suffrage to women in 1916. The history of the suffrage struggle in the rest of Canada need only be summarized here. Constitutionally, the struggle in Canada parallelled that in the United States rather than that of England, since the federal/provincial dichotomy is similar to the federal/state dichotomy. In both countries, it was necessary to fight on two levels, although in Canada the problem was considerably less overwhelming than it was in the States, simply because of the larger number of states involved. In Canada, the Dominion franchise was granted to military women and the wives of relatives in the service in 1917 (this Act was a political manoeuvre on the part of the Borden government). Full Dominion suffrage was granted on May 24, 1918. Women won the provincial franchise in British Columbia and Ontario in 1917, in Nova Scotia in 1918, in New Brunswick in 1919, in Prince Edward Island in 1922, and in Quebec in 1940. (In Newfoundland, the suffrage was granted to women over 25 in 1922. In 1948, when Newfoundland became part of Canada, women were granted the right to vote in provincial elections on an equal basis with men.) The right to hold office was granted on a Dominion level in 1919, but provincially, the dates of this achievement varied, from Manitoba in 1916 (with the suffrage) to New Brunswick in 1934. The right of women to hold certain offices, and specifically to sit in the Canadian Senate, was not of course clarified until the successful outcome of the Persons Case in 1929.

279

Feminism in Canada was characterized by non-hostility, by a spirit of reconciliation which was in striking contrast to the fortunes of the movement elsewhere, especially in Britain. In that country the last phases of the suffrage movement were dominated, in the years leading up to World War I, by the militant Women's Social and Political Union, led by the Pankhursts. The WSPU courted violence from the police, used violence itself, and its members were treated with great brutality by the authorities. From most points of view, Canadian women can consider themselves fortunate to have avoided such violence — violence and confrontation bring harsh consequences. The achievements of the Canadian suffragists were in their own way as taxing of those of the English militant suffragettes. The work of the Canadian women was the sober work of convincing their opposition which more often than not in Canada expressed itself in "women-are-too-good-to-vote" arguments. Yet the violence of the English militants and their milder followers in the United States did achieve something. The most important effects of the militant movement were probably psychological. The spectacle of respectable middle-class ladies courting arrest, defying the law, and undergoing the difficulties and harassment of imprisonment and forcible feeding did much to destroy the image of Victorian ladyhood, and this was very liberating.

The women who were shoved around by hostile crowds and hostile policemen were made to feel the angry hostility of their opposition. And from the point of view of the opposition, the spectacle of women throwing off the mannerisms of respectability, and what is more, risking their lives for their beliefs, convinced many who were opposed to woman suffrage of the seriousness of commitment of the suffragettes.

In contrast, the suffrage movement in Canada did not bring with it the intense emotional and intellectual development that it did in Britain and to a lesser extent in the United States. The issue was discussed and the lives of the suffragists themselves were deeply affected, but the general social and psychological attitudes towards women were not altered by the suffrage struggle because the struggle was not bitter enough. For this no one is to blame: it would surely have been wrong to have resorted to violent tactics where they were not necessary. It would also be wrong to think that the Canadian feminists lacked sympathy for their more militant English sisters. McClung, for instance, was most impressed with Emmeline Pankhurst, and there are indications that she herself would not have opposed the use of similar tactics in Canada had they been necessary. In her autobiography she says: "The visit of Mrs. Emmeline Pankhurst and of Miss Barbara Wiley, also one of the British Militant Suffragettes, created a profound impression." And she tells of a meeting with Roblin in which she said to him that if the government did not give in on the suffrage question, the women would "make a fight for it." McClung was not alone or even unusual in her support for the English militants. Most Canadian equal rights women supported their actions — but at a distance. Their attitude was one of sympathy rather than empathy. They never really believed that they themselves would be involved in such an activity. Because the women didn't really have to "make a fight for it," and because the vote was won in Canada by rational persuasion it was possible for many women to accept the Victorian clichés without question, to accept Maternal Feminism as the ultimate justification for Equal Rights Feminism, to accept the idea that self-sacrifice is central to woman's role, and is the key to woman's psyche. The experience of the militant suffragettes forced English and American women to question the whole idea of self-sacrifice because their experiences showed them that society's idolization of women veiled a determination to restrict them to a severely limited sphere of action, by violent means if necessary. It should be said that the militants themselves sometimes seemed to revel in self-sacrifice; at times militancy appears as Victorian feminine self-sacrifice carried to its ultimate limits. But it produced as a reaction a clear realization of masculine hostility. In some ways Canadian women might have benefited from the experience of being forced to confront the reality of this hostility.

In recent years, the history of the Canadian women's movement (along with the history of the women's movement in other parts of the world) has begun to enter a new phase. In the past, historians of feminism have tended to view the movement in a fairly narrow context. At the same time, historians as a group have tended to ignore the women's movement, if they were not directly concerned with it. Although these weaknesses have not yet been overcome, the situation is improving. Even "general" history is beginning to improve. The new general interpretation of the period by Ramsay Cook and R.C. Brown, *Canada, 1896–1921: A Nation Transformed* (Toronto, 1974), does say quite a lot about women — although it could say *much* more. It is encouraging that the authors include what they have to say about women as an integral part of their text, rather than relegating everything concerning women to one separate chapter. Several new interpretations of the Canadian feminist movement have recently appeared. Since two of the most interesting interpretations (V. Strong-Boag's and Ramsay Cook's) emphasize the role of maternal feminism in Canada, this article will conclude with an examination of some questions relating to the origins of nineteenth-century feminism, in a way that may shed some light on the difference in progress experienced by the movement in the West as contrasted to the East and which may at the same time offer an explanation for the strength of maternal feminism.

281

One constantly recurring explanation put forward by historians to account for the greater success of feminism in both Western Canada and the western United States, as contrasted to the eastern portions of both countries, is that the milieu of the frontier was more conducive to feminism than was the more settled society of the East. The importance of the pioneer tradition, its relationship to the development of the suffrage movement, has in fact become a glib historical cliché, the sort of cliché that does answer a number of questions, but which is nonetheless unsatisfactory, because of the questions it leaves unanswered. The usual statements about the connections between the pioneer mentality and feminist ideas are very much of the same order as the statements made about the connection between the ultimate success of the suffrage movement in England, the United States, and Canada, and the war work done by women during World War I. Women participated in the work of pioneer society, it is said, and that is why their men stood behind them when they demanded their political rights. Speaking of the Canadian movement, Cleverdon puts it this way: " . . . the theory generally prevailed that women as well as men had opened up the country, had shared the experiences of settling a new land and were, therefore, entitled to a voice in making the laws." Ramsay Cook in his introduction to the new edition of Cleverdon's book says that the women of the West "had an advantage: since they had to play the role of equal partner in pioneering conditions, their husbands could hardly fall back on the argument of the different spheres." In writing of the American movement, Eleanor Flexner says essentially the same thing in *Century of Struggle* (Cambridge, 1959): " . . . by the demands it made on human beings for survival, frontier economy established a certain rough egalitarianism which challenged other, long-established concepts of propriety. Women were just as indispensable as men, since a household which lacked their homemaking skills, as well as nursing, sharpshooting, and hunting when needed, was not to be envied."

The undeniable fact that the suffrage was achieved earlier in the West than in the East, in both Canada and the United States, does seem to support the frontier-as-equalizer statements of Cleverdon, Cook, Flexner, and others. Why, then, is the theory not completely satisfactory? Because it implies that in pioneer society, for the first time in human history, women made themselves indispensable, and this is an obvious untruth. The model that Cleverdon, Cook, Flexner, and others have in mind as a contrast to the pioneer woman is the middle-class Victorian lady who did not perform economically valuable work, but whose function was rather to symbolize by her economic uselessness the economic success of her middle-class husband. The Victorian lady was, however, a new phenomenon, a product of industrialization and the rise of a new middle class, and this fact is generally overlooked by those who advocate the pioneer-as-equalizer explanation. Women had performed indispensable work in European society (as they have in every society that has ever existed) before the nineteenth century, and nineteenth-century working-class women, along with their children, were performing indispensable work at lower rates of pay than working-class men. Exploitation served not to raise their status but to lower it. This is of course true of working-class men as a group as well as of working-class women and it is also true of blacks and of any other group which is exploited — indispensability can and does lower one's status rather than raise it, and the tragic plight of the child and female proletariat of the industrial revolution is that they were exploited not only by their capitalist employers, but also by their own men who, for the most part, systematically excluded them from unionization and radical political activity.

It is clear, then, that it could not have been their indispensability that persuaded the husbands of the pioneer women to give them their political rights. But was there no connection between the pioneer tradition and the improvement in the status of women in frontier society? I think that there was a connection, but that the usual statements about the way in which the connection functioned leave out an essential part of the picture. I spoke earlier of the Victorian middle-class lady who was a product of urbanized industrial society: her grandmother, in many cases, might have been a yeoman's wife who performed many functions directly analogous to those of a frontier wife in the North American settlements. Although such a woman was aware of her own usefulness, and was often valued for it, there is no question that institutionally and by custom she was subservient to her husband. Many social historians of the Victorian period have analyzed the metamorphosis that the middle-class woman underwent, as the new industrial middle class emerged. It was not the case that the Victorian lady served no function, but rather that her function had changed. From the bustling manager of the dairy, she became "the angel of the hearth." Her duty was to make of her home a refuge from the world, "a sacred place, a vestal temple," in Ruskin's phrase, and to maintain the moral standard. In his book *Victorian England: Portrait of an Age*, G.M. Young characterized this moral function in a memorable way. "The most influential women of the nineteenth century," he says, "were reared in an atmosphere which made them instinctively Custodians of the Standard." It is this new moral role to which middle-class women were assigned that Kate Millett attacks in her discussion of Ruskin and Tennyson, and which she calls the "separate spheres" answer to the feminist demands which were beginning to emerge in mid-Victorian England. The effectiveness of the "separate-spheres" propaganda was manifest in the fact that middle-class Victorian women, including most middle-class feminists, generally accepted this new stereotype. But this was true not only of the middle-class Victorian lady who remained at home in Britain. It was also true of those women who came to North America as pioneer wives, and I would suggest that it was this new image of themselves as moral guardians and protectors of the hearth that was decisive in changing their status in the new society. It proved especially effective, because as well as maintaining the role of moral guardian and spiritual centre of the home, those women also had to resume their old roles and become once again economically productive. It seems plausible to suggest that it was a combination of the two roles which altered and improved the status of women. An analysis of frontier society and of pioneer family structure in Canada indicates that both men and women believed that women in frontier society performed an essential emotional function, and it would seem reasonable to suggest that it was because they did so that the men of the frontier were able to perceive women as human beings and not simply as work and sex objects.

In her study of the institution of the family as it developed during the period of settlement in Upper Canada, Jean Burnet offers considerable evidence that women were considered an essential part of frontier society, not merely because they were needed to perform useful work but because they provided an emotionally stabilizing influence. Burnet quotes from one commentator on Upper Canadian society who observed of unattached men that "removed from all social intercourse and all influence of opinion, many have become reckless and habitual drunkards.

283

The only salvation of a man here is to have a wife and children." Although the wife and children may benefit the man economically, what is clearly implied is that their chief function is be his moral salvation.

A significant number of the early settler women in Upper Canada came from middle-class households in Britain. Indeed, such women frequently found that one of the most difficult features of adjustment to their new life was that they were forced to give up the culture and leisure to which they had been accustomed. For example, in *Roughing It in the Bush*, Susannah Moodie says: "It was long, very long before I could discipline my mind to learn and practise the menial employments which are necessary to a good settler's wife." One can safely assume that middle-class women like Mrs. Moodie would have been influenced by Victorian ideas about the role of women as moral guardians and keepers of the hearth, and that she and others like her may been sustained by the desire to fulfill this role, and may even have been strengthened by it if they were fortunate enough to have the inner capacity to conform to the pattern. It is possible that the North American frontier was one place where these Victorian ideas about the spiritual function of women may well have served a genuinely useful function. The women who adapted themselves to such a role did so, no doubt, because of cultural pressure — under different circumstances, the women rather than the men might have fallen to pieces. In most cases, it appears that they did not do so. It was the men and not the women who were overcome by the fear of the loneliness of the frontier, while the women were usually able to take hold of themselves and cope with the situation. (This was not universally the case, of course, and there were a few women who could not face the difficulties, the hardships, and the loneliness of the frontier.)

The sort of family that was held together by the successful pioneer wife is of special concern to us, because it was this family pattern which produced many Canadian feminists. It was certainly true of the family pattern in which Nellie McClung grew up. One of the major impressions that emerges from the first part of her autobiography, *Clearing in the West*, is the central role that her mother played in the family. Her mother's moral strength, her capacity for hard work, even her aesthetic sense were obviously central factors in Nellie McClung's upbringing. Here is a description of Nellie McClung's mother's house.

> The floors were pine boards and were scrubbed every week, using very little soap, for soap yellowed the wood. Elbow grease was the thing. . . . The floor had lengths of rag carpet in pale strips and there were red and brown mats, hooked in circles and triangles. . . . the two front windows had hand knitted curtains done by mother, in a fern pattern and paper lace valentines were hung on them. . . .

Those hand-knitted curtains and rag carpets meant something important. They were physical and also spiritual symbols of the fact that the mother in the pioneer family was determined to civilize the bush according to British middle-class standards and not merely to eke out a living from it.

McClung's mother was not a public figure. The task of widening out these virtues into the public sphere belonged to the next generation, but one might venture to suggest that the active creative spirit of her mother which had been used up in the mother's generation by the task of keeping the family together, was in the daughter translated into a wider field. And indeed, as Strong-Boag points out in her introduction to *In Times Like These*, McClung did see women's involvement in politics as an extension of their guardianship and housekeeping role. She put it this way: "Women have cleaned out things since time began; and if women ever get into politics there will be a cleaning out of pigeon holes and forgotten corners, on which the dust of years has fallen, and the sound of the political carpet beater will be heard in the land."

McClung's civic housekeeping and her mother's private housekeeping *285* share a number of features in common. The origins of McClung's maternal feminism were present in her mother's set of private values. With these values, the mother had ordered and strengthened her pioneer home and infused it with moral significance. McClung intended to perform the same functions in the wider society and she set to the task with the efficiency and dedication of a good pioneer wife.

The maternal feminism exemplified by McClung was a powerful force in Canada. But does the idea of maternal feminism provide a complete and totally satisfactory framework for understanding Canadian feminism? The most important new attempts at formulating a conceptual framework (Cook's and Strong-Boag's) seem to assume that it does, and perhaps they both do so because this view accords well with current thinking about movements for social reform in Canada in the first decades of the twentieth century. But we do not in fact have enough information about Canadian feminism to support broad conceptual generalizations. There may have been other motivating forces very different from the disposition to engage in civic housekeeping, and until more is known about a greater number of the women involved, perhaps we should withhold judgement about the universality of this outlook. It would be unfortunate to enclose Canadian feminism in a new orthodoxy at this stage in the discovery of its history.

It is my hope that this brief account of the suffrage movement in Canada will lead some readers to explore women's history further. For women especially, history often seems meaningless and unrelated to the real concerns of life — and indeed for women it often is. Reading history can often make us feel that we never existed, or existed only as an unchanging part of the natural background. But women do have a history: the idea that we've always done the same things in the same way is merely a convenient fiction. Other disciplines (notably anthropology and sociology) are forcing historians to realize that even "natural" institutions like the family are in a constant state of change, and always have been. As women, we have been intimately involved with institutions like the family — much of our history will be rediscovered through a re-examination of these institutions. With this re-examination, better interpretations of more traditional areas of historical enquiry — like the suffrage movement — will be possible. The revival of feminism will, it is to be hoped, make it possible for this re-examination to take place in a way which recognizes the validity of female consciousness.

A Motherhood Issue*

286 ANGUS McLAREN

Only in 1969 was the Criminal Code amended so that the provision of contraceptives ceased to be illegal. The law was also changed to allow medically approved abortions to be performed in hospitals. In defending such changes, Pierre Trudeau came up with one of the most quotable quotes of his political career: "The state has no business in the bedrooms of the nation."

Yet the law was simply catching up with social reality. The Canadian birth rate had been falling for most of the 20th century, and contraceptives of one form or another had been in use for years, even before the appearance of a birth-control movement.

Demographers have discovered that Canadian fertility began its long-term decline at least as far back as the mid-19th century. It dropped about 30 percent between 1851 and 1891. That fall was offset, to an extent, at the turn of the century by the arrival of the prolific immigrants of southern and eastern Europe. Following the First World War, however, the Canadian decline in births matched that of other nations.

The size of "completed" families fell from an average of 4.1 children for parents born in 1871 to 2.9 children for parents born in 1911. The lowest point in the inter-war fertility decline came during the Depression when the possibility of an additional child posed a serious threat to the working-class household. French-Catholic regions did have higher fertility rates than English-Protestant ones, but no group was immune from falling natality.

*From *Horizon Canada* 87 (1986):2072-77. Reprinted by permission.

The "Natural" Way

A great many Canadian couples used some form of birth control in the early 20th century, but few were prepared to defend such practices publicly. Doctors, who might have been expected to best understand the subject, proved, because of their professional caution, among the fiercest opponents of restriction of family size. They were joined by those who saw birth control as both a cause and effect of the modern "threats" of urbanization, rural depopulation, alien immigration, and feminism.

Nevertheless, more and more Canadians sought to limit their fertility. The extension of compulsory education in English Canada was no doubt a key factor inasmuch as it increased the costs of raising children and limited the economic contribution they could make to the household. Also important were the rise in non-domestic work for women, the shift in emphasis in the role of the mother from child bearer to child rearer, and a new idealized image of the family focusing on companionship rather than patriarchy. Fertility limitation was adopted not to undermine the family, but to protect it.

287

Birth-control information was limited then because the Criminal Code of 1892 made it illegal to sell or advertise anything intended for contraceptive or abortive purposes. Considerable reliance was placed on "natural" methods such as abstinence; prolonged nursing, which was widely believed to provide protection against a subsequent conception; and restriction of intercourse to the "safe period" in the woman's ovulation cycle. Unfortunately, 19th-century doctors believed this "safe period" was at mid-month; this inaccurate schedule was widely publicized until the correct cycle was scientifically determined in the 1920s.

Doctors would not discuss the merits of the most reliable forms of contraception — the condom, douche and pessary — because they associated them with the libertine, the prostitute and the midwife. We know, however, that douches were sold by the major department stores as aids to "feminine hygiene."

Recipes for home-made, soluble pessaries (vaginal suppositories) concocted of cocoa butter and boric acid were exchanged by Prairie women. In rubber-goods stores, men purchased condoms, purportedly to protect themselves from venereal disease. And finally, there remained the simplest, oldest and most widespread contraceptive practice — *coitus interruptus*, or the withdrawal method. Well into the 20th century, it was the main way in which Canadian couples sought to "cheat nature."

Hit or Miss

Because all the methods of contraception available were, to a greater or lesser extent, lacking in reliability, many who were firm in their desire to limit family size eventually had to face the serious decision of whether to seek an abortion. In the interwar years, abortion was intimately linked to family planning.

The women who sought abortions were older, married mothers concerned for their own and their families' health and well-being. They resorted to traditional methods. A woman might first seek to "put herself right" by drinking an infusion of some "abortifacient" such as quinine, tansy, pennyroyal, savin, or ergot of rye. If that failed, she could try bleedings, hot baths and violent exercises. After this would come the riskier step of attempting a dilation of the cervix with slippery elm, a sponge tent, or catheter. If none of that worked, the classified columns of local papers listed a variety of patent medicines and the names of nurses and doctors willing to assist women worried by "irregularity."

Because abortion was illegal, women often had to have recourse to ineffective and dangerous methods. A high price was accordingly paid in maternal disease and death. Whereas the infant mortality rate fell dramatically in the first third of this century, the maternal mortality rate actually went up. In 1947, it was noted that while everyone knew that 47,000 Canadians were killed in the Second World War, few knew that 21,000 women had died in childbirth since 1926, 4,000 of them as a result of bungled abortions.

288

Getting Organized

Given the lack of birth-control information in the 1920s and 1930s, many Canadians wrote to Marie Stopes in England or to Margaret Sanger in the U.S. These two remarkable women knew that the middle classes restricted births, so they sought to make contraceptives available to the lower classes. They both stressed the need for government-supported clinics, run by trained personnel.

Most important, they played down the old economic arguments for birth control. They believed that limitation of family size had to be made to appear not just economically necessary, but morally right and socially acceptable. They developed the argument that contraception was not only compatible with pleasure, but essential if the woman's passions were to be allowed full expression. This emotional defence of birth control was to prove immensely successful.

As a result of a cross-Canada lecture tour by Margaret Sanger in 1923, a small group of socialist feminists created the Canadian Birth Control League in Vancouver. This was followed in 1932 by the establishment of a birth-control clinic. Members of the leftist Co-operative Commonwealth Federation such as Dorothy Steeves, Laura Jamieson, Lyle Telford and A.A. Stephen were the most active champions of the right of working men and women to control their own fertility.

Not all socialists or feminists went along, however. Many leftists were wary of taking the population question too seriously for fear of reinforcing the old theory that social improvement could only be achieved by restricting the growth of population. Many feminists also feared that birth control, far from freeing women, would simply further subject them to men's sexual demands.

Once the Depression hit, however, most progressives came to accept birth control as at least offering the prospect of some improvement in the health of mothers and some protection for the working-class family's economy. At the same time, goaded by their fears of working-class unrest and racial degeneration, some businessmen, club women, academics and clergymen joined in supporting a campaign aimed at lowering the fertility of the working class.

From Toronto, the Rev. A.H. Tyrer began in 1930 to send out thousands of tracts for the purpose of having his fellow ministers alert newlyweds that birth-control information was available. With Dr. Rowena Hume and the Rev. Lawrence Skey, he established the Marriage Welfare Bureau, where couples were steered to doctors willing to provide contraceptive instruction.

289

In Hamilton, Ont., club women led by Mrs. Mary Hawkins established a birth-control clinic in 1932, under the direction of Dr. Elizabeth Bagshaw. It was initially opposed by the medical community, but Hawkins soon won over the local elite, arguing like Tyrer that the limitation of working-class births was in the interest of the propertied classes.

A New Tack

A.R. Kaufman, a Kitchener, Ont., businessman, shared the belief that birth control was needed to protect the social status quo.

Hearing of the work of Tyrer and Hawkins, he compared notes with them, and decided to set up the Parent's Information Bureau in Kitchener to spread contraceptive information across Canada. Earlier advocates such as Stopes and Sanger sought to provide women with the best contraceptive — the diaphragm — and this could only be done in a clinic. Kaufman thought the diaphragm too fussy a method for most working-class women to employ regularly, and a clinic too remote an institution for most to visit. He opted for less reliable but simpler forms of protection — contraceptive jelly and the condom. And rather than wait for women to visit clinics, he sent nurses out across the country to track down prospective clients. By 1942, he had over 70 nurses working from Vancouver Island to Newfoundland, contacting families that sent in over 120,000 applications for contraceptive supplies.

There was as yet no birth-control movement in Catholic Quebec, but fertility was declining there too, even if it still appeared frighteningly high to some English Canadians. It would only drop dramatically after the Second World War, when the economy and the prevailing culture no longer encouraged people to have large families. With the dramatic secularization of Quebec society in the "Quiet Revolution" of the early 1960s, when responsibility for schools and hospitals passed from Church to State, contraception became commonplace.

The 1969 reforms of the Criminal Code that officially ended the story of the fight for legal contraception reflected the changes that had taken place in Canadian society as a whole. They also served to open up the debate on the issue of free access to abortion.

The new law permitted abortions to take place only in hospitals, and only when approved by a medical committee. This led to glaring disparities; in some areas, committees readily approved abortions, while in Prince Edward Island, for example, they refused altogether. The campaign for the repeal of the abortion law was launched in 1970. By 1974, it had as its rallying point the defence of the private Montreal abortion clinic set up by Dr. Henry Morgentaler.

The current debate between opponents and supporters of free access to abortion, the so-called pro-life and pro-choice forces, is so fierce that it is easy to forget that women have been controlling their fertility for over a century. It is not a question of whether they will do it, but how — either safely, or at the risk of their lives.

Growing Up Female*

VERONICA STRONG-BOAG

Two images of girls dominate the interwar years. The first to appear, in the 1920s, was the flapper. Women's wartime efforts as suffragists, "farmerettes," munitions workers, army nurses, and volunteers, and feminists' long assault on male privilege in the home, the paid workplace, and public life had, it seemed, borne fruit in liberated youth. Brimming with the promise of adolescence, teenagers, like those in the Canadian Girls in Training (CGIT) in their white midis, or "Girls of the New Day,"[1] as one observer characterized the flapper generation, symbolized that sense of new beginnings for women with which the postwar decade began. The second image, emerging from the 1930s, retreated from the sexual brinkmanship typified by the flapper to return to the innocence of young childhood. This was the girl as "moppet." The Dionne quintuplets, the British princesses Elizabeth and Margaret Rose, and, especially, Shirley Temple were its most visible expression. Their pictures decorated magazines and newsstands and gripped imaginations and hearts from coast

*From Veronica Strong-Boag, *The New Day Recalled: Lives of Girls and Women in English Canada 1919–1939*. Copyright 1988 by Copp Clark Pitman Limited. Reprinted by permission.

290

to coast in the depression decade. While the flapper with her short hair and short skirts was an essentially confrontational figure, poised to contest the conventions of workplace and bedroom, the curly-headed moppet, simultaneously conventionally feminine, touchingly dependent, and often implicitly flirtatious, appeared more calculated to appeal for protection and support, as indeed Ontario's first quints received from Premier Mitch Hepburn's government in 1934. The shift in public attention from flapper to moppet accompanied a retreat from the optimism of the early 1920s, from the essentially liberal faith that women could manage gender politics to the advantage of themselves and their daughters. To be sure, adventurous young women survived the Great Depression and continuing anti-feminism, but tough times robbed them of any certainty that the world would welcome new initiatives from their sex.

The reality behind these two images was complex. Girls had to deal with a world that appeared to offer new experiences but simultaneously retained strong resistance to any significant change in sex roles. In addition, many had to confront the special problems of class and race in an economy that, even in supposedly boom times, kept large numbers in poverty and without power. Yet, whatever the particularities of their situation, whether perhaps as the child of an agricultural labourer or as the offspring of Canada's Native peoples, girls all across the country were distinguished in vital ways from boys. This chapter examines the years from infancy to young adulthood when the outlook of and the options for Canadian women were critically moulded. Individuals and institutions of every sort, from the mother to the police magistrate, from the family to the school, regarded and treated girls differently from boys. With few exceptions, female Canadians were engaged from birth in a series of relationships that finally subordinated them and their interests to male prerogatives. As we shall see, girls and women were not always unconscious of this inequality. In their youthful encounters with a world that was only too likely to value their needs and accomplishments less than those of their brothers, they stored up an experience of self-assertion that remained a powerful component of female culture.

To deal with the challenges facing them, the nation's daughters needed every ounce of the learning, courage, and tolerance that anxious champions such as Agnes Macphail desired for their inheritance.[2] Canada's first female MP went right to the heart of the dilemma facing her sex in observing one of her parliamentary colleagues with his nine-year-old daughter:

> He was getting the funnies for her to read. I said: "Where does she come in the family; the youngest?" He said: "No, the older; I have only two children, a boy and a girl, the boy is the best." I was startled, and this in May 1939. But, controlling my countenance as well as I could . . . I said: "I am very fond of little girls;

291

they are my favourites." I wanted to save that child from a scar she will carry all her life. But the father wouldn't have it. He said to his daughter: "You think the boy is best; don't you?" And she sullenly answered: "Yes." That story illustrates perfectly why women haven't more confidence. I have heard mothers do similar things many a time. It is unforgivable.[3]

And as Macphail found time and time again, the patriarchy that found expression in the preference for sons over daughters was not easily circumvented.

Fortunately, in their reception of children, as in many other matters, Canadians were not unanimous. Many little girls found a hearty welcome. A woman from British Columbia remembered the flood of delight and determination produced by the birth of a daughter. She swore then and there that this "little woman" was not going to suffer as a result of her sex.[4] A strong sense of injustice produced by growing up "in a household where boys were kings and girls scullery maids" moved one Jewish woman married to a marginal shopkeeper to treat her daughters "with a fierce protective joy."[5] When war loomed nearer in the 1930s, the birth of a daughter might be especially desired. A critic of international events summed up her feelings this way: "I wanted a girl badly. I don't want to raise any more cannon fodder."[6]

Such attitudes shaped the consciousness and the experience of little girls across the Dominion. For the lucky there was continued encouragement. Feminist Helen Gregory MacGill, for instance, helped inspire two daughters to pursue graduate degrees in unconventional fields, sociology and aeronautical engineering, in the 1930s.[7] The Jewish mother who repudiated her own family's favouritism to sons prepared Fredelle Bruser to go on for a Ph.D. in English. Close relationships between mothers and daughters, and between several generations of women, as in the MacGill household, laid the foundations for a network of female associations in which girls from their earliest moments would move.[8] Sisters or female relatives of a similar age, as with the novelist Mazo de la Roche and her cousin Caroline or the artist Emily Carr and her sisters, also formed life-long attachments whose intimacy matched or surpassed heterosexual ties.[9] These relationships formed the bedrock of many women's experiences, preparing them to move easily into subsequent female friendships. The resulting female culture may not have offered the prestige of female–male coupling, but it persisted as a vital component of many women's lives and challenged the heterosexual biases that the popular culture of the day celebrated.

Succoured as they might be by a preference for girls and strong female relationships, babies were also marked fundamentally by their particular experience of class, race, culture, and region. Although they did not encounter these factors in precisely the same way as adults, they could not escape their consequences. In many ways, childhood was integrated into adult worlds right from its beginning. An expectant mother's health helped determine the weight and viability of her offspring.[10] Her choice of, or perhaps sole recourse to, midwife, nurse, or doctor, and home, clinic, or hospital, similarly linked infants to a specific set of expectations and possibilities. Babies born in private wards in up-to-date city hospitals with obstetricians in attendance encountered life in a way very different from those delivered in Halifax's black neighbourhood by a Victorian Order Nurse or those helped into the world by fathers on Labrador's north coast.[11]

Although life expectancy remained tied to economic resources, enhanced public health campaigns did help reduce the number of deaths among Canada's young children. Between 1921 and 1939, neonatal mortality fell from 43 to 31 per one thousand live births, and deaths of infants under one year fell from 102 to 61 per thousand.[12] The institution of widespread vaccination and immunization programs meant that children of all classes were less likely to fall victim to smallpox and diptheria.[13] Other commonplace innovations such as "tonsils and adenoids parties," in which doctors found surgical solutions to the problems of chronic illness, were of more questionable benefit. Public health education also enlisted youngsters themselves in nation-wide campaigns. In the elementary schools the Junior Red Cross spread the gospel of good hygiene through the medium of plays such as "The Conversion" on the need for pasteurized milk,[14] "David and the Good Health Elves" on the prevention of TB,[15] and "An Argument in the Kitchen" on the virtues of milk.[16] As one Mother Goose "health rhyme" sung in classrooms across the country put it:

293

I'm little Bo Peep, I need lots of sleep
I go to bed bright and early.
Windows wide are my great pride
For I'm a Fresh Air girlie.[17]

What such admonitions lacked in elegance they undoubtedly made up in the verve with which they were recited. Together with toothbrush drill, handkerchief presentation, and nail inspection, they encouraged pupils to accept higher standards of personal hygiene. For girls this message was hammered home again in domestic science classes. Such instruction not only improved child health, it accorded especially well with patterns of socialization that emphasized that little girls should be neater and cleaner than their brothers.

Such directives notwithstanding, certain groups remained especially vulnerable to illness and physical disability in general. Even in better times, poverty robbed numerous youngsters of good health and security. Such was the case with the Native peoples who confronted challenges that only the hardiest offspring survived.[18] The 1928–29 New Brunswick investigation into child welfare revealed conditions in homes and in poor law institutions throughout the province that would not have been out of place a century or so earlier in Charles Dickens' London.[19] In an impoverished Toronto household a few years later, a little girl stricken with infantile paralysis remained, not untypically for the condition, strapped to her bed all day; every morning revealed fresh bedbug bites.[20] In contrast, additions to the families of the well-to-do, celebrated in the pages of *Saturday Night* and local society columns across the country, did not have to worry about the poor nutrition and unsanitary accommodation that stunted so many young bodies and minds.

Even little girls brought up to attend elite institutions such as Edgehill School for Girls in Windsor, Nova Scotia, or Queen Margaret's School in Duncan, B.C.,[21] did not, however, entirely escape one persisting scourge of childhood. The sexual abuse of children, particularly girls, by male family members and strangers was not limited to any single social or economic group. While some assaults eventually came to trial, most victims had no recourse against the more powerful adults who governed their lives. Such was the case with a thirteen-year-old just before World War II. Many years later she remembered an attempted rape by her forty-six-year-old uncle: "I had no one to talk to and I did not understand. My parents had deceased. He threatened to throw me on the streets."[22] The appearance of very young prostitutes in Canadian cities was only the most visible expression of a more general problem of sexual abuse that afflicted as many as one in two girls.[23]

Although sexual mistreatment of children drew only intermittent attention at best, and its real extent was never acknowledged, the broader and related question of the socialization of girls sparked constant discussion among progressive and conservative commentators alike. Progressives, like one writer published by the B.C. Board of Health, argued for similar treatment of the sexes:

> Remember from the first that boys must be trained to be fathers as well as girls to be mothers. Is it the man who loves and understands children, or the man who does not, that makes the best husband and father and the happiest home? If it is good for your little girl to love babies and help you by minding them, it is good for your little boy, and if it is good for your little boy to play games, climb and run about to make him grow strong and healthy, it is good too for your little girl. God knows she will need all her bodily health and strength and courage if she is to make a worthy mother for the next generation![24]

Some parents, whether they read such advice or not, acted in keeping with the sentiment underlying it. There were daughters who remembered being raised in the 1920s "with the attitude that we had to be independent."[25]

294

While progressive parenting seemed far from rare, feminist critics surveyed the period with general dismay. A contributor to the *Canadian Forum*, the leading social democratic journal in the Dominion, bleakly concluded that girls were still being "brought up to marry."[26] Another critic put it slightly differently:

> Girls usually do a number of things around the house, but it is not such a common thing for boys to undertake responsibility within the home. This is only because they have never been shown that it is as much their duty as their sisters' to help to run the home.[27]

Such complaints point to the widespread resistance to any transformation in sex roles. As far as most Canadians were concerned, the bottom line remained: adult females bore final responsibility for family life and on its success rested the ultimate fate of western civilization.[28] Any style of parenting that questioned this fundamental allocation of duties was at best suspect and, often, fiercely opposed.

295

Despite the fact that mothers clearly had somewhat different feelings about giving birth to girls or boys, the fact that babies came in both sexes was rarely, if ever, explicitly acknowledged in the child care manuals of the day. The dominant pronoun was always masculine, and a young infant was viewed more or less as a *tabula rasa*.[29] Babies were to be shaped by the regular affirmation of good habits in everything from bowel movements to emotions. Subject from their earliest days to strict, clock-regulated regimes in eating, sleeping, and elimination, offspring would be secure enough to be independent and simultaneously habituated to accept the disciplined rhythms of home and workplace. The quints, Yvonne, Annette, Cécile, Emilie, and Marie, the most famous examples of the application of such theories, inspired many imitations, but the artificial situation in which they lived — a hospital separated from parents and other siblings with nurses or early childhood education teachers in attendance — could fortunately not be easily duplicated. Babies, including the "Famous Five," coming with a range of needs and personalities, did not always take easily to up-to-date instruction, even when parents were eager and knowledgeable practitioners of the new behaviouralist psychology.[30] In fact, mothers of every description continued to bring to the task of child rearing a set of assumptions and skills learned from relatives, neighbours, trial and error, and just plain common sense. Raised too, as most mothers and fathers were, to expect different things of daughters and sons, they were hard put not to teach, if only by example, preferred behaviours specific to each sex. Early childhood might resemble that blank slate that many psychologists in these years postulated — and this is very debatable — but what is certain is that most parents assumed without question that girls required somewhat different treatment from boys, in everything from dress to discipline.

In particular, since girls' destiny was generally conceded to be in marriage, their training was often directed more or less explicitly to this end. From the time they could turn to a mirror or another person for confirmation, girls were encouraged to ape the preoccupation with appearance that was believed to characterize the normal adult of their sex. Like Shirley Temple, who inspired a line of dolls fervently desired by little girls in the 1930s, female youngsters might aspire to spunkiness but above all they were to be cute and affectionate. No more than their mothers could they entirely ignore the barrage of advertising directed at female Canadians of all ages that insisted that "You are in a Beauty Contest every day of Your Life."[31] Male admiration was the ultimate goal. Boys and men were routinely portrayed as preferring beauty to brains in their girlfriends and wives, or at least preferring the latter quality to be relatively invisible, thus constituting no threat to their public authority.[32] One adviser in the Junior Red Cross magazine cited modern psychology in explaining that "The boys, and later the men, like the girls and the women who make them feel they are heroes. That is the simple secret of feminine popularity."[33]

More important still, little girls were expected to be mothers in the making. "Little Mother" classes joined homemaking badges in Guides and lectures in CGIT to prompt members to accept special responsibility for and find particular reward in the care of those younger than themselves. Dolls, homemade or store-bought, confirmed the same message. In homes where mothers bore heavy obligations for bearing and rearing children, not to mention housework and paid labour, daughters were also expected to help out regularly. No wonder that the sight of girls wheeling carriages and carrying children not much smaller than themselves was commonplace across the Dominion.[34] The loss of parents, especially mothers, also readily led to daughters like Anna Borisevich, aged eleven, taking on heavy responsibilities for younger siblings.[35] Not all girls enjoyed baby-minding; some regretted the time lost to play or school. For others, however, the social approval they earned as "little mothers" and the affection they might win from those in their care were powerful inducements to nurture. The lesson of such early experiences was difficult to ignore. Even should they be able to reject a maternal role for themselves, girls would be hard put to escape the realization that normalcy for their sex was inextricably linked with mothering, whether biological or social.

Although the forms they took varied tremendously, marriage and children were routinely presented to girls in all walks of life as the fulfilment of every true woman's ambitions. Even exposure for the more fortunate to an ostensibly wider range of career choices could not make much headway against the ubiquitous influence of youthful socialization. One 1938 survey of 167 young women graduating from McGill, Queen's, and Toronto universities, for instance, revealed that 149 preferred marriage to a career and that the vast majority did not intend to keep their jobs after marriage.[36] Anticipating motherhood, 113 respondents desired three or four children and twenty wanted five or more.[37] Girls reached such conclusions despite occasional public recognition that a wedding ring brought no guarantee of security against want and desertion, and children no certainty of love and respect.[38] That breath of harsh reality had trouble penetrating a popular mythology that relentlessly directed girls to wedding vows, childbearing, and child rearing.

The 1920s and 1930s also saw little girls, and children in general, being especially targeted, as were their mothers, by increasingly powerful advertisers. Toys that in the past had been largely restricted to special occasions such as Christmas and birthdays were now available throughout the year, at least for the fortunate. Similarly, where ten- to twelve-year-olds previously were expected to have outgrown playthings, they were now permitted such distractions a few years longer.[39] This expanded market was also reflected in year-round mass advertising campaigns that more than ever before turned to premiums — toys, candy, cards — directed at children.[40] Of course, youngsters did not benefit equally from this potential largesse. Most children relied on a few well-worn favourites and had far fewer possessions than merchandisers would have liked. But if they could not always provoke sales, they could stimulate, as never before, desire for new products.[41] One salesgirl remembered an Eaton's Christmas with Shirley Temple dolls priced at $9 to $16, "a lot more than some families got in a month of relief." She watched

297

> the faces of those little girls, from about four or five right up to about eleven. Some used to come at opening time and just stand there looking at those pink-cheeked, golden-haired lovely Shirley Temples. Little faces, they needed food. You could see a lot who needed a pint of milk a day a thousand times more than they needed a Shirley doll. They'd stare for hours. We tried to shush them away but it didn't do any good. They'd go once around toyland and be back. This, mind you, went on day after day, day after day, until some of the girls thought they would go crazy. One girl had a crying fit just over that, those hundreds of poor kids who would never own a Shirley Temple in a hundred years. They were lucky if they had breakfast that morning, or soup and bread that night.[42]

Shirley Temple dolls were only one of a barrage of new items available to the favoured child in these decades. Shifting fashions in toys were matched by changes in what constituted an up-to-date wardrobe. Here, at least, was the appearance of liberation from old tenets that confined the female form. Most obviously, like women's wear, skirts became shorter and clothes generally somewhat more casual and sporty. In the 1920s pyjamas arrived as alternatives to the traditional nighties.[43] Bare legs, tanned by sun or commercial lotions, succeeded stockings, at least for the summer.[44] Greater physical freedom was also linked to major changes in undergarments. Where previously, respectable young women would be trained early to the restraints of back-laced and, by the beginning of the twentieth century, increasingly front-laced corsets, the 1920s and 1930s saw a major revolution in consumer preference. While the traditional corset industry financed a campaign of disparagement,[45] corselettes and bras and girdles won over their traditional customers. Fears that opposition might extend even to girdles led stores to open up junior sections, to introduce corselettes for twelve to fourteen year olds and to shift to the term "foundation garment" instead of corset, lest an old-fashioned term deter the young buyer.[46] Girls' desire to move freely and to participate in sports was countered by claims that "natural curves were being further enlarged by active games" and that proper girdles held organs in place even for those who were thin and that they would help "keep the figure from getting larger."[47] The strength of resistance to old styles, including some young women buying men's clothing for themselves and complaining that there was no athletic women's underwear available in Canada,[48] was extremely powerful. By the end of the 1920s, bras and girdles had won over all but the most old-fashioned. When combined with silk, cotton, or rayon, new latex with its "two-way stretch" made lighter garments all the more popular.[49] Over the long term, up-to-date manufacturers also benefited. Old corsets had been relatively durable while new model undergarments came in many styles and had to be replaced more regularly, all adding to profits.[50] In part too, as the undergarment controversy demonstrated, the advantage of simpler clothing for children in these decades was countered by the same stress on slenderness, rather than healthiness, that afflicted fashions for adult women. No more than their mothers, could girls easily mould themselves to fit the figure of the day or escape the message that any other body shape ultimately brought into question both their femininity and their ability to compete for boyfriends and husbands.

298

Girls growing up in these decades easily became part of a mass consumer culture that depended on thousands of purchases replacing the homemade and the rarely bought items that had been the norm in years past. Some families consciously resisted the dictates of fashion — religious objectors such as those in the Doukhobor and Mennonite communities being perhaps the most obvious dissenters — but poverty was the more common cause of failure to participate. One B.C. woman remembered, for example, that "we were encouraged not to wear shoes in the summer. . . . The girls were encouraged to wear boys' boots because they wear longer."[51] In such cases a choice between various types of preferred underwear or anything else was obviously irrelevant. For those who could afford to ape fashion, new styles of clothing did offer physical freedom that was absent in long skirts and corsets. They did not, however, ignore the erotic appeal of the female body. Only the focus changed: in the

1920s from the waist and the bottom to the legs and the arms, and in the 1930s to the breasts and hips.[52] Little girls could hardly ignore such visible instruction as to the source of female attractiveness.

Clothing styles told wearers and observers alike an important story about gender differences, but more explicit sexual information was harder to come by. Objections that such knowledge hardened and coarsened "a girl's moral tone" and nipped "in the bud those tender shoots of purity which are a girl's best attributes"[53] remained commonplace after the First World War and never disappeared during these years. To be sure, there was also popular acknowledgement of the need for more education in this area.[54] Some parents became more conscious of the necessity of telling their daughters "the facts of life."[55] Reflecting the lack of consensus about how much advice was appropriate, however, the CGIT, like many organizations dealing with girls, moved cautiously. Under the guise of "Health" or "Family Life" programming, it broached the whole question of female sexuality very carefully.[56] Reticence was not easily overcome. One doctor's daughter was far from untypical in remembering that pregnancies were never mentioned to children or in "polite conversation." At age eleven her mother told her

> that once a month there would be "bleeding" and that I had to wear a napkin while it lasted. I don't think she mentioned what purpose it served, but just said that it was the lot of all women, and we had to accept it. During the "period," she said, we had to be very careful not to catch a cold, and we couldn't take a bath or wash our hair. . . . I was left with the feeling that the whole thing was terribly unjust to females, and with the misconception that the "blood" came from the nipples.[57]

The tendency to greater explicitness in advertising "feminine hygiene" products in these years, as with ads for Kotex and Modess sanitary napkins,[58] and the douches and gels that even the family standby *Eaton's Catalogue* offered,[59] must have countered some ignorance, but many girls remained woefully ill-informed, as later unwanted pregnancies revealed.[60]

While ideally mothers were supposed to communicate both the "facts of life" and the standards for successful femininity to their daughters, children early came into contact with institutions, other than the family, where information could be sought and shared. In these encounters girls tested themselves and their families. Information and skills could stand the challenge or be found wanting. While the great majority of children remained within their parents' homes until they were old enough to attend elementary school, a few could always be found in creches, day nurseries, and orphanages. All of these institutions were the special preserve of the poor. In Halifax, for instance, local charwomen's daughters and sons, from the age of three months on, passed their days in the nursery of the Jost Mission. Here they found the toys, healthy food, and sanitary conditions that their own homes frequently lacked. Little girls also received the domestic lessons that were their special prerogative. For many needy applicants to the mission, the benefits of care outweighed the liabilities of enforced religious instruction and social patronage.[61] In Vancouver, the City Creche performed a function similar to that of the Jost Mission for female day workers. When their mothers had work, babies and preschoolers stayed at the creche from 8 a.m. to 6 p.m. Poverty made them welcome even a creche's monotonous menu: a dinner of soup, pudding, and potatoes at 11 a.m. and a supper of porridge, bread, butter, jam, and milk at 3:30 p.m.[62] Imperfect as such institutional options were, they were frequently superior to the more haphazard arrangements that poor mothers might otherwise have had to make.[63] In any case, they gave children new opportunities to add to their store of knowledge and to understand the highly stratified adult world they would eventually enter.

300   Preschoolers whose parents were more well-to-do normally stayed home. A small minority, however, were beginning to explore other options in these years. Child study centres funded by the Rockefeller Foundation at the universities of McGill and Toronto welcomed trend-setting middle-class youngsters into group settings that promised a further head start on the business of life.[64] In such centres, the domination of behavioural psychology demanded a regularity and simplicity of schedule and nutrition that children in the poor institutions would have recognized. In contrast, however, McGill's and Toronto's privileged situation meant a much more favourable staff-student ratio, immeasurably greater individual attention, and significantly better food and equipment. Their pupils experienced the same advantages in schooling that they knew at home.

In contrast to the situation at the child study centres, inadequate staffing and accommodation was endemic to child care institutions for Canada's poor. Refuges such as New Westminster's Providence Orphanage, Burnaby's United Church Home for Girls, and Vancouver's Salvation Army Maternity Hospital Rescue and Children's Home crowded occupants together in facilities that, whatever the good will of their custodians, could not provide adequate supervision.[65] Despite recognition of their shortcomings for psychological and physical development throughout these decades, orphanages continued to house children whose parents were unable or unwilling to care for them. In 1927, for instance, 180 children came under the care of the Vancouver Children's Aid Society but only nine were placed in paid boarding homes. An unknown but small number of children were sheltered for free by individual families, but the great majority remained in CAS accommodation. For those dubbed defective or delinquent, as with inmates of the Maritime Home for Girls at Truro, Nova Scotia, or the Girls' Cottage Industrial School at Sweetsburg, Quebec, conditions were equally far from ideal. Bereft of what benefits intimate family life could offer, institutionalized children were handicapped from the outset.

Not surprisingly, fostering out became more and more popular, although never universal, as a solution to the dilemmas of institutional care. In many instances, youngsters were readily handed out to whomever would take them. Young girls, like Anne of Green Gables in an earlier period, might very well find themselves expected to perform a multitude of chores in exchange for room and board. Not all such children were Canadians. These years still saw pauper children from Great Britain brought in as home-helpers by emigration societies.[66] The perennial shortage of good foster homes led to attempts by the emerging social work profession and philanthropic women to keep natural families together through state allowances and expert supervision. The modern transformation from institutions to fostering to family case work was well underway during these years, but children remained vulnerable to the stinginess with which public and private authorities undertook their responsibilities.[67] Anne Shirley had many successors in finding herself passed casually from hand to hand, although there is little reason to believe that most orphans finally found a Marilla and Mathew Cuthbert to shelter them. The fate of an illegitimate Vancouver girl who, at age nine, was left behind to shift for herself when foster parents and another child, whom she had believed to be her natural family, moved away, was at least as common.[68]

When they could, most families resisted the permanent loss of their children. Mutual affection was important, and the presence of even very young family members had long been essential to the domestic economy of many Canadians. Such had always been the case with Athabaskan peoples. One Native woman born in 1930 remembered her mother teaching her to sew moccasins when she was eight: "Mom made me start over again if I made a mistake. I watched her tan skin — cut hair, flesh, wash, hang. Dry it and smoke it with rotten wood. Soak in rain water for two or three days, then start to tan."[69] Useful contributions were not unique to those living in the bush or to families in any one culture. Girls of many different backgrounds were regularly kept at home as housekeepers and child-minders. A family's need for such assistance varied with a number of factors. The season, the number, age and sex of siblings, the health and temperament of the mother, and the prosperity of the family all made a difference. At critical times, such as at the birth of a baby or during threshing, even little girls could be called on to lend a hand. An ill or overworked mother meant that duties might begin early, as with Lauretta, born in 1916, who was "busy in the kitchen when she was six years old."[70] In such situations, daughters could well pride themselves on their own accomplishments and their parents' trust. Costs were paid as well. One daughter remembered foregoing a much desired high school education as she was the "only girl and Mother . . . [was] rather sickly."[71] In good times and bad, chances for schooling remained firmly tied to the rhythms of the family economy.

Schools themselves could be a mixed blessing. While some girls found intense friendships on the playground and sought-after learning in the classroom, others found themselves uncomfortably singled out by virtue of their appearance, accents, or ability. Whether they were participant, observer, or intruder, children regularly divided according to sex, age, and social group. Different entrances, play areas, and games affirmed the importance of these distinctions. Girls skipped, played hopscotch and tag, and swung, leaving boys for the most part to rowdier contests. On occasion though, especially when numbers were small, both sexes might engage in spirited games of softball or Red Rover.[72] Chants, songs, and rhymes were also a vital part of this playground culture.[73] Class routines offered further opportunities to discover the world beyond the family. For pupils like the future historian Hilda Neatby in Saskatchewan, education promised release from farm labour and opened up the possibility of a career.[74] Other students, like one resident of small town Ontario, remembered:

302

> I liked all my teachers, and I guess I liked school, though I don't remember being stimulated by it. I worked fairly hard and usually headed my class, but I think I learned only enough to pass exams. I went to school because everyone else went to school.[75]

The less well off had still greater cause for disinclination. A Toronto girl whose family fell on hard times in the 1930s "dreaded hearing that school bell and walking into the hall and into the class" for fear that a classmate would recognize her second-hand clothes.[76]

Such anxieties and aspirations were part of the lives of both boys and girls, but the latter had to contend as well, especially once they entered high school, with resistance to equality in education. Anti-feminists in both decades, but especially in the decade of the 1930s with its reinvigorated fears about the survival of western civilization, the nuclear family, and traditional sex roles, challenged the merits of co-education. A typical critic identified so-called god-given differences between the sexes: "a boy is a boy" and will grow up to be "restless, adventurous, creative, active, a maker, while a girl, under normal conditions, grows calm, homeloving, receptive, passive, a user."[77] Here in a nutshell was the language and thinking that, whether rooted in newer scientific mythology or older misogynist traditions, assigned Canadian girls to a different, and finally subordinate, role in the home and the paid workplace. Denied the option by female nature itself, so it was suggested, of independence, initiative, and ambition, girls were routed, subtly perhaps but nonetheless forcefully, into homes and public employments where their abilities would not directly compete with those of men and, not so incidentally, would prove immediately beneficial to male relatives and bosses. Housewives and secretaries helped nuture male creativity, authority, and independence. In the process their own talents could well be lost sight of.

What seemed equally clear was that many women in these decades believed that men preferred them less educated.[78] As a female observer put it:

> When it comes to leaping off the deep end, beauty has it over brains yesterday, today and forever. Of course, I know the old saw . . . about the beautiful but dumb woman wearing down the resistance and taking the edge off a finely tempered disposition in time, but by that time, there isn't anything to do about it — he's been caught hook, line, and sinker. Meanwhile the brainy prospect isn't a prospect. She is still sitting in somebody's office making pot hooks for a living and maligning fate because she hasn't a pretty face to bewitch it for her. . . . Give me a cute nose and I won't need to know how to spell. Correct spelling will bring me in $25 a week, perhaps, but a cute nose will give me a meal ticket to punch for the rest of my life. . . . An ounce of complexion is worth a pound of grey matter.[79]

303

External beauty was seen as the real secret of female popularity and success.

The prevalence of such views undermined whatever academic talents girls might lay claim to. It also aided and abetted the incursion of home economics or domestic science into school classrooms. This subject had been entering public schools since the end of the nineteenth century,[80] and in the 1920s and 1930s it continued to find new recruits in school systems that could afford the additional expense. In its North American origins, the domestic science movement had raised important questions about just how homes and families could best take advantages of improvements in production, transportation, and services, and simultaneously offer mothers and wives a marked degree of independence, authority, and convenience. Co-operative solutions in everything from cooking to washing and child care, for instance, envisioned a highly sociable future in which women's domestic labour would be valued and alleviated.[81] That co-operative vision faded before corporate capitalism's preference for homemakers who were isolated in single-family residences and who made a host of individual purchases. By the 1920s, domestic science, as institutionalized in Canada's elementary and secondary schools, showed little sign of its radical heritage. Students were groomed to accept the privatization of the household and the strict division of labour between the female homemaker and the male breadwinner.

Yet, for all its evolving conservatism, domestic science remained a poor cousin to more explicitly "masculine" components of the curriculum. In 1922, for example, the province of British Columbia paid only 50 percent of home economics equipment costs while it assumed all the expenses of manual training for boys.[82] Educating girls, even in their "proper" accomplishments, was to be done, as much as possible, on the cheap. Despite such reservations and the onslaught of the Great Depression, which caused towns like Trail, Fernie, Armstrong, and Port Moody to discontinue domestic science classes for a time, the number of B.C. schools offering such classes increased steadily, from 51 domestic science centres in 1919, to 86 in 1929, to 120 in 1939. By 1930, approximately 75 percent of the province's school girls took "home ec," and they would have found much the same opportunity in many other regions of the country.[83]

The exact results of formal instruction are difficult to measure but, taken to their logical conclusion, they meant the homogenizing of domestic culture from one coast to another. As Barbara Riley has observed in her discussion of the situation in B.C. schools:

> In place of family customs in diet, menus, and methods, the girls were introduced to new foods and recipes whose selection was on scientific grounds and whose preparation was taught according to standardized procedures. Finally, many girls may have first been introduced to new consumer goods . . . and new patterns of consumption through domestic science classes.[84]

In the great majority of cases, girls' new information and skills could not contend with the immediate economic and social reality of family life where domestic arrangements in everything from stoves to meals were difficult to update. Over time, however, many girls would seek to apply in their own homes at least some of "the standardized methods, the authoritative cookbooks, and the new technological devices first introduced in the classroom."[85] In this way, budding homemakers helped bring their families into the domestic revolution of modern consumer society.

For students of non-British origins, household science classrooms provided yet one more exposure to the forces of Canadianization. Here they learned that the domestic standards, recipes, and procedures that engaged their mothers were no longer to be preferred. If cookbooks and teachers were any guide, for instance, "real" Canadians ate roast beef and potatoes not spaghetti and tomato sauce. Newcomers were left to cope with what such instruction meant for mothers proud of their traditional skills and daughters encouraged to remake themselves and their "foreign" families into a more acceptable image. Domestic progress in its Canadian form could well be a mixed blessing. Whatever its limitations, instruction in household science raised few unsettling questions about girls or their behaviour in the minds of most observers. As one enthusiast observed, in the somewhat different context of employment security, "As a training for living, Household Science is the safest risk in the list of girls' vocations."[86]

Almost equally safe in terms of its relevance for subsequent employment in these years and almost as good a guarantor of femininity were commercial classes. The private sector had been the first to respond to a massive expansion in clerical occupations that relied on relatively well-educated young women of respectable appearance. Business colleges such as Pitman's and Shaw's were well established by the turn of the century. Public school educators were much slower in meeting the needs of a changing economy, but by 1920 pupils in many towns and cities could take courses in narrowly defined and practically oriented subjects such as typing, shorthand, stenography, and bookkeeping. Applicants for such instruction were overwhelmingly female. In 1923 Toronto's Central High School of Commerce reported 69 percent female enrolment and three years later 74 percent. In Vancouver the Cecil Rhodes High School of Commerce claimed 72.7 percent in 1919 and, ten years later, 74 percent.[87] Such figures reflect the fact that, as Nancy Jackson and Jane Gaskell have argued, "The clientele and raison d'être for commercial programs were increasingly restricted to women and to the limited prospects in the business world that were associated with women's employment."[88] Labour market segmentation on the basis of sex, so that there were in fact two distinct labour markets, meant that young women of very different origins might well be jointly groomed to become secretaries, salesclerks, and banktellers.[89] Background and years of schooling were not finally as important as the structural limitations on women's opportunities. The inauguration in the 1920s of a department of secretarial science at the University of Western Ontario, for instance, implicitly recognized the existence of a dual labour market in which sex was the determining factor.[90] By the 1920s, commercial courses at every level attracted both working- and middle-class girls who found that their presence did not raise unsettling questions about competition with boys and, if they were fortunate, promised stable and respectable occupations before marriage.

Secondary education was girls' surest route to white-collar jobs. The interwar decades, with their elimination in many jurisdictions of tuition, their tighter enforcement of child labour laws, and their increase in school-leaving ages to sixteen in provinces such as Ontario, saw working-class youngsters enter high schools and collegiates in unprecedented numbers. These influences especially benefited girls.[91] Tuition fees, for example, were a special deterrent for girls when their education was widely viewed as less important than that of their brothers. Abolishment of fees allowed for a continuing female majority in secondary educational institutions. In B.C., for example, girls made up 57.3 percent of high school pupils in 1920, 55.1 percent in 1930, and 54.0 percent in 1940.[92] The situation was much the same elsewhere. The school attendance of the fifteen- to nineteen-year-old age group is shown in Table 1. The social and economic advantages of a high school diploma helped counter long-existing prejudices against the education of girls in these years. Toronto's Harbord Collegiate Institute, for example, enrolled increasing numbers of Jewish girls who previously would have been relegated to a formal education far inferior to that of boys of their own age.93

TABLE 1 Percentage of Each Sex Aged 15 to 19 at School			
	1921	1931	1941
Girls	27	36	37
Boys	22	32	35

Source: Jane Gaskell, "Education and Job Opportunities for Women: Patterns of Enrolment and Economic Returns," in *Women and the Canadian Labour Force*, ed. Naomi Hersom and Dorothy Smith (Ottawa: SSHRCC, 1982), 261.

306

Not only were teenage girls more likely than boys to be in school, they were more likely to do well and to graduate.94 Their schooling was further distinguished by different enrolment patterns. Domestic science and commercial classes joined languages and literature in welcoming large numbers of girls; math, sciences, and shop work did not. To an important degree, such segregation meant that high school education was in fact not co-educational for much of the day. Girls and boys learned different skills and information in separate settings. The result, as Jane Gaskell has pointed out, segmented "the labour force by sex on entry to the labour market and on entry to post-secondary education."95 When they graduated from high school, middle-class girls who traditionally had spent their teenage years in the classroom found themselves competing for many of the same kinds of jobs with working-class girls who were likely to be the first generation in their families to complete high school.

For all the disadvantages they faced in entering the labour market, high school graduates were relatively fortunate. Girls with physical and mental handicaps had far fewer opportunities. Although they were more likely than ever before to find a place in public schools, they were also more likely than their luckier sisters to drop out or fail to register, either to remain at home or to begin a desperate search for employment. The Protestant School Board of Montreal had begun work with academically handicapped pupils as early as 1913 but only in the late 1920s were "opportunity classes" formally established. Even then, the marriage of one teacher in 1934, and hence her automatic dismissal, meant the closure of one such class. By 1938, there were eleven "opportunity classes" in nine Montreal schools. There students spent three-fifths of their time on academic work and the rest on handwork.96 Also introduced sporadically across the country wherever jurisdictions were willing to take on the additional expense were habit and guidance clinics for troubled students. In Montreal, a Habit Clinic for Children, established in 1923, assembled two psychologists, a psychiatrist, and a social worker two mornings a week to deal with fifteen to twenty-five children referred by schools, parents, courts, and social agencies.97 In Vancouver, a Provincial Child

Guidance Clinic, established in the 1930s, endeavoured, through IQ testing, home investigations, parental education, and, sometimes, removal from the home, to transform the actually or potentially incorrigible into obedient citizens.[98]

All too frequently, reflecting the belief in women's particular responsibility for children and in the emerging Freudian-influenced psychology of the day, concern focussed on individual causes of behavioural problems, especially the shortcomings of mothers. In Vancouver cases included an eight-year-old girl in 1938 whose extreme stubbornness was linked to the impatience and bad temper of her mother and a teenager whose troubles were blamed on "an irregularity in the personal life of her mother."[99] Whatever outpatient care could be found at the hands of the new generation of psychologists, psychiatrists, and psychiatric social workers was always limited to the very few who could afford such treatment. It was much more likely that girls encountering difficulty in adhering to acceptable patterns of behaviour would find themselves in institutions such as the Mercer Reformatory for Girls in Toronto or the Industrial Home for Girls in Vancouver. Between 1914 and 1937 the latter institution received from all over B.C. 600 admissions ranging in age from seven to twenty years, although the great majority were between fourteen and seventeen.[100] Most inmates were incarcerated for incorrigibility and immorality, but there were also those like eight-year-old Florence. Officially charged with theft, she had in fact been committed more to extract her from an unsuitable home situation than anything else.[101] Not surprisingly, such tragic cases were recruited overwhelmingly from the ranks of the poor. The training in domestic labour that they received in the Dominion's industrial homes and reformatories practically guaranteed that they would return to the same condition.

A very different situation awaited those that could afford the private schools that flourished in these years. In Rosary Hall in Toronto, for example, parents paid $6 to $8 a week in the 1920s to ensure that daughters received the benefits of a good Catholic education and the enjoyment of a pool, library, pianos, and extensive grounds.[102] Schools with such privileges helped to produce a separate upper-class culture and to instil in their well-to-do pupils a sense of the appropriateness of the existing social order. It was all too easy for young women trained in such an environment to ignore the plight of others whose entire family income would not have equalled tuition costs at a prestigious private school. Only a few individuals, like Dorothy Livesay, who attended the select Glen Mawr school in Ontario's capital, were able to make that imaginative leap.[103] For many, a sojourn at a private school merely helped guarantee and publicize their fortunate position in Canada's class hierarchy.

Equally privileged were the small numbers of young women entering university. Women made significant gains in enrolment during the 1920s although they failed by far to catch up with male registration. The 1930s hurt them more than their brothers, especially when one considers how enlistment in the armed forces reduced the number of male students in 1939–40. The repercussions of the dramatic decrease in women's graduate registration would be felt well into the second half of the century in terms of leadership in employment. Equally problematic was the concentration of women in relatively few areas of study. In 1920, 81.62 percent of Canadian co-eds were found in arts and science compared to 48.84 percent of males. The great majority of the remainder of women turned up in such traditional fields as education, nursing, and household science. Twenty years later, 70.09 percent of female undergraduates took arts as compared to 46.46 percent of males, with the remainder of women distributed no more widely than before as teachers, social workers, and the like. In addition, there was a critical decline in the percentage of women enrolled in male-dominated fields between 1920 and 1940. In medicine, their numbers fell from 2.14 percent of undergraduates to 1.97 percent; in law from .40 to .23 percent, and in religion and theology from 1.06 to .44 percent.[104] Explanations for this decline are not yet entirely clear, but it owed something to the absence in these years of an articulate feminist movement that had nurtured the pioneers who had breached male monopolies in the nineteenth century. Lacking both this critical support and the inspiration of an older maternalist ideology that offered women a special role in many professions, women were more ill-equipped than before to challenge the restrictions of their socialization and the hostility of misogynist male preserves.[105] Smaller numbers of female students at every level of postsecondary education reflected the greater unwillingness of parents to invest in the education of daughters and the assumption by both that higher education was less suitable or necessary for girls. Just as in the high schools, patterns of female enrolment reflected the segregated nature of the job market many would enter after graduation. An arts education prepared young women for the career opportunities that existed for their sex, notably as teachers, social workers, librarians, clerical workers, saleswomen, and wives.

The distribution of female enrolment attracted the attention of contemporaries who foresaw overcrowding in female-dominated employments, but women were not necessarily dissatisfied with their lot.[106] A survey of 167 graduates of McGill, Queen's, and Toronto universities, for instance, discovered general approval of an education that fitted them for the segregated labour market. When these women were asked for their job preferences, secretarial work headed the list, teaching took second place, and journalism came in third.[107] Some young women admitted attending university solely because other options in employment, presumably including marriage, looked unattractive.[108] The opportunities that might lure even non-academically inclined co-eds to the halls of scholarship were summed up by one father well satisfied with his daughter's presence in a degree program in household science: "They say you know that when a girl finishes that course, she gets her M.R.S."[109] To an important degree, higher education in general for middle-class girls was

TABLE 2   Full-Time University Enrolment by Sex, Selected Years, for Canada

Year	Female		Male		Women as a percentage of all students	
	undergrad.	graduate	undergrad.	graduate	undergrad.	graduate
1920	3 716	108	19 075	315	16.3	25.5
1925	5 272	221	19 580	625	21.2	26.1
1930	7 428	352	24 148	998	23.5	26.1
1935	7 494	388	26 028	1 198	22.4	24.5
1940	8 107	326	26 710	1 243	23.3	20.8

Source: Series W340–438, *Historical Statistics of Canada.*

TABLE 3   Percentage Changes in Undergraduate and Graduate Enrolment, by Sex, Selected Years, for Canada

Year	Female		Male	
	undergraduate	graduate	undergraduate	graduate
1920–25	+41.8	+104.63	+ 2.65	+98.41
1925–30	+40.9	+ 59.28	+23.33	+59.68
1930–35	+ 0.89	+ 10.23	+ 7.79	+20.04
1935–40	+ 8.13	− 15.98	+ 2.62	+ 3.76

Source: Calculated from Series W340–438, *Historical Statistics of Canada.*

309

acceptable because it did not fundamentally threaten the primacy of the family headed by the male breadwinner. As co-eds' supporters regularly argued,

> homes are all the happier because . . . there is a wife and mother who, in the successful practice of a profession, learned self-control and human nature and how to apply every bit of her powers to her daily problems and who knows that if death should break her marriage she can maintain the independence of herself and her children.[110]

Even when the majority of female students harboured relatively modest ambitions, misogyny continued to flourish on campus. At Dalhousie University in the 1930s, for example, President Carleton Stanley conscientiously favoured young men, funding two scholarships in honours mathematics and classics solely for their benefit.[111] Nor was he alone in this favouritism. A host of awards from the Rhodes on down were formally and informally restricted to males. Prejudice appeared elsewhere as well. In 1935 the head of the University of Alberta's Woman-Haters' Club was elected president of the students' union,[112] and in both decades girls were exposed to instructors like Stephen Leacock in political economy at McGill whose anti-feminism was flaunted in a host of articles.[113] The outcome of such pervasive anti-woman feeling at universities is impossible to measure, but it contributed to undermining intellectual confidence and self-esteem among co-eds just as it no doubt bolstered male egos.

Accustomed as they were to casual anti-feminism, female students managed to find their own pleasures in university life. Here, as in the high schools, a flourishing youth culture emerged. This was often far from sedate. At Hamilton's McMaster, newcomers participated, one supposes more or less willingly, in rites planned for their benefit:

> To the roll-call each freshette replied with the name of that animal which she thought she most resembled, after which her personal appearance was improved by the addition of onion earrings. The various animals were then called upon to perform characteristic stunts, and all joined in an exciting game of leap-frog. Probably the most exciting of all the contests was that of picking up beans with one's nose to which a generous coating of glue had been previously applied. The question was raised, "Why take swimming lessons at the 'Y' when they can be so successfully administered with the aid of a piano stool?" which was followed by enlightening illustration of the same. Dire punishments were meted out to those guilty of ignoring previous orders of the Sophettes.[114]

Such highjinks contributed to the special campus culture that women were beginning to share with men. More than ever before, the term co-ed did not have to be synonymous with the serious-minded. Unlike the committed pioneers of the 1880s and 1890s, this was a successor generation who could afford to take participation, at least in arts, largely for granted.

Like many men, women came to care intensely about campus life, participating in a wide range of athletic, cultural, religious, political, and scholarly activities. Yet their involvement remained distinctive. In many ways the university contained two worlds differentiated by gender. Intercourse of any kind was firmly discouraged by the separation, for the most part, of the two sexes into different programs, an isolation confirmed further by a division of social space within the university. To a large degree, young women and men found separate places to sleep, eat, study, and play. In Toronto, for example, the Students' Administrative Council had two sections, like the washrooms, male and female. Similarly, Hart House, the major athletic building on the Varsity campus, was restricted to men, except for dances when even this bastion of male prerogative could hardly forbid "ladies." At the University of British Columbia, separate English classes for co-eds were the order of the day until 1941. Junior faculty taught the women while male professors set the exams and organized the courses that they personally taught to young men.[115] At the University of Toronto, the long-time chairman of the history department, George M. Wrong, made prevailing prejudices quite clear in his assertion that "What I want is a scholar and a gentleman, and if he knows any history, so much the better."[116] The restriction of membership in the department's prestigious History Club to young men confirmed the lack of welcome for their sisters. No wonder there were few female historians in the country, and none at all at Toronto, for many years. To be sure, young women found countless ways of getting around restrictions, frequently finding ample opportunity to meet the young men of their choice. Dances, teas, and public lectures mingled the sexes for many purposes and provided the highlight of countless lives.

As always, there were outstanding individuals who questioned prevailing views. Those with religious faith often joined the Student Christian Movement (SCM), which espoused a practical Christianity and called into question the inequities of a class society and, more occasionally, sex prejudice.[117] Other radical students repudiated religion altogether. Such was the case with Dorothy Livesay and her friend "Jim" or Jennie Watts at the University of Toronto, both of whom engaged in fierce debates over birth control, free love, Marxism, atheism, and the future of the family. These two rebels later took up the struggle against the right in the 1930s, with Watts going to fight Franco in Spain and Livesay joining the Canadian League Against War and Fascism.[118] Some young women also remained resolutely "career-minded." In her very early teens, for example, Agnes Macphail had done

> a lot of thinking on the subject; men, women, and marriage. I saw that men did a job in the world outside their home and women did not. At fourteen I turned it around in my mind this way; a woman has children, the boys do things and the girls marry and have other children, of which the boys do things and the girls marry and have other children, of which the boys do a job in the world of affairs and the girls do not, but in turn have other children in which family the boys do — , and I asked myself: "Does this thing never end in a woman being a person and making a contribution, in addition to, or in place of having children?"[119]

Brave hopes never disappeared, but the trend of the two decades was against them. Initial research suggests, for instance, that university graduates of the 1920s were substantially more likely to find jobs than co-eds who completed degrees in the 1930s and 1940s. These more limited horizons were in keeping with a significant decrease in the rate of women's entry into university; indeed, in some institutions, such as Dalhousie, there was an absolute reduction in their numbers. Professional careers fell by the wayside for many, confirming the collapse of women's hopes for education that had flourished in the 1920s.[120]

Fortunately, intellectual challenges were not restricted to formal schooling. The poet Adele Wiseman has left an evocative testament to the power of the printed word in inspiring young people to test the boundaries of their society. A voracious appetite for reading helped this Jewish young-

311

ster come to terms with her particular situation in North Winnipeg during the 1930s. Her salvation was shared by readers of every sort. As she explained,

> Books were a route into life and reality and simultaneously an escape from life and reality, from the searing quality of every moment of the raw-nerved child's immediate encounters with existence. Books carved a path through the life into which I was locked, showed possible ways through the jungle of experience to the yearned-for civilization of the happy endings. . . . I belonged where I read, if nowhere else. . . . [121]

Immersion in everything from comic books to classics occupied endless hours for children who discovered their delights. Girls, like other disadvantaged groups — Jews, blacks, workers — rarely, however, found their reality reflected in what they perused. As Wiseman recollected,

> The girls and women I read about in books were usually quite other than what I knew myself and the girls and women I knew to be. But I saw children trying to become the simpering goody girls they read about in books. And didn't I myself practice trying to keep a stiff upper lip, which was the way to be, while simultaneously getting my sensitive lower lip to quiver tremulously which was also the way to be.[122]

Yet for many pages, in their enthralment with literature's pleasures, Adele and her sister "book-molesters" largely managed to ignore the misogyny they encountered. They were not alone in this escape from reality. The burgeoning sales of magazines like *Chatelaine*, with their hefty doses of fiction, spoke volumes for the importance of reading as women's chief leisure and distraction.

Whereas reading was normally a solitary activity, many young women turned to more sociable pastimes. These decades saw the prospering of clubs founded by middle-class women, sometimes at the instigation of potential girl recruits, to channel the energy and character of adolescents into responsible womanhood. In particular, the Canadian Girl Guides, the Canadian Girls in Training, and the Junior Red Cross enrolled thousands in programs from the mundane to the exciting and innovative. Such experiences became commonplace for many youngsters and were important contributors to the evolution of a nation-wide youth culture.

The Guides had been imported from Great Britain just before World War I. Their imperial connections made them especially likely to be sponsored by the Anglican Church, the Salvation Army, the Imperial Order of the Daughters of the Empire, and the Fellowship of the Maple Leaf. The introduction of "Lone Guides" meant that even those far removed from settled communities could participate.[123] Other special groups were served with the introduction of Rangers for older girls, Extension Guiding for the handicapped, and Auxiliary Companies for girls in penitentiaries and prevention and rescue homes. In general, the Guide movement was to engage respectable preteen and teen girls. Leaders in particular were to be above reproach. No supervising Guider, for example, could be recruited from an Auxiliary Company.[124] Attractive camp programs, a strong spirit of international fellowship, a somewhat secular nature, opportunities for good friendship, and, no doubt, the patronage of the British royal princesses kept the movement expanding throughout the interwar years. Badges earned for "Character and Intelligence" (e.g., artist, booklover, homemaker, interpreter, rifle-shot), "Handicrafts, Professions" (e.g., child nurse, carpenter, domestic service, gardener, poultry farmer), "Physical Development and Strength" (e.g., athlete, cyclist, health, pioneer, skater), and "Service for Others" (e.g., fire brigade, pathfinder, sick nurse) were worn with pride and enthusiasm.[125]

Not everyone approved of Guides. By 1920 the YWCA, for instance, had withdrawn from Guides and Brownies in repudiation of their British and non-sectarian orientation.[126] Uniformed Guides, like Scouts, were also vulnerable to charges of militarism.[127] Leaders repeatedly challenged such characterizations: one speaker to B.C.'s South Cowichan Guides insisted that there was "no surer way to secure the world peace . . . than that which the guide movement took as its watchword 'Be Prepared.'"[128] Defenders also endorsed Guiding as "practical Christianity."[129] The first *Canadian Policy, Organization and Rules* manual did not appear until 1945. Prior to that date, Guiders made do with British books with addenda for Canadian leaders.

The maintenance of its imperial connections helped recruit Guides among those of British origin, but another organization believed its own "made-in-Canada" origins to be a source of special appeal. The Canadian Girls in Training was founded in 1917 as an explicitly Canadian and Christian response to the needs of adolescent girls and, incidentally, to the appeal of Guiding, which was distrusted as too competitive, authoritarian, secular, and British.[130] Heavily influenced by "progressive education" with its liberal, child-centred philosophy,[131] the CGIT spoke for a broad-minded, internationalist Christianity in its emphasis on modern biblical criticism. The life of Jesus was believed to offer up-to-date lessons in dealing with the problems of the world. The benefits of Canadian citizenship and the importance of enfranchised women assuming a significant role in national development were also central to CGIT philosophy in a way that recalled suffragists' emphasis on the particular moral responsibility of women. Such qualities often made the early organization appear in direct line of succession to the maternal feminism of an earlier generation. Whatever the attractions of its reform-minded agenda, the CGIT's extensive summer camp, craft, and social programs were critical in keeping membership high throughout the worst years of the Depression. In 1933–34, for instance, there were nearly 40 000 girls enrolled in the CGIT in 1100 communities.[132] Determined as it was to differ from Guiding, the CGIT shared a similar concern to produce an independent and responsible adult who as a mother would serve her family and as a citizen her nation. Strong women leaders in both organizations, many with university degrees and some employment experience, personified what the "Girl of the New Day" might achieve.

In some ways, Guiding and the CGIT represented only a more formal opportunity to participate in a long-existing female culture and cultivate female friendships. Occasionally this tendency sparked some homophobia, as with an article in the *Canadian Guider* by a University of Toronto psychologist who characterized crushes on leaders by young girls as unnatural.[133] For all such negative assessments, intense relationships among girls and women remained an important part of organizational life, fostering co-operation and encouraging leadership. No wonder many graduates of the CGIT, for example, went on to become community leaders, helping to bridge the gap between the first and the second feminist movements with their activities on behalf of peace and consumer protection. In the meantime, both Guides and the CGIT provided girls, mostly of the middle class, with many hours of enjoyment and some experience of the wider world beyond their families. Working-class girls occasionally enrolled, but their time was more fully taken up with contributing to family survival through domestic and paid labour. From time to time, radical organizations such as the Women's Labour Leagues tried to establish working-class children's groups in competition with the Guides and the CGIT, but these floundered, no rivals for the urgent economic pressures on the young people they hoped to reach or the comparatively resource-rich, middle-class initiatives.[134]

After World War I, the Junior Red Cross enlisted teachers, the majority of whom were female, to inculcate in both girls and boys in elementary and, occasionally, high school classrooms across the Dominion the principles of better hygiene and nutrition, good citizenship, and international co-operation. By 1930 there were 236 394 members in the Junior Red Cross, and numbers remained high throughout the decade.[135] Girls shared many aspects of the program with their brothers, but no more than in the organizations devoted to their sex did they escape reminders of their special responsibility for parenting and housework. Lessons in home nursing and care of babies were matters of course. And yet, as with Guides and CGIT, there was a simultaneous emphasis on the new responsibilities of modern citizenship. While that message did not always escape racism and ethnocentrism,[136] it regularly affirmed a "world-mindedness" that was espoused by all three organizations.[137] Such philosophy could only help to make listeners more tolerant and peace-loving. In as much as girls were especially susceptible to such appeals, it also helped differentiate them from their brothers who might be involved in cadet training and competitive rather than co-operative activities.

Not all competitive activity was limited to males. In the 1920s and 1930s, athletics, for instance, developed a special appeal for girls. Liberated from the heavy dresses that had so impeded movement in the past, young women took an unprecedented place in a diverse range of sports. There were individual champions. Toronto resident Gladys Robinsen, in regular practice since she was ten, won a speed skating title in Lake Placid in 1921.[138] Eighteen-year-old Lela Brooks, a skater by five or six years of age, set six world records in speed skating in 1926. In the 1932 Olympics, Jean Wilson, who started on ice at fifteen, won the 500 metre women's speed skating event and was only deprived of a gold medal because this was still an unofficial or demonstration sport.[139] Track and field also produced its stars. Bobbie Rosenfeld, "wearing her brother's 'Y' teeshirt and swim trunks and her father's socks, set Canadian records in the broad jump, the discus and on the track" at the 1928 Amsterdam Olympics.[140] In the same games Ethel Smith took a gold in the 4 × 100 metre relay and a bronze in the 100 metres. Ethel Catherwood, nicknamed "The Saskatoon Lily," brought home a gold medal in the high jump in the same year. Hilda Strike, who won two silver medals in the 100 metres and the 4 × 100 metre relay in the 1932 Olympics, repeated the same feats in the 1934 British Empire Games. Swimming found a champion in Phyllis Dewar, who captured three gold medals at the 1934 British Empire Games and another in the 1938 Games. In golf it was Ada Mackenzie, like Rosenfeld an all-round athlete, who began her winning ways as a teenager and went on to victories throughout the 1920 and 1930s. Such successes came despite a notable absence of facilities, trainers, and, often, encouragement for girls and women. Also significant was the fact that many of these sports "heroines" appear to have come from the working class. Bobbie Rosenfeld worked in a chocolate factory. Ethel Smith left school at fourteen for a job in an embroidery concern. Phyllis Dewar married a CPR conductor. Although more research is needed before we will know for sure, working-class women may have been less intimidated by stereotypical assumptions of what was suitable for their sex and therefore uniquely placed to take advantage of some of the sports opportunities opening up in the 1920s.

Team sports, as the relay wins in the 1928 Olympics suggest, also found recruits in these decades. In 1921, for instance, the University of Manitoba participated in the first interprovincial girls' basketball games against the Universities of Alberta and Saskatchewan.[141] The most famous team was the Edmonton Grads. These basketball players, originally all graduates of Edmonton's McDougall Commercial High School, won steadily from their first game in 1915 to their last in 1940. This included the first Canadian women's championship in 1922 when they beat the London Shamrocks, and a host of other victories against the state champions of Illinois, Missouri, Kansas, Washington, Oklahoma, Iowa, Michigan, Minnesota, Texas, Arkansas, and Ohio. They also went undefeated in games

315

played, unofficially, at the Olympics in 1928, 1932, and 1936. While no other team ever matched this record, their success attracted players in schools all across the Dominion.[142] Softball was another team sport to attract female enthusiasts, although it failed to match basketball's wide appeal.

Not all observers of such developments were positive. One quaint theory held that female athletes produced mainly girl babies or puny boys.[143] More common was the assertion that women's nerves paid the toll of intense physical activity.[144] There was also general agreement that men did not like the look of athletic women. As one opponent put it, "The men want the gals to stay beautiful, graceful, and sightly, not tie their bodies in scrawny, sinewy knots."[145] These chauvinistic views found support from authorities like Dr. A.S. Lamb, of McGill's department of physical education, who opposed women's participation in strenuous sports.[146] Such arguments and experts helped keep numerous events, such as women's speed skating, out of the Olympics for many years.

316

Outspoken female athletes like Bobbie Rosenfeld challenged critics,[147] but still more important in offsetting the stereotypes was the widespread publicity given to women's sports. For the first time, individuals like Rosenfeld, who also edited a newspaper column in the 1930s, became household names. Support from businesses such as Silverwood Dairies in Toronto, which sponsored a basketball club in 1924–25, suggests the generally positive public perception of female athletics. More important still, women became their own promoters. Toronto had its Lakeside Ladies' Athletic Club, which sponsored basketball and softball. Ada Mackenzie founded the same city's Ladies' Golf and Tennis Club. Myrtle Cook, a gold medalist as a member of Canada's "Matchless Six" running team in the Amsterdam Olympics, became an eager supporter of Canadian women four years later in 1932 in Los Angeles.[148] Women athletes decried not only sexual discrimination in sports. Eva Dawes, who won the bronze medal for the high jump at the 1932 Olympics, bluntly repudiated its Berlin sequel for its racism and anti-Semitism: "I'll hang up my spikes rather than take part in an amateur world meet where discrimination is keeping many fine sportsmen from taking part."[149] Such opinions were every bit a match for the idealistic internationalism expressed by the Guides, CGIT, and Red Cross, but the chief impact of female athletes was rarely directly political. It may be, as Nellie McClung argued, that they did "much to widen the conception of beauty. Durability and strength have entered the picture."[150] Finally, the blossoming of women's athletics also permitted girls and women the opportunity, previously limited largely to males, to test their physical mettle, bask in the support of a crowd, and forge the friendships of the playing field. Such opportunities were welcomed by many girls and young women, even if they could not in these years finally lay the myth of the delicate female to rest.

Girls in urban centres during the 1920s and 1930s encountered a wider range of formal activities than ever before. If their labour was not crucial to family survival, their free hours could easily be taken up with clubs and sports. Adults in general preferred the troubling years of adolescence to be occupied and constrained in highly regulated situations. Notwithstanding the suspicions of their elders, girls, particularly those whose families could spare neither the time nor the energy for supervision, flocked to movies, dances, and, occasionally, automobiles, where their behaviour was not so tightly checked. The celluloid world of Mary Pickford, Lillian Gish, Joan Crawford, Katharine Hepburn, Clark Gable, Douglas Fairbanks, and Rudolph Valentino captured girls everywhere who could afford the 5¢ price of admission. In dance halls, big and little bands played the music of the blackbottom and other modern dance crazes that made parents shake their heads. The arrival of radio also meant that it was not always necessary to leave home for entertainment. Young children, for instance, learned early on to tune in to their favourite shows such as the "Sleepy Town Express" on radio CFCY in Charlottetown. Traditional music and dancing also got a boost. Don Messer and the Islanders, initially Don Messer and his New Brunswick Lumberjacks, for instance, got their start in these years.[151] Nor were people shy about making their own music. Agnes Macphail was typical in her enthusiasm for dancing. In her rural community of Grey County, Ontario, "a couple of sleigh-loads of young people, two fiddlers, and a caller" could make up "a party that went on till all hours of the night."[152] Parents had no more reason than usual to worry about such familiar pursuits, but the advent of the automobile — registrations jumped from 196 367 in 1919, to 1 061 500 in 1930, dropped during the worst years of the Great Depression and recovered to reach 1 191 914 in 1939[153] — just like the bicycle in the 1890s fanned consternation among those who feared new opportunities for licence. Critics wondered publicly "What Shall We Do With 'Our' Flapper?"[154] and prescribed stiff doses of hard work, simple living, and early marriage. Yet young people always found their defenders, especially in the 1930s when there seemed to be some agreement that "flaming youth" had "cooled off."[155]

317

Girls in the decade of the Great Depression certainly had ample cause to question the optimism that countenanced experimentation in the 1920s. A very few continued to chance radical solutions, but many more hungered for security and reassurance in traditional social and economic relationships. To some extent at least, Shirley Temple's audiences shared their heroine's essential trust that pluck, helped along by a pretty face, would save the day. And they discovered, when they entered the world of paid work, that they could need all the hope they could muster.

NOTES

[1] Ellen Knox, *The Girl of the New Day* (Toronto: McClelland and Stewart, 1919).

[2] Agnes Macphail, M.P., "Citizenship," *Canadian Mentor* (Feb.–March 1931): 48.

[3] PAC, Agnes Macphail Papers, v. 10, folder, "Speeches, Women's Role in Society," "How Far Can Women Help Solve National Problems," CBC, May 21, 1939 (typescript), 5-6. See also the disappointment of a grandmother at the birth of a girl in "Letters of a Countrywoman," *Canadian Countryman* (April 15, 1922).

[4] SFUA, taped interview with Ruth Bullock by Sara Diamond, 1979.

[5] Fredelle Bruser Maynard, *Raisins and Almonds* (Toronto: Doubleday, 1972), 181-82.

[6] SAB, Violet McNaughton Papers, v. 16, folder 37, Mrs. C. Langerok to McNaughton, Dec. 2, 1936.

[7] See Elsie MacGill, *My Mother the Judge* (Toronto: Ryerson Press, 1955).

[8] For a provocative assessment of the significance of the mother–daughter bond see Nancy Chodorow, *The Reproduction of Mothering: Psychoanalysis and the Sociology of Gender* (Berkeley: University of California Press, 1978).

[9] For a fascinating revelation of these relationships see Mazo de la Roche, *Ringing the Changes: An Autobiography* (Toronto: Macmillan, 1957) and Emily Carr, *The Book of Small* (Toronto: Clarke, Irwin, 1966) and *Growing Pains* (Toronto: Clarke, Irwin, 1971). On the family and female friendships see Margaret Conrad, "'Sundays Always Make Me Think of Home': Time and Place in Canadian Women's History," in *Rethinking Canada: The Promise of Women's History*, ed. Veronica Strong-Boag and Anita Clair Fellman (Toronto: Copp Clark Pitman, 1986).

[10] On the relationship between class, maternal health, and birth weight see W. Peter Ward and Patricia C. Ward, "Infant Birth Weight and Nutrition in Industrializing Montreal," *American Historical Review* (Feb. 1984): 324-45.

[11] See Veronica Strong-Boag and K. McPherson, "The Confinement of Women: Childbirth and Hospitalization in Vancouver, 1919-1939," *B.C. Studies* (Summer 1986): 142-74 for a discussion of treatment of expectant women within hospitals; K. McPherson,"Nurses and Nursing in Early Twentieth-Century Halifax" (M.A. thesis, Dalhousie University, 1982), especially ch. 4 for an assessment of the VON in Nova Scotia's capital, and Elizabeth Goudie, *Woman of Labrador* (Toronto: Peter Martin Associates, 1973) for an autobiographical account of such home births.

[12] Series B51-58, *Historical Statistics of Canada*, 2nd ed., ed. F.H. Leacy (Ottawa: Statistics Canada, 1983).

[13] See Norah Lewis, "Advising the Parents: Child Rearing in British Columbia During the Inter-War Years" (Ph.D. thesis, University of British Columbia, 1980), ch. 6.

[14] *The Junior* (May 1922): 10-11. The outstanding pediatrician of the day, Dr. Alan Brown of the Hospital for Sick Children in Toronto, one of the inventors of Pablum, did not believe that anyone needed tonsils. He was once asked "'At what age do you take tonsils out?'" to which he replied "'Not before the umbilical cord is cut.'" Quoted in Pierre Berton, *The Dionne Years* (Toronto: McClelland and Stewart, 1978), 146.

[15] *The Junior* (March 1923): 13-15.

[16] *The Junior* (March 1926): 8-11.

[17] "Mother Goose in Health Land," *The Junior* (March 1930): 21.

[18] See, for instance, the close relationship between poverty and child distress reported in *Indian Conditions: A Survey* (Ottawa: Indian and Northern Affairs, 1980), *passim*.

[19] New Brunswick Child Welfare Survey, *Report* (1929).

[20] Marjorie Bell, "Are We Exaggerating? Experiences of Visiting Homemakers," *Social Welfare* (June–Sept. 1937): 39.

[21] For a description of such schools see Thomas A. McMaster, "A Study of Private Schools in Canada" (M.Ed. thesis, University of Manitoba, 1940).

[22] Quoted in the Report of the Committee on Sexual Offences Against Children and Youths, *Sexual Offences Against Children* (Ottawa: Queen's Printer, 1984), 1: 192.

[23] *Sexual Offences Against Children* made this estimate based on a National Population Survey of 2008 Canadians. It also concluded that "On the basis of offences reported by adults of all ages, it appears that there has not been a sharp increase in recent years in the incidence of sexual offences" (p. 193). On the kinds of offences reported see ch. 13. Terry Chapman, in "Women, Sex and Marriage in Western Canada, 1890-1920," *Alberta History* (Autumn 1985): 1-12, examines this problem for a slightly earlier period and again the evidence suggests a relatively widespread phenomenon. On youth prostitution see Rebecca Coulter, "The Working Young of Edmonton, 1921-1931," in *Childhood and Family in Canadian History*, ed. Joy Parr (Toronto: McClelland and Stewart, 1982), 143-44.

[24] Mrs. House, "God Saw That It Was Good," *Some Thoughts for Wives and Mothers and Some Teaching to be given to Children by Parents who find it difficult to put their own Thoughts into Words* (B.C. Board of Health, 1936).

[25] SFUA, taped interview with Ruth Bullock by Sara Diamond, 1979.

[26] Gwethalyn Graham, "Women, Are They Human?" *Canadian Forum* (Dec. 1936): 22.

[27] "New Fashioned Chores," *Grain Growers' Guide* (March 21, 1923): 24.

[28] See, for example, Garrett Elliott, "What I Wish for My Daughter," *Chatelaine* (May 1934): 14, 48–49. On the same phenomenon in French Canada see Susan Mann Trofimenkoff, *The Dream of Nation* (Toronto: Gage, 1984), *passim*.

[29] See Alton Goldbloom, *The Care of the Child* (Toronto: Longmans, Green and Co., 1928) and Alan Brown and Frederick Tisdall, *Common Procedures in the Practice of Paediatrics. Being a Detailed Description of Diagnostic, Therapeutic and Dietetic Methods Employed at the Hospital for Sick Children, Toronto* (Toronto: McClelland and Stewart, 1926).

[30] See Veronica Strong-Boag, "Intruders in the Nursery: Childcare Professionals Reshape the Years One to Five, 1920-1940," in *Childhood and Family in Canadian History*, and Berton, *The Dionne Years*.

[31] The title of a full-page ad for Calay Soap, *Chatelaine* (Jan. 1932): 53.

[32] See, for example, Mona E. Clark, "Are Brains a Handicap to a Woman?" *Canadian Magazine* (Feb. 1928): 27.

[33] Margaret I. Laurence, "Romance of the Difficult," *The Junior* (Feb. 1932): 20.

[34] See Jean Barman, "Working Kids," in *Working Lives: Vancouver, 1886-1986*, ed. the Working Lives Collective (Vancouver: New Star Books, 1985).

[35] Helen Potrebenko, *No Streets of Gold: A Social History of Ukrainians in Alberta* (Vancouver: New Star Books, 1977), 227-29.

[36] Alice H. Parsons, "Careers or Marriage?" *Canadian Home Journal* (June 1938), 63.

[37] Parsons, "Careers or Marriage?" 64.

[38] See "Where Are You Going My Pretty Maid?" *Chatelaine* (Feb. 1936): 12-13.

[39] See "Toy Trade Comes Into Its Own," *Dry Goods Review* (June 1920): 106.

[40] See "Experiment Showed Premiums Having Strongest Pull with Children," *Marketing* (June 5, 1937): 4; "Children Can Exert Great Influence on Food Purchases for the Home," *Marketing* (April 22, 1939); and "Appeal to Collector in Every Child Sure Way to Hold Juvenile Market," *Marketing* (Aug. 12, 1939): 2.

[41] On the massive increase in advertising pressure in these years see Stuart Ewen, *Captains of Consciousness* (New York: McGraw-Hill, 1976).

[42] "Does Shirley Temple Know?" in *Ten Lost Years*, ed. Barry Broadfoot (Toronto: Doubleday, 1973).

[43] See "Demand for Pyjamas Steadily Growing," *Marketing* (Jan. 1922): 144, and "Practical Underthings Being Shown," *Marketing* (Aug. 1922): 66-67.

[44] See "Spread of Bare Leg Fancy Would Have Far Reaching Effect," *Dry Goods Review* (Jan. 1929): 14, 52. See also the opposition of the hosiery industry in "More and More . . . It's Less and Less," *Dry Goods Review* (Aug. 1929): 15-16.

[45] See "Campaign to be Waged Against Corsetless Fad," *Dry Goods Review* (Oct. 1921): 105. Some Canadian manufacturers claimed to have learned from the failure of the campaign in the U.S., concluding "There is no use trying to force women's opinion. The abandoning of heavy material and boning for elastic marks a change in women's attitude of mind just as much as the wearing of knickers has done." "Severe Types Unlikely to Return," *Dry Goods Review* (Jan. 1923): 98. They did, however, engage in active publicity campaigns to ward off the threat of the girdleless young girl. See "Teach Girls They Must Wear Corsets," *Dry Goods Review* (Sept. 1923): 81.

[46] See "Junior Section Lays Good Foundation," *Dry Goods Review* (May 1926): 50; " 'Foundation Garment' Replacing 'Corset' as Descriptive Name," *Dry Goods Review* (Oct. 1926): 62; and "A Corset Corner for the Younger Set," *Dry Goods Review* (Nov. 1927): 41.

[47] "The Whys and Hows of Modern Corsetry," *Dry Goods Review* (Sept. 1926): 54; "Thin Women Need Corsets More than Stout Women," *Dry Goods Review* (July 1926): 67; and "Modern Corsets Are Scientific and Healthful," *Dry Goods Review* (Jan. 1927): 64.

[48] "Athletic Underwear for Women," *Dry Goods Review* (April 1922): 76-77.

[49] "Experiments with Two-Way Stretch," *Dry Goods Review* (June 1932): 40, 42.

[50] See "Women Wear a New Type of Corsetry," *Dry Goods Review* (April 1928): 48, and "Ultra-Feminine Fashions Mark Prosperity for Corset Departments," *Dry Goods Review* (March 25, 1938): 16.

[51] SFUA, taped interview with Ruth Bullock by Sara Diamond, 1979.

[52] For an introduction to the fashions of these decades see Jane Dorner, *Fashion in the Twenties & Thirties* (London: Ian Allan, 1973).

[53] Beatrice M. Shaw, "The Age of Uninnocence," *Saturday Night* (May 24, 1919): 31.

[54] See Isabel Dingman. "Your 'Teen Age' Daughter," *Chatelaine* (Oct. 1934): 19, 63.

[55] See, for example, "Teaching Children," *Free Press Prairie Farmer* (Oct. 19, 1932): 4.

[56] Margaret Prang, " 'The Girl God Would Have Me Be': The Canadian Girls in Training," *Canadian Historical Review* (June 1985): 168-69.

[57] TPL "Growing Up in a Small Ontario Town," *We Came to Thornhill*, Interview with Helen Elizabeth Coleman, pp. 31-32, New Horizons Project. See also Mary MacFarlane, "Recollections of A Wrinkled Radical," *Canadian Woman Studies* (Winter 1986): 98-99.

[58] See, for example, "All Doctors Agree on Kotex," *Chatelaine* (March 1928): 65, and "Women are Turning to Modess . . . for Softness," *Chatelaine* (July 1930): 43. *Eaton's Catalogue* also offered a brandless sanitary towel and belt, see (Summer/Spring 1924): 285

[59] See Johnson and Johnson's Ortho-Gynol for feminine hygiene in *Eaton's Catalogue* (Fall/Winter 1934–35): 222, and Wampole's Antiseptic Vaginal Cones (Fall/Winter 1933-34): 204.

[60] We can only guess at the number of these. The number of abortions, for example, is an uncertain guide at best. See Angus McLaren and Arlene Tigar McLaren, "Discoveries and Dissimulations: The Impact of Abortion Deaths on Maternal Mortality in British Columbia," *B.C. Studies* (Winter 1984-85): 3-26. See also the confirmation in a 1922 survey by the Canadian Social Hygiene Council that "Sex education was conspicuous by its absence." Ontario Provincial Archives, Pamphlet 1922, no. 55, Mildred Kensit, *Results of Survey of Venereal Disease Patients in Hospital Clinics in the City of Toronto During the Months of July and August* (1922), 9.

[61] See Christina Simmons, "'Helping the Poorer Sisters': The Women of the Jost Mission, Halifax, 1905-1945," in *Rethinking Canada*.

[62] Mrs. Nelson, "The City Creche," *Western Woman's Weekly* (Dec. 25, 1920): 10-11.

[63] See Simmons, "'Helping the Poorer Sisters,'" 16. On the whole issue of the problems associated with private arrangements see Laura Climenko Johnson, *Taking Care* (Report of the Project Child Care Survey of Caregivers in Metropolitan Toronto, April 1978).

[64] See Strong-Boag, "Intruders in the Nursery" on these schools. McGill's folded with the onset of the Great Depression while Toronto's exists today.

[65] See PAC, Canadian Council on Social Development Papers, v. 43, folder 208, "Report of the B.C. Child Welfare Survey on the Children's Aid Society of Vancouver" [1927], typescript mimeograph.

[66] On the difficult situation facing many immigrant children see Joy Parr, *Labouring Children* (Montreal: McGill-Queen's University Press, 1980).

[67] On these developments see Patricia T. Rooke and R.L. Schnell, *Discarding the Asylum: From Child Rescue to the Welfare State in English Canada (1800-1950)* (New York: University Press of America, 1983), ch. 8.

[68] Jean Archibald Hood, "Some Behaviour Problems and Their Treatment" (M.A. thesis, University of British Columbia, 1937), Case 15, pp. 27-28.

[69] Quoted in Julie Cruikshank, *Athabaskan Women: Lives and Legends*, Canadian Ethnology Service Paper no. 57, National Museum of Man, Mercury Series (Ottawa: Queen's Printer, 1979), 9-10.

[70] Barbara Riley, "Six Saucepans to One: Domestic Science vs. the Home in British Columbia, 1900-1930," in *Not Just Pin Money: Selected Essays on the History of Women's Work in British Columbia*, ed. Barbara Latham and Roberta Pazdro (Victoria: Camosun College, 1984), 161.

[71] "Food Carried In," *Free Press Prairie Farmer* (Oct. 16, 1935): 4. See also the editorial "The Daughter Who Stays Home," *Grain Growers' Guide* (Jan. 10, 1923): 43, and "The Girl Who Stays Home," 12, 20; and Jean Barman, "Working Kids," in *Working Lives*, 121.

[72] For an instructive discussion of child play see Neil Sutherland, "'Everyone Seemed Happy in Those Days': The Culture of Childhood in Vancouver between the 1920s and the 1960s" (Working Paper of the Canadian Childhood History Project, March 1986).

[73] On children's songs see Edith Fowke, *Ring Around the Moon* (Toronto: McClelland and Stewart, 1977) and *Sally Go Round the Sun* (Toronto: McClelland and Stewart, 1969).

[74] See Michael Hayden, ed., *So Much to Do, So Little Time: The Writings of Hilda Neatby* (Vancouver: University of British Columbia Press, 1983).

[75] TPLBR, Coleman, "Growing Up in a Small Ontario Town," 24.

[76] "Lucille, That's My Dress," in *Ten Lost Years*.

[77] A.M. Pratt, "Co-education? No!" *Maclean's* (Oct. 15, 1934): 16. See also G.E. Kingsford, "The System Is Bad," *Saturday Night* (Oct. 27, 1934): 5; Willis J. Ballinger, "Does Education Help Women?" *Maclean's* (Nov. 1, 1932): 28; J.A. Lindsay, "Sex in Education," *Dalhousie Review* (July 1930): 147.

[78] See, for example, the argument put forth in "Co-education," *McMaster University Monthly* (Feb. 1929): 202.

[79] Nan Robins, "I Would Rather Have Beauty Than Brains," *Chatelaine* (Feb. 1931): 3.

[80] See Robert Stamp, "Teaching Girls Their 'God Given Place in Life': The Introduction of Home Economics in the Schools," *Atlantis* (Spring 1977): 18-34, and Marta Danylewycz, Nadia Fahmy-Eid, and Nicole Thivierge, "L'Enseignement ménager et les 'Home Economics' au Québec et en Ontario au début du 20e siècle: une analyse comparée," in *An Imperfect Past: Education and Society in Canadian History*, ed. J. Donald Wilson (Vancouver: Centre for the Study of Curriculum and Instruction, University of British Columbia, 1984).

[81] See Dolores Hayden, *The Grand Domestic Revolution: A History of Feminist Designs for American Homes, Neighborhoods, and Cities* (Cambridge, Mass.: The MIT Press, 1981).

[82] British Columbia, *Public School Report* (1922), 52.

[83] See British Columbia, *Public School Report* (1919-40).

[84] Riley, "Six Saucepans to One," 161.

[85] Riley, "Six Saucepans to One," 176.

[86] Ethel Chapman, "Household Science — The Oldest Profession for Women," *Maclean's* (Oct. 1919): 105.

[87] Nancy S. Jackson and Jane S. Gaskell, "White Collar Vocationalism: The Rise of Commercial Education in Canada" (unpublished paper, 1986), 18.

[88] Jackson and Gaskell, "White Collar Vocationalism," 19.

[89] On the existence of a dual labour market see David M. Gordon, *Theories of Poverty and Underemployment: Orthodox, Radical, and Dual Labor Market Perspectives* (Lexington, Mass.: D.C. Heath,

1972); Richard C. Edwards, Michael Reich, and David M. Gordon, eds., *Labour Market Segmentation* (Lexington, Mass.: D.C. Heath, 1975); Marcia Freedman, *Labour Markets: Segments and Shelters* (Montclair, N.J.: Allanheld, Osmun, 1976); and Graham Lowe, "Women, Work and the Office: The Feminization of Clerical Occupations in Canada, 1901-1931," in *Rethinking Canada*.

90 On the Department of Secretarial Science see Margaret Pennell, "Interesting Canadian Women," *Canadian Magazine* (Aug. 1927): 29-33.

91 See Robert M. Stamp, "Canadian High Schools in the 1920s and 1930s: The Social Challenge to the Academic Tradition," Canadian Historical Association, *Historical Papers* (1978), 79.

92 Jane Gaskell, "Education and Job Opportunities for Women: Patterns of Enrolment and Economic Returns," in *Women and the Canadian Labour Force*, ed. Naomi Hersom and Dorothy E. Smith (Ottawa: SSHRCC, 1982). 295.

93 See Lynne Marks, "Kale Meydelach or Shulamith Girls: Cultural Change and Continuity among Jewish Parents and Daughters — A Case Study of Toronto Harbord Collegiate Institute in the 1920s," *Canadian Woman Studies* (Fall 1986): 85-89.

94 Gaskell, "Education and Job Opportunities for Women," 261.

95 Gaskell, "Education and Job Opportunities for Women," 267.

96 See Norman A. Williams, "Opportunity Classes in the Protestant Schools, Montreal," *School Progress* (Dec. 1938): 7-8.

97 G.S. Mundie, B.A., M.D., "Child Guidance Clinics," *Canadian Medical Association Journal* (June 1924): 508-511.

98 See Hood, "Some Behaviour Problems and Their Treatment."

99 Hood, "Some Behaviour Problems," Case 12, p. 23, and Case 14, pp. 26-27.

100 Indiana Matters, "Sinners or Sinned Against?: Historical Aspects of Female Juvenile Delinquency in British Columbia," in *Not Just Pin Money*, 269.

101 Matters, "Sinners or Sinned Against?" 270.

102 "Rosary Hall, Toronto," *The Canadian League* (May 1923), 10.

103 Dorothy Livesay, *Right Hand Left Hand* (Erin, Ont.: Press Porcepic Ltd., 1977), 20 and *passim*.

104 Series W439-455, *Historical Statistics of Canada*.

105 On feminism and the maternalist ideology, see Veronica Strong-Boag, "'Ever a Crusader': Nellie McClung, First-Wave Feminist," in *Rethinking Canada*, 181.

106 See Elsinore Macpherson, "Careers of Canadian University Women" (M.A. thesis, University of Toronto, 1920), 108.

107 A. Harriet Parsons, "Careers or Marriage?" *Canadian Home Journal* (June 1938): 63.

108 See A. Harriet Parsons, "Varsity or Work?" *Canadian Home Journal* (Aug. 1936): 10-11, 32-33.

109 Quoted in Anne Elizabeth Wilson, "Schools for the Home-Maker — #3," *Maclean's* (Nov. 15, 1927), 63.

110 Ursilla N. MacDonnell, "After University — What?" *Chatelaine* (June 1931): 14.

111 Paul Axelrod, "Moulding the Middle Class: Student Life at Dalhousie University in the 1930s," *Acadiensis* (Autumn 1985), 97.

112 "Woman Hater," *Free Press Prairie Farmer* (April 17, 1935): 6.

113 See Stephen Leacock, "The Woman Question," in *The Social Criticism of Stephen Leacock*, edited and introduced by Alan Bowker (Toronto: University of Toronto Press, 1973). See also the individuals mentioned in Axelrod, "Moulding the Middle Class," and the situation at the University of British Columbia for a slightly earlier period in Lee Stewart, "Women on Campus in British Columbia: Strategies for Survival, Years of War and Peace, 1906-1920," in *Not Just Pin Money*.

114 "Women's Department," *McMaster University Monthly* (Oct. 1922), 28.

115 See Lee Jean Stewart, "The Experience of Women at the University of British Columbia, 1906-56" (M.A. thesis, University of British Columbia, 1986), 136-37, 156-57, note 43.

116 Revealingly, this quote was reproduced without editorial comment in a campaign to increase subscriptions to the largest professional history journal in the country in 1987. See the poster "The Canadian Historical Review" put out by the University of Toronto Press, 1987.

117 On the significance of the SCM for some young people see Stephen Endicott, *James G.: Rebel Out of China* (Toronto: University of Toronto Press, 1980).

118 Livesay, *Right Hand Left Hand*, *passim*.

119 Quoted in Margaret Street and Doris French, *Ask No Quarter: A Biography of Agnes Macphail* (Toronto: Doubleday, 1959), 30.

120 See Axelrod, "Moulding the Middle Class," 93, for a sensitive discussion of these limited opportunities.

121 Adele Wiseman, "Memoirs of a Book-Molesting Childhood," *Canadian Forum* (April 1986): 21-22. See also Mary MacFarlane, "Recollections of a Wrinkled Radical."

122 Wiseman, "Memoirs," 24-25.

123 See the extraordinary efforts on behalf of Guides made by Monica Storrs as a missionary for the Fellowship, in W.L. Morton, ed., with the help of Vera Fast, *God's Galloping Girl: The Peace River Diaries of Monica Storrs, 1929-1931* (Vancouver: U.B.C. Press, 1979). See also IODE, *The Golden Jubilee: 1900-1950* (Toronto: IODE, 1950), 35-36, for a brief mention of the association with Guides and Brownies that lasted until 1946.

124 See Auxiliary Guides, *Policy, Rules and Orders* (1934), no. 11.

[125] See *Policy, Rules and Orders* (1934): 42.

[126] See Diana Pederson, "'Keeping Our Good Girls Good: The Young Women's Christian Association, 1870-1920" (M.A. thesis, Carleton University, 1981), 108. See also her " 'Keeping Our Good Girls Good': The YWCA and the 'Girl Problem,' 1870-1930," *Canadian Woman Studies* (Winter 1986): 20-24.

[127] For an assessment that is in general agreement with the critics see Bonnie MacQueen, "Domesticity and Discipline: The Girl Guides in British Columbia, 1910-1943," in *Not Just Pin Money*.

[128] Vancouver Girl Guides' Headquarters, clipping from the *Victoria Times* (March? 1926).

[129] See VGGH, clipping "The Girl Guide Movement in Relation to Citizenship," Vancouver *Sun* (Nov. 6, 1925).

[130] Prang, "'The Girl God Would Have Me Be,'" 159.

[131] Prang, "'The Girl God Would Have Me Be,'" 163-64.

[132] Prang, "'The Girl God Would Have Me Be,'" 161.

[133] Professor J.D. Ketchum, "Some Emotional Problems," *Canadian Guider* (Jan. 1937): 3.

[134] See Rebecca Coulter, "The Working Young of Edmonton, 1921-1931," 158-59.

[135] "Ten Years of Junior Red Cross," *The Junior* (Jan. 1935): 20-21.

[136] See, for instance, Margaret Isabel Laurence, "The Time of Suffering," *The Junior* (April 1932): 19, with its portrayal of the Japanese as backward and pagan and Europeans as the vanguard of world civilization.

[137] See, for instance, Louise Franklin Bache, "Christmas in Many Lands," *The Junior* (Dec. 1923): 6.

[138] Gladys Robinson, "How I Trained for Speed Skating — and Won Title," *Maclean's* (April 1, 1921): 62.

[139] See David McDonald and Lauren Drewery, *For the Record: Canada's Greatest Women Athletes* (Toronto: Mes Associates, 1981).

[140] McDonald and Drewery, *For the Record*, 10.

[141] See "One of the Beginners," "Western Women Begin Athletics," *Western Home Monthly* (Sept. 1931): 26-27.

[142] See Helen Lenskyj, "We Want to Play . . . We'll Play," *Canadian Woman Studies* (Spring 1983): 16, for an introduction to one Ontario team.

[143] "Should Feminine Athletes be Restrained?" *Saturday Night* (May 28, 1921): 36.

[144] See Andy Lytle, "Girls Shouldn't Do It," *Chatelaine* (May 1933): 12.

[145] Elmer W. Ferguson, "I Don't Like Amazon Athletes," *Maclean's* (Aug. 1, 1938): 9.

[146] Ferguson, "I Don't Like Amazon Athletes," 32.

[147] Bobbie Rosenfeld, " . . . Girls Are in Sports for Good," *Chatelaine* (June 1933): 6-7, 29.

[148] McDonald and Drewery, *For the Record*, 35-37.

[149] "Eva Dawes on U.S.S.R.," *B.C. Workers' News* (Nov. 1, 1935): 2.

[150] N.L. McClung, "'I'll Never Tell My Age Again!!'" *Maclean's* (March 15, 1926): 15.

[151] See "Marianne Morrow," *The Birth of Radio in Canada: Signing On* (Toronto: Doubleday, 1982), 44.

[152] Stewart and French, *Ask No Quarter*, 39.

[153] From Series T147-194, *Historical Statistics of Canada*.

[154] A.N. Plumptre, "What Shall We Do With 'Our' Flapper?" *Maclean's* (June 1, 1922): 64.

[155] Mrs. Rip Van Winkle, "Flaming Youth Cools Off," *Chatelaine* (Aug. 1935): 16, 58-59. See also Judge J. McKinley, "Why Slander Youth?" *Chatelaine* (Nov. 1935): 10-11, 75.

Topic Nine

World War I

In 1914 Canada participated in its first large-scale war. Over the next four years the nation of less than ten million people provided over half a million men as soldiers, sailors, and airmen, as well as several thousand women as nursing sisters, to the Allied war effort. Over 60 000 Canadians died fighting in the struggle, while many more returned to Canada mentally and physically impaired. In "The Great War," Roger Sarty and Brereton Greenhous give a vivid description of Canada's contribution at the front to such battles as the Ypres Salient, the Somme, Vimy Ridge, and Passchendaele.

Not all eligible Canadians volunteered for war service. Two groups in particular were targeted for criticism: French Canadians and pacifists. From the outset French Canadians in Quebec had lagged behind English Canadians in proportion to their enlistment numbers. There were a number of explanations for this discrepancy. French Canadians had no strong attachment to either Britain or France, having lived in North America for three centuries. They also distrusted Britain and suspected imperial ambitions behind Anglo-Canadian enthusiasm for the war. In addition, the Canadian government mismanaged the enlistment effort in Quebec, by failing to give the French language a meaningful place in Canada's armed services. French Canadians had to serve under English-speaking officers in English-speaking units (with the exception of the Royal 22nd Regiment, the famous "Vandoos"). Furthermore, the educational policies of two English-speaking provinces did not help. At a time when the federal government was pressuring French Canadians to fight for democracy in Europe, the provincial governments of Ontario and Manitoba eliminated publicly supported bilingual schools. Two opposing French Canadian viewpoints on the war appear in "An Open Letter from Capt. Talbot Papineau to Mr. Henri Bourassa" and "Mr. Bourassa's Reply."

Canadian pacifists who refused to fight in the war can essentially be divided into two groups: sectarian pacifists, such as the Quakers, Mennonites, and Hutterites, who opposed fighting on religious grounds, and representatives of the liberal peace movement who wanted to achieve order and stability in the world through the use of international arbitration and courts. The outbreak of war fractured this liberal pacifist movement. Some adopted a contradictory position of sympathizing with the war effort while adhering to their pacifist ideals; others came to see the war as the stage upon which Christian ideals must be defended in face of German "barbarism"; still others were consistent in their opposition to both war and what they considered a militarist social and economic order. Thomas Socknat examines and analyses these various pacifist positions in "Canada's Liberal Pacifists and the Great War."

For a compelling account of the war years from the perspective of social history see Desmond Morton and Jack Granatstein, *Marching to Armageddon: Canadians and the Great War, 1914-1919* (Toronto: Lester and Orpen Dennys, 1989). For an overview of the war years see the relevant chapters in R.C. Brown and R. Cook's *Canada, 1896-1921: A Nation Transformed* (Toronto: McClelland and Stewart, 1974). A number of biographies of key politicians during the First World War contain useful discussions of the war years. The most important are R.C. Brown's *Robert Laird Borden: A Biography*, vol. 3, *1914-1937* (Toronto: Macmillan, 1980); J. Schull's *Laurier: The First Canadian* (Toronto: Macmillan, 1965); Robert Rumilly's *Henri Bourassa* (Montreal: Chantecler, 1953); and R. Graham's *Arthur Meighen*, vol. 1, *The Door of Opportunity* (Toronto: Clarke, Irwin, 1960). On Canada's most important military commander in World War I see A.M.J. Hyatt, *General Sir Arthur Currie: A Military Biography* (Toronto: University of Toronto Press, 1987).

324

On the issue of conscription, see Elizabeth Armstrong's *The Crisis of Quebec, 1914-1918* (New York: Columbia University Press, 1937); J.L. Granatstein and J.M. Hitsman's *Broken Promises: A History of Conscription in Canada* (Toronto: Oxford University Press, 1977; new edition, 1984); Brian Cameron's "The Bonne Entente Movement, 1916-17: From Cooperation to Conscription," *Journal of Canadian Studies* 13 (Summer 1978): 1942-55; the relevant chapters in John English, *The Decline of Politics: The Conservatives and the Party System, 1901-1920* (Toronto: University of Toronto Press, 1977); and Jean Pariseau, "La participation des Canadiens français à l'effort des deux guerres mondiales: démarche de ré-interprétation," *Canadian Defence Quarterly/Revue canadienne de défense* 13, 2 (Autumn 1983): 43-48. Henri Bourassa's views are presented in Joseph Levitt, ed., *Henri Bourassa on Imperialism and Bi-culturalism, 1900-1918* (Toronto: Copp Clark, 1970). Thomas Socknat's *Witness against War: Pacifism in Canada, 1900-1945* (Toronto: University of Toronto Press, 1987) reviews the pacifists' response to the war.

Two novels help to re-create the atmosphere of Canada during World War I: Philip Child's *God's Sparrows*, published in 1937 and reprinted in 1978 with an introduction by Dennis Duffy (Toronto: McClelland and Stewart), and Timothy Findley's award-winning *The Wars* (Toronto: Clarke, Irwin, 1977). Grace Morris Craig's *But This Is Our War* (Toronto: University of Toronto Press, 1981) is both her own recollection of the war years at home in Ontario and a collection of letters from her two brothers at the front.

The Great War*

ROGER SARTY and BRERETON GREENHOUS

A distinguished veteran of many 19th-century campaigns once described war as nine-tenths boredom and one-tenth sheer terror. Had he served on the Western Front in the First World War, he would surely have added frustration and squalor to his list of ingredients. It was, in a very literal sense, a filthy war. Mud, rotting corpses, rats, human wastes, and more mud were its principal elements from the perspective of the front-line soldier; and physical exhaustion brought about largely by lack of sleep was the prevailing military condition in the trench lines which extended from the North Sea shore to the Swiss border for most of the war. Especially was it so in the low-lying Flanders fields where the British Expeditionary Force — including the Canadian Corps — held the line.

325

Canadians went to war in 1914 with the simple enthusiasm that was the essence of their meagre military tradition, but even the professionals of European armies had little understanding of the miseries which awaited them. Only a very few theoreticians had fully grasped the potential of modern weapons — machine-guns spitting out 10 bullets a second; "quick-firing" field artillery guns discharging 10 shells a minute, each one exploding into thousands of lethal fragments; and heavy artillery that hurled hundreds of kilos of high explosive over ranges of eight kilometres and more. And none of the generals comprehended the sophisticated tactics that would be required to defeat a resolute, well-entrenched enemy.

In for Keeps

In August 1914, as volunteers enlisted "for the duration," conventional wisdom held that the war would be over by Christmas; some would die, and more would be mutilated, but most would enjoy a moment of adventure to be relished for the rest of their lives. There were long line-ups outside recruiting offices, and men wondered whether the war would be over before they could see action.

In the event, they found themselves engaged in four brutal, bitter years of attrition which cost Canada alone some 50,000 killed and 138,000 wounded — proportionately far more casualties than the country incurred in the Second World War. A good number of the wounded were destined to spend their lives in veterans' hospitals, limbless, blind, or breathing harshly through gas-corroded lungs.

*From *Horizon Canada* 85 (1986): 2017–2023. Reprinted by permission.

Cheerful chaos had attended the raising of the 1st Canadian Division in the late summer of 1914. Scrapping existing mobilization plans, the erratic — some said insane — militia minister, Sam Hughes, issued "a call to arms, like the fiery cross passing through the Highlands of Scotland or the mountains of Ireland in former days." Within weeks 33,000 volunteers gathered at Valcartier, near Quebec City, where a large new camp was carved out of the woods and farmlands as the men arrived.

Hurried to the United Kingdom in a special troopship convoy in October, the Canadians then spent a miserable winter on the windswept, rain-drenched Salisbury Plain. There they trained with the Ross rifle and the MacAdam shovel, both favourites of Sam Hughes, but two of the many pieces of Canadian equipment that quickly proved inadequate for the rigours of trench warfare.

The division arrived in France in February 1915 when the lines had already stabilized, and General Staffs on both sides were puzzling over ways to break the deadlock. How did you get men on foot, wading through deep mud, past artillery fire and barbed wire and machine-guns so that they could close with the enemy? The Canadians soon found themselves in action in the notorious Ypres Salient, where the Allied line still bulged into German-occupied Belgium.

Bent on eliminating the Salient and thus shortening their line, the Germans launched the first serious gas attacks of the war in late April. French colonial troops on the Canadian flank broke and ran before the clouds of chlorine, but the Canadians held the shoulder of the gap and kept the Germans at bay until relieved by British units. "A great wall of green gas about 15 to 20 feet high was on top of us," recalled one officer. "Captain MacLaren gave an order to get handkerchiefs, soak them and tie them around our mouths and noses. Some were able to do that and some just urinated on their handkerchiefs. Some managed to cover their faces. Others did not."

The Brass Turned Green

A British soldier, moving up to relieve the Canadians, remembered how "we stopped at a ditch at a first-aid clearing station. There were about 200 to 300 men lying in that ditch. Some were clawing their throats. Their brass buttons were green. Their bodies were swelled. Some of them were still alive. Some were still writhing on the ground, their tongues hanging out." In three days the Canadians had sustained 3,000 casualties from gas and gunfire.

So desperate was the need for replacements that the Canadian Cavalry Brigade, in England, was dismounted and sent to France to serve as infantry. Trooper W.S. Lighthall of the Royal Canadian Dragoons wrote of going up to the line for the first time: "We filed out of our [reserve] trench and across the open plain towards the east. . . . The entrance to a low walled communication trench showed that it had been used as a first-aid post. Everywhere men were stretched out, apparently asleep, but we soon found they were dead. Hundreds of them, lying in all sorts of postures and conditions, and judging by the stench many had been there for a long time. . . . The trench was about three feet deep and wound across a swamp and every step squelched as one stepped on one of the bodies that floored the trench. The walls were part sandbags and part more bodies — some stiff with *rigor mortis* and others far gone with decay . . . over our heads the continuous crackle of bullets. . . . As we got clear of the low swampland, our trench became deeper and we could stand up, which was a relief. The sounds around us told of the fight that had just died down. We could hear cries of wounded outside the trench and in the bright moonlight we could see the churned-up land on either side, with a maze of trenches running in all directions."

Typically, a tour of the trenches lasted six days, followed by six more in immediate reserve — still within range of the enemy guns, and often taking up supplies to the front every night — and then 12 days "rest" in the rear areas, living in tarpaper barracks, barns, or abandoned villages. In the line, days were spent standing sentry duty, catnapping, and maintaining trenches and dug-outs — always remembering to keep your head down! Men rose above the ground only at night, for patrols

327

Key Dates

- *1914, Aug. 4* — the war begins.
- *1914, Oct. 3* — first Canadian contingent sails for England.
- *1915, Feb.* — Canadians arrive in France.
- *1915, April* — Battle of Ypres.
- *1916, March-April* — Battle of the St. Eloi craters.
- *1916, June* — Battle of Mont Sorrel; 8,000 casualties.
- *1916, July 1* — Newfoundland Regiment suffers devastating losses at Beaumont Hamel.
- *1916, Sept.* — Battle at Courcelette.
- *1917, April 6* — America enters war.
- *1917, Easter* — Battle at Vimy Ridge costs 3,598 lives.
- *1917, May* — conscription announced.
- *1917, Oct.-Nov.* — victory at Passchendaele results in 15,654 casualties.
- *1918, Aug.* — Battle at Amiens.
- *1918, Nov. 11* — war ends.

in "no-man's land," repairing the fire parapet, stringing barbed wire, and bringing up rations and ammunition. Day and night, sporadic fire from the enemy lines plagued existence. The notorious "First Day on the Somme" — July 1, 1916 — cost the British armies 60,000 casualties. Even the quietest of days cost a few dozen.

"Woolly Bears" . . .

Lt. W.B. Foster of Calgary wrote home in the spring of 1916 to tell his family about life in the trenches: "You ask what a 'coal box' is; well, it is a howitzer shell which explodes with a noise like thunder and throws up large volumes of thick black smoke. You can hear it coming quite plainly, and when it is just overhead the noise resembles an express train. . . . 'Woolly bears' are high explosive shrapnel shells which explode in the air. When the shrapnel comes over you the noise is terrific and that is the time we hug the parapet pretty closely. . . . The Huns have a thing they call an aerial torpedo; it is just like a large 14-inch shell and full of high explosive. It goes up to a tremendous height and at first it is very difficult to know just where it may land. This is where good football training stands one in good stead, as very often they come quite close before you can form any idea where they are going to fall. One does not mind a few of these things, but when they amount to 20 or 30 it becomes rather trying on the nerves. . . . Rifle bullets splatter around and occasionally a machine-gun rips off a few rounds. . . . "

. . . and Nightmares

During five such "quiet" months at the front, Foster's battalion lost nearly a quarter of its original strength — 200 killed and wounded. Sleep was grabbed in fits and starts, while squeezed into a hollow in the side of a trench or packed with a dozen others in a wet, musty, stinking dug-out. Private Donald Fraser from Vancouver observed that the strain of war showed most clearly when the soldiers slept; they were full of "groans and sighs," tossing "from side to side as if racked with pain."

Always more men were needed, to replace the casualties and to "thicken up" the front. Eventually there were four Canadian divisions and a cavalry brigade in the field and, in October 1917, the government had to turn to conscription in an attempt to find another 100,000 reinforcements. However, fewer than 25,000 got to France before the war ended.

Each side tried to break the deadlock by blasting away the enemy's line with artillery fire. But, nearly always, enough enemy machine-gunners survived to bring the attacking infantry to a stop, no matter how closely they "leaned" on the moving wall of artillery fire that led the advance. The British introduced tanks, but they were too slow and unreliable to be decisive — blind and deaf armoured monsters easily bogged down on ground that had reverted to primeval swamp. At Loos and Verdun, along the Somme and on the Passchendaele ridge, bone and brain and muscle were ripped apart by steel and high explosive, and millions of casualties were incurred.

Making a Break for Victory

Thorough preparation, good staff work and leadership, exceptional bravery and luck occasionally brought about a small success, as when the Canadians took heavily fortified Vimy Ridge on Easter Monday, 1917. But in the long term, even that was more a political victory than a military one.

All four divisions of the Canadian Corps, more than 70,000 strong, attacked together — fishermen from Cape Breton and Vancouver Island, Ontario loggers and bank clerks, Alberta farmers and cowboys. Their memories of that attack gave the survivors a common bond which linked them together, "from sea to sea" in the post-war era, and it has been argued that Canada really became a nation on Vimy Ridge. If that is true, then the price for nationhood was 3,598 killed and another 7,000 wounded.

Always there was the mud. Captain E.L.M. Burns, a signals officer on the Somme who survived the war to become commander of I Canadian Corps in Italy during the Second World War, remembered how "the overlying clay soil, saturated with rain, was puddled with the chalk turned up by shellfire and trench digging, and became a viscous mass, sticking to our boots in great heavy lumps, covering our clothing, rendering every step a burden, treacherously slippery, causing many falls." When they fell, many men drowned in it. Bugler Vic Syrett found that "a man's clothing became so coated with the half-frozen mud that, together with his boots and puttees, they weighed in the neighbourhood of 120 lbs, and in one case, 145 lbs [66 kg]." Weighed down like that, it was sometimes impossible to get up again.

It took four years for the generals to discover how to break the deadlock. The answer lay in tactics, not technology. Not in gas, or tanks, or everbigger and more prolonged artillery barrages, but in careful, precise coordination of all arms, and the restoration of the element of surprise that had been lost in the frantic search for more firepower.

The great day came on Aug. 8, 1918, when the Canadian and Australian Corps spearheaded an attack in front of Amiens. Lt. R.J. Holmes, who won a Military Cross for his bravery with the 46th (Saskatchewan) Battalion, recorded how: "The night of the 7th/8th we marched fourteen miles to get into battle positions, being loaded down more or less like

329

Christmas trees, with two days' rations, two large water bottles filled, and a large pack, besides all our battle equipment of steel helmet, field-glasses, compasses, gas respirator, revolver, ammunition, and heaven knows what not. We arrived in position at 2:30 a.m. and went over the top [of the trench] at 4:20 a.m. We made seven miles the first day, which was going some after months and months of trench warfare. Thousands of cavalry and hundreds of tanks operated on our front alone, and it was indeed a sight for the gods to see such famous regiments as the Scots Greys, the Bengal Lancers, Strathcona, and Fort Garry Horse going into action at the charge, guns coming up at the gallop, aeroplanes delivering ammunition to the attacking troops."

One Last Shot

330 Casualties were heavy at Amiens too — nearly 12,000 Canadians in 12 days — but this was the way the young men of 1914 had visualized war. And that was the way it remained in the 100 days of fighting that brought the war to an end. Lt. Roscoe Barrett of Toronto, who had come through the slaughter on the Somme and at Passchendaele, wrote home to say that "fighting here has changed completely. . . . There are no longer the extensive trench systems and barbed wire entanglements.

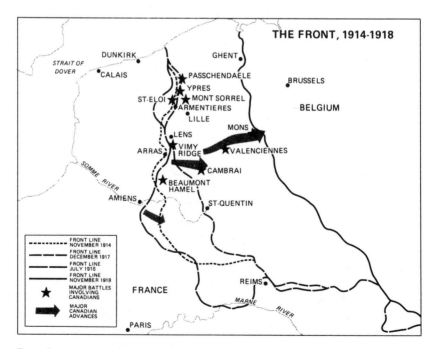

Dept. of cartography, CEGEP de Limoilou, Qué.

The ground is no longer pitted with shell-holes and the villages we capture are no longer razed to the ground and laid desolate. Artillery, except in a few instances, are not used."

The Germans were getting weaker and the Allies were getting stronger — a process accelerated greatly by the arrival of American troops at the front, the United States having come into the war on April 6, 1917 (just three days before the Canadian victory on Vimy Ridge). Finally, the enemy signed an armistice agreement to take effect at 11 a.m. on Nov. 11, 1918. That morning, "we passed through the outskirts of Mons in daylight," recalled Private Harold Wilson of the 28th (North-West) Battalion, many years later. "We were about four or five miles east of Mons. . . . At eleven a.m. we got into a little village. As we approached it, German machine-guns opened up and we got into a ditch. I was in 'B' Company. Another company came up a parallel road. The roads converged. I think it was Corporal Price who didn't get down and walked across the road. He was the last Canadian killed in action in World War One."

The last of 50,000.

An Open Letter from Capt. Talbot Papineau to Mr. Henri Bourassa*

(A copy of this letter was sent to Mr. Bourassa by Mr. Andrew-R. McMaster, K.C., on the 18th of July, 1916. It was published, on the 28th of July, in most Montreal, Quebec, Ottawa, and Toronto papers, both English and French.)

In the Field,
France, March 21, 1916.

To Monsieur Henri Bourassa,
    Editor of Le Devoir,
        Montreal.

My dear Cousin Henri, —

I was sorry before leaving Quebec in 1914 not to have had an opportunity of discussing with you the momentous issues which were raised in Canada by the outbreak of this war.

You and I have had some discussions in the past, and although we have not agreed upon all points, yet I am happy to think that our pleasant friendship, which indeed dates from the time of my birth, has hitherto continued uninjured by our differences of opinion. Nor would I be the first to make it otherwise, for however I may deplore the character of

*From *Canadian Nationalism and the War*. Published in Montreal, 1916.

your views, I have always considered that you held them honestly and-sincerely and that you were singularly free from purely selfish or personal ambitions.

Very possibly nothing that I could have said in August 1914 would have caused you to change your opinions, but I did hope that as events developed and as the great national opportunity of Canada became clearer to all her citizens, you would have been influenced to modify your views and to adopt a different attitude. In that hope I have been disappointed. Deeply involved as the honour and the very national existence of Canada has become, beautiful but terrible as her sacrifices have been, you and you alone of the leaders of Canadian thought appear to have remained unmoved, and your unhappy views unchanged.

Too occupied by immediate events in this country to formulate a protest or to frame a reasoned argument, I have nevertheless followed with intense feeling and deep regret the course of action which you have pursued. Consolation of course I have had in the fact that far from sharing in your views, the vast majority of Canadians, and even many of those who had formerly agreed with you, were now strongly and bitterly op-

332

National Archives of Canada   (C13224).

Major Talbot Papineau exchanged the safety of a staff job for the dangers of the Front. He rejoined his battalion to fight at Passchendaele.

posed to you. With this fact in mind, I would not take the time from my duties here to write you this letter did I not fear that the influence to which your talent, energy, and sincerity of purpose formerly entitled you, might still be exercised upon a small minority of your fellow countrymen, and that your attitude might still be considered by some as representative of the race to which we belong.

Nor can I altogether abandon the hope — presumptuous no doubt but friendly and well-intentioned — that I may so express myself here as to give you a new outlook and a different purpose, and perhaps even win you to the support of a principle which has been proved to be dearer to many Canadians than life itself.

I shall not consider the grounds upon which you base your opposition to Canadian participation in this more than European — in this World War. Rather I wish to begin by pointing out some reasons why on the contrary your whole-hearted support might have been expected.

And the first reason is this. By the declaration of war by Great Britain *333* upon Germany, Canada became "ipso facto" a belligerent, subject to invasion and conquest, her property at sea subject to capture, her coasts subject to bombardment or attack, her citizens in enemy territory subject to imprisonment or detention. This is not a matter of opinion — it is a matter of fact — a question of international law. No arguments of yours at least could have persuaded the Kaiser to the contrary. Whatever your views or theories may be as to future constitutional development of Canada, and in those views I believe I coincide to a large extent, the fact remains that at the time of the outbreak of war Canada was a possession of the British Empire, and as such as much involved in the war as any country in England, and from the German point of view and the point of view of International Law equally subject to all its pains and penalties. Indeed proof may no doubt be made that one of the very purposes of Germany's aggression and German military preparedness was the ambition to secure a part if not the whole of the English possessions in North America.

That being so, surely it was idle and pernicious to continue an academic discussion as to whether the situation was a just one or not, as to whether Canada should or should not have had a voice in ante bellum English diplomacy or in the actual declaration of war. Such a discussion may very properly arise upon a successful conclusion of the war, but so long as national issues are being decided in Prussian fashion, that is, by an appeal to the Power of Might, the liberties of discussion which you enjoyed by virtue of British citizenship were necessarily curtailed and any resulting decisions utterly valueless. If ever there was a time for action and not for theories it was to be found in Canada upon the outbreak of war.

Let us presume for the sake of argument that your attitude had also been adopted by the Government and people of Canada and that we had declared our intention to abstain from active participation in the war until Canada herself was actually attacked. What would have resulted? One of two things. Either the Allies would have been defeated or they would not have been defeated. In the former case Canada would have been called upon either to surrender unconditionally to German domination or to have attempted a resistance against German arms.

You, I feel sure, would have preferred resistance, but as a proper corrective to such a preference I would prescribe a moderate dose of trench bombardment. I have known my own dogmas to be seriously disturbed in the midst of a German artillery concentration. I can assure you that the further you travel from Canada and the nearer you approach the great military power of Germany, the less do you value the unaided strength of Canada. By the time you are within fifteen yards of a German army and know yourself to be holding about one yard out of a line of five hundred miles or more, you are liable to be enquiring very anxiously about the presence and power of British and French forces. Your ideas about charging to Berlin or of ending the war would also have undergone some slight moderation.

No, my dear Cousin, I think you would shortly after the defeat of the Allies have been more worried over the mastery of the German consonants than you are even now over a conflict with the Ontario Anti-bilinguists. Or I can imagine you an unhappy exile in Terra del Fuego eloquently comparing the wrongs of Quebec and Alsace.

But you will doubtless say we would have had the assistance of the Great American Republic! It is quite possible. I will admit that by the time the American fleet had been sunk and the principal buildings in New York destroyed the United States would have declared war upon Europe, but in the meantime Canada might very well have been paying tribute and learning to decline German verbs, probably the only thing German she *could* have declined.

I am, as you know, by descent even more American than I am French, and I am a sincere believer in the future of that magnificent Republic. I cannot forget that more than any other nation in the world's history — England not excepted — she has suffered war solely for the sake of some fine principle of nationality. In 1776 for the principle of national existence. In 1812 for the principle of the inviolability of American citizenship. In 1860 for the preservation of National unity and the suppression of slavery. In 1896 for the protection of her National pride and in sympathy for the wrongs of a neighbouring people.

Nor disappointed as I am at the present inactivity of the States will I ever waiver in my loyal belief that in time to come, perhaps less distant than we realise, her actions will correspond with the lofty expression of her national and international ideals.

I shall continue to anticipate the day when with a clear understanding and a mutual trust we shall by virtue of our united strength and our common purposes be prepared to defend the rights of humanity not only upon the American Continent but throughout the civilised world.

Nevertheless we are not dealing with what may occur in the future but with the actual facts of yesterday and to-day, and I would feign know if you still think that a power which without protest witnesses the ruthless spoliation of Belgium and Serbia, and without effective action the murder of her own citizens, would have interfered to protect the property or the liberties of Canadians. Surely you must at least admit an element of doubt, and even if such interference had been attempted, have we not the admission of the Americans themselves that it could not have been successful against the great naval and military organisations of the Central Powers?

May I be permitted to conclude that had the Allies been defeated Canada must afterwards necessarily have suffered a similar fate.

But there was the other alternative, namely, that the Allies even without the assistance of Canada would *not* have been defeated. What then? Presumably French and English would still have been the official languages of Canada. You might still have edited untrammeled your version of Duty, and Colonel Lavergne might still, publicly and without the restraining fear of death or imprisonment, have spoken seditiously (I mean from the Prussian point of view of course). In fact Canada might still have retained her liberties and might with the same freedom from external influences have continued her progress to material and political strength.

But would you have been satisfied — you who have arrogated to yourself the high term of Nationalist? What of the Soul of Canada? Can a nation's pride or patriotism be built upon the blood and suffering of others or upon the wealth garnered from the coffers of those who in anguish and with blood-sweat are fighting the battles of freedom? If we accept our liberties, our national life, from the hands of the English soldiers, if without sacrifices of our own we profit by the sacrifices of the English citizen, can we hope to ever become a nation ourselves? How could we ever acquire that Soul or create that Pride without which a nation is a dead thing and doomed to speedy decay and disappearance.

If you were truly a Nationalist — if you loved our great country and without smallness longed to see her become the home of a good and united people — surely you would have recognised this as her moment of travail and tribulation. You would have felt that in the agony of her losses in Belgium and France, Canada was suffering the birth pains of her national life. There even more than in Canada herself, her citizens are being knit together into a new existence because when men stand side by side and endure a soldier's life and face together a soldier's death, they are united in bonds almost as strong as the closest of blood-ties.

There was the great opportunity for the true Nationalist! There was the great issue, the great sacrifice, which should have appealed equally

335

to all true citizens of Canada, and should have served to cement them with indissoluble strength — Canada was at war! Canada was attacked! What mattered then internal dissentions and questions of home importance? What mattered the why and wherefore of the war, whether we owed anything to England or not, whether we were Imperialists or not, or whether we were French or English? The one simple commending fact to govern our conduct was that Canada was at war, and Canada and Canadian liberties had to be protected.

To you as a "Nationalist" this fact should have appealed more than to any others. Englishmen, as was natural, returned to fight for England, just as Germans and Austrians and Belgians and Italians returned to fight for their native lands.

But we, Canadians, had we no call just as insistent, just as compelling to fight for Canada? Did not the *Leipzig* and the *Gneisnau* possibly menace Victoria and Vancouver, and did you not feel the patriotism to make sacrifices for the protection of British Columbia? How could you otherwise call yourself Canadian? It is true that Canada did not hear the roar of German guns nor were we visited at night by the murderous Zeppelins, but every shot that was fired in Belgium or France was aimed as much at the heart of Canada as at the bodies of our brave Allies. Could we then wait within the temporary safety of our distant shores until either the Central Powers flushed with victory should come to settle their account or until by the glorious death of millions of our fellowmen in Europe, Canada should remain in inglorious security and a shameful liberty?

I give thanks that that question has been answered not as you would have had it answered but as those Canadians who have already died or are about to die here in this gallant motherland of France have answered it.

It may have been difficult for you at first to have realised the full significance of the situation. You were steeped in your belief that Canada owed no debt to England, was merely a vassal state and entitled to protection without payment. You were deeply imbued with the principle that we should not partake in a war in the declaration of which we had had no say. You believed very sincerely that Canadian soldiers should not be called upon to fight beyond the frontier of Canada itself, and your vision was further obscured by your indignation at the apparent injustice to a French minority in Ontario.

It is conceivable that at first on account of this long held attitude of mind and because it seemed that Canadian aid was hardly necessary, for even we feared that the war would be over before the first Canadian regiment should land in France, you should have failed to adapt your mind to the new situation and should for a while have continued in your former views; — but now — now that Canada has pledged herself body and soul to the successful prosecution of this war — now that we know that only by the exercise of our full and united strength can we achieve a speedy and lasting victory — now that thousands of your fellow citizens have died, and alas! many more must yet be killed — how in the name of all that you hold most sacred can you still maintain your opposition? How can you refrain from using all your influence and your personal magnetism and eloquence to swell the great army of Canada and make it as representative of all classes of our citizens as possible?

Could you have been here yourself to witness in its horrible detail the cruelty of war — to have seen your comrades suddenly struck down in death and lie mangled at your side, even you could not have failed to wish to visit punishment upon those responsible. You too would now wish to see every ounce of our united strength instantly and relentlessly directed to that end. Afterwards, when that end has been accomplished, then and then only can there be honour or profit in the discussion of our domestic or imperial disputes.

337

And so my first reason for your support would be that you should assist in the defence of Canadian territory and Canadian liberties.

And my second would be this: —

Whatever criticism may to-day be properly directed against the Constitutional structure of the British Empire, we are compelled to admit that the *spiritual* union of the self governing portions of the Empire is a most necessary and desirable thing. Surely you will concede that the degree of civilisation which they represent and the standards of individual and national liberty for which they stand are the highest and noblest to which the human race has yet attained and jealously to be protected against destruction by less developed powers. All may not be perfection — grave and serious faults no doubt exist — vast progress must still be made — nevertheless that which has been achieved is good and must not be allowed to disappear. The bonds which unite us for certain great purposes and which have proved so powerful in this common struggle must not be loosened. They may indeed be readjusted, but the great communities which the British Empire has joined together must not be broken asunder. If I thought that the development of a national spirit in Canada meant antagonism to the "spirit" which unites the Empire today, I would utterly repudiate the idea of a Canadian nation and would gladly accept the most exacting of imperial organic unions.

Hitherto I have welcomed your nationalism because I thought it would only mean that you wished Canada to assume national responsibilities as well as to enjoy its privileges.

But your attitude in the present crisis will alienate and antagonise the support which you might otherwise have received. Can you not realise that if any worthy nationality is possible for Canada it must be sympathetic to and must co-operate with the fine spirit of imperial unity?

That spirit was endangered by the outbreak of European war. It could only be preserved by loyal assistance from all those in whom that spirit dwelt.

And so I would also have had you support Canadian participation in the war, *not* in order to maintain a certain political organism of Empire, but to preserve and perpetuate that invaluable *spirit* which alone makes our union possible.

The third reason is this: You and I are so called French-Canadians. We belong to a race that began the conquest of this country long before the days of Wolfe. That race was in its turn conquered, but their personal liberties were not restricted. They were in fact increased. Ultimately as a minority in a great English speaking community we have preserved our racial identity, and we have had freedom to speak or to worship as we wished. I may not be, like yourself, "un pur sang," for I am by birth even more English than French, but I am proud of my French ancestors, I love the French language, and I am as determined as you are that we shall have full liberty to remain French as long as we like. But if we are to preserve this liberty we must recognise that we do not belong entirely to ourselves, but to a mixed population, we must rather seek to find points of contact and of common interest than points of friction and separation. We must make concessions and certain sacrifices of our distinct individuality if we mean to live on amicable terms with our fellow citizens or if we are to expect them to make similar concessions to us. There, in this moment of crisis, was the greatest opportunity which could ever have presented itself for us to show unity of purpose and to prove to our English fellow citizens that, whatever our respective histories may have been, we were actuated by a common love for our country and a mutual wish that in the future we should unite our distinctive talents and energies to create a proud and happy nation.

That was an opportunity which you, my cousin, have failed to grasp, and unfortunately, despite the heroic and able manner in which French Canadian battalions have distinguished themselves here, and despite the whole-hearted support which so many leaders of French Canadian thought have given to the cause, yet the fact remains that the French in Canada have not responded in the same proportion as have other Canadian citizens, and the unhappy impression has been created that French Canadians are not bearing their full share in this great Canadian enterprise. For this fact and this impression you will be held largely responsible. Do you fully realise what such a responsibility will mean, not so much to you personally — for that I believe you would care little — but to the principles which you have advocated, and for many of which I have but the deepest regard. You will have brought them into a disrepute from which they may never recover. Already you have made the fine term of "Nationalist" to stink in the nostrils of our English fellow citizens. Have you caused them to respect your national views?

338

Have you won their admiration or led them to consider with esteem, and toleration your ambitions for the French language? Have you shown yourself worthy of concessions or consideration?

After this war what influence will you enjoy — what good to your country will you be able to accomplish? Wherever you go you will stir up strife and enmity — you will bring disfavour and dishonour upon our race, so that whoever bears a French name in Canada will be an object of suspicion and possibly of hatred.

And so, in the third place, for the honour of French Canada and for the unity of our country, I would have had you favourable to our cause.

I have only two more reasons, and they but need to be mentioned, I think to be appreciated.

Here in this little French town I hear about all me the language I love so well and which recalls so vividly my happy childhood days in Montebello. I see types and faces that are like old friends. I see farm houses like those at home. I notice that our French Canadian soldiers have easy friendships wherever they go. 339

Can you make me believe that there must not always be a bond of blood relationship between the Old France and the New?

And France — more glorious than in all her history — is now in agony straining fearlessly and proudly in a struggle for life or death.

For Old France and French civilisation I would have had your support.

And in the last place, all other considerations aside and even supposing Canada had been a neutral country, I would have had you decide that she should enter the struggle for no other reason than that it is a fight for the freedom of the world — a fight in the result of which like every other country she is herself vitally interested. I will not further speak of the causes of this war, but I should like to think that even if Canada had been an independent and neutral nation she of her own accord would have chosen to follow the same path of glory that she is following to-day.

Perhaps, my cousin, I have been overlong and tedious with my reasons, but I shall be shorter with my warning — and in closing I wish to say this to you.

Those of us in this great army, who may be so fortunate as to return to our Canada, will have faced the grimmest and sincerest issues of life and death — we will have experienced the unhappy strength of brute force — we will have seen our loved comrades die in blood and suffering. Beware lest we return with revengeful feelings, for I say to you that for those who, while we fought and suffered here, remained in safety and comfort in Canada and failed to give us encouragement and support, as well as for those who grew fat with the wealth dishonourably gained by political graft and by dishonest business methods at our expense — we shall demand a heavy day of reckoning. We shall inflict upon them the punishment they deserve — not by physical violence — for we shall have had enough of that — nor by unconstitutional or illegal means — for we are fighting to protect not to destroy justice and freedom — but by the invincible power of our moral influence.

Can you ask us then for sympathy or concession? Will any listen when you speak of pride and patriotism? I think not.

Remember too that if Canada has become a nation respected and self-respecting she owes it to her citizens who have fought and died in this distant land and not to those self-styled Nationalists who have remained at home.

Can I hope that anything I have said here may influence you to consider the situation in a different light and that it is not yet too late for me to be made proud of our relationship?

At this moment, as I write, French and English-Canadians are fighting and dying side by side. Is their sacrifice to go for nothing or will it not cement a foundation for a true Canadian nation, a Canadian nation independent in thought, independent in action, independent even in its political organisation — but in spirit united for high international and humane purposes to the two Motherlands of England and France?

I think that is an ideal in which we shall all equally share. Can we not all play an equal part in its realisation?

I am, as long as may be possible,

Your affectionate Cousin,

TALBOT M. PAPINEAU.

Mr. Bourassa's Reply to Capt. Talbot Papineau's Letter*

Montreal, August 2nd, 1916.

Andrew-R. McMaster, Esq., K.C.,
    189 St. James St.,
       City.

Dear Sir,

On my return from an absence of several weeks, I found your letter of the 18th ult., and the copy of a letter apparently written to me by your partner, Capt. Talbot Papineau, on the 21st of March.

Capt. Papineau's letter, I am informed, appeared simultaneously, Friday last, in a number of papers, in Montreal, Quebec, Ottawa, and elsewhere. You have thus turned it into a kind of political manifesto and

*From *Canadian Nationalism and the War*. Published in Montreal, 1916.

constituted yourself its publisher. Allow me therefore to send you my reply, requesting you to have it transmitted to Capt. Papineau, granting that he is the real author of that document. I can hardly believe it. A brave and active officer as he is has seldom the time to prepare and write such long pieces of political eloquence. Then, why should Capt. Papineau, who writes and speaks French elegantly, who claims so highly his French origin and professes with such ardour his love of France, have written in English to his *"dear cousin Henri"*? How is it that a letter written on the 21st of March has reached me but four months later, through your medium? For what purpose did you keep it so long in portfolio? and why do you send me a copy, instead of the letter itself?

It is, you say, an "open letter." It was, nevertheless, meant to reach me. It opens and ends with forms of language bearing the touch of intimate relationship — more so even than could be expected from the rare intercourse which, in spite of our blood connection, had so far existed between your partner and myself. The whole thing has the appearance *341* of a political manoeuvre executed under the name of a young and gallant officer, who has the advantage or inconvenience of being my cousin. That Capt. Papineau has put his signature at the foot of that document, it is possible; but he would certainly not have written it in cool thought, after due reflexion. It not only expresses opinions radically opposed to

National Archives of Canada   (C 27358).

Henri Bourassa, the founding editor of *Le Devoir*, strongly opposed Canada's involvement in World War I, particularly the conscription of Canadian men to fight in Europe.

those I heard from him before the war; it also contains inaccuracies of fact of which I believe him honourably incapable.

He mentions "some discussions in the past," "differences of opinion," which have left "uninjured" a "pleasant friendship," dating, he says, "from the time of [his] birth." From his childhood to his return from Oxford, I do not think we had ever met, and certainly never to exchange the slightest glimpse of thought or opinion. Of matters of national concern we talked but once in all my life. From that one conversation I gathered the impression that he was still more opposed than myself to any kind of imperial solidarity. He even seemed much disposed to hasten the day of the Independence of Canada. Since, I met him on two or three occasions. We talked of matters indifferent, totally foreign to the numerous questions treated with such eloquent profuseness and so little reasoning in his letter of the 21st of March.

How can he charge me with having expressed "unhappy views" "at the outstart of the war," in August 1914, and held them stubbornly "unchanged" till this day? In August 1914, I was abroad. My first pronouncement on the intervention of Canada in the war is dated September 8th, 1914. In that editorial, while repelling the principles of Imperial solidarity and their consequences, and maintaining the nationalist doctrine in which Capt. Papineau — and you as well — pretends to be still a believer, I pronounced myself in favour of the intervention of Canada, *as a nation*, for the defence of the superior interests uniting Canada with France and Britain. My "unhappy views" were thus analogous to those of your partner. It is but later, long after Capt. Papineau was gone, that my attitude was changed and brought me to condemn the participation of Canada in the war, — or rather the political inspiration of that participation and the many abuses which have resulted therefrom. The reasons of that change are well known to those who have read or heard with attention and good faith all my statements on the matter. To sum them up is now sufficient.

The free and independent participation of Canada — free for the nation and free for the individuals — I had accepted, provided it remained within reasonable bounds, in conformity with the conditions of the country. But the Government, the whole of Parliament, the press, and politicians of both parties all applied themselves systematically to obliterate the free character of Canada's intervention. "Free" enlistment is now carried on by means of blackmailing, intimidation, and threats of all sorts. Advantage has been taken of the emotion caused by the war to assert, with the utmost intensity and intolerance, the doctrine of Imperial solidarity, triumphantly opposed in the past by our statesmen and the whole Canadian people, up to the days of the infamous South African War, concocted by Chamberlain, Rhodes, and the British imperialists with the clear object of drawing the self-governing colonies into "the vortex of European militarism." That phrase of your political leader, Sir Wilfrid Laurier, is undoubtedly fresh in your mind. After having given way to the imperialistic current of 1899, Sir Wilfrid Laurier and the liberal party had come back to the nationalist doctrine. The naval scare of 1909 threw them again under the yoke of imperialism; the war has achieved their enslavement: they united with the tory-jingo-imperialists of all shades to make of the participation of Canada in the war an immense political manoeuvre and thus assure the triumph of British imperialism. You and your partner, like many others, have followed your party through its various evolutions. I have remained firmly attached to the principles I laid down at the time of the South African war and maintained unswervingly ever since.

As early as the month of March 1900, I pointed out the possibility of a conflict between Great Britain and Germany and the danger of laying down in South Africa a precedent, the fatal consequence of which would be to draw Canada into all the wars undertaken by the United Kingdom. Sir Wilfrid Laurier and the liberal leaders laughed at my apprehensions; against my warnings they quoted the childish safeguard of the "no precedent clause" inserted in the Order in Council of the 14th of October 1899. For many years after, till 1912, and 1913, they kept singing the praises of the Kaiser and extolling the peaceful virtues of Germany. They now try to regain time by denouncing vociferously the "barbarity" of the "Huns." To-day, as in 1900, in 1911, and always, I believe that all the nations of Europe are the victims of their own mistakes, of the complacent servility with which they submitted to the dominance of all Imperialists and traders in human flesh, who, in England as in Germany, in France as in Russia, have brought the peoples to slaughter in order to increase their reapings of cursed gold. German Imperialism and British Imperialism, French Militarism and Russian Tsarism, I hate with equal detestation; and I believe as firmly today as in 1899 that Canada, a nation of America, has a nobler mission to fulfil than to bind herself to the fate of the nations of Europe or to any spoliating Empire — whether it be the spoliators of Belgium, Alsace, or Poland, or those of Ireland or the Transvaal, of Greece or the Balkans.

Politicians of both parties, your liberal friends as well as their conservative opponents, feign to be much scandalised at my "treasonable disloyalty." I could well afford to look upon them as a pack of knaves and hypocrites. In 1896, your liberal leaders and friends stumped the whole province of Quebec with the cry "WHY SHOULD WE FIGHT FOR ENGLAND?" From 1902 to 1911, Sir Wilfrid Laurier was acclaimed by them as the indomitable champion of Canada's autonomy against British Imperialism. His resisting attitude at the Imperial Conferences of 1902 and 1907 was praised to the skies. His famous phrase on the "vortex of European militarism", and his determination to keep

Canada far from it, became the party's by-word — always in the Province of Quebec, of course. His Canadian Navy scheme was presented as a step towards the independence of Canada.

Then came the turn of the Conservatives to tread in the footsteps of the Nationalists; they soon outstripped us. A future member of the conservative Cabinet, Mr. Blondin, brought back to life an old saying of Sir Adolphe Chapleau, and suggested to pierce the Union jack with bullets in order to let pass the breeze of liberty. The tory leaders, Sir Robert Borden, Sir George Foster, the virtuous Bob Rogers, and even our national superKitchener, Sir Sam Hughes, while trumpeting the purity of their Imperialism, greeted with undisguised joy the anti-imperialist victory of Drummond-Arthabaska, and used it for all it was worth to win the general elections in 1911.

By what right should those people hold me as a "traitor," because I remain consequent with the principles that I have never ceased to uphold and which both parties have exploited alternately, as long as it suited their purpose and kept them in power or brought them to office?

Let it not be pretended that those principles are out of place, pending the war. To prevent Canada from participating in the war, then foreseen and predicted, was their very object and *raison d'être*. To throw them aside and deny them when the time of test came, would have required a lack of courage and sincerity, of which I feel totally incapable. If this is what they mean by "British loyalty" and "superior civilisation," they had better hang me at once. I will never obey such dictates and will ever hold in deepest contempt the acrobats who lend themselves to all currents of blind popular passion in order to serve their personal or political ends.

This, let it be well understood, does not apply to your partner. His deeds have shown the sincerity of his political turn. Without agreeing with his new opinions, I admired his silent courage in running to the front at the first call. His verbose political manifesto — supposing he is really responsible for it — adds nothing to his merits. Still less does it enhance the dignity and moral worth of the politicians and pressmen of all kinds, who, after having denounced war and imperialism, and while taking great care not to risk their precious body, have become the apostles of war and the upholders of imperialism.

I will not undertake to answer every point of the dithyrambic plea of my gallant cousin. When he says that I am too far away from the trenches to judge of the real meaning of this war, he may be right. On the other hand, his long and diffuse piece of eloquence proves that the excitement of warfare and the distance from home have obliterated in his mind the fundamental realities of his native country. I content myself with touching upon one point, on which he unhappily lends credit to the most mischievous of the many anti-national opinions circulated by the jingo press. He takes the French-Canadians to task and challenges

344

their patriotism, because they enlist in lesser number than the other elements of the population of Canada. Much could be said upon that. It is sufficient to signalise one patent fact: the number of recruits for the European war, in the various Provinces of Canada and from each component element of the population, is in inverse ratio of the enrootment in the soil and the traditional patriotism arising therefrom. The newcomers from the British Isles have enlisted in much larger proportion than English-speaking Canadians born in this country, while these have enlisted more than the French-Canadians. The Western Provinces have given more recruits than Ontario, and Ontario more than Quebec. In each Province, the floating population of the cities, the students, the labourers and clerks, either unemployed or threatened with dismissal, have supplied more soldiers than the farmers. Does it mean that the city dwellers are more patriotic than the country people? or that the newcomers from England are better Canadians than their fellow citizens of British origin, born in Canada? No; it simply means that in Canada, as in every other country, at all times, the citizens of the oldest origin are the least disposed to be stampeded into distant ventures of no direct concern to their native land. It proves also that military service is more repugnant to the rural than the urban populations.

345

There is among the French-Canadians a larger proportion of farmers, fathers of large families, than among any other ethnical element in Canada. Above all, the French-Canadians are the only group exclusively Canadian, in its whole and by each of the individuals of which it is composed. They look upon the perturbations of Europe, even those of England or France, as foreign events. Their sympathies naturally go to France against Germany; but they do not think they have an obligation to fight for France, no more than the French of Europe would hold themselves bound to fight for Canada against the United States or Japan, or even against Germany, in case Germany should attack Canada without threatening France.

English Canada, not counting the *blokes*, contains a considerable proportion of people still in the first period of national incubation. Under the sway of imperialism, a fair number have not yet decided whether their allegiance is to Canada or to the Empire, whether the United Kingdom or the Canadian Confederacy is their country.

As to the newcomers from the United Kingdom, they are not Canadian in any sense. England or Scotland is their sole fatherland. They have enlisted for the European war as naturally as Canadians, either French or English, would take arms to defend Canada against an aggression on the American continent.

Thus it is rigourously correct to say that recruiting has gone in inverse ratio of the development of Canadian patriotism. If English-speaking Canadians have a right to blame the French Canadians for the small number of their recruits, the newcomers from the United Kingdom, who have supplied a much larger proportion of recruits than any other element of the population, would be equally justified in branding the Anglo-Canadians with disloyalty and treason. Enlistment for the European war is supposed to be absolutely free and voluntary. This has been stated right and left from beginning to end. If that statement is honest and sincere, all provocations from one part of the population against the other, and exclusive attacks against the French-Canadians, should cease. Instead of reviling unjustly one-third of the Canadian people — a population so remarkably characterised by its constant loyalty to national institutions and its respect for public order, — those men who claim a right to enlighten and lead public opinion should have enough good faith and intelligence to see facts as they are and to respect the motives of those who persist in their determination to remain more Canadian than English or French.

346

In short, English-speaking Canadians enlist in much smaller number than the newcomers from England, because they are more Canadian; French-Canadians enlist less than English-Canadians because they are totally and exclusively Canadian. To claim that their abstention is due to the "baneful" influence of the Nationalists is a pure nonsense. Should I give way to the suggestion of my gallant cousin, I would be just as powerless as Sir Wilfrid Laurier to induce the French-Canadians to enlist. This is implicitly acknowledged in Capt. Papineau's letter: on the one hand, he asserts that my views on the participation of Canada in the war are denied by my own friends; on the other he charges the mass of the French-Canadian population with a refusal to answer the call of duty. The simple truth is, that the abstention of the French-Canadians is no more the result of the present attitude of the Nationalists than the consequence of the liberal campaign of 1896, or of the conservative appeals of 1911. It relates to deeper causes: hereditary instincts, social and economic conditions, a national tradition of three centuries. It is equally true, however, that those deep and far distant causes have been strengthened by the constant teaching of all our political and social leaders, from Lafontaine, Cartier, Macdonald, Mackenzie, to Laurier inclusively. The only virtue, or crime, of the Nationalists is to persist in believing and practising what they were taught by the men of the past, and even those of to-day. This is precisely what infuriates the politicians, either *blue* or *red*. To please the Imperialists, they have renounced all their traditions and undertaken to bring the French-Canadians under imperial command. Unable to succeed, they try to conceal their fruitless apostasy by denouncing to the hatred of the jingos the obtrusive witnesses of their past professions of faith.

The jingo press and politicians have also undertaken to persuade their gullible followers that the Nationalists hinder the work of recruiters *because* of the persecution meted out to the French minorities in Ontario and Manitoba. This is but another nonsense. My excellent cousin, I am sorry to say, — or his inspirer — has picked it up.

The two questions are essentially distinct, this we have never ceased to assert. One is purely internal; the other affects the international status of Canada and her relations with Great Britain. To the problem of the teaching of languages we ask for a solution in conformity with the spirit of the Federal agreement, the best interests of Confederation, and the principles of pedagogy as applied in civilised countries. Our attitude on the participation of Canada in the war is inspired exclusively by the constant tradition of the country and the agreements concluded half a century ago between Canada and Great Britain. Even if the irritating bilingual question was non-existent, our views on the war would be what they are. The most that can be said is, that the backward and essentially Prussian policy of the rulers of Ontario and Manitoba gives us an additional argument against the intervention of Canada in the European conflict. To speak of fighting for the preservation of French civilisation in Europe while endeavouring to destroy it in America, appears to us as an absurd piece of inconsistency. To preach Holy War for the liberties of the peoples overseas, and to oppress the national minorities in Canada, is, in our opinion, nothing but odious hypocrisy.

347

Is it necessary to add that, in spite of his name, Capt. Papineau is utterly unqualified to judge of the feelings of the French-Canadians? For most part American, he has inherited, with a few drops of French blood, the most *denationalised* instincts of his French origin. From those he calls his compatriots he is separated by his religious belief and his maternal language. Of their traditions, he knows but what he has read in a few books. He was brought up far away from close contact with French-Canadians. His higher studies he pursued in England. His elements of French culture he acquired in France. The complexity of his origin and the diversity of his training would be sufficient to explain his mental hesitations and the contradictions which appear in his letter. Under the sway of his American origin, he glories in the Revolution of 1776; he calls it a war "for the principle of national existence." In good logic, he should approve highly of the tentative rebellion of the Sinn Feiners, and suggest that Canada should rise in arms to break the yoke of Great Britain. His American forefathers, whom he admires so much, fought against England and called upon France and Spain to help them against their mother-country, for lighter motives than those of the Dublin rebels. The Imperial burden they refused to bear was infinitely less ponderous than that which weighs today upon the people of Canada.

With the threat contained in the conclusion of his letter, I need not be concerned. Supposing always that he is truly responsible for that document, I make broad allowance for the excitement and perturbation resulting from his strenuous life. He and many of his comrades will have enough to do in order to help Canada to counteract the disastrous consequences of the war venture in which she has thrown herself headlong. To propagate systematically national discord by quarreling with all Canadians, either French or English, who hold different views as to the theory and practice of their national duty, would be a misuse of time. Moreover, it would be a singular denial of their professions of faith in favour of liberty and civilisation.

As to the scoundrels and bloodsuckers "who have grown fat with the wealth dishonourably gained" in war contracts, I give them up quite willingly to their just indignation. But those worthies are not to be found in nationalist ranks: they are all recruited among the noisiest preachers of the Holy War waged for "civilisation" against "barbarity," for the "protection of small nations," for the "honour" of England and the "salvation" of France.

Yours truly,
Henri BOURASSA

P.S. — I hope this will reach you before you leave for the front: no doubt, you have been the first to respond to the pressing call of your partner.

H.B.

Canada's Liberal Pacifists and the Great War*

THOMAS P. SOCKNAT

On the eve of the Great War many Canadians vaguely thought of themselves as pacifists, causing that perennial observer of Canadian affairs, J. Castell Hopkins, to report that by 1914 "peace had become a habit of thought with many minds in Canada and, in some cases, was almost a religion."[1] Since pacifist rhetoric was "difficult to oppose and hard to discuss," explained Hopkins, it was "easy of presentment and popular acceptance."[2] Indeed, some Canadians expressed alarm that pacifism was actually "sweeping the country." Principal Maurice Hutton of Toronto's University College, for instance, warned a Toronto audience that "the air is so full of pacifism that it is necessary to urge upon the country the duty of national defense."[3]

Pacifists, on the other hand, were pleased with what they considered the "phenomenal advance" of the peace movement, but some were careful not to become complacent just because it appeared that pacifism had been "pretty generally accepted, in theory, at least, by the majority of

*From *Journal of Canadian Studies* 18, 4 (1983–84): 30–44. Reprinted by permission.

thinking persons" in Canada. On the contrary, Arthur G. Dorland, Chairman of the Peace and Arbitration Committee of the Canada Yearly Meeting of the Society of Friends, emphasized that the position adopted by many of the liberal converts to pacifism differed fundamentally from that of Quakers. Although the former condemned the disastrous results of war, he argued, they still believed that, under certain circumstances, wars were justifiable and right, while true pacifists like the Friends believed that since war was inherently immoral it could never be right.[4]

In effect, Dorland was distinguishing between the two different but complementary traditions of pacifism in Canada. One was the historic religious adherence to non-resistance largely confined to sectarian pacifists such as the Quakers, Mennonites, and Hutterites. Their exemption from military obligations had been specifically guaranteed by several Orders-in-Council during the late nineteenth century so that the tradition of religious pacifism was firmly entrenched in Canadian law and custom by 1914. Accordingly, the historic peace sects maintained their quiet pacifist witness throughout the war years.

349

The other tradition and that which was credited with popular appeal before 1914 was the movement for peace and world order motivated by the liberal reform impulse and the social gospel. By the late nineteenth century Quakers had become representative of both the historic and liberal pacifist traditions, but, as Dorland noted, the majority of liberal pacifists were preoccupied with the futility of war. The liberal peace movement, in other words, was largely representative of the progressive attempt to achieve order and stability within the world through the use of international arbitration and an international court. Moreover, it was elevated to a position of key importance since most reformers generally assumed that the success of their attempt to build a new social order depended upon a peaceful international climate. Political, church, farm, and labour spokesmen, and women's groups such as the WCTU and the National Council of Women all endorsed the principle of international arbitration and the peace movement in general. But they gave little thought to the ethics of war and failed to penetrate the relationship between war and the economic order.[5] Rather than pursue the roots of war into the structure of society or formulate a proper response for pacifists in a time of war, the pre-war pacifists merely erected a superficial facade which quickly shattered upon impact with the Great War.

Although this rapid disruption of Canada's peace movement has been noted by historians in the context of other studies,[6] a close examination of the pacifist issue itself reveals that Canadian liberal pacifism ended up taking a radical new turn in its wartime evolution. For instance, rather than unanimously deserting pacifist ideals, the loose reform coalition of liberal pacifists actually splintered into various responses. Some attempted to maintain a moderate stance recognizing the necessity to support the war effort while, at the same time, striving towards pacifist ideals and a progressive post-war era. This was perhaps the most difficult, if not impossible, position to maintain. The majority gradually came to think of the war as the crucible in which Christianity and the ideal of Christian peace were in danger of extinction at the hands of the enemy forces and they joined in the crusade against German "barbarism." At the opposite extreme, however, was a small number who remained ir-revocably opposed to war and militarism as antithetical to a Christian society. In addition, they broadened their attack to include not only war but the whole social and economic system which they believed had pro-duced war in the first place. Contrary to earlier peace advocates of either the historic peace sects or the liberal reform movement, therefore, they began to associate peace with radical, non-violent, socio-economic change at home and abroad.

The general disintegration of the liberal peace movement occurred as the majority of its pre-war membership not only abandoned pacifism but helped build the war effort into a frenzied crusade. Almost all groups of liberal reformers reflected this transition one way or another. Women's groups, for instance, quickly redirected their energies towards more re-spectable pursuits. Indeed, it is ironic that the women who helped pop-ularize the expectation that they would somehow react differently than men to war, because of their moral superiority, were the ones who sub-stantially contributed to the disruption of this myth during the war through their Red Cross work and patriotic activities.

The most vocal expression of this moral transformation, however, was provided by the churches, especially the Methodist Church through its journal *The Christian Guardian*, previously a leading peace organ. Shortly after the outbreak of the war the editor, W.B. Creighton, still condemned war as foolish, costly, and unchristian and reaffirmed his belief that Christian pacifism was still on its way.[7] On the other hand, he also sup-ported the claim by the General Superintendent of the Methodist Church, S.D. Chown, that the war was "just, honorable, and necessary" to really secure a durable peace.[8] Stories of German atrocities in Belgium and government controlled war propaganda, however, eventually trig-gered a more emotional response and raised fears for the future of Chris-tendom itself. As a result, the traditional concept of the just war was transformed into that of an apocalyptic crusade, an eschatological con-frontation between good and evil, between Christianity and the anti-Christ epitomized by Germany.[9] Former pacifists who had found it dif-ficult to rationalize support for a just war with their dedicated faith in the Christian gospel easily accepted the idea of a crusade to save Chris-tianity and liberal democracy from the diabolical German menace.[10] As argued elsewhere, the result was a paradox: idealized Christian pacifism produced an extreme zeal for a holy war.[11] Furthermore, liberal reformers began to think of participation in the war as an act of "national re-generation."[12] The apocalyptic war hysteria demanded a concerted fight against all evil. The demon Hun, the demon rum, the scourge of venereal disease, and other vices affecting society became equal targets of this crusading zeal. Therefore, as the social and moral reform movement joined forces with the war effort, *The Christian Guardian* concluded that "theoretically the church knows no peace — she is always at war with evil."[13]

Given this redefinition of war, many of the pre-war pacifists went full circle and labelled pacifism itself as evil. The shifting perspective could be observed in November 1916, when W.B. Creighton, while praising pacifism as "one of the most hopeful signs of our time," claimed pacifists were guilty of "dull obstinacy," "bitter prejudice," and "plain stupidity" for the manner in which they attempted to apply pacifism to the war with Germany.[14] The conclusion to that line of thinking appeared in the April 3, 1918 issue of the *Guardian*. In a cover page editorial entitled "The vice of Pacifism" Creighton argued that, rather than a virtue, pacifism was "a vice revealing the terrible fact that the conscience has lost its sensitiveness and the soul has lost its courage."[15] The following month Creighton developed his assault further and declared in no uncertain terms that there was no room in the Methodist Church for ministers with a pacifist conscience, even though the church had been pacifist in the past. "If a man cannot conscientiously declare himself a patriot," the editor asserted, "he has no business in any church which prides itself upon its patriotism."[16] Although such sentiments were echoed by the rest of the church press, the *Guardian* came to symbolize the wholesale desertion of the liberal peace movement during the war.[17] Its blanket condemnation of pacifism and denial of the right of conscience either silenced remaining pacifists or drove them further to the socialist camp.

Initially, however, some liberal pacifists tried to maintain moderate support for the war without condoning the extreme transformation of their earlier pacifist stand into a militant crusade. In effect, they attempted to unite a critical acquiescence in the war with a continuing opposition to militarism. Outright pacifist sentiments, on the other hand, were carefully aimed at future post-war society rather than the current conflict in order to avoid contradictions in such a tenuous position.

Two of Toronto's leading newspapermen had called themselves pacifists at the beginning of the war, but within a year both J.E. Atkinson, managing editor of the *Toronto Daily Star*, and J.A. Macdonald, managing editor of the Toronto *Globe*, had more or less succumbed to the patriotic fervor.[18] Macdonald, in particular, had been one of the leading spokesmen of the liberal peace movement in Canada before the war. He was the Canadian representative in various international peace organizations and was a director of the World Peace Foundation, the philanthropic peace research organization endowed by the American publisher, Edwin Ginn.[19] During the war Macdonald attempted to combine the call for patriotic duty with his familiar peace rhetoric, claiming that

351

a time of war was also a time to prepare for peace and disarmament.[20] Following his lead, the *Globe* initially exercised a moderating influence on the public as its editorials protested against the effects of militarism upon society, warned against building anti-German sympathies in Canadian youth, and argued that "no Canadian cadet should be allowed to think of a German or any other man as a target for his marksmanship."[21] But given the circumstances, the two lines of thought were almost impossible to maintain for long and in 1915 Macdonald resigned as editor, thus freeing the *Globe* to assume a more ardent patriotic position. Macdonald himself began a series of patriotic addresses in which he urged young men to enlist. In the end, he joined those liberals who had accepted the war as a means to create a new democratic world order, but the idea of armed peace or preparedness he still denounced as "doomed to the rubbish heap of the world's barbarism."[22]

352

The underlying conflict within the liberal conscience was most clearly reflected by the Canadian Peace and Arbitration Society, the principal liberal peace organization in Canada, as it adjusted to wartime realities. Prior to the war the Society counted over a thousand members, including such prominent Canadian academics as Professor Adam Shortt of Queen's University, Professor J. McCurdy of the University of Toronto, Sir William Mulock, Chief Justice of Ontario, and Lewis E. Horning, Professor of Classics at Victoria College.[23]

As the Society's wartime president, Horning spearheaded an effort to convince a dwindling audience to think "soberly, righteously and fairly" about the events occurring around them and thereby resist the growing war frenzy.[24] The aim of the Society was to combine support for Canada's war effort with some type of constructive action in line with their pacifist principles. As a start in that direction members of the Society made financial contributions, through the Canadian Society of Friends, to the Friends' Ambulance Corps organized in Europe by British Quakers.[25]

Although Horning accepted the war as a just struggle between democracy and militarism, his most perplexing problem was to reconcile it with Christianity. One solution, he proposed, was for peace-loving Christians to waste no time in building a new Christian spirit to supplant war.[26] Accordingly, he hoped the Canadian Peace and Arbitration Society, similar to the League for Democratic Control in Britain, would preserve clarity of thought during the war while working towards the post-war emergence of a new international system in accordance with liberal ideals.

Shortly after the outbreak of war, this position was articulated clearly by Horning in a letter to Dr. T. Albert Moore, Secretary of the General Conference of the Methodist Church. Horning appealed to the Church hierarchy for its "sympathy, whole-hearted co-operation, and active support" in planning that coming generations think "more sanely and soundly than past and present generations."[27] As a course of action, he suggested combatting the martial spirit which had infiltrated daily lives and language by building a new vision of patriotism free from the taint of militarism and war. Horning argued that

> . . . the old Patriotism is altogether too often associated with the soldiers' life. The language of our everyday life and of our past literature smacks very much of the martial, that is, it is a language based upon old ideals and old habits. "Patriotic fund" . . . why not *Soldiers* fund?[28]

Conversely, the word patriotism was to be reserved for references to peace, self-sacrifice, and brave service for one's fellow man. "The New Patriotism," claimed Horning, "calls for life and opportunity for life, not death and destruction, and vandalism and horrors." Pacifists, therefore, could also be viewed as patriots, contrary to the "fallacious arguments" of militarists.[29]

353

The Canadian Peace and Arbitration Society also maintained that its members and sympathetic friends had a special duty to perform regarding Canada's own peculiar problems, such as French–English relations, further complicated by the war, and the question of state ownership and control of the nation's productive wealth. "On all sides," Horning warned, "we need new light, new thought, a new spirit . . . we should believe in another destiny, that of the saving of the nations." In conclusion Horning made a final appeal to the Church:

> Preachers of peace and believers in Goodwill, help us . . . by your heartfelt sympathy, cordial co-operation, and willing openmindedness . . . we can be of great service to each other.[30]

Although the Church ignored Horning's appeal for a "New Patriotism," the Canadian Peace and Arbitration Society continued to sponsor peace meetings and addresses, at least as long as the United States remained neutral, but after 1917 its voice of moderation grew silent.[31] Even Horning ceased his attempt to organize a pacifist program of action and retreated to safer pursuits. In keeping with his personal desire to educate the public, for instance, he delivered a nation-wide series of lectures during the summer of 1918 concerning problems of war and Canadian citizenship.[32] Members of the Society and other frustrated liberals had tried in vain to prevent the development of an over-zealous war mentality but in the end they were not ready to go as far as to endorse radical dissent.

Once the majority of liberal pacifists accepted the war effort, one way or another, there remained only a small minority who maintained a pacifist opposition to the war. But these liberal reformers not only condemned war according to the Christian ethic, they also extended that analysis to social and economic questions, with the result that their views became more socially radical as well as pacifist. This blending of pacifism with social radicalism signified an important transition in the Canadian pacifist tradition: the pacifist initiative had passed from the old coalition of progressive reformers to a developing realignment of committed pacifists with the socialist ideal. The actual shift of some social reformers into more radical ranks was well underway before 1914, but the debate over the war and such measures as conscription further heightened their radicalism as it reinforced a growing awareness that socialists and pacifists shared many common objectives.

One of the earliest expressions of this new pacifist ethic came from a small group of radical feminists. Largely centred in Toronto, they worked through the Women's Social Democratic League and the Toronto Suffrage Association until the summer of 1915 when Elsie Charlton, Alice Chown, and Laura Hughes founded the Canadian Women's Peace Party.[33] Laura Hughes grasped the idea that spring while attending the International Congress of Women at The Hague. Once she learned that women around the world were organizing peace parties she became determined that Canadian women should not lag behind. The conspicuous involvement of Laura Hughes and Alice Chown in wartime pacifism proved to be a matter of some embarrassment to their uncles, S.D. Chown, General Superintendent of the Methodist Church, and Colonel Sam Hughes, the Canadian Minister of Militia, but the two women remained undeterred.[34]

The Canadian Women's Peace Party, later re-christened the Women's International League for Peace and Freedom (WILPF), endorsed the program outlined at The Hague for building a new international order through compulsory arbitration, universal disarmament and a league of democratic nations.[35] Upon closer examination, however, it appeared to be a "stop the war" movement and Laura Hughes actually admitted as much privately although in public she was more discreet in order to avoid the charge of treason.[36] Generally, Hughes moved to an increasingly radical outlook. With the WILPF she directed her wrath at the military-capitalist complex behind the war effort and joined with labour-socialists in their attack on war profiteering by financial trusts and armament makers.

Alice Chown, another founding member, was also no newcomer to radical activities. Somewhat of a free spirit who usually appeared barefoot to emphasize her free will, Chown was active in furthering the cause of women's suffrage and women's trade unions.[37] By 1915 she turned her attention to the war, and, calling herself a "strenuous pacifist," she criticized all violent methods for settling disputes, whether they were strikes, anarchistic actions, or wars, as too costly and only partially successful. Instead she suggested non-violent action was the best alternative and "the only right path for a nation to follow."[38]

Arguing that Christ was a better psychologist than man, Chown proposed that Germany be conquered through a new conception of brotherhood which included, first of all, eliminating injustice and selfishness within Canadian society. Such public declarations as "to conquer your enemy is to love him" insured Chown a hostile reception in a country at war, resulting in public abuse and demands that she be confined in an asylum or a jail.[39] Undaunted, Chown continued to work towards "the brotherhood of nations" and the "abolition of special privileges for individuals and states." "But for the people around me," she recalled, "the most heroic thing that they could do was to throw themselves dis-interestedly into the war."[40] In a letter to her uncle, S.D. Chown, she explained how she had fought all through the war for a knowledge of facts, for justice to the enemy, and for the allies to refrain from acts of unrighteousness in Russia, while he and his associates in the Methodist Church hierarchy had allowed themselves to become "dupes" of the mil-itarists. "I kept my faith in the sermon on the mount," she exclaimed, "and you have put your faith in force and have acquiesced in the lies of the censored press."[41]

Alice Chown also feared the war would have a brutal effect upon Ca-nadian society in general. "I am positive," she wrote, "that the evils we go out to fight with violence we shall graft upon our own nation's life." She explained:

> Starting with hatred of our enemy's cruelty, we shall end by being cruel ourselves; detesting the subservience of the German people to their state, we shall become indifferent to the subservience of our own people to our state. We shall lose our free institutions, free speech, free press, free assemblage, and have to struggle to regain them.[42]

Despite the work of the Toronto based WIL, the centre of pacifist ac-tivity was in Winnipeg where notable reformers like J.S. Woodsworth, William Ivens, F.J. Dixon, A. Vernon Thomas, and Francis Marion Bey-non, some of whom were already known for their social radicalism, had begun to express radical pacifist sentiments as well. As early as the 1912 naval debate, for instance, Dixon had protested strenuously against what he called "creeping militarism" in Canada and during the war years he continued to air his pacifist views.[43] An independent member of the Manitoba legislature since 1914, Dixon was almost the only member of the House to speak out strongly against the war and its infringements on individual rights and freedoms.[44] In 1917 he withstood a movement to have him impeached and thereafter continued to voice anti-war sen-timents, and particularly to publicize the position of radical labour on the war.[45]

It was no coincidence, therefore, that Winnipeg labour leaders were the most active in organizing an anti-conscription campaign. Although sympathetic to pacifism, labour opposition to the war, like that of farmers, was primarily a reaction against conscription and was based more upon economic than pacifist considerations.[46] Outside of a few violent protests and some isolated cases of resistance by western radicals, for instance, Canadian workers and farmers enthusiastically supported the war effort.[47] Nevertheless, what opposition there was had a doctrinal dimension which found suitable expression in the socially radical pacifism Dixon represented. Winnipeg's labour paper, *The Voice*, aired the full views of Dixon and other pacifists throughout the war and, although rejecting the principle of non-violence, urged tolerance for Canadians conscientiously opposed to the war for either socialist or religious reasons.[48]

One of the casualties of the anti-war campaign was the Winnipeg journalist, A. Vernon Thomas. Thomas had been attracted to the *Free Press* from the *Manchester Guardian* and he became involved in Winnipeg reform circles soon after his arrival. His wife, Lillian Beynon, was a prominent Winnipeg reformer and suffragist, as was her sister, Francis Marion Beynon. All three were radical pacifists. For a journalist to express such views publicly was dangerous, however, and in 1916 Thomas was quickly fired from his job at the *Free Press* after he walked onto the floor of the legislature to congratulate F.J. Dixon on one of his anti-war speeches.[49] Shortly afterward the Thomases, bitterly disappointed, left the country and spent the duration of the war in New York.

Writing to Woodsworth from his self-imposed exile, Thomas confessed that the sacrifice in their "little attempt at freedom" seemed contemptible compared to the personal vigil of Woodsworth and other pacifists in Canada.[50] Although Thomas continued to contribute anti-war, anti-racist articles to *The Voice*, he often wondered if he could not make a greater protest. "I don't think the pacifist note of my articles can be mistaken," he wrote. "But it ends there and my position is simply that I am not extolling the war in my daily work, which is a great satisfaction."[51] On the other hand, Thomas maintained there would be plenty to do once the war was over and "immediate fear is removed from the hearts of the people." He looked forward to the day when he could return to Canada and join Woodsworth in the work of "absolutely challenging the present constitution of society and its ideals."[52]

Despite his attempt to remain optimistic about the post-war era, Thomas became depressed over the increasing toll the war was having upon Canadian society. The evil fruits of war, he warned, were growing every day:

> We cannot think the war out of existence. People are not what they were. Their minds have become militarized and we shall have to deal with people of that kind. The workers have not been spared. A good deal of the labor movement is now war. It is all a tragedy and we can only make the best of it.[53]

Thomas's sister-in-law, Francis Marion Beynon, stayed behind in Winnipeg for a time as the editor of the women's page of the *Grain Growers' Guide* and carried on the anti-war struggle. Social discontent was on the rise in wartime Winnipeg and Francis Beynon exemplifies the transition of pre-war liberal into radical. Like most liberals before 1914, Beynon subscribed to the usual anti-militarist, pacifist sentiments. But as Ramsay Cook has explained, the war raised serious questions about fundamental liberal intellectual assumptions, exposing a naive faith in moral progress.[54] Although she believed women had a greater interest in social and ethical questions than men, Beynon questioned the validity of feminist comments on the pacifist influence of women.[55] In a short time her growing skepticism seemed justified by the thorough involvement of women in various war activities and the intolerant, conformist attitude associated with patriotism. Consequently, Beynon accepted the diagnosis that there was something radically wrong with the whole social order that demanded correction.[56] Patriotism and nationalism merely defended the established order, she argued, while its intolerant, militaristic spirit was the same spirit that crucified Christ and continued to threaten those preaching His pacifist doctrine.[57]

357

The super-patriotic atmosphere of the country strengthened Beynon's individual resolve and her radical commitment to pacifism and social reconstruction. Initially, however, the popular association of dissent with subversion cautioned Beynon to restrain her pacifist sentiments in favour of safer demands like the conscription of wealth as well as men. But unlike those who associated this proposal with some form of graduated income tax, Beynon made it clear she favoured the actual "taking over by government of all real property."[58] As she became more outspoken she also echoed the familiar charge that the most fervent patriots were those getting rich from "seated labor and war profiteering."[59] Such regular anti-war statements and the whole radical tone of her column, she suspected, had aroused the wrath of the Press Censor and ultimately placed her at odds with her editor, George F. Chipman, who had moved towards support of conscription and Union government. Consequently, rather than restrain her pacifist and radical beliefs, Beynon resigned in the summer of 1917 and joined the Thomases in exile.[60]

Francis Beynon became convinced that the war was the result of capitalist, economic conflicts and a militant mentality and that it would create more problems than it would solve. Like other radical pacifists, for example, she feared that wartime mobilization was causing Canadian society to become increasingly insensitive to social injustice, as its treatment of enemy aliens testified.[61] The only way to solve world problems and prevent future military conflicts was through a social and intellectual revolution, the fear of which, she asserted, haunted Canadian capitalists by 1918.[62]

Before the war social reformers like Beynon had depended upon the theology of liberal Protestantism, but it now appeared the social gospel lacked the intellectual depth required to support a major movement of social and moral reconstruction.[63] What was necessary, according to socially conscious pacifists, was a synthesis of the ethical aspect of Christianity with a dynamic philosophy for radical change. A radicalized social gospel was partly an attempt in that direction.

Of the social gospel radicals, it was J.S. Woodsworth who most clearly represented the mixture of Christian pacifism and socialism.[64] Although Woodsworth ultimately became Canada's most famous pacifist, his pacifist convictions evolved slowly. It is not clear, for instance, if he was a confirmed pacifist before 1914. In fact, the first two years of the war were a time of confessed "heart searching" for Woodsworth but as he corresponded with numerous pacifists he became increasingly pacifist himself.[65] By June 1916, he was labelled a pacifist by the Manitoba press following an address to a young men's club in which he expressed doubt that moral issues could be settled by force, but it was not until conscription became the issue of the day that Woodsworth openly declared his pacifism.[66]

358   In a letter to the *Free Press* he condemned national registration as a prelude to conscription, a measure he could not conscientiously support.[67] As a result he was dismissed as director of the Bureau of Social Research and the agency itself, which supplied basic research for the social legislation of the three prairie governments, was closed.[68] For a time Woodsworth contemplated joining a Doukhobor community and even made active inquiries in that direction. The Doukhobors were sympathetic but wondered if he could really adapt to their ways.[69] Perhaps Woodsworth agreed, for he finally accepted a charge in Gibson's Landing, British Columbia. His outspoken pacifist views, however, proved to be no more welcome there than in Manitoba and the following year he was removed at the request of the congregation. In response and chagrined over Creighton's anti-pacifist editorial in the *Guardian*, Woodsworth resigned from the ministry entirely, citing the war policy of the Church and the issue of pacifism as his main reasons.[70] For the remainder of the war he worked as a longshoreman on the West Coast while his wife, Lucy, organized the Vancouver chapter of the Women's International League for Peace and Freedom.

Woodsworth's letter of resignation revealed a new socially radical pacifism — a synthesis of absolute Christian social ethics and the socialist critique. For instance, although he claimed war was the "inevitable outcome of the existing social organization with its undemocratic form of government and competitive system of industry," he emphasized that, above all, war was "absolutely irreconcilable" with the spirit and teachings of Jesus. "Christianity may be an impossible idealism," he declared, "but so long as I hold to it, ever so unworthily, I must refuse, as far as may be, to participate in or to influence others to participate in war."[71]

Woodsworth's brand of pacifism was also shared by William Ivens, another renegade in the Methodist Church. Although Ivens refrained from voicing pacifist views from the pulpit of Winnipeg's McDougall

Methodist Church, he felt free to express himself on the outside. Consequently, he contributed regular anti-war articles to *The Voice* and became involved in trade union activities. Ivens' actions split his congregation and by the spring of 1918 an urgent appeal was made to the Manitoba Stationing Committee for his removal. Rather than be intimidated, however, Ivens immediately embarked on a speaking tour of the prairies.[72] Vernon Thomas wrote Woodsworth that it was "greatly encouraging" to see a pacifist such as Ivens speak out publicly and he praised him for fighting a tremendous fight and "winning his way into the hearts of people."[73]

Despite numerous letters and petitions in his support, Ivens was finally removed from McDougall, and, rather than accept a different charge, he assumed the editorship of the *Western Labor News*, the official organ of the Winnipeg Trades and Labor Council.[74] His old friend Vernon Thomas was quick to wish him luck in the new undertaking which, unlike the Methodist Church, might allow him to interpret Christ in his own way — as a pacifist.[75] But Ivens was soon under attack again when the Chief Press Censor, Ernest Chambers, threatened to outlaw the paper unless Ivens purged the publication of revolutionary and pacifist articles.[76] The most visible example of Ivens' radicalism, however, was his labor church founded in July 1918, as a creedless church dedicated to the "establishment of justice and righteousness on earth, among all men and nations."[77] Woodsworth later commented that "the Labor Church was born during the war, as a protest against war."[78]

By 1917, amid mounting casualties at the front and the enactment of the Military Service Act at home, anti-war sentiment in Canada reached its peak. As a catalyst, conscription not only resulted in the Quebec crisis and farm and labour protests but it necessitated pacifist resistance as well. Both Woodsworth and Ivens had begun to publicize their pacifism in response to the conscription issue and it remained the central stimulus to pacifist protests throughout the balance of the war. In the first instance, conscription brought conscientious objection into the open in a new way and exposed objectors to a new degree of maltreatment. The torture of Jehovah's Witnesses at the Minto Street Barracks in Winnipeg was a sensational example of this and fueled the protest of pacifist spokesmen.[79] F.J. Dixon raised the matter in the Manitoba legislature and demanded an immediate investigation, arguing that "the day of torture should be past."[80] Likewise, Ivens led a public outcry over the death of a conscientious objector in Stoney Mountain Penitentiary. Ivens used the incident to reiterate the radical pacifist demand that individual conscience be given full and proper respect rather than the type of maltreatment that led to the death of the young Pentecostal pacifist. "It may be that his death was necessary," Ivens argued, "to convince the Government that there are Conscientious Objectors in the Dominion outside of Pacifist Churches and Organizations who are pre-

359

pared to die for their convictions rather than submit to perform military service."[81]

The young Canadians who conscientiously objected to military service were largely sectarian pacifists from the historic peace sects and the more recent pacifist groups like Jehovah's Witnesses. The majority of these religious pacifists, such as Mennonites and Hutterites, maintained an adamant isolation from war and society alike; nevertheless, their staunch resistance to compulsory military service reinforced the principle of conscientious objection and pacifist dissent in general within Canadian society.

The Society of Friends, on the other hand, had abandoned their old quietistic ways and had become an important part of the liberal reform movement. In effect, Quakers bridged the gap between traditional religious non-resistance and the liberal faith in social action. Accordingly, they attempted to maintain a program of pacifist activity, from assisting conscientious objectors to supporting war relief programs. It was the view of Friends that all pacifists should assume the role of reconcilers in the war and help suppress the feeling of bitterness and hatred intensified in society.[82]

Like other liberal pacifists during the war, Quakers also moved towards social radicalism. They began by examining the conditions that made for war and their own complicity in them. "Have we," Friends asked, "either as Christians or as responsible citizens of our respective countries, done all that we might or should to remove these conditions?"[83] Once they discovered the seeds of war sown within the established social order, the Quakers replaced their historic emphasis upon mercy in a static society with an increasingly radical commitment to change the social order.[84] Canadian Friends, for instance, began to endorse government control and possible ownership of all industries manufacturing war-related articles.[85] Furthermore, by the war's end they equated the causes of international war with those of the social struggle, something which was central to the new socially radical pacifism the war had bred.

J.S. Woodsworth was among the first to notice that Friends were "beginning to abandon their old rather negative and abstract position with regard to war and to attack the evils which are responsible for modern wars." Although expressing surprise to find Quakers advocating "scientific socialism," he was encouraged by their new line of thinking.[86] In 1919, for example, Friends warned that "the crime, the wickedness, the deceit, the hypocrisy that stood at the back of the conditions that produced the first war" remained, resulting in the post-war unrest which threatened to erupt in a violent social revolt, equal to the war in horror, unless there was a radical reconstruction of Canadian society. What was needed, they claimed, was a "revolution, not necessarily violent, and an edifice of new design" which would guarantee labour "shorter hours, more of the product it produces, larger opportunities, a different interpretation of justice."[87]

The Quakers and the other radical pacifists from feminist and social gospel ranks had moved a long way from the old progressive call for peace, order and stability. The war had changed that. It had confronted the liberal peace movement with an insurmountable challenge, resulting in its disruption and disintegration as the majority of its members deserted pacifism in favour of a new means to achieve their desired ends — a holy war. Even the few liberals who attempted to maintain a moderately realistic position were smothered in the process. Certainly, the ease and enthusiasm with which this reversal was made betrayed the rather ambiguous nature of pre-war pacifism.

But the death of the progressive peace movement early in the war was not the end of liberal pacifism in Canada. It would re-emerge in the post-war years among such groups as the League of Nations Society and, once again, attempt to ensure world peace without directly challenging the state. Amid the pressures of the escalating wartime crusade, however, liberal pacifism proved to be utterly untenable. Those who wished to maintain their pacifist protest found it necessary to adopt a radical critique of the social and economic roots of war and in doing so abandon their liberal reformism for some variant of the socialist creed. For some, that too became almost an eschatological warfare against the established social order, not entirely unlike their erstwhile colleagues who sought the reign of peace via the war to end war. Furthermore, just as the democratic socialist movement in the English-speaking world built upon and incorporated historic tenets of liberalism, so, too, the socially radical pacifism forged during the war retained a glimmer of its liberal past.

361

Although not fully articulated during the war, the new pacifist ethic would ultimately gain support in the post-war era and encourage a temporary alliance between a resurgent peace movement, democratic socialists, and elements of the far left. In 1919, however, socially radical pacifists failed to foresee a serious dilemma awaiting them beyond the horizon: their momentum towards radical reform and social change to secure peace and justice was on a long-term collision course with their pacifist rejection of the use of violence in any cause.

NOTES

[1] J.C. Hopkins, *The Canadian Annual Review* (1914), 132.
[2] Hopkins, *The Canadian Annual Review* (1914), 133.
[3] Hopkins, *The Canadian Annual Review* (1914), 135.
[4] Arthur G. Dorland, "Militarism in Canada," *The Canadian Friend* (July 1913), 14. Dorland was a history professor at the University of Western Ontario from 1920 to 1955.
[5] Peter Brock, *Twentieth-Century Pacifism* (Toronto, 1970), 10. See also Michael Howard, *War and the Liberal Conscience* (Rutgers, 1978).
[6] Those studies, by Richard Allen, J.M. Bliss, Ramsay Cook, Kenneth McNaught, Donald Page, and John H. Thompson, are cited below.
[7] *The Christian Guardian*, 19 August 1914, p. 5.
[8] *The Christian Guardian*, 26 August 1914, p. 5, and 16 September 1914.
[9] J.M. Bliss, "The Methodist Church and World War 1," *Canadian Historical Review* (September 1968), reprinted in *Conscription 1917*, ed. Carl Berger (Toronto, 1969), 42; Albert Marrin, *The Last Crusade: The Church of England in the First World War* (Durham, North Carolina, 1974), 124–25.

[10] *The Presbyterian Record*, June 1918.

[11] Bliss, "The Methodist Church and World War I," 57.

[12] John H. Thompson, "'The Beginning of Our Regeneration': The Great War and Western Canadian Reform Movements," Canadian Historical Association, *Historical Papers* (1972), 238–39.

[13] *The Christian Guardian*, 25 November 1914, p. 8.

[14] *The Christian Guardian*, 1 November 1916, p. 5.

[15] *The Christian Guardian*, 3 April 1918, p. 1.

[16] *The Christian Guardian*, 1 May 1918, p. 5.

[17] The Presbyterian press, for instance, published very closely worded statements. See *The Presbyterian Record*, October 1914, p. 433; June 1918, p. 161; *The Presbyterian*, 12 November 1914, p. 436. Strong support for the war was also voiced by the Anglicans and Baptists. See Colm Brannigan, "The Anglican Church in Canada and the Great War" (graduate seminar paper for Professor A. R. Allen, Department of History, McMaster University, 1978), and Steven R. Ramlochan, "The Baptists of Ontario and World War I, 1914–1918" (undergraduate paper for Professor C.M. Johnston, Department of History, McMaster University, 1973).

[18] Atkinson finally claimed the war was a crusade to save Christianity itself. J.E. Atkinson, "The Aftermath of the War," *Canadian Club of Toronto, 1915–1916* (Toronto, 1916), 60–61.

[19] C. Roland Marchand, *The American Peace Movement and Social Reform, 1898–1918* (Princeton, 1972), 19.

[20] *The Globe* (Toronto), 21 August 1914, p. 4.

[21] Hopkins, *Canadian Annual Review* (1914), 136.

[22] *Canadian Annual Review* (1915), 351.

[23] Henry James Morgan, ed., *The Canadian Men and Women of the Time* (Toronto, 1912), 833.

[24] Victoria University Archives (VUA), Lewis E. Horning Papers, Lewis E. Horning, "The New Citizenship" (unpublished manuscript).

[25] *Minutes of the Genesee Yearly Meeting of the Society of Friends in Canada*, 1915 (Toronto, 1915), 25.

[26] Horning, "The New Citizenship."

[27] United Church Achives (UCA), The Methodist Church of Canada, General Conference Office, General Correspondence, 1914, Box 3, file 59, Lewis E. Horning to T.A. Moore, 26 September 1914.

[28] UCA, General Correspondence, 1914, Horning to Moore, 26 September 1914.

[29] UCA, General Correspondence, 1914, Horning to Moore, 26 September 1914.

[30] UCA, General Correspondence, 1914, Horning to Moore, 26 September 1914.

[31] Sometimes they sponsored well-known pacifist speakers such as the British pacifist, Chrystal MacMillan. Hopkins, *Canadian Annual Review* (1915), 350.

[32] VUA, Horning Papers, Vault, 12E. W566TP.

[33] Saskatchewan Archives Board, Saskatoon (SAB), S.V. Haight, n.d.

[34] Colonel Hughes even attempted to bribe his niece in order to remove the disgrace. Donald Page, "Canadians and the League of Nations before the Manchurian Crisis" (Ph.D. thesis, University of Toronto, 1972), 30.

[35] Page, "Canadians and the League of Nations," 30.

[36] Page, "Canadians and the League of Nations," 31.

[37] Alice Chown, *The Stairway* (Boston, 1921), 81, 103, 126. Chown's philosophy was heavily influenced by theosophy. See Michèle Lacombe, "Theosophy and the Canadian Idealist Tradition: A Preliminary Exploration," *Journal of Canadian Studies* 17 (Summer 1982): 100–118.

[38] Chown, *The Stairway*, 294.

[39] Chown, *The Stairway*, 260, 263.

[40] Chown, *The Stairway*, 296.

[41] UCA, S.D. Chown Papers, Box 10, file 214, Alice Chown to S.D. Chown, 17 December 1918.

[42] Chown, *The Stairway*, 261.

[43] Roy St. George Stubbs, *Prairie Portraits* (Toronto, 1965), 99.

[44] *Manitoba Free Press*, 19 January 1917, p. 1.

[45] *Manitoba Free Press*, 19 January 1917, p. 2; David J. Bercuson, *Confrontation at Winnipeg* (Montreal, 1974), 42.

[46] A. Ross McCormack, *Reformers, Rebels, and Revolutionaries: The Western Canadian Radical Movement, 1899–1919* (Toronto, 1977), 129.

[47] McCormack, *Reformers, Rebels, and Revolutionaries*, 158; John H. Thompson, *The Harvest of War: The Prairie West, 1914–1918* (Toronto, 1978), 117.

[48] *The Voice*, 10 November 1916, p. 1; 19 January 1917, p. 13; 13 July 1917, p. 5; *Western Labor News*, 9 August 1918, p. 5. One pacifist later praised *The Voice* for its priceless wartime service of providing an open forum for the "bludgeoned minority," *Western Labor News*, 9 August 1918, p. 5.

[49] *Western Labour News*, 9 August 1918, p. 5; Ramsay Cook, "Francis Marion Beynon and the Crisis of Christian Reformism" *The West and the Nation: Essays in Honour of W.L. Morton*, ed. Carl Berger and Ramsay Cook (Toronto, 1976), 190–98.

[50] Public Archives of Canada (PAC), J.S. Woodsworth Papers, Manuscript Group 27, Correspondence v. 2, A.V. Thomas to J.S. Woodsworth, 18 June 1918.

[51] PAC, J.S. Woodsworth Papers, MG 27, Corr. v. 2, Thomas to Woodsworth, 18 June 1918.

[52] PAC, J.S. Woodsworth Papers, MG 27, Corr. v. 2, Thomas to Woodsworth, 24 April 1918.

[53] PAC, J.S. Woodsworth Papers, MG 27, Corr. v. 2, Thomas to Woodsworth, 16 January 1919.

[54] Cook, "Francis Marion Beynon," 197–99.

[55] *Grain Growers' Guide*, 24 November 1915, p. 10.

[56] *Grain Growers' Guide*, 3 March 1915, p. 10.

[57] *Grain Growers' Guide*, 7 March 1917, p. 10.

[58] *Grain Growers' Guide*, 2 July 1917, p. 9.

[59] *Grain Growers' Guide*, 13 June 1917, p. 10

[60] *Grain Growers' Guide*, 27 June 1917, p. 10; Cook, "Francis Marion Beynon," 200.

[61] For Beynon's reaction to the treatment of enemy aliens see: *Grain Growers' Guide*, 6 June 1917, p. 9.

[62] *Western Labor News*, 29 November 1918, p. 2.

[63] Cook, "Francis Marion Beynon," 203.

[64] I am in agreement with Kenneth McNaught, *A Prophet in Politics: A Biography of J.S. Woodsworth* (Toronto, 1959), 67.

[65] J.S. Woodsworth, "My Convictions About War," *Vox* (December 1939), 5.

[66] McNaught, *A Prophet in Politics*, 75.

[67] *Manitoba Free Press*, 28 December 1916, p. 5.

[68] I support Allen's assertion that Woodsworth's dismissal was due to his pacifism rather than to his social and economic radicalism. His pacifism represented an "unknown potential," especially since there was talk in labour circles of passive resistance to the registration scheme. See Richard Allen, *The Social Passion: Religion and Social Reform in Canada, 1914–28* (Toronto, 1973), 47–48.

[69] I am indebted to Richard Allen for this information.

[70] J.S. Woodsworth, *Following the Gleam* (Ottawa, 1926), 9.

[71] Woodsworth, *Following the Gleam*, 9.

[72] Allen, *The Social Passion*, 51.

[73] PAC, Woodsworth Papers, Correspondence, v. 2, A.V. Thomas to J.S. Woodsworth, 24 April 1918; 18 June 1918.

[74] Allen, *The Social Passion*, 53; McCormack, *Reformers, Rebels, and Revolutionaries*, 153.

[75] *Western Labor News*, 9 August 1918, p. 5.

[76] McCormack, *Reformers, Rebels, and Revolutionaries*, 153.

[77] J.S. Woodsworth, *The First Story of the Labor Church* (Winnipeg, 1920), 7–8.

[78] Woodsworth, *The First Story*, 12–13.

[79] *The Voice*, 15 January 1918, p. 1. M. James Penton's *Jehovah's Witnesses in Canada* (Toronto, 1976) also provides a detailed account of the incident.

[80] *Winnipeg Evening Tribune*, 24 January 1918, p. 1; PAC, Department of National Defence, Record Group 24, Vol. 2028, HQ 1064-30-67, T.A. Crerar to Major-General S.C. Mewburn, 28 January 1918.

[81] PAC, Sir Robert Borden Papers, RLB 2309, William Ivens to T. A. Crerar, 25 February 1918; *The Voice*, 1 March 1918, p. 1.

[82] *Minutes of the Genesee Yearly Meeting of Friends, 1915*, 24, 33.

[83] *Minutes of the Genesee Yearly Meeting of Friends, 1915*, 41.

[84] Charles Chatfield, *For Peace and Justice: Pacifism in America, 1914–1941* (Knoxville, 1971), 54.

[85] *Minutes of the Genesee Yearly Meeting of Friends, 1915*, 33.

[86] *Western Labor News*, 5 September 1919, p. 6.

[87] *Minutes of the Genesee Yearly Meeting of Friends, 1919*, 21.

363

Topic Ten

Post-War Unrest

Labour quickly became unhappy with post-war conditions. Workers believed that they had made greater sacrifices than their employers during the war years, and they now awaited their just reward. With their expectations unfulfilled, they turned to radical action.

Western workers were particularly militant and dissatisfied. High unemployment and inflation, together with a tradition of radicalism, made the West the most likely Canadian region for unrest. In 1919, Winnipeg, the largest and most economically advanced of the western cities, became the focal point of western labour strife. David Bercuson explains the historical context, the events, and the significance of 1919 in "The Winnipeg General Strike."

Western farmers joined labour in revolt. The farmers' protest had a history that dated back to the time of the region's inclusion in the Canadian Confederation. The western farmers hated the high-tariff National Policy of 1879, which, they argued, favoured eastern manufacturers and industrialists. In an effort to fight back, they had formed co-operatives, which became effective economic organizations as well as powerful political bodies. In the early 1920s western dissatisfaction emerged not only as a full-scale political protest movement, but as a powerful third party, known as the Progressives. From the beginning, however, this movement/party faced innumerable problems, including serious internal dissension between two leading factions. Walter Young discusses the tensions that emerged, and the lessons to be learned from them, in "The Progressives."

The Maritimes also had a history of protest since Confederation. The post-war years proved a particularly disquieting period, as Maritimers re-examined their position in Confederation and compared their region's slow rate of growth to that of central Canada and the West. Their complaints, like those of the western farmers, centred on the prevailing system of freight rates. In "The Origins of the Maritime Rights Movement," E.R. Forbes analyses the motives of the different groups that participated in this effective protest group.

Labour radicalism in the West can be examined further in D.J. Bercuson's *Confrontation at Winnipeg: Labour, Industrial Relations and the General Strike* (Montreal: McGill-Queen's University Press, 1974) and *Fools and Wise Men: The Rise and Fall of the One Big Union* (Toronto: McGraw-Hill Ryerson, 1978), as well as in A.R. McCormack's *Reformers, Rebels, and Revolutionaries: The Western Canadian Radical Movement: 1899–1919* (Toronto: University of Toronto Press, 1977). Kenneth McNaught and David J. Bercuson's *The Winnipeg General Strike: 1919* (Don Mills, Ontario: Longman Canada, 1974) is a popular study of the incident. For an overview of the western Canadian working class see "Capital and Labour, 1900–1940: Cities, Resource Towns, and Frontier Camps," in Gerald Friesen, *The Canadian Prairies: A History* (Toronto: University of Toronto Press, 1984), 274–300.

W.L. Morton's *The Progressive Party in Canada* (Toronto: University of Toronto Press, 1950) remains the definitive study of the farmers' protest movement. For background leading up to the rise of the Progressive party see Morton's "The Western Progressive Movement, 1919–1921," Canadian Historical Association, *Report* (1946), 41–55. The link between the Progressive movement and the social gospel movement is shown in R. Allen's "The Social Gospel as the Religion of the Agrarian Revolt," in *The West and the Nation: Essays in Honour of W.L. Morton*, ed. C. Berger and R. Cook (Toronto: McClelland and Stewart, 1976), 174–86.

365

A more comprehensive treatment of the post-war protest in the Maritimes can be found in E.R. Forbes' *The Maritime Rights Movement, 1919–27* (Montreal: McGill-Queen's University Press, 1979). Students will find the essays on the Maritimes in *Canada and the Burden of Unity*, ed. D. Bercuson (Toronto: Macmillan, 1977) of value in placing the Maritime Rights movement in a broader perspective.

The Winnipeg General Strike*

DAVID BERCUSON

General strikes are cataclysmic events; they are, by their nature, unlikely to be created in a day. The first moments of a general strike take place against a background of many years of bitter relationships, class polarization, frustrated ambitions, and real or imagined oppression. The Winnipeg General Strike of May and June 1919 fits snugly into this well-established pattern because its taproots may be found growing into the very bedrock of Winnipeg's development as a booming modern industrial centre. The attitudes and conditions that created the general strike were an integral part of the Winnipeg scene almost from its beginnings, although they were compounded by the effects of the Great War. Winnipeg was ripe for a general strike in the spring of 1919 because the division of the city into two separate and increasingly hostile camps had started so long before and had reached a point of no return.

*From *On Strike: Six Key Labour Struggles in Canada, 1919–1949*, ed. I. Abella. Copyright 1974 by James Lorimer and Company. Reprinted by permission.

Winnipeg was destined to be a boom town, the new Chicago of North America. The analogy was to be used many times to describe the future of the city, particularly after civic leaders had succeeded in capturing the Canadian Pacific Railway route from the town of Selkirk in the early 1880s. Over the course of the next forty years, Winnipeg endured several periods of boom and bust, liberally watered by speculation dollars. This atmosphere of expected prosperity but realized chaos acted on the serious-minded men who had come to Manitoba to make their fortunes, and prompted them to assume leadership of the community, not only in business matters but in politics as well. They believed in the great future of their city but became convinced that it could only be realized if certain conditions prevailed: a rational and efficient city administration, a beneficent climate in which business could grow and prosper, and the absence of any factor which could, if allowed to develop unchecked, disrupt the peace and prosperity of the business community. Unions fell within this last category.

366

Business in Winnipeg was anti-union from the beginning, but this was no different from the situation in other cities. What did make Winnipeg different was both the extent to which the business community ran the city — assuring the political powerlessness of the working class — and certain economic factors that affected Winnipeg to a greater extent than other cities. Winnipeg had the potential to become a great manufacturing and marketing centre, especially after all three Canadian transcontinental railroads established their repair shops, marshalling yards, and roundhouses in and around the city, but it was distant from its sources of supply and its industrial markets. As long as the business community was content to allow Winnipeg to remain a trans-shipment point and distribution centre for the thousands of new prairie farmers who began to flood the plains after 1895, Winnipeg was not at any disadvantage. When they raised their sights to larger markets, however, they felt the pressures of higher transportation costs. When they began to think in terms of manufacturing for a national and even international market, they had to consider the price of bringing the raw materials in and shipping the finished goods out. To balance these higher costs they would try to keep other costs as low as possible, and this invariably affected wages.

There was yet another factor behind the long history of intransigent anti-unionism that developed early in Winnipeg's history: the myth of the self-made man.[1] Many of Winnipeg's political and industrial leaders were men of poor or humble origins who had made their way west to find their fortunes. They believed that they were destined to lead, having demonstrated their superior abilities by their rise through the social strata. Social Darwinism was a strong religion, diligently and consistently worshipped by many of the *nouveaux riches*, who were not yet confident or secure in their new-found wealth and station. These individualists scorned those whom they considered weaker than themselves — the men who were forced to resort to combination and organization to protect their jobs and living standards. Here workers and their unions stood indicted.

Trade unions did not play a passive role in this situation. Unions began to develop early in Winnipeg and grew quickly in the years prior to World War I. These organizations were led by strong-willed, tough-minded men, many of whom were immigrants from the industrial heartland of the British Isles and who had received their training in hard-knock schools such as Birmingham, Leeds, the Clydeside or the black mines of Wales.[2] They were fervent believers in the necessity of trade-union organization and many were followers of one socialist school or another, self-educated in the intricacies of Marxian analysis and rhetoric. These men were never timid in their assertion of labour's rights and challenged the power and prerogatives of management at every opportunity. Each victory confirmed them in their belief that theirs was the correct path; each defeat convinced them that society itself would have to be changed before the worker would ever receive his due.

367

Patterns of political and social separation developed early and were aggravated by physical separation. As new immigrants began to pour into Winnipeg they tended to settle in certain districts, usually together, seeking the security that new arrivals in a strange land crave. For the most part they gravitated to the area immediately north of the CPR main-line — the "north end."[3] This became Winnipeg's version of "the wrong side of the tracks," which it was in fact, clearly marked off from the new areas being opened up by Winnipeg's wealthier citizens. The rich and the aspiring to be rich settled along the river banks to the south, in locales such as River Heights and Wellington Crescent,[4] where they built magnificent mansions with long, broad driveways, well-manicured lawns and large stables or garages. The "south end" became as strongly symbolic in its own right of a bastion of privilege as the "north end" was of the home of the worker and the immigrant.

The results were almost predictable — Winnipeg was wracked by bitter strikes from the turn of the century, many involving the use of strike-breakers, court injunctions, and even the armed militia on one occasion.[5] In most instances the issues were the same, the demand of workers that their unions be recognized and collective agreements entered into, and the absolute refusal of employers to allow unions in their plants or stores. The class polarization inherent in the city was heightened by these strikes because in most cases the very existence of the unions was at stake and courts and governments invariably sided with the employers. During the last boom period before World War I, some of the bitterness was dissipated as men with skills were able to wrench higher wages and better working conditions from their employers, but it never disappeared entirely because the basic attitudes creating it remained unchanged. By

1919, in addition to those attitudes, there was a history of bitterness, hatred, and mistrust, and a martyrology to support it.

In August 1914 Canada entered the first large-scale war of her history ill-prepared for the hardships and trials that would test the national mettle in the next four years and three months. The effort involved in raising and equipping an army of over half a million men would have been monumental enough, but it was compounded by Canada's role as a breadbasket and arsenal for the allies. Within a short time the national economy began to suffer from manpower shortages, rapid cost-of-living increases, imbalances of supply and production, and the machinations of unscrupulous men who tried to reap large and undeserved profits from munitions and war-supply contracts. Given these conditions, it is not surprising that labour–management relations began to break down on a national scale after 1917 and that deterioration greatly affected areas such as Winnipeg, where conditions were already ripe for industrial strife.

368 Inflation was, without doubt, the single most important factor causing industrial strife in the war and immediate postwar period. Though few reliable statistics are available to give an exact measurement of the increasing cost of living during the war, it is safe to estimate, on the basis of what data was collected by the federal Department of Labour and published monthly in *Labour Gazette*, that it increased from fifty to seventy-five per cent between 1914 and 1918–19.[6] Increased demands for all manner of manufactured and semi-manufactured commodities, as well as foodstuffs and raw materials, drove prices skyward. This was coupled with shortages of skilled manpower and, consequently, higher wages in certain industries, which furthered the inflationary trend. The net result was that tens of thousands of Canadians who were not in any position to earn substantial wage increases saw their already low standards of living further decline. The only worker groups able to stay ahead of the rising cost of living, and then only barely, were those in great demand for war industries and munitions production — machinists, tool and die makers, shipyard workers. The majority of workers in Winnipeg, however, did not fit into this category.

One group of workers in the city that was able to keep ahead of the rising cost of living was, at the same time, the most radical — the railway machinists. The machinists were in great demand throughout the war both in the maintenance and repair of railway equipment and in the manufacture of shells. They were irked, however, by a constant failure to organize their colleagues in the other machine shops and considered that the long hours of work and low wage scales in those shops posed a dangerous example for other metal workers in the city. They were frustrated also by the knowledge that their unions were strong enough to face Canada's powerful transcontinental railways across the bargaining table, but were still thwarted locally by the owners of three small contract shops which together employed fewer than five hundred men.[7]

In early 1917 the government of Prime Minister Robert Borden decided that conscription should be instituted to meet Canada's moral commitments to total support of the allied war effort. Labour leaders in western Canada were almost unanimous in their intense and unwavering opposition to this measure and led the forces inside the Trades and Labour Congress of Canada advocating a national general strike against compulsory military service.[8] In the end, they could not garner adequate support and the idea of a strike was shelved, but the bitter anti-government feelings created by the campaign prompted many union men to decide that the government, rather than employers, was their greatest enemy. This, in turn, strengthened the influence of those labour leaders who were affiliated to one or another of the many socialist parties flourishing in the West at that time and resulted in a general shift to the left throughout the Prairies. The two main centres of this radical shift were Vancouver and Winnipeg.

War created labour shortages in hundreds of industries. Tens of thousands of skilled Canadians volunteered their services to the armed forces at the same time as the new war industries were exerting greater demands for manpower. Conditions for trade-union growth were better than they had been in many years and labour leaders were not slow to take advantage of them. In 1917 and 1918, vast organizing drives were launched throughout the country in almost every conceivable industry, and many new workers were brought into the fold. Even areas hitherto considered sacrosanct were entered: policemen, firemen, civic employees, and provincial government employees, among others, became union members.[9] This growth process was bound to create industrial tensions as a byproduct.

In the days before the closed or union shop, automatic checkoff, labour-relations boards, and certification votes, union organizing could be a hazardous business. In fact, union membership itself was sometimes hardly any safer. Unions were forced to battle tremendous odds, often including the forces of government and the judiciary, to sign members and thus had to demonstrate to prospective adherents the great advantages of affiliation. This could only be done by winning significant improvements in wage rates and working conditions, by demonstrating that the union was respected by employers and governments and by assuring prospective members that the union could protect them against arbitrary and unjust actions of management. This meant, in turn, that as the organizing campaign wore on, union leaders demanded more and were unwilling to settle for less — a situation creating militancy. When these unions confronted employers who were determined that workers and unions should not benefit from the labour situation created by the war, an irresistible force had met its immovable object.

Winnipeg was the scene of several such meetings in 1917. Three times in the year employers defeated strikes by applying for and receiving *ex*

369

parte injunctions against picketing. In each case packinghouse workers, store clerks, and contract-shop employees were unable to continue their respective strikes and suffered defeat.[10] The effect upon industrial relations in the city was traumatic; workers were forced to realize that very little had changed since the original use of injunctions in the city in 1906. All their organizing could come to naught if employers still had the ability to defeat recognition strikes by getting anti-picketing court orders and then bringing in scab labour. Labour leaders were forced to conclude that unions would have to band together and pool their resources if they hoped to force intransigent employers to the bargaining table. The formation of the Metal Trades Council in the spring of the following year was at least one result of the 1917 experiences.

In April 1918, three unions of civic employees struck for a new and higher wage schedule after having been offered a war bonus by city authorities. Almost immediately the straight dollars-and-cents issue was

370

obscured by the question, posed by the *Free Press* and echoed by business leaders, of whether civic employees should have any right to strike. The atmosphere became further charged when sister unions rushed to the defence of the strikers and began to discuss the possibility of a sympathetic walkout of all civic workers. Even city firemen were in a fighting mood and issued an ultimatum threatening to strike unless their own pay demands were quickly met.

The city council reacted by appointing a committee of six, including the mayor and two Labour aldermen, to negotiate with the striking unions. The two sides settled down to serious bargaining and within a few days hammered out the rudiments of a settlement. On Monday, May 13, they presented the terms of the agreement to a full meeting of city council but were stunned when the council, led by Alderman F.O. Fowler, amended their proposal and added a proviso that all civic employees undertake to pledge that they would not strike at all in future but would have their grievances settled by arbitration. In effect this "Fowler Amendment," named after its sponsor, put the city council on record as opposing any right to strike for civic employees.

The new measure did not come out of the clear blue sky. It was clearly an accurate reflection of a new mood of toughness in business and city government circles and was strongly supported by the *Free Press* and the Winnipeg Board of Trade. It was a naked challenge to the Winnipeg Trades and Labour Council and was accepted as such. At this point, after the successful organizing drives and the frustrating strikes of 1917, labour was not about to turn from a fight on so fundamental an issue. The effects of the amendment were immediate and electrifying.

On Tuesday morning, May 14, city firemen walked off their jobs. Within the next ten days ten other unions joined the strike as the city government, supported by volunteer help supplied by the Board of Trade, attempted to continue the operation of civic services. By Friday, May

24, thirteen trades, totalling about seven thousand workers in government and industry, had met Fowler's challenge. Fire, water, light and power, public transportation, telephone service, and railway maintenance were directly and drastically affected and there was every sign that the movement would continue to grow.

At this point the city government had become virtually paralyzed by indecision and passed responsibility for negotiations to a new, private body, formed for the purpose of helping to maintain essential services and bring about a settlement with the unions — the Citizens' Committee of One Hundred. On May 19 the first meeting between this group and the strikers took place and negotiations continued for the next few days. The two parties eventually succeeded in working out an agreement on almost all major points and were helped to the final solution by the intervention of Senator Gideon Robertson, newly appointed to the upper House and, at the time, special assistant to the federal minister of Labour, who travelled to Winnipeg at the behest of Prime Minister Robert Borden. *371* The agreement was essentially the same one that had been presented to the city council on May 13 but this time it was accepted by that council, largely because of Robertson's prodding. On Friday evening, May 24, the settlement was agreed to and the strike was over. The workers' victory was almost complete.[11]

The 1918 general strike strengthened the hand of the radicals in the city and pushed the labour movement further left. Labour leaders concluded that the combined power of the unions acting together was irresistible and was responsible for the crushing defeat inflicted upon the city government. Almost every commentator underlined the plain fact that the original striking unions would surely have been defeated if they had not been supported by the rest of the city's labour movement.[12] When this was contrasted, publicly and privately, with the events of the previous year, the lesson appeared to be obvious — individual unions could not face tough employers supported by governments and/or the courts, but a combination of unions could and had defeated an enemy just as powerful. From this point on labour men began to think of the general strike as a necessary adjunct to individual strikes, to be used when those individual strikes failed or showed signs of failure.

One concrete result of the metal workers' defeat in 1917 had been the creation of the Metal Trades Council. The reasoning was simple — since individual unions had no chance of defeating the contract-shop employers or forcing them to the bargaining table, perhaps a combination of unions could. A Metal Trades Council would bargain for all those workers in the plant and would, if necessary, have the authority to call all those workers out on strike. This was not industrial unionism, although many of the supporters of the Metal Trades Council clearly believed in industrial unionism as opposed to craft organization; it was, rather, modelled on the type of bargaining conducted by railway-shop craft workers in the United States and metal workers in other Canadian cities, such as Vancouver and Victoria shipyard workers.

In July of 1918 the Metal Trades Council struck the contract shops after failing to receive recognition following a long and apparently fruitless mediation procedure involving the federal government and a royal commission. The Winnipeg Trades and Labour Council threatened a general strike to support the contract-shop employees but did not act. By the end of September the strike had petered out and the workers had suffered yet another defeat. R.B. Russell bluntly attributed the failure to the fact that the rest of the city's workers did not back the Metal Trades Council adequately in its fight.[13]

The lesson of 1918 was now clearer than ever. Not only was it increasingly difficult for individual unions to win fights against intransigent employers; it was growing harder for combinations of unions in a single industry — such as the Metal Trades Council — to achieve victory. The civic workers, on the other hand, had achieved one of the most clear-cut victories in many years and only because they were promptly and adequately supported by workers in *every* industry. Where the workers had not been radical enough they had lost; where they had been, they had won. This finalized the trend towards the use of general strikes in industrial disputes and made the general strike in the spring of 1919 necessary in the eyes of many labour leaders in the city, radical or otherwise. The experiences of 1918 convinced them that a general strike was just like any other kind of strike, only larger, and that it enabled labour to bring its full power to bear in circumstances where that power was necessary. The Trades and Labour Council capped this process in December 1918 when it passed a motion giving itself the power to call out every union member in the city if a motion for a general strike was approved by a simple majority of all Winnipeg's union members.[14]

By the end of the war, labour leaders in the city were ready to reach for new objectives and were prepared to utilize new tactics in the effort. At the same time, the arrival of peace released the pent-up hope of many thousands of Canadians that the great sacrifices of the war would not have been in vain and that a new, more just, more equitable society would be fashioned out of the ruins of war. Men and women all over the country had worked ceaselessly to assure the victory while sixty thousand men, approximately one out of every ten Canadians in uniform, would never return. When it became increasingly apparent that there would be precious little forward movement and that the government's reconstruction efforts would, for the most part, be confined to dismantling the regulatory and managerial agencies established during the war, those who sought change grew more vociferous in their opposition to the status quo. By the end of 1918 the winds of change were already sweeping the rest of the world. Revolutions in Russia and Germany appeared to confirm that those who called for rapid social change were not isolated but, on the contrary, were the heralds of a great, globe-spanning move towards true reconstruction.

Western Canadian workers had always felt that their situation was somewhat different from that of their fellow labourers in central Canada and in the populous regions of the United States. They were numerically weaker, were, for the most part, engaged in extractive, resource industries, and were physically isolated from each other in small population centres scattered over the Prairies, in the British Columbia interior, and on the Pacific Coast. These conditions, combined with the ideological leadership provided by former American progressives and British socialists who moved to Canada during the periods of great immigration, prompted western workers to call for trade-union participation in politics, organization of the tens of thousands of unorganized workers in extractive and mass industries all over the country, and establishment of industrial unions which would group workers together on an industrial rather than a craft basis.[15] All these ambitions were in direct conflict with the ideological foundations of North American trade unionism, which was guided in thought and action by the principles of the founder of the American Federation of Labor, Samuel Gompers.

373

Gompers and his supporters believed that trade unions should not enter directly into politics, but should throw their support to the candidates or parties that favoured pro-labour principles. In addition, Gompers firmly believed in the necessity of keeping the labour movement relatively small and confined to the highly skilled, who had the best chance of wringing concessions from employers. Thus the principles of the AFL and its Canadian affiliate, the Trades and Labour Congress of Canada, contrasted sharply with the ideas held by western Canadian labour leaders, ideas which they believed had to be acted upon if the labour movement in the West was to survive.

These traditional points of contention had caused sharp disagreements in the TLC before the war — the numerically inferior West was almost always defeated. But three major inter-union squabbles during the war widened the gap between East and West and laid the groundwork for a western assault on the eastern bastions at the 1918 TLC convention. In the fight against conscription, westerners had been much more vociferous in their opposition and many believed they were being sold out by the congress's predominantly eastern leadership. This crisis in 1917 opened the first breach. The negotiations between Canada's railway-shop craft workers and the major Canadian railroads in 1918 made it almost permanent.

By the summer of 1918 negotiation procedures for railway-shop craft workers in Canada had been radically altered. The unions had joined in a loose bargaining federation known as Division 4 while management was combined into the Canadian Railway War Board. These two bodies met for the first time in late April 1918 to work out one contract to

cover over fifty thousand railway workers. The unions demanded substantial wage increases, pointing to the greatly increased cost of living
as justification, and threatened to pull every railway maintenance worker
in Canada off the job if their demands were not met. Since this would
eventually paralyze all national transportation, the government took a
hand in the bargaining and prompted the railway managers to offer wage
parity with American shop craft workers.

The move created a split in union ranks. Eastern labour leaders, heavily
supported by the leadership of the AFL and the head offices of the shop
craft unions in the United States, pressed for acceptance. They had no
intention of forcing or risking a nation-wide rail strike against the opposition of the employers and the government, which was threatening
to draft all railway maintenance workers and work them at military pay
rates should they walk out. Western union leaders were disgusted at this
attitude and, when they realized they could not prevail, called their negotiators home.[16] There was both anger and consternation directed not
only at the government, but against the leadership of the international
unions and their central Canadian supporters.

The third East–West split took place during Canada's first national
postal strike in August. Once again eastern union leaders were prepared
to order their men to accept compromise arrangements while westerners
dissented. This time, however, the westerners continued their strike after
the eastern postal employees returned to work; they were not only able
to wrench more concessions from the government, but also secured pay
for the time they had been on strike.[17] Another Canadian union had
split geographically because the westerners were more daring and perhaps
more radical than the easterners.

Thus the stage was set for the September 1918 convention of the TLC
in Quebec City. Westerners were sorely outnumbered but went ahead
to present several resolutions demanding a reorganization of the TLC
as an industrial congress, and the removal of civil-liberties restrictions
imposed during the war — the release of political prisoners and the ending of government-imposed censorship. Each time they were defeated
both on the floor of the convention and in committee rooms; when they
appealed committee rulings they were defeated again. Recorded votes
were called and they were defeated yet again; the eastern establishment
controlled the steamroller and the westerners were flattened. To add insult to injury, the president of the TLC, James Watters, a westerner,
was defeated in his bid for re-election by Tom Moore, a conservative
and a friend and admirer of Samuel Gompers, in one of the very few
contested presidential elections yet held by the congress. The West's defeat was total.[18]

The TLC convention was absolute proof that wars and industrial strife
might come and go but things would never change for westerners within
the congress. If their demands were to be satisfied, extraordinary meas-

ures would have to be taken. With this in mind several western delegates met in caucus at Quebec City and decided to hold a meeting of all western representatives prior to the next TLC convention to plan strategy and decide on a unified program. This was the objective of the man responsible for calling the meeting, Dave Rees, a United Mine Workers official from British Columbia and a TLC vice-president, but it was not shared by all.

The Socialist Party of Canada was a small, closely knit organization that proclaimed itself to be the only ideologically pure guardian of Marxist theory in Canada. Its members were dedicated, hard-working, and had met rather exacting standards before they were admitted to membership. The party was the most uncompromising of a plethora of socialist parties that had grown up in the West since before the turn of the century and it frequently ran candidates against other left-wing and labour political groups. Ordinarily it might not have achieved any significant influence in labour affairs but for the radical temper of the postwar period and the adherence of some of the best-known trade unionists in western Canada, including R.B. Russell, R.J. Johns, Victor Midgley, and W.A. Pritchard.

375

SPC members were determined to seize the opportunity that now presented itself to build a new labour centre in Canada. Ostensibly they were interested in fulfilling the desires of western workers for industrial unionism and more intensified political action. These men had no intention of allowing the conference of western labour representatives to move in the direction Rees wished it to go, but prepared, instead, to begin a secessionist movement from the TLC and the AFL. They pressed for and were successful in securing a meeting not directly prior to the 1919 TLC convention, but in the very early spring in Calgary.

The Western Labour Conference opened in the foothills city on March 16, 1919. Rees reiterated his desire to forge a united policy for presentation to the next TLC convention, but at this point there was little possibility of the meeting following his suggestions. The British Columbia Federation of Labour, meeting the previous three days in the same city, had just opted for a program of unmitigated radicalism. Over some objections from moderate delegates, the federation had supported the idea of a new secessionist movement, attacked the federal government for allowing censorship and imprisonment of political dissenters to continue and sent greetings to the Bolshevik government in Moscow.

From the very beginning of the western conference, then, the moderates were outmanoeuvered. The meeting declared itself in favour of a nation-wide vote of all TLC-affiliated unionists on the question of secession and adherence to a new organization to be laid out along "industrial" lines. The policy committee, headed by Winnipeger R.J. Johns, suggested that the new body be called the One Big Union and that a five-man committee be elected to popularize the OBU, raise funds and organize the referendum. These men were subsequently chosen, along with provincial executives, to act in conjunction with the new Central Committee.

The referendum decided upon was not to be a simple poll of all union members in Canada, since the ballots were to be divided between those from east of Port Arthur and those from the West. In addition, the question was to be decided by a majority vote of those organizations considered to be vital trades — transportation, metal trades, mining, etc. Locals of other trades were also to be polled with those members not voting to be counted in the affirmative. A second vote was to be taken in conjunction with the referendum to determine if Canadian workers favoured a nation-wide general strike on June 1 to institute the thirty-hour week.[19]

The Western Labour Conference did not actually launch the One Big Union; it was a declaration of intent to do so. But it reflected the mood of militancy that had been growing in the West for some time. Resolutions sending greetings to the new Soviet government in Russia, demanding Allied withdrawal from the Soviet Union, and an end to government restrictions on civil liberties were only the outward manifestations of the new radicalism. The significant part of the three-day meeting was the delegates' decision to take secessionist action.

376

The One Big Union did not officially come into existence until the first week of June, when its founding convention was held in Calgary. By that time the Winnipeg strike was already over two weeks old and not a single member of the Winnipeg Trades and Labour Council was able to attend.[20] Nevertheless, the announced intention to found a radical Marxist labour union, industrial or syndicalist in nature and sympathetic to the aims and aspirations of the Bolsheviks, provided the enemies of the strike with a focal point for their deepest fears. Governments and employers asserted that the OBU was behind the strike, that the strike was a test of OBU tactics and that its defeat would prove to be a knockout blow against the One Big Union. In fact there was no connection between the events in Winnipeg and the One Big Union except that the Calgary convention formed part of the backdrop and contributed to the atmosphere in which events immediately leading to the strike took place.

The general strike was touched off by disputes in the metal and building trades that surfaced in April and May. The inability of the unions in these two industries to win concessions from management — higher wages in the case of the building trades, union recognition in the metal trades — prompted them to turn to the Trades and Labour Council for help. A sufficient number of workers believed the issues to be important enough to the welfare of all organized labour to enable the supporters of radical action to push a general strike vote through the Trades Council.

The Winnipeg Building Trades Council, uniting all the city's construction unions in one organization, had taken on a new task in the spring of 1919 — henceforth it would negotiate working agreements to cover all of its constituent trades directly with the employers' organization, the Winnipeg Builders' Exchange. This arrangement was welcomed by all since it meant that both sides would be unable to take advantage of disunity in their opponents, while the employers were particularly pleased since they would only have to negotiate one agreement to cover the entire industry. The discussions were difficult, because the unions were determined to win large wage increases to make up for the small gains they had made during the war. The employers, however, would not agree to anything better than half the amounts sought by the unions. They knew this was not sufficient and conceded the fairness of the unions' demands, but claimed it was all they could pay to avoid bankruptcy. Half a loaf was better than none, they pointed out, and a strike would only mean that no wages at all would go into their workers' pockets.

377

The workers' claim to large increases was buttressed by statistics showing they had been left behind in the race to keep wages ahead of the rising cost of living. This had increased by approximately seventy-five per cent since 1913, although the average wage in the building trades had only risen by about thirteen per cent. The employers, however, were actually in a real bind because the depression of 1913 had killed Winnipeg's construction boom while the war served to keep it dead. War priorities kept building at an all-time low and the builders were hard pressed to keep out of debt. Though many expected construction to pick up in the summer of 1919, these hopes had not yet been realized and the employers were no better off than they had been in the previous five years. These conditions created an impasse in the negotiations and prompted the Building Trades Council to call a strike for Thursday morning, May 1, 1919.[21]

While the crisis in the building trades was mounting, another impasse was developing in the city's metal trades. The Metal Trades Council, an amalgam of various metal craft unions whose members worked in the city's independent contract shops, automobile repair establishments, and so on, had been formed in the spring of 1918 to increase the power of the individual unions in their attempt to gain recognition from the owners and managers of the contract shops. These unions had been trying to win recognition since 1906 and had fought and lost three bitter strikes in 1906, 1917, and July 1918, which saw the use of *ex parte* injunctions, damage suits, and professional strikebreaking agencies. In April 1919, the Metal Trades Council prepared to do battle once again and sent letters to the contract-shop owners asking for a higher wage schedule and the forty-four-hour work week. It did not ask for recognition, since all parties realized that the acceptance or negotiation of the Metal Trades Council's demands would have amounted to *de facto* recognition. The contract-shop owners had successfully resisted the unions in the past, and again studiously ignored the letters from the Metal Trades Council.

One of the contract shops, Vulcan Iron Works, was owned and managed by E.G. and L.R. Barrett, brothers who had been in the forefront of opposition to union recognition for over thirteen years. In the third week of April they sent letters to each of their employees setting out their position on the question of union recognition; they claimed that although they would meet individual workers or a committee of workers they would not, under any circumstances, negotiate with the Metal Trades Council. They were running "an absolutely open shop" and would never bargain with any group or organization which contained members or representatives from other shops or factories. This letter was the only reply of any sort from the largest three of the contract shops; only three of the smaller establishments in the city signified their willingness to negotiate with the union.[22]

378

On the last night of April, metal-trade union members crowded into a room in the Labour Temple on James Street to hear the news that the council's approach to the contract shops had been spurned and that the executive was left with little choice but to turn matters over to the membership for some sort of decision. The meeting then voted overwhelmingly to begin a strike the next morning at eleven but was persuaded by the executive to postpone action for another twenty-four hours. The extra day of grace brought no response from the "Big Three" and on Friday, May 2, at eleven A.M., Winnipeg's third metal-trades strike in three years closed the factories down. The issues were familiar ones to this troubled industry: union recognition, a shorter work week, and wage parity with metal workers in the city's railway repair and maintenance shops.

At this point many union members in Winnipeg were ripe to respond to a call of support for the two striking trades since several other unions were involved in disputes of their own. In the last week of April a strike of telephone operators was narrowly averted when the provincial government met demands for a pay increase scant days before the deadline ran out. At the same time, the policemen's union was also involved in negotiations and had a great deal of trouble squeezing higher wages out of the civic administration. The men had voted overwhelmingly to strike but received a new contract with higher wages in the last days of April. The street-railway employees had begun negotiations with their employer on April 21; after reaching an impasse, they had voted 900 to 79 in favour of strike action. They held off, however, until receiving the report of a conciliation commission appointed under the federal Industrial Disputes Investigation Act.[23]

Thus, when the metal-trades delegates entered the Labour Temple for the regular weekly Trades Council meeting of May 6, there was already widespread labour unrest in the city. Two trades were on strike, one was threatening to strike and two had just concluded bitter and protracted negotiations which had almost broken down. Metal-trades delegates were instructed by their locals to bring the matter of their own strike before the council and to ask for the council's support. They intended to tell the meeting that a defeat would now jeopardize the gains of the entire union movement and would set labour back many years.

The meeting hall in the temple was crowded to capacity as the Metal and Building Trades Councils reported on the lack of progress in their struggles. Delegate James Lovett told the meeting that union recognition had never before been an issue in the construction strike but that the Builders' Exchange was threatening to withdraw its recognition of the Building Trades Council unless the employers' offer was accepted. Lovett added the charge that the bankers were behind the current impasse since they would not allow the builders to increase wages to the levels sought by the workers. Lovett asked the Trades Council to help the construction trades because the Building Trades Council's strike had not been sanctioned by international union headquarters and the members were not receiving strike pay.

379

As the meeting progressed someone handed a note to Secretary Ernie Robertson informing him that a worker of German origin, who had been visiting metal-trades shops at the instruction of his local, had been arrested. A number of delegates immediately volunteered to go to the police station and returned shortly with the worker in tow. His impromptu speech, charging government support for the employers, was a sensation. It was nothing, however, to the one delivered by R.B. Russell, secretary and acknowledged leader of the Metal Trades Council. The fiery Scot was the centre of attention as he reviewed the dispute thus far and charged the Barretts with responsibility for the stiffening employer opposition. Winnipeg, he warned, must stand firm for the sake of labour everywhere. This strike was made necessary by the defeat of 1918, he claimed, and there must be no more defeats.

Finally Harry Veitch, former Trades Council president, told the delegates of the great progress that had been made in previous weeks in organizing non-union workers in the city, and claimed that a general strike would tie Winnipeg up completely. This was the final argument. The meeting voted to take a poll of every union member in the city and to make a final decision by May 13.[24] In accordance with action taken by the council the previous December, a simple majority of all union members in the city would suffice to instruct council delegates to call the walkout.

The next few days were feverish with activity as Robinson arranged the printing and distribution of eighteen thousand ballots. In a few cases, such as that of the letter carriers, the vote was taken by an open show of hands but in most instances ballots were simply filled out at work and returned to Robinson. Ballot boxes were rarely used and votes were added up as they came into the Labour Temple. The Typographical Union was the only organization affiliated with the Trades Council that refused to participate in the voting and it was bitterly attacked by other unions who charged that the typos were afraid to lose their funeral expenses and old-age homes.

On Tuesday evening, May 13, excited delegates gathered in the Labour Temple to hear further reports on the course of the building and metal-trades strikes and to receive the results of the general strike ballot. Lovett told the meeting that the Builders Exchange had carried out their threat and were now refusing to deal with the Building Trades Council. Delegates were also told that Premier Norris had met with the contract-shop employers and the Metal Trades Council earlier in the day in an attempt to work out a compromise. The Big Three told him they might form an employers' association in the future and would, at this point, consider union recognition, but discussions with the unions at the moment were definitely out. Undaunted, Norris appointed Russell and Trades Council solicitor T.J. Murray to an *ad hoc* conciliation committee. The union men ridiculed independent arbitration at this point, however, since their precondition for any settlement, union recognition, was not even being considered by management.

Robinson then read the results of the vote to the meeting. Union members in Winnipeg had demonstrated solid support for a general strike — over eleven thousand endorsed the idea while a mere five hundred were opposed. The council thus set Thursday, May 15, as the day and eleven A.M. the hour in which the general strike was to begin. In addition, Lovett, A. Scoble of the street railwaymen's union, Veitch, Russell, and W. Logan of the machinists' union were appointed to act as the nucleus of the Strike Committee, which eventually consisted of three delegates from each of the unions represented on the council, to act on behalf of the strikers in all future negotiations.[25]

Several abortive attempts were made to avoid the strike in the seventy-two hours preceding the Thursday morning deadline. Both the premier and Mayor Gray tried unsuccessfully to bring the two sides together. In almost all cases it was apparent that the building-trades workers and their employers were not far removed from an agreement, but the relative lack of disharmony here was overshadowed by the total absence of any spirit of compromise in the metal trades. The unions continued to demand recognition for the Metal Trades Council while the Big Three refused to recognize unions in any form.

On Wednesday night, May 14, Gray, Norris, and the provincial attorney-general made an eleventh hour attempt to stop the strike. Gray telephoned James Winning, president of the Trades Council, and asked him if there was a chance of abandoning the strike should the ironmasters be persuaded to adopt a more reasonable approach. Winning, a moderate, was probably somewhat dazed by the rapidly developing events of the previous two weeks, but he was astute enough to realize that the movement towards a general strike had generated a momentum of its own. "It might help," he answered, "but it is too late to discuss that now."[26] The stage was set for the walkout to begin.

At precisely eleven o'clock the next morning, Winnipeg ceased to work. The strike was complete and overwhelming in its proportions as over twenty-two thousand workers answered the call within the first twenty-four hours. Ninety-four of ninety-six unions participated to a man. Firemen left their stations, telephones were shut down, the city's electrical workers left turbines and transmission equipment unattended; telegraphers and others responsible for keeping a modern city in touch with the world refused to work. At the waterworks a skeleton staff remained behind at the request of the Trades Council to provide a meagre thirty pounds pressure, sufficient for single-storey dwellings. Commercial establishments of every sort, from moving-picture houses to restaurants, were closed.[27]

381

The general strike was called in a moment of intense and hopeful enthusiasm amidst the certainty that labour would win this fight even more decisively than the strike of 1918. The duration of the strike and its completeness is only explained, however, by the fact that this was the culmination of over twenty years of struggle for the city's unions. This was to be the final battle in which nothing would be held in reserve. Years of despair and frustration fuelled the intense hostility of workers towards the employers and governments who had foiled their ambitions for so long. In this battle labour would win or lose all — the unions knew it, and so did the employers. This was a challenge to traditional ideas and methods that labour's opponents could not ignore and to which they responded in tough and decisive fashion.

From the first days of the walkout the strikers faced the powerful opposition of employers, governments, and the Citizens' Committee of One Thousand. The last-named organization was loosely patterned after the Committee of One Hundred which had taken so active a role in the 1918 strike. Though it purportedly voiced the interests of the city's "neutral" citizens, it was strongly anti-strike, supported the employers, labelled the union leaders Bolsheviks, and provided thousands of volunteers to run the services and equipment the strikers had abandoned. Citizens' Committee representatives sat in on secret government policy conferences and advised the contract-shop owners throughout the six-week period of the strike.

The new Citizens' Committee was an amalgamation of the old committee and individual members of organizations such as the Board of Trade, the Manufacturers' Association, and the Winnipeg bar. Of several names that appeared most frequently, for example, H.B. Lyall was an official of Manitoba Bridge and a member of the Board of Trade. A.L. Crossin was a broker with Oldfield, Kirby and Gardner, a firm dealing in insurance and loans, and also a member of the Board of Trade. A.K. Godfrey, chairman of the Citizens' Committee of One Thousand, was the 1917–18 president of the Board of Trade and an executive of the Canadian Elevator Company. J.E. Botterell was a senior partner in the grain- and stock-brokerage firm of Baird & Botterell and also a member of the Board of Trade. Isaac Pitblado, KC, was a senior partner in the law firm of Pitblado, Hoskin & Co., which handled the personal business of the Hon. Arthur Meighen, federal minister of the Interior.[28]

Direct anti-strike involvement by the Citizens' Committee added an element not present in the 1918 sympathetic walkout, but it was not as serious as the intervention by the federal and provincial governments. When the political leaders of the country and the province opted to intervene on the side of the employers, the strikers were faced with the choice of having the massive political, legal, and military power of those governments levelled against them, or ending the strike. Though this was not immediately apparent, it became more evident as the strike dragged on that the governments were playing an active and interested role in events.

Within a week of the outbreak of the new strike, Gideon Robertson and Arthur Meighen were on their way to Winnipeg. Even before they reached the city they met with several members of the Citizens' Committee and heard biased accounts of what was going on in Winnipeg. Robertson, as a former labour man and an ardent supporter of the conservative craft-union status quo in the AFL and TLC, launched an immediate and all-out verbal assault against the OBU as soon as he arrived in the city, charging that the strike was a One Big Union affair aimed at revolution and the destruction of the international craft-union movement. Robertson and Meighen also decided to take post-office matters into hand and get the men back to work as quickly as possible. Robertson fixed a deadline for all post-office employees to return to work, under threat of dismissal if they did not show up. When the deadline passed, the vast majority of postal workers in the city were fired and replaced with volunteers.[29]

The ultimatum soon became the accepted method of dealing with government employees at every level. Robertson used it with great effect to end a one-day strike of railway mail clerks while the provincial government utilized it in an effort to force its telephone employees back to their jobs. Even the city got into the act and issued ultimatums to its firemen, clerks, and waterworks employees. In most cases, employees did not heed their deadlines and lost their jobs.

Meighen and Robertson represented the government in body and in spirit. Their anti-strike views accurately reflected the beliefs and attitudes of the cabinet to which they belonged. From lesser luminaries such as C.C. Ballantyne, minister of Fisheries, up to Prime Minister Borden

382

himself, the government was uniform in its condemnation of the strike, its assertion that the strike was revolutionary in origin and intent, and its firm resolve that the workers could not be allowed to win. Though they tried hard to convince some of the more hysterical voices, such as the New York *Times*, that Winnipeg was not in the midst of a revolution and that legitimate government authority still prevailed, they spoke in the House of Commons and to the newspapers of threats to constituted authority and of the strikers' desire to smash the traditional order of labour–management relations. Meighen revealed the innermost fears of the government when he attacked the general strike in the House in early June. If unions were going to be allowed to combine into larger unions, he asked, where was the logical end to the process going to be? Eventually there would be only one union capable of calling one tremendous strike which would bring anarchy to the country. This, he warned, could not and would not be allowed to happen.[30]

While talk of revolution surged and ebbed around their heads, the strike leaders bent every effort to keep the streets peaceful and to convince their followers to keep out of trouble. In most cases they even refused to grant permission for peaceful picketing. Though incidents involving strikebreakers did occur on occasion, they were usually initiated spontaneously by hotheads. The strike leaders had asked the police to remain at work and asked their followers to do nothing because they feared that the least provocation would bring the armed forces into the streets of Winnipeg, assuring defeat of the general strike.

What the strike leaders failed to realize was that the type of campaign they had embarked upon was different from any they had known before and was bound to present great difficulties which could not be easily resolved. An entire city had been paralyzed, but no one had taken the time to think about the ramifications of this beforehand. Workers too had families, let alone those people who sided neither with strikers or employers, and they also had to be fed and heated, their garbage collected, and their milk, bread, and ice delivered. The maintenance of essential services was of the utmost importance and was one of the most difficult problems wrestled with by the strikers.

On May 16 the intense and hostile public reaction to the termination of bread and milk deliveries forced the Strike Committee to begin to think about and attempt to find a solution to the problem of staples distribution. The strikers approached a sub-committee of the city council, a meeting also attended by A.J. Andrews, W.J. Botterell, representing the Committee of One Thousand, and J.W. Carruthers, owner of the Crescent Creamery Company. Carruthers suggested that the problem of staples distribution could be solved if special cards were issued to delivery wagons notifying the public that the men delivering bread and milk were not scabs. This was accepted by the meeting and approved by the Strike Committee, which soon issued cards reading "Permitted by authority of Strike Committee" to bakeries, dairies, and other establishments.[31]

A degree of normalcy returned as businesses deemed essential to the well-being of the city reopened under the protection of the permits. The arrangement, however, made certain people uneasy. Mayor Gray was moved to point out that people should not think the necessities of life were now being supplied by an authority other than the legitimate elected government of the city. This did not stop the mounting criticism of those who charged that the administration of Winnipeg had now passed to the hands of the strikers. The strikers, for their part, claimed that they had no intention of assuming government authority and had merely issued the cards to protect their own men.

Pressure began to mount for the removal of the cards only a few days after their use had begun. Gray and Premier Norris told the strikers they objected to the cards, even though they knew why they had been issued in the first place. On Monday, May 20, Gray told the strikers that the permit cards would have to be removed before any effort could be made to solve the root causes of the walkout. The following day the mayor brought the issue before city council and demanded the removal of the permits since they had outlived their usefulness. Many people all over the country, he asserted, were under the false impression that their use signified the erosion of constitutional authority in Winnipeg. The result was a heated debate between the mayor's supporters and the Labour aldermen who claimed that the cards were absolutely necessary for the continuation of essential services. A.J. Andrews explained that, even though he too knew and understood why the permit cards had been decided upon, he believed that the city's necessities were being supplied by permission of the strikers and this was an erosion of constituted authority, whether intended as such or not. When the debate cooled, the council voted seven to four to have the cards taken down. The following day the Strike Committee complied.[32]

The permit episode cast a heavy shadow over the Strike Committee. Though the permits were not decided upon unilaterally and in fact were approved by two representatives of the Citizens' Committee and a subcommittee of city council, their wording created the impression that the strikers alone were responsible for the maintenance of essential services in the city. This naturally lead to a belief in some minds that the government of Winnipeg had passed to the Labour Temple, which now had the power to operate or shut down these facilities. From there it was but a small step to the assumption that the Labour Temple was now the "James Street Soviet." This cry reinforced the opinions and spurred the activities of those who claimed the strike was nothing but a revolutionary plot in the first place. Foremost among this group was the federal government.

The Borden administration led a coalition of forces which opposed the strike and could accept only two solutions — a total and complete collapse of the strike, or a compromise settlement that would leave little doubt that the strikers were accepting terms dictated by management. If the latter could not be accomplished, the former was necessary because in no way could the general strike be allowed to succeed or even to have the appearance of success. Agents of the federal government, in the persons of Robertson and Meighen, Brigadier-General H.D.B. Ketchen, officer commanding the Manitoba military district, Commissioner A.B. Perry of the RNWMP, and A.J. Andrews, worked long and hard to see that the government's purpose was accomplished. The federal government was thus deeply involved in each of the five major steps which led to the disintegration of the strike in the last week of June.

At the request of the Strike Committee, the members of the city police force had remained at their posts on May 15, but anti-strike forces, convinced that the police were either under the control of or were sympathetic to the strikers, found the situation intolerable. Anti-strike members of city council tried to rectify this by presenting the members of the force with an ultimatum: they were asked to sign a pledge dissociating themselves from the Trades and Labour Council and promising not to participate in any future sympathetic strikes. The police were nearly unanimous in their rejection of the ultimatum and the city council was left in the difficult position of having to ignore its own ultimatum or doing what the strikers had not dared to do — leave the city devoid of police protection.

385

The solution was provided by General Ketchen, who suggested the employment of an alternative force of "special police" to supplement or replace the regular constables. Supported by Ketchen and the Citizens' Committee, the city began to recruit special police, mostly from amongst anti-strike veterans and students, and paid them six dollars per day, a higher wage than that earned by the regular police. When a force of close to two thousand had been successfully recruited, the council repeated its earlier demands that members of the force sign the pledges. When they refused as they had on the first occasion, 240 of them, almost the entire force, were fired.[33] From June 10 the city was in the hands of a large group of men who were, with few exceptions and without pretence, hostile to the strike and the strikers. The fact that they were also inept was demonstrated on several occasions when fights and disturbances broke out due to the inability of these untrained men to conduct themselves properly.

The first afternoon of their service, a group of mounted specials rode down Main Street to a point near the junction with Portage where a crowd had gathered to hear a man speaking from a parked car. The specials, armed with clubs, attempted to disperse this group and rode up on the sidewalk. As they began to walk their horses slowly into the crowd, swinging their batons to force the group to scatter, one of their number was thrown from his horse and badly beaten. Sergeant Major F.G. Coppins, VC, was riding his horse slowly along the sidewalk when someone cupped his hands under Coppins's stirrup and heaved upward, unseating him. As this happened several men grabbed Coppins, helped pull him off the horse, and began to beat him. Coppins, already injured, jumped to his feet swinging his club and had to be rescued from the crowd by other specials. He was subsequently taken to Tuxedo Military Hospital suffering from severe bruises.[34]

Ketchen was instrumental in setting up the force of special police, but he did not intend to rely solely on them should he have to use force to maintain order or put down the strike. From the beginning of the walkout he directed the buildup of a large military force in the Winnipeg area and, with the help of his superiors in Ottawa, the Mounted Police, and the Citizens' Committee, did it without bringing a single regular soldier to the city. By co-ordinating his activities with the Mounties and initiating a training program using newly recruited citizen volunteers for the militia, Ketchen was able to build a large force in a relatively short time. To direct this group he called on former officers residing in the city, and to transport the militia he arranged for the use of trucks supplied by the Citizens' Committee to augment those already on hand. From outside the city a secret shipment of machine guns was forwarded by Ottawa, marked "regimental baggage" and included in the freight of the 27th Battalion, travelling to Winnipeg to demobilize. In addition he had an armoured car available which was regularly stationed in the city.

By Tuesday, June 17, Ketchen had a formidable group of Mounties, militia, and civilian auxiliary volunteers at his disposal. At Fort Osborne Barracks an armoured car equipped with three machine guns and manned by three officers, two drivers, and six riflemen was kept in readiness. The Citizens' Committee had completed the organization of an auxiliary motor-transport service and placed it under Ketchen's command. The Mounties, in addition to a reinforced complement of officers and men, had been issued four machine guns mounted on motor trucks and could put sixty men on horses into the streets in a matter of minutes. Two mobile militia groups had been placed in readiness, one stationed at Fort Osborne Barracks, the other at Minto Barracks. Each consisted of a troop of the Fort Garry Horse, one motor machine-gun section with two guns apiece, infantry escorts in motor trucks and one company of motorized infantry. The total force immediately available in an emergency numbered eight hundred and Ketchen had worked out special arrangements to call the rest of the militia into action at a moment's notice.[35] If necessary, the government had all the armed force it might require ready and available.

In the last few days of May a committee representing six railway running-trades unions approached the unions and the contract-shops employers with an offer to mediate the dispute. The offer was accepted and the committee got down to work inviting proposals from both sides. The Metal Trades Council and the contract-shop owners stuck close to their original positions, but the mediation committee saw nothing extraordinary about the unions' desire to gain recognition for a Metal Trades Council. They thus worked out what they believed was a compromise solution, which included recognition of the Metal Trades Council, and offered it to both sides. The unions accepted the settlement, the employers rejected it, and the committee prepared to announce that its efforts had failed.[36]

At this point Senator Robertson arrived in the city once again. There were, at that point, ominous rumblings from the railway yards to the effect that train crews, including locomotive engineers, firemen, and carmen, would join the general strike, paralyzing East–West rail transportation at its most vital point in the national communications network. Robertson could not let this happen and determined to find some immediate solution to the strike. The best opportunity appeared to be to use the offices of the mediation committee and to put pressure on the mediators to accept a solution, short of recognition of the Metal Trades Council, that they could bless. This task was relatively simple because Robertson was of the same ilk as the mediators, probably knew them all personally, and played on their fears of the rising power of the One Big Union.

387

On Sunday evening, June 15, Robertson finally succeeded in forcing the contract-shop employers to offer to recognize individual craft unions in their plants — there was no thought or mention of the recognition of the Metal Trades Council — and had the offer published in the newspapers the next morning.[37] He believed that this offer, containing part of the recognition the unions had sought for many years, might confuse the strikers and weaken their resolve to continue — the strike was already over four weeks old — and give the moderates on the Strike Committee a platform from which to advocate the end of the general strike. To insure that the radical hold on the Strike Committee was weakened at this crucial point, he ordered the arrest of Russell, Johns, and the other radicals on Monday night.[38]

In the early hours of June 18, six Anglo-Saxon strike leaders along with a token handful of "enemy aliens" were arrested under authority of a new Immigration Act amendment which had been passed through Parliament in less than one hour on June 6.[39] They were taken straight to Stony Mountain penitentiary and placed in cells while the government decided their fate. Meighen wanted them deported immediately, while A.J. Andrews believed this would alienate the public and therefore argued for their release on bail. By early Friday, June 20, it was decided to release the men if they promised to take no further part in the strike.[40] By then deportation had become completely unnecessary since the moderates had taken Robertson's bait and were preparing to negotiate an end to the strike on the basis of the offer of June 16.

At this point control of events slipped from the Strike Committee's hands. Since the last days of May, several thousand veterans who supported the aims and tactics of the strikers had grown increasingly vocal and militant in their demonstrations of solidarity. On the final day of May, and for some days after, they had paraded in large numbers in the downtown streets of Winnipeg, to the city hall and legislative buildings and in front of Citizens' Committee headquarters. On days when they did not take to the streets they held boisterous meetings in Victoria Park, listening to speeches and reports from their leaders and members of the Strike Committee. To counter this new element, anti-strike veterans organized parades of their own; on one occasion the two groups narrowly missed each other while marching near the legislature. To avoid the possibility of a massive and violent confrontation the mayor issued a ban against parades and twice repeated the order during the course of the strike.[41] On June 20, however, the pro-strike veterans held a mass meeting in a park across from city hall and declared their intention to demonstrate the next day because of the arrests of the strike leaders and the resumption of streetcar service.

At 10:30 the next morning, a hurried meeting convened in Robertson's suite in the Royal Alexandra Hotel. Three veterans' delegates had come to present their terms for cancellation of the planned parade to Robertson, Gray, Andrews, and Commissioner A.B. Perry of the Mounted Police. The returned men planned to march from city hall to the Royal Alexandra, where they hoped to be addressed by Senator Robertson, return down Main Street, and take possession of the Industrial Bureau, headquarters of the Citizens' Committee. Government and city officials could avert the demonstration, the veterans claimed, if the streetcars were removed from the streets, the strike settled within the next four hours, and Robertson agreed to speak to the men in the Industrial Bureau. Gray retorted that it would be impossible to bring about a negotiated end to the strike within the time limit indicated and he had no intention of sending the streetcars back to their barns. They would, however, try to fulfil the third of the conditions and, at that point, Andrews left immediately for the bureau to line up meeting space for the afternoon. By the time he was able to report back to the hotel, events had already passed him by.

The meeting continued after Andrews's hurried departure as Gray tried to dissuade the veterans from precipitating a crisis by going ahead with a demonstration that would violate three proclamations. He would stop the demonstration peacefully if possible, he declared, but would resort to "other measures" if they insisted on forcing his hand. While the mayor and the veterans continued to argue, crowds were already gathering in Main Street, across from the city hall, in anticipation of the parade's 2:30 starting time. At fifteen minutes to two Acting Police Chief Newton telephoned the mayor to inform him of the crowds. Gray hurriedly left the hotel and rushed through back streets to city hall where Newton told him he thought the situation was already out of hand and that his force of special police could not restore order. Gray suggested that the RNWMP be called in, Newton concurred, and the mayor drove to Mounted Police headquarters to ask Commissioner Perry to send his men out to patrol the streets. Perry complied and dispatched fifty-four men on horses and thirty-six in trucks.

By 2:30 the gathering crowds were filling the east side of Main Street between William and Rupert. A streetcar moving slowly north along Main was surrounded by several hundred people who tried unsuccessfully to stop it. When it forced its way through, they turned their attention to a southbound car, pulled its trolley off the wires and began to smash its windows. The crowd, now almost completely out of control, rocked the car back and forth, trying to tip it on its side, but when the task proved too great they broke the rest of the windows, slashed the seats, and set the interior ablaze. While the attack on the streetcar was in progress, the Mounted Police arrived on the scene.

389

They swung north along Main from Portage Avenue, half in khaki coats and half in the traditional scarlet, batons in hand. Twice they charged north through the crowd and both times they met with flying stones and bottles. After the second charge one Mountie's horse tripped over a piece of streetcar fender lying in the street, threw its rider to the ground, and began to drag him wildly, his foot caught in the stirrup. Within moments several men separated themselves from the mob, grabbed the officer and began to beat him. When the rest of the force caught sight of their comrade they wheeled north once again, this time with revolvers cocked in their hands. Mayor Gray, watching anxiously from a parapet in front of city hall, decided to take further action and formally read the Riot Act. The time was now 2:35 and the crowd was given thirty minutes to get off the streets or be arrested. As Gray turned to go inside the building, he heard gunfire in the street below.[42]

The officer commanding the Mounted Police detachment, Inspector Mead, had concluded after the second charge that his men could not handle the large and excited crowd without extraordinary measures and ordered them to fire a volley into the throng. The command was given only moments after the Riot Act had been read and shooting continued intermittently for several minutes afterwards. One man was killed instantly and many others were wounded. It was claimed afterwards by Mayor Gray, the Manitoba *Free Press*, and the Mounties that the order to fire was only given after the Mounties themselves had been shot at by unknown assailants in the crowd. They had certainly come under vigorous attack from bricks, stones, and bottles, but the only shots fired that day came from police revolvers. Newspaper casualty lists published in following days listed all serious wounds suffered in the riot, including those of the RNWMP officers, not one of whom had been hit by a bullet.[43] Mayor Gray told reporters that he had not heard shots until shortly after he read the Riot Act and "presumed" they came from the crowd but, in fact, this was almost the exact moment when Mead was ordering his men to shoot. Mead himself, in early reports of the day's events, explained that he had ordered his men to use their sidearms only after he realized how hard pressed they were; he made no mention at all of being fired upon.

Panic swept the crowd as the bullets spattered and ricocheted against the streets and walls and people fell where they stood. Hundreds trying to escape police bullets swept down back alleys and ran up the streets where they met cordons of special police, armed with clubs and revolvers, thrown across Main Street and other streets and alleys in the vicinity of city hall. Now vicious fights broke out and many were arrested as Mounties and specials started to clear the downtown area. Meanwhile, Gray had driven to Fort Osborne Barracks when he heard the gunfire and asked General Ketchen to turn out the militia. The general complied, dispatched an emergency force and within minutes a mixed group of cavalry and the motor machine-gun section began to move into the downtown area in the auxiliary transport so obligingly provided by the Citizens' Committee.

By this time most of the crowd was trying in every way possible to escape the scene. Over eighty who were not successful were caught in the dragnet and arrested. The special police and the militia, aided by the Mounties, threw up cordons to block access to Portage and Main from Garry in the south to the CPR station in the north and remained on duty until midnight. Soon all was quiet; the day known to history as Bloody Saturday was over.[44]

The events of June 21 climaxed the Winnipeg strike. The dénouement came four days later when the Strike Committee called off the walkout effective Thursday morning, June 26. The strikers had failed to achieve any of their objectives, and after six weeks of effort, the futility of the strike had become painfully clear. All that the strikers were able to gain was an agreement on the part of the provincial government to appoint a royal commission to conduct an impartial investigation into the causes of the dispute.[45]

In embarking on the course taken in the spring of 1919, the workers of Winnipeg were travelling a path few North American wage earners had trod before. There had been other attempted general strikes, the most complete in Seattle, Washington, in February 1919 involving sixty thousand workers, but they were either of short duration (Seattle's strike lasted four days) or incomplete. There were thus almost no campaign histories that could have been consulted and no previous successes or failures to guide the Winnipeg strikers. Therein lies the source of their failure to examine fully the consequences of what they were planning and to prepare themselves and their city for the days and weeks to come. This, more than anything else, assured the defeat of the strike and the resultant grave weakening of the city's labour movement.

Workers in Winnipeg and western Canada had spoken increasingly of general strikes since mid-1917, but rarely gave any consideration as to what a general strike would involve. They talked and wrote about general strikes either as political weapons to oppose conscription or as the ultimate manifestation of industrial conflict, this being especially true following the 1918 Winnipeg civic workers' victory. There was, however, never any thought given as to which essential services should be maintained, if any, and how this might be done. Workers were quite blind to the fact that they were going to be forced to assume some responsibility for the maintenance of society in the event they were to launch an open-ended general strike. This held true whether or not they were planning to create a revolutionary situation, since they could never separate themselves and their families from the rest of society.

Trapped into a situation in which they appeared to be assuming government authority, the Winnipeg strikers were not equipped or prepared to cope with the political and military implications of this new situation. By launching a general strike the workers had embarked on a radical course, but they were not radical enough to escape the consequences of their action. Once the unions had decided to shut down the entire city and keep it shut until they won, they ran directly into the power of three levels of government. And when the federal government decided to involve itself in countering a revolution that never existed, the workers were lost: their only choice was between unacceptable compromise, complete defeat, or direct, perhaps armed, resistance.

The Winnipeg General Strike was not a revolution and was never planned to be one. It did, however, raise basic questions concerning the nature and composition of "constituted authority" as well as what qualifies as a *bona fide* challenge to that authority. There can be no doubt that the strikers intended to enhance their own position at the expense of the normal political and economic power of capital. In using as blunt an instrument as a general strike, however, they also ran the risk of challenging the *de facto* power of at least one level of government. General strikes are intended to bring the normal functions and activities of society to a standstill and they therefore transfer to the workers part of the option of what will continue to operate and what will not — this is inevitable if anarchy is to be avoided. To this degree the existing order *is* undermined, whether by accident or design and whether on a purely local level or a more national one.

391

The rapid increase of labour's power in Winnipeg was a shock to the cosy arrangements and alliances that had existed between capital and government for at least four decades. This threat to the status quo was compounded by the belief in some quarters that the workers were embarked on a campaign to supplant the municipal and even the provincial and national governments. The charge was not true, but it did reflect the unions' rapid rise to new positions of power. The leaders of the strike urged their followers to hold to a non-violent course so they could avoid open confrontation with the government and its police and military forces. They did not realize that this confrontation actually began at eleven A.M. the morning of May 15. Many years of mostly unsuccessful industrial struggles and the victorious sympathetic strike of 1918 had convinced them that a general strike would enable them to bring their full power to bear in an industrial dispute. This was a basic flaw in their thinking, however, because a general strike was not and could not be just another larger strike. By its very nature it is a political weapon and must, to a certain degree, challenge areas of authority of legally constituted governments. The strikers were, therefore, caught in a dilemma of their own making and the result was a crushing defeat.

In a very real sense the Winnipeg General Strike marked the end of an era in Winnipeg and western Canada. The Winnipeg strikers had manned the battle lines for their western brothers and their loss seriously undermined the strength of all western labour. The defeat of the strike assured the weakening of those unions and labour leaders who had championed its use and who had called it. The strike was, therefore, a key event in the climactic happenings of a postwar era of turmoil. Much of the vitality of a labour movement grown powerful and energetic during four years of war was sapped in the grinding and hopeless struggle of the six-week confrontation at Winnipeg.

NOTES

[1] See, for example, Testimony of T.R. Deacon, Evidence Presented to the Royal Commission on Industrial Relations, Winnipeg, 10 & 12 May 1919, Department of Labour Library, Ottawa.

[2] D.C. Masters, *The Winnipeg General Strike* (Toronto: University of Toronto Press, 1950), 8–10.

[3] Masters, *Winnipeg General Strike*, 7.

[4] Masters, *Winnipeg General Strike*, 7.

[5] D.J. Bercuson, "Labour in Winnipeg: The Great War and the General Strike" (Ph.D. dissertation, University of Toronto, 1971), 17–37.

[6] See Canada Department of Labour, *Eighth Annual Report on Wholesale Prices in Canada, 1917,* and monthly tables in *Labour Gazette* for 1918 and 1919.

[7] Bercuson, "Labour in Winnipeg," 101–102, 105.

[8] Martin Robin, "Registration, Conscription and Independent Labour Politics, 1916–1917," *Canadian Historical Review* 47 (June 1966): 101–118.

[9] Bercuson, "Labour in Winnipeg," 189–90.

[10] Bercuson, "Labour in Winnipeg," 175–78.

[11] Bercuson, "Labour in Winnipeg," 200–217.

[12] T.J. Murray to Rigg, 28 May 1919, Rigg/Rees Papers, Public Archives of Manitoba; Manitoba *Free Press*, 25 May 1918.

[13] *Western Labor News*, 4 October 1918.

[14] *Western Labor News*, 13 December 1918.

[15] See P. Phillips, "The National Policy and the Development of the Western Canadian Labour Movement," in *Prairie Perspectives* 2, ed. A. Rasporich and H. Klassen (Toronto: Holt, Rinehart and Winston, 1973), 41–61.

[16] Bercuson, "Labour in Winnipeg," 134.

[17] Bercuson, "Labour in Winnipeg," 227–28.

[18] Trades and Labour Congress of Canada, *Proceedings of the 34th Annual Convention* (Ottawa, 1918), 32–33, 128–31.

[19] Masters, *Winnipeg General Strike*, 38.

[20] *Western Labor News*, 16 June 1919.

[21] *Western Labor News*, 2 May 1919.

[22] Bercuson, "Labour in Winnipeg," 289.

[23] Bercuson, "Labour in Winnipeg," 291.

[24] *Western Labor News*, 9 May 1919.

[25] *Western Labor News*, 16 May 1919.

[26] *Western Labor News*, 4 June 1919; Winnipeg *Citizen*, 20 May 1919.

[27] *Western Labor News*, 17 May 1919.

[28] Bercuson, "Labour in Winnipeg," 312–14.

[29] Bercuson, "Labour in Winnipeg," 330–31.

[30] Canada House of Commons, *Debates* (2 June 1919), 3035–43.

[31] *Western Labor News*, 17 May 1919.

[32] *Western Labor News*, 22 May 1919.

[33] Winnipeg *Citizen*, 10 June 1919.

[34] Manitoba *Free Press*, 11 June 1919.

[35] Ketchen to Ottawa, 17 June 1919, Department of National Defence Papers, File 5678, Public Archives of Canada (PAC).

[36] *Western Labor News*, 12 June 1919.

[37] Manitoba *Free Press*, 16 June 1919.

[38] Robertson to Borden, 17 June 1919, Borden Papers, PAC.

[39] Masters, *Winnipeg General Strike*, 103–104.

[40] *Western Labor News*, 20 June 1919.

[41] Manitoba *Free Press*, 23 June 1919.

[42] Manitoba *Free Press*, 23 June 1919.

[43] Manitoba *Free Press*, 23 June 1919.

[44] Manitoba *Free Press*, 23 June 1919; *Western Labor News*, 23 June 1919.

[45] *Enlightener (Western Labor News)*, 25 June 1919.

The Progressives*

WALTER YOUNG

The Progressives entered the campaign of 1921 with considerable enthusiasm. True to their philosophical origins, they did not campaign as a national party, although their leader, T.A. Crerar, did tour most of Canada. Instead, they campaigned almost exclusively in individual constituencies. Each electoral district was an autonomous unit in the party and as a result there was neither a national campaign nor an overall campaign strategy.

A national campaign would have been rather awkward, for there was a split within the movement. It was not serious in the beginning, but as the Progressives edged further into politics it grew and deepened. The division was between the Alberta wing and the Manitoba wing, or, more specifically, between Crerar and Henry Wise Wood. Crerar saw the election as an opportunity to bring the Liberal party to its senses, and to force a tariff reduction and free trade in agricultural products.

*From *Democracy and Discontent*, 2nd ed., by Walter D. Young. Copyright McGraw-Hill Ryerson Limited, 1978. Reprinted by permission.

He was not fundamentally opposed to the party system. He had been in the Borden cabinet and was no stranger to cabinet solidarity and party discipline. Wood, understandably, said of the 1921 election: "The issue is between the old party system and the system we have built up."[1] Progressives of his persuasion characterised the old system as the tool by which the big interests had corrupted the electorate and had run the country to serve their own selfish ends.

A further bone of contention was the question of free trade versus government control in the marketing of grain. During the war the federal government had assumed control of the marketing of wheat. A board was established that fixed the price of wheat and controlled the marketing of the crops in 1917 and 1918. In 1919 the Canadian Wheat Board was set up to handle the selling of that year's crop, but the legislation was not renewed for 1920. The Manitoba wing of the Progressives was more interested in free trade and not much concerned about the demise of the wheat board. The Saskatchewan farmers, on the other hand, were well pleased with the effects of the wheat board and wanted to see the federal government stay in the business of marketing wheat. They believed this policy would result in stable prices and secure markets.

Of the two leaders of the "old line parties," as the farmers called them, Mackenzie King of the Liberals was the most shrewd. Prime Minister Arthur Meighen of the Conservatives displayed the short-sighted arrogance that became his trademark in politics and contributed materially to his lack of success. King saw the Progressives as impatient Liberals and attempted to placate the western farmers by telling them things about his tariff policy that he did not dare say in eastern Canada. Meighen either ignored the farmers' demands or referred to them as "Socialistic, Bolshevistic and Soviet nonsense." He described the governments they had formed in Ontario and Alberta as "freaks."

Meighen and King were campaigning to form a government — they were seeking power. The Progressives did not want power, they merely wanted representation. This fitted well their constituency by constituency campaign. The voters were not asked to elect a Progressive government, they were simply asked to elect a Progressive to represent them in Ottawa — an important distinction.

The Progressives at Ottawa

The election of sixty-five Progressives might appear to be a great start for a party but the results were actually a disappointment. Only one Progressive was elected east of the Ottawa river; the majority were from the prairies, with twenty-four from Ontario and five from British Columbia. They constituted a western block dedicated to the interests of the wheat farmer.

Although his party was the largest group in the House of Commons, Mackenzie King did not have a majority. Soon after the election he set about to bring the Progressives into some sort of alliance. The Progressives viewed his advances with mixed feelings. The Alberta wing, strongly committed to the idea of constituency autonomy and opposed to party politics, condemned any arrangement with the Liberals. The Manitoba wing wanted only to reform the Liberal party and would have entered into some agreement without much difficulty. But King did not have complete unanimity in his own party. The conservative wing represented by Sir Lomer Gouin and his Quebec colleagues, despised Progressivism and opposed any alliance.

King first offered cabinet representation to the Progressives in return for some kind of coalition arrangement. The offer was ultimately denied by King and, in any case, it was turned down by the Progressives. As a result of the reticence of the Albertans, the most the Progressives would agree to was conditional support of the Liberals. They recognized that there was likely to be more for them to support in the program of a Liberal administration than in that of the Conservatives.

In the discussions that took place before the opening of the new parliament, the division in the ranks of the radicals was evident. Crerar, as an experienced parliamentarian, was concerned about establishing the machinery of parliamentary discipline to ensure that the Progressives voted as a single unit, as a party, in fact. This involved the institution of a caucus, party whip, and reasonable adherence to the direction of the parliamentary leaders. The Alberta Progressives opposed this approach, for they saw themselves as spokesmen for their constituents, not as subordinate members of a political party. Despite his efforts and conditional agreement from his followers, Crerar never achieved the kind of solidarity necessary to enable the Progressives to operate effectively in a parliamentary setting.

Although they were the second largest group in parliament, the Progressives did not choose to form the official opposition. This right they yielded to Meighen's Conservatives. The Progressives did not see themselves as an alternative government. They were a kind of pressure group, sitting in parliament to chastise the unfeeling and to assist those who wanted to help the farmers. By refusing responsibility and, by implication, demonstrating their lack of interest in forming a government, they made it possible for other politicians and the rest of the country to refuse to take them seriously. They rejected the opportunity to achieve the cohesion they so desperately needed to reach their goals.

The Progressives could not become the official opposition because of their principles. The Manitoba Progressives did not want to oppose the Liberals — they only wanted to reform them. The Alberta Progressives did not want to engage in the competitive processes of party government — they wanted to eradicate party government. For opposite reasons,

395

therefore, the two wings of the Progressive group combined to pass up a chance to become a political party.

The Progressives were determined to demonstrate that they were an independent body, free to support the government or to oppose it in the light of their principles and the needs of their constituents. As Professor Morton has remarked:

> It was a brave experiment, inspired by political naiveté, and marked by a curious over-emphasis on the importance of legislation and an ill-advised indifference to the importance of administration.[2]

It was a difficult position for the group to maintain, particularly as they lacked the unity such a role demanded. They were, in Morton's phrase, a "restive and unreliable band." Mackenzie King could count on Progressive support, however, for as much as the westerners disliked the Liberals, they liked the Conservatives even less. "Only the Albertan Progressives could regard the two old parties as indifferently steeped in iniquity."[3]

The rules of the House of Commons at that time were designed to facilitate the operation of a two-party parliament, composed of government and opposition. The Progressives did not fit the pattern. Because of the rules of the Commons, they found themselves unable to move a sub-amendment to the Conservative amendment to the government's budget. Thus they were deprived of a prime opportunity to criticise government fiscal policy, their chief concern at the time. Unable to get their own proposals before the House, they were forced to vote with the Conservatives. Their most significant achievement in the 1922 session was in gaining the government's agreement to reinstate the 1918 Crowsnest Pass rates on the shipment of grain and flour — to the advantage of the farmer.

Tension and Disintegration

By the end of 1922 cracks in the Progressive ranks were widening. Two Progressives slipped away to become Liberals. Crerar tried toward the end of the parliamentary session to bring his group closer to the Liberals by proposing some kind of working agreement between the two. The proposal was turned down and Crerar resigned as leader, to be replaced by Robert Forke. Forke was no less liberal than Crerar. His initial actions were toward establishing a national Progressive *party*. This move was opposed by the Alberta members and failed to succeed. Forke's failure in this regard — really the failure of the Progressives — marked the beginning of the end. There was nothing for them to do.

The two views on the movement's purpose turned the Progressives into a body of dissidents, in danger of disintegration. The Alberta view of the Member of Parliament as a delegate was simply inconsistent with the structure of parliament. The views of the Manitoba moderates were inconsistent with the radical strain in Progressive thought. Progressivism began to disintegrate through the centrifugal forces generated by the inconsistency and contradiction in its doctrine and composition.

In 1923 the Conservative party allowed the Progressives to make the major amendment to the budget motion. Forke made a frontal assault on Liberal tariff policy, calling for a reduction in the tariff on the necessities of life, more favourable terms of trade with Britain, reciprocity in trade with the United States, and increased taxation on unearned incomes and luxury items. The ringing presentation of the bare bones of their policy united the Progressives as never before. The combination of the Progressive and Conservative assault on the Liberal budget reduced King's combined majority to 8. This was the Progressive's finest hour. Their course was downhill thereafter. In particular, they were beaten to a standstill in their attempt to amend the Bank Act in 1923 — although *397* some of the reforms they advocated were later enacted.

The major break in Progressive ranks occurred in 1924. During the debate on the budget of that session, J.S. Woodsworth, Labour MP from Winnipeg North, moved an amendment that was substantially the same as that moved by Forke the previous year. The Progressives were in a difficult position. If they supported Woodsworth's amendment, the Liberal government could conceivably be defeated. If they opposed it, they would be repudiating their own principles. One of the main criticisms the Progressives made of the old parties was that they seldom stood by their principles.

Forke led most of his followers in opposition to Woodsworth's amendment on the grounds that there was more likelihood of a Liberal government enacting Progressive reforms than would ever be the case with the Conservatives. To defeat the government would, then, be folly. Fourteen Progressives disagreed and supported the Woodsworth amendment. As E.J. Garland of the breakaway group of Progressives declared on the floor of the House, his constituents would be:

> . . . encouraged to know that even though our efforts are largely nullified by the attitudes of opposing interests, they have at least representatives who are pleading their cause without fear of party or press, and who will not be silent while injustice still stands.[4]

Six of the fourteen renegades left the Progressive party shortly after, constituting what became known as the "Ginger Group." In an open letter to Robert Forke they said:

> As we see it there are two species of political organization — one the "Political Party" that aspires to power, and in so doing, inevitably perpetuates that competitive spirit in matters of legislation and gov-

ernment generally which has brought the world wellnigh to ruin; the other is the democratically organized group which aims to co-operate with other groups to secure justice rather than to compete with them for power. It is as representatives of this latter type that we take our stand. . . . [5]

The Ginger Group was later joined by three more Progressives.

By 1925 the Progressive party was shattered beyond repair. Seventeen broke with the caucus and voted with the Liberals on the 1925 budget. When the election was called that year there was little to hold the group together. They had no funds and no national organization. Only 24 Progressive MP's were left when the votes had been counted. The Conservatives under Meighen had the most seats this time, but not a clear majority.

In the constitutional crises which followed, the Progressives played the part of makeweight and were responsible first for the defeat of King's administration and finally for the defeat of Arthur Meighen's. In the 1926 election Liberals and Progressives reached an agreement not to oppose one another in several ridings; in others "Liberal-Progressives" appeared. When the 1926 session of parliament opened there were only nine "pure" Progressives left.

398

The Lesson of Progressive Experience

To some extent the Progressives had achieved their goals. The eastern politicians and magnates had been jolted into an awareness of the needs of the farmers, even if these demands were not entirely met. The general spirit of reform, which had fostered the farmers' movements and had led to the creation of the Progressive party, had achieved some results in increasing the amount of social welfare legislation at the provincial level. But prosperity helped to take some of the steam from the movement, and the manifest failure of the party in parliament aided the process of diminution. Third parties, it seemed, had no place in the context of parliamentary government, and if they could not effect changes in the rules — as the Progressives had tried and failed to do — then they remained both vulnerable and impotent. This factor and the concessions Mackenzie King made to the west in the election of 1926, effectively brought an end to the career of the Progressive party. The Liberal-Progressives in the House of Commons insisted on keeping their dual identity but they attended the Liberal caucus and were seated in the House with the Liberals. Slowly but surely they were absorbed and digested by the Liberals.

The left-overs — those who sat as UFA members or Independent Progressives — were themselves absorbed in a different way by a different group. When the Progressives flared into prominence in the 1921 election, two Labour MP's were also elected: J.S. Woodsworth for Winnipeg North Centre and William Irvine for East Calgary. By 1923 Woodsworth had established his right to speak after Robert Forke as the leader of a party. Earlier Irvine had referred in debate to the presence of a "Labour Group" in the Commons; "Mr. Woodsworth is the leader," he said, "and I am the group."[6]

The Labour group had met occasionally with the more radical of the Progressives. After the Ginger Group had separated itself from the decaying carcass of the Progressive party, meetings of this group with the Labour group were more frequent and collaboration was the rule rather than the exception. By 1930 co-operation had proceeded to the stage that more formal arrangements could be considered. A document was drawn up which stated that the groups were "engaged in the common fight against a strongly entrenched system of special privilege," and affirmed the decision to work in unison to develop "a co-operative system of administration."[7] Each group was to retain its identity, and there was no intention to form another political party. A steering committee was elected, a secretary appointed, and a chairman was elected to act on behalf of all groups in the event that there was insufficient time for a conference. In effect, therefore, the document did lay the groundwork for a political party. Two years later the "co-operating groups" were to agree to begin building a new political party.

Much had happened between 1926 and 1932 to convince J.S. Woodsworth and his colleagues in the House of Commons that there was enough support in the country to spell success for another organized attempt to break the two-party monopoly. The onset of the depression and a series of crop failures once again brought the farmer up against the precarious nature of his occupation. There had been increased activity on the part of the various labour and socialist parties in the cities in the west. The failure of the Progressive party had certainly dampened the political ambitions of the farmers' organizations, but they had not disappeared.

What the Progressive experience had shown was the impossibility of effective parliamentary action by a loosely linked body of independents. The Progressives had assumed that government was essentially the process of law-making and that as long as you had a seat or two in the House of Commons you have a voice in making the laws. They had not understood the mechanism of parliament, nor had they realized that the centre of power was the executive, not the legislature.

The cabinet governs the country through the civil service, and cabinets are only interested in parties other than their own if those parties constitute a threat in the House of Commons. Had the Progressives been a single, united party, and had they been willing to play the parliamentary game with the Conservatives, they could have forced Mackenzie King

399

to do more for the farmers — by threatening to defeat his government. But they had not been united and could never have been because the Alberta group at least, and certainly several from the other provinces, had championed the view that the Member of Parliament ought not to be subordinate to the party. They had held that his first duty was to his constituents and his principles. It would have been odd, indeed, if having been elected because they opposed "partyism" the Progressives had turned around and adopted it.

If everyone playing a game follows one set of rules, those who join under their own different rules soon discover they have no hope of achieving any of their goals. It did not matter how valid the cause of the Progressives was, nor how accurate their criticism of the "old line" parties; they achieved little because they had not played the party game.

The Progressives had erred in thinking that it was parliament and the party system that were at fault and causing their trouble. To some extent the influence of American reform ideas and American experience had led to this misapprehension, for in the American Congress the individual member does have more influence than his counterpart in the Canadian House of Commons. Leadership in the Canadian House lies with the cabinet. Members, in effect, merely approve cabinet proposals or oppose them. The cabinet retains its right to lead the Commons and govern the country by virtue of the support it has in the House of Commons. Generally, this support is guaranteed because the prime minister and his cabinet colleagues are the leaders of the majority party in the Commons and that party, through strict party discipline, votes as a bloc. The addition of sixty-five undisciplined Progressives had alerted the Liberal and Conservative parties to the discontent of the farmers, but it did not force the government to make the concessions the Progressives had assumed their victory would bring.

When the CCF was established it appeared the lesson of the Progressive experience had been learned. Unlike the Progressives, the CCF was a vigorous champion of the parliamentary system and its members became particularly adept in using the institution to achieve the goals of the socialist movement. Social Credit, on the other hand, never demonstrated any great fondness for the institution, and on more than one occasion its members indicated that they considered it a nuisance. J.S. Woodsworth, M.J. Coldwell, and Stanley Knowles of the CCF were all, at various times, described as great parliamentarians. William Aberhart of the Social Credit party rarely spoke in the Alberta legislature and W.A.C. Bennett of the B.C. Social Credit party considered that there was altogether too much talk in the chamber.

From the Progressive experience in the twenties and the agrarian opposition to "partyism," these two strands, the CCF and Social Credit, branch off, each running in different directions from the same source.

In neither case was the position of the Member of Parliament — or of the provincial legislator — reconsidered in the light of Progressive ideas. For the CCF, the MP remained a representative and a party member; for the Social Credit party, he was an adjunct to the cabinet and the civil service, with a much more reduced role in the legislative process than even the normal parliamentary system envisaged. The Progressive ideal of members as delegates from their constituencies or from their economic groups languished and died, killed by the necessity of party unity that the cabinet system of parliamentary government demanded.

NOTES

[1] Cited in W.L. Morton, *The Progressive Party in Canada* (Toronto: University of Toronto Press, 1950), 116-17, from *The Grain Growers's Guide* (Winnipeg), October 5, 1921, p. 27.
[2] Morton, *Progressive Party*, 152-53.
[3] Morton, *Progressive Party*, 153.
[4] Cited in Morton, *Progressive Party*, 193, from House of Commons *Debates* (1924), 2214.
[5] Cited in Morton, *Progressive Party*, 195.
[6] Cited in K.W. McNaught, *A Prophet in Politics: A Biography of J.S. Woodsworth* (Toronto: University of Toronto Press, 1959), 167.
[7] PAC, Manuscript in Henry Spencer Papers (n.d.).

The Origins of the Maritime Rights Movement*

E.R. FORBES

Canadian historians have devoted considerable attention to post-war agitation on the Prairies: they have virtually ignored similar agitation in the Maritimes, the regional protest movement which became known by the slogan "Maritime Rights." The few comments it has received, in biographical literature or in sweeping analyses of long periods of history, have been largely concerned with its political manifestations.[1] Such a preoccupation is not surprising. Both Liberals and Conservatives were vociferous in their efforts to portray themselves as the champions of the movement. Shortly before the Antigonish-Guysborough by-election of 1927 a Protestant clergyman set out to review the issues of the campaign from the pulpit. Both candidates, he noted, were clamouring for attention as the defenders of "Maritime Rights." This aspect of their campaign, he said, reminded him of the behaviour of his own young children one evening when he and his wife were getting ready to go visiting. The little girl set up an awful howl from the moment the babysitter arrived. She bawled and bawled. Finally, just as her parents were going out the

*Reprinted with permission from *Acadiensis: Journal of the History of the Atlantic Region* 5, 1 (Autumn 1975): 54-66.

door, her brother turned, slapped her sharply, and declared, "Shut up, I wanna cry."

There was much more to "Maritime Rights" than the conspicuous wail of the politicians. One cannot begin to tell here the story of the movement — the intensive organizational campaign with its delegations to Ottawa, economic conferences, and country-wide speaking tours; the erratic swings in the popular vote from one party to another as Maritimers searched desperately for solutions to their problems; and the inevitable royal commissions sent in to defuse the agitation[2] — but one can at least attempt a more basic introduction through the analysis of the motives of the different social groups which participated in it. Their behaviour suggests that the issues involved went much deeper than mere political manoeuvering or even, as Professor G.A. Rawlyk has suggested, the attempt by the local "Establishment" to undercut other forms of social protest.[3] All classes in the region, although often in conflict on other issues, were united in their support of Maritime Rights. Each was aware that its own particular aspirations were incapable of realization until the region's declining influence was checked or reversed.

402

The social categories employed here will be those used by the people themselves. Maritimers spoke frequently in this period of their "classes." They were not referring to any clear Marxian structure nor did they imply the status-based stratification of the modern sociologist. Essentially they were talking about broad occupational interest groups. Such divisions were partly theoretical: the members of each group or "class" were assumed to have interests in common of which not all might be conscious. But they also had an empirical basis through such exclusively occupational organizations as the Maritime Division of the Canadian Manufacturers Association, retail merchants' associations, the United Farmers, federations of labour and, by the end of the decade, the Maritime Fishermen's Union. These were the kinds of groupings to which New Brunswick Premier P.J. Veniot referred early in 1923 when he reported to Mackenzie King that, after looking "carefully into the [Maritime Rights] movement," he had found it was "purely non-political and embraces [the] efforts of all classes to obtain what is sincerely considered fair play for [the] Maritime Provinces."[4]

The development of Maritime regionalism, of which the Maritime Rights movement formed the climax, took place largely in the first two decades of the century. Previously, popular loyalties had been focused upon larger imperial or national entities or upon smaller political, cultural, or geographical units. The shift was dictated by a growing realization of the need for co-operation. Co-operation was essential if the three Atlantic Provinces were to counteract the eclipse of their influence which resulted from the rise of the West and the growing metropolitan dominance of Central Canada. Another factor contributing to the growth of regionalism was the progressive ideology of the period, which increased the pressure upon the small governments for expensive reforms while at the same time suggesting the possibility of limitless achievement through a strategy of unity, organization, and agitation. Consequently, regional awareness increased sharply in the three provinces. Their leaders joined forces to fight losses in representation, which followed every census after 1891; to increase their subsidies, which had fallen far behind those of the Prairies; and to defend the Intercolonial Railway, whose pro-Maritime policies came under attack from both the Prairies and Central Canada.[5]

The manufacturers' stake in the regionalization of the Maritimes was most obvious, particularly for the defense of the Intercolonial Railway. By the end of the 19th century that railway had become an important agent of industrialization in the region. Its management had accepted the principle that half a loaf was better than none and had reduced rates to develop traffic. It created a basic freight rate structure which was between 20 and 50 percent lower than that in force in Ontario and offered in addition special rate concessions based upon "what the traffic would bear."[6] Built into the structure was a system of "arbitraries" or especially low rates between the Maritimes and Montreal on goods destined for points further west. These rates enabled the secondary manufacturers in the Maritimes to penetrate markets in Western and Central Canada to obtain the sales volume necessary for competitive production.[7] With such encouragement, capital investment in manufacturing in the Maritimes quadrupled between 1900 and 1920.[8] The old dream of some Nova Scotian entrepreneurs that their province would play the role of a great industrial metropolis to a Canadian hinterland was far from realization. But the Maritimers' optimism for their manufacturing potential persisted. The Halifax *Morning Chronicle* in 1906 explicitly touted Nova Scotia's pioneer programme in technical education as encouraging the industrialization which would reverse the region's declining status in Confederation. The Saint John *Standard* in 1916 enthused about a hydro-electric project to harness the Bay of Fundy tides, which, by providing cheaper energy for manufacturing, would raise the Maritimes "to a position of commercial supremacy as compared with any other part of the Dominion."[9]

Such aspirations received a severe check with the integration of the Intercolonial into a national system. The happy partnership between the Intercolonial management and the local producers had come under attack both from competing Central Canadian manufacturers and Prairie farmers preoccupied with their demand for the equalization of freight rates.[10] The Borden government apparently decided to get rid of the anomaly of a Maritime-oriented railway once and for all. In November, 1918, it shifted the Intercolonial's headquarters to Toronto, transferred its senior officials to other lines and replaced them with appointees from the Canadian Northern. The following year, the Intercolonial was placed under the *de facto* jurisdiction of the Board of Railway Commissioners which raised the rates to the Ontario level.[11] The process was completed in time to provide an inflated base for the 40 per cent general rate increase of 1920. In Ontario and Quebec freight rates increased 111 percent between 1916 and September 1920; in the Maritimes basic rates rose between 140 and 216 percent and the simultaneous cancellation of special rates, such as the special commodity rate on sugar, led to still greater increases.[12]

The rate changes not only threatened the local entrepreneurs' dreams of industrial grandeur, but left them seriously exposed to the pressure for metropolitan consolidation. For many, the campaign for Maritime Rights became a struggle for survival. In 1919 a group of manufacturers mounted a delegation to Ottawa, demanded the restoration of the Intercolonial to independent management, and revived the Maritime Board of Trade as a channel for their agitation.[13] They continued to play a prominent role in the leadership of the movement through such representatives as W.S. Fisher of Saint John, a former Canadian Manufacturers' Association president, who served as a spokesman for another delegation to Ottawa in 1921, and D.R. Turnbull, managing-director of the Acadia Sugar Corporation, who, in 1925, became Nova Scotia's representative on the newly formed Maritime Rights Transportation Committee.[14]

Maritime merchants were also seriously affected by the integration of the Intercolonial into a national system. The wholesalers were injured by the shift in supply purchasing for the railway from the Maritimes to Toronto.[15] They were weakened further, in relation to their metropolitan competitors, by the sharp increase in "town distributing rates" — especially low rates which had enabled them to import quantities of goods from Central Canada, break them up, and send them out to individual towns and villages at little more than the cost of direct shipment. Similarly higher rates on the Intercolonial accelerated the shift away from Maritime ports as distributing points for products entering from abroad. H.R. Silver, a commission merchant, reported a decline in molasses shipments out of Halifax from 130 carloads in 1916 to 17 in 1921.[16] Retailers were also adversely affected. They had to pay more for their goods and had difficulty in passing the full charge on to their customers. The Halifax *Maritime Merchant* commented tersely in 1920 upon the general effect of the increase: "Added to the handicap already suffered by firms seeking western business, the new rate will be hard on the merchants and add materially to the cost the local consumer must pay."[17]

The issue which generated the greatest heat from the merchant and commercial interests of Halifax and Saint John was the development of their ports as entrepôts for Canada's winter trade. The two cities were engaged in a Darwinian struggle with the American seaports and with each other. The key to victory was volume and variety of traffic. The more traffic, the lower the port charges and ocean rates; the lower the rates, the greater the traffic. The Maritime ports were most conscious of their rivalry with Portland, Maine, which had traditionally enjoyed the advantage of a very active canvass for trade from the Grand Trunk Railway.[18] The Maritime ports' aspirations for Canadian trade, aroused initially by Confederation, had blossomed under the "national policy" of the Laurier Government. Laurier had promised that the National Transcontinental Railway would channel exports, particularly grain, through national ports. In 1903, he appointed a Royal Commission to investigate other means of routing trade through "all-Canadian channels," and in 1911, he pledged that his government would restrict the Imperial preference to goods entering through Canadian ports.[19]

Such expectations were rudely shaken by the federal take-over of the Grand Trunk. With it, the Canadian government inherited a strong vested interest in the commercial success of Portland. At Halifax, prominent Liberals urged the return of a Conservative cabinet minister in the by-election of 1920 to give the Maritimes at least a voice in defending their port's interest.[20] Early in 1922 the Halifax and Saint John boards of trade appointed a joint committee, consisting largely of merchants and manufacturers, to co-ordinate their agitation on such issues as the restoration of the Intercolonial and the routing of trade through Maritime ports.[21] The merchants' position in the Maritime Rights movement continued to be a prominent one through the organized activities of boards of trade and the role of individuals such as W.A. Black, of the leading merchant-shipping firm of Pickford and Black. At seventy-six years of age, against "his physicians' advice, his wife's fears and his family's opposition," Black came out of retirement to fight the Halifax by-election of 1923 on a platform of Maritime Rights.[22]

Another business group, the lumbermen, also joined the agitation. For them, the impact of the increased freight charges was compounded in 1921 by increased American duty on timber products under the Fordney tariff. Angus MacLean of The Bathurst Company, later president of the New Brunswick Lumberman's Association, appealed to Mackenzie King for relief on both issues.[23] When none was forthcoming he and other so-called "Lumber lords" of New Brunswick, such as Archie and Donald Fraser, owners of the second largest lumber company in the Maritimes, threw their very considerable support behind the Conservative "Maritime Rights" candidates in the federal election of 1925.[24] In that year, MacLean became the titular leader of the protest movement as president of the Maritime Board of Trade.

Although labour in the Maritimes was at the peak of its "class" consciousness in 1919, it joined with the business groups in the agitation. Between 1916 and 1920, reported union membership in the Maritimes had quadrupled to about 40 000.[25] Spurred by the anticipation of a "new

405

era" to follow the War[26] and beset by the grim reality of galloping inflation,[27] the workers attempted new techniques in organization and challenged their employers in a series of strikes in 1919 and 1920. At the
same time they were conscious that their aspirations for a greater share
of the fruits of their labour could not be achieved if their industries
were destroyed from other causes. Early in 1919 the *Eastern Federationist*,
published by the Trades and Labour Council of Pictou County, argued
that the freight rate increases violated the "rights of the Maritime Provinces' people under the terms of Confederation."[28] After the Amherst
"General Strike" in May and June of 1919, the *Federationist* was particularly incensed by reports that the Canada Car Company was planning
to transfer its Amherst operation to Montreal. The thrust of the editor's
bitterness was directed at both the capitalists involved and the trend
towards metropolitan consolidation which posed a continual threat to
Maritime industry and jobs.[29] Similarly the Halifax *Citizen*, the organ
of the local Trades and Labour Council, severely criticized the removal
of the railway headquarters from Moncton and commended the activities
of the Maritime Board of Trade president, Hance J. Logan, in seeking
Maritime union as a counterweight to the declining political influence
of the region. Bemoaning the unfair treatment accorded the Maritimes
by the rest of the country, the *Citizen* concluded that there was "very
little hope of any justice for us under present conditions."[30] The journal
periodically returned to this theme and remained a consistent supporter
of Maritime Rights.

The Railway Brotherhoods, which, after the United Mineworkers, constituted the largest bloc of organized labour in the region, were directly
involved in the Maritime Rights campaign. During the first decade of
the century the brotherhoods had won the acceptance of the principle
of seniority in promotions and lay-offs on the Intercolonial.[31] In theory
at least, the humblest employee could aspire to the highest office on
the road. Under the new regime after 1918, that principle went by the
board. According to one estimate, 400 employees were transferred out
of the Moncton headquarters and any replacements came from other
government roads. In addition, the repair shops declined and staff was
reduced all along the line. To some workers it seemed the principle of
seniority had been replaced by the principle that no Maritimer need
apply.[32]

Labour did not need to be coaxed into the Maritime Rights movement
by the Halifax *Herald* or other politically oriented journals in the 1920's;
large segments were already there, drawn by a consideration of their
own immediate interest. The railway centres provided the most consistent
voting support for Maritime Rights candidates throughout the 1920's.
F.B. McCurdy attributed his victory in the important Colchester by-
election of 1920 to the railway workers' belief that in the cabinet he
would "be strong enough to afford some relief in the railway grievance."

He blamed his defeat in the general election of 1921 on his inability to do so.[33] Labour also threw its support behind W.A. Black in the Halifax by-election of 1923.[34] Neil Herman, labour organizer, Social Gospel clergyman, and sometime editor of the Halifax *Citizen* was a founder and executive member of the Halifax Maritime Club.[35] He later accompanied its president, H.S. Congdon, in a tour of Central Canada to drum up newspaper support for the movement. When the so-called "Great" Maritime Rights delegation went to Ottawa in February 1925, J.E. Tighe, president of the Saint John local of the International Longshoreman's Association, was one of four speakers who addressed the Members of Parliament on Maritime problems.[36]

The farmers were only slightly behind labour in their support for Maritime Rights. They too had expected to play a greater role in the new society which was supposed to follow the war; instead they were con-

407

Acadia University Archives.

In the 1920s many Maritimers became concerned about their region's declining position in Confederation. In this cartoon, Maritimers are promised greater wealth if they board the "Maritime Rights train to prosperity." They did elect a number of Maritime Rights advocates to the federal parliament in the election of 1925.

fronted by the realities of rural depopulation and community disintegration.[37] They challenged the business groups with new or intensified political, occupational, and economic organization. But their problems were in part those of the region. The new freight rates hit them, both as producers and consumers. Some were also angered by federal policies which seemed not only to encourage new immigrants to by-pass their region but also to promote westward migration at their expense. As much as they might resent the growth of industrial towns and their own relative loss in status, the farmers were conscious of their dependence on these towns for their markets. Even those who sold their apples or potatoes in Great Britain or the West Indies usually earned a significant proportion of their income in local markets — an important hedge against the sometimes widely fluctuating international prices.[38]

For a brief period the farmers' regional concern was obscured by their participation in what they believed was a national "class" movement. But their organizations, such as the Canadian Council of Agriculture, were dominated by the Prairies. Manitobans, T.A. Crerar and George Chipman, also sought to direct the movement in the Maritimes through the *United Farmers' Guide*. The *Guide*, theoretically the organ of the New Brunswick and Nova Scotia United Farmers Associations, was in fact a subsidiary of the *Grain Growers' Guide*.[39] The two regionalisms were soon in conflict. Western organizers tried in vain to get unequivocal statements against the tariff from the United Farmers of Nova Scotia and were cool to suggestions that "necessary" protection for local industries should be retained.[40] At the same time they offered no support for the Maritime positions on such issues as the Intercolonial, freight rates, and subsidies. Most Maritime farmers realized they could not achieve their regional goals through a movement which was, in federal politics at least, "an agrarian and sectional bloc from the continental West, the representation of the monolithic wheat economy."[41] In 1921 support for the western-affiliated United Farmers Associations rapidly dwindled. By mid-summer "a majority" in the Maritime Co-operative Companies was reported anxious to dispose of the *United Farmers Guide* in which they had initially invested but were unable to control.[42]

The agricultural interests of Prince Edward Island had been involved in the Maritime Rights movement from the outset. At the Maritime Board of Trade meeting in 1919 they were happy to associate with the broader issues of the movement their own special problems. These were two: the need for a second car ferry and the completion of the widening of their narrow gauge railways to permit a more rapid, reliable, and cheaper delivery of their products to mainland markets.[43] In 1921 the Mainland farmers met in conference with representatives of manufacturing, merchant, and shipping groups to launch a delegation to Ottawa to demand the return of the Intercolonial to independent management.[44] Thereafter, farm leaders assumed an increasingly important role in the

Maritime Rights agitation. In 1923, for example, A.E. McMahon, president of the United Fruit Companies and a former vice-president of the United Farmers of Nova Scotia, became president of the Maritime Board of Trade, and, a year later, of the Maritime Development Association. One of the primary purposes of the latter organization was the rehabilitation of the rural areas through immigration and colonization.[45]

The fishermen's contribution to the Maritime Rights movement was largely restricted to the intensification of the discontent which underlay it. Their aspirations had been relatively moderate. The victims of a declining salt fish trade with the West Indies, they hoped to restore their industry through the expansion of their sales of fresh fish in Central Canada and New England. The former had been encouraged by a federal subsidy of one third of the express rate to Montreal on less than carload lots, the latter by a *modus vivendi* with the United States which had permitted them to land and sell their catches directly at American ports.[46] In 1919, the federal subsidies on fresh fish were terminated just as the trade was hit by the higher freight rates.[47] Needless to say, the fish merchants passed on their losses to the largely unorganized fishermen. Meanwhile, the door to the New England market was slammed shut by the American cancellation of the *modus vivendi* and the introduction of the Fordney tariff.

In the election of 1921, some fishermen seem to have accepted the Liberal promises of reciprocity to restore the American markets.[48] When this failed to materialize, their desperate plight led many (for example, the Yarmouth halibut fleet) to pack up and move to the United States.[49] Those who remained formed one group in Maritime society which seemed genuinely prepared to contemplate secession in their frantic search for markets. It was surely no coincidence that both Howard Corning, who proposed the famous secession resolution of 1923, and the lawyer Robert Blauveldt, self-proclaimed secessionist and Maritime Rights publicist,[50] were both residents of Yarmouth county.

The role of professional classes in the Maritime Rights movement was prominent, but their motivation ambiguous. It is often difficult to discern whether lawyers, doctors, clergymen, academics, and journalists were speaking for themselves or for the other groups in society by whom they were directly or indirectly employed. Certainly they played an important function in articulating and rationalizing the aspirations of the other groups. This role was explicit in some cases. The Nova Scotia government retained H.F. Munro of Dalhousie University to aid in the preparation of its submission to the Duncan Commission. The boards of trade hired freight rate experts, professional organizers, and lawyers to prepare, publicize, and help present their cases before the federal government and its various commissions. Significant also was the relationship between Maritime Rights journalists and the interests who paid their salaries, or patronized their newspapers through advertising and subscriptions.

The lumberman-industrialist Angus MacLean, for example, was reportedly "the principal owner" of the Saint John *Telegraph Journal*.[51] That paper in 1925 promoted the cross-country speaking-tours of president J.D. McKenna and editor A.B. Belding as part of its campaign for Maritime Rights. Similarly C.W. Lunn, who was credited with the initial popularization of the defence of the Intercolonial as guaranteed under the "compact of confederation," aspired to a labour readership and was even hired for a brief period to write for the *Eastern Federationist*.[52] More tenuous but still significant was the relationship between clergymen and the congregations which they represented. It is clear, for example, that the priests who protested the Duncan Commission's failure to help the fishermen were acting as agents for the fishermen in their parishes. Their intervention resulted in the Royal Commission investigation of the fisheries in 1928.[53]

In articulating the progressive reform ideology, which provided an important element in the developing Maritime regionalism, the professionals' motivation was also ambiguous. As various American scholars have pointed out, "progressivism," with its optimism, social criticism, and focus on government as an agent of reform, might be inspired by many and mixed motives.[54] To farmers, labour, and their representatives, "progressivism" could be the desire to improve the lot of the weak and exploited, namely themselves. On the part of the business-oriented it might be concern for efficiency, the replacement of old-fashioned party structures, and the development of a more dynamic role by government which might more effectively serve the interests of the entrepreneur. To the professionals, besides any humanitarian concern, "progressivism" might mean an improved status or an expansion of their role in society in social work, health services, or the government bureaucracy.

In the Maritimes, the clergy and academics were most prominent in articulating the various strains of an amorphous progressive ideology. The clergy, imbued with the social gospel, promoted a variety of reforms ranging from prohibition to widows' pensions and occasionally engaged in wholesale attacks on the capitalist system.[55] Academics used a more secular terminology but they too championed a wide range of reforms for the welfare of the community. Dr. F.H. Sexton hailed Nova Scotia's programme of technical education — he happened to be its superintendent — as a valuable means of "social service" in improving the lot of the miners and industrial workers.[56] That it was also a service for local industry went without saying. Dr. Melville Cummings of the Truro Agricultural College and Rev. Hugh MacPherson of Saint Francis Xavier University displayed a similar zeal for agricultural education and farmers' co-operatives as the means of rural regeneration. President George B. Cutten of Acadia University, having failed to persuade governments to undertake the hydro-electric development of the Bay of Fundy, organized the Cape Split Development Company in an attempt to interest private capital in the scheme.[57]

410

All these progressive proposals placed strong pressure upon provincial governments to inaugurate or expand programmes for which revenue was not readily available. This fact led progressive elements into an ephemeral campaign for Maritime union, which was expected to provide a more efficient use of available resources,[58] and into a more substantive campaign for Maritime unity, one object of which was to wrest from the Federal Government a "fair" share of Dominion revenues.

Increased federal subsidies were sought, for example, by professionals concerned about the declining quality of instruction in the schools as higher salaries drew experienced teachers westward. But, since fiscal need had never been accepted as a justification for higher subsidies, Maritime governments developed the claim that they were entitled to monetary compensation for grants of land from the public domain — grants such as had been given to Ontario, Manitoba, and Quebec in the boundary settlements of 1912. They also demanded subsidies in lieu of the increasingly lucrative "school lands" funds held in trust by the federal government for the Prairie Provinces. The Maritime Educational Convention at Moncton in 1918 and a Catholic educational conference at Antigonish a year later both discussed the subsidy claims as a matter vital to educational reform.[59] In the latter year the Conservative Halifax *Herald* enthusiastically endorsed a Liberal resolution which outlined the Maritime claims in the Nova Scotian Legislature. The "serious material injustice" inflicted upon the Maritimes through "the unfair distribution which has been made of federal assets by successive governments" had, according to the *Herald*, starved local government services or supplied them "in such a niggardly manner that progress is almost impossible." The *Herald* advocated the launching of "a concerted movement and [*sic*] properly directed activity. *We suggest that a maritime popular league should be forthwith organized, with provincial and county and town and village branches in all parts of the Maritime provinces, until the whole country has been enlightened, aroused and arrayed in a support of the resolution unanimously adopted by the Nova Scotia legislature.*"[60] Although as their problems increased, Maritimers sought more fundamental solutions, the subsidy claims remained one of the basic components of the campaign for Maritime rights.

411

The Maritime Rights agitation which had emerged by 1919 was a regional protest movement which saw all classes united in their demands upon the rest of the country. This did not mean that different classes did not have distinct aspirations of their own; on the contrary, they were probably more conscious of them in 1919 than in any other period before or since. Each held a dream of progressive development in which its own collective interests were directly involved: for the manufacturers, their growth as the major industrial suppliers of the country; for the urban merchants, the final attainment of their communities' status as the entrepots of Canada's trade; for labour and farmers, the emergence of a new, more democratic, society in which they would break the economic and political dominance of the business classes; for the fishermen, the chance to rehabilitate their industry through the new fresh fish trade; and for the professionals, the elevation of Maritime society through education. But none of these aspirations was capable of realization with the continued decline of the economic and political status of the Maritimes in the Dominion. Just as electricity might channel the usually conflicting molecular energies of an iron bar to produce a magnetic force, so the federal government's adverse policies served to re-align the various "classes" in the Maritimes to produce a powerful social force — regionalism. This force, dressed up in a variety of complex rationalizations, became the Maritime Rights movement of the 1920's.

NOTES

1 See J.M. Beck, *The Government of Nova Scotia* (Toronto, 1957), 338-40; W.R. Graham, *Arthur Meighen*, vol. 2, *And Fortune Fled* (Toronto, 1963), ch. 11; H.B. Neatby, *William Lyon Mackenzie King: 1924-1932; The Lonely Heights* (Toronto, 1963), 67 and 220-24; K.A. MacKirdy, "Regionalism: Canada and Australia" (Ph.D. thesis, University of Toronto, 1959), 245-50; and G.A. Rawlyk, "The Maritimes and the Canadian Community," in M. Wade, ed., *Regionalism in the Canadian Community, 1867-1967*,(Toronto, 1969), 113-15. The only previous study which focused directly on Maritime Rights was Michael Hatfield, "J.B. Baxter and the Maritime Rights Movement" (B.A. honours essay, Mount Allison University, 1969).

2 E.R. Forbes, "The Maritime Rights Movement, 1919-1927: A Study in Canadian Regionalism" (Ph.D. thesis, Queens University, 1975).

3 G.A. Rawlyk "The Farmer–Labour Movement and the Failure of Socialism in Nova Scotia," in Laurier LaPierre et al., eds., *Essays on the Left* (Toronto, 1971), 37-38.

4 P.J. Veniot to W.L.M. King, 27 February 1923, W.L.M. King Papers, Public Archives of Canada (hereafter PAC).

5 See Canada, *Sessional Papers* (1910), no. 100; Halifax *Wesleyan*, 12 May 1909; Saint John *Standard*, 30 October 1913; W. Eggleston and C.T. Kraft, *Dominion Provincial Subsidies and Grants* (Ottawa, 1939), 188-89; and the "Presentation to His Royal Highness in Council of the claims of the Provinces of New Brunswick, Nova Scotia and Prince Edward Island, for Compensation in Respect of the Public Lands of Canada, transferred to Certain Provinces of Canada or held in trust for their Benefit, January 29, 1913," R.L. Borden Papers, p. 5249, PAC.

6 R.A.C. Henry and Associates, *Railway Freight Rates in Canada* (Ottawa, 1939), 266 and 268, and Transcripts of the hearings of the Royal Commission on Maritime Claims, 462-65, Atlantic Provinces Transportation Commission (hereafter APTC).

7 See S.A. Saunders, *The Economic History of the Maritime Provinces* (Ottawa, 1939), 27.

8 *Canada Year Book* (1922-23), 220, 415-16.

9 Halifax *Morning Chronicle*, 17 August 1906, and Saint John *Standard*, 25 March 1916.

10 Judgement of the Board of Railway Commissioners, 15 March 1919, R.L. Borden Papers, pp. 131067-9, PAC; Canada, *Debates* (1917), 787, 4339-77.

11 Transcript of hearings of the Board of Railway Commissioners [BRC], 1920, p. 11703, PAC.

12 Calculated from percentages in BRC transcripts 1926, p. 6602, and from "standard mileage rates" in R.A.C. Henry, *Railway Freight Rates.*

13 *The Busy East of Canada* (Sackville), September 1919.

14 "Report of Meeting with the Prime Minister and the members of the Government, Delegation from the Maritime Province," 1 June 1921, R.B. Bennett Papers, p. 10142, PAC, and F.C. Cornell to H.D. Cartwright, 12 October 1925, Maritime Provinces Freight Rate Commission Papers, APTC.

15 E.M. Macdonald to Mackenzie King, 8 December 1922, W.L.M. King Papers, PAC.

16 F.C. Cornell "Memorandum re the Transportation Problems and Freight Rate Structure of the Province of Nova Scotia," 1926, p. 10, and Transcripts, BRC, 1926, pp. 6765-67, PAC.

17 *Maritime Merchant*, 16 September 1920, p. 104.

18 Transcripts, Royal Commission on Maritime Claims, p. 2173, APTC.

19 "Report of the Royal Commission on Transportation . . . 1903," Canada, *Sessional Papers* (1906), no. 19a; Canada, *Debates* (1922), 708-10.

20 Halifax *Herald*, 18 September 1920.

21 Minutes of the Council of the Saint John Board of Trade, 13 July 1922, New Brunswick Museum.

22 Hector McInnes to Arthur Meighen, November 1923, Arthur Meighen Papers, p. 051956, PAC.

23 A. MacLean to W.L.M. King, 25 April 1922 and 8 October 1924, W.L.M. King Papers, PAC.

[24] J.C. Webster to Arthur Meighen, 26 September 1925, and R. O'Leary to Meighen, 3 September 1925, Arthur Meighen Papers, PAC.

[25] *The Fifth Annual Report on Labour Organization in Canada, 1916* (Ottawa, 1917), 206–207, and the *Tenth Annual Report on Labour Organization in Canada, 1920* (Ottawa, 1921), 279.

[26] For examples of their optimistic rhetoric see the Sydney *Canadian Labour Leader*, 8 February 1918; the New Glasgow *Eastern Federationist*, 19, 26 April 1919; and the Moncton *Union Worker*, February 1920.

[27] *Labour Gazette*, January 1921, p. 117.

[28] *Eastern Federationist*, 8 March 1919.

[29] *Eastern Federationist*, 7 June 1919.

[30] Halifax *Citizen*, 21 May and 10 September 1920.

[31] "Being an address by Mr. Geo. W. Yates, Assistant Deputy Minister of Railways, Before the History and Political Science Club of Western Ontario, Feb. 16, 1923," Arthur Meighen Papers, pp. 157485–9, PAC.

[32] *The Busy East*, June and July 1923.

[33] F.B. McCurdy to Robert Borden, 21 December 1921, Robert Meighen Papers, PAC.

[34] H.L. Stewart to W.L.M. King, 9 December 1923, W.L.M. King Papers, PAC.

[35] "Minutes of the Maritime Club of Halifax," 11 February 1924, H.S. Congdon Papers (courtesy of Mr. H.H. Congdon, Huntsville, Ontario).

[36] Saint John *Telegraph Journal*, 27 February 1925.

[37] See A.A. Mackenzie, "The Rise and Fall of the Farmer–Labour Party in Nova Scotia" (M.A. thesis, Dalhousie University, 1969), and L.A. Wood, *A History of Farmer Movements in Canada* (Toronto, 1924).

[38] *Proceedings of the Select Special Committee of the House of Commons to inquire into Agricultural Conditions* (Ottawa, 1924), 475.

[39] Three of the five members of the directorate were Manitobans. C.F. Chipman to "The Editor," *Maritime Farmer*, 13 March 1920, T.A. Crerar Papers, The Douglas Library, Queen's University.

[40] J.M. Pratt to T.A. Crerar, 9 November 1920, and G.G. Archibald to T.A. Crerar, 4 October 1920, T.A. Crerar Papers, The Douglas Library, Queen's University.

[41] W.L. Morton, *The Progressive Party in Canada* (Toronto, 1950), 129.

[42] S.H. Hagerman to G.F. Chipman, 18 June 1921, T.A. Crerar Papers, Douglas Library, Queen's University.

[43] *The Busy East*, September 1919. See also M.K. Cullen, "The Transportation Issue, 1873–1973," in F.W.P. Bolger, ed., *Canada's Smallest Province: A History of Prince Edward Island* (Charlottetown, 1973), 255–57.

[44] *The Busy East*, May 1921.

[45] Charlottetown *Evening Patriot*, 23 January 1925.

[46] *Report of the Royal Commission Investigating the Fisheries of the Maritime Provinces and the Magdalen Islands* (Ottawa, 1928), 32, 61–65.

[47] "Fifty-third Annual Report of the Fisheries Branch . . . 1919," *Sessional Papers* (1919), no. 44, p. 11.

[48] G.B. Kenny reported to Hector MacInnes after a trip along the Eastern Shore that the Liberal candidates had "actually got many people to believe that real free trade with the U.S. is in sight." 21 November 1921, Hector MacInnes Papers (courtesy of Donald MacInnes, Halifax, N.S.).

[49] Transcripts of the hearings of the Royal Commission Investigating the Fisheries . . . 1928, p. 3476, APTC.

[50] R. Blauveldt to H.S. Congdon, 30 September 1924, H.S. Congdon Papers.

[51] J.H. McGaffigan to Arthur Meighen, 28 February 1924, Arthur Meighen Papers, PAC.

[52] See Halifax *Morning Chronicle*, 16 November 1921; C.W. Lunn to H.S. Congdon, 13 April 1929, H.S. Congdon Papers.

[53] Transcripts, Royal Commission to investigate the Fisheries . . . 1927, p. 6.

[54] See for example R.H. Wiebe, *The Search for Order, 1877–1920* (New York, 1967); Gabriel Kolko, *The Triumph of Conservatism* (New York, 1963); and D.W. Noble, *The Progressive Mind, 1890–1917* (Chicago, 1970).

[55] See E.R. Forbes "Prohibition and the Social Gospel in Nova Scotia," *Acadiensis* 1, 1 (Autumn 1971): 15–19, and his review of Richard Allen, *The Social Passion*, in *Acadiensis* 2, I (Autumn 1972): 98.

[56] Halifax *Daily Echo*, 24 May 1913.

[57] *Industrial Canada*, August 1918.

[58] See J.M. Beck, *The History of Maritime Union: A Study in Frustration*, 31–44.

[59] O.T. Daniels, *The Claims of the Maritime Provinces for Federal Subsidies in Lieu of Western Lands* (Halifax, 1918) and *Proceedings of the Second Annual Educational Conference, Antigonish* (1919).

[60] Halifax *Herald*, 10 May 1919.

413

Topic Eleven

The Great Depression

In the 1930s, Canadians faced their worst economic depression in modern history. The Great Depression affected Canada severely because of the nation's reliance on foreign trade of primary commodities in what had become a nationalistic and protectionist era. Wheat prices, for example, fell from two dollars a bushel in the late 1920s to thirty-four cents a bushel in 1932. The resulting economic decline affected secondary and service industries. Between 1929 and 1933 Canada's gross national expenditure fell by nearly a third. Unemployment reached as high as thirty-five percent in some regions. Thousands endured the humiliation of going on relief — a last, desperate solution to their critical situation. James Gray adds a personal dimension to the depression in "Our World Stopped and We Got Off," an excerpt from his book *The Winter Years,* in which he recalls his own desperate search for work and the humiliation of going on relief when that search failed.

At first Canadians expected the depression to be a temporary phenomenon that would end as suddenly as it had begun. Such hopes were soon frustrated. The Conservatives had come to power in 1930, and it remained for R.B. Bennett, the prime minister, to find a solution. Initially he tried to create "work and wages" for the unemployed through higher tariffs, unemployment relief, and public works. Yet the jobless rate kept increasing. Frustrated and fearful of social upheaval, Bennett became less sympathetic to the unemployed, seeing them as an unnecessary drain on the state.

In the 1935 election, the Liberals defeated the Conservatives, and William Lyon Mackenzie King was returned to office. Although he came with essentially no new policies, he did — under pressure — appoint both a National Employment Commission to investigate the unemployment and relief situation and a Royal Commission on Dominion–Provincial Relations. Both strongly recommended that the federal government take responsibility for unemployment relief by setting up a national employment service and a nationwide unemployment-insurance system. James Struthers outlines the rationale behind the attitudes of the Bennett and Mackenzie King governments towards unemployment and relief projects, and their disastrous results, in "Canadian Unemployment Policy in the 1930s."

Students interested in the Great Depression in Canada should begin with *The Dirty Thirties: Canadians in the Great Depression,* ed. M. Horn

(Toronto: Copp Clark, 1972), a collection of primary and secondary sources on the social and political repercussions of the depression, and *The Depression in Canada: Response to Economic Crisis*, ed. M. Horn (Toronto: Copp Clark, 1988). See as well H.B. Neatby's *The Politics of Chaos: Canada in the Thirties*, which contains biographical sketches of the political leaders. The second and third volumes of the official biography of Mackenzie King, also by H.B. Neatby, cover the depression years: *The Lonely Heights: 1924-1932* (Toronto: University of Toronto Press, 1963) and *The Prism of Unity* (Toronto: University of Toronto Press, 1976). James Struthers' work on unemployment relief in the thirties is presented in greater detail in *No Fault of Their Own: Unemployment and the Canadian Welfare State, 1914-1941* (Toronto: University of Toronto Press, 1983). Also useful is Dennis Guest's *The Emergence of Social Security in Canada* (Vancouver: University of British Columbia Press, 1980). On the role of Charlotte Whitton see P.T. Rooke and R.L. Schnell, *No Bleeding Heart: Charlotte Whitton: A Feminist on the Right* (Vancouver: University of British Columbia Press, 1987).

415

There are a number of excellent studies of third parties during the depression era. For the CCF see Walter Young's *The Anatomy of a Party: The National CCF* (Toronto: University of Toronto Press, 1969) and Kenneth McNaught's *A Prophet in Politics* (Toronto: University of Toronto Press, 1959), the only scholarly study of the party's first leader, J.S. Woodsworth. Joan Sangster discusses the role of women in the CCF and in the Communist party in *Dream of Equality: Women on the Canadian Left, 1920-1950* (Toronto: McClelland and Stewart, 1987). Social Credit is the subject of a series published in the 1950s by the University of Toronto Press; students should examine in particular John Irving's *The Social Credit Movement in Alberta* (1959) and C.B. Macpherson's *Democracy in Alberta: Social Credit and the Party System* (1953). Also of interest is John Barr's popularly written *The Dynasty: The Rise and Fall of Social Credit in Alberta* (Toronto: McClelland and Stewart, 1974). William Aberhart, the founder and first leader of the Social Credit party, is the subject of David Elliott and Iris Miller's *Bible Bill: A Biography of William Aberhart* (Edmonton: Reidmore Books, 1987).

Our World Stopped and We Got Off*

JAMES GRAY

From our home on Ruby Street in Winnipeg to the relief office at the corner of Xante Street and Elgin Avenue was less than three miles. It could be walked easily in an hour, but I didn't complete the journey

*From *The Winter Years* by James Gray, copyright 1966. Reprinted by permission of Macmillan of Canada, A Division of Canada Publishing Corporation.

the first time I set out, or the second. If I had not been driven by the direst necessity, the third trip would have ended as the first two had done. I would have veered sharply to the right, somewhere en route, to head down town in one last attempt to find a job. But on the third trip the truth could no longer be dodged by any such pointless manoeuvre.

We were almost out of food, we were almost out of fuel, and our rent was two months in arrears. At home were my wife and daughter, and my mother, father, and two younger brothers. Applying for relief might prove the most humiliating experience of my life (it did); but it had to be done, and I had to do it. The deep-down realization that I had nobody to blame but myself made the journey doubly difficult. In mid-February 1931 I was not yet twenty-five, but I could look back on ten years of psychopathic concentration on getting ahead in life. Then my number had come up and I was confronted with the ego-shattering discovery that there wasn't a single employer in all Winnipeg who would give me a job.

I had been out of work since the end of November, and I was already deeply in debt when my job disappeared. I canvassed the Grain Exchange, where I had worked, from top to bottom every week. I tried door-to-door selling, attempted to leave my application with department stores and the Post Office, but nobody was even taking applications, let alone dispensing jobs. There was no alternative to applying for relief.

At that moment, I was a fitting subject for a sermon on frugality and thrift. Ten years before, at fifteen, I had started out to make my fortune. In our family, the idea of any of us pursuing a higher education was never considered because it was naturally assumed that, as the oldest of four brothers, I would leave school to help support the family as soon as it was legally possible. If I had an educational goal, it was to go as far as I could as quickly as I could before I had to quit. I made it to Grade 10 and then got my first job in 1921 delivering groceries for $5 a week. From that I moved up to delivering engravings for $7 a week. When I landed a job as an office boy in the Grain Exchange at $10 in the early fall, I was convinced I was on the sure road to success. The Grain Exchange was synonymous with unmitigated affluence and was the status place to work in post-war Winnipeg. No one knew this better than I, for I had delivered morning papers to the baronial houses of wealthy Grain Exchangers. Inside these houses lived the men who had come west with nothing and made their fortunes in Winnipeg. If they could do it, I would some day do it. Spinning day-dreams helped take some of the sting from the cold winter mornings.

Money has an overweening importance to anybody who grows up in poverty, and our family knew nothing but poverty in Winnipeg during the First World War. From the time I was nine, and my brother Walter was six, we sold papers, ran messages, delivered groceries and laundry after school. If we never went hungry, there was never a time when what was wrong with our family could not have been repaired with $25 or $50.

The Winnipeg Grain Exchange in 1921 was on the threshold of its last great fling. The brokerage offices were crowded with speculators who bought and sold grain futures on margin. Outside, work was starting on a ten-storey addition that was to make it the biggest office building in the British Empire. The trading floor itself was a forest of temporary wooden beams and scaffolds, for it, too, was being enlarged. Here the shrieking voices of a hundred pit-traders created a din that, when the windows were open, could be heard clear over to Portage and Main. Behind the Monte Carlo façade was the actual business of warehousing, transporting, and marketing the western grain crops. Incidental to the frenzy of speculation, the wheat crops did get marketed. It so happened that the company I went to work for was actually engaged in the marketing business, and my employer never went into the wheat-pit. He was one of half a dozen vessel-brokers who obtained lake freighters for grain exporters and found exporters to charter the vessels.

417

My first job was running messages back and forth between our office and the telegraph offices on the trading floor. Soon I was helping with the books and learning eagerly how to run a typewriter, operate an adding machine, and make out insurance policies and invoices. The office opened at nine and closed whenever the day's work was done, usually along towards midnight. My job was as exhausting as it was exhilarating and at Christmas time I was amply rewarded with a $100 bonus. I ran all the way home clutching my envelope full of $5 bills.

When navigation ended on the Great Lakes in December, the vessel-brokerage business came to a dead stop. My employer went off to California; I enrolled in a correspondence course in accounting and picked up some extra money as a part-time bookkeeper in an option brokerage across the hall. Thereafter, promotions and pay raises came rapidly. By the time I was nineteen, there was nothing about the business I did not know or could not do, I was making $150 a month, and my Christmas bonus reached $500. Only experienced bricklayers made more, and most bank accountants made less. In those days the banks refused to permit their employees to marry until they were earning $1,000 a year, a level that usually took ten years to reach.

The success I achieved only whetted my appetite for more. I bought a half interest in a couple of race-horses, fell for one swindle after another, sent good money after bad to promoters of oil wells in Louisiana, gold mines in Colorado, and silver mines in Ontario. In between times I took losing fliers in the grain market. That I did nothing but lose never concerned me, because ultimately I would make an investment that would repay all my losses. Besides, by 1926, I was otherwise preoccupied. I had acquired a nearly-new Ford sedan, smoked two-for-a-quarter cigars, and was squiring one of Eaton's prettiest cashiers. Her name was Kathleen Burns, and by that Christmas we were so much in love that we could discover no reason for not getting married. We did so, and I had a further incentive to get on with my fortune-making. Instead of buying furniture or a house, we bought a race-horse, with my employer as silent partner, and for the next year I coupled horse-training with my Grain Exchange employment. As a horse-trainer I was a monumental bust, but it was great fun.

Our daughter Patricia was born in 1928, and her arrival gave me still another incentive. But somehow I had slipped into a rut. My salary had stopped going up, my employer had brought his brother into the company, and my position steadily deteriorated. When a group of grain-brokers decided to finance a new stock-brokerage office on Portage Avenue, I hired on as margin clerk, statistician, and general factotum. Not a single partner or employee knew anything about the stock market or the brokerage business. We even had to bring in employees of other brokers to train us in the simplest procedures such as computing margins. On the basis of this all-pervading ignorance, we were prepared to advise everybody in town how to make and manage investments in the stock market. In the logic of 1928, we should have been eminently successful, but the project never got off the ground and the business closed a full year before the crash.

Instead of going back to the Grain Exchange, I decided the time had come to get into business for myself. The first chance that came along was a candy franchise, and for the first half of 1929 I was in the candy business. I worked eighteen hours a day servicing the candy stands and Kay worked almost as long filling bags with candy. We went broke in six months and I returned to the vessel-brokerage business with a different employer. A few months after the Wall Street crash I was offered a much better job as manager of the grain department of a new brokerage firm that was opening an office in Lethbridge.

I arrived in Lethbridge just before the Solloway Mills scandal broke. Brokers were being arrested all across the country for "bucketing" their customers' orders during the mining boom. They were more victims of circumstances than anything else. The banks would not lend money on mining shares, and this prevented the brokers from financing their customers' margin purchases at a time when the customers were clamouring for mining stocks on margin. So the brokers sold stock on the exchange against their customers' purchases, a highly illegal action for which they went to jail.

By the time Kay had sold our furniture and brought Patty to Lethbridge, I had discovered some highly unsavoury things about an oil company my employers were floating. The more I probed into it, the more certain I became that the investors would lose their money. I quit in a panic, for fear I too would go to jail, and went back to Winnipeg to the job I had quit only a few months before. It was not until much later that I realized how lucky I was to get any kind of a job then. The brokerage failures turned hundreds out of jobs in Winnipeg. The break of the wheat market below a dollar and then below ninety cents brought hard times for the Grain Exchange, and, outside, the secondary effects of the stock-market crashes were becoming clear. But not to me.

That was the year of the miniature-golf craze. Like millions of others, Kay and I took up the game. The trouble was that the nearest course was miles away from home, and it was always crowded.

"You know," I said, "a guy could make a lot of money with a course like this near our place."

Kay pointed out that she could act as cashier during the day, if my mother would look after Patty, and I could run it at night. Our overhead would be small, and, if we got a quarter of the business the pioneer course was getting, we could clean up. We talked ourselves into it in no time. There was a small impediment. We had no money, or relatively little, compared to the capital required. The original operator egged us on.

419

"Why," he said, "there's nothing to it. Do it on credit! Your course will cost you $2,000. You might even do it for $1,500, and all you need is a couple of hundred in cash. Right now I'm taking in better than $200 a day. You won't do that good. But you could figure on a minimum of $100 a day. In fifteen days you'll pay for the course and you'll be set for next year."

It sounded wonderful. And it was as easy as that — almost. We rented a vacant lot, installed lights and a shack, and bought clubs and balls. No one demanded payment for the supplies. We were astounded at how good our credit was. Nevertheless, we spent all the money we had and borrowed more before the thing was finished. During the first week business was wonderful and we took in well over $500. Then came Labour Day, and nothing collapsed as quickly as miniature golf in September 1930. We closed the course in October with creditors clamouring for their money. So much of my pay was earmarked to repay loans that there was little left to live on.

Then the blow fell. On November 30 my employer went out of business. Nor was this all. By one of those queer twists of fate, two of my brothers were laid off on the same day. By a momentary stroke of good fortune, I managed to find a buyer for the golf course and he paid me enough to clean up most of my debts. But I still owed better than $300, which was more than I could have repaid even if I had had a job. And I had no job.

I have told this story in detail to make this point: I was a typical "child of the Twenties." What happened to me happened to everybody, more or less. What you became in life depended upon the job you settled into. You left school when you had to, though no earlier than fourteen, the legal limit. Then you got whatever extra education you needed at night schools or by correspondence courses. If your first job lacked opportunity for advancement, you quit and went elsewhere. It was not uncommon to make three or four false starts before settling into a permanent position, and no stigma attached to rolling stones.

Lack of education was no handicap in obtaining employment, and it was no bar to advancement for the eager and industrious youth of the Twenties. My educational attainments were at least equal to those of my contemporaries who rose to lofty eminence in Canadian banking and industry. Arnold Hart was fresh out of high school when he joined the Bank of Montreal at eighteen. A.T. Lambert reached the top of the Toronto-Dominion Bank by getting an early start at fourteen. At sixteen, H.G. Welsford got the job that led ultimately to the presidency of Dominion Bridge; James Pearson was only fourteen when he hired on at National Steel Car; G.H. Sheppard got to the top of IBM by starting as a fifteen-year-old office boy in 1929.

Harry Sellers parlayed a teen-age job in a Fort William grain elevator into the presidency of a dozen western grain companies. His feat was matched by K.A. Powell, who began as a minor clerk in the Grain Exchange. George McKeag made it from office boy to the head of Security Storage, western Canada's biggest forwarding enterprise. T.O. Peterson detoured from rural Saskatchewan through the Bank of Montreal to the presidency of Investors' Syndicate. W.M. Currie began as an office boy in Medicine Hat at seventeen and was elected president of the Canadian Imperial Bank of Commerce in 1965.

Rapid advancement was possible on ability alone. The so-called professions had not yet become government-sheltered monopolies, and professional unions were not yet blockading the avenues of advancement. Ours was a boot-strap economy in which you learned by doing. Young men became accountants by enduring the starvation wages of the banks for two or three years. They became mechanics by getting jobs in garages, became carpenters by carrying lumber around construction sites, became railway engineers by starting as wipers in the shops. If they were Harts, Sheppards, or Welsfords, they settled into their first jobs and made them their life work. If they were James Grays, who were driven to running before they could walk, they were willing to try anything once, again and again. There was nothing either in our experience or in our history that prepared us for the Dirty Thirties. Booms and busts there had been — four major depressions in the previous thirty years. But they had passed quickly; and the assumption everywhere was that this, too, would pass quickly. The Dirty Thirties were almost over before governments recognized that a hard core of unemployment had become a permanent fact of economic life. The Dirty Thirties were almost over, too, before the young adults of the Roaring Twenties realized that the world they had known was gone forever; that they had emerged from it equipped only to blunder and flounder through a pathless wilderness.

420

In the transition between the 1920s and the 1930s, the most persistent and widely held delusion of all was that unemployment was a temporary thing that would soon pass. As I walked to the Elgin Avenue relief office I believed it; the hundred-odd other applicants I found waiting in line believed it. It was a delusion that encompassed all governments and it was the foundation on which the entire system of unemployment relief was erected. The governments simply adopted whatever method there was in existence for dispensing temporary assistance and extended it *ad infinitum.*

The Winnipeg system, like that of all other prairie cities, was designed only to bridge the winter for those who were seasonally unemployed and could prove they were completely destitute. Those who were aided — a few hundred families each winter — worked off their relief sawing cordwood into stove lengths at the city Woodyard. The city Relief Department was an adjunct of the Woodyard — departmentally and physically. Cordwood from the tamarack forests was still a staple fuel in Winnipeg. The city brought it in by the trainload and stored it in great piles twelve feet high and six rows deep around the two city blocks that the yard occupied. At an open corner in the stockade was the yard office, to which the relief office was attached. Least adequate of all the Relief Department facilities was the building itself. It was shaped like a flattened, stretched-out U. The centre section was some sixty feet long and contained the office. At one end an extension, some thirty feet long, jutted out at a right angle and was used as a store-room. The waiting-room was another extension from the other end and it was about fifty feet long and twenty feet wide. Over a door at the corner was a sign:

421

RELIEF OFFICE

A crowd of several hundred milled around in the yard and I elbowed my way through to the shed. Inside, at the far end of the shed, were three doors leading into the main office. One was marked APPLICATIONS. The next was marked RENT AND FUEL, and a third was marked GROCERIES. There were long lines in front of each door and the APPLICATIONS line extended the full length of the shack and out into the yard. I found the end of it and huddled against the wall with a dozen others while we waited for the line to move up and let us inside. After half an hour in the shack, the one thing we wanted most was to escape into the fresh air, regardless of the temperature.

Winnipeg's North End was home to Canada's largest blocs of unassimilated immigrants, many of whom had only lately arrived. Because of the language barrier they were the last hired and the first fired, so it naturally followed that the bulk of the first applicants for relief were New Canadians. In addition to their arts, music, dancing, and literature, they brought to Canada a folk cookery based upon highly aromatic herbs and spices. Garlic, to race-proud Anglo-Saxons, was something to touch gently to a salad bowl. To the Galicians — a derisive generic term Winnipeggers applied to all foreigners — garlic was an anti-toxin, a medicine, a gargle, a liniment, and a confection to chew while waiting for streetcars. The Woodyard waiting-room that day swam in an aroma of garlic, to which was added the smells of stale tobacco, wet leather, perspiration, and singed rubber and wool from those who stood too close to the intermittently smoking stove.

Overpowering as the atmosphere became, it never reached a sufficient potency to drive anybody out of his place in line. Perhaps it was the narcotic effect of the air, but as time passed so did my panic about going on relief. The closer I got to the door, the more anxious I became to get the thing over and done with. It was as if some impersonal force was moving me inexorably to some mysterious fate. I relaxed and waited, almost impatiently, for the next adventure. The terrible aloneness of the long walk to the relief office was gone. Nobody was alone any more.

I was feeling a lot better when I reached the end of the line that afternoon and a harried clerk took my application and explained the system to me. I became entangled in the regulations before we even got on relief. When we returned from Lethbridge, Kay and I had rented a house with my parents and brothers. The clerk said I could apply for relief for Kay and Patty, but my father would have to apply for his own family. Nobody could get relief for relatives. I explained that my father was partly crippled and could not walk all the way to the Woodyard. In that case, he said, there was no point in his coming. Being unemployable, he was only eligible for social welfare, which was something different and dispensed by the City Hall. I answered that my father was perfectly capable of doing clerical work, only his legs were arthritic.

The clerk went off for a long conference with a supervisor. In the end the supervisor let me apply for everybody, and I went home to await the arrival of an investigator who would come around to inspect us. Two days later an investigator turned up, made a few perfunctory inquiries, and approved my application. He also took the time to make out a special form for my father to sign, scribbled his approval on the bottom of it, and said he would turn the form in at the office and the vouchers would be sent out by mail on a temporary basis. I was to take my approved application back to the Woodyard on Tuesday. Thereafter, save when sickness intervened, I was a regular Tuesday visitor to the Woodyard for the next two years.

When I arrived on the first Tuesday, the system had been somewhat reorganized from the week before. There was now a "NEW CARD" line parallel to the "APPLICATIONS" line. The end of the line for new cards was again outside the shack and it took the better part of an hour to get in out of the cold. Eventually I reached the clerk who was handing out the cards. He took the slip the investigator had given me and laboriously copied the particulars onto a printed card somewhat larger than a driver's licence.

Across the top of the card were a number of headings, viz.: "Groceries," "Bread," "Meat," "Milk," "Rent." Under each the clerk inserted code numbers after I had named the store, bakery, meat market, and creamery with which we dealt. I spent the rest of the day going from line to line picking up vouchers. One qualified me to receive seven quarts and seven pints of milk, a second provided for seven loaves of bread, a third was worth sixty-five cents at the butcher's, and the fourth was for $2.38 in groceries. This was the new world of vouchers in which no cash ever passed from hand to hand.

In some cities a different system was used. Regina and Saskatoon gave out food supplies from a central depot. Edmonton and Calgary used vouchers. Regardless of the system, the allowances were about the same everywhere, varying naturally with the size of families. A family of three such as ours was allowed $16 a month for food and $10 to $13 a month for rent. Householders got a winter allowance of $6 to $10 a month in cordwood for fuel. It was possible to live on these allowances because of the collapse in the price structure. Indeed, as prices dropped even these relief allowances were reduced. Regina once cut the food allowance from $16 to $14 a month, until a near-riot changed the city council's mind. Any such episode naturally got economy-minded aldermen in other cities thinking about making similar reductions, "in view of the drop in food prices."

423

In the late winter of 1931, milk was ten cents a quart, bread six cents a loaf, chuck roasts sold for ten cents a pound, hamburger was nine cents, a rib roast was twelve cents, sausage was three pounds for a quarter, and potatoes forty-five cents a bushel. Even these prices would seem high a year later, when milk sold for six cents a quart in Winnipeg, bread was three loaves for a dime, butter sold for fifteen and twenty cents a pound, and eggs were fifteen cents a dozen.

For people accustomed to shopping with money, operating a household with vouchers took a lot of getting used to. Everything had to be bought in small quantities. If we had been given our grocery allowance for the month in a single voucher, instead of once a week, advantage could have been taken of quantity buying. But many months were to pass before the fact was recognized and allowances were distributed on a fortnightly basis. While becoming accustomed to voucher shopping was slow, people settled into the relief system itself with little difficulty. We had lived in a continuing food-and-shelter crisis for a month, and once these problems were solved by going on relief we were freed from the feeling of being incessantly driven. We relaxed and made a start at sorting out our family problems. On an invitation from relatives, my father and brothers emigrated via cattle train to Ontario to look for work in the textile mills. My mother stayed on with us until they could send her transportation. We found a house we could rent for the $13 a month the relief department would allow and settled down to wait for spring and a job. Two months later I came down with tuberculosis.

Canadian Unemployment Policy in the 1930s*

JAMES STRUTHERS

I

One of the problems of discussing unemployment during the Great Depression is the danger of becoming overcome by a sense of déja vu. Today unemployment officially stands at over 12% of the workforce; perhaps as many as 2,000,000 Canadians are without work and according to the Economic Council of Canada the jobless total is unlikely to drop below 10% until 1987. Yet despite these appalling figures, our government, as in the 1930s, tells us it cannot act to create jobs because its first priority must be to reduce the deficit in order to restore business confidence.

Although the arguments behind today's economic policies are certainly different from those of the 1930s, many of the essential moral homilies remain unchanged. Canadians in the 1980s, like their parents and grandparents of the 1930s, are being told they can't expect to hope for recovery without practising severe restraint, self-discipline, hard work, and much tightening of belts. Despite these frightening parallels, however, we haven't yet been surrounded by soup kitchens, relief camps, food vouchers, bankrupt provincial governments, and trainloads of hungry single men "riding the rods" in search of work or relief. Yet all these sights and problems were characteristic of the failure of governments to respond to unemployment during the 1930s. Why this was so I'll attempt to explain in this paper.

To a large extent the unemployment policies pursued by R.B. Bennett and Mackenzie King in the 1930s were continuations of approaches and attitudes towards joblessness that had been widespread in Canada before 1930. Canadians had become well acquainted with cyclical unemployment — or trade depressions as they were then called — well before the "dirty thirties." The 1870s, the early 1890s, and the years 1907–08, 1913–15, and 1920–25, were all periods of heavy unemployment in this country. From this perspective it's best to think of the Great Depression as simply the most intense and long-lasting of a series of "waves" of unemployment which battered all western industrial economies during the last half of the 19th and first third of the 20th centuries.

Because of our climate we were also quite familiar with seasonal unemployment. Canada is infamous for being an "eight months country."

*Windy Pine Occasional Paper no. 1, by James Struthers. Copyright 1984 by the Canadian Studies Program, Trent University. Reprinted by permission.

Each winter tens of thousands of Canadians working in the country's great outdoors industries — construction, agriculture, forestry, fishing, and transportation — routinely lost their jobs, often for up to six months of the year due to bad weather. Even in the boom years of the so-called "roaring twenties" (1926–29), winter unemployment rates averaged well over 10% of the workforce. So the sight of hungry, jobless men walking the streets in search of work or relief was quite familiar to most urban-dwellers in Canada.

Why, then, did the Great Depression take us so much by surprise? Why, for example, didn't Canada follow Great Britain's lead in 1911 by devising new institutions and policies, such as a national system of unemployment insurance and a state employment service, to cope with the problem of joblessness? There were a number of reasons for our unpreparedness but three were particularly important. In the first place, seasonal unemployment was predictable. Winter was a fact of Canadian life; therefore, newspapers, politicians, businessmen, and others argued that workingmen should save up enough money during the summer to tide themselves and their families over the winter. Moreover, it was simply assumed (without any evidence) that wages for seasonal labour were high enough to allow them to do so. To provide the seasonally unemployed with relief, it was argued, would discourage habits of thrift, frugality, and self-reliance.

As for cyclical unemployment, attitudes towards this problem were shaped by two factors. First, recovery in the past had always occurred eventually. The market did correct itself. Therefore, all a country could do was to "tough it out" by practising restraint and doing nothing to discourage business confidence, especially on the part of foreign investors. Secondly, Canada was a New World society with a developing farm frontier. It was also a country which, in the three decades before 1930, had become increasingly preoccupied with rural depopulation. And it was a country in which farmers were still politically powerful and were continually complaining about the shortage of farm help at affordable wages. For these reasons, legislation such as unemployment insurance, which might be appropriate in more crowded, congested, and highly urbanized societies such as Great Britain, was deemed by business and farm leaders to be inappropriate for Canada. There was always work for the unemployed, even if only for room and board and little more, they argued, on the nation's farms during the winter. If life in the city was made too easy through doles and unemployment insurance for the idle, might not even more men and women be encouraged to leave the land altogether?

Finally, working-class political pressure, in the form of strong trade unions and labour parties, was extremely weak in Canada before World War II. Farmers and businessmen, on the other hand, were politically powerful. Hence governments responded to their views on the unemployment question and not to the views of those who were most likely to become unemployed.

As a result of these attitudes, Canadian governments, although well acquainted with unemployment before 1930, were hopelessly ill-equipped for dealing with it. No one kept unemployment statistics; there was no efficient state employment service; no public welfare departments existed at the federal or provincial level and there were only four at the municipal level. In all of Canada before 1930 there were less than 400 trained social workers. Relief, where available, was granted by private religious charities or by 19th century poor law "Houses of Industry," both of which operated at the local level. In Toronto as late as 1932, jobless men still had to line up at the local House of Industry, first built in the 1830s, to get a bag of groceries or a basket of coal and were expected to saw wood or break rocks in exchange for this miserly relief. Moreover, with the brief exception of the years 1920–21, when the threat of unemployed World War I veterans loomed large throughout Canada, provincial governments along with Ottawa denied any responsibility for coming to the aid of the jobless. Public relief where given was an exclusively local matter financed solely out of local taxes, chiefly on property. One of the sad ironies of the "dirty thirties" was that although no other country, except perhaps the United States, was more economically devastated by the Great Depression than Canada, no other country was as ill-prepared for dealing with its consequences. On the eve of 1930 we lacked even the bare bones of a permanent welfare structure for relieving those in need.

II

The origins of Canadian unemployment policy in the Depression lie within the 1930 federal election. On the one hand Mackenzie King went into the election — at a time when unemployment was about 12% — denying that there was a jobless problem and bragging that he would not give a "five cent piece" to any Tory provincial government for unemployment relief. King also claimed that the whole idea of an unemployment crisis was simply a Conservative pre-election plot.

Bennett, on the other hand, made what from our perspective today seem like recklessly extravagant promises. He claimed he would "end unemployment," "abolish the dole," and provide "work and wages for all who wanted it." Not surprisingly, Bennett won the election, largely on the strength of his promises to do something about the unemployment crisis.

Despite the boldness of his rhetoric, however, (which reflected his egotism, arrogance, and over-confidence in his own abilities) Bennett really had very traditional ideas about how to deal with unemployment. Like King, he believed the problem in 1930 was largely a seasonal and temporary phenomenon which would quickly right itself. Unlike King, Bennett as a good Tory, also believed that sharply boosting the protective tariff would stimulate investor confidence, create jobs by reducing reliance upon imports, and ultimately force other nations to lower their trading barriers against Canadian exports. It was through these tariff hikes that Bennett hoped to "end unemployment."

But these hikes would take time to produce results. Since Bennett had promised to provide jobs immediately, he also introduced a $20,000,000 emergency relief act in the summer of 1930 to tide people over with what was expected to be a difficult winter. $16,000,000 was to be spent on public works and, most significantly, the projects were to be administered by local and provincial governments who together were expected to contribute 75% of their cost. Unemployment relief, Bennett insisted like King before him, was primarily a local responsibility. Ottawa's help was on a temporary, emergency basis only, and would last only until the effects of his tariff hike were felt.

427

Through providing money for relief projects such as provincial roadbuilding Bennett also hoped to deal with another pressing problem. Transient, unemployed single men, largely immigrants, were trapped in Canadian cities because the lumber, construction, and agricultural industries which normally drew them out of cities were closed down. Such men, cut off from family ties, coming from different cultural backgrounds, and with nothing to lose, were considered to be a serious menace to law and order. Bennett's relief projects would draw them out of the cities and put money into their pockets for the winter months ahead.

Between the fall of 1930, when he first took office, and the spring of 1932, Bennett adhered to this policy of using public works or relief works as they were called, to fight unemployment. Indeed, throughout the fiscal year 1931–32 his government spent almost $50,000,000 or more than twice as much as it had the previous year on this approach. Nevertheless, by the spring of 1932 unemployment stood above 20% of the workforce and the federal deficit was over $151,000,000, almost half of total government revenue for that year. As a result, Bennett quickly became disillusioned with public works as a means of relieving unemployment.

In the first place, he had used this approach only as a temporary stopgap expedient. Neither he nor anyone in his government were believers in Keynesian deficit-spending as a way out of depression; therefore there was no expectation that public employment could be used in itself as a recovery strategy. Moreover, by 1932 it had become obvious that the Depression was more than a "temporary" problem. Secondly, by 1932, local and provincial governments, especially in the west, could no longer afford to pay their 75% share of the cost of these increasingly expensive relief works and Bennett had no intention of assuming a larger share of the cost. Finally, Bennett and Canadian businessmen were increasingly alarmed at the size of the federal deficit and the level of taxation which in themselves appeared to be a threat to investor confidence, and hence a barrier to recovery.

For all these reasons, then, Bennett reversed his unemployment policy in the spring of 1932 virtually abandoning reliance on public works and instead depended almost solely upon direct relief or the provision of a "dole" to tide the unemployed over the worst of the Depression until recovery began. His chief unemployment policy, now that tariffs and public works had failed, was to attempt to eliminate the deficit and to balance the federal budget. This meant keeping expenditure on the job-less down to the lowest level consistent with their physical survival. At the same time, Bennett also refused to modify his policy that unem-ployment relief was primarily a provincial and local responsibility. His government would pay only one-third the cost of direct relief in any town or city and would contribute nothing to the costs of its administration.

428

III

Once Bennett opted for a policy of direct relief as his sole remaining means of dealing with unemployment, he entered into a nightmare of contradictions, ironies, and paradoxes which he had never anticipated

Glenbow Archives, Calgary.

A crowd of unemployed gather at the Army and Navy store in Edmonton in response to an advertisement for six store clerks, August 1931.

and which would ultimately destroy his administration. Five such anomalies were of particular importance. The first was the paradox of residency requirements for relief. Since local governments, under Bennett's policy, had to assume anywhere from one-third to one-half the cost of relief on a rapidly diminishing and highly regressive property tax base, they attempted to limit their own relief costs in the only way possible, namely by restricting eligibility for relief to their own municipal residents. Only those who could prove anywhere from six months to, in some cases, three years continuous residence in a city before applying for the dole were deemed eligible to receive it. In a country like Canada with a geographically diverse and highly mobile labour market, many of the unemployed who had been on the road looking for work could not qualify for relief when they needed it. To get the dole they had to return to their home town which they had left in the first place because there was no work. Bennett's policy, then, discouraged the unemployed from looking for work outside their town or city for fear of becoming ineligible for relief.

429

Transients also posed a contradiction. Tens of thousands of Canada's unemployed were immigrant, seasonal workers — bunkhouse men — who by the very nature of their work on the frontier could not qualify for relief in any city. Bennett's earlier public works policy had, in part, been intended once again to get them out of urban areas. Now, without public works, they had no choice but to drift back into Canadian cites where they could find neither relief nor work. As a result, transient single men "riding the rods" from town to town were quickly recognized as a serious menace to law and order. Since the cities refused to assume responsibility for them, and since Bennett refused to assume responsibility for relief, he decided upon another alternative suggested to him by General Andrew McNaughton of the Canadian army — relief camps, run by the Defense Department. Here the men could be kept out of the cities, provided with room, board, and clothing and put to work on useful projects to preserve their morale. There was only one hitch. Since Bennett had already abandoned public works as a relief policy, the men couldn't be paid a wage, not without arousing serious unrest from married unemployed men on direct relief. Instead they were paid a 20¢ daily "allowance" in return for their labour in the camps.

Why would single men go into such camps for 20¢ a day? Cut off from direct relief in the cities, they had no choice except starvation, which is why the 20,000 men in the camps after 1933 quickly referred to them as "slave camps" and ultimately organized the relief camp strike and "On to Ottawa Trek" of 1935, which ended in a bloody two hour riot with the RCMP in Regina. As one camp inhabitant cynically put it in 1933, "You come in broke, work all winter and still you are broke. It looks like they want to keep us bums all our lives."

Relief standards posed a third source of contention. By insisting on primary local and provincial responsibility for the financing of relief, and by assuming no share in the cost of administering relief, Bennett's government ensured that relief scales — that is, how much money or its equivalent in food vouchers a family would receive — varied dramatically from city to city, depending upon the health of local economies and the political complexion of local city councils. A survey by the Canadian Welfare Council of relief standards in 50 Canadian cities during September 1936 showed just how far such scales of aid could differ. In London, Ontario, a family of five could receive no more than $40.39 a month for food, fuel, and shelter costs. That same family in Toronto could get $58.87; in Hamilton $34.40; in Ottawa $45.32; in Quebec City $26.66; in Calgary $60.00; and in Halifax a mere $18.86. Such gross variations in support within cities of comparable living costs was, of course, morally indefensible. Within Ontario, the Canadian Association of Social Workers discovered, in a survey of 107 municipalities, that not one provided the food allowance recommended by the Ontario Medical Association as the minimum necessary to maintain nutritional health. Food allowances in Toronto alone were 40% below the minimum standard which the League of Nations defined as necessary to maintain health. Since Bennett had promised, when elected in 1930, to "abolish the dole," such gross variations and substandard levels of support in a policy of direct relief which his administration had initiated, was political catastrophe.

430

The bankruptcy of first local and then provincial governments was the fourth disastrous consequence of Bennett's relief policy. By insisting that local and provincial governments were to be held primarily responsible for the cost of relief, Bennett's unemployment policy concentrated the fiscal cost of the Depression where its impact was greatest — that is, in western Canada. By 1932, all four western provinces were technically bankrupt because of the cost of paying their two-thirds share of direct relief and were only kept solvent by continual federal loans and grants. By 1937 Ottawa would be paying 85% of all relief costs in Saskatchewan; 71% in Alberta; 69% in British Columbia; and 68% in Manitoba; while still insisting that relief was a local responsibility. In Ontario and Quebec, in contrast, Ottawa paid only 29% and 32% respectively of relief costs.

To give an equally paradoxical example of the contradictions of this policy, in Forest Hill, a very wealthy area of Toronto with few unemployed, per capita relief costs to taxpayers averaged only $4.00 a month in 1934. In East York, a working-class borough only a few miles away, with almost 50% of its population on relief, the cost of the dole averaged $25.00 a month per taxpayer. Yet the people of Forest Hill, in many cases, were the employers of those living in East York. By drawing municipal boundary lines around themselves, they could enjoy the lowest relief taxes in Canada and shove the burden of the Depression onto their unfortunate employees.

The final irony of direct relief was the fact that you had to be totally destitute to receive it. Insurance policies, bank savings, home equity, automobiles, everything of value had to be liquidated in many municipalities before a family could become eligible for the dole. Hence, what was the point of saving for a rainy day if you knew beforehand that all your assets would be confiscated before you could become eligible for aid? Far better to spend your money while you had it, since if you lost your job you would soon be just as badly off as the man down the road who had saved nothing.

IV

Because of contradictions such as these, by 1933–34 Bennett was desperately looking for alternatives to his relief policy. There were two directions he could go. The first, urged increasingly by the provinces, the municipalities, organized labour, some social workers, and the unemployed, was to take over total responsibility for unemployment relief instead of continuing to contribute on a one-third basis. Had Bennett followed this option, residency requirements for relief could have been abolished; the provinces, particularly in the west, and the municipalities would once again have been fiscally solvent; and most importantly the levels of assistance for families on the dole across Canada could have been raised to a national minimum standard sufficient to ensure that everyone received at least enough food, shelter, and clothing to remain healthy and to enjoy reasonably decent living standards.

Bennett had absolutely no interest in taking this route, however. In the first place, it would have cost far more to the federal government, already concerned primarily in reducing, not increasing, its deficit. Secondly, it would have necessitated the creation of a permanent federal welfare bureaucracy at a time when Bennett was still convinced that the unemployment crisis was temporary. Finally, and most importantly, Bennett and his advisors believed that a national minimum standard of relief would increase the numbers of those unemployed. Why? Because wage rates for those already working in Canada, particularly unskilled labourers, had been so lowered by the Depression (clothing workers in Montreal and Toronto, for example, often made only $10.00 for a 60 hour work week) that for a large segment of Canada's working-class a dole which provided healthy and decent living standards would be preferable to work.

This was certainly the conclusion of Charlotte Whitton, Canada's most well-known social worker, an arch social conservative, and Bennett's key advisor on relief policy in the 1930s. In a 1932 report to the government on relief in western Canada, Whitton told Bennett that 40% of those living off the dole on the prairies didn't really need it; that the very existence of direct relief in the west was drawing tens of thousands of farm families into the western cities during the winter, thus artificially boosting the unemployment rate; and that by contributing to local and provincial relief efforts, Bennett's government had only succeeded in making thousands of immigrant and poor rural families "permanently dependent at a scale of living which they never had and never will be able to provide for themselves."

With this kind of advice coming from the chief executive of the Canadian Welfare Council it was small wonder that Bennett himself concluded in 1934 that the people had become "more or less relief-conscious and were determined to get out of the Government, whether it be municipal, provincial, or federal, all they could." Instead of opting to take over total responsibility for unemployment relief, Bennett decided over the winter of 1934 to move in exactly the opposite direction: to sever all of Ottawa's ties with the dole and turn the whole ugly, embarrassing business completely back to the provinces and municipalities.

From this perspective, unemployment insurance, which the British had pioneered in 1911, began to appear more and more attractive as a policy alternative for the Bennett government. In the first place, at a time when unemployment still hovered at 20% of the workforce, Bennett simply could not withdraw from direct relief and abdicate all responsibility for the jobless. He had to have some political alternative to put in its place. Unemployment insurance fit the bill nicely for a number of reasons. Businessmen, particularly bankers and insurance company and real estate executives, favoured such a measure by 1934. These financial organizations now held many worthless municipal and provincial bonds and had become convinced that direct municipal relief was a highly inefficient way to finance the costs of unemployment. Far better, such businessmen argued, to build up an unemployment fund in good times through insurance premiums which could be used to aid the jobless during depressions. Better yet, unemployment insurance seemed to reinforce thrift. Since the premiums were compulsory, it forced workers to defer part of their incomes for a rainy day. Thus, unlike the dole, it didn't reduce everyone to complete and utter destitution before they could become eligible for aid. Moreover, because 80% of the cost of unemployment insurance could be financed by compulsory premiums paid by workers and employers, it would cost the federal government only a fraction of what was presently being spent on relief. As a result, unlike the dole, unemployment insurance would not interfere as directly with the widely shared desire among businessmen to see a balanced federal budget.

Finally, precisely because it was called unemployment "insurance," actuarial science, not nutritional standards of human need, could provide an arbitrary ceiling on benefits which in any case would always be kept to a fixed percentage of existing wage rates. In this way unemployment insurance seemed to pose no threat to the market-determined distribution

432

of income. Under the legislation Bennett eventually introduced in the early months of 1935, Canadians had to work a minimum of forty weeks over two years to be eligible for any benefits whatsoever, which in any case were set at a maximum of $11.40 a week for a family of five, almost 40% below the $17.30 a week which the Montreal Council of Social Agencies recommended as the minimum amount necessary to maintain health.

Under Bennett's unemployment insurance act, then, only those workers who were most regularly employed could qualify for benefits and the levels were set low enough to ensure that in no case would life on unemployment insurance be preferable to any form of work offered by Canadian employers anywhere in the country. In other words, unemployment insurance, as drafted by Bennett's advisors, was designed to reinforce the work ethic and to provide a perfect political cover for a federal withdrawal from relief. It was not designed to reduce poverty or to provide unemployed Canadians with a level of support adequate to maintain health and decency.

433

Most importantly, unemployment insurance offered nothing to the 1.2 million Canadians who were already on relief in 1935. Since their family breadwinners were obviously not working, they could not pay any premiums or qualify for benefits. It was a good idea for future depressions, but unemployment insurance really provided no solution to the problems of the 1930s.

Nevertheless, Bennett proceeded with his strategy. In June 1934, he told the premiers that all federal support for relief would be cut off on August 1st. After tremendous political pressure, he subsequently modified this policy to a 22% federal cut-back in relief spending. Then, in September, Bennett asked the provinces whether they would be willing to surrender their exclusive jurisdiction over unemployment insurance to Ottawa. Outraged by his high-handed pressure tactics and unilateral cut-backs, the premiers understandably refused. As a result, faced with an election and almost certain defeat in 1935, Bennett simply introduced his unemployment insurance bill in Parliament as part of his package of New Deal reforms, knowing full well that without provincial agreement the bill was probably unconstitutional and hence useless, as indeed it turned out to be.

After five years in office, Bennett went down to spectacular defeat in the 1935 election, his party losing all but 39 seats. He also left a very meagre legacy for his successor, the Liberal leader Mackenzie King. The attempt to provide work for the jobless had been abandoned after 1932; relief standards across Canada were grossly inadequate everywhere; four provincial governments were technically bankrupt; single unemployed men in the relief camps had walked out and rioted in their attempt to reach Ottawa; and unemployment insurance, the only creative piece of legislation on the jobless crisis to emerge from Bennett's administration, was clearly unconstitutional.

V

In what ways, if any, did Mackenzie King pursue different policies for the remainder of the Depression? Unlike Bennett in 1930, King made no promises in the 1935 election beyond pledging to provide sober, orderly government. As a result, he had no political I.O.U.'s to redeem. In fact, the most striking aspect of King's unemployment policy is that from December 1935 until the spring of 1938 it was virtually a carbon copy of Bennett's. In the first place, he continued to insist that the jobless were primarily a local and provincial responsibility. Secondly, after a quick hike in federal relief contributions immediately after the election, King began systematically to cut back on Ottawa's support of the dole to such an extent that by 1931, in cities such as Winnipeg, Ottawa was paying only 20% of relief costs and on a national basis, only 30%, compared to the one-third share Bennett had paid throughout most years of his administration. Like the Tory prime minister, King's first priority was to balance the budget.

King's administration also refused to define any national minimum standard of relief, based on medical or nutritional standards. Instead, his government defined a national *maximum*. In October 1937 King's minister of labour, Norman Rogers, announced that Ottawa would in no province pay more than 30% of the dole's cost, and in every city the standard of living on relief had to be kept below the average going rate for unskilled labour in the surrounding area, in order that "work incentives" could be enforced. This policy was adopted at a time when most provinces had no minimum wage for men.

Although King did abolish Bennett's hated relief camps for single men in 1936, the alternative he put in their place was, in many ways, much worse. This was a farm placement scheme which paid about 45,000 of Canada's single unemployed $5.00 a month to work on farms across the country. This was less than the infamous 20¢ daily "allowance" the men had received in the camps, and there was no guarantee that food, clothing, shelter, and medical care provided by individual impoverished farmers across Canada would be comparable to what the army had offered in the relief camps. As one army commander pointed out when the camps were shut down in 1936 and many men refused to leave, "the men prefer to stay where they have 'regular hours' and good food, rather than leave for farms, where they have to work harder, longer hours, and for lower wages, with a possibility that they may not collect their wages in the fall." Although cynical in its conception, King's farm placement scheme nonetheless did solve the problem of chronic unrest among transients. Spread out individually across Canada rather than concentrated in the camps, single men proved almost impossible to organize politically after 1936.

King's overall unemployment strategy duplicated Bennett's in two other ways. As Bennett had done after 1932, until the severe recession of 1938, King rejected public works as an antidote to unemployment, in marked contrast to the massive works schemes pioneered by Franklin Roosevelt's New Deal south of the border. Instead, King relied totally on direct relief as a means of caring for the jobless. King also refused to enact an unemployment insurance plan, claiming that the political opposition to the measure by New Brunswick, Quebec, and Alberta made impossible the unanimous consent which he claimed was necessary for a constitutional amendment.

In only two areas did King take actions significantly different from Bennett's. In April 1936 he appointed a National Employment Commission, chaired by Montreal industrialist Arthur Purvis, to investigate the unemployment and relief situation and to come up with recommendations for reform. Secondly, in August 1937, he appointed a Royal Commission on Dominion–Provincial Relations, chaired by Supreme Court justice Newton Rowell, to investigate and attempt to straighten out the tangled web of federal–provincial financial relations, particularly the continuing inability of the western provinces to stay fiscally solvent without federal loans and grants.

435

The most significant result of both these commissions is that they ended up saying the same thing. The NEC, which reported in January 1938, and the Rowell-Sirois Commission, as it came to be called, which reported in May 1940, both argued that the first step in combatting unemployment and restoring fiscal solvency to the provinces and local governments was for Ottawa to put in place immediately a national employment service and system of unemployment insurance, and to assume total financial and administrative responsibility for unemployment relief. In short, both commissions argued that Ottawa should take the route both Bennett and King had rejected throughout the entire depression, namely to accept primary responsibility for unemployment. The jobless crisis, both commissions argued, was a *national* problem, reflecting Canada's national economy; consequently, relief to those without work should be first and foremost a national responsibility. Only Ottawa through its unlimited taxing power, they argued further, possessed the fiscal strength to pay for these relief costs. Finally, reflecting the new Keynesian sophistication being developed within the department of finance, both commissions concluded that only Ottawa could inject enough purchasing power into the economy through insurance and relief payments and public works to push levels of demand up high enough to stimulate economic growth and thus ultimately to eliminate unemployment.

It would be pleasant to report that after receiving this sensible advice, King realized the error of his ways and reversed his economic policies. In fact, he did no such thing. When he discovered that the NEC was about to recommend federal control of relief, King pulled out every stop he could to kill the Commission's final report. When that proved impossible, thanks to Arthur Purvis' integrity, King simply ignored it. Why? The reason was best expressed by Mary Sutherland, King's closest confidant on the NEC and the author of a dissenting minority report. In it, Sutherland articulated the basis for Ottawa's continued resistance throughout the 1930s to accepting primary responsibility for the jobless. "No matter which government is responsible for and administers relief . . . ," Sutherland wrote, "there will be constant pressure to increase the benefits and to enlarge the base of admittance to benefits. If responsibility is centralized in the Dominion government, the counter-pressure from local taxpayers will be eased. The irksome, unwelcome, and hard check provided by necessity, by municipal officials, harassed by mounting demands on diminishing revenues, will be removed."

In short, Sutherland, like King and R.B. Bennett, believed that national responsibility for relief would cost too much and would erode the work ethic. If Ottawa controlled relief, it would have to define a national minimum standard of support, or in effect a national poverty line, across the country. In a country like Canada with widely diverse regional wage rates and living standards, such a national minimum would inevitably be higher than existing wage rates for many of the working poor. The result would be to attract this class out of work and onto relief, thus increasing unemployment. Sutherland's argument was, in this sense, almost identical to the one first put forward by Charlotte Whitton in her 1932 report on relief in western Canada. Only by keeping relief a local responsibility and local governments on the edge of bankruptcy could relief costs and benefit levels be kept to the barest minimum.

Ironically, putting more purchasing power directly into the hands of the jobless and their families in the form of higher relief benefits was exactly what *was* needed in order to push up consumption and effective demand to levels that would in turn encourage investment and employment. But as long as the Bennett and King administrations continued to approach the relief question from the angle of its effects upon the work ethic of individuals rather than upon the purchasing power of all the unemployed, they simply could not see this. As a result, in their relief policy, as in their wider economic policies of balanced budgets, a sound dollar, and regressive taxation, Bennett and King inhibited the chances of recovery.

VI

In 1940, after World War II had begun, Canadians finally did see enacted a constitutionally valid scheme of unemployment insurance. The pressures of war and the need for national unity had dissolved the political objections of the three dissenting provinces. More importantly, King's own fear of post-war unemployment, and of how jobless veterans would respond to relief of the 1930s variety, now galvanized him into making unemployment insurance a first priority of the government, particularly with an election looming on the horizon in 1940. Wartime mobilization and the potential labour shortage also gave the federal government a vital need for creating a national employment service, motive which had not been present during the heavy labour surplus of the 1930s. Finally, the necessity for massive war expenditures gave Ottawa an overpowering political argument for trying out new Keynesian ideas such as deliberately incurring large deficits, a policy which would have left most Canadian businessmen aghast in the Depression.

The tragedy of unemployment policy in the 1930s is that strategies for dealing with joblessness which *were* politically possible, indeed essential in the context of the war, were not deemed possible, given Canada's political landscape in the Depression. The essential continuity and the essential failure of the policies pursued by both R.B. Bennett and Mackenzie King lay in their refusal to accept that the unemployed were a national responsibility. This refusal, in turn, was rooted in what might be termed the dilemma of "less eligibility" in a market economy. In a private enterprise system, business and the market set wage levels and living standards. During the 1930s, for many *working* Canadians, these standards and wages were below what was necessary to ensure a decent and healthy standard of living. As a result, both the Bennett and King governments believed they could not provide higher relief benefits for the jobless without attracting many of the working population onto the dole. Without direct state intervention or trade union pressure to improve working conditions and living standards for low income Canadians, or in other words, without massive intervention into the marketplace, the government felt limited in the benefits it could provide for the unemployed. And in the political context of the 1930s, given the absence of a serious political threat from the left or a strong labour movement, the pressure simply was not there for either Bennett or King to move in a direction that would have been regarded by Canadian businessmen as serious meddling in their affairs.

Only war, with the full employment it would bring and the strong labour union organization it would permit, could create a political climate in which it would be possible to effect these kinds of permanent structural reforms to underpin working-class incomes. By 1945, then, Canadians were finally ready to fight the Great Depression of the 1930s.

437

World War II

On September 10, 1939, the Canadian Parliament declared war on Germany. It was the first time in its history that Canada had entered a war as an independent country, not a colony. The Canadian government had waited one week after Britain entered the war before obtaining parliamentary approval for its own declaration. Yet no sooner had Canada weakened its military and economic ties with Britain than it strengthened them with the United States. Canada, it has been said, went from colony to nation to satellite.

Canada, the only country in the Americas at war, had entered unprepared. It had initially seemed that Britain and France would be able to defeat Germany on their own, and the danger of a German invasion seemed remote. But this confidence was shattered with the Germans' lightning sweep, the *blitzkrieg*, which led to the defeat of the Low Countries and, in June of 1940, the fall of France. When the Canadian government recognized the vulnerability of Canada's position, it looked to the United States for protection and direction. The Ogdensburg Agreement of August 1940, which provided for the mutual defence of North America, symbolized the real beginning of American influence in Canada.

The war brought many changes on the home front as well. The increased demand for manpower in the armed forces and in war-production industries led to a new demand for women, both married and single, in the workplace and in military-related activities. For the first time, women were recruited into the armed forces, although most were assigned to traditionally "feminine" jobs. Women responded with vigour to the wartime demands, and contributed greatly to Canada's war effort. In "The 'Bren Gun Girl' and the Housewife Heroine," a chapter from *Canadian Women: A History*, the authors outline the role of women during the war years and their return to domesticity in the immediate postwar era.

The war affected all Canadians at home, but particularly those from countries that were at war with Canada — such as the Japanese Canadians living on the West Coast. Their very presence raised a cry of alarm among a white population already prone to racial intolerance. The Canadian government responded to the popular outcry by evicting Japanese Canadians to inland British Columbia or points further east, disregarding the fact that the majority of them were born in Canada or had become Canadian citizens. Peter Ward recounts the expulsion in "British Columbia and the Japanese Evacuation."

Desmond Morton and J.L. Granatstein's *Forged in Fire: Canadians and the Second World War, 1939–1945* (Toronto: Lester and Orpen Dennys, 1989) is an up-to-date and interesting review of Canada's participation in World War II. A good primary source of the war is J.W. Pickersgill's *The Mackenzie King Record* (Toronto: University of Toronto Press, 1960–70), a four-volume collection of excerpts from the Mackenzie King diaries. C.P. Stacey, the Canadian military historian, discusses the war years in *Arms, Men and Governments: The War Policies of Canada, 1930–1945* (Ottawa: Information Canada, 1970), as do W.A.B. Douglas and Brereton Greenhous in *Out of the Shadows* (Toronto: Oxford, 1977). For an understanding of the conscription crisis in World War II, see J.L. Granatstein, *Canada's War: The Politics of the Mackenzie King Government, 1939–1945* (Toronto: Oxford University Press, 1975); J.L. Granatstein, *Conscription in the Second World War, 1939–1945* (Toronto: Ryerson, 1969); J.L. Granatstein and J.M. Hitsman, *Broken Promises: A History of Conscription in Canada* (Toronto: Oxford University Press, 1977; new edition, 1984); and Jean Pariseau, "La participation des Canadiens français à l'effort des deux guerres mondiales: démarche de réinterprétation," *Canadian Defence Quarterly/Revue canadienne de défense* 13, 2 (Autumn 1983): 43–48. R.D. Cuff and J.L. Granatstein's *Ties That Bind: Canadian–American Relations in Wartime from the Great War to the Cold War* (Toronto: Samuel Stevens Hakkert and Co., 1977) contains essays relevant to the World War II period.

439

Ruth Pierson discusses women's roles during the war in her book *They're Still Women After All: The Second World War and Canadian Womanhood* (Toronto: McClelland and Stewart, 1986) as well as in "The Double Bind of the Double Standard: Venereal Disease Control and the CWAC in World War II," *Canadian Historical Review* 62 (March 1981): 31–58, "Jill Canuck: CWAC of All Trades, But No Pistol-Packing Momma," Canadian Historical Association, *Historical Papers* (1978), 106–133, and "Women's Emancipation and the Recruitment of Women into the Canadian Labour Force in World War II," Canadian Historical Association, *Historical Papers* (1976), 141–74.

Peter Ward's *White Canada Forever: Popular Attitudes and Public Policies towards Orientals in British Columbia* (Montreal: McGill-Queen's University Press, 1978) is a comprehensive study of the British Columbia response to Asian immigration. For an alternative view, see Patricia Roy's "British Columbia's Fear of Asians, 1900–1950," *Histoire sociale/Social History* 13 (May 1980): 161–72. Ann Gomer Sunahara, *The Politics of Racism: The Uprooting of Japanese Canadians during the Second World War* (Toronto: Lorimer, 1981) is a carefully documented study of this same issue; it should be read in conjunction with Ward's study. A popular summary is Thomas Berger's "The Banished Canadians: Mackenzie

King and the Japanese Canadians," in his *Fragile Freedoms: Human Rights and Dissent in Canada* (Toronto: Clarke, Irwin, 1981), 93–126.

The "Bren Gun Girl" and the Housewife Heroine*

ALISON PRENTICE, PAULA BOURNE, GAIL CUTHBERT BRANDT, BETH LIGHT, WENDY MITCHINSON, and NAOMI BLACK

By 1939 the Dominion was slowly recovering from the devastating impact of the Depression. On September 17, however, Canadians found themselves yet again engaged in an overseas conflict not of their own making. And once more Canadian women played a key role in the war effort through their domestic activities, voluntary organizations, and participation in war-related industries. In addition, they were recruited for the first time into that most venerated of male establishments, the quintessential expression of patriarchal power — the armed forces.

440

After the war, government and media focussed on the need to get women back into the home. But the structures of Canadian women's lives changed rapidly by the late 1950s. Earlier age at marriage, reduced fertility rates, and earlier completion of childbearing combined with increased longevity and economic opportunities to promote women's participation in the labour force. Most Canadian women with pre-school children continued to withdraw from the labour force to devote themselves solely to their families, but the average length of time spent doing so contracted. Though few noticed it, a new era had begun for women.

War Work

Women were indispensable to the Canadian war effort, and most contributed in the familiar surroundings of the household, the family farm, or women's voluntary organizations. As individuals and in their associations, women initiated extensive and varied war work, as they had in the Great War. This time, however, their activities came to be closely co-ordinated and controlled by the federal government through the Women's Voluntary Services Division, created in the autumn of 1941. Since they had already begun their own programs, some women's organizations were irked by what they considered government intervention.[1] The Department of National War Services ran an extensive publicity campaign

*From *Canadian Women: A History*, by Alison Prentice, Paula Bourne, Gail Cuthbert Brandt, Beth Light, Wendy Mitchinson, Naomi Black. Copyright 1988 by Harcourt Brace Jovanovich Canada, Inc. Reprinted by permission.

in both French and English to involve Canadian housewives in the war effort. One advertisement entitled "From the frying pan to the firing line," depicted three women pouring a panful of grease, which magically turned into bombs, over an enemy ship. "Work at munitions production in your own kitchen," the accompanying copy exhorted.[2] In response, thousands of women collected fats, paper, glass, metals, rubber, rags, and bones for recycling in war production.

The government's management of the war economy depended on women: some 2 285 000 homemakers were responsible for over 80 percent of the nation's retail purchases.[3] For many Canadians, the war effectively ended the Depression. As wartime production expanded, employment levels soared, and the average Canadian's purchasing power grew rapidly. At the same time, there were fewer civilian goods available, resulting in shortages, a sharp increase in the cost of living, and the spectre of an uncontrollable price–wage spiral. To control inflation, as soon as war was declared the federal government created the Wartime Prices and Trade Board to establish production quotas and maximum prices for many civilian goods. Various women's organizations, such as the National and Local Councils of Women, made it their responsibility to see that the board's price guidelines were followed. Impressed by their price-monitoring activities, the board moved to create a Consumer Branch with the well-known editor of *Chatelaine*, Bryne Hope Saunders, as its head. Subsequently fourteen regional committees co-ordinated the efforts of over 10 000 liaison officers supplied by women's voluntary organizations; these women informed consumers of the board's regulations, policed prices, and laid the basis for the establishment of the Canadian Consumers' Association when the war ended.

441

The federal government also relied on women to support its rationing system and wartime savings program, and to maintain the nation's nutritional standards. In addition, hundreds of thousands of women planted victory gardens, knitted and sewed articles of clothing for the troops, made up parcels for prisoners of war, ran hospitality centres and canteens for members of the armed forces, organized blood banks, practised civil defence procedures, or acted as spotters of enemy aircraft.

In the rural areas the Women's Institutes were especially active in promoting women's war services, and in mobilizing women for agricultural production. Across the nation wives and daughters supplemented the declining male agricultural workforce, as men signed up for military service or gravitated to more attractive industrial work. In British Columbia and Ontario, dominion–provincial programs were established to mobilize farm labour, and in Ontario three separate women's groups were created. The Farm Girls' Brigade included farm women under the age of twenty-six; the Women's Land Brigade recruited working women and housewives to help whenever they could; and the Farmerette Brigade brought together students and teachers to help out during the summer months. In 1943 nearly 13 000 women were enrolled in the three group.[4] For some farm wives, the war years brought not only an increased burden of work and responsibility, but also new opportunities for personal growth and accomplishment. "Dorothy," for example, tackled the heavy farm work during her husband's absence overseas, maintained the equipment, looked after the house and children, taught Sunday school, and still found time for curling and hunting. On her husband's return, she handed him the family bankbook and proudly declared, "There is more money in there than we ever had in our lives."[5]

The recruitment of women for agricultural production was part of a federal government campaign to manage the wartime labour force and to cope with labour shortages. Initially little government intervention was required, for there were some 900 000 unemployed Canadians when the war broke out. By 1942, however, this labour pool had been depleted as both industry and the armed forces expanded. In March of that year, Mackenzie King's government established the National Selective Service agency to oversee the recruitment and allocation of labour. Two months later, the Women's Division of the Selective Service agency was created under the direction of Fraudena Eaton of Vancouver, and in September 1942 it undertook a national registration of women aged twenty to twenty-four. The primary objective was to identify young single women who could be recruited into war industry. Although married women in this age category were also required to register, the federal government hoped that, by creating a pool of single workers, wives could be kept at home. Once the registration exercise was complete, the National Selective Service initiated programs to relocate single women from the Prairies and Maritimes to central Canada to work in war industry. In order to accomplish this, massive publicity campaigns were also launched to encourage single women to participate in war production. By June 1943, some 255 000 women were employed in war industry, and thousands more had entered military service.

The urgent demand for workers continued to grow, however, particularly in those industries that had traditionally employed large numbers of women. Workers were exchanging low-paying positions in garment and textile factories, in hotels, restaurants, hospitals, and private homes, in laundries and dry cleaning establishments, for the high wages offered by war industries. Now there was no choice but to turn to married women to take up the slack. Throughout the summer of 1943, with the help of Local Councils of Women, Selective Service mounted ambitious drives to recruit married women for part-time work in service industries. Housewives were also asked to work evening shifts created specially for them in essential war industries. Still the labour shortage remained acute, and the government in Ottawa was compelled to widen the scope of its recruitment plans to include full-time employment for married women. Yet another extensive campaign was undertaken, and the King government agreed to offer a few incentives: in July 1942, the Income Tax Act was amended so that working wives were treated as full dependents no matter how much they earned. Previously a wife could only earn up to $750 before her husband lost the married status exemption.[6]

The other major initiative was the provision of government-funded daycare services. Well before the promotion of employment for married women with children had begun, many mothers had availed themselves of the unprecedented job opportunities, despite the absence of adequate childcare services. In Ontario, where there was growing public concern over the lack of proper supervision for children, the blame for juvenile delinquency was laid squarely on the mothers of "latch-key children."[7] In July 1942, the federal government acknowledged the need for institutional childcare by introducing the dominion–provincial Wartime Day Nurseries Agreement. It provided for the two senior levels of government to share equally the costs of daycare services for children whose mothers were employed in war industries. However, only three provinces signed the accord — Ontario, Quebec, and Alberta — and after further study Alberta decided not to implement the program. Eventually, twenty-eight day nurseries were established in Ontario and six in Quebec. These nurseries accommodated children between two and six years of age, and in Ontario, homecare was arranged for children under the age of two and after-school daycare for those between the ages of six and sixteen. In keeping with the government's commitment to provide such services strictly to cope with the wartime emergency, only one-quarter of the available spaces could be given to the children of working mothers not employed in war industries. Eventually public pressure forced the government to amend the legislation to provide services for the children of all working mothers, but priority was still assigned to war industry employees.

In Quebec, the few day nurseries established under the program primarily served the anglophone population, a situation that reflected the vocal opposition of French Canadian Catholic leaders in that province to the employment of mothers. French Canadians now appeared to be among the most prejudiced against daycare centres, even though some childcare services had been available since the nineteenth century when the Grey Nuns opened their *salles d'asile*. Part of this negative reaction was the result of opposition to the war itself, particularly after conscription for home service was introduced in June 1940. In the national plebiscite that released the King government from its pledge not to institute conscription for overseas duty, the overwhelming majority of French-speaking Quebeckers had voted "No." Well before the implementation of the Day Nurseries' Agreement, which occurred three months later, French Canadian opposition to the war effort had solidified. Religious leaders and nationalists in Quebec roundly condemned those married women who "deserted" their families for lucrative work in munitions

443

plants, and articles published in the influential Jesuit publication *Relations* branded government-sponsored daycare facilities as communistic and destructive of the family. Provocative but unfounded reports of thousands of abandoned children in Montreal, and of infant deaths occurring in unlicensed nurseries, flooded the newspapers. In an impassioned speech, one member of the Quebec Assembly condemned all women's work outside the home. Such work, he claimed, created a desire for emancipation; it was destroying the family and "sabotaging what is most precious to us."[8]

Despite these vehement denunciations, thousands of French Canadian mothers took on paid employment. Their primary reasons for doing so were economic, according to Florence Martel, Fraudena Eaton's Quebec assistant:

> We were coming out of the Depression. There were no longer sheets on the beds, the children had no shoes and there were no more kitchen utensils. . . . Women lacked everything for a long time and they did not go to work to buy luxuries, as certain people accused them of doing.[9]

Indeed, Canadian women themselves indicated that an improved standard of living, not the call to loyalty and service, was their primary motivation for entering paid employment. In a 1943 survey conducted among married women over the age of thirty-five who were applying for paid work, only one in ten gave patriotism as their prime object, while well over half said they wanted to add to the family income. The rest cited "personal needs."[10]

By July 1, 1944, some 42 000 women in Quebec and Ontario were engaged in munitions works, where their much-vaunted ability to perform repetitive, precise work was fully exploited. One male journalist explained why women were able to persist at such work long after men had grown weary from the monotony — after all, they had long been accustomed to the boring routine of daily housekeeping! Analogies between women's war work and domestic tasks were rife: running a lathe was even easier than operating a vacuum cleaner, while filling a shell was no more difficult than making a cake.[11] Although working conditions had improved substantially compared to those endured by munitions workers during World War I, hours were long and the work often dangerous. Average wages for women workers were 10 cents an hour less than for men. Although women employed in the dangerous explosives department were paid from 5 to 13 cents an hour more than other female munitions workers, the amount seemed small for the additional risk.[12]

As the labour shortage grew, women were admitted in increasing numbers into the dominion–provincial War Emergency Training Program, and into non-traditional employments. By the end of 1942, nearly half of all full-time participants in pre-employment training were women who were being taught skills normally reserved for men, such as machineshop work, welding, aircraft assembly, shipbuilding, electronics, drafting, and industrial chemistry.[13] The aircraft industry, which by itself provided employment to 33 000 women, contained the largest proportion of women employed in any war industry.[14] But these apparent opportunities were only of limited value. Government training programs were shorter for women than for men, and most women received only two to six weeks' instruction. Women who entered directly into industry without such training were often expected to acquire the skills they would need during their first shift. Consequently there was little opportunity for them to secure the specialized training that would ensure long-term employment or upward mobility.

A few women did assume positions of authority; they immediately became the focus of media attention and were held up as living examples of the emancipating effects of the war. Such was the case of Elsie Gregory MacGill, who was put in charge of all engineering work for Canadian production of the Hurricane and Helldiver fighter planes. The daughter of Helen Gregory MacGill, Elsie MacGill had been the first woman to graduate in electrical engineering in Canada. Far more typical of war workers were young women like Veronica Foster, the 1941 "Bren gun girl," who worked on the assembly lines.[15] If, like Foster, they worked in war industry, they too might be singled out and glamourized for publicity purposes.

445

"You're in the Army Now!"

The image of the emancipated woman was further enhanced by the entry of women into the armed forces, but here, as in war industry, equality was never gained. Even before war began, women across the nation had organized themselves into paramilitary groups. One of the earliest and largest was the Victoria Women's Service Club, created in October 1938. Subsequently other units were formed in British Columbia, and by 1940 such groups boasted a total of 1200 members. The movement spread eastwards to other Canadian cities, and by 1941 nearly 7000 women were enrolled. Modelled on the women's auxiliary of the British army, these organizations taught their members military drill, first aid, map reading, signalling, and transport driving; some even included rifle practice. Shortly after their formation, the women's corps lobbied vigorously for official recognition from the Department of National Defence, but this was withheld. Only when the manpower shortage grew serious did the government decide to form the Canadian Women's Army Corps (CWAC). Established in August 1941, it provided only partial recognition of the existing women's corps, which were used primarily as a source of recruits.

Once again women's war initiatives were taken over and directed by a male-dominated bureaucracy. Since the CWAC was initially not integrated into the army, but comprised a separate organization, its officers did not enjoy the same ranks, authority, or insignia as men in the army. The women officers' ranks were indicated on their uniforms by an array of beavers and maple leaves. Only in March 1942 was the Canadian Women's Army Corps integrated into the Canadian armed forces, and its members entitled to use the usual military titles and insignia.[16] In the same year as CWAC was formed, the federal government established the Canadian Women's Auxiliary Air Force, largely as a result of British inquiries about recruiting women to assist at Commonwealth Air Training Plan centres; in February 1942, the auxiliary was transformed into the Women's Division, Royal Canadian Air Force. In the following July, the Women's Royal Canadian Naval Service was created.

Women who entered the armed forces encountered many of the obstructive attitudes and practices confronting women in civilian life. In all ranks, the women received only two-thirds of the basic pay of men with equivalent rank. Initially, there was no provision for servicewomen to receive dependents' allowances, and women recruits married to military personnel were not eligible for a separation allowance. Confronted by vehement protests against these practices by servicewomen themselves and the National Council of Women, and by the negative impact the poor pay was having on female recruitment, the Department of National Defence raised women's basic pay to 80 percent of that received by men of similar rank. In addition, women were to receive the same trades pay as men in each category, and a servicewoman with a husband in the military was to receive a separation allowance — provided her annual income did not exceed $2100. Dependents' allowances for parents and siblings were also to be provided on the same basis as to servicemen, but women continued to be denied such allowances for spouses or children.

Job segregation also remained a fact of life in the armed forces. It was understood that only the war emergency and the necessity to release able-bodied men for active duty justified the creation of the women's services. From the beginning, military authorities intended to use female recruits to replace support personnel such as clerks, cooks, telephone operators, drivers, mess waiters, and canteen helpers. In all areas men remained firmly in charge. In the CWAC, for example, eventually close to fifty occupations were opened to women recruits, but the vast majority worked at typically female jobs: of nearly 6000 CWAC tradeswomen surveyed in March 1945, 62 percent were working as clerks. Although most women who enlisted hoped to satisfy their spirit of adventure through an overseas posting, only one in nine servicewomen served outside Canada, with the exception of the nursing sisters. We can well imagine the anger and disappointment felt by one group of WDs (Women's Division,

RCAF) at Rockcliffe, who found themselves scrubbing the floors in the governor-general's residence. When they did manage to make it overseas, most CWACs found themselves assigned to work as clerks, laundresses, and cooks; in fact, the first call for Canadian servicewomen to serve overseas came when Canadian Headquarters in London was unable to find sufficient laundresses, and requested 150 CWACs to make up the shortfall.[17] The sexual division of labour remained intact.

Indeed, traditional attitudes towards women were ultimately reinforced during the war, in spite of initial challenges. The sight of women dressed in overalls and bandanas, swinging lunch pails on the way to work, or of women in trim military uniforms, caused many Canadians considerable consternation. Those responsible for recruiting women into the labour force and the armed forces felt called upon to reassure the public that the new tasks women were undertaking were short-term, necessitated by the current emergency, and did not constitute any real threat to existing gender roles. Military authorities undertook a massive educational and publicity campaign to reassure Canadians that the femininity of the women recruits was not being jeopardized, emphasizing the attractive uniforms and the homey atmosphere of the women's barracks. Female recruits were allowed to wear make-up, were encouraged to be attractive and feminine, and were reminded "at all times to act in a becoming and lady-like manner."[18]

447

As part of their campaign, the authorities also had to reassure the public about the respectability of the women under their command. There was a persistent belief that servicewomen were promiscuous; rumours abounded that some were former prostitutes, that many were getting pregnant, and that a large proportion were suffering from venereal disease. Despite the fact that venereal disease was far more common among Canadian servicemen, who also accounted for nearly 90 percent of the fathers named by CWACs discharged for pregnancy, the reputations of the men were unaffected. Indeed, it is only too evident that a double standard of sexual behaviour was transferred from civilian to military life. Servicewomen who contracted venereal disease were much more likely to be discharged than servicemen with the same condition, and much greater effort was expended on setting up preventive programs for men. The latter were constantly reminded that it was predatory, un-principled women who caused venereal infection.[19]

By the war's end, more than 43 000 women had enlisted in the armed forces: 21 000 in the Women's Army Corps, 16 000 in the Women's Div-ision of the air force, and 6600 in the Women's Naval Service. In addition, some 2500 women joined the Nursing Service and 38 women doctors signed up for medical duty. Despite the limitations and discrimination that women in the services frequently encountered, for many their war-time experience was exhilarating. "When you passed your exams and you received your flags," one member of the Women's Naval Service recalled, "it was like getting your degree. It had a big effect on our lives. We were proud of ourselves as individuals as well as women, for we succeeded under the same conditions as the men, and for many this changed our outlook toward our place within society."[20] Nonetheless, the official mottoes of the women's services — "We are the Women behind the men behind the guns"; "We serve that men might fly"; "We serve that men might fight" — cast them in a subsidiary role. Although the women's naval and military units played a crucial role in the war effort, and considerable pressure was exerted on the government to maintain them as part of Canada's reserve forces, once the hostilities ceased they were promptly disbanded. Concurrently, the government abandoned the wartime incentives to attract women into paid employment. Women were expected to return to their primary sphere of activity — the home.

448 What Should Women Do after the War?

Canadian policy makers were merely reflecting prevailing public opinion — that women's labour force participation during the war was a temporary phenomenon. Even before peace was achieved, most Canadians expected women, especially those who were married, to rededicate themselves to work in the home. In 1944 Dorise Nielsen, CCF member from Saskatchewan, gave Parliament a sardonic summary of men's attitudes towards women's appropriate role: "Well, girls, you have done a nice job; you looked very cute in your overalls and we appreciate what you have done for us; but just run along; go home; we can get along without you very easily."[21]

A Gallup poll conducted in 1944 indicated that 75 percent of the Canadian men polled, as well as 68 percent of the women, believed men should be given preference in post-war employment.[22] Given the limited opportunities for women to move out of female work ghettos during the war, the physical and emotional strain endured by those who combined paid employment with domestic labour, the aggravation of wartime shortages, and the anxiety caused by the absence of loved ones, many Canadian women themselves looked forward to a return to full-time home life at war's end. "When the Johnnys and Joes come marching home," a woman journalist noted, "just shopping for ham to cook ham and eggs — if she can get eggs — is apt to be important to a woman . . . even if she drops an odd pay envelope along the way."[23] Not surprisingly, both governments and industry quickly adjusted their policies and practices to encourage women to stay at home.

Planning for the post-war economy and society began well before the Allied victory in Europe in May 1945. Many Canadians feared a resumption of the severe recession and massive unemployment of the 1930s, or of the inflation and social unrest of the years immediately following

World War I. Spurred on by these concerns, in March 1941 the Liberal government named an Advisory Committee on Reconstruction, consisting of six prominent men, with Principal Cyril E. James of McGill University as chairman. Almost immediately, women began to petition for representatives of their sex in the planning exercise, on the basis of women's important contribution to the war effort. Finally, in January 1943, the government bowed to the women's lobby, and established a new subcommittee to deal with the problems women in war industry were likely to encounter once war ended. This subcommittee, whose terms of reference were soon expanded to allow it to report on post-war problems for all Canadian women, was headed by Margaret Stovel McWilliams, journalist, Winnipeg councillor, and prominent women's organization activist, and included nine other women from across the nation.[24] They were all well-educated, almost exclusively of British Protestant background, middle-aged, and mostly upper middle class. Although these women had considerable experience and expertise as a result of the organizational work in which nearly all were involved, several were clearly chosen because of their husbands' prominent positions and political connections.

449

At its initial meeting, the subcommittee adopted as its first principle the precept that women's war work entitled them to the same possibilities as men for post-war training and employment. Each woman, its members believed, should have the right not only to choose her work, but also to obtain equal remuneration, working conditions, and opportunity for advancement as men. Although the subcommittee's effectiveness was undermined by being ordered to avoid publicity, and by the sudden shortening of its term to eight months, it produced a comprehensive report.

The report itself was a mixture of old and new. Assuming that marriage would greatly reduce potential female unemployment, the subcommittee nevertheless recommended that the federal government assume responsibility for the training and retraining of women workers, and to provide low interest loans to help needy women upgrade their skills. Training should be available to women on the same basis as it was to men, but most women would be trained in distinctive women's occupations, such as domestic service, nursing, teaching, and social work; to avoid duplicating the work of another subcommittee, proposals on training programs were given only for domestic workers. Somewhat radically the subcommittee proposed that "household workers" be included in any national labour code that might be forthcoming, including minimum wage legislation, unemployment insurance, and workmen's compensation. Such workers were to be protected further by means of written contracts with their employers. The subcommittee echoed again the hope that domestic work would be raised to the status of a vocation, a development that would benefit housewives as well as their employees. In respect to married women at home, the subcommittee members proposed measures intended to improve their status: they should be viewed as economic partners with their husbands, be included in social security schemes such as health insurance, receive family allowances, and have access to government-funded morning nursery schools. Hoping that the rural way of life would attract back to the countryside many of the 95 000 women who had left the farm during the war, they urged governments to extend electricity to rural areas, supply household appliances at cost, improve communication networks, and expand rural educational, health, and recreational facilities.

The important new elements in the subcommittee's recommendations led some journalists to describe their report as a "charter of rights" or a "bill of rights" for Canadian women.[25] Yet, despite its innovative character, the report received little public attention apart from a few press accounts that were usually consigned to the "women's pages." The federal government ignored most of its recommendations, as it did most of the recommendations of the Advisory Committee's other subcommittees.

Instead, governments now moved to cancel the incentives they had created to draw women into the workforce. The Quebec government discontinued its participation in the Day Nurseries Agreement in October 1945, and the federal government ended its agreement with Ontario in June 1946. Although the total number of children accommodated in these nurseries was small — some 1000 in the pre-school programs and 2500 in the school-age programs — their existence had been extremely significant symbolically. The federal government also amended income tax regulations so that after January 1, 1947, if a wife earned more than $250 — not the pre-war $750 — her husband could no longer claim the full married status exemption.[26] Although the tax amendments appear to have had little effect on married women's employment in some regions, in others they were reported as having a significant negative impact. In Prince George, British Columbia, the local employment office manager noted that no fewer than eight married women had indicated their intent to resign their nursing positions at the local hospital owing to the new tax regulations, aggravating an already "grim" shortage of trained nurses. There were also reports that labour shortages were occurring in the fruit packing and canning industry in the Okanagan Valley because married women were quitting work once they had earned $250.[27]

Another post-war policy that worked to women's disadvantage was "veterans' preference," giving priority in government employment to Canadians who had performed active duty overseas. Relatively few women met this criterion, since only 7000 Canadian women had served overseas.[28] There was a general effort to limit women's employment in the public service. The prime minister went so far as to request his cabinet ministers not to employ female secretaries. The Minister of Agriculture, W.R. Motherwell, is reported to have responded "To —— with him. I couldn't get along without her."[29] Within the public service, the married women who had been implored to help run the burgeoning wartime bureaucracy were now discharged. Married women continued to be barred from the federal civil service until 1955.

When the government disbanded the women's military services in 1946, post-war training programs for discharged members paid lipservice to the principle of equal opportunity for training for women and men, but in reality focussed on "suitable" occupations such as stenography, home-making, dressmaking, and nursing. Of the female veterans who took vocational training, over half took commercial training courses.[30] For young women who had learned a trade in the armed forces, the return to civilian employment was often frustrating. The experience of one French Canadian telegraphist was typical. Since railway companies and airlines gave preference to men, Monique Comeau Gauthier was counselled to take a course in how to use an adding machine; eventually she found work as a telephone operator.[31]

451

For women who had been engaged in war industry, there were few opportunities to retain the skilled jobs or the high wages of the war years. The National Employment Service considered that low-paid, unskilled labour was suitable for female war workers: in one case brought to the attention of the House of Commons in July 1946, the service was accused of offering an elevator operator's job that paid $15.30 per week to a woman who had been earning $30.80 per week as an instrument mechanic in an aircraft factory. The new wage was below the prevailing minimum wage.[32] Moreover, women were to be redirected from manufacturing, where their continued presence might constitute a threat to male employment, into domestic service, where there was a dearth of workers. By going into domestic service, women also lost the opportunity to receive unemployment insurance benefits. The 1941 unemployment insurance legislation did not include domestic servants, teachers, or nurses, although some categories of nurses were included in 1944. The oft-repeated but unrealistic objective of attracting throngs of women into paid domestic work by improving the status and wages was tried once more under the label of the "Home Aide" program. And once again, Canadian women workers responded by virtually ignoring the program.[33]

Disillusioned by public failure to recognize women's contribution to the war effort adequately, one female reporter wondered whether married women would "go to war" again:

> We made munitions, served overseas or at home, whenever we were needed. And loved doing it. Then what happened when the war was over? We were patted on the head and told, "Good show, girls, but now back to kinder, küche and kirche. . . . " If married women are people in emergencies, why can't they be people when there isn't an emergency?[34]

Once more, women's role as a "reserve army of labour" was unmistakable. When workers were urgently needed, even married women were encouraged to take on paid employment; once male labour became more plentiful, women were encouraged to shift back to traditional female occupations or to the home.

Media Messages

The Canadian government's massive campaign to encourage women to enter the labour force and military service during World War II made use of newspapers, periodicals, radio, and the newly created National Film Board to modify the image of the ideal Canadian woman. At war's end, the image changed again: women's productive role disappeared, and it was domestic duties that were the central feature of the idealized woman's life. Canadian media portrayals of women in the post-war years stressed an all-pervasive stereotype of women as happy homemakers, winsome wives, and magnanimous mothers. Woman's role as consumer was re-emphasized.[35] In *Maclean's* magazine between 1939 and 1950, the proportion of all advertisments that directly appealed to women as homemakers rose from about 40 percent in the period 1939–43 to over 70 percent in 1950. And the emphasis shifted. No longer did the advertisements merely offer to free the housewife from the drudgery and boredom of her work; now they promised her a life of personal fulfillment — provided she wisely purchased the right products.[36]

The Francophone media followed a similar pattern, but adopted an even more traditional version. The representation of the ideal French Canadian woman was thoroughly unidimensional: she was portrayed as a fervent Catholic, a devoted wife and mother, and attached to the rural way of life. This characterization was consistently presented in *La Terre et le Foyer*, the official organ of the *Cercles de fermières* after 1945. Designed for women in the smaller urban centres as well as farm women, most of the articles in this magazine discussed women's handicrafts (*artisanat*), and promoted the primary objective of the *cercles*: the professionalization of country women's work. *La Terre et le Foyer* made it clear that it adhered closely to church directives. During the 1950s, articles dealing with women and the family thoroughly reflected the ideas of the Catholic church that nature destined women to perform domestic work, and that women's paid employment outside the home was a negative influence.

The media did not question whether or not the normal and desired fate of most women was marriage and motherhood. Although a rare editorial in *Chatelaine* did champion a woman's right to remain single, and some articles in Canadian mass-circulation magazines such as *Saturday Night* strongly advocated education for women that would enable them to pursue certain "women's careers," spinsterhood was not a highly regarded state. Advertisements aimed at the single young woman counselled her on how to catch a man, and glamour was decreed her most highly prized attribute. The 1950s were the decade of Yves St. Laurent's "New Look," the sweater girl, and Marilyn Monroe. St. Laurent designed clothes, he said, "for flowerlike women, clothes with rounded shoulders, full feminine busts, and willowy waists above enormous spreading skirts."[37] For many women, such feminine appearance required encasing themselves in padded bras and waist-cinchers. In addition, the essential requirement for a glamorous image was impeccable personal hygiene. Advertisements for soaps, deodorants, and sanitary napkins were numerous: one deodorant advertisement showed a tearful young woman under the caption, "She lost her man because of *that*." It was not enough, however, to be clean and odour-free; a woman's chances of romantic success depended on improving her appearance by using the plethora of products the cosmetic industry had to offer her.

453

Once she had used her beauty to effect the desired change in marital status, it was a woman's duty to continue to be sexually attractive to her husband. An advertisement for disinfectant showed a distraught wife whose husband was walking out the door, suitcase in hand; if only she had used Lysol in her douche to keep herself fresh and dainty! The married woman's role as a tension manager was also highlighted in the advertisements. Under a picture of a beaming middle-aged couple, the manufacturers of Ovaltine proclaimed that this twosome was "still in love after years of marriage." But it had taken "more than love to reach this blissful state of trust and devotion." The "thoughtful wife" had made a cup of Ovaltine their "nightly custom," thereby "melting away the nervous tensions of the day."[38]

It was still only with her transformation into mother, however, that a woman was able to reach her full potential. Weston's Bakery paid tribute to the Canadian mother as the "heart of her home," responsible for the moral and civic training of her children.[39] The message of this advertisement is remarkably similar to that delivered by Dr. Hilda Neatby, Canada's pre-eminent woman historian of the 1950s. A professor at the University of Saskatchewan and member of the Massey Commission on cultural affairs, Dr. Neatby never married. However, she confidently assured other women that the establishment of "a moral tone and moral practices in her family is a woman's first obligation to society. . . . Women, gifted and otherwise, are the individuals who in the present state of society have a large, perhaps the largest share in determining the cultural atmosphere of the home."[40] Neatby's arguments were echoed by many others who sought to expand opportunities in higher education for Canada's future mothers.

The belief that marriage and motherhood were the normal goals for women was reinforced by medical experts. As Freudian views about women became more widespread in the 1950s, as did the psychosomatic approach to medicine, doctors stressed the importance of women's reproductive and maternal roles. The growing tendency for women to work outside the home fuelled concern about the preservation of the family. Women suffering from gynecological disorders were considered to have rejected their traditional roles. According to the *Canadian Medical Association Journal* in 1958, women who experienced pre-menstrual tension tended to resent their femininity and to envy men. Another doctor asserted that women exaggerated the extent of their menstrual pain "in order to get revenge on men for their easy lot in life and to shirk their own work responsibilities." Specialists in obstetrics and gynecology were advised to determine the extent to which their patients accepted themselves as women.[41]

454   For those women who did become mothers, feature articles and regular columns appearing in the women's magazines offered advice — frequently conflicting — about how to deal with the myriad problems inherent in raising a child. The expansion of the middle class in the prosperity of the post-war years created an enlarged audience of well-educated parents receptive to childrearing advice. Childcare experts emphasized the emotional bonds between mother and child, and as infant mortality rates for the general population continued to decline, middle class mothers could be increasingly confident that this emotional investment would not be destroyed by the untimely death of their children.

Many mothers were anxious about their abilities as parents, increasingly so with the popularization of the work of child psychologists such as Dr. John Bowlby. Bowlby was the British psychologist who coined the phrase "maternal deprivation," a notion central to his book *Child Care and the Growth of Love*, and discussed widely in women's magazines in North America. On the basis of a study of orphaned children who had to be cared for in institutional settings or foster homes, Bowlby argued that irreparable damage was done to young children when they were separated from their mothers for a prolonged period. He counselled mothers not to leave children under three years of age in the care of others except for the most urgent reasons. Even "the holiday whilst granny looks after the baby" was "best kept to a week or ten days." Many mothers interpreted Bowlby's dictum about the "absolute need of infants and toddlers for the continuous care of their mothers" as meaning they should always be on call for their children.[42]

The conflicting advice mothers of infants received further complicated their lives: should they feed baby according to a strict time schedule, as their own mothers had done, or when baby demanded it? Although infant care experts pointed out the advantages of breast feeding, and counselled mothers to try it, they assigned an inordinate amount of space in the literature to describing the procedures to be followed in bottle feeding. Given the overwhelming importance accorded motherhood, and the confusion about how best to meet the demands of this role, it is small wonder that Canadian women relied on books such as the free government publication, *The Canadian Mother and Child* (1940), and Dr. Benjamin Spock's *Baby and Child Care* (1945) for authoritative answers. By 1953 Canadian public health nurses had handed out to new mothers over 2 000 000 copies of the former; by 1975 it was in its third edition.

Although the image of women as homemakers and mothers was all-pervasive and powerful, and undoubtedly exercised a considerable influence, increasing numbers of Canadian women did not conform to its fundamental specifications. Once again, it is important to underline the gap that existed between what women were told they should do and what women actually did. The very vigour with which the "happy home-maker" image was promoted by the media may well have been a reaction to women's growing involvement in activities outside the home.

What Women Really Did

Immediately after the war, there was little apparent discrepancy between the image and the reality of women's lives. Canadians' desire to return to familiar roles combined with the reduced opportunities for women in paid employment to produce a sharp decrease in the female participation rate in the labour force. By September 1945, nearly 80 000 women in war industry had been laid off and thousands of servicewomen discharged.[43] In 1944, at the peak of wartime employment, one-third of all women over the age of 15 were in the paid labour force. Two years later, only one-quarter were working for pay. Only in 1967 did women's participation rate surpass the 1944 level. However, the decline in the period immediately after the war appears to have been caused less by the withdrawal of women already in the workforce than by the lower participation rate of younger women. Prolonged education, earlier age at marriage, and earlier age for starting a family together produced this result. One estimate placed the number of women who withdrew from the workplace at war's end at approximately 102 000, under 10 percent of all female war workers.[44] In the United States, women's labour force participation rate had reached even higher levels during the war, only to drop by 19 percent between 1945 and 1947. The decline in Canada was much less pronounced — less than 9 percent during the same period.[45]

After the war, marriage rates soared, especially among younger women. For those aged 15 to 19, the rate more than doubled, climbing from 30 per 1000 in 1937 to 62 per 1000 in 1954.[46] Canadian women were also marrying earlier. The average age of brides at first marriage fell from 25.4 years in 1941 to 22 years by 1961.[47] In addition, they were having more children, and having them earlier than women of the previous generation. There was a sharp increase in the number of births per 1000 population, which rose from 20.1 in 1937 to 28.9 in 1947. It is important to note, however, that significant increases in the birth rate were recorded only among married women under 30, and most strikingly among those under 25. As one observer pithily commented, "Young girls are more interested in raising families than jobs; not-so-young girls like jobs better than children."[48] In the younger groups of married women, birth rates continued to climb until 1956; for women over 40, the rates continued to decline compared to those established by women in the same age category during previous generations.[49] These patterns initially produced the renowned post-war "baby boom" in the late 1940s and early 1950s, the result of a combination of earlier age at marriage, earlier births of first children, and larger completed families. In 1956, nearly one-half of all live births consisted of third or later children.[50] Nevertheless, after 1956, substantial declines in birth rates were recorded for all age groups.

456

Despite the general absence of young mothers from the workforce in the post-war era, the proportion of married women among paid female workers continued to rise. In part, this was owing to the lower age at marriage and the growing acceptance of young married women working, providing that they did not have children; in part, to the presence in the labour force of older women with school-age or older children. In 1941 only slightly more than 10 percent of all employed women were married; during the war the estimated proportion was from 25 to 35 percent. By 1951 the percentage had dropped slightly, but by 1961 nearly half of all female workers were married. This dramatic increase can also be measured by looking at the proportion of wives who were in the paid labour force: from only one in twenty-five in 1941, the figure changed in twenty years to a remarkable one in five. Changes such as these led the Dominion Chief Statistician to declare in 1954, "The woman's place is no longer in the home, and the Canadian home is no longer what it used to be."[51]

In spite of the initial post-war setbacks, women's involvement in the labour force increased steadily from the mid-1950s on. For the first time in Canadian history, the number of women entering the workforce was greater than the number of men.[52] During the recession from 1957 to 1961, a *Financial Post* reporter noted that married women's wages were being used to supplement their husbands' unemployment benefits. He concluded, "This is a woman's world all right and getting more so. More and more married women are going to work and they are quickly being snapped into jobs. . . . Keep your eye on Mom."[53] Unemployment rates were lower for women than men owing to the rapid expansion of clerical and service positions, largely filled by women.[54] With the post-war baby boom and the failure of teachers' salaries to keep pace with inflation, an acute teacher shortage developed, and once more women, including married women, were actively recruited. To cope with the unprecedented numbers of students crowding into schools in Ontario, the provincial government dropped the entrance requirement for teachers' college from grade 13 to grade 12, and encouraged high school graduates to "qualify" as teachers by taking a brief, five-week summer course. Other provinces adopted similar policies: in Nova Scotia, for example, in a practice reminiscent of the nineteenth century, women as young as sixteen were recruited for rural schools.[55]

The increasing numbers of working mothers became the source of much controversy and, possibly as a result, in 1955 the Department of Labour conducted a survey of employed married women in eight Canadian cities. Over 50 percent of those interviewed had dependent children, and some 80 percent worked full-time. They had evidently taken jobs for economic reasons: only 15 percent of their husbands earned a relatively high income of $4000, but when the wives' wages were included, over half of the families reached this income level. One-third of the workers in the Department of Labour survey were born outside Canada.[56] For some immigrant groups such as the southern Italians, married women's paid employment was central to the family's strategy for improving its financial situation.[57] The higher labour force participation rate of married women in the late 1950s compared to the immediate post-war years was, it seems, owing in part to the massive post-war wave of immigration. The authors of the eight-city survey were eager to refute the public perception that most married working women had children who were being neglected — so eager that, instead of stating that 56 percent of the women interviewed had dependent children, they declared that 44 percent had none.[58]

457

Women workers with pre-school children had to make their own childcare arrangements, and generally preferred family or friends. Highly placed women such as Marion Royce, director of the Women's Bureau of the federal Department of Labour created in 1954, persistently argued the need for better daycare facilities and more part-time work for married women with children.[59] However, no level of government felt an obligation to provide such facilities, and most Canadians continued to believe that married women with young children should not be employed outside the home. It was still assumed that the vast majority of women could not successfully combine work and family. In 1955 one woman who tried but failed concluded vehemently,

> I don't care who you are or how well organized you are, you can't be a good wife and mother, hostess and housekeeper, and also do a good job for your employer all at the same time. When you try, someone is bound to get cheated — your husband, your child or your boss — and in most cases, all three.

Her solution: quit your job to save your marriage.[60]

Most married women in the paid labour force could not choose to quit their jobs. It was essential for them to work to maintain their families' standard of living in an increasingly consumer-oriented society. The strong desire of Canadians to improve their material situations, frustrated by years of depression and war, was not to be denied. In the 1950s, television revolutionized mass advertising techniques, stimulating the demand for major consumer items such as cars, appliances, and furniture. To purchase these things, which most Canadians now considered essential, and to ensure access to higher education and better health care for their children, many married women had to supplement their husbands' wages through paid employment.

The pronounced emphasis on consumption may also have increased the workload of most homemakers. As the standard of living rose, and the volume and diversity of consumer goods increased, the tasks associated with household management became more complex. The work entailed in managing the family budget, trying to balance family income against family needs, was even more difficult in the new suburbs that mushroomed on the fringes of Canadian urban communities. Frequently isolated and without transportation, suburban housewives had little opportunity to engage in comparison shopping or to buy at the lowest prices. Shopping plazas, the first of which was constructed in Toronto in 1946, were somewhat helpful, but they provided only a limited choice of shops. Women were also responsible for dealing with the countless salesmen, repairmen, public officials, and community representatives who showed up on their doorsteps.[61]

For women who continued to participate in the workforce, there were some significant attempts at organization, a consequence of the continuation of labour militancy generated during World War II. During the war, as the demand for workers expanded, so did workers' bargaining power; union membership soared, especially with the expansion of industrial unionism. Even the more conservative international unions became involved in organizing semi-skilled and unskilled workers, within whose ranks were to be found thousands of women. In the textile industry, Madeleine Parent and her future husband, Kent Rowley, made impressive inroads. Parent, the daughter of a prosperous French Canadian retail manager, graduated from McGill in 1940 and became a labour activist while still a very young woman. In 1942 Parent and Rowley started to organize Quebec cottonmill workers in Valleyfield and Montreal. They faced formidable odds, for they had to confront not only the might of the textile cartel headed by Dominion Textile, but also the overt hostility of the Roman Catholic church, which branded them Communists. Because of the wartime ban on strikes, the workers had to wait until 1945 before they could walk off the job an attempt to win union recognition, a shorter work week, and improved benefits.

In June 1946, some 3000 workers at Dominion Textile's Montreal mills and an additional 3000 workers at the Valleyfield mill staged a walkout. Approximately one-third of the workers were women. Although the

Montreal strike was grudgingly accepted as legal by the blatantly pro-business government of Maurice Duplessis, it declared the Valleyfield strike illegal since not all the bargaining procedures required by law had been followed. The authorities made a concerted effort to break the strike, using the provincial police to protect strikebreakers and intimidate the workers. The Valleyfield strike was long, bitter, punctuated by violence, and marked by the arrest of the union leaders, including both Parent and Rowley. However, it finally terminated in September and resulted in a first contract, improved wages, and other benefits for the workers.

There was another effort in 1946, equally concerted but less successful, to unionize a segment of the workforce containing a large proportion of female wage earners — the campaign undertaken by the Retail, Whole-sale and Department Store Union to organize the 15 000 T.E. Eaton Co. workers in Toronto. A key figure in this drive was Eileen Tallman, a Toronto CCF activist and crack organizer for the United Steelworkers. One of the major obstacles in recruiting workers to the union was their high rate of turnover, over one in four leaving each year. It took one and a half years of painstaking efforts to contact Eaton's employees working at various outlets throughout Toronto before the first union meeting could be held. Equal pay for equal work became a principal objective: the starting salary for married women was $20 per week, while it was $24 to $26 for single men and $30 for married men.[62] Although the Canadian Congress of Labour created a special organizing committee to support the union in this monumental task, and there was a prolonged attempt to win certification, the drive was unsuccessful. It was finally called off in 1952. The company managed to undercut the strength of the campaign by improving wages and establishing pensions for some long-term employees. The failure of the Eaton's drive was a clear indicator of how difficult it was, and would continue to be, to organize white collar workers. And this was the sector where women workers were increasingly to be found.

The importance of women's support for the trade union movements grew during and after World War II, as production workers saw many of their material gains threatened by the rising cost of living, and women's consumer roles expanded. Some women's auxiliaries were also involved in the bitter internal struggles between local Communist union leaders and their international leadership that bedevilled many unions after the war; such a situation occurred in Lake Cowichan, British Columbia, where the ladies' auxiliary supported the local "red" faction of the International Woodworkers of America. The political activities of this auxiliary also led it to support the "rolling pin brigade," a protest movement largely composed of housewife consumers, which culminated in a march on Ottawa after the war to demand price and rent controls, low-cost housing, and the establishment of a peacetime agency to regulate prices. More importantly, on an individual level women active in the auxiliary

459

acquired a greater awareness of the interconnections between men's paid labour and women's unpaid domestic labour. One delegate to a 1947 district auxiliary convention aptly summarized the relationship:

> I didn't just marry a meal ticket, and that's what it amounts to if my husband works more than forty hours a week! Wives also need a shorter work week and the only way that most of us can get it is if our husbands pitch in at home to give us a break, spend a little time with the children and (incidentally) learn a bit of housekeeping.[63]

By the end of the 1950s, it should have been clear that women were in the workplace to stay. Instead, what was mainly noticed was the continuing emphasis on women's role in the home. Certainly, wartime did not have any "liberating" effect for the Japanese Canadian women who spent the war years imprisoned in internment camps, or "resettled" thousands of kilometres away from their homes. Nor was the war a period of personal fulfillment for those who lost sons, husbands, or lovers. Nevertheless, a more optimistic assessment may be in order. For some Canadian women, the opportunity to expand their activities did have a positive impact. According to one woman,

> The war killed all this servant business, being a maid, and I think it did a lot to finish off the idea that a woman's place and her only place was in the home. . . . The war and working in plants so changed me I became an entirely different person. I wish I'd kept a diary.[64]

Such women gained an increased sense of self-worth, leading them to chafe at the more traditional and limited notions of women's appropriate roles that re-emerged at war's end.

NOTES

[1] Ruth Roach Pierson, *"They're Still Women After All": The Second World War and Canadian Womanhood* (Toronto: McClelland and Stewart, 1986), 36–37.

[2] Geneviève Auger and Raymonde Lamothe, *De la poêle à frire à ligne de feu* (Montréal: Boréal Express, 1981), frontispiece (authors' translation).

[3] Auger et Lamothe, *De la poêle à frire*, 53.

[4] Pierson, *"They're Still Women,"* 33.

[5] Barry Broadfoot, *Six War Years, 1939–1945: Memories of Canadians at Home and Abroad* (Toronto: Paperjacks, 1974), 355–56.

[6] Pierson, *"They're Still Women,"* 48.

[7] Pierson, *"They're Still Women,"* 50.

[8] Auger and Lamothe, *De la poêle à frire*, 128 (authors' translation).

[9] Auger and Lamothe, *De la poêle à frire*, 128 (authors' translation).

[10] Pierson, *"They're Still Women,"* 47.

[11] Pierson, *"They're Still Women,"* 71.

[12] National Archives of Canada, RG 3614, vol. 135, McTague Commission Inquiry, *Proceedings*, 2263–79.

[13] Pierson, *"They're Still Women,"* 71.

[14] *Financial Post*, February 24, 1951.

[15] Sheila Kieran, *The Family Matters: Two Centuries of Family Law and Life in Ontario* (Toronto: Key Porter Books, 1986), 125.

[16] This discussion of women in the armed forces relies extensively on Pierson, *"They're Still Women,"* ch. 3.

[17] Carolyn M. Gossage, "Never the Same Again: Canada's Women in the Armed Forces, 1939–45" (unpublished manuscript, 1985), 116–17, 192.

[18] Gossage, "Never the Same Again," 123.

[19] Pierson, *They're Still Women,* chs. 5 and 6.

[20] Paul Ward, "Women in World War II: Focus on the Women's Royal Canadian Naval Service" (unpublished paper, April 1987), 27.

[21] Canada, House of Commons, *Debates* (1944), 2629.

[22] Clare Booth Luce, "Women Can Win the Peace," *Chatelaine* (February 1944), 3.

[23] "Will Women Go Back to the Kitchen?" *Canadian Home Journal* 40 (January 1944): 3.

[24] The other members included Margaret Mackenzie (Fredericton), Thaïs Lacoste Frémont (Quebec City), Margaret Wherry (Montreal), Dr. A. Vibert Douglas (Kingston), Helen Smith Agnew and Marion Findlay (Toronto), Susan Gunn (Lloydminster), Grace MacInnis and Evelyn Lett (Vancouver); see Gail Cuthbert Brandt, " 'Pigeon-Holed and Forgotten': The Work of the Subcommittee on the Post-War Problems of Women, 1943," *Histoire sociale/Social History* 15, 29 (March–May 1982): 239–59.

[25] *Saturday Night* (June 24, 1944), 6; *Halifax Herald,* February 2, 1944, p. 8.

[26] Pierson, *They're Still Women,* 49.

[27] National Archives of Canada, MG 28, 1–10, vol. 104, file 777, 1947.

[28] Pierson, *They're Still Women,* 82.

[29] Agnes Macphail, "Men Want to Hog Everything," *Maclean's* (September 15, 1949), 71–72.

[30] Pierson, *They're Still Women,* 91.

[31] Auger and Lamothe, *De la poêle à frire,* 215.

[32] Canada, House of Commons, *Debates* (July 4, 1946), 3182.

[33] Ruth Pierson, " 'Home Aide': A Solution to Women's Unemployment after World War II," *Atlantis* 2, 2 (Spring 1977): 85–96.

[34] M.A.C. Francis, "Will Married Women Go To War Again?" *Saturday Night* 66 (January 30, 1951): 21–22.

[35] Yvonne Mathews-Klein, "How They Saw Us: Images of Women in National Film Board Films of the 1940s and 1950s," *Atlantis* 4, 2 (1979): 26.

[36] M. Susan Bland, "Henrietta the Homemaker, and Rosie the Riveter: Images of Women in Advertising in Maclean's Magazine, 1939–50," *Atlantis* 8, 2 (Spring 1983): 70.

[37] Susan M. Hartmann, *The Homefront and Beyond: American Women in the 1940s* (Boston: Twain Publishers, 1982), 203.

[38] *Chatelaine* (August 1951); *Chatelaine* (October 1948), 59; *Chatelaine* (March 1958), 78.

[39] *Maclean's* (June 15, 1951).

[40] Hilda Neatby, "Are Women Fulfilling Their Obligations to Society?" *Food for Thought* 13 (November 1952): 20–21.

[41] Deborah Findlay, "Professional Interests in Medicine's Construction of Women's Reproductive Health" (a paper presented to the Canadian Sociology and Anthropology Association, Winnipeg, 1986), 29, 10, 21.

[42] Ruth Adam, *A Woman's Place, 1910–1975* (London: Chatto and Windus, 1975), 165–67.

[43] Pierson, *They're Still Women,* 215.

[44] Victor Koby, "The Ladies, Bless 'Em, Can Ease the Squeeze," *Financial Post,* February 24, 1951.

[45] Alice Kessler-Harris, *Out to Work* (New York: Oxford University Press, 1985), 277.

[46] Pierson, *They're Still Women,* 216.

[47] Monica Boyd, Margrit Eichler, John R. Hofley, "Family: Functions, Formations, and Fertility," in Gail Cook, ed., *Opportunity for Choice* (Ottawa: Statistics Canada, 1976), 18.

[48] "You'll Hire Older Women, Miss Giggles Will Marry," *Financial Post,* May 4, 1957, p. 1.

[49] Warren E. Kalbach and Wayne W. McVey, *The Demographic Bases of Canadian Society* (Toronto: McGraw-Hill 1971), 61.

[50] *Canada Yearbook, 1976–77, Special Edition* (Ottawa: Ministry of Supplies and Services, 1977), Table 4.35.

[51] Omer Leroux, "All This and Suffrage Too," *Financial Post,* September 4, 1954, p. 22.

[52] Pat Armstrong and Hugh Armstrong, *The Double Ghetto,* rev. ed. (Toronto: McClelland and Stewart, 1984), 20–21.

[53] "Save Your Tears — Watch the Girls," *Financial Post,* November 16, 1957, p. 1.

[54] Patricia Marchak, "Rational Capitalism and Women as Labour," in Heather Jon Maroney and Meg Luxton. eds., *Feminism and Political Economy: Women's Work, Women's Struggles* (Toronto: Methuen, 1987), 197–212.

[55] Interview with Florence Mowatt, former school teacher in Hants County, Nova Scotia, March 10, 1987.

[56] Canada, Department of Labour, *Married Women Working for Pay in Eight Canadian Cities* (Ottawa, 1958), 52.

[57] Franca Iacovetta, "From *Contadina* to Worker: Southern Italian Immigrant Women Working in Toronto, 1947–62," in Jean Burnet, ed., *Looking Into My Sisters' Eyes: An Exploration in Women's History* (Toronto: The Multicultural History Society of Ontario, 1986), 209–211.

[58] Canada, Department of Labour, *Married Women Working for Pay,* 52.

[59] Canada, Department of Labour, *Labour Gazette* (1954), 1513.

461

[60] Dorothy Manning, "I Quit My Job to Save My Marriage," *Chatelaine* (June 1955).

[61] John Kenneth Galbraith, *Economics and the Public Purpose* (New York: New American Library, 1973), 29–37.

[62] Wayne Roberts, ed., *Where Angels Fear to Tread: Eileen Tallman and the Labour Movement* (Hamilton: McMaster University, n.d.), 23; Eileen Sufrin, *The Eaton Drive: The Campaign to Organize Canada's Largest Department Store, 1948 to 1952* (Toronto: Fitzhenry and Whiteside, 1982).

[63] Sara Diamond, "A Union Man's Wife: The Ladies' Auxiliary Movement in the IWA, the Lake Cowichan Experience," in Barbara K. Latham and Roberta J. Pazdro, eds., *Not Just Pin Money: Selected Essays on the History of Women's Work in British Columbia* (Victoria: Camosun College, 1984), 287.

[64] Broadfoot, *Six War Years*, 358.

British Columbia and the Japanese Evacuation*

W. PETER WARD

462

On 27 February 1942 the Canadian government announced plans to remove all persons of Japanese ancestry from the coastal region of British Columbia. During the seven months which followed more than 22,000 Japanese, aliens and Canadian citizens alike, were forced to abandon their homes and move eastward under government supervision. The majority were sent to settlements in the interior of the province, while others went to more distant points beyond the Rockies. Yet when war with Japan was first declared, on 7 December 1941, the federal government saw no need for such drastic action. Left to their own devices Prime Minister King and his cabinet would not have compelled most of the Japanese to leave the coast. After war's outbreak, however, the Liberal government could not resist the swelling tide of anti-Japanese feeling on the Pacific. Ultimately, King and his government concluded that only evacuation would quiet the popular outcry and avert public disorder.

But if the expulsion was a direct result of wartime stress, it was also the consequence of strained race relations in British Columbia. Since the late 1850s west-coast society had been divided by a deep racial cleavage and, over the years, only limited integration had occurred in patterns of work, residential accommodation, and social contact. The white community had vented its persistent anti-Asian sentiments through petty discrimination, verbal abuse, and even mob violence. Driven by economic threats (both real and apparent) as well as cultural conflicts and psychological tensions, politicians, editors, farm and business organizations, patriotic clubs, and nativistic societies had all assailed the Asian immigrant at one time or another. Periodically, federal, provincial, and municipal governments had also approved legislation and enforced covenants which discriminated against Orientals. These official measures served to legitimate popular prejudice. In sum, long before Canada went to war with Japan, British Columbians had passively tolerated and actively promoted hostility toward their Asian minorities.[1]

*From *Canadian Historical Review* 57, 3 (September 1976): 289–309. Reprinted by permission of the author and the University of Toronto Press.

Many whites who peered across this racial cleft viewed Orientals through a haze of prejudice, for their images of Asians were drawn from a few widely accepted negative stereotypes.[2] In the case of the Japanese these stereotyped attitudes, which hardened perceptibly during the interwar years, emphasized four characteristics: their unassimilability, their economic competitiveness, their high birth rate, and their lingering loyalty to Japan. None of these stereotypes was particularly accurate, although some did contain at least a kernel of truth. But it was their substance, not their accuracy, that mattered most to British Columbians.

During the early and middle 1930s anti-Japanese feeling was not particularly intense in British Columbia. But in the closing months of 1937 a new source of strain bore down upon the west coast's racial cleavage. Japan attacked China once again and, in Canada, reports of this aggression provoked the first strong outburst of anti-Japanese feeling in a decade. Much of it was directed at Japan herself. Across the nation indignant Canadians boycotted Japan's products and protested her war atrocities.[3] At the same time British Columbians aimed new barbs at the local Japanese. Animus was most intense in coastal centres — especially Vancouver, Victoria, and their surrounding districts — where provincial xenophobia traditionally had been strong. In part, at least, Canada's Japanese merely became the scapegoats of Japan's militarism. But some whites saw them as a separate cause for concern. Japan's military adventures had roused anxiety on the coast by stirring up the re-

463

National Archives of Canada.

Japanese Canadian internees arrive at Slocan City internment camp, 1942. The internees could bring to the camps no more than they could carry. The remainder of their property was sold at ridiculously low prices to other British Columbians.

gion's traditional fears of isolation and vulnerability, and this new, tense atmosphere breathed fresh life into the community's dormant animus. Moreover, it confirmed the threatening impression left by the popular Japanese image. Older Japanese stereotypes, like those which emphasized low standards-of-living and unfair competition, were burnished anew by abrasive racial tension. They shone even more brightly in the menacing light of Japanese militarism, for Japan was presumed to have designs upon British Columbia. It was rumoured that hundreds of illegal Japanese immigrants were present on the coast, that Japanese spies and military officers lived surreptitiously in the community, and that a Japanese fifth column potential was growing in the province. Thus in 1937, when old antipathies fused with new anxieties, another wave of anti-Asian sentiment surged over the province.

Archdeacon F.G. Scott, a former popular Anglican wartime padre, precipitated the new outbreak in mid-November 1937, one week after the Japanese had taken Shanghai. In a widely reported interview with the *Toronto Daily Star* he suggested that Japanese officers were living, disguised, in Japanese fishing villages along the west coast.[4] A few coastal residents ridiculed Scott's claims. Others, however, vouched for their truth, and his supporters won the day, for a public outcry followed his remarks. Captain MacGregor Macintosh, a Conservative member of the legislature of British Columbia, first endorsed Scott's report and then, early in 1938, raised charges of widespread illegal Japanese immigration.[5] Led by A.W. Neill, an Independent and perennial foe of the Oriental immigrant, provincial members of Parliament from all major parties demanded a halt to Japanese immigration.[6] Simultaneously, in Vancouver, Alderman Halford Wilson urged City Council to limit the number of licences for Japanese merchants and to impose zoning restrictions upon them.[7] Meanwhile, Vancouver's major daily newspapers launched their own anti-Japanese campaigns.[8] In Ottawa the prime minister received a flurry of protest notes while the outspoken Alderman Wilson's mail brought him letters of support.[9]

Judged in the light of past anti-Oriental incidents, this was not a major outburst. Its central figures, Wilson and Macintosh, made no attempt to organize a protest movement. They merely spent their energies in making public demands for more restrictive legislation. Nor was popular hostility as intense as it had been during the mid-1880s or the summer of 1907, when anti-Asian riots had occured in Vancouver. Because the level of social strain was relatively low and dynamic organizational leadership was absent, this precluded the development of a major racial crisis. Nevertheless, signs still pointed to increasing public tension, and the weight of this concern was soon felt in Ottawa.

But Prime Minister Mackenzie King was loath to grasp the nettle. King probably wished to placate British Columbia's xenophobes, or at least quiet them, if he could. At the same time, however, he was subject to countervailing pressures. He was anxious not to embarrass British interests in Asia by taking any initiative which might provoke Japanese ire. Japan's renewed militarism had heightened his own inherent sense of caution. But pressure from the west coast grew so intense that, ultimately, he could not ignore it. Urged first by Premier T.D. Pattullo of British Columbia and then by Ian Mackenzie, the only west-coast representative in the cabinet, King early in March 1938 promised a public enquiry into rumours of illegal Japanese immigration.[10]

But the mere promise of an investigation did not still the insistent demands for an end to Japanese immigration. Macintosh even called for the repatriation of all Japanese residents in Canada, regardless of their citizenship.[11] Then on 24 March the Board of Review charged with the investigation held its first public hearing in Vancouver. Over the next seven weeks it conducted a series of further meetings in major centres throughout the province and, once the hearings commenced, popular unease appeared to dissipate. The hearings themselves put an end to scattered public protest by offering a forum to the vociferous. Furthermore, the meetings forced critics to prove their allegations or remain silent, and many chose the latter refuge. In fact, public concern subsided to such an extent that, when the board's findings were published early in 1939, the report scarcely attracted notice.[12]

But while hostility ebbed appreciably it was not completely dispelled, and over the next two years the west-coast Japanese remained the targets of rumours, suspicion, and criticism. Then in the spring of 1940, a wave of animosity began to well up once again. The anxious wartime atmosphere shaped by Canada's recent belligerency once more heightened traditional prejudices and aggravated racial tensions in west-coast society. At the same time, and for the same reason, Japan's Asian military campaign again began to rouse concern. The growth of general unease once more strengthened feelings of vulnerability and insecurity in the community. Prompted by mounting anxiety, the cry again went up that illegal Japanese immigrants were infiltrating the country; renewed demands were made for an end to all Japanese immigration as well as for stronger Pacific coast defences.

It was Alderman Halford Wilson who headed this new campaign of protest. Throughout the summer of 1940 he warned of Japanese subversion and called for closer restrictions on all Japanese residents.[13] Wilson still made no attempt to organize a popular movement but he did remain the most insistent of the Japanese community's critics. Himself aside, it is difficult to know for whom Wilson actually spoke. Few British Columbians in 1940 were willing to follow his lead in public. Yet undoubtedly there were many who endorsed the general thrust of his remarks, if not their specific aim. Certainly his crusade was a measure of the times, for anti-Japanese nativism was once more on the rise.[14] And in Ottawa as well as Victoria this resurgence soon became a source

465

of some concern.[15] The worry was that Wilson's comments might put the torch to public opinion and touch off racial disorder.

While provincial and federal authorities grew increasingly alarmed at the prospect of racial turmoil, senior military officers in British Columbia were also concerned by the presence of Japanese on the coast. Intelligence officers had kept watch on the Japanese community since 1937 and, from the outset, they had accepted the prevailing assumption that Japanese residents, regardless of their citizenship, would endanger national security in time of war. As early as June 1938 the Department of National Defence had explored the prospect of widespread Japanese wartime internment.[16] In 1940, during the summer's crest of popular anti-Japanese feeling, the Pacific Command's joint Service Committee approved contingency plans to meet both an external Japanese attack and an internal Japanese insurrection. The committee also endorsed an intelligence report which warned of possible sabotage from the west-coast Japanese fishing fleet. Japanese residents, it reported, "could very easily make themselves a potent force and threaten the vital industries of British Columbia." If war broke out, the committee believed, every Japanese resident in British Columbia should be considered a potential enemy.[17]

In contrast the RCMP tended to minimize the Japanese threat. Since 1938 officers in "E" Division, stationed in Vancouver, had also kept the Japanese under surveillance. In 1940 they assigned three constables to observe the community and also employed Japanese informants. Through continual investigation the force concluded that Japanese residents posed no real threat to Canada. On the contrary, it observed what it believed to be convincing evidence of Japanese loyalty to Canada. Signs of this were especially clear in the community's strong support for Victory bond drives and Red Cross work, the Nisei desire to volunteer for military service, and the widespread wish amongst Japanese not to arouse white antagonism. "This office," the officer commanding at Vancouver reported late in October 1940, "does not consider that the Japanese of British Columbia constitute a menace to the State."[18]

Was there substance to this apparent threat of Japanese subversion? The Board of Review in 1938 had found no proof of wholesale illegal immigration. Nor had the RCMP discovered any indication of serious danger and, surely, this was the organization best able to judge.[19] It had scrutinized the Japanese community more carefully than had any other agency. Neither military intelligence nor popular rumour was founded on such close observation, and the claims of each should be judged accordingly. All available signs pointed in one direction only: no significant evidence of Japanese treachery could be seen at this time. Nor would any be discovered at a later date. The threat of Japanese subversion was in essence a fiction based on xenophobic traditions and perceptions clouded by fears and anxieties. Yet despite its insubstantial basis, the threat was real enough to many British Columbians and it was the goad which stirred popular animus to life once more.

466

This resurgence of anti-Japanese sentiment again placed the King government in an uncomfortable position. Whatever it felt about the demands of west-coast nativists, more than ever, in the summer of 1940, it wished to avoid irritating Japan as this might jeopardize British interests in the Pacific, if not induce war itself. As well, by this time Canada was preoccupied by European conflict and presumably the federal government wished to avoid distractions. Therefore it hesitated as long as seemed possible before taking action. But by September 1940, when rumours first were heard that Oriental Canadians would be included in the first call for military service, the question could no longer be ignored. Just as Japan announced her alliance with the Axis powers, these reports provoked a sharp cry of protest. Bowing before the rising winds of criticism, the Cabinet War Committee omitted Asian Canadians from the first draft and then formed a special committee to investigate the question of Orientals and British Columbia's security.[20]

The committee soon confirmed that anti-Japanese feeling was running high in the province and that this, rather than Japanese subversion, was the greatest potential source of danger to the community. Its major recommendations were therefore aimed at reducing public tension. In order to scotch persistent rumours of illegal Japanese immigration, it urged a new registration of all Japanese residents, both citizens and aliens alike. It also proposed the creation of a standing committee to advise the government on problems relating to Orientals in British Columbia.[21] King and his cabinet, because of the delicate state of Anglo-Japanese relations, were anxious to avoid even the threat of civil disorder in British Columbia. Thus they implemented these suggestions in the hope that they would promote public calm. Intent on disarming British Columbia's xenophobes, the government included MacGregor Macintosh on the Standing Committee. And in order to reassure the Japanese it nominated Professor H.F. Angus, a long-time champion of civil rights for Japanese Canadians.[22]

If the King government hoped its new initiative would calm popular fears, it must soon have been disabused of its optimism. During the first half of 1941 the public temper remained aroused. A few signs indicated, in fact, that some British Columbians were growing even more suspicious of the Japanese. Agitation thus continued, even though still no credible leadership had emerged to give protest a focus. Halford Wilson kept up his one-man campaign, repeatedly urging that, in the interest of national security, all Japanese fishing boats should be sequestered.[23] Furthermore, ongoing tension remained a source of concern to federal officials who still feared a racial incident. Wilson was singled out as the chief cause for alarm and unsuccessful efforts were made to persuade him to keep silent.[24] Meanwhile, in military circles, fear of public disturbance was matched by continued suspicion of the Japanese themselves. As an intelligence report noted in July 1941, widespread Japanese sabotage was unlikely in the event of war but it remained a pos-

467

sibility unless proper security precautions were taken and the Japanese themselves were protected from white provocation.[25]

In the final months before Pearl Harbor was bombed, racial tensions began to abate. But even then conditions favoured a new anti-Japanese outburst. Influenced by the community's xenophobia, its traditional racial cleavage, and its anxieties born of war and isolation, British Columbians continued to suspect their Japanese neighbours. The west-coast Japanese could not be trusted. Their allegiance was in doubt. Given the opportunity, it was assumed, some among them would betray the province to the enemy. The federal government, while alarmed by British Columbia's Japanese problem, was ill prepared to meet the issue head on. It feared that Japan might use a racial disturbance as a *casus belli*, but aside from forming the Standing Committee, it had done very little to prevent an outbreak.

Canada declared war on Japan on 7 December 1941, within hours of Pearl Harbor. The King government immediately recognized the likelihood of violent anti-Japanese demonstrations in British Columbia. At the same time it had to deal with a new enemy alien problem, for war's outbreak altered the status of many Canadian residents of Japanese origin.[26] Faced with the prospect of racial incidents as well as an alien menace, the dominion government quickly took pre-emptive action. Thirty-eight Japanese nationals were interned on the grounds that they might endanger the community and the west-coast Japanese fishing fleet was immobilized. On the advice of the RCMP, all Japanese-language newspapers and schools voluntarily closed their doors. Meanwhile, Prime Minister King, senior police and military officers, and Vancouver's major newspapers all reassured the public and called for calm. As King declared in a radio address to the nation on 8 December: "the competent authorities are satisfied that the security situation is well in hand. They are confident of the correct and loyal behaviour of Canadian residents of Japanese origin."[27]

But many west-coast whites were not so easily mollified. Neither prompt federal action nor loyal protestations from leading Japanese did much to assuage their fears. War's outbreak had once more opened the floodgates of fear and hostility. Roused by war on the Pacific, the west coast resumed its attack on the province's Japanese. Again, enmity was strongest in and around Vancouver and Victoria, long the province's two focal points of anti-Asian sentiment. In the week following Pearl Harbor some Japanese in Vancouver were victimized by scattered acts of vandalism. Several firms began discharging their Japanese employees. Fear of Japanese subversion again spread in the province.[28] In private, British Columbians began protesting to their members of Parliament. The weight of public concern also bore down on provincial newspapers. Columnist Bruce Hutchison informed the Prime Minister's office that, at the *Vancouver Sun,* "we are under extraordinary pressure from our readers to advocate a pogrom of Japs. We told the people to be calm. Their reply was a bombardment of letters that the Japs all be interned."[29]

To encourage calm, police, government, and military officials issued further assurances that the Japanese problem was well in hand.[30] But their statements seemed to have little effect. Popular protest continued to grow and, in response, alarm in government and military circles increased too. On 20 December, F.J. Hume, chairman of the Standing Committee, told King: "in British Columbia particularly, the successes of the Japanese to date in the Pacific have to a great extent inflamed public opinion against the local Japanese. People here are in a very excited condition and it would require a very small local incident to bring about most unfortunate conditions between the whites and Japanese."[31] Major General R.O. Alexander, commander in chief of the Pacific Command, was also concerned: "The situation with regard to the Japanese resident in British Columbia is assuming a serious aspect. Public feeling is becoming very insistent, especially in Vancouver, that local Japanese should be either interned or removed from the coast. Letters are being written continually to the press and I am being bombarded by individuals, both calm and hysterical, demanding that something should be done."[32] Alexander feared that public demonstrations, to be held in the near future according to rumour, might lead to racial violence.

After a brief lull over Christmas the public outcry grew more strident than ever. Increasing numbers of west-coast whites, regardless of all reassurance, were certain that the local Japanese community endangered west-coast security. By early January 1942 patriotic societies, service clubs, town and city councils, and air-raid precaution units, most of them on Vancouver Island or in the Vancouver area, had begun to voice protest.[33] Repeatedly they urged that all Japanese, regardless of citizenship, be interned, as quickly as possible. Other spokesmen suggested somewhat less drastic action, but whatever the precise demands of the public they all assumed the need for some form of Japanese evacuation. And with each passing day opinion seemed to grow more volatile. Even moderates like J.G. Turgeon, the Liberal MP from the Cariboo, were alarmed at the seeming danger. On 6 January he warned the prime minister:

> the condition of this province is dangerous, so far as the Japanese are concerned. If the Government do not take drastic action, the situation will get out-of-hand. The Government will suffer, and so will the Japanese, personally and through destruction of property.
>
> I am therefore forced to recommend that very strong measures to [sic] taken, and quickly. Either delay, or lack of thorough action, may cause violence.[34]

Beneath this new hostile outburst, which war with Japan had precipitated, lay two primary social strains.[35] The first was British Columbia's traditional racial cleavage, one marked in recent years by strong anti-

469

Japanese prejudice. This permanent gulf between whites and Asians had created enduring social tensions which perpetually tended towards outbreaks of racial animosity. The structure of west-coast race relations was conducive to such an end. The second strain was the growing sense of anxiety which accompanied war's outbreak, a condition created by the atmosphere of ambiguity which surrounded the Pacific war. In the weeks following Pearl Harbor the level of generalized public anxiety created by war increased appreciably. In itself the opening of a new theatre of war was a new source of unease because it raised new uncertainties in an already war-troubled world. More specifically, the ambiguity which enveloped Japan's military activities in the weeks after 7 December also conditioned the growth of anxiety. The startling number of her targets, the suddenness of her assaults, the speed of her military expansion, and the seeming ease of her victories surprised and frightened many west-coast whites. The enemy seemed everywhere in the Pacific. No one knew where he might next attack and some feared it would be British Columbia. In such conditions civil defence preparations themselves became a source of unease for they reflected the assumption that a Japanese attack was indeed imminent. During the first week of war air raid precaution units were called for duty, defence regulations were posted, and nightly blackouts were enforced. Far from offering reassurance these activities further unsettled an already apprehensive public.

470

In the years since the expulsion it has occasionally been suggested that two economic motives caused the anti-Japanese outburst: one the desire of some British Columbians to acquire Japanese property at bargain prices, the other a wish to rid the province, once and for all, of Japanese economic competition. These conclusions, however, are informed by little more than hindsight. There is no body of evidence to indicate that either factor significantly shaped public opinion or government policy. In the Fraser and Okanagan valleys some residents did request stringent restrictions on Japanese landholding, a proposal which reflected inter-racial tensions of economic origin. But the great majority of those who protested had no obvious economic interest to defend against Japanese encroachment and, evidently, no strong desire to profit at the expense of evacuees.[36]

It was because of wartime social strains that a sense of crisis mounted in British Columbia. And as these tensions grew they sharpened the coast's hostility toward the Japanese minority. Japanese militarism and the province's legacy of racial tension combined to cast the old image of the Yellow Peril in a new and lurid light. As many British Columbians peered through the fog of their anxieties they saw little but the menacing outline of Japanese subversion. Furthermore, while the growing sense of crisis narrowed whites' perceptions, these perceptions, in turn, intensified public unease. Thus, social tensions and racial imagery were mutually reinforcing. Had British Columbians seen their Japanese neighbours clearly, they would have observed an isolated, defenceless minority, gravely alarmed by its plight and anxious to demonstrate its loyalty to Canada. But fear and prejudice prevented them from taking a closer look. Consequently, the Japanese appeared nothing but a threat and therefore the call went up for their expulsion.

In addition, aroused public opinion pressed down upon a group of politicians particularly susceptible to prejudice against Asians. On a personal level most political leaders in British Columbia probably shared the stereotyped attitudes of their constituents. Furthermore, ever since Confederation anti-Orientalism had pervaded the provincial political culture. Over the years conservatives, liberals, and socialists alike had freely employed the rhetoric of racialism. The Conservative and Liberal parties had regularly nailed anti-Oriental planks to their election platforms, both federal and provincial, and after 1933 the CCF, despite its professed concern for civil liberties, had been divided on the question. Seldom, if ever, had the anti-Asian cry been a decisive issue in electoral contests: the broad consensus amongst west-coast politicians had prevented that. Yet, by World War II racial prejudice had long been common currency in political discourse. Some politicians merely dealt in the small change of petty racialism; others, like Wilson and Macintosh, traded in larger denominations — nativism and xenophobia. Ian Mackenzie, upon whom the weight of west-coast opinion fell in 1942, stood between the two extremes. He was undoubtedly confirmed in his anti-Asian sentiments, yet not outspokenly so. Certainly, on the eve of war in the Pacific, most British Columbian politicians shared some of Mackenzie's convictions. Consequently, when anti-Japanese feeling welled up after Pearl Harbor, they also shared the public's growing concern and responded sympathetically to popular pressure.

471

In Ottawa Mackenzie King was also a target of rising protest. His experience with west-coast hostility toward Asians had been longer and more intimate than that of any other federal politician. In 1907 and 1908 he had held three royal commissions to investigate Oriental immigration and racial disturbances in Vancouver. Throughout the 1920s and 1930s, as prime minister, the issue confronted him repeatedly. As was usual with King, his comments on the Oriental problem were always extremely circumspect. Prior to his premiership he concluded that the roots of west-coast tensions were economic, not racial, and he saw their satisfactory resolution in negotiation with Asian nations to seek mutually acceptable immigration levels.[37] In office his government used both diplomacy and legislation to enforce restrictions on immigration from China and Japan. During the later 1930s, however, when anti-Japanese feeling increased on the west coast, King felt constrained from any further restrictive action by international tensions. His view of the issue after the outbreak of war with Japan remains unclear. He did not share the anxieties of west-coast residents yet he ultimately accepted the possibility of a Japanese invasion of British Columbia.[38] Probably his primary concern was for the instability of west-coast opinion and the threat to public order which it posed. If subsequent government policy was any measure of King's thought, he was willing to accept any expedient solution to reduce public tension.

Under heavy popular pressure the federal government ordered yet another review of the Japanese problem in British Columbia. On 8 and 9 January 1942 a committee of federal and provincial government, police, and military officials met in Ottawa to discuss means of allaying west-coast alarm. The central question explored was whether or not the Japanese should be removed from coastal areas; but the meeting could not agree on an answer. Several representatives who had just arrived from British Columbia, together with Ian Mackenzie, the meeting's chairman, argued that all able-bodied male Japanese nationals should immediately be removed. The majority of the delegates, however, few of whom had recently been in British Columbia, opposed such drastic action. Consequently the meeting submitted a moderate report which suggested both an extension of existing minor restrictions on the liberties of all Japanese and the creation of a quasi-military work corps for Canadian Japanese who wished to support the war effort.[39]

But the conference's report was only one opinion. From British Columbia there came ever more insistent demands for an evacuation programme and within the cabinet Ian Mackenzie, King's closest political friend from the province, pressed for such a solution.[40] Consequently, when the government announced its revised plans on 14 January, the new policy bore the unmistakable imprint of west-coast opinion. The King government accepted most of the Ottawa conference's proposals but in addition it proposed to remove all enemy aliens, regardless of age, sex, or nationality, from protected areas soon to be defined in British Columbia. The programme was aimed primarily at Japanese nationals although it embraced Germans and Italians as well. The statement also promised that a Japanese Civilian Corps would soon be formed for work on projects deemed in the national interest.[41] The covert hope was that Japanese-Canadian men would volunteer for it in large numbers, thus permitting the government to remove them from the protected areas without an unpleasant resort to compulsion.[42]

It was felt that, by yielding to some of the west coast's demands, the partial evacuation policy would calm British Columbian fears. Concerned for the safety of Canadian prisoners in Japan's hands, anxious to avoid needless expense and disruption in time of war, and touched with a lingering sense of justice and humanity, the King government refused to make further concessions. But the plan was also rather equivocal in that it neither defined the protected areas nor promised when evacuation would begin. In effect it still gave the federal government considerable freedom of action. For a few brief moments the gesture seemed satisfactory. Premier John Hart of British Columbia, whose government had already demanded similar measures, applauded the decision and the *Vancouver Sun* praised the King government's common sense. The storm of protest abated temporarily.[43]

Within ten days, however, agitation began to increase once again. The public outcry mounted throughout February until, during the last week of the month, it reached unprecedented volume. Pressed by the fear of enemy subversion, thousands of west-coast whites petitioned Ottawa for the immediate evacuation of all Japanese. Individuals, farm organizations, municipal councils, civil defence units, constituency associations, service clubs, patriotic societies, trades unions, citizens committees, chambers of commerce — even the Vancouver and District Lawn Bowling Association — all demanded the total evacuation of Japanese from coastal areas.[44] One group of prominent Vancouver residents telegraphed Ian Mackenzie that, "owing to wide spread public alarm over enemy aliens on the Pacific coast and especially respecting those astride vital defence points and with a view to stabilizing public opinion and in the interest of public safety," they urged the immediate evacuation of all Japanese.[45] Never before had west-coast race relations been so seriously strained.

473

By and large British Columbians appear to have reached their conclusions about the Japanese menace with little prompting. More or less simultaneously thousands recognized an obvious threat and identified the equally obvious solution. In the generation of this consensus neither popular leaders nor popular journalism played a predominant role. Halford Wilson and MacGregor Macintosh, once the two chief critics of the west-coast Japanese, were submerged beneath the rising tide of hostility. In fact the protest movement had no pre-eminent leaders whatsoever. Nor did provincial papers become leaders of opinion, even though some took up the popular cry. During the crisis west-coast journalism helped sustain the prevailing mood, but most papers merely reflected the popular mind. Agitation was the product of a widespread outburst of hostility, one which was rooted in longstanding antipathies as well as immediate wartime pressures.

The very structure of the protest movement supports this contention for it clearly revealed how extensive was the anti-Japanese consensus. Although public anxiety had flared up immediately after Pearl Harbor, no effective anti-Japanese movement had begun to emerge until late January. In its earliest stage protest was random; it had no central leadership and no institutional focus. But when the movement began to take form, protest was mobilized by a broad range of the traditional social, economic, administrative, and political organizations already entrenched in British Columbia. The Provincial Council of Women, the Vancouver Real Estate Exchange, the Canadian Legion in Gibson's Landing, the Kinsmen's Club of Victoria, the North Burnaby Liberal Association, the B.C. Poultry Industries Committee, the Corporation of the District of Saanich, the

National Union of Machinists, Fitters, and Helpers (Victoria Local Number 2), and scores of other similar groups all pressed their demands for evacuation. These organizations not only represented major interest groups in the province but their influence cut across most social, economic, and political bounds in west-coast society. They represented the interests and opinions, the fears and hostilities of tens of thousands of British Columbians. If there were some who did not share prevailing attitudes, they remained largely silent when confronted by the tyranny of the consensus.

One further sign of mounting social pressure was the growing incidence of rumours of Japanese subversion. Some told of Japanese who owned high-powered vehicles and short-wave equipment, who lived near sites of great strategic value, who swelled with insolent pride at Japan's successive victories. Others hinted at active Japanese disloyalty — and, in the hothouse atmosphere of growing public tension, stories grew to outlandish proportions. Military intelligence officers were informed in mid-January that Japanese in Vancouver had fixed infra-red and ultra-violet beacons on their roofs, devices which, when viewed through special binoculars, would guide enemy flights over the city.[46] Rumour itself is usually the product of serious social strain.[47] These persistent rumours were one more indication of the growing racial crisis on Canada's west coast. The outbreak of war with Japan had spread a grave sense of looming threat amongst west-coast whites. Yet for all its immediacy this threat remained somewhat vague and nebulous. The enemy was identified, his whereabouts were not. Rumours helped resolve this ambiguity. They suggested that some of the enemy were very close at hand. While this in itself was cause for concern, it also helped to clarify the confusions of war with a distant, elusive power. Because rumours singled out the nearest available enemy they helped reduce the ambiguity which had spawned them in the first place. And, once in circulation, they, too, stirred the ever-widening eddies of hostility and alarm.

It seemed clear, as well, that one immediate reason for the renewed upsurge of protest in February was that many British Columbians, anxious for total evacuation, had misinterpreted the government's policy announcement of 14 January. The *Vancouver Sun* had taken it to mean that "all Japanese and other enemy aliens" were to be removed from protected areas, an assumption shared by several provincial members of Parliament. "My understanding," wrote Ian MacKenzie, "was that all able-bodied, adult enemy aliens would have to be removed from protected areas. My further understanding was also that all able-bodied *Canadian nationals* would have to be moved, but that *first* they should be given an opportunity to volunteer in the Civilian Corps."[48] This confusion aside, the federal government also failed to implement its programme immediately. Neither the evacuation plans nor the designated

474

protected areas were announced until 23 January, and the delay itself provoked some concern. Furthermore, when finally announced, the plans indicated that evacuation was not to be completed before 1 April, a date which seemed far too remote to those who believed the Japanese threat was imminent. Once the plans were made public there was a further delay while the relocation machinery was set up. The task of arranging to move, house, and care for several thousand Japanese proved a time-consuming one and it was complicated further by the strong opposition of residents in the British Columbian interior, especially the Okanagan Valley, to proposals that the Japanese all be settled inland.[49] Several times the immediate departure of Japanese from Vancouver was announced and then postponed. Consequently, few, if any, Japanese left their homes before mid-February. In the eyes of concerned west-coast whites the government's partial evacuation policy increasingly seemed a mixture of confusion, delay, and prevarication. It appeared that Ottawa did not understand, let alone sympathize with, British Columbia's predicament.

475

Japan's startling military success continued to play on west-coast fears as well. By mid-January Japanese troops had overrun much of Malaya, the Philippines, Burma, and British North Borneo. They had occupied Thailand, captured Hong Kong (taking more than 1600 Canadian troops prisoner), sunk Britain's most modern battleship, and crippled her Pacific fleet. Late in January they had laid siege to the island of Singapore. News of this swift succession of decisive victories dominated the front pages of the provincial press. Furthermore, these accounts repeatedly emphasized that Japanese subversion and fifth-column activity had played a central role in Japan's programme of conquest. Already convinced of their own vulnerability, British Columbians grew more alarmed when worse news succeeded bad. As the military crisis deepened across the Pacific, so public tension grew on Canada's west coast.

Parliament reconvened on 22 January as the racial crisis mounted. Members of Parliament from British Columbia, no doubt as concerned as their protesting constituents, themselves began to press for total evacuation. Howard Green, the Conservative member from Vancouver South, opened the attack in the Commons on 29 January.[50] The threat of Japanese treachery confronted the Pacific coast, he said, and therefore all Japanese should be removed from the province. Other British Columbian members made similar claims before the House over the next three weeks. In private they were even more insistent. On 28 January British Columbians in the Liberal caucus demanded that Japanese Canadians who failed to volunteer for the Civilian Corps be evacuated as quickly as possible. In succeeding weeks, as popular protest reached its greatest heights, King faced successive demands for relocation from provincial politicians — Conservative, Liberal, and Independent alike.[51]

Meanwhile, government officials in British Columbia sustained their pressure as well. At the height of the popular outcry the attorney-general of British Columbia told Ian Mackenzie:

> Events have transpired recently which add to the danger we have already been subjected to by the presence of Japanese on this Coast.
>
> I cannot urge too strongly the seriousness of this situation and the danger the people of British Columbia feel upon this matter.
>
> Nothing short of immediate removal of the Japanese will meet the dangers which we feel in this Province.[52]

At the same time the minister of labour campaigned for total evacuation. The lieutenant-governor informed Mackenzie King that he had "rarely felt so keenly about any impending danger as I do about the Japanese on this coast being allowed to live in our midst." He suggested that, at very least, Japanese males be quickly interned. Since mid-January senior officers of the Pacific Command had grown more concerned as well. By the time public protest reached its peak, they, too, subscribed to demands for total evacuation.[53]

476

It was Ian Mackenzie who ultimately bore the brunt of this storm of protest. First he received warnings and notes of alarm, then petitions urging evacuation, and finally demands that he resign. But Mackenzie shared the concerns of his west-coast constituents. In the first weeks after the outbreak of war he grew convinced that all able-bodied Japanese men should be removed from strategic areas. In consequence, he considered the partial evacuation policy inadequate. He also believed that the 1 April deadline was too remote. Furthermore, as pressure upon him grew, Mackenzie's alarm at the instability of public opinion increased in like proportion. On 22 February, when news reached him of a series of mass protest meetings planned for 1 March, his anxiety heightened further.[54] Two days later he informed cabinet colleagues of the heated state of west-coast opinion and of a call for his own resignation. As he told the minister of justice:

> The feeling in British Columbia in regard to the Japanese is so aflame that I consider we should take the necessary powers (if we have not got them now) to remove Canadian Nationals, as well as Japanese Nationals, from the protected areas.
>
> I have no report on how the Vancouver Corps has succeeded, but I greatly fear *disorder* from reports actually received, unless all able-bodied males of Japanese origin are immediately evacuated.[55]

Publicly Mackenzie appeared unperturbed, urging calm on his west-coast correspondents, but privately he was extremely exercised.[56]

Within the cabinet others shared something of Mackenzie's alarm, particularly his concern for possible public disturbances. The prime minister agreed that there was "every possibility of riots" on the west coast, and feared that in such an event there would be "repercussions in the Far

East against our own prisoners." The situation was awkward, he recognized, because "public prejudice is so strong in B.C. that it is going to be difficult to control."[57] Thus, under heavy external pressure and alarmed by the evident danger of racial violence, the federal government finally took decisive action. On 24 February, only hours after Mackenzie had written his warning to cabinet colleagues, the government approved an enabling measure which permitted total evacuation. Three days later the announcement was made that all persons of Japanese ancestry would have to leave the protected zones.[58] In the hope of reducing social tensions the King government had finally capitulated to public pressure.

The province did not all at once breathe a sigh of collective relief. Tension remained high for several days thereafter. From Ottawa Ian Mackenzie believed that public disorder was still possible. Hostility surged onward in the Okanagan Valley, where many local residents feared that the new federal policy would bring a large Japanese influx. Slowly, however, the strain of racial crisis began to ease. The two mass meetings held on 1 March were quiet and orderly. Mackenzie received a note of praise from supporters in Vancouver. The flood of protests to Ottawa began to recede.[59]

477

When the cabinet approved the order which permitted evacuation, the editors of the *Sun* looked forward to the day the move would be complete. They hoped that the coast was "Saying Goodbye, Not Au Revoir" to the Japanese.[60] But while some had undoubtedly seen the crisis as a chance to solve the province's Japanese problem for all time, this scarcely explains the previous weeks' outburst of hostility. War with Japan had sharpened the animus, narrowed the vision, and roused the fears of a community already deeply divided along racial lines. In the minds of west-coast whites intimations of vulnerability and isolation had long nursed a sense of insecurity, and after Pearl Harbor many British Columbians had felt themselves exposed as never before to attack from Japan. In addition they had grown convinced that the resident Japanese were a threat to the community's security. These beliefs had virtually no foundation in fact. In essence they were facets of the traditional Japanese image held by white British Columbians, stereotypes further distorted in the heat of war. Its fears fed by these perceptions, the west coast loosed a torrent of hostility. Sensitive to the public temper, and alarmed by the prospect of racial disturbance, the federal government attempted preventative action. But neither minor restrictions on civil liberties nor the promise of partial relocation could satisfy the west-coast public for long. It demanded total Japanese evacuation. In the end its wishes were met.[61]

NOTES

[1] The major works on Orientals in Canada are Tien-fang Cheng, *Oriental Immigration in Canada* (Shanghai, 1931); Charles H. Young and Helen R.Y. Reid, *The Japanese Canadians* (Toronto, 1938); Charles James Woodsworth, *Canada and the Orient: A Study in International Relations* (Toronto, 1941); Forrest

E. LaViolette, *The Canadian Japanese and World War II: A Sociological and Psychological Account* (Toronto, 1948); William Peter Ward, "White Canada Forever: British Columbia's Response to Orientals, 1858-1914" (Ph.D. thesis, Queen's University, 1972).

2 On the nature and significance of Oriental stereotypes see Ward, "White Canada Forever," 37-67 and 132-48, and LaViolette, *The Canadian Japanese*, 3-28.

3 A.R.M. Lower, *Canada and the Far East — 1940*, Institution of Pacific Research Inquiry Series (New York, 1940), 23-28.

4 *Vancouver Sun*, 17 Nov. 1937.

5 *Vancouver Sun*, 24 Nov. 1937; *The Colonist* (Victoria), 19 Jan. 1938.

6 Canada, House of Commons, *Debates* (17 Feb. 1938), 550-75.

7 *The Province* (Vancouver), 22 Feb. 1938.

8 *The Province*, 2, 17, 18, and 24 Feb. 1938; *Vancouver Sun*, 10, 12, 14, and 28 Feb. 1938.

9 Two representative letters to King are: R.S. Hanna to King, 14 Feb. 1938, William Lyon Mackenzie King Papers, MG 26, J2, vol. 147, file 1-209, Public Archives of Canada [PAC]; Forgotten Native of Japanada to King, n.d., King Papers. Letters to Wilson in 1938 can be found in the Halford Wilson Papers, vol. 1, file 1, Public Archives of British Columbia [PABC].

10 T.D. Pattullo to King, 26 Jan. 1938, King Papers, MG 26, JI, vol. 256, 218388-9; Ian Mackenzie to King, 26 Feb. 1938, King Papers, vol. 253, 216060; King to Mackenzie, 1 March 1938, King Papers, vol. 253, 216062-3A. At this time Mackenzie was the minister of national defence. After the outbreak of war he was transferred to Pensions and National Health.

11 *Vancouver Sun*, 23 March 1938.

12 The Board of Review concluded that rumours of illegal Japanese immigration had been greatly exaggerated. It estimated that about 120 Japanese were living illegally in the province. Board of Review [Immigration], *Final Report*, 29 Sept. 1938, 38.

13 H.L. K[eenleyside], Memorandum, 11 June 1940, Department of External Affairs Records, RG, G-1, vol. 2007, file 212, part 1, PAC; *The Province*, 7 and 15 Aug. 1940.

14 See also Wilson Papers, vol. 1, file 4; *Vancouver Sun*, 29 June and 10 Aug. 1940; *The Province*, 21 and 24 Aug. 1940.

15 K[eenleyside], Memorandum, 11 June 1940, External Affairs Records, vol. 2007, file 212, part 1, PAC; Gray Turgeon to King, 7 Aug. 1940, King Papers, MG 26, JI, vol. 297, 252824-5; King to Lapointe, 8 Aug. 1940, King Papers, vol. 297, 252828.

16 Extract from Report on Japanese Activities on the West Coast of Canada, 10 March 1937, External Affairs Records, vol. 1803, file 729, PAC; Major General E.C. Ashton, Chief of the General Staff, Memorandum, Acquisition by Japanese Interests of Timberland and Mineral Concessions on the Pacific Coast, 13 Nov. 1937, Ian Mackenzie Papers, MG 27, 3-B-5, vol. 30, file X-23, PAC; L.R. LaFlèche, deputy minister, Department of National Defence, to F.C. Blair, director of immigration, 2 June 1938, Department of National Defence, to F.C. Blair, director of immigration, 2 June 1938, Department of National Defence Records, file HQ 6-0-7, Department of National Defence Archives.

17 Brigadier C.V. Stockwell, district officer commanding Military District 11, to the secretary, Department of National Defence, 4 Sept. 1940, Defence Records, file HQS, vs 38-1-1, vol. 5.

18 Superintendent C.E. Hill, "E" Division, RCMP, to the Commissioner, 25 Aug. 1938, Government of Canada, Immigration Branch Records, RG 76, vol. 86, file 9309, vol. 16, PAC; R.R. Tait, assistant commissioner, RCMP, to Keenleyside, 28 Oct. 1940, External Affairs Records, vol. 2007, file 212, part 1, PAC. The entire contents of this file substantiate the observations made in this paragraph.

19 The RCMP did, however, identify a small number of Japanese who might endanger the state in time of war and these individuals were arrested and detained immediately after war on Japan was declared.

20 Pattullo to King, 23 Sept. 1940, King Papers, MG 26, JI, vol. 293, 248363; King to Pattullo, 27 Sept. 1940, T.D. Pattullo Papers, Vol. 70, file 4, 21, PABC; Wilson to the Finance Committee, City of Vancouver, 24 Sept. 1940, Wilson Papers, vol. 1, file 4; A.D.P. Heeney, Memorandum for the Prime Minister, 27 Sept. 1940, King Papers, MG 26, J4, vol. 361, file 3849.

21 Report and Recommendations of the Special Committee on Orientals in British Columbia, Dec. 1940, typescript, King Papers. The committee also recommended that, because testimony before it almost unanimously favoured a complete end to Japanese immigration, the government should forbid it when the international situation permitted. This recommendation was not published because King feared it might strain existing relations with Japan and inflame anti-Oriental opinion in British Columbia. Government of Canada, Privy Council, Minutes and Documents of the Cabinet War Committee, RG 2, 7C, vol. 4, Minutes, 2 Jan. 1941, 8-9, PAC; Keenleyside to Sansom, [3 Jan. 1941], External Affairs Records, vol. 1868, file 263, part 4, PAC; Additional Statement by the Members of the Special Committee on Orientals in British Columbia for consideration by the Prime Minister and members of the Cabinet War Committee, n.d., King Papers, MG 26, JI, vol. 307, 259432-3.

22 Keenleyside to King, 2 Dec. 1940, King Papers, MG 26, JI, vol. 289, 244808-10.

23 *The Province*, 9 Jan. and 11 Feb. 1941; *Victoria Times*, 26 Feb. 1941; *Vancouver Sun*, 8 April and 26 July 1941. One sign of growing suspicion was the increasing sensitivity of west-coast whites to Japanese using cameras. For example see *Nanaimo Free Press*, 8 Feb. 1941.

24 Keenleyside to S.T. Wood, commissioner, RCMP, 20 Feb. 1941, External Affairs Records, vol. 2007, file 212, part 2, PAC; F.J. Mead, assistant commissioner, RCMP, to the commissioner, 28 Feb. 1941, External Affairs Records, vol. 2007; H.F. Angus to Mayor F.J. Hume, chairman, Standing Committee on Orientals, 25 July 1941, External Affairs Records, vol. 2007.

[25] Flying Officer W.A. Nield, Report on the State of Intelligence on the Pacific Coast with Particular Reference to the Problem of the Japanese Minority, 27 July 1941, Defence Records, file HQ S67-3, vol. 1.

[26] All Japanese nationals immediately became enemy aliens and, in addition, restrictions imposed upon them were also imposed upon all Japanese Canadians naturalized after 1922.

[27] LaViolette, *The Canadian Japanese*, 44; Declaration of the Existence of a State of War Between Canada and Japan, 8 Dec. 1941, King Papers, MG 26, J5, D58190-4; *Vancouver Sun*, 8 Dec. 1941; *Nanaimo Free Press*, 8 Dec. 1941; *The Province*, 8 Dec. 1941.

[28] After Pearl Harbor the major daily newspapers in Vancouver and Victoria published steady streams of letters on the Japanese problem, most of which voiced suspicion of the west coast Japanese and demanded federal action to remove the threat which they posed. For reports of vandalism see *The Province*, 8, 9, and 11 Dec. 1941. For rumours of Japanese subversion see Weekly Internal Security Intelligence Report, 13 Dec. 1941, Western Air Command, Defence Records, file HQ S67-3, vol. 1. With the exception of fishermen, those Japanese who lost their jobs were soon reabsorbed by the labour market. C.H. Hill, assistant commissioner, RCMP, Intelligence Report, 16 Dec. 1941 and 13 Jan. 1942, External Affairs Records, file 3464-G-40, Department of External Affairs, Archives Branch [EAA].

[29] Hutchison to Pickersgill, [16 Dec. 1941], King Papers, MG 26, J4, vol. 347, 239219-20.

[30] *The Province*, 19 Dec. 1941; Hill to the commissioner, RCMP, 20 Dec. 1941, External Affairs Records, file 3464-H-40C, EAA.

[31] Hume to King, 20 Dec. 1941, External Affairs Records, vol. 1868, file 263, part 4, PAC.

[32] Alexander to chief of the General Staff, 30 Dec. 1941, Defence Records, file HQ 6-0-7. Alexander's concern was shared by those officers commanding Canada's Pacific coast naval and air forces. Commodore W.J.R. Beech to the general officer commanding-in-chief, Pacific Command, 27 Dec. 1941, Defence Records; L.S. Stevenson to the secretary, Department of National Defence for Air, 2 Jan. 1941, Defence Records, file HQ S67-3, vol. 1. In Ottawa the chief of the General Staff did not subscribe to these fears. Lt.-Gen. K. Stuart to Keenleyside, 26 Dec. 1941, External Affairs Papers, file 3464-H-40C, EAA.

[33] Petitions to the federal government can be found in King Papers, MG 26, J2, vol. 294, file p-309, vol. 14; Mackenzie Papers, vol. 24, file 70-25, vol. 1, vol. 25, file 70-25, vols. 2 and 3, vol. 25, file 70-25E; External Affairs Records, file 773-B 1-40, parts 1 and 2, EAA.

[34] Turgeon to King, 6 Jan, 1942, External Affairs Records, file 773-b-1-40, part 1.

[35] For a useful theoretical discussion of the hostile outburst as a social phenomenon see Neil J. Smelser, *Theory of Collective Behaviour* (New York 1962), especially ch. 8.

[36] *Langley Advance*, 15 and 22 Jan. 1942; see also note 49.

[37] W.L. Mackenzie King, *Industry and Humanity: A Study in the Principles Underlying Industrial Reconstruction* (Toronto, 1918), 75–76.

[38] King Diary, 20, 23, and 24 Feb. 1942, King Papers, MG 26, J13.

[39] Conference on the Japanese Problem in British Columbia, Minutes, 8 and 9 Jan. 1942, External Affairs Records, vol. 1868, file 263, part 4, PAC; Mackenzie to King, 10 Jan. 1942, Mackenzie Papers, vol. 32, file x-81; Keenleyside to Mackenzie 10 Jan. 1942, Mackenzie Papers. The minority recommendation for partial evacuation was appended to the report.

[40] Pacific Command to National Defence Headquarters, 12 Jan. 1942, telegram, Defence Papers, file HQ 6-0-7; Mackenzie to King, 10 Jan. 1942, Mackenzie Papers, vol. 32, file x-81.

[41] Statement of the prime minister, 14 Jan. 1942, Mackenzie Papers, vol. 24, file 70-25, vol. 1.

[42] Mackenzie to Bryce M. Stewart, deputy minister of labour, 23 Jan. 1942, Mackenzie Papers, vol. 32, file x-81, vol. 2; Keenleyside to Mackenzie, 26 Jan. 1942, Mackenzie Papers; Keenleyside, The Japanese Problem in British Columbia, Memorandum to Mr. Robertson, 27 Jan. 1942, Mackenzie Papers.

[43] *Vancouver Sun*, 14 Jan. 1942; the lull was obvious to military intelligence officers in British Columbia. Major C.H. Bray, Intelligence, Pacific Command, to the director, Military Operations and Intelligence, National Defence Headquarters, 29 Jan. 1942, Department of Labour Papers, RG 27, Lacelle Files, vol. 174, file 614.02:11-1, vol. 1, PAC.

[44] See above note 33.

[45] M.C. Robinson and others to Mackenzie, 23 Feb. 1942, Mackenzie Papers, vol. 25, file 70-25, vol. 2.

[46] Weekly Internal Security Intelligence Report, 17 Jan. 1942, Western Air Command, Defence Records, file HQ S67-3, vol. 1. For another example of rumour see Gwen Cash, *A Million Miles from Ottawa* (Toronto, 1942), 25–26.

[47] On the nature and significance of rumour see Gordon W. Allport and Leo Postman, *The Psychology of Rumor* (New York, 1965), especially ch. 2.

[48] *Vancouver Sun*, 14 Jan. 1942; Mackenzie to Stewart, 23 Jan. 1942, Mackenzie Papers, vol. 32, file x-81, vol. 2. The emphasis was Mackenzie's.

[49] Although some fruit and vegetable growers in the Okanagan Valley requested Japanese workers for the duration of the war in order to ease the wartime labour shortage, the proposal roused a strong outburst of bitter opposition in the valley. Protest was channeled through municipal councils, newspapers, boards of trade, and dissenting farm organizations. In addition, proposals that the Japanese be moved east of the Rockies met opposition from several provincial governments. *Penticton Herald*,

479

15, 22, and 29 Jan. 1942; *Kelowna Courier*, 22 Jan. and 12 Feb. 1942; Keenleyside, Memorandum for Mr. Robertson, 4 Feb. 1942, External Affairs Records, file 3464-G-40, [EAA].

[50] House of Commons, *Debates* (29 Jan. 1942), 156–58.

[51] Mackenzie to Robertson, 28 Jan. 1942, Mackenzie Papers, vol. 32, file x-81, vol. 2; R.W Mayhew to King, 12 Feb. 1942, King Papers, MG 26, J1 vol. 330; G. McGeer to King, 13 Feb. 1942, Gerald Grattan McGeer Papers, box 2, file 9, PABC; Olaf Hanson and others to King, 21 Feb. 1942, King Papers, MG 26, J1, vol. 336.

[52] R.L. Maitland to Mackenzie, 17 Feb. 1942, Mackenzie Papers, vol. 32, file x-81, vol. 2.

[53] *Vancouver Sun*, 16 Feb. 1942; Pearson to A. MacNamara, associate deputy minister of Labour, 17 Feb. 1942, Labour Records, RG 27, Lacelle Files, vol. 174, file 614.02: 11-1, vol. 1; W.C. Woodward, lieutenant-governor, to King, 11 Feb. 1942, King Papers, MG 26, J1, vol. 336; Alexander to the secretary, Chiefs of Staff Committee, Department of National Defence, 13 Feb. 1942, Defence Records, Chiefs of Staff Committee, Miscellaneous Memoranda, vol. 3, Feb. 1942; Joint Services Committee, Pacific Coast, Minutes, 19 and 20 Feb. 1942, Defence Records.

[54] Mackenzie to L. St. Laurent, 14 Feb. 1942, Mackenzie Papers, vol. 24, file 70-25, vol. 1; Mackenzie to King, 22 Feb. 1942, King Papers, MG 26, J1, vol. 328.

[55] Mackenzie to St. Laurent, 24 Feb. 1942, Mackenzie Papers, vol. 25, file 70-25, vol. 2. At the same time Mackenzie sent similar letters to colleagues King, Power, Ralston, Macdonald, and Mitchell.

[56] Mackenzie to J.R. Bowler, dominion secretary, Canadian Legion, 26 Feb. 1942, Mackenzie Papers, vol. 25.

[57] King Diary, 19 Feb. 1942.

[58] Order-in-Council PC 1486, 24 Feb. 1942; House of Commons, *Debates* (27 Feb. 1942), 917–20.

[59] Cash, *A Million Miles from Ottawa*, 33; *The Province*, 2 March 1942; *The Colonist*, 3 March 1942; Ann Thompson, Vancouver Liberal Council to C.N. Senior [private secretary to Mackenzie], 27 Feb. 1942, Mackenzie Papers, vol. 25, file 70-25, vol. 2.

[60] *Vancouver Sun*, 26 Feb. 1942.

[61] While racial tensions swelled in British Columbia after Pearl Harbor, a similar crisis occurred on the American Pacific Coast. There, as in Canada, residents in coastal areas who were of Japanese origin were forced to move inland to camps constructed for their reception. The American decision for evacuation, however, was based solely on military considerations and was taken by military officers who had been given a free hand by President Roosevelt. There was no collaboration between the Canadian and American governments in the decision-making process and, while the events of the two evacuations ran in close parallel, neither country's policy appears to have influenced the other. For accounts of the American evacuation see Morton Grodzins, *Americans Betrayed: Politics and the Japanese Evacuation* (Chicago, 1949); Stetson Conn, "The Decision to Evacuate the Japanese from the Pacific Coast (1942)," *Command Decisions*, ed. Kent Roberts Greenfield, Prepared by the office of the Chief of Military History, Department of the Army (New York, 1959); Roger Daniels, *Concentration Camps USA: Japanese Americans and World War II* (New York, 1972).

Topic Thirteen

Canadian Foreign Policy

Although a nation in name, Canada after 1867 allowed Britain to direct its relations with other nations, including the United States. For nearly half a century, many English-speaking Canadians saw themselves as Britons overseas, part of the greatest empire the world had ever known. Only slowly and gradually did Canada evolve into an independent nation, assuming responsibility for its own foreign policy. John R. English traces the steps "from colony to nation" in his article "Getting On in the World."

No sooner had Canada achieved independence, as symbolized by the signing of the Statute of Westminster in 1931, than it faced the dilemma of maintaining its autonomy from Britain in a world aligning itself once again for war. Indeed, in its obsession with maintaining independence, Canada overlooked the serious international situation of the 1930s which led to World War II. Independence became the rationale for refusing to support the League of Nations, the only international organization capable of controlling European aggression. In "'A Low Dishonest Decade': Aspects of Canadian External Policy, 1931–1939," James Eayrs critically reviews Canada's foreign policy in the 1930s.

After the Second World War, Canada abandoned its misguided policy of isolationism and assumed a new responsibility as a peacemaker in the world, through such organizations as the United Nations, the Commonwealth of Nations, and NATO. J.L. Granatstein examines both the image and the reality of Canada as peacekeeper during the so-called "golden age of Canadian diplomacy" in the 1950s and 1960s in his article "Canada and Peacekeeping: Image and Reality."

Canadian Foreign Policy: Historical Readings, ed. J.L. Granatstein (Toronto: Copp Clark, 1986) is a useful collection of articles. James Eayrs, in *In Defence of Canada*, vol. 2, *Appeasement and Rearmament* (Toronto: University of Toronto Press, 1965), provides an exhaustive analysis of Canadian foreign policy in the late 1930s. Two alternatives to Eayrs' critical views of Canada's position of isolationism are H. Blair Neatby's "Mackenzie King and National Unity," in H.L. Dyck and H.P. Krosby, *Empire and Nations: Essays in Honour of Frederic H. Soward* (Toronto: University of Toronto Press, 1969), 54–70, and J.L. Granatstein and R. Bothwell's "'A Self-Evident National Duty': Canadian Foreign Policy,

1935–1939," *Journal of Imperial and Commonwealth History* 3 (1975): 212–33. A good documentary collection on the 1930s is R. Bothwell and G.N. Hillmer, *'The In-Between Time': Canadian External Policy in the 1930's* (Toronto: Copp Clark, 1975). For an overview of the interwar years see C.P. Stacey, *Canada and the Age of Conflict*, vol. 2, *1921–1948: The Mackenzie King Era* (Toronto: University of Toronto Press, 1981). I. Abella and H. Troper, *None Is Too Many: Canada and the Jews of Europe, 1933–1948* (Toronto: Lester and Orpen Dennys, 1982) deals with Canada's failure to allow European Jews into Canada.

On the cold war era, see James Eayrs' *In Defence of Canada*, vol. 3, *Peacemaking and Deterrence* (Toronto: University of Toronto Press, 1972) and vol. 4, *Growing Up Allied* (1980), as well as Denis Smith's *Diplomacy of Fear: Canada and the Cold War, 1941–1948* (Toronto: University of Toronto Press, 1988). The critical question of Canadian–American relations in the post-war years is dealt with in John W. Holmes, *Life with Uncle: The Canadian–American Relationship* (Toronto: University of Toronto Press, 1981) and his *The Better Part of Valour* (Toronto: McClelland and Stewart, 1975). See also: *Partners Nevertheless: Canadian–American Relations in the Twentieth Century*, ed. Norman Hillmer (Toronto: Copp Clark, 1989); Allan E. Gotlieb, "Power and Vulnerability: Canadian and American Perspectives on International Affairs," in *The Future of North America: Canada, The United States and Quebec Nationalism*, ed. E. Feldman and N. Nevitte (Montreal: Institute for Research on Public Policy, 1979), 109–131; and Stephen Clarkson, ed., *An Independent Foreign Policy for Canada?* (Toronto: McClelland and Stewart, 1968), and his *Canada and the Reagan Challenge: Crisis and Adjustment, 1981–1985* (Toronto: Lorimer, 1985). Two special issues of *International Journal* should be examined: the Summer 1967 issue offers retrospective looks at Canadian foreign policy and the Summer 1976 issue concerns "The U.S. and Us." Students should also consult the relevant sections of R. Bothwell, I. Drummond, and J. English's *Canada since 1945: Power, Politics, and Provincialism* (Toronto: University of Toronto Press, 1981).

Canada's involvment in NATO is discussed in Tom Keating and Larry Pratt, *Canada, Nato and the Bomb: The Western Alliance in Crisis* (Edmonton: Hurtig Publishers Ltd., 1988) and in D.W. Middlemiss and J.J. Sokolsky, *Canadian Defence: Decisions and Determinants* (Toronto: Harcourt Brace Jovanovich, Canada, 1989), while events leading up to the NORAD agreement are covered in Joseph T. Jockel, *No Boundaries Upstairs: Canada, The United States and the Origins of North American Air Defence, 1945–1958* (Vancouver: University of British Columbia Press, 1987). For an account of one man's role in Canada's peacekeeping efforts, see George Ignatieff, *The Making of a Peacemaker: The Memoirs of George Ignatieff* (New York: Penguin Books, 1987). On Lester Pearson, see his memoirs, entitled *Mike*, 3 vols. (Toronto: University of Toronto Press, vol. 1, 1972; vol. 2, 1973; vol. 3, 1975). On Diefenbaker's foreign policy, see H. Basil Robinson, *Diefenbaker's World: A Populist in World Affairs* (Toronto: University of Toronto Press, 1989).

Getting On in the World*

JOHN R. ENGLISH

When the victors gathered in Paris in 1919 to sort out the debris left by the First World War, several statesmen claimed they were baffled by the peculiar arguments of the Canadians. How, U.S. President Woodrow Wilson asked, could Canada and the other British Dominions have a separate seat at the peace table? They had no diplomats abroad. Their head of state was the King of England. They had never signed a treaty with a foreign nation. Moreover, they had agreed that their aim was a common British Empire foreign policy. Why, then, should they have votes separate from Britain's in the crucial decisions facing the peacemakers? Would not these British Dominions simply multiply British influence? Why, some Americans asked, should not Texas and some other states have a separate vote? They were as sovereign as the British Dominions, at least in terms of their international presence.

483

These arguments angered Sir Robert Borden, Canada's wartime prime minister. He became more determined to secure Canada's right to a voice in the peacemaking. Canada, Borden believed, could get nothing out of the dividing of the victor's spoils, except recognition. But for him and for many other Canadians in 1919, recognition meant a lot.

A "Nation" More or Less

Canadians may have been angered by the disposition of others to regard their nation as simply a part of the British whole. Looking back, however, we can see why so many were confused. The British North America Act of 1867 said nothing about Canada's relationship with the world beyond the British Empire. They British government retained responsibility for, and control of, Canada's contacts with other nations. And yet Canada proclaimed itself a new nation, and the Confederation Debates and much of the popular press were filled with references to nationhood.

Canada's first prime minister, Sir John A. Macdonald, accepted that Canada, as a part of the British Empire, must deal with other nations through the British diplomatic service. He realized that the British connection had a deep emotional importance to many (although certainly

*From *Horizon Canada* 95 (1987): 2257–63. Reprinted by permission.

not all) Canadians. Furthermore, the British link was a guarantee for Canada against threats from the United States.

By permitting the British to handle its external relations, Canada gained not only a sense of security but also the great experience and the worldwide range of British diplomacy. For a small struggling nation, it was a good bargain. All Canadians were British subjects and thus shared the rights and privileges bestowed upon the citizens of that country's greatest empire.

Yet the fact that Canada was a nation with more limited authority than most others did create difficulties and Canadian complaints. Macdonald sensed the contradictions when he joined the British negotiating team for the Treaty of Washington in 1871. British interests were not always Canadian interests, and for British negotiators the broader imperial interests naturally came first.

Macdonald could accept these priorities albeit grudgingly, but by the 1870s there were other Canadians who believed that Canada's own interests should come first. Edward Blake, the prominent Liberal politician, strongly complained in 1874 that Canadians were "four millions of Britons who are not free" because they lacked a voice in the formation of imperial foreign policy. He and others formed Canada First, a political group which expressed the new English-Canadian nationalism and which, as the name suggests, wanted Canada to be more assertive in its dealings within and without the Empire.

The members of Canada First had various answers to the problem. Some wanted an Imperial Federation; others wanted a closer union with the United States; a few wanted an independent Canada. Not surprisingly, the group disintegrated. Although the debate about Canada's international position continued, Canada's actual position had changed very little by 1896 when Sir Wilfrid Laurier became prime minister.

The Call of Empire

Laurier took office when the British were more eager than ever before to draw the colonies closer to them. Facing economic and military challenges from France, Germany, and the United States, the British saw the Empire as a unique resource in their competition with others. Laurier, however, feared this pressure because he knew that many Canadians, especially his fellow francophones, would not support British imperialist adventures. Always proclaiming his loyalty to the British tie and his deep respect for the British heritage, Laurier nevertheless resisted all attempts to snare Canada into a formal imperial federation. He could not, however, prevent Canadian involvement in the Boer War in 1899. His English-Canadian colleagues prevailed upon the government to send a contingent to faraway South Africa. The decision divided the cabinet, and an important precedent was set.

After 1900, all Canadians knew that Canada's Britishness meant that Canada would likely become involved in future wars which the British fought. French Canadians generally feared this; many English Canadians, however, argued that this meant that Canada should have a voice in the making of British foreign policy since British decisions could have, literally, a life-or-death impact on Canadians. Laurier chose to be ambiguous in public utterances, but he resisted strongly all attempts to join British councils. He also used occasions where British imperial interests took precedence over Canadian interests in British decision-making to rouse Canadian nationalist feeling.

By the time Laurier left office in 1911, Canada was dealing directly with the United States on an International Joint Commission, and it had its own Department of External Affairs which had been established in 1909. It still had no foreign ambassadors and could not sign treaties independently. Nor could it make independently the most important decision — to go to war or not.

485

Thus when Britain declared war on Germany in August 1914, Canada was automatically at war. Neither Laurier nor his Conservative successor, Borden, disagreed with this constitutional practice. As Canada poured men and money into the war effort, however, Borden grew to resent Canada's exclusion from the British councils where the war was planned. In 1917, the war's most horrible year, the British, desperately needing Dominion support, finally called the Dominions to their councils. Canada, it seemed, had gained a voice in London, one which the British promised would survive the war. It did not.

Many Canadians, appalled by the losses of World War One, no longer wanted to have that voice because they no longer wanted to be committed to fight British wars. Moreover, the war had intensified not only French-Canadian opposition to imperial entanglements but also English-Canadian nationalism. Borden reflected this latter sentiment at Versailles in 1919. While he still clung to the notion of a common imperial policy, younger politicians were increasingly doubtful.

The Path to Autonomy

In the aftermath of war, Canadian nationalism proved a potent political brew, one which the Liberals of William Lyon Mackenzie King dispensed freely at election time. In the 1920s and 1930s, a series of actions and events suggested that Canada, along with the other British Dominions, was moving toward autonomy; that is, the right to conduct its own foreign policy. The path, however, was not straight, and the goal was generally obscure.

By the beginning of the 1920s, the notion of a common imperial foreign policy was collapsing. The test of Canadian post-war opinion came in 1922 when the British asked for support against Turkey in the so-called Chanak Crisis, arising out of the settlement of the war in that part of the world. News that Britain wanted Canada's help in what might turn out to be a war first came to King through the newspapers. King was incensed, as was his cabinet.

The Canadian response was cold: Before any commitment could be made, Parliament must be summoned, and it alone must decide about Canadian participation. Conservative leader Arthur Meighen disagreed. "When Britain's message came," he argued, "then Canada should have said: 'Ready, aye ready; we stand by you.'" But the Conservative opposition soon began to modify its stand when it became obvious that Canadians agreed with the government.

486 In 1923, Justice Minister Ernest Lapointe signed the Halibut Treaty with the United States, and this marked the first Canadian independent treaty-making. In that same year, the Imperial Conference recognized that all hope for a common imperial foreign policy had died. Not only the Canadians had reservations; the South Africans and the Irish were even more vociferously opposed to any automatic commitments to follow the results of British imperial decisions. Canada, in fact, was in a comfortable middle position among the Dominions, with the Australians and the New Zealanders continuing to cling to the view that a united Empire policy would be best. The Imperial Conference of 1926 formally recognized the autonomy of the Dominions.

Playing the Nationalist Card

The so-called nationalist actions of the King government won widespread support among French Canadians and among younger English Canadians. This was clearly revealed in the election campaign of 1926 when King used this nationalist appeal to defeat the Conservatives. The year before, the Liberals' rather sorry domestic record had led to the Conservatives winning more seats than any other party in the House of Commons. King tried to govern with help from the Progressive Party, but found himself unable to do so. He asked Gov. Gen. Lord Byng for a dissolution of Parliament, which Byng refused. Byng instead asked Meighen to form a government. Meighen could not maintain a parliamentary majority either, and his government fell. King now had the issue he wanted: the interference of a British governor general in Canadian politics.

On the hustings in 1926, King often sounded as if he were fighting a battle of liberation. In reality, King did not want an "independent" Canada which had no links with Britain. His appeal to Canadian nationalist sentiment, however, was most effective, if rather dishonest. Lord Byng became a symbol of all that Canadians disliked about the British: their arrogance, their class system, and their willingness to commit Canadians to decisions in which they had no part. Western Canada as well as Quebec found this appeal most pleasing. The Conservatives argued that the issue was phoney, but too few listened. King's appeal and his party carried the day.

After 1926, Canada began to adopt the appearance of a nation with an independent foreign policy. Embassies appeared, the first being established in Washington in 1927. A few others followed, but the economy-minded governments of the interwar years did not want a large-scale diplomatic establishment. The Department of External Affairs, under the powerful undersecretary O.D. Skelton, began to gain influence within Canadian government councils. The department attracted some brilliant young Canadians, but in terms of policy, Skelton's opinions were not always followed. He had a deep distrust of the United Kingdom, and a strong desire to link Canada's foreign policy with that of the isolationist United States. Canada, in his view, must be a North American nation.

487

How Independent Is Independent?

But the old garments could not be cast away so easily. Canadians may have wanted to be recognized as a distinct nation not under the control of the British government. The Statute of Westminster of 1931 recognized this fact. Nevertheless, most Canadians retained strong emotional ties to their British heritage. Some continued to favour stronger imperial links. The Conservative R.B. Bennett, who became prime minister at the beginning of the Depression in 1930, called for closer imperial economic ties. He even managed to push the British government to agree to a system of imperial customs preferences which did serve to direct more Canadian trade along Empire lines. Bennett also tended to trust the British in their conduct of foreign policy. Despite his imperial outlook, he wandered little from the path followed by King. He was, however, more aware of the dilemma Canadian foreign policy faced in the 1930s as Europe once again began to teeter toward war.

Although Canadians talked about an independent foreign policy in the 1930s, they could not manage to agree on what independence should mean. The result was considerable confusion about what would happen if Britain went to war. After Mackenzie King returned to power in 1935, he adopted a policy of extreme caution. He would make no commitment; he would issue no declarations. Ambiguity was his refuge. He tried to keep his distance from the British, except when the British tried to avoid war through appeasing the Italian and German dictators Mussolini and Hitler.

In the last few years before World War Two, independence brought more embarrassment than exhilaration. And how independent was Canada? Would not Canada once again go to war if Britain were threatened? If that was the case, should Canada not try to influence British policy rather than wait to be drawn into the European cauldron once more?

Canada, of course, did go to war in 1939, not because it lacked autonomy as in 1914, but because most Canadians wanted to fight again at Britain's side. By World War Two, Canada could conduct its own foreign policy and make its own decisions. With this new autonomy, Canada often found the international winds cold, and the danger near. It learned that independence had a limited meaning in the modern world. Nevertheless, the mistakes Canada made would now be its own.

---

488   "A Low Dishonest Decade": Aspects of Canadian External Policy, 1931–1939*

JAMES EAYRS

There has not yet taken place in Canada that debate on the wisdom of appeasement in which British statesmen and scholars have been engaged since the appearance of Professor Feiling's *Life of Neville Chamberlain*. If this seems a remarkable fact, it is not hard to explain. Had the Canadian government of that day urged a more sturdy resistance to the Nazi tyranny, it is doubtful that events would have taken a significantly different course. German policy was unresponsive to the action or inaction of the Dominions; and it seems unlikely that Chamberlain would have been deflected from the path of the appeaser any more by the Prime Minister of Canada than he was by the Prime Minister of New Zealand, which is to say not at all. Canada's external policy during the years 1931–1939, so far from requiring extended apology, appears to most of its historians to possess the self-evident vindication of having brought a united and determined nation to Britain's side on September 10, 1939. The evidence which might sustain a contrary interpretation is still scanty. Documents from the files of the Department of External Affairs have yet to be published; the private papers of the Prime Ministers of the period are withheld from the scholar's domain;[1] both R.B. Bennett and Mackenzie King retained a jealous hold upon the External Affairs portfolio and conducted foreign policy possessively, even stealthily, so that few of their colleagues and subordinates have been able to throw strong light upon shadowy though crucial episodes; and a tradition unlike that prevailing at Westminster (where politics and literature — or politics

*From *The Growth of Canadian Policies in External Affairs*, ed. H.L. Keenleyside. Copyright © 1960 by Duke University Press. Reprinted by permission.

and journalism — honorably combine) assists in their concealment. These are some (but by no means all) of the circumstances accounting for the remarkable early appearance of an Authorized Version of events not yet three decades removed.

The time is now approaching when a revisionist interpretation will be possible; one or two significant steps in this direction have already been taken.[2] The present paper has a more modest purpose. It attempts to discuss some aspects of Canadian external policy during the 1930's to which insufficient attention has perhaps been paid, and to bring to more familiar themes evidence previously overlooked. Although the title[3] may suggest an excess of moral indignation, its point of view is rather that of Lord Vansittart, who, writing of Dominion policies during the period in which he labored with such prescience and to such little avail, remarked, perhaps too generously: "One could not blame them, one could not admire them, one could not admire anybody."[4]

489

1. The New World and the Old

In 1919 Canadians turned away from Europe, leaving behind their dead. However misguided it might appear to those of a later generation drawn as their fathers had been into "the vortex of militarism," isolationism in Canada was a natural response to the four-year ordeal on the Western front. The Great War remade the map, but left unchanged the scale and the projection. How could a conflict in which major gains were measured by hundreds of yards, and a million lives exchanged for a few desolated acres of mud, affect in any way the traditional concepts of geography? It brought half a million Canadians to Europe but Europe no closer to Canada. The world was still wide. To the Oceans and the Fleet might now be added as purveyor of security the great and friendly guardian to the South. Canada was a "fire-proof house, far from inflammable materials";[5] and its fortunate inhabitants peered indistinctly at the distant continent from which invasion seemed so improbable. "At present danger of attack upon Canada is minor in degree and second-hand in origin," Mackenzie King had insisted as late as 1938;[6] and although his military advisers were less certain of Canada's immunity,[7] their misgivings were not allowed to disturb unduly the complacency of the public or the size of the defense estimates.

Isolationism was the product of geography; it was shaped by distrust, a distrust born of the Great War and confirmed at the council tables of Paris. "It was European policy, European statesmanship, European ambition, that drenched this world with blood," N.W. Rowell told the First Assembly of the League of Nations. "Fifty thousand Canadians under the soil of France and Flanders is what Canada has paid for European statesmanship trying to settle European problems. I place responsibility on a few; I would not distribute it over many; but nevertheless it is European."[8] These bluntly accusing words, an official of the Canadian delegation wrote privately at the time, "hurt and stung many people," and in his view "marred the performance."[9] But they conveyed, however tactlessly, the sense of Canadian feeling; and the Prime Minister wrote to their author to express his "appreciation of the stand you took in stating to the Conference, as frankly as you did, the price the world has paid for the European diplomacy of the last hundred years."[10] Nor, as it seemed, had the trauma of the trenches changed Europe for the better. Ancient enmities and grievances arose once more, or were replaced or supplemented by new disorders; the scope for intrigue and for disaster was if anything enhanced. "Everywhere there are signs of trouble," wrote one of Canada's representatives at the Paris Peace Conference in 1919. "Egypt is now disturbed with the fever for self govt. — the vicious results of Wilson's doctrine of ill or nondefined self determination. Asia Minor and Turkey are disorganized — Roumanians threatened on three sides by Bolshevists and Hungarians — Russia poisoned and poisoning — Hungary communist and Germany in near chaos. 'Tis surely a sad mess out of which to evolve a new Europe."[11]

490

Distrust and disapproval of Europe's statecraft and statesmen passed easily into an assertion of North American moral superiority. In Canada as in the United States there was nourished the conviction that the New World in its national life and international behavior exhibited standards above and beyond those of the Old. Like Mr. Herbert Hoover, Canadians

> returned in 1919 from several years abroad . . . steeped with two ideas: first, that through three hundred years [North] America had developed something new in a way of life of a people, which transcended all others of history; and second, that out of the boiling social and economic cauldron of Europe, with its hates and fears, rose miasmic infections which might greatly harm or even destroy . . . the hope of the world.[12]

Rare was the Canadian who, addressing himself at Geneva or at home to the theme of his country's place in world affairs, did not elaborate this contrast. " . . . [W]e think in terms of peace," remarked Senator Dandurand in 1924, "while Europe, an armed camp, thinks in terms of war."[13] "After listening to and participating in the proceedings of the League," Mackenzie King declared in 1928, "I have come back to Canada with a more profound conviction than ever that there is no land on the face of the globe in which the lot of men, women and children is cast in a pleasanter place than in this Dominion."[14] In 1936 he referred to Canada's "tremendous, absorbing and paramount tasks of achieving economic development and national unity, which with us take the place of the preoccupation with the fear of attack and the dreams of glory which beset older and more crowded countries";[15] a few weeks later, at

Geneva, he contrasted his country's friendly relations with the United States and Europe's "violent . . . propaganda and recriminations hurled incessantly across the frontiers, the endeavours [in Europe] to draw all countries into one or other extremist camp, the feverish race for rearmament, the hurrying to and fro of diplomats, the ceaseless weaving and unravelling of understandings and alliances, and the consequent fear and uncertainty of the peoples";[16] and in March 1939, soon after Hitler's seizure of Czechoslovakia, he referred despairingly to the "continent that cannot run itself," in implied contrast to that North American continent which could.[17]

Such comparisons were frequently joined to moral exhortation. The rostrum of the Palais des Nations became for successive Canadian spokesmen a pulpit from which Europe was urged to forswear her foolish ways, to abandon intrigue, violence, hostility, to adopt those institutions which (they claimed) had brought a century of peace to North America. Canada and the United States, Mackenzie King informed the Ninth Assembly of the League of Nations, had ceased "to rely upon force, we have looked to reason as the method of solving our differences, and reason has supplied us from time to time with conference, conciliation or arbitration in a form . . . sufficient to settle our various differences as they have arisen."[18] Let there be a European Rush-Bagot Treaty, a European International Joint Commission — tranquility would follow for a hundred years. As a prescription for Old World ills, these New World remedies were altogether inadequate, arising as they did from a wholly different situation.

491

> The toad beneath the harrow knows
> Exactly where each tooth-point goes;
> The butterfly upon the road
> Preaches contentment to that toad.

Moreover, they were compounded of a series of fictions unrelated to things as they were. "Not a single soldier, not a single cannon," the Canadian delegate had told the Fifth Assembly of the League, faced the famous frontier. This was simple falsehood. The International Joint Commission had been able to function without major difficulty only because each government had refrained from submitting disputes other than those over waterways. As for the Rush-Bagot Agreement, "the truth is," Mackenzie King had written privately in 1922, "our American friends have been steadily evading [it], until it has become more or less of a mockery to speak of its terms in the manner in which we do."[19]

However ill-justified, Canada's moralizing at Europe led logically not to isolation but engagement. Ought not the practitioners of the New World's higher mortality try by more active participation in the affairs of the Old to lead it into the paths of righteousness? That is not what happened. More potent than the zeal of the missionary was the desire to escape contamination. The less the New World came in contact with the Old, the better; the more, the greater the chance of succumbing to those "miasmic infections" which threatened to invade and to destroy the healthy bodies politic of North America. "Bolshevism," wrote the editor of the *Canadian Annual Review* in 1918, "had a basis wherever Russians and Jews and other foreigners gathered together" in Canada's cities; if foreigners brought Bolshevism, Canadians should keep clear of foreigners. "We are told there are enormous numbers of people on the continent of Europe who want to come [here]," remarked a former Minister of Immigration in 1922. "I want to say I regard it of the dimensions of a national menace that there is any danger whatever of the bars being let down."[20] Questioned in 1920 on Canada's readiness to accept a mandate for Armenia, the Leader of the Opposition wrote that the proposal "would provoke general protest from one end of the Dominion to the other," for "a sort of reaction has set in . . . with respect to interference by the Governments of this Continent with European Affairs."[21] As the twenty years' crisis developed and deepened, isolationism became if anything more firmly rooted in the Canadian people and their governors. Early in 1922 the Canadian government refused to contribute funds in the form of an interest-free loan for the relief of famine in Russia, and turned down a Soviet request for credit to buy Canadian seed wheat. In 1924 it ignored an appeal to contribute to the relief of famine in Albania. In 1925 it refused the invitation to sign the Geneva Protocol, and it was largely at Canada's insistence that an article was inserted in the text of the Locarno Agreements specifically exempting the Dominions from their provisions. " . . . I do not see," Ernest Lapointe observed some years later, "that Canada should assume obligations in connection with the boundaries between France and Germany . . . [or] guarantee any boundaries in central Europe or elsewhere. . . . "[22] And an influential member of the Canadian government wrote before sailing for the Imperial Conference in the spring of 1937:

> The conference will be interesting, and probably in some ways revealing; but the more I see of the whole thing, the more I am certain that our destiny is on the North American continent and that if Europe is going to insist on destroying itself, it is no part of our mission to destroy ourselves in attempting to prevent it. . . . [23]

2. The League and the Nation

If other countries entered the League of Nations in something of the spirit expressed by Smuts' phrase — "the tents have been struck and the great caravan of humanity is once more on the march" — Canada may be said to have been mainly concerned lest she be called upon to do more than her share of the work in breaking camp or be compelled to march without the consent of her Parliament. It is usual to attribute the reserve with which Canadians watched the Geneva experiment to the coercive characteristics of the Covenant, and to suppose that so long as the League confined itself to conciliatory methods it could count upon Canadian approval. This view has the weighty support of Professor Mansergh, who writes that "from the first the League was welcomed as a means of furthering international co-operation, as a forum for debate and discussion," and that it was only "as a means for enforcing, as distinct from maintaining, peace" that it aroused the suspicion and censure of successive Canadian governments.[24] Certainly it is difficult to overestimate the agitated concern lest through Articles X and XVI of the Covenant the newly independent Dominion be placed at "the beck and call of a Council not responsible to the nation for its actions," or, even worse, become involved "in conflicts in some far-away section of Europe, or in some distant portion of South America."[25] Fears such as these lead to that policy; "remarkable," as Professor Mansergh observes, "for its consistency," by which Canada tried at first to have Article X removed entirely from the Covenant; that proving unsuccessful, introduced an interpretative resolution which, though it failed by one vote to receive the unanimous support required for adoption, had the desired effect of weakening the obligations of League membership; and finally, when the League was confronted with the two decisive tests of its procedures for collective security, did what could be done to weaken the effectiveness of sanctions.

493

But this interpretation may be misleading. It implies a degree of attachment to the League as a non-coercive agency for peaceful conciliation which, whatever might be said in public, no Canadian Minister really felt. For Canadian suspicion of Geneva derived basically from Canadian distrust of Europe; and it was as a European institution that the League appeared from Canada. "The League was born ostensibly as a world League," commented a former official of the Department of External Affairs in 1926, "but really is a European League with the non-Europeans tacked on. The most distinctive and powerful New World people went out of it." A Canadian had no more legitimate concern "with the administration of Danzig or of the Saar Valley" than had "a Nova Scotian . . . [with] the municipal government of Vancouver."[26] "Let us . . . conciliate Quebec and Ontario," remarked a member of Parliament in 1923, "before we start conciliating Roumania and Ukrainia."[27] "The League of Nations is a preposterous and expensive farce," wrote Sir Clifford Sifton, "and amounts to nothing more than a part of a machine designed to involve us in European and Imperialistic complications. Canada ought to call a halt on this business."[28] The views of those in office were much the same. Sir Joseph Pope, the Under Secretary of State for External Affairs until 1925, dismissed the Covenant as "not worth the paper it is written on," and wrote in his diary: "Our reps are making a great stir at the League of Nations, advertizing Canada and incidentally themselves. I think it all absurd, and am convinced that Canada's true policy right now is to develop her resources and to leave European questions such as the Bessarabian frontier &c to our Imperial statesmen and the trained experts of Downing Street."[29] His successor, O.D. Skelton, while holding "the trained experts of Downing Street" in somewhat lesser regard, was no more sympathetic to the Geneva experiment. Mackenzie King, as his official biographer remarks, "was the type of uplifter who might have been expected to give the League his full and enthusiastic support," but his attitude towards the League in its formative years "was one of studied neglect."[30] In the 1930's this was to develop into an attitude of profound hostility, especially after the "Riddell incident" of November 1935. W.A. Riddell, the Canadian Permanent Delegate at Geneva, left in some perplexity as a consequence of the General Election a few days earlier, proposed on his own initiative the imposition of certain sanctions against Italy, and in the brief period until his action was repudiated by the Canadian government, set Canada's policy upon a course it had never before taken. In his published recollection of this celebrated episode, Dr. Riddell attributes his repudiation partly to the fact that the Prime Minister and the Under Secretary of State for External Affairs were at the time out of the country, leaving the Department of External Affairs in charge of "two French Canadians," Ernest Lapointe and Laurent Beaudry. On reporting to Mackenzie King in Ottawa, Dr. Riddell writes, he found him, "as always, most gracious," while Lapointe seemed "cold, critical and overbearing."[31] But beneath a mask of practiced cordiality King was no less angered than Lapointe, probably more so, by Riddell's initiative. A Canadian newspaperman has recorded an interview with the Prime Minister soon after the event:

> Had a few words with Mr. King re the Italo-Ethiopian settlement and he spoke with surprising frankness. I never knew before Mr. King's general attitude towards the League and foreign affairs. King complained angrily about Dr. Riddell's gasoline [sic], steel and coal proposal. "I am certainly going to give him a good spanking", was the way he put it. . . . He said that excessive idealism in politics should be avoided. Canada's policy, he believed, should be dictated by considerations of geographical location and population. After all we are but 10 millions on the north end of a continent and we should not strive to over-play our part. . . . He is very dubious about foreign commitments, and, also, about getting into the League too deeply. He said that the only real difference of opinion he had ever had with Lapointe was with regard to Canada's acceptance of the presidency of the League Assembly [in 1925]. He had opposed it on the ground that it would stimulate League thought in Canada, tend

494

to lead us more deeply into League affairs and, possibly, foreign commitments.[32]

"We should not strive to over-play our part." This theme was henceforth to be heard in nearly all of the Prime Minister's infrequent public statements on the European crisis until the outbreak of war, a refrain in praise of diffidence. "After all, . . . there is such a thing as a sense of proportion in international affairs," he said in the House of Commons in February 1936. "Do hon. members think that it is Canada's role at Geneva to attempt to regulate a European war . . . ?" If he had not disavowed Riddell's proposal, "the whole of Europe might have been aflame today."[33] A few days later he added: "Our country is being drawn into international situations to a degree that I myself think is alarming."[34] Within a fortnight Hitler was to invade the Rhineland.

3. The Law and the Jungle

495

If distrust of European politics contributed to isolationist sentiment in Canada in the years between the wars, it also helped to thwart understanding of what was happening to Europe during the deepening crisis of the later 1930's. With a very few exceptions, notably J.W. Dafoe,[35] Canadians did not recognize Fascist Italy and Nazi Germany for what they were. Totalitarianism was thought to be merely an aggravation of that *malaise* from which Europe traditionally suffered; there was little if any suspicion that it might be a distinctively twentieth-century phenomenon arising from the tensions and insecurities of twentieth-century man. The fascist apparition was no new menace for which the old responses would no longer suffice, but a rebirth of the intrigues, the rivalries, the nationalisms of prewar European diplomacy. Thus it required no special explanation; created no new problems; needed no exceptional precautions.

A significant section of the Canadian public was indeed disposed to view fascism in its Mediterranean setting not merely without alarm but with undisguised approval. The lofty sentiments of Fascist doctrine elaborated by Mussolini's publicists, with their apotheosis of order, discipline, family, nation, their pseudo-syndicalist remedies for industrial unrest, gained powerful support among the elite of French Canada. "The work of Mussolini and of the Fascist Party finds among a certain number of my compatriots admirers," remarked Mr. Paul Gouin in 1938. "They have the same attitude towards the corporative movement of Salazar. . . . We may ask ourselves if it would not be to the advantage of our Province and of Canada to borrow what is best in these different formulae, while naturally avoiding their excesses."[36] Few French-speaking Canadians saw anything for adverse comment in the description of General Franco's forces offered by the newly appointed Papal Delegate to Canada and Newfoundland as that "army of heroes, justly called Christ's militia,"[37] any more than they resented the valedictory pronounced by Maxime Raymond in the House of Commons on the occasion of the departure of the Mackenzie-Papineau Brigade: "This, I admit, does not give me any sorrow; it will rid us of these undesirable people, provided they do not return home here."[38] If there was no emulation in French Canada of General O'Duffy's Blueshirts, who went from Eire to fight in Spain for Franco, it was due not to want of sympathy for the Nationalist cause but to the even stronger hold of isolationism.

National Socialism was something else again. No religious or ideological link could bind Quebec to a regime which had so soon and so obviously singled out the Catholic Church for brutal destruction. But diagnosis of the Nazi movement was hindered in Canada by the magnitude of domestic crisis and by the isolationist tradition. Events in Germany were consistently misconstrued as a nationalist revival of the conventional type, distinguished, perhaps, by the odd fanaticism of its leaders, by the strut and swagger of its rank and file, but for all that a movement which might be comprehended in traditional terms, appeased and contained by traditional methods. When Hitler entered the Rhineland there was aroused among English-speaking Canadians little of the emotion produced by Mussolini's attack on Ethiopia. On the contrary, there was a widely held conviction that in reoccupying the demilitarized zone Hitler was only avenging the wrongs of Versailles, taking possession of what rightfully belonged to Germany. Why shouldn't a man walk into his own backyard? With the significant exception of Dafoe's *Free Press*, nearly all Canadian newspapers urged, on March 9, 1936, a sympathetic understanding of Hitler's position. "Canadians who do not allow themselves to be swayed by a personal dislike for Hitler and his unpleasant colleagues," wrote the editor of the Vancouver *Sun*, "will feel a measure of sympathy for this new attitude of the German people. . . . Canada is only a spectator. There are not enough moral principles at stake to induce her to become otherwise. . . . Whatever morality lies in the scales seems to be, this time, on Germany's side of the balance." "After eighteen years," the Edmonton *Bulletin* observed, "Europe can afford to restore Germany to full standing in the concert of nations." "Nothing can ever be gained," argued the editor of the Montreal *Gazette*, "by persistently treating Germany as though she were national enemy No. 1 in perpetuity. It would likewise be dangerous and futile to regard Adolf Hitler in no other light than as one whose designs are wilfully antagonistic to forces that hate war."

It is possible that had Canada been represented in Germany by a diplomat of insight and influence, a less reassuring image of National Socialism would have reached its government and people. As it was, the Canadian government, having no diplomatic mission at Berlin, necessarily relied on whatever Whitehall might select for its instruction from the despatches of Sir Nevile Henderson — despatches which conveyed a sadly erroneous interpretation of Nazi policy.[39] This unhelpful source was supplemented by the assessment of the Canadian High Commissioner at London, so closely associated with the group which moved with such great and disastrous effect between Cliveden, Printing House Square, and Downing Street that nothing he learned from its members seems likely to have provided a useful corrective to the misleading despatches passed on by the Dominions Office. "Walked about the grounds in the forenoon with Vincent Massey, talking politics," wrote Thomas Jones in his diary on June 7, 1936. "I begged him to stress the urgency of dealing with Germany and not to wait upon France."[40]

But the most misleading impression was derived more directly. In 1937 Mackenzie King decided to go from the Imperial Conference to Germany. There he met and talked with Hitler and other leading personalities of the Third Reich. It was not a wholly useful confrontation. It is true that King did not allow so unique an opportunity to pass without stressing in Berlin what he felt unable to disclose in London, namely, that in the event of "a war of aggression, nothing in the world would keep the Canadian people from being at the side of Britain."[41] Heeded or not heeded, this message was at least delivered, and more valuable service could hardly have been rendered. But its value was diminished by the way in which the Canadian Prime Minister fell victim to the Führer's remarkable capacity for mesmerizing his visitors. "There is no doubt that Hitler had a power of fascinating men," Mr. Churchill wrote in his memoirs; and added the sage advice: "Unless the terms are equal, it is better to keep away."[42] And between the Prime Minister of Canada and the perpetrator of the Nazi *Schrecklichkeit* the terms were far from equal. The extent of Hitler's advantage may be measured by the opinions with which King returned to Canada. According to Mr. Bruce Hutchison, to whom he related them soon afterward, King found Hitler

497

> a simple sort of peasant, not very intelligent and no serious danger to anyone . . . obsessed with the recovery of neighboring territory inhabited by Germans, a natural feeling. When he had brought these territories into the Reich . . . he would be satisfied . . . he would not risk a large war. His ambitions were centered entirely in Germany and the narrow irredentist regions beside it. For this reason [there would be] . . . no early trouble in Europe. . . .[43]

And to the Canadian people Mackenzie King declared, three weeks after his talks with the German leaders:

> Despite every appearance to the contrary, I believe the nations of Europe have a better understanding of each other's problems today than they have had for some years past. Moreover, despite all

appearances, they are prepared, I believe, in an effort to work out a solution, to co-operate to a greater degree than has been the case for a long while. . . . Of this I am certain . . . that neither the governments nor the peoples of any of the countries I have visited desire war, or view the possibility of war between each other, as other than likely to end in self-destruction, and the destruction of Europe civilization itself.[44]

That the destruction of European civilization was precisely the object of the man he had so recently talked with in the Reichskanzlei was a thought unlikely to have crossed the mind of the Canadian Prime Minister; for, as was remarked of him in a different connection, "Mr. King never quite got it into his head during his economic studies at Toronto and Harvard that our civilization is dominated by carnivorous animals."[45]

498 4. Empire and Reich

In 1923 the Prime Minister of Canada had protested vigorously and decisively against the Imperial Conference "assuming the rights of a cabinet in the determination of foreign policy . . . expressing approval of the present [British] Government's foreign policy . . . , trying to shape the affairs of Europe."[46] By 1937 Mackenzie King's suspicions of "Downing Street domination" had been sufficiently allayed to allow him to do what he had never done before — to endorse at an Imperial Conference a united Commonwealth policy on international affairs. As it happened, the policy for which the Dominions offered their collective approval and support was the ill-fated policy of appeasement. " . . . [T]he settlement of differences that may arise between nations," asserted the section of the *Proceedings* of the Conference dealing with foreign affairs, " . . . should be sought by methods of co-operation, joint enquiry and conciliation . . . differences of political creed should be no obstacle to friendly relations between Governments and countries . . . nothing would be more damaging to the hopes of international appeasement than the division, real or apparent, of the world into opposing groups."[47] These sentiments, which, as Professor Mansergh rightly remarks, are "hardly consistent with the dignity of a great Commonwealth confronted with the shameless aggression of European tyrants unmatched for their cruelty and faithlessness since the Dark Ages,"[48] continued to be uttered by Mackenzie King during the interval between the end of the Conference and the beginning of war. For the first time since becoming Prime Minister in 1921 he found himself able to pay public tribute to "the unremitting care and anxiety which those responsible for the foreign policy of Britain have devoted to their task"; he spoke of "their strong and determined effort to establish peace."[49] This was followed by a series of press statements in praise of British policy. When the news of the proposed mission to Berchtesgaden reached him, Mackenzie King announced that he had "conveyed to Mr. Neville Chamberlain the deep satisfaction with which my colleagues and I have learned that his proposal for a personal conference with Herr Hitler . . . has been agreed to" and described "this far-seeing and truly noble action on the part of Mr. Chamberlain" as "emphatically the right step." A further statement issued after the British Cabinet's decision to support the principle of self-determination for Sudeten Germans referred to the "courage and vision" displayed by the Government of the United Kingdom in seeking "to avert recourse to force by finding a peaceful and agreed solution of the present clash of interests in Central Europe." Following Chamberlain's radio address of September 27, 1938 ("How horrible, fantastic, incredible it is that we should be digging trenches and fitting gas-masks because of a quarrel in a far away country"), Mackenzie King proclaimed the Canadian government's "complete accord with the statement Mr. Chamberlain has made to the world today." Word of the impending visit to Munich called forth the most ecstatic endorsement of all:

499

> The heart of Canada is rejoicing tonight at the success which has crowned your unremitting efforts for peace. . . . My colleagues in the Government join with me in unbounded admiration at the service you have rendered mankind. . . . On the very brink of chaos, with passions flaming, and armies marching, the voice of Reason has found a way out of the conflict.

It may be safely assumed that these utterances were carefully noted and transmitted to Berlin by the German Consul General at Ottawa, Herr Windels; and to the extent that the disordered diplomatic apparatus at the Wilhelmstrasse was capable of bringing them to the attention of the Führer they can only have reinforced his belief that the British Empire was too weak and too craven to oppose his plans for the subjugation of Eastern Europe as a prelude to the destruction of the West. Appeasement, the only foreign policy on which the Commonwealth has ever been in substantial agreement, thus came close to accomplishing its ruin. Offered in the hope of peace, it led it straight to war.

Yet while Mackenzie King had by 1937 become able to support Britain's appeasement of Germany, his earlier fear of centralized control persisted in the realm of defense. All attempts on the part of the United Kingdom to co-operate militarily and industrially with Canada in advance of the outbreak of war were rebuffed. "From 1936 onwards," the official history of the Royal Air Force recalls reproachfully, "Canada, which enjoyed an ideal strategic position and a convenient proximity to the vast industrial resources of the United States, was repeatedly approached [with the request to make facilities available for training of pilots and aircrew]; but the Canadians, largely for domestic reasons, felt unable to accept our proposals. . . . "[50] At the Imperial Conference of 1937 "the principal Supply Officers' Committee tried to pilot through . . . an agreement with Canada about wartime supplies of bauxite and aluminium," but failed largely because of Canadian opposition.[51] In the summer of 1938 the Board of Trade entered into negotiations with the Canadian government to make provision in advance of war for adequate supplies of certain strategic materials; but Ottawa being unwilling to assume such commitments, by September 1939 "virtually no preparations had been made for the war-time purchase of raw materials in North America."[52] Munitions fared little better; with the exception of a contract for Bren machine guns, nothing was done by the Canadian government to assist United Kingdom defense officials in their effort to stimulate the manufacture of arms in the overseas Dominions.[53]

It is thus a major irony of Commonwealth history that Canadian influence on British policy was at this stage brought to bear in the worst of all possible ways. In external policy, as Professor Mansergh observes, "what was most of all required was not a greater consensus of Commonwealth opinion but the more vigourous expression of independent and conflicting opinion";[54] in defense policy what was most of all required was a united effort to create a deterrent of imperial power. The Canadian response was to voice with unaccustomed fervor approval of British statecraft while resisting Britain's efforts to improve the Empire's defenses. While "No evidence so far published suggests that doubts about the unity of the Commonwealth were a major factor in encouraging German aggression,"[55] a firmer signification of the Commonwealth's will to resist might have given Hitler pause; in any event the opportunity was both too good and too rare to be squandered. Certain it is that a fuller measure of defense preparation would have made his defeat less costly and precarious. The margin of superiority with which Britain faced the Axis in the summer of 1940 remained excruciatingly narrow. Had the R.A.F. failed, for want of aircraft or of pilots, to deflect and defeat the Luftwaffe, would not those responsible for Canadian policy during the prewar years have to share the blame?

5. Statecraft and Unity

On January 20, 1937, the Canadian Prime Minister spoke in confidence to a meeting of his parliamentary supporters. He urged them to reject the views of Mr. Arthur Meighen, the Conservative Leader in the Senate, "that the amount in the [defense] estimates was not enough, that we were concerned with the defence of the Empire as a whole; that the first line of our defence was the Empire's boundaries." Equally he urged them to reject the alternative offered by J.S. Woodsworth, the leader of the socialist group in the House of Commons, who, he said, "would do nothing at all" for defense. "The safe policy is the middle course between these two views. . . . Let us explain that policy to our people and let us above all strive at all times to keep Canada *united*."[56] This insistence upon the overriding importance of national unity appears again and again in Mackenzie King's statements on external policy during the years immediately preceding World War II. It served to explain his reluctance to participate in projects or pronouncements likely to deter potential aggressors. To do so, as he remarked in the House of Commons on May 24, 1938, "would bring out deep and in some cases fundamental differences of opinion, [and] would lead to further strain upon the unity of a country already strained by economic depression and other consequences of the last war and its aftermath."[57] Of the wisdom of this policy its architect betrayed neither doubt nor misgiving, and believed it fully vindicated by events. On September 8, 1939, he spoke as follows in the House of Commons:

> I have made it, therefore, the supreme endeavour of my leadership of my party, and my leadership of the government of this country, to let no hasty or premature threat or pronouncement create mistrust and divisions between the different elements that compose the population of our vast dominion, so that when the moment of decision came all should so see the issue itself that our national effort might be marked by unity of purpose, of heart and of endeavour.[58]

501

It is a matter for debate whether this "supreme endeavour" was not altogether too restricted. Politics is the art of the possible. But how much was possible during the years before the war? More, perhaps, than the Prime Minister of Canada allowed the nation, or himself, to believe. Never was Mackenzie King more satisfied than when enunciating the dictum that his country was difficult to govern. It was, and is, difficult to govern, in the sense that government is at all times and in all places an exacting and complicated craft. Compared to the ordeals which nearly every twentieth-century nation has undergone — destruction and occupation in war, civil conflict, malevolent and scouring tyrannies — Canadians might consider their situation extraordinarily favorable. Nor were those wearying comparisons between the continent of the undefended frontier and "the continent which cannot run itself" too easily reconciled with plaintive references to exceptional domestic difficulties invoked to justify inaction. So much harping upon the need for unity and the obstacles in its path exaggerated the degree of internal discord, just as repetition of the difficulties encountered in governing the country obscured the fact that it was a good deal less difficult to govern than most. Was it not misleading "to emphasize the precariousness of Canada's export markets, but not the value of her exports; to speak of regional and cultural tensions within but not of the growing sense of unity; of the conflicting pulls of geography and history to which indeed every 'settled' country is subject, but not of the immense strength of Canada's position in the heart of the English-speaking world"?[59] When the history of these years is set out in detail, many of the portents of disunity in the Dominion will be seen to have been greatly overdrawn. For example, it is commonly believed that had the United Kingdom gone to war over Czechoslovakia in September 1938, the C.C.F. (Socialist) party in Canada would have demanded a policy of neutrality. But Professor McNaught has discovered that "correspondence in the Saskatchewan C.C.F. files . . . leaves no doubt that the C.C.F. leaders who defeated the Woodsworth–Farmer neutrality motion in the emergency National Council meeting in [September] 1939 had concluded at least as early as September, 1938, that 'it is already decided that if Britain declares war, Canada must accept the situation.'"[60]

A direct result of reducing Canadian policy to the lowest common denominator of public agreement was the condition of the nation's defenses, "utterly inadequate," as the official historian of the Canadian Army observes, "by comparison with the scale of the coming emergency."[61] Another harmful consequence was the effect upon United Kingdom policy. Just as the Canadian government seized with alacrity upon stress and strain in the Dominion's domestic affairs as an excuse for passivity in all external policies save that of appeasement, so the British government fastened upon the difficulties of members of the overseas Commonwealth to justify its own cautious conduct. Disunity in the Dominions plays a major part in the arguments of apologists for Britain's prewar policy. "The fact remains that the Commonwealth Governments were unwilling to go to war on the issue of Czechoslovakia," a former British Foreign Secretary has written of that period. "Dominion opinion was at the time overwhelmingly against a world war. This opposition was continually in our minds. Time after time we were reminded of it, either by the High Commissioners in London, or by Malcolm Mac-Donald, the Secretary of State for the Dominions. As early as March 18, 1938, we had been told that South Africa and Canada would not join us in a war to prevent certain Germans from rejoining their Fatherland."[62] While "The actual policy Mr. Chamberlain followed in September 1938 owed little or nothing to dominion inspiration,"[63] there can be no doubt that dispiriting responses from the Dominions were used by him to discourage those within the British Cabinet who urged a less cowardly posture in the face of German threats.[64] In Canada's case their effect was the more damaging for their misrepresentation of the real intention of its government. For had war broken out at the time of Munich, the Prime Minister "was prepared to call Parliament within two weeks and submit to it a policy of Canadian participation. . . . The Cabinet was unanimous."[65]

Over half a century ago the French historian André Siegfried had noted the timidity of Canada's political leaders. "They seem . . . ," he wrote, "to stand in fear of great movements of public opinion, and to seek to lull them rather than to encourage them and bring them to political

502

fruition."[66] It will be observed that Canadian political leadership at the time of M. Siegfried's examination was provided by Sir Wilfrid Laurier; and that it was upon Sir Wilfrid Laurier's leadership that Mackenzie King had faithfully modeled his own. "You do Sir Wilfrid Laurier an injustice in regarding him as an opportunist," King had written a friend during the controversy over naval policy in 1909. "He is other than that. . . . We have had no man in Canada who had done as much to reconcile differences of race and creed and to make of the people one nation. If he hesitates to go to the length that some desire, it is because he does not wish disruption and believes that a united progressive Canada is a more valuable asset to the Empire, and will be so through time, than a Canada divided in opinion, or professing an obligation it is not in a position to meet."[67] But hesitation for the sake of unity was not the inevitable response of all Canadian leaders to the tensions of their plural society; there were those to whom its tensions the more insistently demanded bold and imaginative statecraft. "In our Dominion where sections abound," Mr. Arthur Meighen once declared, "a Dominion of races, of classes and of creeds, of many languages and many origins, there are times when no Prime Minister can be true to his trust to the nation he has sworn to serve, save at the temporary sacrifice of the party he is appointed to lead."[68] Faithfully practicing this doctrine, Mr. Meighen was compelled to retire from public life. Mackenzie King's very different concept of political leadership, no less faithfully practiced and resulting in political longevity only once surpassed in the history of the Commonwealth, must face a very different kind of criticism. It "would have been improved," his official biographer has conceded,

503

> had he been more venturesome and more willing to offer forthright advice to the nation. King's tactics enabled him to secure and retain office — the indispensable first step. But King, too frequently, stopped right there; and because he was reluctant to press on and try to realize some independent conception of the national interest, his policies slipped into the mire of pure expediency. King was always reluctant to venture into the unknown. He avoided taking risks, and he would postpone action, if by so doing he could ensure a greater degree of safety. He dreaded unnecessary discussion which might lead to disagreement and even threaten the existing party solidarity on which the whole security of his position rested. He was not prepared to use his own power extensively in an effort to modify the character and scope of those common elements on which he sought to base his policy. He was too willing at times to yield his own judgment when confronted with opposing opinion. He was slow to admit that he had a duty as leader to exert a moderate pressure in the direction in which he believed the country should move.[69]

This verdict is the more severe coming as it does from "one who is in general sympathy with Mr. King and his work and career."[70] There is no part of Mackenzie King's long responsibility for Canadian affairs to which it may with more justice be applied than to his conduct of external policy during that "low dishonest decade" when the world lay "defenceless under the night" and so few free men in power dared to "show an affirming flame."

NOTES

[1] The Bennett Papers have been deposited by Lord Beaverbrook, their owner, at the Library of the University of New Brunswick. The King Papers are in the Public Archives of Canada and became the property of the Crown in 1975. The present writer, having assisted in the preparation of the official biography of W.L. Mackenzie King, has had access to this immense collection; he has permission from Mr. King's Literary Executors to quote from the King correspondence to the end of 1923, the period covered by the published first volume of the official biography.

[2] See K.W. McNaught, "Canadian Foreign Policy and the Whig Interpretation: 1936–1939," Canadian Historical Association, *Report of the Annual Meeting* (1957), 43–54.

[3] It is taken from the poem by W.H. Auden, "September 1, 1939": "As the clever hopes expire/ Of a low dishonest decade."

[4] *The Mist Procession: The Autobiography of Lord Vansittart* (London, 1958), 529.

[5] League of Nations, Official Journal, Special Supplement no. 23, *Records of the Fifth Assembly* (1924), 222. It is interesting that this most celebrated of Canadian utterances on foreign affairs goes unremarked in the unpublished autobiography of Senator Raoul Dandurand, its author.

[6] Canada, *House of Commons Debates* (1938), 3: 3179.

[7] See Colonel C.P. Stacey, *Six Years of War: The Army in Canada, Britain and the Pacific* (Ottawa, 1955), 10.

[8] League of Nations, *Records of the First Assembly* (1920), 379.

[9] Loring C. Christie to Sir Robert Borden, Dec. 12, 1920, Borden Papers (Public Archives of Canada).

[10] Arthur Meighen to N.W. Rowell, Jan. 10, 1921, Rowell Papers (PAC).

[11] Diary of Sir George Foster, entry for April 7, 1919 (PAC).

[12] *The Memoirs of Herbert Hoover: The Cabinet and the Presidency, 1920–1933* (New York, 1951), v.

[13] League of Nations, Official Journal, Special Supplement no. 23, *Records of the Fifth Assembly* (1924), 221.

[14] "Address Delivered by the Right Hon. W.L. Mackenzie King on November 9th, 1928, at a Banquet of the League of Nations Society in Canada" (Ottawa, 1928), 22.

[15] Canada, *H. of C. Debates* (1936), 4: 3862.

[16] League of Nations, *Verbatim Record of the Seventeenth Ordinary Session of the Assembly*, Sept. 29, 1936, p. 1.

[17] Canada, *H. of C. Debates* (1939), 3: 2419.

[18] League of Nations, Official Journal, Special Supplement no. 64, *Records of the Ninth Assembly* (1928), 60.

[19] Mackenzie King to Wallace Nesbitt, Oct. 2, 1922, King Papers.

[20] Sir Clifford Sifton, "Immigration," in *Addresses Delivered before the Canadian Club of Toronto, 1921–2* (Toronto, 1923), 185–86.

[21] Mackenzie King to Aneuran Williams, Feb. 18, 1920, King Papers. A portion of this letter is quoted in R. MacGregor Dawson, *William Lyon Mackenzie King: A Political Biography*, vol. 1, *1874–1923* (Toronto, 1958), 404.

[22] Canada, *H. of C. Debates* (1928), 2: 1960.

[23] T.A. Crerar to J.W Dafoe, April 17, 1937, Dafoe Papers (PAC).

[24] Nicholas Mansergh, *Survey of British Commonwealth Affairs: Problems of External Policy, 1931–1939* (London, 1952), 112.

[25] Canada, *H. of C. Debates* (1919, Special Session), 102, 103.

[26] Loring C. Christie, "Notes on the League of Nations Meeting of March, 1926," April 14,1926, Borden Papers.

[27] Canada, *H. of C. Debates* (1923), 4: 4001.

[28] Sir Clifford Sifton to J.W. Dafoe, Nov. 19, 1920, Dafoe Papers.

[29] Entry for Dec. 11, 1920, Pope Papers (PAC).

[30] Dawson, *William Lyon Mackenzie King*, 1: 403.

[31] W.A. Riddell, *World Security by Conference* (Toronto, 1947), 140.

[32] Grant Dexter to J.W. Dafoe, Dec. 17, 1935, Dafoe Papers.

[33] Canada, *H. of C. Debates* (1936), 1: 97, 98.

504

[34] Quoted in F.H. Soward et al., *Canada in World Affairs: The Pre-War Years* (Toronto, 1941), 23.

[35] Of whose newspaper it was well remarked that "what the *Free Press* thinks today, Western Canada will think tomorrow and the intelligent part of Eastern Canada will think a few years hence." Frank H. Underhill, "J.W. Dafoe," *Canadian Forum* 13 (Oct. 1932): 22.

[36] Quoted in Henri Saint-Denis, "Fascism in Quebec: A False Alarm," *Revue de l'université d'Ottawa* (Jan. 1939), 4. See also "S," "Embryo Fascism in Quebec," *Foreign Affairs* 16 (April 1938): 454–66.

[37] *Le Devoir* (Montreal), July 14, 1938.

[38] Canada, *H. of C. Debates* (1937), 1: 910.

[39] During the Munich crisis in the fall of 1938, Henderson wrote of "Hitler's own love for peace, dislike of dead Germans and hesitation of risking his regime on a gambler's throw." Quoted in Felix Gilbert, "Two British Ambassadors: Perth and Henderson," in Gordon A. Craig and Felix Gilbert, *The Diplomats, 1919–1939* (Princeton, 1953), 543.

[40] Thomas Jones, *A Diary with Letters, 1931–1950* (London, 1954), 218. See also Thomas Jones to Lady Grigg, March 8, 1936, Jones, *A Diary*, 179–81; *The History of 'The Times': The 150th Anniversary and Beyond, 1912–1948*, part 2, *1921–1948* (London, 1952), 938; John Evelyn Wrench, *Geoffrey Dawson and Our Times* (London, 1955), 369.

[41] Canada, *H. of C. Debates* (1944), 6: 6275.

[42] Winston S. Churchill, *The Second World War*, vol. 1, *The Gathering Storm* (London, 1949), 250.

[43] Bruce Hutchison, *The Incredible Canadian* (Toronto, 1953), 226.

[44] Speech given over the National Network of the Canadian Broadcasting Corporation, July 19, 1937.

[45] Frank H. Underhill, "The Close of an Era: Twenty-five Years of Mr. Mackenzie King," *Canadian Forum* 24 (Sept. 1944): 125.

[46] Quoted in Dawson, *William Lyon Mackenzie King*, 1: 474.

[47] Imperial Conference, 1937, *Summary of Proceedings*, pp. 14, 16.

[48] Mansergh, *Survey . . . : Problems of External Policy*, 89.

[49] Canada, *H. of C. Debates* (1938), 3: 3182.

[50] Denis Richards, *Royal Air Force, 1939–1945*, vol. 1, *The Fight at Odds* (London, 1953), 72–73.

[51] *History of the Second World War*, United Kingdom Civil Series, M.M. Postan, *British War Production* (London, 1952), 89.

[52] *History of the Second World War*, United Kingdom Civil Series, J. Hurstfield, *The Control of Raw Materials* (London, 1955), 254.

[53] See *History of the Second World War*, United Kingdom Civil Series, H. Duncan Hall, *North American Supply* (London, 1954).

[54] Nicholas Mansergh, *Survey of British Commonwealth Affairs: Problems of Wartime Co-operation and Post-War Change, 1939–1952* (London, 1958), 17.

[55] Mansergh, *Survey . . . : Problems of External Policy*, 446.

[56] Quoted in Stacey, *Six Years of War*, 14.

[57] Canada, *H. of C. Debates* (1938), 3: 3184.

[58] Canada, *H. of C. Debates* (1939, Special War Session), 1: 25.

[59] Mansergh, *Survey . . . : Problems of External Policy*, 111.

[60] McNaught, "Canadian Foreign Policy," 54 n. 40.

[61] Stacey, *Six Years of War*, 35.

[62] Viscount Templewood, *Nine Troubled Years* (London, 1954), 323.

[63] Mansergh, *Survey . . . : Problems of External Policy*, 439.

[64] See *Old Men Forget: The Autobiography of Duff Cooper* (London, 1954), 239–40.

[65] "Back Stage in Ottawa," *Maclean's Magazine* 2 (Nov. 1, 1938).

[66] André Siegfried, *The Race Question in Canada* (London, 1907), 142.

[67] Mackenzie King to Lord Stanhope, July 23, 1909. Quoted in Dawson, *William Lyon Mackenzie King*, 1: 215.

[68] Arthur Meighen, *Unrevised and Unrepented: Debating Speeches and Others* (Toronto, 1949), 319.

[69] Dawson, *William Lyon Mackenzie King*, 1: 417–18.

[70] Dawson, *William Lyon Mackenzie King*, 1: viii.

Canada and Peacekeeping: Image and Reality*

J.L. GRANATSTEIN

"The art and science" of peacekeeping, John Holmes of the Canadian Institute of International Affairs wrote in 1967, is of special interest to

*From *Canadian Forum* 54, 643 (August 1974). Reprinted by permission of the author.

Canadians "because we have been involved in it more than almost any other country, and it has, in fact, been incorporated into our image of our role in the world."[1] So it was just a few years ago. The proudest boast of Canadian foreign policy was that Canada's servicemen had done duty in each of the United Nations peacekeeping operations and in Indochina on the International Control Commissions. The acronyms of peacekeeping — UNTSO, UNMOGIP, UNEF, ONUC, UNOGIL, UNFICYP, UNTEA, UNYOM, UNIPOM, and ICC — were never part of the public's everyday vocabulary, but the record was popularly considered to be an excellent one, an unselfish one, a record worthy of a nation committed to peace.

Peacekeeping seemed to be the perfect middle-sized responsibility for a middle power in the late 1950's and early 1960's. Canada was tied to the American chariot wheels in the North American Air Defence Command and in the North Atlantic Treaty Organization, to be sure, but peacekeeping at the same time somehow smacked of independence from the United States, of a more-Canadian Canadian foreign policy. Peacekeeping was useful too, something that seemed increasingly difficult to say about NORAD and NATO service. Equally important, peacekeeping did not require nuclear weapons or expensive equipment, nor did it demand large military forces. It was the ideal role for Canada: responsible, useful, inexpensive, and satisfying.

The satisfaction, in particular, was intensive. As John Holmes noted, peacekeeping was part of Canada's world image. All too often Canadians had found themselves regarded as American, when they travelled abroad, but peacekeeping helped to differentiate them. The Americans, after all, with their wild west, shoot first image, their huge military forces, and their world-wide net of bases, advisors, and arms sales had a very different style from peaceful Canadians. Canadians were middlemen, honest brokers, helpful fixers in a world where these qualities were rare. Peacekeeping made us different and somehow better.

Colonel Charles Stacey has argued very convincingly that war shaped the nationalism of Canadians.[2] In the post-war period, peacekeeping bolstered and refined that nationalism. The image of the peacekeeper dominated the Canadian mind from the formation of the United Nations Energy Force and Lester Pearson's subsequent Nobel Peace Prize in 1956 and 1957 until the expulsion of UNEF from Egypt by President Nasser just before the Six Day War in 1967. Today, notwithstanding new forces in Vietnam and in Egypt, the image appears much dimmer if not totally faded.

Was it ever substance? This paper is an attempt to examine the peacekeeping image from emergence to decline. Where did it come from? Who fostered it and accepted it? Why did it dissolve into nothing?

Canada emerged from the Second World War in 1945 as something close to a great power. We had the fourth largest air force, the fifth largest navy, and a well-trained, splendidly equipped army of almost half a million men and women. We had demonstrated our capacity to produce the material of war and to grow food in abundance. We had shown that our society could be mobilized from being a nation of unemployed in 1939 to a society with full employment in 1945, a society that could produce the goods not only for its own people and armies, but also for those of its allies.

The triumph of Canadian achievement in the war effectively squelched the "little Canadianism" of non-internationalism and isolationism that seemingly had dominated Canadian policy in the interwar years. "Parliament will decide" had been the watchword for this era of supposed non-policy, but Parliament never did. The postwar Canada demanded something different and better, and the new men who were responsible for the making of policy were determined to give it to them. The change in attitude was highlighted by the emergence of Louis St. Laurent as Prime Minister in 1948 and of Lester Pearson as his Secretary of State for External Affairs in the same year. These two men were the architects of policy for the postwar era, and the policy would be that of involvement and responsibility.

507

As an idea, involvement was not new in Canada; as policy it was a radical departure. At the turn of the century, imperialists in Canada had demanded that Canada do its bit in helping to maintain the Empire. If Canadians could assume some responsibility in the world, then their nationalism would grow strong. Only by participation could Canada demonstrate that they were prepared for ever greater responsibilities, and if all proceeded according to plan eventually a truly strong Canada would be ready to inherit Britain's world-wide role.

By the time that Canadian nationalism had developed, however, there was no longer any Empire worth inheriting. But the idea of fostering nationalism through service was still alive. Canadians could show the world that they were prepared to do their part. As Lester Pearson said, "we must convince the United States, by action rather than merely by words, that we are, in fact, pulling our weight in this international team."[3] Out of this responsible internationalism would grow a greater pride in Canada and in its place in the world. This attitude seems to have been at the root of the eagerness with which Canadians seized on responsibility after the war. Canadian diplomats had pressed for a strong United Nations, and when the world body by 1948 seemed to be a weak reed, they pressed with equal vigour for the formation of NATO. We met our commitments; we accepted our responsibilities. Canadians did not want power without responsibility — Rudyard Kipling had called that the privilege of the harlot through the ages. They wanted power and responsibility and for a time they had both.

In practice, this internationalism was sometimes little more than co-operation with the United States clothed in multilateral garb. But so long as the threat of Communist aggression seemed real, there was public support for this role. Canada's airmen and soldiers served in Europe and in North America while the navy patrolled the North Atlantic and the Pacific Oceans. Lester Pearson was our spokesman in New York, in Washington, in London, and in Moscow, everywhere the manifold interests of Canadian diplomacy took him. And in the respect and attention accorded Pearson wherever he went, Canadians took pride.

But throughout Canada during the early 1950's there was an undercurrent of grumbling at Canada's apparent willingness to hew to the American line. Already there were signs of concern at the huge amount of American capital invested in Canada, and on the political left the view was taking form that perhaps the simplistic Cold War tale of right and wrong was not the entire story. In this area, as in social policy, the Co-operative Commonwealth Federation was the forerunner. The public was being prepared to accept new initiatives.

The opportunity came with the Suez Crisis in 1956. The crisis marked the high water line of Canadian influence in the world, the last time that Canada could use the accrued prestige and influence with which she had emerged from the Second World War in 1945. Suez sundered the Western alliance, and Britain and France pursued a course diametrically opposite to that advocated by the United States — and Canada. For a few critical weeks, discourse between London–Paris and Washington ceased, and Canada seized the opportunity to become the channel of communication between the old world and the new. The linch-pin, the bridge, the interpreter — the hoary clichés suddenly came true. It would never happen again.

Under Pearson's leadership Canada suddenly found itself promising to serve on a major United Nations force in the Middle East, a force that Pearson himself suggested and in a few days of inspired work with Dag Hammarskjold, the UN Secretary-General, largely created. It was a triumph on two fronts at once, and the Canadian reputation was high indeed. And when Pearson was awarded the Nobel Prize for Peace in 1957 this put the cap on Canada's newly minted image of itself.

Suddenly the locus of action for Canada had shifted back to the United Nations. Canada had been involved in sending peacekeepers to Palestine after 1948, to the India–Pakistan borders, and to Indochina in 1954, but there had been no public or official enthusiasm for these chores. After Suez, however, the enthusiasm was very strong, even among the Tory press and public that had felt qualms at Ottawa's reaction to the Anglo-French invasion of Egypt.

Surprisingly, the public satisfaction at Canada's new-found role survived Egypt's reluctance to accept Canadian troops as part of the United Nations Emergency Force. The uniforms worn by the Canadians were too similar to those of the invaders, the Egyptian spokesmen argued, and the unfortunate name of the regiment chosen for Sinai service — the Queen's Own Rifles of Canada — added to the potential confusion.

Moreover, Canada was a Commonwealth partner of Britain, a NATO ally of Britain and France, and Canadian Jews were strong in their support of Israel. Those were all valid complaints, and the Egyptians were by no means wrong to object.

The upshot was that Canadian infantry did not go to Suez after all. What Canada did supply to UNEF was service and transport troops, aircraft and pilots, and an armoured reconnaissance squadron. Canada had the technical expertise and equipment of a nation with overseas defence commitments, and there were no other states acceptable to the Egyptians that did. Egypt did not want Canadians, but if UNEF was to function it had to accept them.

These vicissitudes notwithstanding, UNEF was still a Canadian triumph. And so strong was the reaction in Canada to this success that even when the government changed in 1957 there was no apparent alteration in Canada's new-found delight with peacekeeping. John Diefenbaker and many of his colleagues in the Conservative front bench had criticized the Liberals for letting down Britain in 1956, but few had criticized peacekeeping itself. When in 1958 another crisis erupted in the Middle East, therefore, the Conservatives were quick off the mark in sending a large contingent of observers to serve with the United Nations Observer Group in Lebanon. The public response was again strong and even newspapers that had bitterly criticized Canada's part in 1956 demonstrated a changed attitude.

509

The public's desire that Canada should serve the United Nations was so strong indeed that it could force the government's hand. This became clear in 1960 when the Congo won its independence and almost immediately sank into chaos. The UN decided to intervene with a new peacekeeping force to preserve order, and Canada was invited to contribute signallers and pilots. For the Diefenbaker government, well launched into its own time of troubles, the Congo was the wrong crisis at the wrong time. The country was hard hit by unemployment and budgetary problems, and there were in addition very few signalmen free in the army. The government stalled. But the press soon began to ask "Why is Canada not represented?" The *Ottawa Journal*, a good Tory newspaper, demanded a "most imaginative and wide-visioned and generous consideration" of UN requests. And even after the government caved in and agreed to send the men in a month, the Vancouver *Province* pointed out sharply that Ireland and Sweden had had their men underway in 48 hours.[4]

The response of press and Parliament had been quite extraordinary. The Congo was certainly not an area to which Canada had historic ties; there was no aggression involved; and until a few months after the UN decision there were not even any Communists suspected of trying to usurp the government. None of the usual triggers for public response were there. Except that Canadians clearly expected that their government would be eager and willing to assist the United Nations with any new peacekeeping forces. Peacekeeping was the Canadian role, and the Canadian people demanded the right to play it. The national self-image required it.

Small numbers of servicemen went abroad again in 1962 to West Irian and in 1963 to the Yemen. Both of these operations were small but relatively successful, and neither did anything to harm the growing conviction that peacekeeping was the proper policy. Nor did the Cyprus operation of 1964. The UN Force in Cyprus was largely the creation of Paul Martin, Secretary of State for External Affairs in the Pearson government that had taken office in 1963. Martin had wheeled and dealed and successfully interposed a UN presence, for a time largely Canadian, between Greek- and Turkish-Cypriots. In the process he headed off a threatening war between Greece and Turkey and earned substantial American gratitude.

510   Cyprus was the last peacekeeping victory. In May, 1967, President Nasser expelled UNEF from Egypt and set in train the events that precipitated Israel's blitzkrieg invasion and conquest of the Sinai. Most important for Canadian opinion, Nasser singled out the Canadian component of UNEF and demanded immediate departure. Public reaction was stunned. "Peacekeeping has become the foundation on which much

Canadian Forces Photo / WO Vic Johnson   (ISC 84–358).

Canadian soldiers of the United Nations peacekeeping force in Cyprus patrol along the "Green Line" in Nicosia.

of Canada's foreign and defence policy is built," the Montreal *Gazette* said. "If the foundation is undermined . . . the superstructure built on that foundation will not last very long." The *Toronto Star* wondered: "Can UN peacekeeping survive the Sinai Crisis?" And as the *Canadian Annual Review* for 1967 noted, "It is not an exaggeration to say that the Canadian press was as concerned, if not more so, with the effect the UNEF withdrawal would have on one of the main 'cornerstones' of Canadian foreign policy than it was with the possible catastrophes that might befall both Jew and Arab in the region."[5]

The cornerstone had crumbled, and the Canadian government was forced to recognize this. Peacekeeping had held a very high priority through the 1960's and had been cited as one of the justifications for imposing unification on the armed forces after 1964. But after the Six Day War, peacekeeping was relegated further down the list of priorities. The new stress for the military would be to defend Canadian sovereignty and to maintain order in the streets of the big cities. The internationalism of 1948 and the idealism of 1956 had been superseded by the neo-isolationism of 1968. The concept of nationalism through international responsibility that had motivated the foreign policy of St. Laurent and Pearson had been replaced by a foreign and defence policy of unabashed self-interest.

511

Peacekeeping at no time was a very important military role for the country. At most perhaps 2200 servicemen were employed at any one time on UN operations, and while this was not an inconsiderable number or a minor expense, the commitment probably did not warrant the barrage of publicity or the weight of prestige that became attached to it. More men supported NORAD in Canada and the United States. More troops were stationed in Europe with NATO. More were on anti-submarine patrols off the coasts. Peacekeeping was only a minor role performed by the military forces of a minor power.

Of course it did not seem so from 1956 to 1967.

Peacekeeping fostered the Canadian sense of self-importance. What could be more important than to be the mediator between Britain and the United States in 1956? What could be more important than to restore order in the Congo in 1960? What could be more vital to the West than to help prevent war between Greece and Turkey, ostensible NATO allies, in 1956? What could be more important than to keep the peace?

The questions were the right ones, but the answers did not demand Canadian participation. Few Canadians ever realized that peacekeeping, in most instances, would have been impossible without the direct logistical support of the United States. American aircraft, for example, had to be used to fly the Canadians' signal equipment to the Congo in 1960. American supplies were needed to get UNEF started in 1956. And Britain, though no longer a great power, provided most of the back-up support for the Cyprus force in 1964. Peacekeeping was not as independent as it seemed.

Moreover, on at least one occasion Canada was put onto an observer force precisely because she was attached to the Western alliance. In 1954 when the International Control Commissions were established in Indochina, Canada was the Western delegate, India the neutral, and Poland the Communist nominee. The same kind of reasoning held true in 1973 when new international commissions were established in Viet Nam.

Canadians similarly failed to grasp the fact that peacekeeping was fundamentally a political act that would have been impossible without support in the UN Security Council or in the General Assembly. Political consensus, not Canadian participation, was the *sine qua non* of peacekeeping. The great powers had to agree to establish a force, or at the least not to oppose it, before peacekeeping could start. The nations in the area of the proposed intervention had to be receptive. The politics of the situation had to be right. In other words, Canada's role, however creditable, was usually a minor one and one that was mainly confined to the military side of the operation. Suez 1956 is the exception that proves the rule.

This should not be surprising because after 1956 Canada's power relative to the rest of the world was in decline. Europe had re-built itself and Japan was becoming a giant industrial power. The United Nations was in the process of tripling in size. Power had returned where it belonged, and Canada once again was simply a country with large territory and few people. The world had changed and Canada could not keep up. There was no way in which it could have been different.

Pearson's triumph in 1956 then has to be seen as the last hurrah of the golden age of Canadian diplomacy rather than as the beginning of a new era of influence. As such, it acquired a mythology of its own, and the accession of Pearson to the leadership of the Liberal Party in 1958 ensured that this would be so. The managers of Canadian Liberalism traded on Pearson's world repute as a marketable asset that could be used to restore the fortunes of the party. For a time in fact Pearson's reputation seemed to be the only asset on which the party could draw. To his great credit Pearson tried very hard to live up to the things that were said about him. After he became Prime Minister in 1963, be supported peacekeeping as much as possible. His speech in Philadelphia denouncing the United States for its bombing in Viet Nam was a courageous act, and one that fit well within the image of Pearson as peacekeeper pre-eminent. Peacekeeping was a satisfactory role for Pearson, one can surmise, because it was inherently useful, because it had good public relations value in Canada and abroad, and because it struck a responsive chord in Pearson's and the national soul.

Peacekeeping indeed should be viewed as analogous to the missionary impulse that was so much a part of Canada before the 1939 war. Almost every church in both England and French Canada helped to support a missionary family or an order of nuns somewhere in Latin America, Asia, or Africa. Regularly the letters home would tell of the joys and hardships of bringing Christianity and God's peace to the unenlightened. The missionary impulse to service abroad was enormously strong and genuine, and nowhere did it live on in deeper form than among the officers in the Department of External Affairs. Sometimes it seemed as if every post had at least one or two sons of missionaries on staff. The Department sprang full blown from the church and its outposts.

While Pearson was not the son of missionaries, he was the child of the manse. As a boy he travelled around Ontario with his parents, moving from parish to parish, and exposed to the nascent social gospel idealism that characterized Canadian Methodism at the time. Who can doubt the strength of this upbringing in shaping the statesman? in shaping the course and character of Canadian policy?

So much of it bears this stamp. One can readily argue that Canadian foreign policy has been characterized by a mixture of idealism and realism. It was idealistic to want to bring peace to a divided world, but eminently realistic to offer to serve in the troubled parts of the globe. This is uplift, of course, but committed uplift. It resembles nothing so much as J.S. Woodsworth establishing his All Peoples' Mission among the immigrant poor of North Winnipeg. It smacks not at all of the antiseptic and businesslike Christianity of Toronto's Timothy Eaton Memorial church.

513

If uplift had its roots in the Canadian past, so too did a passion for order. Canada was a land of peace, order, and good government. There was change, but always conservative and orderly change. There was no political violence, no real radicalism. This was never true, of course, but it was what Canadians were taught and what they seemed to believe. And peacekeeping fit right into this image. Had Sir John A. Macdonald not despatched a few red-coated Mounties to the untamed West? And had these strong men not imposed order on the land? Law and order was the Canadian way. If Canadians could help the United Nations in transferring this image to the world outside our borders, that would be a worthy goal. Peacekeeping was Canada's attempt to do this, but it failed.

The failure was not Canada's. The United Nations failed in its task of bringing the powers together. Peacekeeping was something that almost every nation could accept because it bought time, because it froze situations, and because it created a breathing space for negotiation. Unfortunately, all too often the negotiations never took place or got nowhere. Peacemaking almost never followed peacekeeping. The result was a decay in world morale, a lessening of faith in the UN. The disillusion was felt in Canada, too. Suez 1956 had stirred hope but Suez 1967 destroyed it. Suddenly Canadians began to question why peace had not followed peacekeeping. Suddenly they began to wonder why their troops should ever have been exposed to difficulty, hardship, and danger in a thankless desert. The sense of futility was very sharp.

Nowhere was this more pronounced than among the Canadian military, for the very instruments of Canadian peacekeeping had never been sympathetic to the idea. The generals had never liked UN service and the political emphasis it received in Canada. To train for the UN's duties was to take time away from the important task of preparing to fight the Russians. For the rank and file, peacekeeping was simply boring, a dull duty away from home among people whose culture was too different to enjoy. The job was done and done well but it was never liked. And the dislike increased among all ranks when Paul Hellyer, the Minister of National Defence in the Pearson administration, imposed unification on the reluctant three services, in part because it facilitated peacekeeping. If peacekeeping implied unification then the military wanted none of it.

514

The military's reaction was not entirely unfounded. Peacekeeping probably should have been recognized for what it was, a temporary expedient that met the needs of a period, not as a long-term reality upon which equipment and force structure could be based. Possibly the instinctive military response was more correct than the politicians', although for the wrong reasons. To be lukewarm about peacekeeping because it clashed with the military's idea of Cold War imperatives was wrong; to oppose peacekeeping as an international fad might not have been.

Significantly, perhaps, the fad of peacekeeping had caught on least among French Canadians, traditionally the segment of the population most suspicious of foreign commitments. Part of the problem for Quebec was that it could not identify with the armed forces, for like other elements of Canadian society before 1968 they were grotesquely imbalanced in linguistic composition. Few officers at any level were French-speaking, and only among the most junior ranks was there anything approaching the national percentages of English- and French-speaking citizens. There was little in the armed forces to which *Québécois* could identify, for the military, like Confederation itself, was flawed.

This does not mean that Quebec was opposed to peacekeeping for the United Nations. It was not. But although the evidence of opinion sampling is perhaps questionable, there seems to be enough evidence to support the generalization that French Canadians were markedly less enthusiastic than their English-speaking compatriots in supporting the sending of troops abroad for any purpose. Significantly, only the Suez Crisis, 1956, stirred any genuine enthusiasm in Quebec. At best, the national consensus for peacekeeping was a fragile one; at worst, it was only an English-Canadian consensus.

Another final factor needs to be mentioned. By the time Pierre Trudeau arrived on the stage as Prime Minister in 1968, domestic peace and order had begun to break down. Bombings had first occurred in Quebec early in the 1960's, and the sense of impending violence had developed ever since. The riot in Montreal just before the 1968 general election was a sign, as was the intervention of troops to maintain order in Montreal when the police went on strike in 1969. The significant shock of course, was the kidnapping of James Cross, the British Trade Commissioner, and Pierre Laporte, the Quebec Minister of Labour, in the fall of 1970. The federal government's imposition of the War Measures Act just before Laporte's corpse was discovered resulted in the despatch of 10,000 troops to Montreal and Ottawa. The idea of Canada as an ordered, conservative society had been severely shaken.

For the government the lesson of October, 1970, seemed to be that the barrel of available, reliable military force had been scraped. Just enough troops for the task had been available. If more had been necessary, Ottawa might have been forced to bring the boys home from NATO duty or from Cyprus peacekeeping. The lesson was clear enough, and already discredited peacekeeping abroad was replaced by the necessity for peacekeeping at home. At National Defence Headquarters, aid to the civil power was priority number one.

So pronounced was this shift that when in 1972 it first seemed likely that Canadians would be called on to serve in a new International Control Commission in Viet Nam, there was a marked disinclination in Ottawa, in the press, and so far as one can tell among the public, to take on any such task. American pressure presumably became intense, and the government apparently felt itself obliged to yield. A wide-ranging series of conditions were laid down, however, and the public response, while somewhat mollified, still seemed to be that no conditions went far enough if they permitted any Canadians to go to Viet Nam. Certainly when the Canadians withdrew from the ICC at the end of July, 1973, 84 per cent of those questioned by the Canadian Institute of Public Opinion approved. The times had changed. In 1960 the public had forced the government to send troops to the Congo. In 1972–1973, if the public had had its way no troops would have gone to Viet Nam. Nor after the fourth Arab–Israeli War was there any evident public support for Canadian participation in a new UN force. Mitchell Sharp was initially wary in his comments in mid-October, but within a week or less he and his officials in New York and Washington were preaching for a call yet again. Just why is still unclear, but as the *Globe and Mail* noted,

> The desultory applause and comments in the House of Commons when External Affairs Minister Sharp made the announcement that Canadians would return to Suez are indicative enough that Cana-

515

dians are skeptical about the whole idea of international peacekeep-ing. . . . [6]

Presumably Canadians now recognized that peacekeeping was just a dirty thankless job.

As an exportable and Canadian-designed commodity, then, peacekeep-ing had gone off the market almost completely, barely fifteen years after its introduction. But the concept had been useful to the United Nations and the world, if only because a frozen crisis was less dangerous than an uncontrolled one. For Canadians, too, peacekeeping had served a pur-pose, even if that was only to provide symbols and images for a nation that needed them.

NOTES

This article was prepared before the Cyprus crisis of July [1974] but the initial public response seems to support the conclusions expressed here.

[1] Preface to Alistair Taylor et al., *Peacekeeping: International Challenge and Canadian Response* (Toronto, 1968), n.p.

[2] C.P. Stacey, "Nationality: The Experience of Canada," Canadian Historical Association, *Historical Papers* (1967).

[3] See Lester B. Pearson, *Words and Occasions* (Cambridge, Mass., 1970), 106.

[4] Toronto, *Globe and Mail*, July 20, 1960.

[5] Montreal *Gazette*, May 19, 1967; *Toronto Star*, May 24, 1967; John Saywell, ed., *The Canadian Annual Review for 1967* (Toronto, 1968), 230–31.

[6] *Globe and Mail*, October 31, 1973.

Topic Fourteen

Quebec/Canada

In the early 1960s the Quebec government began to take an active interventionist role in the province's economic, social, and cultural affairs. The hydroelectric industry was nationalized, the educational system restructured and brought under government control, the civil service reformed and broadened, and a new labour code instituted. These changes have been called Quebec's "Quiet Revolution," as they mark such a dramatic departure from its previous policies.

A new bureaucratic middle class arose to direct social and economic development. In addition, a French Canadian nationalism, identified with Quebec rather than Canada, gained strength. At the same time another group of liberal-minded French Canadians still looked to Ottawa for a renewed Canadian federalism as Quebec's answer. Michael Behiels presents the two opposing ideologies in his article "Quebec: Social Transformation and Ideological Renewal, 1940–1976."

Throughout the 1960s and 1970s all major Quebec provincial political parties sought to strengthen Quebec's position in its relations with the federal government. A vocal and popular-based party, the Parti Québécois, arose in the late 1960s under René Lévesque, the former minister of national resources in the Quebec Liberal government of Jean Lesage. Lévesque and his party favoured Quebec separatism through a peaceful and democratic process. In 1976, the party won its first electoral victory, after a campaign fought on the promise that it would negotiate a form of "sovereignty-association" with the rest of Canada. The Lévesque government held a plebiscite on the issue of sovereignty-association in May 1980. In "Maybe Yes, or Maybe No," Robert Boily explains what happened on that historic night in Quebec, and the meaning of the vote for the province.

For overviews of Quebec in the last half century, see Kenneth McRoberts, *Quebec: Social Change and Political Crisis*, 3rd ed. (Toronto: McClelland and Stewart, 1988); Susan Mann Trofimenkoff, *The Dream of Nation: A Social and Intellectual History of Quebec* (Toronto: Gage, 1982), ch. 17–20; and Paul-André Linteau, René Durocher, Jean-Claude Robert, and François Ricard, *Histoire du Québec contemporain*, vol. 2, *Le Québec depuis 1930* (Montreal: Boréal, 1986). *Quebec since 1945: Selected Readings*, ed. M. Behiels (Toronto: Copp Clark, 1987) contains useful articles and documents.

On the Duplessis era, see Conrad Black, *Duplessis* (Toronto: McClelland and Stewart, 1977) and Richard Jones' brief overview in *Duplessis and the Union Nationale Administration*, Canadian Historical Association, Historical Booklet no. 25 (Ottawa: CHA, 1983). The opposition to Premier Maurice Duplessis in the late 1940s and 1950s is analysed in M. Behiels, *Prelude to Quebec's Quiet Revolution: Liberalism versus Neo-Nationalism, 1945-1960* (Montreal and Kingston: McGill-Queen's University Press, 1985).

For an overview of the Quiet Revolution, see Dale C. Thomson, *Jean Lesage and the Quiet Revolution* (Toronto: Macmillan, 1984) and articles by Ramsay Cook in his collection *Canada, Quebec, and the Uses of Nationalism* (Toronto: McClelland and Stewart, 1986). On the Parti Québécois, see Graham Fraser, *PQ: Rene Lévesque and the Parti Québécois in Power* (Toronto: Macmillan, 1985). Peter Desbarats' *René* (Toronto: McClelland and Stewart, 1976) reviews the life of the founder of the Parti Québécois. See also Lévesque's *Memoirs* (Toronto: McClelland and Stewart, 1986). On Pierre Elliott Trudeau, see Richard Gwyn, *The Northern Magus* (Toronto: McClelland and Stewart, 1980) and George Radwanski, *Trudeau* (Toronto: Macmillan, 1978). The October Crisis of 1970 is discussed in Francis Simard, *Talking It Out: The October Crisis from Inside*, translated by David Homel (Montreal: Guernica, 1987). The views of sociologist Hubert Guindon, a leading analyst of modern Quebec politics and society, appear in *Tradition, Modernity, and Nationhood: Essays on Quebec Society* (Toronto: University of Toronto Press, 1988).

Edward McWhinney analyses the constitutional crisis in *Quebec and the Constitution, 1960-1978* (Toronto: University of Toronto Press, 1979) and in his *Canada and the Constitution, 1979-1982: Patriation and the Charter of Rights* (Toronto: University of Toronto Press, 1982). The aftermath of the Quebec referendum and the patriation of the BNA Act are discussed in *And No One Cheered: Federalism, Democracy and the Constitutional Act*, ed. Keith Banting and Richard Simeon (Toronto: Methuen, 1983).

518

Quebec: Social Transformation and Ideological Renewal, 1940–1976*

MICHAEL D. BEHIELS

Despite the steady migration of rural French Canadians to the towns and cities of Quebec, New England, and Ontario since the 1870's, the myth of French Canada being an agrarian society remained prevalent

*From *Modern Canada, 1930-1980's*, ed. Michael S. Cross and Gregory S. Kealy. Used by permission of the Canadian Publishers, McClelland and Stewart, Toronto.

until World War II. Many outside observers retained the outmoded impression of a pleasantly quaint and stable community steeped in the values of Catholicism and a rural life cycle that had remained in their essentials unchanged for over two centuries. Few could foresee the fundamental changes this society would experience as a result of a new round of industrialization and urbanization initiated by the war and prolonged by post-war economic expansion. The emergence of the social welfare state in Ottawa, coupled with the creation of a consumer-oriented society, was to have profound social, economic, ideological, and political implications for all classes of the French-Canadian society, in particular the established clerical and secular elites.

Just what were the major socio-economic changes experienced by the Francophone society of Quebec in the three decades following the outbreak of the war in 1939? These changes will be examined along with the critical responses of a growing number of individuals, groups, and associations. In the first stage these individuals and groups articulated a critique of the prevalent ideology of conservative, clerical nationalism. They then proceeded to propose alternate ideologies based on welfare-state liberalism, social democracy, and eventually, democratic socialism. The Francophone intelligentsia was to become increasingly divided on the question of whether or not their respective liberal, social democratic, or socialist visions of society should be structured according to neo-nationalist imperatives, that is, oriented primarily toward the development of a dynamic and powerful Québécois nation-state. The neo-nationalists were divided over whether or not the achievement of their nationalist-imbued objectives could be attained within a renewed Canadian federal system or via the acquisition of full political independence.

519

Demographic, Economic, and Social Transformation

Since 1940 Quebec has experienced social change on an unprecedented scale. In the mid-1950's this upheaval prompted the director of *Le Devoir*, Gérard Filion, to remark that the province of Quebec was undergoing a degree of socio-economic change unparallelled in any other Western industrialized country.[1] A great deal of the pressure for change was prompted by a considerable increase in Quebec's population. Most of the growth was due to natural increase but this was supplemented by the influx of immigrants in the post-war years. Furthermore, immigration to the United States had remained difficult for most Quebecers, thereby forcing them to seek employment at home or in other parts of Canada. As a result of this pattern, Quebec witnessed a 22-per-cent increase in its population in the 1940's, a 30-per-cent increase in the 1950's, and another 15 per cent in the 1960's. In 1971 over 6 million people lived in "la belle Province" compared with 3.3 million three decades earlier.[2]

The renewal of industrial and urban expansion brought about a precipitous decline of agriculture both as an economic activity and as a way of life for what remained of the rural society. Widespread rural depopulation, caused by a sharp decline in agricultural commodity prices, became one of the dominant features of post-war Quebec. Not only were one out of every two sons leaving the ancestral home as in the past, but entire families were abandoning farming in pursuit of employment in the factories in and around metropolitan Montreal or in the towns associated with such resource industries as mining and pulp and paper. Within a generation the number of French Canadians on farms declined from 1.1 million to 285,000, that is, from 41 per cent of the Francophone community in 1941 to 6 per cent in 1971. The number of French Canadians living in urban centres rose from 1.5 million in 1941 to over 3.7 million or 78 per cent of the Francophone population by 1971. Metropolitan Montreal, with 40 per cent of Quebec's population by 1961, dominated the economic and cultural life of the province. Montreal became the new home for two-thirds of those French Canadians leaving their farms as well as for virtually all the post-war immigrants. Because Montreal's Anglo-Scottish financial, commercial, and industrial elite dominated the Canadian and Quebec economies, the language of work and, to a degree, social intercourse inevitably was English. It was just as predictable perhaps that Montreal, the point of contact between Francophone and Anglophone communities, would emerge as the centre of contemporary French-Canadian neo-nationalism in the 1950's.[3]

Quebec was able to absorb the vast majority of its native-born sons and daughters as well as thousands of immigrants largely because of the rapid growth in the provincial economy. Between 1946 and 1956 the gross provincial product grew by 45 per cent in constant dollars. The traditional manufacturing sectors, such as food, textiles, clothing, tobacco, rubber, leather, and wood, all increased their production. But the newly created or expanded high-technology and capital-intensive industries, such as non-ferrous metals, non-metallic minerals, iron, transportation, electrical appliances, and chemical and petrochemical products, experienced the strongest growth in production and employment. Quebec entered the 1950's with a bullish and diversified economy.[4] The vibrant domestic and American demand for Quebec's mineral resources and forest products and relatively cheap hydroelectricity spurred the rapid development of these resources. The spin-offs for the industrial and service sectors were tremendous.

One of the most significant social aspects of the expansion and diversification of Quebec's economy has been the dramatic shift in employment from the primary sector to the tertiary or service sector. The dramatic decline of agriculture and the ever-increasing mechanization of the resource sector explain the drop in proportion of employment in the primary sector from 32.4 per cent in 1941 to 7.5 per cent in 1971.

Employment in the manufacturing sector grew only slightly in this period, but the proportion of Quebecers employed in the service sector — utilities, transportation, public services, commerce, and professions — rose from 41 per cent to 62.9 per cent of the labour force.

This shift to jobs in some cases requiring a higher degree of education, and therefore providing higher economic remuneration, has not been as extensive for French Canadians as for Quebec's other ethnic groups. While French Canadians are now slightly overrepresented in manufacturing jobs and have made significant gains in the clerical and sales category, in 1971 they remained significantly underrepresented in managerial and administrative positions.[5] Because the growth in prosperity has not been distributed very evenly, with managerial, administrative, and highly skilled unionized employees reaping the highest rewards, French Canadians as a collectivity were found by the Royal Commission on Bilingualism and Biculturalism to rank near the bottom of the income scale in 1961.[6] This situation has improved to some extent during the past two decades.[7] Nevertheless, the growing awareness of this ethnic cleavage during the 1950's and 1960's undermined the perception of growing class distinctions in contemporary Quebec. More importantly, this ethnic cleavage contributed to the re-emergence of strong neo-nationalist sentiments among well-educated, middle-class French Canadians whose aspirations for upward mobility were being thwarted.

521

Perhaps the most significant ideological and political development emanating from this rapid process of socio-economic change was the emergence of an expanded and diversified middle class in French Canada. The traditional French-Canadian professional petty bourgeoisie of doctors, lawyers, notaries, journalists, clerics, and small entrepreneurial businessmen was expanded to incorporate social scientists, scientists, engineers, technicians, and private and public managers and administrators. This was due in large measure to the partial modernization of French Canada's educational institutions.[8]

Deeply concerned with the serious problems facing the French-Canadian *petite et moyenne bourgeoisies* in competing with the Anglo-Canadian and American financiers and industrialists, the Liberal government of Lomer Gouin created in 1907 the *Ecoles des hautes études commerciales* in Montreal as well as encouraged the expansion of several commercial academies at the secondary level. Nearly half of the Francophone economic elite by the 1940's had been educated in these or similar institutions in order to maintain and hopefully extend their role in the development of the Quebec economy. Concerns with overcrowding and serious competition from other ethnic groups prompted the Francophone professional petty bourgeoisie to advocate the creation of faculties of science at Laval and the Université de Montréal in the 1920's.[9] Similar concerns, coupled with the emergence of a liberal interpretation of Catholic social doctrine and social action, led to the creation of faculties of social science at both Francophone universities in the 1930's and 1940's.[10] Hampered by the unwillingness and, often, the inability of classical college graduates to pursue careers in these new faculties, as well as by the non-existence of a Francophone public secondary system providing its successful graduates with automatic access to university faculties, the growth of the new faculties of pure and applied sciences was slow and the social sciences even slower.

This situation changed dramatically during and after World War II. By the academic year 1952–53, the number of Laval and Montréal students enrolled in the faculties of science and commerce was almost on par with those enrolled in medicine, law, and dentistry. Furthermore, nearly 40 per cent of these students did not have a classical college degree but had been recruited from the *écoles primaire supérieur* or the commercial academies.[11] As a result of this expansion considerable numbers of graduates from these non-traditional faculties were on the job market by the 1950's. Most of them faced two difficult choices. French-Canadian scientists, engineers, and business managers had to seek employment primarily in the private sector, which was largely dominated by Anglo-Canadian and American companies. These French Canadians found the competition with Anglophones particularly tough, and when they were hired it was usually "in sales, public relations, and personnel work rather than in production and general administration."[12] French-Canadian social scientists, administrators, and educators sought employment in the health, social welfare, and educational institutions, but this meant they had to work under the direction of religious personnel since the Catholic church owned and operated the vast majority of these institutions. Indeed, this process of co-opting members of French Canada's new middle class strengthened momentarily the position of the traditional political and clerical elites.[13]

With the arrival in 1960 of the Liberal Party led by Jean Lesage and the beginning of the process of political modernization, this new middle class became the most vociferous advocate of the ideology of neo-nationalism. It would use effectively a rejuvenated and modernized Quebec state to wrestle control from the Catholic church over all health, social welfare, and educational institutions, as well as to begin to challenge the Anglophone elite's control over Quebec's economy.[14]

Ideological Renewal

Quebec's "quiet revolution" originated during the depression, gained momentum in the 1940's and 1950's, and eventually found political expression in the 1960's and 1970's. In retrospect, it was primarily an ideological revolution. It was initiated by a renewed and reinvigorated Francophone intelligentsia intent on instituting a social revolution that would install it as the dominant ruling class in contemporary Quebec. Prior to 1940, ideological pluralism existed in Quebec, but the Francophone intelligentsia was committed pretty exclusively to the ideology of traditional French-Canadian nationalism. With the exception of a small handful of outspoken individuals, such as the journalist Jean-Charles Harvey and Senator T.D. Bouchard, economic and social liberalism did not find favour with French Canada's clerical or professional petty-bourgeois elites. Liberalism found a forum only in the ranks of international unions, the commercial and industrial *petite et moyenne bourgeoisies*, and the Quebec Liberal Party of Premier Alexandre Taschereau.[15]

During the 1940's and 1950's the Francophone intelligentsia became quite diversified, thereby ending its long-standing monolithic outlook. This occurred in the face of a Catholic church intent on preserving the only rural and Catholic nationality in North America as well as in the climate of the socially regressive political regime of Maurice Duplessis. His Union Nationale administration, while co-operating with the traditional clerical and petty-bourgeois elites, encouraged the rapid exploitation of Quebec's natural resources by American capital for American needs. Neither Duplessis nor his clerical and secular supporters showed much insight into or sympathy for the problems of the burgeoning proletariat created by the economic boom.

523

CITÉ LIBRE LIBERALISM

Since the late 1930's the Francophone Catholic labour movement of Quebec, faced with the threat of being undermined by the American industrial unions, became increasingly militant and aggressive in its demands and collective bargaining tactics. This process culminated in the famous 1949 Asbestos Strike. In the aftermath of this turbulent strike during which over 5,000 French-Canadian workers courageously defied an anti-labour coalition of the Duplessis government and American mining interests, a young, dynamic group of Francophone liberals, social democrats, and democratic socialists came together in June 1950 to found a new periodical entitled appropriately *Cité libre* or "open society." Co-edited by Pierre Elliott Trudeau and Gérard Pelletier, *Cité libre* served as a focal point for labour advisers and militants, such as Charles Lussier, Réginald Boisvert, and Pierre Vadeboncoeur, and such literary critics and journalists as Maurice Blain, Guy Cormier, and Jean Le Moyne, as well as a number of social scientists, namely Marcel Rioux, Fernand Dumont, Jean-Charles Falardeau, and Léon Dion. *Citélibristes*, as they came to be called, undertook a wide-ranging, in-depth analysis of Quebec's socio-economic and political institutions and of the ideology of traditional French-Canadian nationalism they saw being used by the established clerical and professional petty-bourgeois intelligentsia to retain its control over the Francophone society. *Citélibristes* were ardent French

Canadians and practising Catholics who wanted to modernize and democratize Quebec's Francophone and Catholic institutions at all levels and in all areas of activity.

The first prominent institution to be challenged by *Cité libre* was the Catholic church in Quebec. Many of *Cité libre*'s members had participated actively in the anti-nationalist and social-oriented Catholic action movements established in Quebec during the 1930's. Most members had also absorbed the "liberating" and inspiring personalist philosophy of France's left-wing Catholicism as articulated by Jacques Maritain, author of *Humanisme intégrale*, and Emmanuel Mounier, editor of *Esprit*.[16]

As a result of these influences and their own experience with growing up in Catholic institutions, *Citélibristes* called for three reforms. First, the church had to democratize its internal operations by allowing lay participation in its councils. This step would help rid it of its excessive authoritarianism, dogmatism, and social conservatism.[17] Second, there had to be a separation of church and state. The administrative clericalism that stemmed from the church's control over health, social welfare, and educational institutions threatened to compromise severely the church's spiritual mission. Only a complete separation of church and state in these areas would enable the French-Canadian society to modernize and expand these essential services without jeopardizing the Catholic church's autonomy and its spiritual role.[18] This reform would also undermine the more insidious form of social clericalism whereby church officials and priests used the power and the influence they garnered in the spiritual realm to impose their views on social and political issues. The church, *Citélibristes* contended, had no right to determine the nature and extent of social and political debate in Quebec society. French Canada was no longer a "sacralized" society. It had become a secular society in which the relationships between human beings were considered just as important as those between an individual and his Creator. For democracy and pluralism to flourish in Quebec, French Canadians had to realize that they, not some distant providential power, were responsible for the development of the temporal City.[19] Third, the Catholic church in Quebec had to end its long-standing practice of censuring public debate on important secular issues, such as education and political morality. It must also end its historic intolerance of other religious groups and allow French Canadians freedom of choice. Freedom of thought and expression coupled with an acceptance of religious pluralism were essential if the French-Canadian society were to become genuinely open, pluralistic, and democratic.[20]

The second major impediment to the political and social modernization of Quebec was the prevalence of the ideology of traditional French-Canadian nationalism. "What had nationalism and the nationalists given Quebec?" was the rhetorical question posed by Trudeau in his celebrated introduction to a monograph on the Asbestos Strike. By the 1950's French

Canadians faced an anti-social, anti-democratic, anti-labour, and excessively pro-capitalist regime. Premier Maurice Duplessis spoke the rhetoric of traditional French-Canadian nationalism and never failed to denounce the federal government for its "centralist" social welfare policies. Yet in the same breath Duplessis would deny the need to reform Quebec's anachronistic health, social welfare, and educational institutions on the grounds that they were uniquely French and Catholic. He would then go on to extol the virtues of selling off Quebec's natural resources at ridiculously low prices without thinking that this policy might well be against the best interests of French Canadians.[21]

Trudeau and several of his colleagues, Blain, Vadeboncoeur, Dumont, and Rioux, advanced the thesis that an ever-growing credibility gap had developed between the realities of modern French Canada and the dominant clerical and petty-bourgeois vision of nationalism that had prevailed since the mid-nineteenth century. Traditional French-Canadian nationalists had, out of their desire to create a distinct society, construed an ideal society that was totally unprogressive, anti-modern, and destructive of the individual. In a post-war Quebec deeply transformed by successive waves of industrialization and urbanization, this vision of a homogeneous rural society no longer corresponded to the new realities.[22]

Citélibristes, led by Trudeau, argued effectively that traditional French-Canadian nationalism had prevented French-Canadian intellectuals from drawing on new developments in the modern social sciences and had led to a reactionary interpretation of the social thought of the Catholic church. The pervasiveness of this nationalism on the political level had made it impossible to implement solutions to socio-economic problems proven successful for the Protestant and "materialistic" Anglo-Saxons. The traditional nationalists' equation of state intervention with communism and socialism had made the implementation of a meaningful provincial autonomy impossible and impeded the growth of a democratic concept of authority and the role of the state. The solutions proposed by nationalists since the early part of the century, such as return to the land, small businesses, co-operatives, Catholic labour unions, and Christian corporatism, were all, in Trudeau's estimation, conservative and even reactionary programs intended to impede the necessary secularization and democratization of French Canada's values and institutions. Unfortunately, many of French Canada's most important institutions — the Société Saint-Jean Baptiste, the *Ecole sociale populaire*, the classical colleges, the universities, the church, and the Catholic unions — had been imbued so thoroughly with traditional French-Canadian nationalism that it was virtually impossible for them to make the transition to the modern secular world.[23]

Since nationalism had served the French-Canadian society so poorly, *Cité libre* proposed that only a widespread and genuine commitment to the ideology of liberal democracy would bring about the urgently required

525

regeneration and modernization of French Canada. *Citélibristes* were convinced that the persistence of an authoritarian, conformist, and patronage-ridden political regime led by Duplessis was largely because French Canadians were anti-democratic. Out of historical necessity and a devotion to national survival, French Canadians had learned early on to use democracy rather than adhere to it as political philosophy to be fought for and cherished in its own right.[24] Hence the rallying cry for *Citélibristes* became "democracy first."

They set out, after the notorious dirty-tricks provincial election of 1956, to create a political movement, called *le Rassemblement*, to help establish genuine parliamentary democracy in Quebec.[25] In doing so, *Citélibristes* were opting for a society that placed its priority on the defence and development of individual rights and freedoms via liberal democratic institutions. *Cité libre* called for the creation of a ministry of education as soon as possible, for the creation of a modern educational system would allow the full and effective realization of every individual's potential. The ministry should undertake the building of a Francophone public secondary system administered by new regional school boards. This system would replace the elitist church-controlled classical college system and the truncated *Ecole primaire supèrieur* thereby providing all Francophones with equal access to all levels of post-secondary education.[26] *Citélibristes* also supported the eventual secularization of Quebec's Catholic universities and colleges and strongly opposed the church's plans to allow the Jesuit order to build a new university in Montreal.[27]

The revenues for necessary reforms could be obtained, according to *Cité libre*, from a more rational development of Quebec's vast natural resources. The modern neo-liberal state had a clear responsibility to intervene in the economy to ensure high employment, orderly and planned development, and a reasonable return for the treasury from the exploitation of publicly owned resources.[28] The wholesale sell-out of iron-ore deposits in Ungava for one cent per ton was considered a violation of the public's right to equitable resource rents and detrimental to the overall development of Quebec's economy. Natural resources had to be processed within the province to increase the quantity and quality of jobs in the manufacturing sector. A more productive and diversified economy would enhance the revenues accruing to the treasury, making more funds available for social programs and education reforms.[29]

Finally, *Cité libre*'s perception of federalism and federal–provincial relations was determined by its strong advocacy of liberal and social democratic policies and practices. *Cité libre* vigorously opposed not the social objectives but the fiscal and monetary goals of the "new federalism" that emerged in the federal bureaucracy during and after the war. Following Trudeau's assessments of post-war economic developments in Ottawa, *Cité libre* rejected Maurice Lamontagne's plea that French Canada accept the imperatives of the modern world and participate in a lucid integration of Quebec into the new federalism.[30]

526

As a result of this line of thinking, Trudeau on behalf of *Cité libre* objected strongly to the federal government's decision in 1951 to grant subsidies to Canadian universities as recommended in the Massey Commission Report. Trudeau maintained that federal grants to universities violated the spirit and the law of the constitution. Agreeing with neo-nationalists at *Le Devoir*, he was adamant in his belief that the federal government should not use its general taxing powers to encroach on provincial responsibilities. It was up to Quebec voters to pressure their provincial government to provide a better financial deal for post-secondary education because this area was a provincial, not a federal, responsibility. It was only logical, given this conception of federalism, that Trudeau and his colleagues supported the imposition of a provincial income tax by the Duplessis government in 1954. Most of the revenue was slated for education and the legislation was a perfect example of the government responding to public pressure.[31]

The provincial income tax created quite a row with Prime Minister St. Laurent and the federal bureaucrats. Following several months of verbal bombast Ottawa consented, albeit reluctantly, to share in a minor way the personal income tax field. While *Citélibristes* rejected the nationalists' claim that the provinces had an exclusive or priority right in the area of direct taxation, they supported their proposal that Quebec taxpayers be allowed to deduct, to a certain level, provincial income tax from their federal taxes. In short, there should be a sharing of the taxing resource base to serve both levels of government in proportion to their respective constitutional responsibilities. Among Ottawa's responsibilities Trudeau included financial equalization between the have and have-not provinces, economic stabilization, and full employment programs. Canada, *Citélibristes* firmly believed, could have strong autonomous provinces financing their own responsibilities as well as a strong federal government capable of directing and regulating a rapidly expanding industrial and technological society.[32] *Citélibristes* did not believe that constitutional changes pertaining to the division of powers between both levels of government were necessary or advisable. French Canadians had all the provincial powers they required to build an open, democratic, and pluralistic society under their control. Given this perspective, it was only natural that *Cité libre* would characterize the re-emergence of separatism in the early 1960's as the new treason of the intellectuals and would denounce the separatists as political counter-revolutionaries.[33]

527

THE BIRTH OF NEO-NATIONALISM

Indeed, the neo-nationalism formulated by a small contingent of French Canada's intelligentsia during the 1940's and 1950's could easily be given a separatist orientation by disgruntled and ambitious members of French Canada's rapidly expanding new middle class. In fact, neo-nationalist historians at the Université de Montréal — Michel Brunet, Maurice

Séguin, and Guy Frégault — were developing a secular nationalist interpretation of Quebec's past that weighed heavily in favour of political independence as the only viable guarantee of the survival of the French-Canadian nationality in North America. In the 1950's most neo-nationalists were not yet willing to accept this interpretation. Yet in 1952, to his rhetorical question "Is there a crisis of Nationalism?" André Laurendeau responded with a categorical yes. In the wake of the demise of the *Bloc populaire canadien* in 1947, the creation of Ottawa's welfare state, and the growing identification of nationalism with the regressive policies and practices of the Duplessis administration, nationalists had become terribly confused. In fact, as Laurendeau was quickly discovering, much to his chagrin, many were indifferent and some were hostile to nationalism.[34]

528

French Canadians generally, but in particular the rural professional petty-bourgeoisie and the clerical leaders, rejected an abrupt departure from past practice. Consequently the Union Nationale, with its vigorous defence of the rural way of life, of the strong presence of the Catholic church in education, health, and welfare, and of the constitutional prerogatives of the province against an ever-encroaching Ottawa bureaucracy, was able to regain and retain power with relative ease for a decade and a half following its defeat of the Liberal and *Bloc* parties in the 1944 election.[35]

If French-Canadian nationalism, argued André Laurendeau and Gérard Filion, were to become once again an effective ideological force in contemporary Quebec, capable of influencing the direction of government policies and programs, it would have to be reformulated to reflect the needs and aspirations of an urban/industrial society. The neo-nationalist leaders, Filion and Laurendeau, were well placed to undertake this task. In April 1947 Filion had become director of *Le Devoir*, French Canada's most influential nationalist daily. He then hired Laurendeau as editor-in-chief. This was an inspired move because Laurendeau had impeccable nationalist credentials and, despite his liberal-reformist leanings, was generally acceptable to the more traditional nationalists. In 1948 Laurendeau was also reappointed for a second five-year term as director of French Canada's leading nationalist periodical, *l'Action nationale*. During the 1950's *Le Devoir*'s editorial staff included Paul Sauriol, Pierre Vigeant, Pierre Laporte, and Jean-Marc Léger. *Le Devoir* quickly became the centre of the debate about the future of the Francophone society and its role in Canada.

At the very heart of the political and ideological crisis facing French-Canadian nationalism was its inability to win over the hearts and minds of French Canada's dominant social class, the urban working class.[36] There were a number of divergent reasons for this: the homogenizing nature of the industrialization process; the lack of an urban French-Canadian culture and institutions; the foreign domination of Quebec's economy.[37] But the most important reason, according to neo-nationalists, was that the traditional nationalists had simply lost touch with the people by failing to elaborate a realistic and meaningful doctrine and program of action. A group of Université de Montréal students, who had created the *Equipe de recherches sociales* in 1947 to inculcate a social conscience in their fellow students, contended that the traditional nationalist elite of petty-bourgeois professionals and clerics was more concerned with defending its own particular class interests than with advancing the collective interests of the French-Canadian nation.[38] Somewhat surprisingly, the students found immediate support for their interpretation from abbé Gérard Dion and Joseph Pelchat of the Department of Industrial Relations at Laval, as well as from Claude Ryan, an organizer in the Catholic action movement, and Jean-Paul Robillard, a former *Bloc* militant. André Laurendeau gave the interpretation qualified support while encouraging the group to pursue its activities.[39]

The solution to the crisis was not, as the *Citélibristes* proposed, to abandon nationalism but rather to reorient and redefine it to meet the needs of contemporary Quebec. French-Canadian neo-nationalists accepted the fact that their society was no longer rural and agricultural but urban and industrial. The challenge confronting the French-Canadian people was to assimilate the new urban/industrial order and turn it to the advantage of a revitalized French-Canadian nation.[40] Neo-nationalists set out with considerable determination to break the identification of nationalism with anti-social, anti-labour, xenophobic, and petty-bourgeois values and interests. Nationalism, for them, was to become an ideology of socio-economic reforms, an ideology that would help undermine the dehumanizing and depersonalizing aspects of the urban/industrial social order. With the revitalization of such institutions as the family and the community and the acquisition of greater autonomy for the individual, perhaps nationalism might well become a valued ideology among French Canada's working-class majority.[41]

529

The neo-nationalists' concern with the integration of the French-Canadian working class into the nationalist mainstream was reinforced by a growing awareness that the social, political, and economic interests of the French-Canadian middle class, old and new, were in serious jeopardy. This predicament was the natural outgrowth of the ever-increasing economic inferiority of French Canadians as individuals and as a collectivity. This issue was at the very centre of the neo-nationalists' concerns throughout the 1950's. It contributed directly to their decision to look toward the Quebec state as the key to the creation of a modern, secular society under the leadership of a new Francophone middle class.

Neo-nationalists observed the post-war economic boom with considerable trepidation. While Duplessis's laissez-faire economic policies and strong encouragement of foreign investment certainly created plenty of jobs and profit in the resource sector of the economy, they also accelerated the economic inferiority of French Canada's financial, commercial, and industrial *petite et moyenne* bourgeoisies. It was painfully apparent that French Canada lacked a financial and industrial *haute* bourgeoisie to compete with Montreal's Anglo-Canadian and American capitalists who dominated the most crucial sectors of Quebec's economy.[42] French Canadians, who constituted 30 per cent of Canada's population, could lay claim to only 8 per cent of the country's wealth. In Quebec, where they formed 80 per cent of the population, they could lay claim to merely 25 per cent of the wealth. Little wonder that only 5 per cent (400) of the 8,000 company directorships listed in the 1954 *Directory of Directories* were French Canadians and only a small proportion of these held sizable stock portfolios.[43]

In general, neo-nationalists accepted the standard explanations for the absence of a French-Canadian bourgeoisie. While it remained true that French-Canadian family-based businesses feared the risks of going to the open market for expansion funds, it was no longer true that French Canada lacked internal capital resources. The real challenge was how to marshal those resources in an effective and efficient manner to enable the emergence of a Francophone *haute* bourgeoisie.[44] Laurendeau, Filion, Léger, and Laporte all had been convinced for some time that the Francophone majority's only effective method of achieving control over the provincial economy was to create a dynamic, interventionist, and secular nation-state. Consequently, they were very receptive to a reinterpretation of French Canada's past proffered by the Université de Montréal's neo-nationalist historians. Michel Brunet, Guy Frégault, and Maurice Séguin were contending that the Conquest of 1760 was the single most important event explaining the absence of a modern secular bourgeoisie in French Canada.[45] In short, their political explanation for French Canada's position of economic subservience encouraged other neo-nationalists to believe that a political solution was an important element in the attempt to redress an untenable situation.

Extensive government intervention, it was believed, was needed in the planning and development of the economy. To become economic masters in their own house, French Canadians must start by regaining control over their vast natural resources — hydroelectricity, pulp and paper, and mining. If private companies refused to allow French Canadians to become the majority stockholders and managers of the resource corporations or to provide the citizens of Quebec an equitable share of the economic rents of their resources, the Quebec state had no alternative but to nationalize the companies.[46] Neo-nationalists were particularly incensed at the Duplessis government's decision in 1946 to grant the Iron Ore Company, a consortium of several American steel companies, the right to develop the iron ore deposits in northern Quebec for a fixed annual royalty of $100,000. This amounted to little more than one cent per ton of ore! Certainly jobs were created but the public's share was meagre indeed. They might also have added that Francophones were conspicuous by their absence in the upper echelons of the corporation. Duplessis's resource policy appeared particularly galling when he proclaimed time and time again that his government lacked the revenue to improve educational and social services. It was also imperative, argued neo-nationalists, for the government to create, as soon as possible, a state-controlled steel corporation to mine and process Quebec's iron ore.[47]

After initially resisting the call for increased provincial activity in the social welfare and health fields for fear of alienating the church, neo-nationalists by the late 1950's supported organized labour's pleas for provincial medicare and hospitalization programs. Neo-nationalists perceived the reform of Quebec's anachronistic and unco-ordinated education institutions as the central element in their drive to create a modern, secular, French-Canadian nation-state.[48] Indeed, the pressures for educational reform were quite widespread by the 1950's, a fact that was clearly demonstrated by the 140 briefs on education presented to the Tremblay Commission on Quebec's constitutional problems (1953-55). Over fifty organizations also participated in a highly publicized provincial conference on educational reform in June 1958 to deal with such urgent problems as the low participation rate of Francophones at the secondary and postsecondary levels, the abysmal lack of funding at all levels, the persistence of undemocratic structures and procedures, poorly qualified and underpaid teachers, and finally, the total lack of co-ordination between the various levels.[49]

531

Neo-nationalists, led by the work of Arthur Tremblay, a Laval education specialist and the moving force behind the 1958 conference, supported raising the compulsory age of attendance from fourteen to sixteen to ensure that French Canadians were better prepared to face the demands of the work world and to pursue, if qualified, further education at the post-secondary level.[50] Neo-nationalists also wanted school boards and the *Conseil de l'instruction publique* to become fully secularized and democratized — all lay members were to be elected by universal suffrage.[51] They also came to realize that French Canada's private secondary and post-secondary system of classical colleges was totally inadequate to serve the needs of a modern society. Unlike the *Citélibristes* who wanted to scrap the system in its entirety, the neo-nationalists wanted to make the classical Latin-science curriculum available to all qualified students through a network of secular, state-supported regional high schools. This would democratize access to secondary education and provide the universities with well-prepared recruits for the science and social science faculties and the professional schools. Only in this manner could French Canada provide itself with a modern, secular middle class capable of managing the apparatus of an interventionist state and thereby gain control over Quebec's foreign-dominated economy.[52]

Much of the reform at the primary and secondary levels was dependent on the modernization of Quebec's three French-language universities run by the church. Well-funded, dynamic, secular Francophone universities were seen by neo-nationalists as a *sine qua non* for the flourishing of an autonomous Québécois nationality.[53] Neo-nationalists in the late 1950's still remained cautious about demanding the reinstatement of a ministry of education for fear of arousing the wrath of the church, thereby endangering the growing consensus for reform at the other levels. Laurendeau recommended in 1960 that the newly elected Liberal government of Jean Lesage establish a Royal Commission to investigate all aspects of education and prepare the groundwork for long overdue reforms.[54] Lesage agreed and created the Parent Commission, named after its neo-nationalist chairman, Monsignor Alphonse-Marie Parent, former rector of Laval. With Filion and Arthur Tremblay appointed to the Commission, neo-nationalists were in an excellent position to influence the direction of education reform in contemporary Quebec.

Inevitably, the neo-nationalists' campaign for a dynamic, interventionist nation-state was to have serious implications for their perception of Quebec's role within the Canadian federal system. Their initial reaction was to demand that Ottawa respect the provincial and cultural compacts nationalists argued were inherent in the British North America Act of 1867. In due course they came to feel that fundamental constitutional revisions to entrench the equality of the French-Canadian nation and to accommodate the urgent requirements of the "new" Quebec were imperative.

This shift was consolidated by two full-scale battles between Ottawa and Quebec over taxing powers and education. The first struggle entailed the Duplessis government's rejection of the tax-rental scheme Premier Godbout had signed in 1942, which expired in 1947. While Duplessis refused to sign a new agreement his government also refused to take any decisive action to counter this fiscal centralization. The neo-nationalists campaigned aggressively for the province to exercise its taxing powers by imposing a personal income tax. This action would produce one of two effects. The federal government might conceivably allow Quebec citizens to deduct their provincial tax from their federal tax or Ottawa could choose to reduce its personal tax level by an amount equivalent to the provincial tax. If Ottawa refused to budge, Quebec's politicians could effectively blame it for imposing double taxation.

Thanks to the co-ordinated efforts of the neo-nationalists, the *Chambre de Commerce de la Province de Québec*, and the *Chambre de Commerce de Montréal*, the Tremblay Commission was able to persuade a very reluctant Duplessis to implement a provincial income tax in 1954. When the federal government agreed after several months of turmoil to share in a very small way the personal income tax field the neo-nationalists were elated.[55] As subsequent events demonstrated, Ottawa's decision marked the effective demise of the tax-rental system and the beginning of a new era of fiscal sharing. While Duplessis refused to press his hard-won advantage, the neo-nationalists, having seen their strategy of aggressive provincial autonomy reinforced by success, expressed the view that this was merely the beginning. Just think, they wondered out loud, what the province could accomplish if its political leaders subscribed wholeheartedly to a policy of state-building!

The second issue to arouse the ire of nationalists, old and new, was the federal government's decision to provide direct grants to universities as recommended by the Report of the Royal Commission on National Development in the Arts, Letters and Sciences (1951). The scheme was a direct challenge to the neo-nationalists' campaign to develop a dynamic Quebec state because it involved the federal government in an area of provincial jurisdiction. That area, education, was considered sacred to the survival and development of a distinct French-Canadian nationality. No national minority could allow central government bureaucrats and politicians, who mostly represented the values and aspirations of Canada's English-speaking majority, to control its educational institutions. In the words of the *Ligue d'Action Nationale* and Michel Brunet, Quebec City, not Ottawa, was the capital of the French-Canadian nation.[56] The Duplessis government accepted the federal grants for 1951-52 but the vociferous reaction of all nationalists forced it to reject all future subsidy proposals of the federal government. Neo-nationalists kept pressuring the Duplessis administration to put its money where its mouth was and start providing the necessary financial support to Quebec's hard-pressed universities, especially the Francophone universities, which were facing rapidly increasing enrolments and enduring antiquated and totally inadequate facilities. They proposed that Ottawa, as an alternative, provide Quebec with a larger slice of direct taxes, personal or corporate, or increase the province's equalization grant by two million dollars. Pressure could then be put on Duplessis to spend this money on post-secondary education.[57] In fact, after several years of wrangling and continued poverty for Quebec's Francophone universities, the first proposal was precisely the solution that Ottawa and Quebec adopted after lengthy negotiations between Premiers Paul Sauvé and Jean Lesage and the Diefenbaker government.

The significance of these federal-provincial disputes was that they prompted neo-nationalists to consider seriously the need to revise the constitution. Two constitutional options emerged. The *Ligue d'Action Nationale* in its brief to the Tremblay Commission, authored by Jean-Marc Léger, proposed the creation of a highly decentralized confederal system in which the provinces had expanded prerogatives, including all residual powers, while the central government retained only limited and specific economic, military, and political responsibilities. Maximum decentralization was imperative if the French-Canadian nation, which had its homeland in Quebec, was going to survive and achieve equality with the English-Canadian nation.[58] The second option was proposed by the *Société Saint-Jean-Baptiste de Montréal* in its brief, authored by Michel

533

Brunet, to the Tremblay Commission. Since it appeared that English Canadians considered Ottawa to be their national government it was not likely that they would support a highly decentralized system. If the French-Canadian nation, in its view, was to survive and achieve equality, it required its own highly autonomous nation-state. That state could be none other than Quebec. A revised constitution had to recognize the "special role" of Quebec by granting it greater taxing powers than other Canadian provinces as well as complete control over all social security, health, education, and cultural responsibilities. In short, Quebec required a constitutionally entrenched "special status."[59] The Tremblay Report sanctioned both of these proposals while suggesting a couple of practical methods of moving toward greater fiscal decentralization and provincial control over all social programs. To facilitate intergovernmental relations the commissioners proposed the creation of a Federal–Provincial Relations Secretariat and a Permanent Council of the Provinces.[60]

534

Laurendeau and Filion strongly favoured the special-status option and *Le Devoir* would become, in the 1960's, one of the most strident voices for a renewed constitution entrenching this special status. The emergence of a bureaucratic middle class intent on establishing its control over the urban/industrial French-Canadian society had focused considerable attention on the powers and prerogatives of the Quebec state. It was only a matter of time before some members of this new middle class would begin to question the serious constraints of federalism and North American monopoly capitalism.

PARTI PRIS: QUEST FOR A SOCIALIST AND INDEPENDENT QUEBEC

The Quiet Revolution of the 1960's symbolized more than a political changing of the guard from the conservative, rural notables of the Union Nationale to the progressive, urban technocrats of the Liberal team of Jean Lesage. For many young French Canadians it marked the end of the *ancien régime* and the beginning of a cultural and ideological revolution whereby a new intelligentsia, with the support of a progressive middle class, would bring about a wholesale social revolution. Just as the *Cité libre* and neo-nationalist movements had developed, in part, as response to the policies and practices of the Duplessis régime, the various movements for an independent and socialist Quebec were, to a large degree, a response to the perceived shortcomings of liberal neo-nationalism and its proponents, the Liberal Party. The *Rassemblement pour l'indépendance nationale* (RIN), created in September 1960 as a political movement, became a centre-left political party in March 1963 under the leadership of Pierre Bourgault. While right-wing separatist groups also flourished — the *Alliance Laurentienne* (1957), the *Parti Républicain du Québec* (1962), and the *Ralliement Nationale* (1964) — it was the combination of secessionist nationalism and socialism that provided the most innovative and politically challenging ideological development of the 1960's.

In 1963–64 three periodicals, *Partis pris, Socialisme,* and *Révolution québécoise,* appeared on the scene to articulate and disseminate the ideology of socialist nationalism. *Parti pris* proved to be the most dynamic and influential of the three because of the composition of its editorial team and its strong neo-nationalist orientation. The five founders of *Parti pris,* Pierre Maheu, Jean-Marc Piotte, Paul Chamberland, André Brochu, and André Major, were all in their early twenties. All except Major, the poet, were university-educated and were heavily influenced by the socialist-nationalist theories pertaining to the decolonization movement of Third World countries, such as Frantz Fanon's *Les damnés de la terre* (1961), Albert Memmi's *Portrait du Colonisé* (1957), and Jacques Bergue's work on Arab countries.[61]

Parti pris militants and ideologues set themselves the challenge of creating an independent, secular, and socialist Quebec.[62] The tremendous difficulties of reconciling the "class" imperatives of their socialism with the "nationalist" imperatives of their commitment to independence for the Québécois nation plagued *Parti pris* throughout the entire five-year period of its existence. *Parti pris* members were caught in a dilemma not entirely of their own making. A genuine working-class consciousness did not, as of the mid-1960's, exist among the vast majority of French-Canadian workers, as was clearly demonstrated by the total lack of political success of the *Parti socialiste du Québec* or the Quebec wing of the New Democratic Party. Quebec's labour leaders were simply unable or unwilling to ensure that unionists would vote for a working-class party devoted to a socialist and independent Quebec. Socialism had been anathema to the French-Canadian society for several generations. Nationalism, on the other hand, had been part of the ideological and political landscape since the early nineteenth century. In the 1960's and 1970's, neo-nationalism dominated the political, cultural, and social environment even to the point of becoming, perhaps for the first time, a genuine mass, as opposed to a middle-class, ideology. This historical development helps to explain, in part, why nationalism prevailed so easily over socialism in the *Parti pris* elaboration of its ideas and its strategy of political action.[63]

The commitment to political independence for Quebec was paramount. Relying on the revisionist work of the neo-nationalist historians at the Université de Montréal, *Parti pris* members argued that the Québécois nation had become, since the Conquest of 1760, a colonized nation, first by Great Britain and then by English Canada. This imperialism had debilitating and destructive effects on the French-Canadian people, such as creating a deep sense of inferiority and alienation.[64] Only complete political independence would destroy the persistent colonial subordination of the French-Canadian nation by the English-Canadian nation.[65]

535

It was imperative, given the Marxist view of society elaborated by *Parti pris*, that the national revolution not be controlled and monopolized by the neo-bourgeoisie to create a powerful national bourgeoisie that would merely perpetuate the exploitation of the working class under new political structures. French-Canadian workers could achieve complete decolonization of themselves and their society only if the political revolution was followed by an economic and social revolution.[66]

The *Parti pris* assessment of the nature and extent of the social reforms required in Quebec was based on a neo-nationalist rather than a socialist interpretation of the crisis facing their society. Following the theory of several Quebec sociologists, *Parti pris* viewed the French-Canadian society essentially as a proletarian nation — an ethnic class — because the exploited and dominated French-Canadian working class constituted the vast majority of the French-Canadian nation.[67] The French-Canadian bourgeoisie, old and new, was weak and ineffectual and, largely, beholden to the dominant Anglophone community for its minor political, social, and economic privileges. Given this reality it was only natural that French-Canadian workers, in attempting to come to grips with their sense of alienation and inferiority, did so in ethnic rather than class terms.[68] The struggle for the survival of the French-Canadian national culture — essentially a working-class culture — entailed, according to the *Parti pris* manifesto of 1965–66, an overthrow of the Anglo-Canadian and American colonial and capitalist dominations, which had brought a foreign "mass culture" to Quebec.[69] In an independent Quebec, the working class could secularize all institutions and end the negative effects of an authoritarian Catholicism on the family and the individual. It could also ensure that education at all levels served the needs of the working people rather than the interest of the bourgeoisies. Finally, the working class could create the institutions needed to develop a genuine and humanistic Québécois culture, one allowing for the achievement of an individual's full potential within the framework of the nation.[70]

The *Parti pris* assessments of industrial capitalism and the role of the state were also influenced by its neo-nationalist outlook rather than by a genuine socialist analysis. Quebec had a neo-capitalist industrialized economy that exploited and alienated workers, but this had not created a class reaction. Instead, it had fostered a sense of greater ethnic cleavage, especially among ambitious middle-class professionals, managers, industrialists, and businessmen because the development of the province's natural resources and a large part of the manufacturing sector were controlled by foreigners. Quebec's economy was underdeveloped because it relied on the export of primary products and the importation of manufactured goods, thus ensuring that the standard of living was considerably lower for French Canadians than for Canadians in general.[71] Finally, the existing system of neo-capitalism fostered a petty-bourgeois business unionism that concentrated on economic gains while refusing to develop a working-class consciousness and a working-class party.

Hence, the unions were not in a position to lead either the national or the social revolutions.[72] The Quebec state, argued *Parti pris*, was controlled by a ruling class comprising a foreign bourgeoisie and a subservient French-Canadian neo-bourgeoisie. The increased role of the Quebec state in the 1960's, such as the nationalization of hydroelectricity and the modernization of the education system, served primarily the interests of the foreign bourgeoisie by creating better-educated workers. The process also enhanced the political power of, and job opportunities for, the French-Canadian neo-bourgeoisie, which controlled the state apparatus.[73]

Parti pris, nevertheless, rejected the logic of its fairly crude Marxian analysis of Quebec society. Instead, its neo-nationalism brought it to argue that its priority was to achieve independence because, with the use of the modern state being established in Quebec by the bureaucratic middle class, it would be possible to create a new society. Chamberland contended that the French-Canadian petty bourgeoisie lacked internal cohesion. This would enable the working class to gain control eventually of the state and use it as a tool for its own liberation.[74] This meant, of course, that *Parti pris* would, for what it argued were tactical and strategic reasons, support all reformist elements of the new petty bourgeoisie that supported the cause of independence. The acquisition of an independent, democratic, and bourgeois state was a great gain because it allowed the working class to conquer "selon le mot de Marx, *le terrain de la lutte*."[75]

537

By the summer of 1965 it appeared that the thrust had gone out of the Quiet Revolution as the conservative forces within the Liberal government were gaining the upper hand. It also appeared to some members of *Parti pris* that organized labour was finally becoming militant and even showing signs of political action. They formed the *Mouvement de Libération populaire*, developed a "minimum" program that would appeal to the working class, and joined forces in March 1966 with the *Parti Socialiste du Québec (PSQ)* to contest unsuccessfully a handful of seats in the 1966 provincial election. The PSQ was lukewarm at best on the issue of independence and the projected ties with organized labour never materialized.[76] *Parti pris* quickly abandoned its support for the PSQ. Piotte, in the fall of 1966, called for a return to the former strategy of revolution by stages, that is, a tactical support for the progressive wing of the French-Canadian petty bourgeoisie.[77] Other members, including Gabriel Gagnon, Luc Racine, and Gilles Bourque, disagreed strongly with this strategy. Any attempt to consolidate the power of the French-Canadian petty bourgeoisie would, they maintained, be suicidal for all socialist groups and would undermine any chance of building a genuine socialist labour party.[78]

The "independence first" faction, led by Piotte, retained the upper hand in this ideological dispute. Since the Liberal Party was out of office and its progressive wing had abandoned it, *Parti pris* decided to support the RIN, a petty-bourgeois party devoted to an independent, socialist Quebec.[79] In the fall of 1968, the RIN was swallowed up in the vortex of the newly created Parti Québécois and this reopened the ideological crisis within *Parti pris*. The socialist faction led by Bourque and Racine rejected the concept of sovereignty-association because it denied both the socialist and nationalist revolutions and they decided to quit *Parti pris* in the summer of 1968.[80] The neo-nationalist faction defended the strategy of "independence first" and joined forces with the emerging Parti Québécois. *Parti pris* disappeared from the scene, a victim of the ideological struggle between left-wing neo-nationalists who gave their priority to independence and the ardent socialists who wanted to achieve their revolution through a working-class party founded on a militant organized labour movement.

538   The Impact of Ideological Renewal

By the mid-1960's the ideological landscape of Quebec was certainly a lot more pluralistic and complex than had been the case some thirty years earlier. This was largely a reflection of the expansion and diversification of the Francophone middle class. Each sector of this new middle class — public- and private-sector middle managers and administrators, unionized professionals and semi-professionals, and organized labour leaders — developed its own particular ideological outlook to attain control over the levers of power represented by the recently expanded state. The three groups represented the neo-liberal, the social-democratic, and the socialist wings of the new middle class. Nevertheless, these three groups overlapped considerably depending on what issues were being debated.

The ideological evolution of the Catholic labour movement demonstrates well the impact of changing socio-economic and political structures. Thanks to *Cité libre*, welfare-state liberalism found a small but vocal intelligentsia willing and able to articulate and disseminate a societal model based on neo-liberal assumptions and tenets. Under the influence of liberal social Catholicism and encouraged by *Cité libre* activists, the Catholic labour movement abandoned its long-standing commitment to social corporatism and campaigned for the establishment of industrial democracy in Quebec through a system of co-management, profit-sharing, and co-ownership of industry. The emphasis was placed on the democratization and humanization of the workplace as a prelude to the democratization and humanization of contemporary society.[81] This step was particularly important because it encouraged the Catholic labour movement, led by Gérard Picard and Jean Marchand, to come to terms with the welfare state and, by 1958, to support the creation of national hospitalization and medicare systems administered concurrently by Ottawa and the provinces.[82]

The Catholic labour movement's commitment to neo-liberalism was also symbolized by the gradual secularization of its outlook and its operations during the 1940's and 1950's. This process culminated by 1960 in the adoption of a new set of principles and a new name, *Confédération des syndicats nationaux (CSN)*. During the first half of the 1960's, the CSN actively supported the Liberal administration's reforms of the social service systems, the provincial bureaucracy, the political institutions and process, and the labour code, as well as its attempts to gain control over the Quebec economy through government planning, regional economic development, and direct intervention, such as nationalization of the private hydroelectric companies after the 1962 election.[83]

While the Lesage government was no doubt motivated by its commitment to the creation of a liberal democratic society, the most pervasive and influential ideological force behind the Quiet Revolution proved to be neo-nationalism because the various sectors of the new middle class quickly perceived that if the modernization of Quebec society was accomplished by the state under the aegis of nationalist goals and aspirations it was imperative to gain firm control over the levers of power. Only then would the new middle class, or at least one segment of it, emerge as the dominant social class, displacing the traditional Francophone petty bourgeoisie, the church, and, it might be hoped, the Anglo-Canadian and American bourgeoisies who controlled the economy. Neo-nationalism was a perfect ideology to appeal to the masses for the political support essential in a system of parliamentary democracy. Moreover, the emergence of a powerful new class (and the internal struggle between its various elements) was camouflaged by the rhetoric of collective rights and aspirations.

By the mid-1960's disenchantment set in over the limitations of the Quiet Revolution. The three groups of the new middle class parted ways. The public-sector managers and administrators and the unionized professionals whose power was based on knowledge and the private-sector petty bourgeoisie and emerging Francophone bourgeoisie clashed over the issue of political sovereignty for Quebec as well as over the question of the kind of society that should be created in Quebec — a neo-capitalist welfare state or a decentralized social-democratic society with a high degree of public ownership of important sectors of the economy. After the Liberal defeat in 1966, René Lévesque led a small radical wing out of the party and created the *Mouvement Souveraineté-Association* which several months later became the Parti Québécois. The Parti Québécois articulated the national and social vision of the middle-class technocrats, bureaucrats, and professionals — the men of knowledge, such as Arthur Tremblay, Deputy Minister of Education, Claude Morin, Deputy Minister of Intergovernmental Relations, and Jacques Parizeau, an economist. These state managers and professionals formed part of a bureaucracy that expanded dramatically in the 1960's, from 2,103 professionals in 1964 to 4,646 in 1971. The vast majority were committed to using the

539

powers of a politically independent Quebec state to create a modern Québécois society controlled increasingly by them.[84]

After considerable wrangling, the Quebec Liberal Party of Jean Lesage, who was replaced by Robert Bourassa in 1970, rejected both the special-status and sovereignty-association options and argued for a strong Quebec within a renewed federal system. The various Anglophone and Francophone private-sector bourgeoisies that supported the Liberal Party wanted no further economic expansion of the Quebec state. Bourassa agreed and put the emphasis on encouraging the private sector to create urgently needed jobs for the fastest growing labour force in the western world. Increasingly under pressure from neo-nationalists in all quarters, Bourassa introduced language legislation, known as Bill 22, which made French the official language of the province, limited the choice of schooling for new Quebecers, and encouraged the use of French in the work world. These measures, it was felt, would help stem the integration of immigrants into the Anglophone community and would in time open the English-dominated sectors of the economy to newly educated Francophones. Bourassa, encouraged by his party's landslide victory in 1973, pursued these policies until his government was defeated by the Parti Québécois on November 15, 1976.[85]

540

Organized labour also became increasingly disenchanted with what it considered to be the petty-bourgeois limitations of the Quiet Revolution. The recently expanded public and para-public unions, most of them affiliated with the CSN, found the bourgeois-dominated governments, be they Union Nationale or Liberal, to be extremely hard-nosed, even provocative, in negotiations. After 1968 organized labour found itself confronting what some authors have called the coercive or disciplinary state.[86] Of course, the emergence of a socialist-imbued, neo-nationalist intelligentsia, albeit fractious and immature, helped to create an ideological and psychological climate conducive to the radicalization of the labour movement.

Both Quebec centrals, the CSN and the FTQ, responded to these circumstances by adopting a neo-Marxist interpretation of the working class's continued exploitation and subordination. The CSN, in its 1971 pamphlet *Ne comptons que sur nos propres moyens*, denounced the powerful American economic elite — supported by its Anglo- and French-Canadian compradors — that controlled the federal and provincial governments. The CSN and its fiery president, Marcel Pépin, called upon the workers to carry out a program of co-ordinated direct action to overthrow the existing neo-capitalist system and establish a democratic socialist society in Quebec. The FTQ, not wanting to be left behind in the struggle for new members and under the leadership of the dynamic Louis Laberge, followed the road to democratic socialism after 1965. In its 1971 pamphlet *L'Etat, rouage de notre exploitation*, the FTQ denounced the bourgeois liberal states, federal and provincial, for serving primarily the interests of American economic imperialists and of the English- and French-speaking bourgeoisies. The bourgeois liberal state confiscated public capital and transformed it into private capital, thus reinforcing all forms of exploitive capitalism. In 1971 Laberge called for a Common Front (*Un seul front*) of all progressive forces to liberate Quebec society from the bondage of neo-capitalism and the bourgeois liberal state and to create a democratic socialist society.[87]

The CSN and the FTQ leaders organized a general strike of over 200,000 public and para-public workers in the spring of 1972. The Common Front campaigned for an expansion of the collective bargaining parameters — the right to negotiate at a central table the amount of the government budget to be devoted to salaries. In particular, the Common Front wanted a minimum wage of $100 per week for all public employees. The Bourassa government stonewalled the labour leaders with delays, court injunctions, and, finally, Bill 19, which forced all public-sector employees back to work. The leaders, Pépin, Laberge, and Charbonneau, advocated civil disobedience of the Bill — for which they were later charged and jailed — but the Common Front disintegrated as the majority of strikers returned to work. While the CSN lost some members over the strike, the general outcome was the further radicalization of labour's ideological outlook and a toughening of its resolve to gain greater powers.[88]

541

Public-sector bargaining became the central focus of conflict between competing elements of the new Francophone middle class. By the mid-1970's organized labour leaders and militants felt that perhaps public-sector negotiations might become more successful if the incumbent Liberal government of Bourassa was replaced by the Parti Québécois. While the CSN refused to endorse officially the PQ, the FTQ decided to support the party, despite the fact that the PQ was not a working-class but rather a petty-bourgeois party. Laberge proposed to radicalize the PQ from within. In reality, the force of neo-nationalism and a common class interest were slowly eroding organized labour's distrust of the bourgeois state. An internal class conflict, reflected in divergent ideological perspectives, was being overshadowed by an ethnic conflict as reflected in the struggle over language and the role of the Québécois nation within the Canadian federal system.

Conclusion

The relationship between social transformation and ideological renewal was, in the case of Quebec, quite direct. *Cité libre*'s liberalism, *Le Devoir*'s and *l'Action nationale*'s neo-nationalism, and *Parti pris*' socialist neo-nationalism articulated the aspirations of various wings of the new Francophone middle class. In time, Quebec's political parties came to represent some of these divergent ideologies. But the re-emergence of an ethnic conflict between this new middle class and the Anglophone economic elite that controlled Quebec's economy fuelled the fires of neo-nationalism and camouflaged the internal struggle over which sector of this middle class was going to control the power levers of the newly expanded state. The Lesage Liberal Party made a valiant attempt to bring liberals and neo-nationalists together but the latter gained the upper hand, forcing such *Citélibristes* as Pierre Trudeau and Gérard Pelletier to turn to the national Liberal Party to fight separatism and restore democracy to Quebec. After the Liberal defeat in 1966, those neo-nationalists favouring political independence for Quebec followed René Lévesque out of the party and helped found the Parti Québécois, a party committed to political independence and the creation of a social-democratic society in Quebec under the aegis of a Francophone bureaucratic and technocratic middle class that controlled the state. Even CSN and FTQ labour leaders and militants, committed ostensibly to socialism, eventually supported the "petty-bourgeois" Parti Québécois and helped it defeat the Liberal Party of Bourassa.

542

The question that some authors have been asking is: "Were the real needs of the people being served by this process of political modernization symbolized by the Quiet Revolution which has been underway in Quebec since the defeat of the Union Nationale in 1960?"[89] The answer to the question is at best a qualified yes for some and a categorical no for others. Most commentators remain cautiously optimistic. A dynamic, creative, and increasingly autonomous Quebec will survive and prosper, argues one social critic, if the various elements of the new middle class recognize and set aside their self-serving ways and a new pragmatic collective ethic comes to prevail.[90] Others feel that neo-nationalism, as demonstrated by the defeat of the sovereignty-association option in the 1980 referendum, is on the wane while liberalism and individualism are once again back in vogue throughout much of Quebec society, including the new middle class.[91] While no one can predict the final outcome of what has been a very complex process of social change, ideological renewal, and incessant struggle for political hegemony, it is always helpful to try to understand a little better the historical process of change and continuity.

NOTES

[1] Gérard Filion, "Un avertissement sévère," *Le Devoir*, 9 janvier 1954.
[2] *Annuaire du Québec, 1974*, 226, tableau 3.
[3] Kenneth McRoberts and Dale Posgate, *Quebec: Social Change and Political Crisis* (Toronto, 1980), 52, table 7.
[4] Jean Hamelin et Jean-Paul Montminy, "La mutation de la société Québécoise, 1939–1976: Temps, ruptures, continuités," in Fernand Dumont et al., *Idéologies au Canada français, 1940–1976* (Québec, 1981), 1: 34–35.
[5] McRoberts and Posgate, *Quebec*, 40–43.
[6] *Report of the Royal Commission on Bilingualism and Biculturalism* (Ottawa, 1969), 3B: 23.

[7] F. Vaillancourt, "La situation démographique et socio-économique des francophones du Québec: une revue," *Canadian Public Policy* 5 (Autumn 1979): 542-52.

[8] Hubert Guindon, "Social Unrest, Social Class and Quebec's Bureaucratic Revolution," *Queen's Quarterly* 71 (1964): 153.

[9] Pierre Dandurand et Marcel Fournier, "Développement de l'enseignement supérieur, classes sociales et luttes nationale au Québec," *Sociologie et sociétés* 12 (avril 1980): 103-107.

[10] Michael Behiels, "Le père Georges-Henri Lévesque et l'établissement des sciences sociales à Laval, 1938-1955," *Revue de l'Université d'Ottawa/University of Ottawa Quarterly* 52 (juillet-septembre 1982): 355-76.

[11] Arthur Tremblay, *Les Colleges et les écoles publiques: Conflict où coordination?* (Québec, 1954), 11-12, 15-18.

[12] Jacques Brazeau, "Quebec's Emerging Middle Class," in Marcel Rioux and Yves Martin, eds., *French-Canadian Society* (Toronto, 1964), 322.

[13] Guindon, "The Social Evolution of Quebec Reconsidered," in Rioux and Martin, eds., *French-Canadian Society*, 157-58.

[14] Brazeau, "Les nouvelles classes moyennes," *Recherches sociographiques* 7 (janvier-août 1966): 157.

[15] Yves Roby, *Les Québécois el les investissements américains (1918-1929)*, (Quebec, 1976), 207-220.

[16] Gérard Pelletier, "Trois paroles d'Emmanuel Mounier," *Cité libre* 3 (mai 1951): 45-46.

[17] Jean LeMoyne, "L'atmosphère religieuse au Canada français," *Cité libre* 12 (mai 1955): 1-12; Maurice Blain, "Sur la liberté de l'esprit," *Esprit* 20 (août-septembre 1952): 243-44.

[18] Gérard Pelletier, "Crise d'autorité ou crise de liberté," *Cité libre* 5 (juin-juillet 1952): 6-7.

[19] LeMoyne, "Jeunesse de l'homme," *Cité libre* 2 (février 1951): 10-12; Pierre Vadeboncoeur, "Réflexions sur la foi," *Cité libre*, 12 (mai 1955): 21.

[20] Vadeboncoeur, "Réflexions sur la foi," 3-4; Pierre Elliott Trudeau, "Matériaux pour servir à une enquete sur le cléricalisme, I," *Cité libre* 7 (mai 1953): 31-32.

[21] Trudeau, "La province de Québec au moment de la grève," in *La grève de l'amiante* (Montréal, 1970), 19-37.

[22] Vadeboncoeur, "L'irréalisme de notre culture," *Cité libre* 4 (décembre 1951): 20-21; M. Rioux, "Idéologie et crise de conscience du Canada français," *Cité libre* 14 (décembre 1955): 3-14.

[23] Trudeau, "La province de Québec," 14-37, 88.

[24] This theme was developed primarily by Trudeau with the full support of his colleagues. Trudeau, "Réflexions sur la politique au Canada français," *Cité libre* 6 (décembre 1952): 53-57; "Some Obstacles to Democracy in Quebec," *Canadian Journal of Economics and Political Science* 24 (August 1958), reprinted in his *Federalism and the French Canadians* (Toronto: Macmillan, 1968), 103-23.

[25] Trudeau, "Un manifest démocratique," *Cité libre* 22 (octobre 1958): 2-29.

[26] Léon Lortie et al., *L'éducation* (Rapport de la troisième conférence annuelle de l'Institut canadien des affairs publique, 1956).

[27] Lortie et al., *L'éducation*; G. Pelletier, "Visite aux supérieurs, I-III," *Le Devoir*, 11-12 janvier 1949; Roger Rolland, "La lettre contre l'esprit: Un témoignage sur l'enseignement secondaire, I-III," *Le Devoir*, 13, 20, 27 septembre 1952; M. Rioux, "Remarques sur l'éducation et la culture canadienne-française," *Cité libre* 8 (novembre 1953): 40-42.

[28] P. Charbonneau, "Défense et illustration de la gauche," *Cité libre* 18 (1958): 37-39.

[29] Trudeau, "*Le Devoir* doit il préparer ses lectures au socialisme?" *Le Devoir*, 2 février 1955; "Les Canadiens français rateront (encore une fois) le tournant . . . ," *Le Devoir*, 29 janvier 1960.

[30] Maurice Lamontagne, *Le fédéralisme canadien: évolution et problèmes* (Québec, 1954).

[31] Trudeau, "De libro, tributo et quibusdam aliis," *Cité libre* (octobre 1954), in *Federalism and the French Canadians*, 63-78.

[32] Trudeau, "Federal grants to Universities," *Cité libre* (février 1957), in *Federalism and the French Canadians*, 79-102.

[33] Trudeau, "La nouvelle trahison des clers," *Cité libre* 46 (avril 1962): 3-16; "Les séparatists: des contre-révolutionnaires," *Cité libre* 67 (mai 1964): 2-6.

[34] Laurendeau, "Y a-t-il une cris du nationalisme? I," *Action Nationale* 40 (décembre 1952): 208. Cited hereafter as AN.

[35] Richard Jones, *Duplessis and the Union Nationale Administration* (Ottawa, 1983), 12-17.

[36] Laurendeau, "Le quatrième état dans la nation," AN 30 (octobre 1947): 83-88.

[37] Laurendeau, "Conclusions très provisoires," AN 31 (juin 1948): 414-16; "Y a-t-il une crise du nationalisme? I," 215-17.

[38] Jean-Marc Léger, d'Iberville Fortier, Pierre Lefebvre, et Camille Laurin, "L'ennemi dans nos murs," AN 31 (février 1948): 107.

[39] G. Dion et J. Pelchat, "Repenser le nationalisme," AN 31 (juin 1948): 408-411; C. Ryan, "Le sens du national dans les milieux populaires," AN 31 (mars 1948): 171-73; J.-P. Robillard, "Pour un nationalisme social," AN 31 (avril 1948), 286-88; Laurendeau, "Conclusions très provisoires," 413-24.

[40] Léger, "Le Canada français à la recherche de son avenir," *Esprit* 20 (septembre 1952): 261.

[41] Léger, "Urgence d'une doctrine nationale," AN 46 (octobre 1956): 137-38.

[42] Filion, "Une double tentation," *Le Devoir*, 12 mai 1954.

[43] Léger, *Notre situation économique: progrès ou stagnation* (Montréal, 1957), 1-21. Studies for the Royal Commission on Bilingualism and Biculturalism based on the 1961 census data confirmed the economic

543

inferiority of French Canadians as individuals as well as the desperate plight of the Francophone private sector (*Report* 3B: 11-60).

44 Roland Parenteau, "Quelques raisons de la faiblesse économique de la nation canadienne-française," *AN* 45 (décembre 1955): 320-25; Laporte, "L'enjeu: notre survivance ou notre disparition," *Le Devoir*, 23 août 1957.

45 Cf. Dale Miquelon, ed., *Society and Conquest: The Debate on the Bourgeoisie and Social Change in French Canada, 1700-1850* (Toronto, 1977).

46 Filion, "La reprise de nos richesses naturelles," *Le Devoir*, 25 novembre 1953; Paul Sauriol, "Entre la servitude économique et la nationalisation," *Le Devoir*, 20 octobre 1958.

47 Laporte, "Une province qui se contente des miettes, I-VIII," *Le Devoir*, 24-25, 27-30 janvier, 1, 3 février 1958.

48 Sauriol, "*Le Devoir* et la libération de notre groupe," *Le Devoir*, 29 janvier 1960; Laurendeau, "A l'heure des réformes," *Le Devoir*, 15 mars 1958.

49 Cf. Jean-Louis Roy, *La marche des Québécois: le temps des ruptures (1945-1960)* (Montréal, 1976), 245-308.

50 Arthur Tremblay, "La conjoncture actuelle de l'éducation," in *L'éducation au Québec face au problèmes contemporains* (Saint-Hyacinthe, 1958), 39-40.

51 Filion, "Crise scolaire," *Le Devoir*, 26 novembre 1955; "Il ne faut pas faire des éveques des boucs émissaires," *Le Devoir*, 9 novembre 1960.

52 Filion, "Il faut des techniciens, on nous donne des plaideurs," *Le Devoir*, 1 juin 1955; Laurendeau, "Le cours classique a l'école publique," *Le Devoir*, 25 avril 1955.

53 Laurendeau, "Premier but: l'université," *Le Devoir*, 10 juin 1955; "Où va le canada français? XIII," *Le Devoir*, 21 mai 1959.

54 Laurendeau, "Pour une enquete royale sur l'éducation," *Le Devoir*, 15 novembre 1960.

55 Filion, "Le fédéralisme canadien I-IV," *Le Devoir*, 21-24 juillet 1954; "Un accord, non une capitulation," *Le Devoir*, 29 février 1956.

56 Ligue d'Action Nationale, "Conditions d'un Etat Français dans la Confédération canadienne: Mémoire à la Commission royale d'enquete sur les relations fédérales-provinciales," *AN* 43 (mars-avril 1954): 312-16.

57 Filion, "L'aide fédérale à l'enseignement, III," *Le Devoir*, 1 avril 1952; "Le devoir du Québec envers ses universités," *Le Devoir*, 27 octobre 1956; "L'aide fédérale aux universités," *Le Devoir*, 13 octobre 1956.

58 Ligue d'Action Nationale, "Conditions d'un Etat Français," 328-44.

59 Société Saint-Jean Baptiste de Montréal, *Canada français et union canadienne* (Montréal, 1954), 54-125.

60 *Tremblay Report*, vol. 3, book 2, 227-28, 233-37, 255-72, 294-95.

61 Pierrette Bouchard-Saint-Amant, "L'idéologie de la revue *Parti pris*: le nationalisme socialiste," in Dumont et al., *Idéologies au Canada français, 1940-1976*, 1: 315-17; Roch Denis, *Lutte des classes et question nationale au Québec, 1948-1968* (Montréal, 1979), 359-62.

62 "Présentation," *Parti pris* 1 (octobre 1963): 2-3.

63 Bouchard-Saint-Amant, "L'idéologie de la revue *Parti pris*," 317-19. The author argues that the *Parti pris* demise can be explained by the review's inability to develop a rigorous theory of the relationship between social classes and the nation. Nationalism and socialism, in her view, can only be reconciled if they are both authentic products of the working class.

64 Paul Chamberland, "De la domination à la liberté," *Parti pris* 1 (juin-août 1964): 64-81; Pierre Maheu, "L'oedipe colonial," *Parti pris* 1 (juin-août 1964): 20.

65 Chamberland, "Aliénation culturelle et révolution nationale," *Parti pris* 1 (novembre 1963): 15-16.

66 "Manifeste 65-66," *Parti pris* 3 (septembre 1965): 7-41; "Jean Lesage et l'Etat béquille," *Parti pris* 2 (février 1965): 4; Chamberland, "Aliénation culturelle," 16.

67 Jacques Dofny et Marcel Rioux, "Les classes sociales au Canada français," *Revue française de sociologie* 3 (juillet-septembre 1962): 290-300; Guy Rocher, "Les recherches sur les occupations et la stratification," *Recherches sociographiques* 3 (1962): 183-84.

68 Jean-Marc Piotte, "Sens et limites du néo-nationalisme," *Parti pris* 4 (septembre-octobre 1966): 29; Maheu, "Québec politique," *Parti pris* 5 (avril 1968): 11.

69 "Manifeste 65-66," 17.

70 Maheu, "Le dieu canadien-français," *Parti pris* 4 (novembre-décembre 1966): 45-48; "Le rapport Parent," *Parti pris* 2 (mars 1965): 7.

71 Maheu, "Que faire?" *Parti pris* 2 (mars 1965): 54; Piotte, "Sens et limites," 28.

72 "Manifeste 65-66," 20.

73 "Manifeste 65-66," 16; Piotte, "Ou allons-nous?" *Parti pris* 3 (août-septembre 1965), 68-69.

74 Chamberland, "Les contradictions de la révolution tranquille," *Parti pris* 1 (février 1964): 4.

75 "Manifeste 64-65," *Parti pris* 2 (1964): 14.

76 Denis, *Lutte des classes*, 467-503.

77 Piotte, "Sens et limites," 36-37.

78 Gabriel Gagnon, "Vraie ou fausse indépendance," *Parti pris* 4 (novembre-décembre 1966): 9-10; Gilles Bourque et al., "Organisations syndicale, néo-capitalisme et planification," *Parti pris* 4 (mars-avril 1967): 5-27.

[79] Gaetan Tremblay and Pierre Maheu, "L'indépendance au plus vite!" *Parti pris* 4 (janvier-février 1967): 2–5.

[80] Bourque et al., "Pour un mouvement," *Parti pris* 5 (été 1968): 30–34.

[81] Jacques Rouillard, *Histoire de la CSN, 1921–1981* (Montréal, 1981), 198.

[82] CTCC et FTQ, "Les centrales ouvrières du Québec et l'assurance santé," *Relations industrielles* 13 (1958): 175–208.

[83] Rouillard, *Histoire de la CSN*, 198; Denis, *Lutte des classes*, ch. 12, 287–308.

[84] J.-J. Simard, "La longue marche des technocrates," *Recherches sociographiques* 18 (1977): 112–17, 129–32.

[85] Réjean Pelletier, "Les parties politiques et l'Etat," in G.and A. Bergeron, *L'Etat du Québec en devenir* (Montréal, Boréal, 1980): 241–61.

[86] Carla Lipsig-Mummé, "Quebec Unions and the State: Conflict and Dependence," *Studies in Political Economy* 3 (Spring 1980): 136–37; Carol Levasseur, "De l'Etat-Providence a l'Etat-disciplinaire," in *L'Etat du Québec en devenir*, 315–25.

[87] Bernard Solasse, "Les idéologies de la Fédération des travailleurs du Québec et de la Confédération des Syndicats Nationaux 1960–1978," in Dumont et al., *Idéologies au Canada français, 1940–1976* 2: 233–44, 255–67.

[88] Levasseur, "De l'Etat-Providence," 317–22; Rouillard, *Histoire de la CSN*, 236–42.

[89] Cf. Edmond Orban, *La modernisation politique du Québec* (Montréal, 1976), 15.

[90] Jacques Grand'Maison, *La nouvelle classe et l'avenir du Québec* (Montréal, 1979), 263–72.

[91] Cf. Dominique Clift, *Quebec Nationalism in Crisis* (Montreal, 1980).

Maybe Yes, or Maybe No*

ROBERT BOILY

Quebecers went to the polls in droves on May 20, 1980, as they had in the election of 1976 which had brought the Parti Québécois to power. Then, 85.3 percent of eligible voters had turned out. Now, the turnout was 85.6 percent, not for an election, but for the first province-wide referendum in Quebec, held under the new referendum law passed in 1978.

If Quebec held its breath that day, so did the rest of Canada. For all, the stakes were high, in this referendum campaign in which the PQ government was asking the public's support to begin negotiations aimed at making Quebec politically independent and linked to Canada in a purely economic alliance. The campaign had been launched officially on April 15, but in fact, it had been in full swing since Nov. 15, 1976, when the PQ had come to power, committed to hold a referendum on its goal of "sovereignty-association."

Around 8 p.m. on that fateful May 20, the suspense of several years came to an end: The vote against giving the government a mandate to negotiate sovereignty-association was 59.6 percent, the vote in favor, 40.4 percent. The Nays had it, but what exactly was "it"?

Truth and Consequences

As Premier René Lévesque had repeated throughout the campaign, a majority Yes vote would not have suddenly changed Quebec's status

*From *Horizon Canada* 117 (1987): 2785–91. Reprinted by permission.

within Confederation. It would simply have paved the way for the province to invite the rest of Canada to negotiate the recognition of Quebec's political sovereignty, and the establishment of an economic association whose features would include a common currency, the free circulation of capital, goods and persons between the two countries, and joint institutions to administer the association.

Sovereignty-association was thus something less than full independence, and something more than "special status" for Quebec in Canada. This was the vision Lévesque had maintained since his days as a novice Liberal politician and cabinet minister in the 1960s, as founding leader of the Mouvement Souveraineté-Association (MSA) in 1967, then as founding leader of the PQ in 1968.

In the months leading up to referendum day, it was explained that the fruit of the negotiations on sovereignty-association with the rest of Canada would be the subject of a second referendum. Should the Ayes then carry the day, Quebec would become its own country, standing between the Atlantic provinces and the rest of Canada.

But supposing the rest of Canada refused to negotiate the kind of deal Lévesque was after? Were not the premiers of the nine other provinces and Prime Minister Pierre Trudeau saying just that — that they had no intention of entering into such negotiations? In that case, the PQ would have no choice but to call a second referendum and push for full independence . . . or backtrack.

All this became somewhat academic on the evening of May 20, because a majority of Quebecers voted No. What would be the consequences? While the result was not legally binding on the government, it was conclusive in one sense: From the downcast appearance of Lévesque and his supporters — the cracked voices, the tears — as soon as the vote results were announced, it was clear that they considered the path to sovereignty-association blocked. This was defeat.

Who Said What?

To grasp the true significance of the vote for the future of Quebec and Canada, however, it was important to determine who exactly had voted Yes, who No, and to what.

First, the who. It turned out that the French-speaking population had voted more or less half for, half against; English speakers and others had voted No overwhelmingly — 96 percent in the case of the former, and 90 percent in the latter. Still, as the referendum was one of the milestones in the affirmation of French Quebec, the fact that nearly half the French-speaking voters had cast their ballots for the Yes made it difficult to speak of the results as a stunning victory or a definitive defeat for either side.

546

The split in the French-speaking population was not so much according to sex, occupation, income, or geographical area. It had more to do with whether people were born before or after 1945, whether they worked in the private or public sector, whether they were unionized, and how strong were their religious convictions. The Yes vote was that much stronger in areas where the presence of young people, public employees, union members, and those of lax religious observance was most marked. The opposition, then, seemed to be between new and traditional values, between the Québécois nationalism that had developed since the Quiet Revolution of the 1960s, and the old French-Canadian nationalism.

As for what people had voted Yes or No to, the views of political analysts were varied, and sometimes contradictory. To understand this, it is necessary to look at how the idea of a referendum was born, and at the strategies and views expressed in the referendum campaign.

The Go-Slow Strategy

In its early years, the PQ had taken the position that victory in a general election would authorize it to take the steps leading to the declaration of Quebec's political sovereignty. The idea of separating the sovereignty issue from an election and making it the subject of a referendum, first broached in the general election of 1973, was enshrined in the party program at a convention in November 1974.

The decision was based on strategic and ideological reasons. There had to be no doubt that when it came, the declaration of independence reflected the clearly and freely expressed will of the majority. This was hardly possible in an election, where, in choosing a government, voters had to weigh a variety of candidates and issues. Besides, the electoral system was such that a political party could collect a lower percentage of votes than its opponents, and still win a majority of seats. By focusing on a single, clear question, a referendum, it was thought, would eliminate all ambiguity.

To call a referendum, however, the PQ had to be in power. To gain the confidence of voters and win power, it had to show that it was not the separatist bogeyman that opponents made it out to be. Thus, the party was well advised to reassure voters in an election that the issue was "good government," and that the question of independence would be settled later. This step-by-step strategy, known as *étapisme*, was seen as the brainchild of Claude Morin, a specialist in federal–provincial relations who became Intergovernmental Affairs Minister in the first PQ government in 1976.

As the time for the referendum approached, another step was added to the strategy. It was decided that voters would not be asked to say Yes or No to sovereignty-association, but to give the government "the mandate to negotiate the proposed agreement between Quebec and Canada." A second referendum would then be called to ratify the outcome of these negotiations. The idea was to gain time to win more converts to the cause, and to avoid spooking people in the first referendum. As Morin liked to say, "You don't make a flower grow faster by pulling on it."

Part of the PQ's strategy in office was to point up the frustrations of working under the federal system. It was not hard. History offered countless examples, as did current affairs. In the matter of constitutional reform, successive Quebec governments had been at loggerheads with Ottawa, particularly since the election of Pierre Trudeau as prime minister in 1968. The threat that Ottawa might act unilaterally on constitutional reform remained a distinct possibility. The bane of Quebec nationalists, Trudeau was beaten at the polls in 1979, only to be returned to power nine months later, in February 1980, just in time for the referendum.

548

There were federalists, deeply attached to Quebec, who found the constitutional stance of the federal government under Trudeau highly objectionable. The PQ sought to convince them that only a strong Yes vote in the referendum could force Ottawa to budge: They had nothing to

Key Dates

- *1968* — Founding of Parti Québécois (PQ).
- *1974* — Pledge to hold referendum on sovereignty-association becomes part of PQ program.
- *1976* — PQ comes to power in Nov. 15 election, with 41 percent of the vote and 71 seats (of 110).
- *1978* — Prime Minister Trudeau publishes his government's constitutional position, *A Time for Action*, in March; on June 23, the Quebec legislature adopts the Referendum law.
- *1979* — Premier Lévesque publishes his government's white paper on sovereignty-association, *La Nouvelle Entente Québec–Canada* (Quebec–Canada: A New Deal), on Nov. 1; the referendum question is made public Dec. 20.
- *1980* — Quebec Liberal party publishes its constitutional position, *A New Canadian Federation*, on Jan. 10; the text of the referendum question is adopted by the legislature on March 20.
- *1980, April 15* — Referendum campaign begins.
- *1980, May 20* — Referendum day.
- *1981* — PQ re-elected April 13, with 80 seats (of 122).

lose, it was said, since they were just being asked to give the Quebec government a "mandate to negotiate."

The PQ's strategy thus led it to tailor its appeal to the various target audiences. Supporters of Quebec sovereignty were told: "Give us a mandate to negotiate sovereignty-association." The more timorous were told: "Don't worry; if you're not sure now, you'll be able to state your definitive

A Mandate to Negotiate

Le Gouvernement du Québec a fait con-naître sa proposition d'en arriver, avec le reste du Canada, à une nouvelle entente fondée sur le principe de l'égalité des peuples;

cette entente permettrait au Québec d'ac-quérir le pouvoir exclusif de faire ses lois, de percevoir ses impôts et d'établir ses relations extérieures, ce qui est la souveraineté — et, en même temps, de maintenir avec le Canada une association économique comportant l'uti-lisation de la même monnaie;

aucun changement de statut politique résultant de ces négociations ne sera réalisé sans l'accord de la population lors d'un autre référendum;

en conséquence, accordez-vous au Gou-vernement du Québec le mandat de négocier l'entente proposée entre le Québec et le Cana-da?

The Government of Québec has made public its proposal to negotiate a new agree-ment with the rest of Canada, based on the equality of nations;

this agreement would enable Québec to acquire the exclusive power to make its laws, levy its taxes and establish relations abroad — in other words, sovereignty — and at the same time, to maintain with Canada an economic association including a common currency;

no change in political status resulting from these negotiations will be effected with-out approval by the people through another referendum;

on these terms, do you give the Govern-ment of Québec the mandate to negotiate the proposed agreement between Québec and Canada?

OUI YES ▢

NON NO ▢

The ballot. This was the question put to Quebecers in the referendum.

549

The question, as it appeared on the ballot, was complicated, to say the least. It asked not for a decision on separation, but for a "mandate to negotiate" a new arrangement between Quebec and the rest of Canada.

If the question was compli-cated, so was the answer. Of the 3,738,854 votes cast, 40.4 per-cent said yes, while 59.6 percent said no. But these figures tell only a part of the story. A poll taken after voting day suggests that 78 percent of English-speaking people who voted *"Non"* in the referendum nev-ertheless wanted to see some kind of change. And 22 percent of French-speakers voting *"Oui"* were not for independ-ence at all, but were trying to encourage a "renewed federal-ism."

One thing that was clear: The status quo was the choice of only a small minority. Quebecers wanted change.

choice in a second referendum." Federalists favouring greater autonomy for Quebec were told that the stronger the Yes vote, the greater the chances of a "renewed federalism."

Maybe Yes, Maybe No, Maybe Maybe

Quebec's Referendum Act had been designed to establish democratic rules, to place the Yeas and Nays on the same footing as regards the financing of their campaigns, and to ensure that the matter was settled among Quebecers. It was thought that in the absence of such rules, the Nays, with all of the rest of Canada behind them, might keep the Yeas from getting a fair hearing. Under the law, each side had to set up an umbrella committee to conduct its campaign. All individuals, parties, or groups wishing to take an active part in the campaign had to work under the one committee or the other, as all campaign spending had to be authorized by these committees. Lévesque headed the Yes committee, while Claude Ryan, leader of the Quebec Liberal party, headed the No. Besides these two committees, however, there was a third big player — the federal government. It set up its own committee to give support to the official No committee, distributing copies of speeches made in the House of Commons attacking the "*oui*" side and using Federal advertising for partisan purposes. Unbound by the rules made in Quebec, the Trudeau government quickly became the dominant partner on the No side.

The basic argument used by the No camp was that the Quebec–Canada economic association proposed by the PQ would never come about, because neither Ottawa nor the other provinces were prepared to negotiate it. Take the association out of sovereignty-association, and what is left? Sovereignty, pure and simple. In other words, an independent Quebec is what voters were opting for if they voted Yes in the first referendum. Never mind the PQ's promise of a second referendum — this was it, the moment of decision. Scare tactics were used to convince voters that this would be disastrous: On its own, Quebec would be unable to meet its energy needs, particularly in fossil fuels, nor would it have the financial resources to fulfill its obligations to the old, the unemployed, and the sick.

On a more positive note, the No side appealed to voters' dual loyalty to Quebec and Canada. Keenly aware of the strong desire for constitutional change among Quebecers, Ryan's forces came to stress more and more that a No vote in the referendum would really mean Yes to "renewed federalism." At the very end of the campaign, Trudeau solemnly pledged himself and the other Liberal MPs from Quebec to set the process of change in train as soon as the referendum was past. But "renewed federalism" was left largely undefined.

On one side, then, voters were told that even if they opposed sovereignty-association or were unsure, they could vote Yes in order to force changes in the federal system. But the other side claimed the same results could be achieved by voting No. A Yes vote could mean No to the status quo; a No vote could mean Yes to reform. Is it any wonder, then, that the answers given in the referendum were more tangled than the simple words Yes and No would suggest?

An Open Question

It is clear that on the whole, a majority of Quebecers asserted their desire for constitutional change. In all the public opinion polls, the defenders of the status quo were in a minority; they alone saw themselves as Canadians first and foremost, while others considered themselves Quebecers first, or as strongly attached to Canada as to Quebec.

551

The complexity was most marked in the responses of French-speaking voters. Among those who voted Yes were people who wished to express their clear, unambiguous support for sovereignty-association, as well as others who meant to signify that they wanted to give federalism one more chance. Among the latter were some who, before the vote, were hesitant, leaning to the Yes side, and prepared, so they said, to vote eventually for sovereignty-association; a smaller proportion of this group remained federalist, but strongly believed that voting Yes was the only way to give Quebec a strong hand and to force Ottawa to embark on a renovation of the federal system.

Even if they sought change, the vast majority of those who voted No while favouring "renewed federalism" did not view things in the same way. They did not share the visceral belief in the primacy of Quebec, nor did their dissatisfaction with the federal system take on the same intensity.

The result of the referendum cannot be interpreted as a great victory for Canada and the end of the independence issue in Quebec. Still less did it mean that all obstacles to harmony between Quebec and Ottawa had been removed, or that Quebec's sense of grievance had suddenly subsided. The strains and soul-searching within the PQ after the referendum, the splintering of the independence movement, and the PQ's loss of power in 1985 may tend to suggest this. But it must not be forgotten that in 1981, the year after the referendum, Quebecers re-elected the PQ; that even after the PQ's loss of power four years later, Quebec refused to endorse the Canadian Constitution that was patriated in 1982; and finally, that the language conflict, a longstanding issue that had contributed to the PQ's rise to power, flared anew in the mid-1980s when the party was beaten at the polls. It was almost as if nothing had been settled.

Topic Fifteen

Contemporary Canada

Canadians today face challenges unknown to those who lived in the Confederation era. But although these challenges result in part from the unique circumstances of the present, their roots extend back in the nation's history.

In "Native History, Native Claims, and Self-Determination," Thomas Berger explores a challenge as old as Canadian history itself: to find a means to enable the native people — the Indians, Métis, and Inuit — to maintain their cultural identity within the larger, dominant society. In recent times, native people have sought constitutional guarantees to protect their distinct identity, and have tried to secure native land rights. In his article, Thomas Berger discusses these issues and the response of Canadians to them.

In contemporary English–French relations in Canada, the fundamental concern is the same as that raised by the native people: to define and secure the rights of a minority in a majoritarian democracy. Many federalist French Canadians have sought to protect Quebec's distinctive French Canadian culture and society through political and constitutional guarantees. Most recently Premier Robert Bourassa and the Quebec Liberal Party demanded that Quebec be recognized as "a distinct society" in the Constitutional Act of 1982, and put forward four other recommendations designed to strengthen Quebec's provincial role in Canada. By granting Quebec's demands, and by extending most of them to the other nine provinces, Prime Minister Brian Mulroney succeeded in persuading the provincial premiers to agree on the Meech Lake Accord. But before Parliament and the ten provincial governments ratified the agreement, strong opposition arose. The excerpt from Kenneth McRoberts' *Quebec: Social Change and Political Crisis* examines the general question of Quebec–Canada relations in light of the post-1980 referendum. He notes how the defeat of the referendum put the Parti Québécois government on the defensive in its negotiations with Trudeau and federal government on "renewed federalism." The broader political and constitutional context of the Meech Lake Accord, and its possible implications for Canada, are outlined in Roger Gibbins' "The Constitutional Politics of Meech Lake," an excerpt from his *Meech Lake and Canada: Perspectives from the West*.

The Berger Report, *Northern Frontier, Northern Homeland: Report of the Mackenzie Valley Pipeline Inquiry* (Ottawa: Minister of Supply and Services Canada, 1977; reprinted, Vancouver: Douglas and McIntyre, 1988) outlines the history of native claims in Canada, and presents the native peoples' case for self-determination. A supplement to the Berger Report is *The Modern North: People, Politics and the Struggle against Colonialism,* ed. Kenneth Coates and Judith Powell (Toronto: James Lorimer, 1989). Allan D. McMillan provides an overview of contemporary native issues in the last chapter of *Native Peoples and Cultures of Canada: An Anthropological Overview* (Vancouver: Douglas and McIntyre, 1988), 287-307. J.R. Miller has recently published *Skyscrapers Hide the Heavens: A History of Indian-White Relations in Canada* (Toronto: University of Toronto Press, 1989).

On the Meech Lake Accord students can consult ed. Michael D. Behiels' *The Meech Lake Primer: Conflicting Views of the 1987 Constitutional Accord* (Ottawa: University of Ottawa Press, 1989) as well as the articles in R. Gibbins' ed. *Meech Lake and Canada: Perspectives from the West* (Edmonton: Academic Printing and Publishing, 1988). Also useful are K.E. Swinton and C.J. Rogerson, ed. *Competing Constitutional Visions — The Meech Lake Accord* (Toronto: Carswell, 1988); P. Hogg, *Meech Lake Constitutional Accord Annotated* (Toronto: Carswell, 1988); and "The Meech Lake Accord — L'Accord du Lac Meech" in a special issue of *Canadian Public Policy/Analyse de Politiques* 14 (September/septembre 1988).

553

Native History, Native Claims, and Self-Determination*

THOMAS R. BERGER

We think of native claims as something that has only come to the fore in the last decade, particularly in the recent constitutional debate. In fact native claims present the oldest question of human rights in Canada — indeed, in the whole new world, for the question goes back to the Spanish conquest of the Indies, Mexico, and Peru. Columbus may at first have thought he had reached India, but the Spanish soon realized that they had discovered a new world, a world already inhabited by another race having its own languages, cultures, and civilizations.

In Spain, lawyers and clerics struggled with the questions of law and morals that this epochal discovery presented. By what right did the Europeans conquer these people, take their land, and subjugate them? There were two views. Juan Gines de Sepulvèda, the greatest Aristotelian philosopher of the day, relied on the doctrine propounded by Aristotle

*From *B.C. Studies* 57 (Spring 1983): 10-23. Reprinted by permission.

in his *Politics*, that some races are inferior to others, that some men are born to slavery. By this reasoning, the Europeans, a superior race, were justified in subjugating the Indians, an inferior race. On the other hand, there was the view propounded by Bartolomé de Las Casas, God's angry man of the sixteenth century. He argued that all men are endowed with natural rights, that the Europeans had no right to enslave the Indians, that according to natural law the Indians were entitled to live as free men, under their own rulers and their own laws.

In 1550, Charles V, King of Spain and Holy Roman Emperor, directed that a junta of theologians, judges, and court officials — fifteen in all — assemble at the University of Valladolid to consider the arguments on either side. This they did and, as Lewis Hanke has said, "Then for the first, and doubtless for the last, time a colonizing nation organized a formal enquiry into the justice of the methods used to extend its empire."[1]

The question on which the King sought advice from the junta was: "How can conquests, discoveries and settlements be made to accord with justice and reason?" Here is Hanke's account of the argument advanced by Sepulvèda. Sepulvèda said that the Indians

> require, by their own nature and in their own interests, to be placed under the authority of civilized and virtuous princes or nations, so that they may learn, from the might, wisdom and law of their conquerors, to practise better morals, worthier customs and a more civilized way of life.[2]
>
> Compare then those blessings enjoyed by Spaniards of prudence, genius, magnanimity, temperance, humanity, and religion with those of the *homunculi* [little men] in whom you will scarcely find even vestiges of humanity, who not only possess no science but who also lack letters and preserve no monument of their history except certain vague and obscure reminiscences of some things in certain paintings. Neither do they have written laws, but barbaric institutions and customs. They do not even have private property.[3]
>
> The bringing of iron alone compensates for all the gold and silver taken from America. To the immensely valuable iron may be added other Spanish contributions such as wheat, barley, other cereals and vegetables, horses, mules, asses, oxen, sheep, goats, pigs, and an infinite variety of trees. Any one of these greatly exceeds the usefulness the barbarians derived from gold and silver taken by the Spaniards. All these blessings are in addition to writing, books, culture, excellent laws, and that one supreme benefit which is worth more than all others combined: the Christian religion.[4]

Las Casas' views were already well known. He regarded the Indians as people with an evolved culture, possessing their own social, economic, and religious institutions.[5] (He had, in fact, been instrumental in securing the passage of the New Laws of 1542 abolishing the *encomienda* under which Indians were allotted to the Spaniards together with land — the New Laws, however, were never enforced because of the outcry from the colonists.) According to Las Casas, the Indians were rational beings, fit to be compared to the Greeks and Romans. In fact, as Hanke recounts it, Las Casas said that the Indians

> are superior to the ancient peoples in rearing and educating their children. Their marriage arrangements are reasonable and conform to natural law and the law of nations. Indian women are devout workers, even labouring with their hands if necessary to comply fully with divine law, a trait which Las Casas feels many Spanish matrons might well adopt. Las Casas is not intimidated by the authority of the ancient world, and he maintains that the temples in Yucatan are not less worthy of admiration than the pyramids, thus anticipating the judgment of twentieth-century archaeologists.[6]

555

Las Casas discussed the Indian economy, architecture, and religion. (He seems not to have been aware of the achievements of the Indians in such fields as mathematics or even agriculture.) He sought to demonstrate that Indian culture, customs, and institutions deserved respect on their own terms. "All the peoples of the world are men," he said. Sepulvèda and Las Casas addressed the junta in turn. The debate apparently went on for weeks, after which the junta adjourned to consider what advice to give the King. Unfortunately it is not now known what decision the junta came to, and there is still controversy as to whether or not they ever did deliver an opinion to the King. In any event, Charles V soon abdicated and entered a monastery, to be succeeded by his son, Philip II. Thereafter events overtook the Indians and the other native peoples of the New World.

The great debate at Valladolid took place in 1550. Yet it still moves us today. Why should this be so? I think it is because our own history goes back to that earliest encounter between the Europeans and the indigenous peoples of the Americas. It was an encounter that was repeated throughout the New World. Here, in what is now Canada, it was an encounter first between French and native people, then between British and native people. It is in encounter that has ramified throughout our history, and its consequences are with us today. It was a brutal encounter. The Beothuks were exterminated, the Hurons were overwhelmed, the Cree were displaced, the Salish were dispossessed. But those were the bad old days. They have been replaced by the welfare state. Our view has been, for many years now, that the native "problem" can be solved by education and by industry. With schooling, with vocational training, native people will be able to hold down any job. To secure them a place in the labour market, employers will be encouraged — if need be required — to employ native people. Has the native "problem" been solved? No one can be unaware of the poverty, violence, and degradation which disfigure life in many native communities. The problems have not gone away; if anything, they appear to have been aggravated. The penetration of industry has resulted in increased violence, social disarray, and even increased unemployment. Why? Because the problems of native people are not simply problems of poverty, but of a people trying desperately to preserve their cultural identity. The white presence — from the missions and the fur trade to the advent of industry and the proliferation of government institutions — represented, and continues to represent, a domination of native society. There is an intrinsic relationship between this domination and the cluster of social pathologies and economic difficulties that afflict native communities.

We have pursued policies designed to suppress native languages, native culture, and the native economy. Our attitude has been founded on the belief that native society is moribund, that their "culture" consists of crafts and carvings, dances and drinking — that it is at best a colourful reminder of the past, and that what we observe today is no more than a pathetic and diminishing remnant of what existed long ago. Man puts his unique stamp on the world around him. His values, ideas, language, and institutions exhibit his understanding of himself and his world. These things are his culture. All people seek to ensure that these things are transmitted from one generation to another, to ensure a continuity of the beliefs and knowledge that a people hold in common. We sought to erase the collective memory of the native people — their history, language, religion, and philosophy — and to replace it with our own. The astonishing thing is that the drive to assimilate native people, whether by draconian or liberal measures, has never succeeded. The native people have clung to their own beliefs, their own ideas of themselves, of who they are and where they came from.

The great debate at Valladolid has been rejoined in Canada. The arguments Sepulvèda and Las Casas addressed to the junta in 1550 are still before us today.[7] How far has the debate progressed since 1550? Do we really recognize the place of native history, of native culture? Many people are inclined to view the extension of the commercial and industrial system as the very definition of progress; accordingly they regard native societies as poor and acutely disadvantaged. It is not a long step from there to dismiss native culture as having no place in the modern world. Then there are those who see the aboriginal past of native peoples as a time of happiness and social cohesion, if not necessarily of economic prosperity. They wish to see native people protected in a kind of living folk museum. These two ideas, the idea of Progress and the idea of the Noble Savage, are both products of the Western imagination. J.E. Chamberlin has said:

What was done becomes clear enough. What people thought that they were doing is much less clear, but often much more important.

556

The attitudes towards the Indian and "the Indian problem" of generations of explorers, traders, missionaries, settlers, military personnel and government administrators are as critical as the actions which these attitudes precipitated. The idea of the noble savage and the idea of progress together conspired to create a very confused and ambivalent response to the native, combined as it was with personal and national ambitions and dreams.[8]

Both ideas assume that native culture is static and unchanging. The native people are seen as people locked into their past. Such an assumption becomes self-fulfilling. If we do not allow native people the means to deal with their present problems on their own terms, their culture may, in fact, tend to become degraded and static.

It comes down to our attitude toward native culture. That was what Las Casas believed. And our attitude, whether we have sought to preserve native culture or to eradicate it, has been a patronizing one. Those on *557* both sides of the argument have too often rejected the notion that native culture is viable in the contemporary context, believing that it has no place in an urban, industrial society. This is the crux. For native people insist that their culture is still a vital force in their lives. It informs their view of themselves, of the world about them, and of the dominant white society. The culture and the values of native people amount to more than crafts and carvings. Their tradition of decision-making by consensus, their respect for the wisdom of their elders, their concept of the extended family, their belief in a special relationship with the land, their regard for the environment, their willingness to share — all of these values persist in one form or another within their own culture, even though there has been unremitting pressure to abandon them.

We have sought to make over these people in our own image. But this pronounced, consistent, and well-intentioned effort at assimilation has failed. The Indians, the Inuit, and the Metis survive, determined to be themselves. In the past their refusal to be assimilated was usually passive, even covert. Today it is plain and unmistakable, a fact of life which cannot be ignored. Canadians generally — and the descendants of Europeans whose institutions predominate not only in Canada but throughout the Western Hemisphere — must be prepared to accept the distinct place of native people in our midst. What measures, then, are required to provide a distinct place for native people within the larger society, in the modern context? How are they to defend their economic mode? How are they to defend their languages, their art, their history? How are they to be enabled to defend their right to a future of their own? This is what native claims are all about.

The native people claim a special status under the Constitution of Canada. They have always had special status. Indian treaties, Indian reserves, the *Indian Act* — all of these are special institutions devised by us for native people. Now they seek to devise a future of their own fashioning. Native self-determination is the contemporary expression of special status.

In 1867, the Fathers of Confederation provided in the Constitution that native people should come under the exclusive legislative jurisdiction of Parliament. Why should the native people of Canada be given special consideration? No such provision has been offered to the Ukrainians, the Swedes, the Italians, or any other race, ethnic group, or nationality. The answer is simple enough: the native people did not immigrate to Canada as individuals or families expecting to assimilate. Immigrants chose to come to submit to Canadian government and institutions; their choices were individual choices. But the Indians and the Inuit were already here, and were forced to submit to the government and institutions imposed upon them. They were here with their own languages, cultures, and institutions before the arrival of the French or English. They, together with the Metis, are the original peoples of Canada.

558   There are many instances of our history which show how easy it is for the dominant society in Canada, whether anglophone or francophone, to discount native aspirations whenever they are inconveniently opposed to cultural, political, or industrial imperatives. Today the dominant society is largely — and increasingly — urban, industrial, and bureaucratic. It is the same in every province. Native claims are the means by which native people seek to defend their interest against encroachments.

At the heart of native claims lies the concept of aboriginal title and aboriginal rights. In the *Statement of the Government of Canada on Indian Policy, 1969*, the government said: "Aboriginal claims to land . . . are so general and undefined that it is not realistic to think of them as specific claims capable of remedy except through a policy and program that will end injustice to Indians as members of the Canadian community." Prime Minister Trudeau, speaking in Vancouver on August 8, 1969, said: "Our answer is no. We can't recognize aboriginal rights because no society can be built on historical 'might have beens.'" In saying this, the Prime Minister spoke for all of us. Yet the policy of the government was soon overthrown by the vehemence of the native people's reaction. The belief that their future lay in the assertion of their own common identity and the defence of their own common interests proved stronger than any of us had realized. They forced the government to reverse its policy on aboriginal rights.

One of the means by which this reversal was achieved was the lawsuit brought by the Nishga tribe against the Province of B.C., *Calder* v. *AGBC*, (1973), 34 D.L.R. (3d) 145 (S.C.C.). In that case Mr. Justice Wilfred Judson, speaking for three judges, found that the Nishgas, before the coming of the white man, had aboriginal title, a title recognized under English law. But, he went on to say, this title had been extinguished by pre-Confederation enactments of the old colony of British Columbia. Mr. Justice Emmett Hall, speaking for three judges, found that the Nishgas, before the coming of the white man, had aboriginal title, that it had never been lawfully extinguished, and that this title could be asserted even today. On this reckoning, the court was tied. Mr. Justice Louis-Philippe Pigeon, the seventh judge, expressed no opinion on the main issue. He held against the Nishgas on the ground that they had proceeded by issuing a writ against the Province of British Columbia. They should, he said, have proceeded by way of a petition of right. (This procedure, however, was in fact unavailable to them since it was in those days necessary to have the consent of the province to bring any proceedings by way of petition of right.) Mr. Justice Pigeon's vote meant that the Nishgas had lost, four to three.

Here is the crucial point. All of the six judges who had addressed the main question supported the view that English law in force in British Columbia when colonization began had recognized Indian title to the land. For the first time, Canada's highest court had unequivocally affirmed the concept of aboriginal title. Mr. Justice Judson, in describing the nature of Indian title, concluded at p. 156:

> The fact is that when the settlers came the Indians were there, organized in societies and occupying the land as their forefathers had done for centuries. This is what Indian title means. . . . What they are asserting in this action is that they had a right to continue to live on their lands as their forefathers had lived and that this right has never been lawfully extinguished.

Although Mr. Justice Judson went on to hold that the old colony of British Columbia had effectively extinguished the aboriginal title of the Nishga Indians, his view of Indian title affirmed the legal concept of aboriginal title. Mr. Justice Hall, speaking for the three judges who were prepared to uphold the Nishgas' claim, urged that the court should adopt a contemporary view and not be bound by past and mistaken notions about Indians and Indian culture. Mr. Justice Hall tried to look at the idea of aboriginal rights and to see it as the Indian people see it. This required some idea of the place of Indian history in our own history. In 1970 the B.C. Court of Appeal had (13 D.L.R. (3d) 64) rejected the notion of aboriginal title. Chief Justice Davey, in asserting that the Nishgas were at the time of European settlement "a very primitive people with few of the institutions of civilized society, and none at all of our notions of private property" had assessed the Indian culture by the same standards that the Europeans had applied to the Indians of North America when colonization began. Mr. Justice Hall, at p. 169, rejected this approach:

> The assessment and interpretation of the historical documents and enactments tendered in evidence must be approached in the light of present-day research and knowledge disregarding ancient concepts

559

formulated when understanding of customs and culture of our original people was rudimentary and incomplete and when they were thought to be wholly without cohesion, laws or culture, in effect a subhuman species. This concept of the original inhabitants of America led Chief Justice Marshall in his otherwise enlightened judgment in *Johnson* v. *McIntosh*, (1823) 8 Wheaton 543, which is the outstanding judicial pronouncement on the subject of Indian rights, to say: "But the tribes of Indians inhabiting this country were fierce savages whose occupation was war. . . . " We now know that the assessment was ill-founded. The Indians did in fact at times engage in some tribal wars but war was not their vocation and it can be said that their pre-occupation with war pales into insignificance when compared to the religious and dynastic wars of "civilized" Europe of the 16th and 17th centuries.

560

Mr. Justice Hall concluded that the Nishgas had their own concept of aboriginal title before the coming of the white man and were still entitled to assert it today. He said, at p. 190:

> What emerges from the . . . evidence is that the Nishgas in fact are and were from the time immemorial a distinctive cultural entity with concepts of ownership indigenous to their culture and capable of articulation under the common law, having "developed their cultures to higher peaks in many respects than in any other part of the continent north of Mexico."

As a result, at p. 223, he upheld the claim to a declaration

> that the appellants' [the Nishga tribe's] right to possession of the lands delineated . . . and their right to enjoy the fruits of the soil of the forest, and of the rivers and streams within the boundaries of said lands have not been extinguished by the Province of British Columbia or by its predecessor, the Colony of British Columbia, or by the Governors of that Colony.

Native claims, whether founded on aboriginal rights or treaty rights, begin with the land; but they do not end there. They extend to renewable and non-renewable resources, education, health and social services, public order and, overarching all of these, the future shape and composition of political institutions. Many of the proposals that native people are making are far reaching. (Consider, for instance, the proposals by the Dene and the Inuit for two new northern territories, Denendeh and Nunavut.) Some regard such proposals as a threat to established institutions, while others look on them as an opportunity to affirm our commitment to the human rights of indigenous minorities. It might be thought, however, that it is all very well for native people in rural and frontier areas in British Columbia and elsewhere in Canada to strengthen their society and their economy, but that native claims can mean nothing to the many native people who live in urban, industrial areas and who cannot return to the past. The reply is, of course, that native people do not wish to return to the past. They do not wish to be the objects of mere sentimentality. They do not say that native culture, native communities, and the native economy should be preserved in amber for our amusement and edification. Rather, they wish to ensure that their culture can continue to grow and change — in directions they choose for themselves. Their determination to retain their identity as native people does not mean that they want to return to live in tents or igloos. Because the native people use the technology of the dominant society does not mean that they must learn no language in school except English or French, and learn of no one's past but ours, and be governed by no institutions except those of our sole devising.

It will take time for them to limn these claims, especially as regards their implications for native people entering urban life. Nevertheless, some elements are clear enough. For instance, native people say that their children are taught about the kings and queens of England, and about the brave band of settlers who established the colony of New France on the banks of the St. Lawrence. "This," they say, "is your history — what about our history?" They say that they want schools where their children can learn native history, native languages, native lore, and native rights. Of course they want their children to learn to speak English or French, as the case may be, and to learn the history of our European antecedents, and to study mathematics, science, and all the subjects that they need to know in order to function in the dominant society, but they must have schools where they can learn about who they are, as well as who we are. These proposals are not limited to a rural or a frontier context. Anyone who says that responding to these proposals is out of the question should be aware that it is already happening. Since 1973 the federal government has accepted the right of native communities to have their own schools, their own teachers, and their own curriculum. Today, in province after province, programs are being established to train native teachers to teach in native communities.[9] The same thing is happening in other fields. The federal government's new Indian Health Policy, adopted on 19 September 1979, is founded on the principle that Indian people ought gradually to assume responsibility for health care and health care programs in native communities. Indian health councils and Indian health boards are being established in Alberta, British Columbia, and Saskatchewan.[10] The native people say that the key to native claims is aboriginal rights. On 29 January 1981, the Joint Committee of the Senate and the House of Commons on the Constitution agreed to recommend an amendment to the new Constitution which would provide: "The aboriginal rights and treaty rights of the aboriginal peoples of Canada are hereby recognized and affirmed." The Prime Minister

561

and the Premiers agreed, on 5 November 1981, to delete this provision. But within little more than a week they were forced by public opinion to agree to its restoration, although they did so in a qualified fashion. Now, it is "existing" aboriginal and treaty rights that are recognized and affirmed. None of the other measures in the Constitution and the Charter is limited in this way. Nevertheless, explicit recognition of aboriginal and treaty rights may have its uses. These words appear now in the Constitution. They will be binding not only on the federal government but also on the provinces. They may provide the means by which the provinces will be brought to negotiations on native claims. (Section 25 should not be overlooked. It says that nothing in the Charter shall abrogate or derogate from any aboriginal, treaty, or other rights of the aboriginal peoples, including those recognized by the Royal Proclamation of 1763, and any that may be acquired under future land claims settlements.)

562   Ever since British Columbia entered Confederation, the province has refused to acknowledge aboriginal rights. This has been the policy of governments of all parties: Liberal and Conservative in earlier times, Social Credit and NDP in our own time. A shift in governmental attitudes and policies under both Social Credit and NDP administrations can, however, be observed within the past decade. Sometimes concessions have been made, agreements reached, even changes in governmental arrangements decided upon, which profoundly affect native communities and which serve the same purposes as native claims. In 1975 the government of British Columbia agreed that the Nishga Indians were entitled to their own school district. Formerly they had been included in the Terrace School District. As a minority within that district they had little or no control over the schooling of their children. Now that a new district, consisting of their four villages along the Nass, has been carved out of the Terrace district, the Nishga can adopt their own curriculum, hire and fire their own teachers, and control other aspects of the education of their children. They have begun to implement a bilingual, bicultural program in the schools. In this way they are able to ensure that their children grow up knowing about their own people and their own past, as well as learning all that the conventional curriculum requires. In early 1982 the province of B.C. awarded a tree farm licence to the Stuart-Trembleur band in northern B.C. In the past, tree farm licences have been granted only to forest companies. The licence gives to the licensee the right to cut timber within the licensed area, to saw it, and to sell it; the licensee is responsible for fire control and is obliged to replant the forest on a perpetual yield basis. The Stuart-Trembleur licence, the first of its kind, gives the band an expanded resource base, and the opportunity to develop its own resources and to provide employment for band members. Nobody calls this native claims or land claims, but what else is it? Just as the Nishga school district protects Indian culture, so

the Stuart-Trembleur tree farm licence gives to the band a measure of control over resources the Indians claim.

Nor is this all. At its spring session in 1982, the British Columbia legislature passed Bill 58, the *Indian Cut-off Lands Disputes Act*. The Act authorizes the provincial government to enter into agreements with Indian bands and the federal government to resolve long-standing grievances over the loss of reserve lands in the early part of the century. As the result of the recommendations of the McKenna-McBride Commission, which reported in 1916, much valuable acreage was "cut off" Indian reserves laid out in the latter part of the nineteenth century. These claims affect twenty-two bands throughout the province. With federal co-operation, 12,000 acres of reserve lands cut off from the Penticton Indian Band have been restored. In addition, the band received $14.2 million. The legislation should allow this process to continue.

In September 1982 a royal commission of inquiry into Canada's fishing industry recommended that Indian claims on fish should be acknowledged. Dr. Peter Pearse, the Commissioner, proposed that the fisheries department allocate a specific quantity of fish to each band involved in the Indian fishery, the quantity and kind of fish to be determined through negotiations with the bands. The catch allocated to bands should, he urged, have priority over commercial and sports fisheries and, if in any year a band fails to harvest its allocation because of conservation measures, they should be compensated with bonus quotas in future years. No royalties should be levied on these catches. The department should enter into 10-year fishery agreements with bands and the agreements should specify the band's allocation of fish and authorize the band to harvest its allocation according to an annual fishing plan determined jointly by the band and the department. There should be no restrictions on the sale of fish.

These changes, in little more than a decade, in public attitudes and official perceptions are remarkable. They have not come as fast or gone as far as native people wish, but they represent progress that will not, I think, be turned back.

The settlement of native claims ought to provide to native people what has been denied them in the past: the means to enable them to thrive and to develop their culture; the means to ensure that they know who they are and where they came from. They can become hunters, trappers, fishermen, sawmill workers, loggers, doctors, nurses, lawyers, or teachers. But most important of all, the collective fabric of native life will be strengthened.

It is my conviction that if, in working out a settlement of native claims, we try to force native social and economic development into moulds that we have cast, the whole process will be a failure. No governmental ukase will settle the matter once and for all; no tidy bureaucratic chart will be of any use. There must be an affirmation of the right of native people to a distinct and contemporary place in the life of our country. At the same time they must have access to the social, economic, and political institutions of the dominant society. At times it is suggested that native claims are based on the idea of apartheid. This suggestion misses the whole point of native demands. In South Africa the blacks are confined to "homelands," without any right to citizenship in South Africa itself and without any right to live, work, or own property in South Africa. Blacks who live and work in South Africa do so on sufferance. The native people in Canada are seeking access to the social, economic, and political institutions of the dominant society. What they are seeking is the exact opposite of apartheid. Only if we were to deny them that access could it be said that we were guilty of apartheid.

Nevertheless, the argument may be made that the entrenchment of the rights of the native people is anomalous, since no group should have rights not enjoyed by other Canadians. Put another way, some believe that to provide a formal place within the Constitution for aboriginal peoples is an affront to the conventions of liberal democracy. The new Constitution, however, recognizes and affirms the existing rights of aboriginal peoples. While this may be said to be only qualified recognition, there can nevertheless be no turning back. The recognition of such anomalies may in time constitute Canada's principal contribution to the legal and political order. J.E. Chamberlin has said that "Canada is Canada not only because of its unique commitment to French and English cultures, but because of its unique commitment to native nations." Constitutional protection of French and English makes the way easier for other languages, because it negates the idea of a monolithic culture. In the same way constitutional guarantees to the Indians, the Inuit, and the Metis (imperfectly rendered though they may be) exemplify the Canadian belief in diversity.

Pierre Trudeau once said:

> Canada could be the envied seat of a form of federalism that belongs to tomorrow's world. . . . Canada could offer an example to all those new Asian and African states who must discover how to govern their polyethnic populations with proper regard for justice and liberty.[11]

The Canadian experience may also be useful to the other countries of our own hemisphere. It is not only we in Canada who must face the challenge that the presence of native peoples with their own languages and their own cultures presents. In the Western Hemisphere there are many other countries with indigenous minorities — peoples who will not be assimilated, and whose fierce wish to retain their own culture is intensifying as industry, technology, and communications force a larger and larger mass culture, excluding diversity.

It is, in fact, in our relations with the people from whom we took this land that we can discover the truth about ourselves and the society we have built, and gain a larger view of the world itself. It is worth reminding ourselves of what Claude Lévi-Strauss said, in *Tristes Tropiques*, when discussing "confrontation between the Old World and the New":

> Enthusiastic partisans of the idea of progress are in danger of failing to recognize — because they set so little store by them — the immense riches accumulated by the human race on either side of the narrow furrow on which they keep their eyes fixed; by underrating the achievements of the past, they devalue all those which still remain to be accomplished.[12]

NOTES

[1] Lewis Hanke, *Aristotle and the American Indians* (Indiana University Press, 1959), ix–x.
[2] Hanke, *Aristotle*, 47.
[3] Hanke, *Aristotle*, 47.
[4] Hanke, *Aristotle*, 52–53.
[5] Las Casas' views were compendiously set out in his *History of the Indies*, trans. Andree M. Collard (Harper Torchbooks, 1971).
[6] Hanke, *Aristotle*, 54–55.
[7] The very arguments advanced in 1550 were reflected in the submissions I heard as Commissioner of the Mackenzie Valley Pipeline Inquiry at the hearings I held in the Northwest Territories and the Yukon in 1975 and 1976. The Inquiry was held to examine the impact of a proposed pipeline from the Arctic to the mid-continent. The Inquiry visited all of the cities, towns, villages, and settlements in the Mackenzie Valley and the Western Arctic. A thousand northern residents of all races gave evidence largely opposed to the construction of the pipeline without a prior settlement of their claims.
[8] J.E. Chamberlin, *The Harrowing of Eden: White Attitudes Toward North American Natives* (Fitzhenry and Whiteside, 1975), 11.
[9] Special teacher training programs for native persons, designed to enable them to teach in native communities, have been undertaken in every province. All of the native Indian teacher education projects in Canada are surveyed in More and Wallis, *Native Teacher Education*, produced in cooperation with the Canadian Indian Teacher Education Projects (CITEP) Conference, September 1979.
[10] I have reviewed recent developments in the field of Indian and Inuit health care and health care programs in my Report on *Indian and Inuit Health Consultation*, Ottawa, Ontario, 28 February 1980.
[11] Pierre Trudeau, "Canada and French Canadian Nationalism," (1962), in *The Peaceable Kingdom*, ed. William Kilbourn (Macmillan of Canada, 1970), 16.
[12] Claude Lévi-Strauss, *Tristes Tropiques*, trans. John and Doreen Wightman (Atheneum, 1974), 393.

Quebec: Social Change and Political Crisis*

KENNETH McROBERTS

Explaining Quebec's Defeat

In large part, this outright failure of constitutional revision to address the demands of Quebec nationalists stemmed directly, and quite logically,

*From *Quebec: Social Change and Political Crisis*, 3rd ed., by Kenneth McRoberts. Used by permission of the Canadian Publishers, McClelland and Stewart, Toronto.

from the referendum outcome, and the way in which it so weakened Quebec's bargaining position. With the defeat of the *souverainiste* option, Quebec nationalists lost their essential tool for influencing English Canadians and federalists in general. English-Canadian readiness to consider Quebec's constitutional demands had always hinged on the belief that some accommodation of Quebec was necessary to head off the possibility of Quebec deciding to disengage itself from Canada altogether. In the last analysis, this fear of "rupture," vastly heightened by the accession of the Parti québécois to power in 1976, had spurred the sudden interest in "renewed federalism" and had led to the preparation of such blueprints for "renewal" as *A New Canadian Federation* and *A Future Together*. With the massive rejection of sovereignty in the referendum, Quebec nationalists could no longer credibly raise the spectre of "rupture." For twenty years, Quebec nationalists had been able to claim that the forces of secession were steadily growing, requiring an urgent response on the part of the rest of Canada. Through the referendum, the Quebec government had sought to give this argument even greater strength. Instead, it did exactly the opposite. In the eyes of many English Canadians, the "Quebec problem" had simply resolved itself.

566

For those who were concerned, nonetheless, that there be some fulfilment of the pre-referendum commitment to "renewed federalism," the federal government offered its limited package of reform. While totally ignoring the demands of Quebec nationalists as well as most notions of "renewed federalism," the proposals were invested with the moral authority of Pierre Trudeau, who not only was himself a French Canadian but, in the eyes of many, had personally secured the strong "No" vote.

English-Canadian sentiment was perhaps best exemplified by Richard Hatfield when, during a televised discussion in the summer of 1980, he grew impatient with an elaboration of Quebec's constitutional position by Daniel Latouche, constitutional adviser to the Lévesque government. Even though Quebec's proposals for an enhancement of its powers were very much along the lines of the models of "renewed federalism" that had been circulating in the late 1970s, Hatfield declared, "We don't have to listen to this anymore — this is over. . . . There was a referendum which settled all that."[1]

Yet, beyond Quebec's weakened bargaining position, the constitutional outcome also reflects the fierce determination of the federal government to take full advantage of this and every other opportunity to assert federal power. Through the late 1970s a growing sense had developed among officials in Ottawa that federal power had declined, and provincial power increased, to such an extent that Ottawa could no longer properly discharge its responsibilities as the government of all Canadians. On this basis, they mounted a concerted attack on the pretensions of the provincial governments, in general, and the aspirations of Quebec nationalists, in particular. Once the referendum had been defeated, a result for which federal officials gave themselves full credit, this determination was given full rein.[2] In the process, the whole of intergovernmental relations between Ottawa and Quebec City came into much greater conflict than they had ever been before the referendum.

The federal government's unprecedented threat in the fall of 1980 to send its package of constitutional reforms to Westminster even without the approval of the provincial governments was, in fact, only one of several instances of a new federal disposition to act unilaterally in areas where in the past it had always sought the collaboration and consent of the provincial governments. In October of the same year, Ottawa announced the National Energy Policy through which, for the first time, it would impose a pricing and taxation regime for oil and gas without first securing the consent of the producer provinces. And in the fall of 1981 federal officials announced radical reductions in federal transfers to the provinces without allowing time for the extensive consultation of the provincial governments, which had always preceded Ottawa's determination of the five-year fiscal arrangements in the past.

567

By the same token, the federal government sought in several ways to provide direct services and benefits to citizens and institutions that in the past, out of deference to provincial jurisdiction, it had funnelled through the provincial governments. For instance, in June, 1983, the Ministry of Employment and Immigration established a direct job creation program through which funds were made available to a variety of recipients, including municipal governments. More significantly, in January, 1982, Prime Minister Trudeau announced a radically different approach to regional development policy through which, in some cases, the federal government would retain exclusive responsibility for projects rather than allowing provincial management of them as had been the case in the past.[3]

Also striking are several federal initiatives that fell on Quebec alone. In 1981, the federal government amended the National Energy Act to authorize it to draw on the rarely used declaratory power to create a right-of-way across Quebec territory for the transmission to the United States of Labrador electrical power. This was intended to undermine Hydro-Québec's long-standing contract with Newfoundland — a contract Newfoundland had been seeking in vain to renegotiate.[4] In 1983, the government introduced to the Senate a bill, S-31, to restrict provincial ownership in enterprises engaged in interprovincial transportation. By all reports, the bill was aimed at Quebec's Caisse de dépôt et de placement, which was alleged to be seeking a controlling interest in Canadian Pacific.[5] Also, two major regional economic development projects were undertaken unilaterally by the federal government. In May, 1983, a massive $224 million five-year program was announced for the Gaspé and Lower St. Lawrence and in June, 1984, a $109 million project for the province as a whole was announced. Federal officials justified these unilateral moves in terms of difficulties in negotiating a new comprehensive agreement (ERDA) with Quebec. Nonetheless, negotiations were also lagging with Ontario and British Columbia, yet no projects had been declared unilaterally for these provinces.[6]

A variety of factors could be cited to explain the rise of this extraordinary determination to assert federal power. It may have been engendered in part by institutional changes within the federal government itself. The introduction of new rationalized decision-making procedures, and concomitant concern with measuring the effectiveness of expenditures in terms of clearly defined policy objectives, may have helped to trigger the disaffection with federal–provincial collaboration. Also, with the shift of power within the federal government from line departments to the new central agencies, the alliances between federal and provincial program officials that had supported federal–provincial collaboration in the past may have been undermined.[7]

568

Beyond such institutional changes, one might also point to changes in the international political economy and Canada's place within it to account for the new federal assertiveness. Yet, while these changes may have provided ready rationales for federal action, it is not clear that they can explain it. For instance, the prolonged recession of the early 1980s was cited by federal officials to explain their determination to reduce federal transfers to the provinces. They contended that funds had to be diverted to reduce the spiralling federal deficit. Yet, it appears that the real purpose was to free up funds for new, highly "visible" forms of direct spending by Ottawa: in its own projections, the government's financial requirements were to fall from $10 billion in 1980–81 to $5.5 billion in 1983–84.[8] Likewise, the movement of economic activity to western Canada, in response to the soaring world price for oil, was cited as justification for the National Energy Policy. Officials argued that economic activity had to be stimulated in other parts of Canada, such as the North and offshore, in order to avoid important dislocative effects on the distribution of capital and labour. A more persuasive explanation of federal intervention, however, lies in the fact that these areas were outside provincial jurisdiction, were dubbed the "Canada Lands" by Ottawa, and thus economic activity would be taxed by the federal government alone.

In the last analysis, the new federal assertiveness was more than simply the result of the reorganization of federal institutions or an attempt to redress the problems of the Canadian economy. Its roots were fundamentally ideological. For Trudeau and for many of his colleagues, the primary purpose of political life always had been to implant a new conception of the Canadian political community and of the role the federal government should play as a "national government," the government of all Canadians. With their victory in the Quebec referendum, they had an unprecedented opportunity to put their ideas into effect. The past conventions of collaboration with the provinces could now be safely ignored.

Thus, in 1981 Trudeau declared that federal transfers to the provinces had to be radically altered so that Ottawa could undertake new projects of its own. On this basis, he declared, "We have stopped the momentum that would turn Canada into, in everything but name only, ten countries."[9] It was time, he said, to:

reassert in our national policies that Canada is one country which must be capable of moving with unity of spirit and purpose towards shared goals. If Canada is indeed to be a nation, there must be a national will which is something more than the lowest common denominator among the desires of the provincial governments.[10]

It is clear that for Trudeau, as for many of his colleagues, the obstacle to such a Canadian "national will" lay first and foremost in Quebec and in the counter-project of a Quebec nation. Thus, it is not surprising that the new unilateral initiatives were aimed most frequently at Quebec. By the same token, it is not surprising that a primary concern of Ottawa's new initiatives was to establish a closer relationship between citizens and the federal government. Ottawa had long been preoccupied with its "visibility" in Quebec, fearing that through "opting out" and other arrangements that heightened the role of the Quebec government, Québécois had become estranged from the federal government.[11] Flush with a referendum victory based in part on media campaigns that extolled the many benefits of federal activity, federal officials were determined that this estrangement should never occur again. Any renewal of the federal system had to be compatible with this fundamental objective. The ultimate accord faithfully reflected this premise.

Finally, however, beyond the very heavy constraints that were placed on Quebec, the outcome also reflected the ineffective way the Quebec government itself handled the constitutional negotiations. The Lévesque government's position was, to be sure, an exceedingly awkward one in the post-referendum negotiations. Having sought without success to persuade Québécois that their collective aspirations could be met only if Quebec were to become a sovereign state, it now had to define and defend Quebec's interests within the Canadian federation.

Initially, it did so by turning to the positions on constitutional change articulated by previous Quebec governments. Accordingly, as negotiations got under way in the summer of 1980, Quebec insisted that repatriation must be linked to a substantial revision of the division of powers, including provincial ownership of offshore resources and control of communications. In addition, Quebec maintained, any constitutional declaration of principles must contain a recognition of Quebec's distinctiveness, there must be no entrenchment of linguistic rights (at least with respect to Quebec), and the Supreme Court should be reorganized to give Quebec justices equality within a constitutional bench or "near equality" within the Court as a whole.[12]

However, in April, 1981, apparently out of the fear that the federal government might otherwise be able to persuade the British House of Commons to approve its package of constitutional revision, thus diminishing provincial power with an entrenched charter, Quebec joined the seven other dissenting provinces in formally supporting repatriation if it were to be accompanied simply by a modified version of what had become known as "the Vancouver formula."[13] Under this formula, Quebec would not have a veto: constitutional amendment would require the support of any seven provinces, representing 50 per cent of the Canadian population. To be sure, under the formula, a dissenting province could opt out of any transfer of jurisdiction to the federal level, and still receive financial compensation. Nonetheless, never before had a Quebec government publicly endorsed an amendment formula in which Quebec did not have a veto over all forms of change in the constitution. Moreover, no previous Quebec government, at least within recent decades, had ever approved repatriation without an accompanying change in the division of powers.

In effect, through its actions the Lévesque government had itself sanctioned a "renewal" of the federal system in which the longstanding aspirations of Quebec nationalists were totally ignored. To be sure, the "common front" position to which it had subscribed had not entailed any curtailment of provincial jurisdiction through an entrenched charter. However, reflecting the priorities of the other provinces, neither had it involved an enhancement of provincial power. Having thus assimilated its position to that of the other provinces, the Quebec government was poorly placed to object when the other provinces readied their accord with the federal government. The deviations they accepted from the original interprovincial position do not seem to have transcending significance. With respect to the amending formula, the other provinces accepted that while a province could opt out of transfers of jurisdiction to the federal level, compensation would be restricted to transfers that involve "education and culture." (As it happens, transfers of any kind are unlikely in any event within the foreseeable future.) They did agree to a Charter of Rights and Freedoms, which restricts provincial governments' actions. Nonetheless, most of these provisions are subject to the "notwithstanding" clause. In the case of Quebec, many of these provisions bear restrictions that Quebec governments had already imposed on themselves through the Quebec Human Rights Act. The main exception is, of course, the provision for minority-language education. Yet, in its application to Quebec, this provision generally approximates the terms of Bill 101's "Canada clause."[14] As for the mobility provision, it will not, in any event, apply to Quebec within the foreseeable future given the exemption of provinces whose level of employment falls below the national average.

In terms of the historical aspirations of Quebec nationalists, the problem with the amendment formula is not the scope of "compensation" if Quebec opts out of transfers of jurisdiction but the absence of a Quebec veto over all forms of constitutional change: the Lévesque government had already conceded this. More generally, the failure of the constitutional revision, as "renewal" of Canadian federalism, is not so much in what it accomplished as in what it did not accomplish: to enhance the position of the Quebec government. This objective had been recognized, to varying degrees, by all previous Quebec governments in their proposals for constitutional reform just as it had been central to the Lévesque government's post-referendum proposals for a renewed federalism. But in subscribing to the "common front" position, the Lévesque government had itself renounced this goal, in the process making it easier for Ottawa and the other provinces to claim that they could fulfil "the promise" to Quebec with a constitutional revision that does nothing to enhance the status and powers of the Quebec government, let alone recognize it as a "national" state.

In the face of both the extent of its defeat and the evident contradictions of its own tactics, the Lévesque government had difficulty formulating a new strategy for defending Quebec's interests, even as a provincial government. Four years passed before, with an apparently more sympathetic government in Ottawa, the Lévesque government presented a new package for constitutional revision. There would be recognition of Quebec's existence as a people. Quebec would have exclusive jurisdiction over language, with statutory protection of English-language rights. With respect to the Charter of Rights and Freedoms, Quebec would be bound only by the "democratic rights." Quebec would have power of veto over modifications of federal institutions and the establishment of new provinces and would have a veto or receive full compensation with respect to changes in the division of powers. The federal spending power would be limited and the federal powers of disallowance and reservation eliminated. With respect to the division of powers, Quebec (and other interested provinces) would have: primary responsibility for manpower policy, economic development, and selection and settlement of immigrants; increased powers pertaining to communication; exclusive jurisdiction over marriage and divorce; and the right to international dealings on matters falling within its jurisdiction. Finally, with respect to the Supreme Court, three of the nine justices would come from Quebec, with sole authority in matters of civil law, and the Quebec government would participate in the appointment of Quebec judges. Also, the Quebec government would have authority to appoint judges to Quebec superior courts.[15]

It was hardly a radical document. By and large, Quebec was simply reintroducing notions of reform that had already surfaced in the discussions of "renewed federalism" of the late 1970s. Virtually all of Quebec's proposals could be found in either the Task Force on National

Unity's *A Future Together* or the Quebec Liberal Party's *A New Canadian Federation*, or in both.[16] Nonetheless, times had changed: if English Canada had had some disposition to discuss such reforms in the late 1970s, by the mid-1980s it clearly did not. The Quebec question and constitutional revision in general were viewed as closed.

In sum, during its second term in office the government of a party formally committed to Quebec independence had instead focused its efforts on trying to secure an improved position for Quebec within the existing political order. Even this reduced objective had continued to elude the PQ government, only in part because of its own ineptness. This result seemed to reinforce the conclusion that many neo-nationalists had already drawn from the referendum defeat: the dream of making Quebec a truly "national" state was effectively dead. As we shall see later, many militants began to vent their frustration on the party leadership, claiming that it had in effect traded the goal of independence for a "renewal" of the federal system. For these militants, a party founded on the ideal of Quebec sovereignty could legitimately pursue nothing else, however bleak may be the immediate prospects of success. Before examining these developments within the party, however, we first need to explore how the second PQ government dealt with the other premise of the neo-nationalist project: the ideal of an interventionist, even social democratic, state.

572

NOTES

[1] Graham Fraser, *P.Q.: René Levesque and the Parti Québécois in Power* (Toronto: Macmillan, 1984), 239.

[2] This new approach of the federal government to dealings with the provinces is documented and analysed at much greater length in Kenneth McRoberts, "Unilateralism, Bilateralism and Multilateralism: Approaches to Canadian Federalism," in Richard Simeon, ed., *Intergovernmental Relations*, vol. 63, Collected Research Studies of the Royal Commission on the Economic Union and Development Prospects for Canada (Toronto: University of Toronto Press, 1985), 71–129.

[3] This shift in policy is analysed in Michael Jenkin, *The Challenge of Diversity: Industrial Policy in the Canadian Federation*, Science Council of Canada, Background Study 50 (Ottawa: Supply and Services Canada, 1983); and Peter Aucoin and Herman Bakvis, "Organizational Differentiation and Integration: The Case of Regional Economic Development Policy in Canada," paper presented to the Canadian Political Science Association, June 1983.

[4] See *Globe and Mail*, June 24, 1981; *Le Devoir*, June 26, 1981; plus the analysis by Marc Laurendeau, *La Presse*, June 27, 1981.

[5] This initiative is examined at length in Allan Tupper, *Bill s-31 and Federalism of State Capitalism* (Kingston: Queen's University, Institute of Intergovernmental Relations, 1983).

[6] Accounts of these measures appear in *Globe and Mail*, May 7, 1983; *Le Devoir*, June 5, 1984.

[7] See J. Stefan Dupré, "Reflections on the Workability of Executive Federalism," in Simeon, ed., *Intergovernmental Relations*, 1–31. Donald Smiley has taken this argument one step further, contending that central agencies responsible for managing and co-ordinating intergovernmental relations have had an especially deleterious effect (Donald V. Smiley, *Canada in Question*, 3rd ed. [Toronto: McGraw-Hill Ryerson, 1980], 113). Nonetheless, a study of the federal government's Federal–Provincial Relations Office found that during the 1970s personnel were divided in their conception of the agency's role, with some seeing it as one of facilitating federal–provincial collaboration (Timothy B. Woolstencroft, "Organizing Intergovernmental Relations," Discussion Paper 12 [Kingston: Queen's University, Institute of Intergovernmental Relations, 1982], 52). To be sure, by the 1980s the agency had clearly moved to an openly adversarial role.

[8] On this basis, Gillespie and Maslove contend that the publicly stated concern with the deficit was "more smokescreen than substance." W. Irwin Gillespie and Allan M. Maslove, "Volatility and Vis-

ibility: The Federal Revenue and Expenditure Plan," in G. Bruce Doern, ed., *How Ottawa Spends Your Tax Dollars, 1982* (Toronto: James Lorimer, 1982),56.

9 *Globe and Mail*, November 25, 1981.

10 As quoted in Sharon Dunn, "Federalism, Constitutional Reform and the Economy: The Canadian experience," *Publius* 13, 2 (Spring, 1983): 134.

11 R.M. Burns recounts that in 1945 Louis St. Laurent feared that Duplessis, recently returned to power, would seek aggressively to mobilize public support behind the Quebec government. Feeling that the provinces had the advantage in such a campaign since they provided more services directly to the people than did Ottawa, he advocated new federal programs such as family allowances. (R.M. Burns, *The Acceptable Mean: The Tax Rental Agreements, 1941-1962*, Financing Canadian Federation 3 [Toronto: Canadian Tax Foundation, 1980], 46–47.) For an account of the role that fear of Quebec separatism played in stimulating the federal government's concern with visibility in the 1960s, see Anthony Careless, *Initiative and Response* (Montreal: McGill-Queen's University Press, 1977), 177.

12 The Quebec government's position was reproduced in a two-page ad in *La Presse*, August 21, 1980.

13 This interpretation is advanced in Fraser, *P.Q.*, 283. See also René Lévesque, *Attendez que je me rappelle* (Montréal: Québec/Amérique, 1986), 436. Yet, the actual impact of this should be minor. As Lévesque himself wrote of the set of revisions: "The only truly serious worry that it created for us is that Ottawa would now have the power to reduce the scope of Bill 101, to the benefit of Anglo-Québécois. However, in no way to the point of endangering our fundamental position. Much more than the content, it was the procedure which was intolerable." Lévesque, *Attendez*, 448 (our translation).

14 The provision does go beyond the "Canada clause" to the extent that in addition to children whose parents were educated in English in Canada it also covers children who have received, or have a sibling who has received, education in English anywhere in Canada — whatever the status of the parent. Lévesque recounted that even Quebec public opinion was beginning to respond to the federal argument that it was intolerable that constitutional amendment should depend on the British Parliament. As for Quebec's loss of a veto, Lévesque contended that in the hands of other provinces a veto could be used to frustrate Quebec's own development. If Quebec is to have one, then Ontario and the other provinces would insist on one, too. Yet, he also acknowledged that in extremely serious instances, a veto would indeed be necessary. Lévesque, *Attendez*, 440.

15 Quebec, *Draft Agreement on the Constitution: Proposals by the Government of Quebec*, May 1985.

16 Both documents called for the changes in federal powers and in the division of powers. The Task Force study, but not the Liberal document, had called for full control over language matters within provincial jurisdiction. The Liberal document would have given Quebec a total veto over constitutional change, while the Task Force provided for a provincial referendum. The Task Force report proposed that a new constitutional preamble should include recognition of Quebec as a "distinct society"; the Liberal document did not propose a preamble.

573

The Constitutional Politics of Meech Lake*

ROGER GIBBINS

The Meech Lake Accord represents the second major set of revisions to Canada's constitutional structure to have taken place during the 1980s. Although one might argue that the Constitution Act of 1982, and more specifically the Charter of Rights and Freedoms embedded with the Act, will have a greater impact on the daily lives of Canadian citizens, the Meech Lake Accord has the potential to transform the shape of government in Canada. Whereas the Constitution Act primarily addressed the relationship between citizens and their governments, the Accord attempts to redefine the relationship among governments in the Canadian federal state. In the long run, changes to that relationship could have

*From *Meech Lake and Canada: Perspectives from the West*, ed. Roger Gibbins et al. Reprinted by permission of Academic Printing and Publishing.

a profound impact on the character of Canadian political life, and thus on the lives of Canadians.

The Meech Lake Accord merits close examination as much for the process of constitutional change that it embodies as it does for its written text. In the analysis which follows [in Gibbins, ed., *Meech Lake and Can-*

574

S.S.C. Photo Centre A.S.C. / D. Burcsik.

Queen Elizabeth II signs the Canadian constitution document as Prime Minister Pierre Trudeau, Michael Pitfield, and Michael Kirby look on. Ottawa, April 1982.

ada], the political process surrounding the origins and ratification of the Accord receives as much attention as the Accord's formal content. In part this reflects a growing unease with the emerging style and form of constitutional politics in Canada; in part it reflects an unease with the impact of the Accord on the Canadian political process in the years ahead. It may also reflect the famous observation by Marshall McLuhan that "the medium is the message." For many of the contributors to this collection, the message to be drawn from the Meech Lake medium is as unsettling as anything contained within the Accord itself. That message, the vision of the Canadian political community projected by the Accord, is a troublesome one for many western Canadians reflecting upon their region, their country, and the interplay between the two.

The Meech Lake Accord is the product of a long, even tortuous process of constitutional change that finds its roots in the 1960s. At that time a constellation of factors opened up the Canadian constitution to intensive scrutiny and emotional political debate. An increasingly assertive nationalist movement in Quebec, resurgent regional unrest in western Canada, a growing concern with the protection of individual rights associated in part with the American civil rights movement, the nationalism associated with Canada's centennial celebrations in 1967, dramatic legislative initiatives to redefine and restructure the linguistic character of Canada and Quebec, regionally unbalanced federal governments, and incessant intergovernmental conflict across a broad front were just some of the factors which led Canadians to question existing constitutional arrangements.

575

Thus for close to twenty years Canadians both inside and outside government were involved in a wide-ranging and frequently acrimonious constitutional debate that touched virtually all aspects of Canadian political life. That debate was finally brought to a head by the 1980 sovereignty-association referendum in Quebec, and by the commitment of the federal Liberal government to pursue a "renewed federalism" should Quebec voters defeat the referendum. When the federalist option prevailed, Ottawa and the ten provincial governments were plunged into an intensive set of constitutional negotiations which ultimately culminated in the Constitution Act, proclaimed by Queen Elizabeth on April 17, 1982. However, on that rainy day in Ottawa, only ten of the country's eleven first ministers were on hand to sign the Act. Quebec's Premier René Lévesque refused to sign and, in this symbolic gesture, left the constitutional settlement incomplete. Although the Constitution Act was legally binding on the Quebec government and public, its legitimacy within Quebec had not been secured.

By entrenching language rights which had first been expressed in the Official Languages Act of 1969, the Constitution Act shored up the rights of francophone minorities outside Quebec and the anglophone minority inside Quebec in a way consistent with the liberal, individualistic tenor of the Charter of Rights and Freedoms. However, the Constitution Act did not address the constitutional position of Quebec within the Canadian federal state, and for that matter said very little about intergovernmental relations and the constitutional division of powers among governments. In this sense, and in its failure to define the Aboriginal rights which it entrenched, the Constitution Act was incomplete. Although one could argue that the Act's silence on Quebec was in itself a constitutional statement reflecting Pierre Trudeau's stress on individual rights and his consistent opposition to any special constitutional status for Quebec, the fact remains that the major source of political instability within the Canadian federal state since the mid 1960s — the constitutional status of Quebec — had not been addressed.

It was this loose end that was taken up by the governments of Canada after the retirements of Pierre Trudeau and René Lévesque, and after the defeat of the federal Liberals in 1984 and the Parti Québécois in 1985. Brian Mulroney's election in 1984 brought a leader to the federal government who had not been a central or even active player in the prolonged constitutional debate leading up to the Constitution Act, and who was not committed to the national and political vision upon which the Act had been constructed. Robert Bourassa's election in 1985 brought to the Quebec government a premier committed to federalism, but also one determined to achieve nationalist objectives for Quebec which his predecessor had not achieved in the negotiations leading up to the Constitution Act.

While these changes in leadership put in place the preconditions for the Meech Lake Accord, the eleven First Ministers were brought back to the negotiating table by a number of more pragmatic considerations. Quebec's refusal to participate in constitutional conferences made any future fine-tuning of the constitution very difficult to accomplish, a matter of some considerable concern to those interested in, for example, the further constitutional entrenchment of Aboriginal rights or the reform of federal institutions such as the Senate. Quebec's blanket use of the section 33 notwithstanding clause threatened to undermine the political legitimacy of the Charter in Quebec, while the Act's amending formula coupled with Quebec's refusal to participate gave Ontario in effect a veto on constitutional change. There is also little question that Prime Minister Mulroney was determined to show that he could deliver in Quebec where Trudeau had failed, that he could bring Quebec into the constitutional family and, in doing so, cement his party's newly found electoral grip on Quebec. For his part, Premier Robert Bourassa was determined to prove to nationalist forces in Quebec that a federalist premier could deliver, that he could secure a place for Quebec in Canada while at the same time projecting and enhancing the political autonomy of Quebec. Thus with the First Ministers of Canada and Quebec ready to deal, the other premiers were lured back to constitutional negotiations,

576

albeit rather low-keyed negotiations kept well away from public light until success was assured.

In June 1985, the Bourassa government set out five conditions which, if met, would enable Quebec to sign the Constitution Act. The conditions were the recognition of Quebec as a distinct society, a restriction on the federal government's spending power in areas of exclusive provincial jurisdiction, a Quebec veto on constitutional change, Quebec's participation in appointments to the Supreme Court of Canada, and constitutional entrenchment of Quebec's existing role in immigration. In August, 1986, the ten provincial premiers stated in the Edmonton Declaration that their first constitutional priority was to commence negotiations on the five conditions set out by Quebec. These negotiations, which were conducted with little public knowledge much less fanfare, led to a meeting of the First Ministers at Meech Lake, Quebec, on April 30, 1987.

At that time the basics of the constitutional agreement were put in place and, at the conclusion of the meeting, the Meech Lake Accord was announced to the public. After limited public discussion and parliamentary debate, the First Ministers met in Ottawa on June 2nd and 3rd to consider a number of modifications to the initial text. In an all-night session in the Langevin Block, and after a number of amendments to the initial Accord were hammered out, an agreement was reached and signed by Prime Minister Mulroney and the ten provincial premiers. As this volume goes to press, that agreement has now been ratified by Parliament, over the objections of the Senate, and by the legislative assemblies of Alberta, Nova Scotia, Prince Edward Island, Saskatchewan, and Quebec. The Accord will become part of the constitutional fabric of the Canadian federal state if it is ratified by the remaining five provinces by June, 1990.

In one sense, the Accord can be seen as the endpoint in a long and often tortuous constitutional journey, one that ties up a number of "loose ends" left hanging by the Constitution Act. In another sense, however, the Meech Lake Accord should be seen as a waystation on a longer constitutional journey that stretches back to Confederation and, in all likelihood, forward into the next century. While the Accord will, if ratified, settle several constitutional issues, it will also open up a new constitutional agenda with its provisions for annual constitutional conferences dealing with, among other things, Senate reform and "the roles and responsibilities in relation to fisheries." From this perspective, then, the Accord is part of the evolving constitutional framework for the Canadian federal state, a constitutional journey without end but not without form and structure.

While there might be some concern about presenting an analysis of the Accord before it has even been ratified, we would argue that the Accord is too important a development to wait. As many of the essays

577

in this collection point out, much of what is important about the Accord is the process through which it was created and through which it is being ratified, an importance which will persist no matter what the eventual fate of the Accord might be. It should also be stressed that the Accord is important for what it says about Canada, about the nature of both the national community and the provincial communities which are embedded within it. Regardless of its eventual fate, the Accord demands examination for the vision of Canada which it embodies, a vision that invites debate.

In a fundamental way, the Meech Lake Accord challenges the vision of Canada expounded by Pierre Elliott Trudeau, a vision that not only guided Trudeau's political career but which also found partial embodiment in the 1982 Constitution Act. Not surprisingly, Trudeau was drawn out of political retirement to defend his vision and to attack the Accord, first in his article in *La Presse* and *The Toronto Star*, then in his August 1987 testimony before the Parliamentary hearings on the Accord, and finally in his March 1988 testimony before the Senate hearings on the Accord in which he argued that if the Accord was not "put out in the dustbin," then "in vain we would have dreamt the dream of one Canada."[1] Trudeau's outspoken opposition played an important role in galvanizing those groups — women, ethnic and linguistic minorities, natives, and some Liberals — who had doubts about the Accord but were hesitant to break with the governmental consensus on Meech Lake.

While Trudeau's attack on the Accord is thus worthy of note in its own right, it has also played a role in shaping regional perceptions of the Accord in Western Canada. Note, for example, an Edmonton speech by Alberta Premier Don Getty to the annual convention of the provincial Progressive Conservative party. "While I knew the accord was good," Getty told approximately 2,400 convention delegates, "after Mr. Trudeau's intervention I'm certain it's one hell of a deal."[2] In this sense, Trudeau's participation in the debate over the Meech Lake Accord has done little to promote rational discourse on the Accord in western Canada.

However, Mr. Getty's conclusion that whatever Mr. Trudeau dislikes must be "one hell of a deal" for the West has not been universally shared across western Canada. For some observers in the West, the Accord suffers from significant blemishes although the broad outlines of the Accord, and ratification, are still supported for a variety of reasons. Other observers in the West see the Accord as more fundamentally flawed, and thus not only question its ratification but express serious concern over the potential impact of the Accord on Canadian political life. In short, there is considerable regional dissensus on the Accord, dissensus that this volume hopes to explore.

Constitutional documents are more than sets of procedural rules and institutional formalities. They are also important as political symbols,

578

as statements which expound and codify the political essence of national communities. Constitutions in this sense are a distillation of a nation's political culture. We might ask, then, what the Meech Lake Accord says about Canada, and to Canadians. More specifically, we might ask what the Accord says about the place of the West within the Canadian federal state, and what the Accord says to western Canadians about the nature of their regional and national communities. Do western Canadians find their vision of Canada reflected in Meech Lake? Or is the reflection distorted, pulled out of shape by currents somewhat at odds with western interests and aspirations? It is these questions which are addressed in this collection.

Yet in addressing these questions, we must never lose sight of the fact that the Meech Lake Accord is a national constitutional statement, and that western Canadians are very much a part of the national political community. To examine the Accord from a western Canadian perspective means that we must also examine it from a national perspective; a perspective too narrowly circumscribed by regional self-interest would fail to capture the ongoing effort of western Canadians to participate fully within the national community, to use that community rather than the region alone as the primary vehicle for western aspirations.

NOTES

[1] *Globe and Mail*, March 31, 1988, p. A1.
[2] Kathy Kerr, "Getty Rallies Tory Troops on Strong Keynote Speech," *Calgary Herald*, April 10, 1988, p. A2.

Contributors

T.W. Acheson is a member of the Department of History at the University of New Brunswick in Fredericton.

Harry Baglole is Director of the Institute of Island Studies at the University of Prince Edward Island.

Michael D. Behiels is in the Department of History, University of Ottawa.

David Bercuson teaches history at the University of Calgary.

Carl Berger teaches history at the University of Toronto.

Thomas R. Berger, the former Commissioner of the Mackenzie Valley Pipeline Inquiry, practises law in Vancouver.

Naomi Black teaches in the Department of Political Science at York University, Toronto.

Robert Boily teaches in the Political Science Department at the Université de Montréal.

Paula Bourne is a research associate at the OISE Centre for Women's Studies in Toronto.

Gail Cuthbert Brandt teaches in the Department of History at Glendon College, York University, Toronto.

Craig Brown is a member of the Department of History, University of Toronto.

John Dales has retired from the Department of Political Economy at the University of Toronto, St. George Campus.

René Durocher is a professor of history at the Université de Montréal.

James Eayrs is the Eric Dennis Memorial Professor of Political Science and Government at Dalhousie University in Halifax.

John R. English teaches in the Department of History, University of Waterloo.

E.R. Forbes teaches history at the University of New Brunswick in Fredericton.

Roger Gibbins teaches political science at the University of Calgary.

Deborah Gorham teaches history at Carleton University, Ottawa.

Jack L. Granatstein teaches Canadian history at York University, Toronto.

James Gray is a writer who lives in Calgary.

Brereton Greenhous is with the Directorate of History, Department of National Defence, Ottawa.

Joseph Levitt taught history at the University of Ottawa. He is currently retired.

581

Beth Light is a research associate at the OISE Centre for Women's Studies in Toronto.

Paul-André Linteau is a professor of history at the Université du Québec à Montréal.

Peter DeLottinville is an archivist at the Public Archives of Canada.

Angus McLaren teaches history at the University of Victoria.

Kenneth McRoberts teaches political science at York University in Toronto.

John Marlyn is a novelist living in Ottawa.

J.R. Miller is in the Department of History at the University of Saskatchewan.

Wendy Mitchinson teaches history at the University of Waterloo.

Douglas Owram teaches history at the University of Alberta in Edmonton.

Howard Palmer teaches in the Department of History at the University of Calgary.

Alison Prentice teaches history at the Ontario Institute for Studies in Education (OISE), Toronto.

Jean-Claude Robert is a professor of history at the Université du Québec à Montréal.

Walter N. Sage (1888–1963) taught history at the University of British Columbia.

Roger Sarty is with the Directorate of History, Department of National Defence, Ottawa.

Thomas P. Socknat teaches history at the University of Toronto.

Veronica Strong-Boag teaches in the Women's Studies program at Simon Fraser University in Vancouver.

James Struthers teaches in the Canadian Studies program at Trent University, Peterborough.

Donald Swainson teaches in the Department of History at Queen's University in Kingston, Ontario.

John L. Tobias teaches history at Red Deer College, Alberta.

W. Peter Ward is a professor of history at the University of British Columbia.

Donald F. Warner taught history at Macalester College, St. Paul, Minnesota.

David Weale is a history professor at the University of Prince Edward Island.

Walter Young (1933–1984) taught political science at the University of Victoria.

To the Student:

We are interested in your reaction to *Readings in Canadian History: Post-Confederation, 3rd ed.*, by Douglas Francis and Donald Smith. Through feedback from you, we can improve this book in future editions.

1. What was your reason for using this book?

   _____ university course   _____ continuing education course
   _____ college course   _____ personal interest

2. Approximately how much of the book did you use?

   ___ ¼   ___ ½   ___ ¾   ___ all

3. Which article did you like best? _____

   Least? _____ Why? _____

4. Have you any suggestions for improvement?

Fold here

To the Instructor:

We are interested in your reaction to *Readings in Canadian History: Post-Confederation, 3rd ed.*, by Douglas Francis and Donald Smith. Through feedback from you, we can improve this book in future editions. Please help us by completing this questionnaire:

1. Type of school: Comm. coll. _____ University _____

2. Type of course: One ____ Two ____ semester; Other: ____

3. Size of class: _____

4. Total *annual* enrolment for *all* sections of this course: _____

5. Which articles did you like best/assign most often?

   _____

6. Which articles did you like least/assign least often? Why?

   _____

7. Any suggestions for readings/topics for future editions?

   _____

8. What are the strongest features of the book?

   _____

9. How could this book be improved?

   _____

Fold here